BISHOP G. BROMLEY

OXNAM

PALADIN OF LIBERAL PROTESTANTISM

BISHOP G. BROMLEY OXNAM

PALADIN OF LIBERAL PROTESTANTISM

Robert Moats Miller

Abingdon Press

Nashville

BISHOP G. BROMLEY OXNAM
Paladin of Liberal Protestantism

This book is printed on acid-free paper.

Library of Congress Cataloging-in-Publication Data

Miller, Robert Moats.
Bishop G. Bromley Oxnam : paladin of liberal Protestantism / Robert Moats Miller.
p. cm.
Includes bibliographical references and index.
ISBN 0-687-03564-3 (alk. paper)
1. Oxnam, G. Bromley (Garfield Bromley), 1891-1963. Methodist Church—United States—Bishops—Biography. 3. Methodist Church (U.S.)—Bishops—Biography. 4. Liberalism (Religion)—Methodist Church—History—20th century. I. Title.
BX8495.093M54 1990
287'.6'092—dc20
[B] 90-42071
CIP

MANUFACTURED IN THE UNITED STATES OF AMERICA

In Loving Dedication
To
Mary June Miller Burd and Lawrence Hull Burd
(1915-1983)
David Sears Miller
(1918-1939)
John Tuttle Miller and
Gwendolyn Morgan Miller

C O N T E N T S

PREFACE

This big book is not for the faint of heart or short of wind. Garfield Bromley Oxnam was a large man physically. By the time of his retirement in 1960 he was almost certainly the most powerful (and imaginative) bishop in The Methodist Church, then the largest and most muscular Protestant church in the United States. He was a mighty force in the affairs of the Federal Council of Churches and the subsequent National Council of Churches and World Council of Churches. There are those (including vexed members of my family) who say that I am constitutionally incapable of writing with brevity. They are probably right. Still, though I may be kidding myself, I truly believe that it would be impossible in a slim volume to do justice to Oxnam's massive presence in the American Protestant Establishment, a family of denominations, agencies, and individuals tilting toward religious and social liberalism but embracing "moderate middlers" as well.

This book is not in any *special* sense intended for Methodist or even other Protestant readers. In truth, such was the range and depth of Oxnam's involvement in matters political, diplomatic, economic, and social, it may well be that readers with similar concerns, rather than formally religious ones, will be the readers least likely to doze off. This point bears emphasis. Oxnam's interest in public affairs was joined with action. If there was any person holding such a high denominational position who was more deeply implicated in public issues, that individual's name does not come easily to mind. "Relevant" is the most hackneyed word in our current vocabulary, yet no other word suggests itself to describe the meaning for today of Oxnam's public life. Many of the issues troubling and engaging him continue to haunt the world to this moment.

At the same time, the admission must be made that the American religious scene has changed dramatically since Oxnam's death. The triumphalism then felt, especially in the 1940s and 1950s, by the older, established, "mainline" Protestant denominations, such as The Methodist Church, and agencies, such as the National Council, has been replaced by a mood of chastened concern. Declining membership, prestige, and authority in the secular world are facts, although even in the nineteenth century the perception of mainline Protestant hegemany did not fully accord with the reality of religious pluralism. Oxnam passed from center stage almost at the precise moment that an era was ending in the religious history of the American people. Establishment Protestantism in general and Methodism in particular are not what they were a generation or half a generation ago. This need not be and is not for many good Methodists a cause for despair. Indeed, the absence of triumphalism may be a sign of returning health. It is the antiestablishment religious forces who today need to worry about the perils of hubris. Oxnam symbolizes much that was good, vital, true, and humane—and recoverable. His life endures as an inspiration to those Christians today who share as he did the conviction of the Jewish seer Martin Buber: "The true meaning of love of one's neighbor is not that it is a command from God which we are to fulfill, but that through it and in it we meet God." If Oxnam's life may be read as an inspirational tale, it must, alas, also be seen as a cautionary one. There are things he did and things left undone, it seems to me, that religious liberals today would do well not to seek to recover. But either way—for weal or for woe—Oxnam speaks to us as this most awesome of all centuries draws to a close.

This book is not for those who prize blandness and eschew controversy. Oxnam possessed a puissant personality. He held strong convictions. He expressed them endlessly, publicly, and forcefully. Ideas were weapons to be used in the service of the coming Kingdom. He inspired both adulation and acrimony. He was constantly embroiled in contention, especially with religious and secular conservatives. He was not a J. Alfred Prufrock, T. S. Eliot's ineffectual man, who after "tea and cakes and ices" could never find "the strength to force the moment to its crisis."

This book is not for those who assume that the biography of a religious figure must be a moist memorial, with all tics and traumas piously veiled. I like to think that this volume does not fall into the hagiographic genre.

My concern, in fact, is quite the opposite. There are things about the mature Oxnam that I find disquieting, though these things emphatically do *not* relate to his splendid performance as husband, father, and friend. I fear that my disquietude is revealed in the stern tone of too many passages, especially as the biography deepens. I further fear that after completing a reading of this volume some individuals—perhaps members of the Oxnam family, United Methodist bishops and ministers and lay persons, and Abingdon Press editors—will judge me a worthy candidate for a modern auto-da-fé. If so, I would not blame these readers. I suppose my only answer to them would be that inevitably—or so it seems to me—the biographer reveals himself as he proceeds in attempting to reveal his subject. If in the readers' eyes I have proven myself, not Oxnam, as the flawed one, would this not be an exquisite illustration of "poetic justice"?

On more instances than I care to count I have awakened from a nightmare clammy as a Scottish moor at midnight. In the recurring dream I am being confronted by Oxnam in the hereafter. (The exact location need not be named.) Biography in hand, the bishop looms over me and begins to speak in his powerful voice. . . . It is at that moment that I rise up in bed trembling. In order to coax sleep's return, I hug the following comforting thought as Linus hugs his blanket. Oxnam relished an honest, challenging fight. He would use all of his impressive powers of persuasion to set me straight where in the biography I had been unfairly critical of him. Yet, even though I might not relent on all counts, in the end I like to think he would offer to shake hands and say, "Brother Miller, you have misunderstood me and many of my positions, but I bear no grudge because I discern no conscious malice in your motivation, and I appreciate the fact that you have been just to my beloved wife and children."

Once again I have failed to provide citation footnotes and I expect some reviewers, not without reason, will again box my ears, as several did following the publication of my unfootnoted biography of Harry Emerson Fosdick. Ultimately, however, I would prefer to have ringing ears than barnacle the biography with hundreds and hundreds of citations. If a reader is interested in knowing the source of a statement or quotation, I would be happy to lend an assist.

The dedication comes from a grateful heart.

R.M.M.
Chapel Hill, N.C.
June 1989

ACKNOWLEDGMENTS

As surely many of these pages will make painfully clear to the reader, this volume is not in any sense a family-commissioned, family-authorized biography. Nevertheless, for good reasons the Oxnams merit heading the list of those individuals to whom I am profoundly indebted. The second son, Philip Holmes Oxnam, and his wife, Louise Magee Oxnam, in Florida shared with me their memories and also significant documents in their personal possession. I truly liked them both enormously. (They also thoughtfully asked their two daughters, Judith Louise and Elizabeth Catherine, to record in writing their childhood recollections of their grandfather.) The sole Oxnam daughter, Mrs. Bette Ruth McCormack, was equally forthright and generous in sharing memories, lending personal possessions, and providing warm hospitality, although we were together a matter of hours rather than of days as was the case with Philip and Louise. Mrs. Dalys Houts Oxnam, the widow of the oldest son Robert Fisher Oxnam, traveled from her home as a convenience to me in order to talk about her father-in-law and to provide copies of the letters of condolence received by her husband at the time of the bishop's death and also letters written to the bishop from world leaders during his lifetime. Robert Bromley Oxnam stole an hour from his busy schedule as president of the Asia Society in New York to recall his vividly remembered grandfather.

These Oxnams lead in the acknowledgments for a second reason as important as their friendly cooperation. Once they had agreed to be interviewed and opened their hearts and personal documents to me, they maintained a hands-off posture. At no time have they attempted to influence my judgments or sought to censor the manuscript in advance of publication. For this restraint I am eternally grateful, all the more because most certainly they will be disturbed by some of the critical and controversial things said here about their father, father-in-law, and grandfather.

Bishop Earl G. Hunt, Jr., has been in the truest sense my mentor in this entire enterprise. He it was, under authorization of the Council of Bishops of The United Methodist Church, who invited me to undertake the biography, and who over the long years has sustained me with his encouragement and friendship. At the time I write these words, June 1989, Bishop Hunt has not had the opportunity to read the completed manuscript. I pray that when that opportunity soon arises his disappointment will not be too grievous, though I am as confident (alas) as a Christian with four aces (to steal Mark Twain's naughty words) that neither he nor other members of the Council will be in total agreement with my interpretations of Oxnam's life.

Gerhard E. Lenski and Chester A. Pennington are two scholars who did read the penultimate draft of the manuscript and I am immeasureably grateful for their searching critiques. To absolve them of complicity in my sins it must be frankly admitted that I was too mulish to accept *all* their suggestions. The members of the CUSHWA Center for the Study of American Catholicism at the University of Notre Dame suffered through the original, longer draft of chapter 11 without *obvious* whimpering.

Two wise and willing graduate students, Rob Gilbert and Stuart Leibiger, lent a helping hand in editing the opening ten chapters. The History Department secretaries, Mrs. Linda Stephenson, Miss Pamela Fesmire, Mrs. Mattie Hackney, Mrs. Mary Woodall, and especially Mrs. Eunice Hernandez, added to their normal duties the typing of eleven initial chapters. Mrs. Molly Dearing typed the bulk of the final manuscript with thoroughly professional skill and dispatch.

This project would not have been possible without substantial monetary contributions. I am most grateful for support from the Park Avenue United Methodist Church Trust Fund, New York City; Mr. John Ruan of the Iowa Annual Conference; The National Methodist Foundation; the Chicago Area; the New York Annual Conference; the Oregon-Idaho Annual Conference; the Ohio East Area; the Monk Bryan Bishop's Fund; Bishop Wayne K. Clymer; Bishop and Mrs. T. Otto Nall; and Bishop Earl G. Hunt, Jr.

A generous grant of $1,300 from the American Philosophical Society made possible four research trips in 1986 and a welcome grant of $500 from the National Endowment for the Humanities underwrote a research trip in 1985. Grant sums totaling $3,700 from the Faculty Research Council of the University of North Carolina at Chapel Hill, awarded between 1983 and 1986, were a godsend in facilitating out-of-state research. Thanks to my then departmental chairman, Gillian T. Cell, the History Department cooperated with United Methodist Church sources in making it possible for us to spend the entire academic year 1984–85 in Washington. Thanks to my then departmental chairman, Colin A. Palmer, the History Department in conjunction with a University Kenan Leave permitted devoting the entire academic year 1988–89 to pressing the completion of the manuscript. My wife, Carol Herter Miller, merits a word of gratitude because despite the generous financial assistance from the sources named above, the truth is these months of research travel and living and considerable mailing and professional typing expenses hit our family budget pretty hard. My last book was dedicated to our children, David, Abigail, and Amanda, "The Hope of the World." Well, they were then and continue to be just that.

ESSAY ON SOURCES

PERSONAL INTERVIEWS

In addition to members of the Oxnam family, a number of individuals shared their memories in interviews and great is my gratitude to them. Inasmuch as Oxnam died in 1963 it is self-evident that many of the key persons in his career were no longer living at the onset of my researches in 1983 or died before interviews could be consummated. I thank again:

Mary Anderson, Baltimore; Glenn Archer, Silver Spring; Bishop A. James Armstrong, Washington; E. Mallary Binns, Silver Spring; William Bishop, Baltimore; Paul Blackwood, Baltimore; Roger Burgess, Baltimore; Douglas Chandler, Washington; Ottilie De Simone, New York City; Avery Dulles, S.J. (by phone), Washington; Philip Edwards, Baltimore; John Tracy Ellis, S.J. (by phone), Washington; Glen Everrett (by phone), Washington; James Findlay, Washington; Gerald Fogarty, S.J., Washington; C. C. Goen, Washington; Robert Green, Washington; Edward Hart (by phone), Washington; Msgr. George G. Higgins, Washington; Bishop Earl Hunt, Jr., Nashville and Raleigh; Roland Kircher, Washington; Peter Krogh, Washington; Joseph Lash, Washington; Douglass Lewis, Washington; Louise Link, Bethesda; Dorothy McConnell, New York City; Mr. and Mrs. John McLaughlin, Gaithersburg; Bishop and Mrs. James Mathews, Washington; Albert J. Menendez, Silver Spring; Ralph Minker (by phone), Baltimore; Mr. and Mrs. Foster Montgomery, Bethesda; Walter G. Muelder, Boston; Bishop T. Otto Nall,

Baltimore; Albert C. Outler, Washington; Charles C. Parlin, Jr., New York City; Dr. and Mrs. Jed Pearson, Bethesda; Mr. and Mrs. Chester Pennington, Chapel Hill; R. Bruce Poynter, Washington; Kenneth Rose, Madison (N.J.); Edwin Schell, Baltimore; Delores Shaw, Baltimore; Charles Shepard (by phone), Washington; Bishop Roy Short, Baltimore; William Skinner (by phone), Washington; Mrs. and Mrs. Asbury Smith, Gaithersburg; William Stansbury, Jr., Baltimore; Mr. and Mrs. Mike Szpak, Washington; Harry Taylor (by tape), Jacksonville; Bishop Lloyd Wicke, Baltimore; Morrell Williams, Bethesda; Harvey Woodbury, Baltimore; Bishop Joseph Yeakel, Baltimore.

LETTERS TO THE AUTHOR

In response to petitions placed in the *New York Times, Washington Post, Christian Century,* and numerous and varied Methodist publications, and also in response to specific letters of inquiry, a number of individuals wrote to me about their associations with Oxnam or knowledge of him. In many instances these individuals included correspondence they had had with the bishop or materials related to his career. I thank again:

Norman Amtower; Gerald Anderson; Hurst Anderson; Bishop A. James Armstrong; Lloyd Averill; Clarence Avery; Raymond Balcom; V. Nelle Bellamy; Roger Burgess; J. Edward Carothers; Grady Carroll; Raymond Cooke; Bishop Fred Corson; Marion Creeger; Robert Crist; Ann Daly; Kenneth Dole; Tom Driver; James Findlay; Richard Fox; R. Benjamin Garrison; Joseph Grostephan; Robert T. Handy; Edward Hart; Stuart Henry; Steward Herman; Msg. George G. Higgins; Robert Hohner; Ivan Lee Holt, Jr.; Darrell Hoyle; James Hupp; William Hutchinson; Charles Jack; Thomas Karnes; Robert Kelley; Bishop Peter Lee; Paul Lewis; George Lortz; Ralph Luker; Donald Macleod; Claude Mahoney; Karen McClure; William McGaughey; Michael McIntyre; Mrs. Jack R. McMichael; Edward Michelson; John Millett; Louise Montgomery; Arthur Moore; Kathleen Morehouse; Bishop T. Otto Nall; J. Robert Nelson; Margaret Newton; Martha Olejar; Charles C. Parlin, Jr.; Chester Pennington; Eleanor Ragsdale; Helen Rosan; Francis B. Sayre; Edwin

Schell; Charles Shephard; Roger Shinn; Bishop Roy Short; Eugene Smith; Dieter Splinter; Karen Stone; Richard Stonesifer; Mike Szpak; Lawrence Tagg; Henry Taylor; Laurel and Esther Turk; Vivencio Vinluan; William Waters; Harold Wells; Herman Will; L. Allyn Welliver; Morrell Williams; Robert Wilson; Wesley Wilson; Hanford Wright; Robert Young, Jr.

ARCHIVE AND LIBRARY HOLDINGS

However valuable personal interviews and personal correspondence are in enriching an understanding of an individual, nothing is quite so satisfying to a biographer as the chance to work with primary documents. Fortunately the lode is rich surrounding Oxnam's public and private life. Archivists and librarians are the nonfiction writer's best friends (if indeed biography may be said to be nonfiction). The roll call of those professional and invariably cooperative keepers of records who lent me a helping hand is long. If they remain unnamed here it is not because I feel any less admiration and gratitude than I did at the times when I spent hours or days or weeks or months in their repositories.

We know that when Oxnam moved from Area to Area he was obligated to leave behind or discard materials in his possession. When he retired he was forced to throw out even larger quantities of records. Nevertheless, upon his death, Mrs. Oxnam presented his papers as a gift to the Library of Congress, Manuscript Division. This Oxnam Collection is massive: 16,000 items housed in 137 containers occupying 55.2 linear feet of shelf space. Its contents have been detailed in a 23-page brochure prepared by the Manuscript Division and available upon request. Some suggestion of its richness and variety is from time to time found in the preceding text of the biography. To read every item and take notes on many of them chewed up the entire academic year of September 1984–June 1985—and two additional vacation periods as well. Happily, the research conditions in the Manuscript Room are ideal; the friendliness of the staff nonpareil; and the Metro efficiently carried me from and back to our modest two rooms in the Wesley Theological Seminary married students' dorm.

The second major location of Oxnam materials is the Library of Wesley Theological Seminary. Some of these materials duplicate those in the Library of Congress, but this is not always the case. Among the Wesley holdings are: Oxnam's bound volumes of the *Minutes* of the Council of Bishops and earlier Board of Bishops; Oxnam's bound volumes of the minutes and journals of the Annual and Jurisdictional Conferences he served; Oxnam's records of weddings, baptisms, funerals, ordinations, transfers, and personal notes on pastors; files of *The Modern Samaritan* and *In Days To Come*; scores of his addresses and articles in both printed and manuscript form; the between four thousand and six thousand books in his personal library he gave to the seminary; and other materials. The seminary's Oxnam Collection is not nearly as formidable as the Library of Congress's, but neither is it insignificant.

Every biographer must be aware of a perilous trap: namely, that of becoming a victim of his or her sources. A full account of Oxnam's life could certainly be constructed from the materials in the two Oxnam Collections just cited. But that would be seeing things from Oxnam's angle of vision. This, of course, the sympathetic biographer must attempt to do. Yet a broader vision requires the examination of a wider range of sources. And so, during spring, summer, and Christmas vacation periods I visited the following archives and libraries. (They are mostly listed in the order of chronological visitation.)

Library of Congress, Manuscript Division, Washington, D.C.: Charles P. Taft Papers; Myron C. Taylor Papers. [1]

Americans United for Separation of Church and State Headquarters, Silver Spring, Maryland: Important materials relating to the history of the organization, including the generous gift of books and a bound file of *Church and State*, 1948–60, for my personal library.

United Methodist Historical Society, Baltimore, Maryland: Significant materials relating to Oxnam specifically and Methodism generally in the Oxnam era.

Princeton University, Seeley G. Mudd Manuscript Library, Princeton, New Jersey: John Foster Dulles Papers; Louis Fischer Papers; David E. Lilienthal Papers. [2]

Archives and History Center, United Methodist Church, Drew University, Madison, New Jersey: Significant materials relating to Oxnam specifically and Methodism generally in the Oxnam era, and also relating to Robert Oxnam's presidency of Drew.

Union Theological Seminary Library, New York City: Henry Sloane Coffin Papers; Henry Pitney Van Dusen Papers; Harry F. Ward Papers.

National Council of Churches Headquarters, Interchurch Center, New York City: Very helpful for annual and biennial reports, minutes of executive committee meetings and other meetings, and files of *Information Service* and *National Council Outlook.*

World Council of Churches Library, Interchurch Center, New York City: Very helpful for reports, minutes of meetings, press releases, and Council publications.

The Methodist Library, Interchurch Center, New York City: Contains now little relating to Oxnam.

B'nai B'rith, Anti-Defamation League Records Department, New York City.

National Conference of Christians and Jews Headquarters, New York City.

National Broadcasting Company Headquarters, New York City: Unfortunately an honest search by the staff failed to turn up either in the archives here or in the New Jersey satellite archives NBC's television coverage of Oxnam's famed appearance before the House Un-American Activities Committee on July 21, 1953.

Boston University School of Theology Library/New England Methodist Historical Society Library, Boston, Massachusetts: Fairly significant for both Oxnam's student years and his one later year as professor at the School of Theology.

Boston University, Mugar Memorial Library, Boston, Massachusetts: Edgar Sheffield Brightman Papers; Allan Knight Chalmers Papers; Daniel L. Marsh Papers; miscellaneous materials.

Archdiocese of Boston Archives, Brighton, Massachusetts: William Henry Cardinal O'Connell Papers; Richard Cardinal Cushing Papers; "Chancery Central Subject File."

John Fitzgerald Kennedy Library, Boston, Massachusetts: Pre-Presidential Papers; John Cogley Oral Interview; Hugh Sidey Oral Interview.

Yale Divinity School Library and Archives, New Haven, Connecticut: John R. Mott Papers; Liston Pope Papers; Henry Knox Sherrill Papers.

Harry S. Truman Library, Independence, Missouri: See text for elaboration.

Dwight D. Eisenhower Library, Abilene, Kansas: See text for elaboration.

Duke University Library, Manuscript Department, Durham, North Carolina: Graham A. Barden Papers.

University of North Carolina, Southern Historical Collection, Chapel Hill, North Carolina: Edwin McNeill Poteat Papers.

Duke University Divinity School Library, Durham, North Carolina: Invaluable for the standard sources of Methodism such as the quadrenially published *Doctrines and Discipline*, the *Journal of the General Conference*, and the *Daily Christian Advocate*; and for Annual Conference and Jurisdictional Conference minutes and journals; and for files of Methodist periodicals such as the *Christian Advocate* and *Zion's Herald*; and for a mountain of other Methodist materials.

University of North Carolina, Walter Davis Library, Chapel Hill, North Carolina: Indispensable for unpublished dissertations; magazine and journal articles; files of the *New York Times* and *Washington Post*; biographies and autobiographies; monographs; reference works.

The papers of several churchmen I examined in researching my earlier books are relevant to Oxnam's life and were tapped in writing this biography. They are: Ernest Fremont Tittle Papers, Garrett-Evangelical Seminary, Evanston, Illinois; Harry Emerson Fosdick Papers, Union Theological Seminary, New York City; Reinhold Niebuhr Papers and John Haynes Holmes Papers, Library of Congress, Manuscript Division, Washington, D.C. (The Bishop James Cannon, Jr., Papers, Duke University

Library, Manuscript Department, Durham, North Carolina, are of little relevance to Oxnam's life. [3])

Thanks to the Freedom of Information Act and the cooperation of the United States Department of Justice, I received copies of the great majority of the over four hundred pages in the Federal Bureau of Investigations's file on Oxnam. The text assesses that file.

Two unpublished works fully merit mentioning. David E. Gillingham's "The Politics of Piety. G. Bromley Oxnam and the Un-American Activities Committee" (senior thesis, Princeton University, 1967) is a brief, incisive, critical work that forced me to do some hard thinking. Wayne Lowell Miller's "A Critical Analysis of the Speaking Career of Bishop G. Bromley Oxnam (Ph.D. dissertation, University of Southern California, 1961) is a substantial, well-researched study which I found helpful. It does not, however, purport to be a biography. (William C. Logan's M.S.T. thesis, Wesley Theological Seminary, 1968, "Bishop G. Bromley Oxnam: A Study of His Views on Communism and the Consequences of These Views," proved of limited value to me.)

I will now bring to a close this brief essay on sources holding the hope, as the Quakers say, that the text will confirm the enforced depth and breadth of the research.

---

[1] In Washington, the United Methodist Building does not now possess records relating to the Oxnam era; nor does Bishop Joseph Yeakel's headquarters (in Silver Spring). The B'nai B'rith headquarters has nothing on Oxnam. I was not permitted access to the National Catholic News Service holdings located in the National Conference of Catholic Bishops headquarters.

[2] The Princeton Theological Seminary Library houses the John A. Mackay Papers, but as of July 1986 the collection remained closed to examination.

[3] Indeed, Professor Robert A. Hohner, who for over two decades has been writing the biography of Cannon, informs me that he did not come across any material on Oxnam in his examination of the papers of Bishops Candler, Denny, Harrell, Mouzon, Moore, or Leete.

CHAPTER 1

YOUNG BROMLEY OF THE WEST

One wintry night in 1942 a Methodist bishop named Garfield Bromley Oxnam slipped into a Chicago theater to indulge in a favorite form of relaxation. He anticipated the movie's plot, for earlier he had read *How Green Was My Valley,* an evocative tale of danger and death, singing and joy, in a Welsh mining village. He was not, however, prepared for the intensity of his emotional reaction to the film. Returning to his hotel, he confided his thoughts to his faithfully kept diary: "I was strangely moved. I felt that I had lived that life, but knew I had not. I had been in those mines, but I had not. The Welsh and the Cornish are of Celtic blood. And the religion, the music, the labor, the tragedy, the glory of the workers must be in my blood. I felt father was present, and his father's father." Perhaps as he drifted off to sleep, the mystic chords of memory pulled the bishop back to his boyhood visits to Cornwall with his father, Thomas Henry Oxnam, and his stories of those bygone days working in the tin mines, of adventures in Africa, and of the decision to migrate to the American West and win his way in her gold and silver mines.

Thomas Henry Oxnam, named after his own father, a tinner, was born in 1854 in the village of Pool in the district of Carn Brea, Cornwall. The little stone house was crowded with eight children. At age seven, Tom followed his father into the mines. In time he learned the uses of dynamite and powder and witnessed "bread riots" by families driven beyond endurance. Tom stubbornly refused to attend the village's Wesleyan chapel. Instead of wrestling with the Devil, he won the wrestling championship of Cornwall.

Nine years later, while Tom worked alongside his father and younger brother hundreds of feet below the ground in the famous Dolcoath tin mine, the largest in Cornwall, disaster struck. As falling rocks smashed one another and lit the mine with flashes as bright as day, Tom carried his brother to safety. Finally the roaring gave way to silence and darkness. "Strike a light, Father!" cried Tom. When no reply came, he knew. Two days later, the father's mangled body was removed from the rubble.

The following Sunday the youth went to the chapel and heard a simple sermon. When the preacher asked those who would accept Christ as Savior to come and kneel at the altar, Tom responded to the summons. Tom's conversion was to that peculiar form of Christianity known as Methodism thanks to the heroic labors among the Cornish miners by John and Charles Wesley a century earlier. Methodism now entered the heart and soul of Thomas as deeply as mining was in his muscles and mind.

When the mines of Cornwall showed signs of exhaustion, he, like so many other Cornishmen, sought work elsewhere, first in Scotland, then South Africa. He returned home only long enough to spill a bag of gold sovereigns into his widowed mother's apron before sailing for America. In the raw West he toiled in mines by day and studied by night. He avoided the carnal pleasures afforded in the mining camps of Nevada, Montana, and California. His was another passion: to build with his own hands little churches and preach in them.

Not surprisingly, Thomas rose in rank and reputation in the worlds of mining and religion. On June 6, 1882, in Trenton, Illinois, he married Mary Ann (Mamie) Jobe, eight years his junior. The bride had been born in Illinois and raised in Wisconsin before returning to Illinois with her parents, Jonathan and Faith Jobe. Surely it was more than a matter of good joss that Mamie was a devout Methodist, active in the local church, a charter member of the Woman's Christian Temperance Union, and the daughter of a man who had once mined out West.

After the wedding the young couple headed west, moving by stagecoach from one rough mining district to the next. Little wonder that an expectant Mamie returned to Illinois in July 1883 to await the arrival of their first child, Thomas Henry, Jr. The new family then struck roots, first in Marysville, Montana, a boom town of eight thousand, where they lived in a little house high on the hill overlooking the valley. As was his custom, Oxnam personally purchased the property for a Methodist church, built much of the structure with his own hands, and raised the initial salary for a minister. As was the cruel fate of so many women of the era, Mamie lost twin babes at birth in 1886, and then an infant daughter two years later. As Thomas carved wooden markers and erected a picket fence to identify their graves in the little cemetery in neighboring Silver City, anxiety over his wife's impaired health compounded his grief. For her sake he decided to move the family to California's milder climate.

In California, Thomas found work in the mines surrounding Sonora, including the rich Confidence Gold Mine. Mamie was placed under the care of Dr. Robert I. Bromley, who decided to operate. During surgery, Mamie ceased to breathe; the assisting surgeon pronounced her gone. Dr. Bromley, somehow, staved off death. Three years later, on August 14, 1891, Mamie gave birth to another child. They baptized him Garfield Bromley—Garfield, after the Republican president; Bromley, after the life-saving physician. Considering his later politics, Bromley seems the more appropriate of the given names. At any rate, that is what he was always called. In 1894 Bromley was joined by a baby sister, Lois. The arrival of infant William in 1899 completed the family.

By the time Bromley was four, the Oxnams had established a permanent residence in Los Angeles, a city with which Bromley would be intimately associated until 1928. At the turn of the century, Los Angeles was a metropolitan form of kudzu. Between Bromley's birth and his entrance into college, its population swelled from 50,000 to over 300,000, many of the newcomers being Midwestern Methodists. The Oxnam homes, first on Wall Street and later on Westlake Avenue, stood in comfortable neighborhoods. The help of immigrant girls eased Mamie's domestic chores, while Thomas enjoyed the luxury of a telephone, although it shared a ten-party line. Thomas also owned one of the first automobiles in Los Angeles. Bromley saw his first airplane, piloted by a daring Frenchman, in 1910. "I expect in a few years we will all be flying around as gay as birds," he predicted.

"In fact is there any one who, faced with the choice between death and a second childhood, would not shrink in dread from the latter prospect and elect to die?" inquires Saint Augustine in his *City of God*. Acknowledging the universality of childhood experience, which transcends time and geographic location, one nevertheless questions whether Bromley Oxnam would have agreed with Augustine. About Bromley's childhood, one might reasonably say, "It was the best of times, it was the worst of times"—with emphasis on the former.

Bromley earned respectable grades at both the public grade schools and at Los Angeles High School, where he completed his freshman year. In eighth grade he gave a school oration, an experience which he relished despite his initial nervousness—a matter of some consequence to his future career. Being both good looking and sturdy, he was popular with both teachers and classmates. Although forbidden the playing of games on Sunday by his Methodist parents, the boy was not totally hobbled by a moral ball-and-chain. He rode the city's famed electric "crimson chariots" to local beaches and parks, enjoyed "café parfaits" at the Alexandria Hotel, played baseball in a neighboring lot, heard dirty stories from the local barber, and, along with the rest of his gang, "rocked the monkeys"—that is, stoned the Chinese vegetable vendors. When he was seventeen, Bromley began seeing a girl named Blanche. A year later he recalled that they had kissed often.

In atonement for his "sins," Bromley joined the young people's activities at the "old First Street" Church, the one attended by his parents. In 1900 it moved to a new location and became the First Methodist Episcopal Church of Los Angeles. The boy contributed his entire savings to help raise the seventy-three thousand dollars needed to build the new structure. "One Sunday morning soon after the dedication of the Church," he recalled, "I was seated in the pew and put my feet, contrary to all the training of my family, up against the back of the pew in front of me. An usher came down the aisle and told me to put my feet down. I informed him that I had paid fifty dollars to that church and intended to put my feet where I pleased."

Among Oxnam's memories of his childhood, none were more fond than those of Christmases past. Christmas had been the "gladdest time of the year"; "the happiest time of our lives"; "I'd give anything on earth to have back again the Christmases of the past."

On Christmas Eve Bromley's anticipation would build, until at four the next morning "we would hear father and mother sing 'Joy to the world, the Lord has come, Let earth proclaim her king.'" The family would then carol, and finally, "rush to the fireplace, while father read the names and gave out the presents."

Only trips, perhaps, matched the excitement of Christmas. Bromley accompanied his father on journeys to Catalina, Yellowstone, and Mexico. The boy kept an enchanting journal of the family excursion to England in 1900, which he skillfully illustrated with pen, pencil, and crayon. He pridefully reported that none of the family was sick during the Atlantic crossing. The English trains, however, shook "us out of our seats." The Oxnams spent their two months in England visiting relatives, seeing the sights, and even catching a glimpse of the "Prince of Whales."

Sibling rivalry is real and may often be critical, but in the case of Bromley there is little to flutter the dovecotes. Tom, older by eight years and who became an engineer living for years abroad, appears in Bromley's diary and later recollections as a distant figure. Bromley mentions that he and Tom made an unbeatable doubles tennis team, but not much else, save for a diary passage written when Bromley was twenty-two which hints at a strained relationship: "I would give a great deal if he could somehow get away from his partial superficiality, get a great purpose into him and then fight for it. But I am not to judge and he may be rated far higher than I."

Lois, younger by nearly three years, was a lovely, sensitive, artistic girl who idolized Brom, and his attitude toward her was that of a lovingly protective older brother. Of course, as all brothers, he was quite capable of teasing, ruefully reporting in 1910: "Still mean and cranky. Lois is ill on account of it."

In that same diary entry he confessed to bullying Willie, whose incessant chatter vexed him. Nevertheless, Brom took his younger brother to ball games and the circus and protected him on the school yard.

Such are the mysteries of heredity: the four Oxnam children appear to be a veritable briar patch of paradoxes: Tom, the pertinacious, politically conservative engineer; Lois, the sweet, idealistic, dutiful daughter who, remaining unmarried, devoted her adult life to the care of her widowed mother; Willie, the fun-loving, musically inclined chap, dreaming of an acting career that would bring less than stardom; and Bromley, a most fascinating compound of the characteristics found in his siblings.

If Bromley's early years held their joys, it is but a bromide to add that no childhood is free from moments of interior hell. Exteriorly, the "worst of times" appear to have been the consequences of his father's fluctuating economic fortunes.

"Examining and Reporting on Mines a Specialty" announced Thomas Oxnam's business letterhead. Despite the volatility of the era in general and of the mining occupation in particular, Thomas had done well since migrating to America, his skills being in demand in the American West, Mexico, and other foreign lands. In 1906, success took its toll, however. Failing health induced him to take the whole family to Europe for a year. Although Tom would resume his engineering studies at Columbia in the fall, the younger children were to enter schools in England. Sailing in July, the family again toured England and then visited France, the Low Countries, and Germany. In the fall three events caused them suddenly to return to America. First, Thomas had to settle the estate of his deceased brother William. Second, a warehouse fire had destroyed most of the family's stored goods. Third, Thomas was offered the position of vice-president and general manager of the Consolidated Arizona Smelting Company in Humbolt. Bromley would work in the office.

The Panic of 1907 brought a drop in the price of copper. As a result, the smelter was closed down and the family returned to Los Angeles. His father's continuing poor health and bleak business prospects combined with brother Tom's education at Columbia convinced the dutiful Bromley that he ought to take a job rather than continue to be a financial burden to the family by returning to high school. His father wanted Bromley to enter the Los Angeles Business College. And so he did.

Bromley completed the courses of study at the Business College in nine months rather than the normal twelve. He acquired technical skills including shorthand, typing, and bookkeeping. After three months as an instructor of accounting at the Business College, Bromley took a job as a stenographer for the Pacific Electric Railroad. In return for the comfortable salary of $60 a month, he agreed to provide his own typewriter, sign a "Yellow Dog" contract (pledging not to join a labor union), and work a full Saturday. Shortly thereafter, Bromley took a similar position in the office of the Union Oil Company. Two years later, on June 29, 1909, a company official wrote the following laudatory words: "It gives me great pleasure to speak a word of commendation regarding the bearer, Mr. G. B. Oxnam, who, while in the service of Union Oil Company of California, has endeared himself to the management of the corporation, and whose fidelity and aptitude in corporation matters have proven his worth and eventual success were he to follow commercial lines." While this tribute is somewhat fulsome, it ought not to be forgotten that it was paid to a mere teenager. Clearly, Oxnam's subsequent career was anchored in a firm foundation of conscientious, industrious, youthful accomplishment.

While working for Pacific Electric and Union Oil (and for a year or two subsequently), Bromley assisted his father professionally. Prior to 1909, he accompanied his father to Mexico on business at least twice. "I was intimately associated in a business way with my father while he was general manager and director of large mining interests," Bromley recalled in 1923. His 1910 diary contains countless intriguing entries: "I was present at the Directors meeting of the Bonanza Gold Mining and Milling Company," reads one. "I am Secretary and Treasurer of the company." Or again, "I closed the Bonanza Gold M. & M. Co.'s books today and reports sent to Washington." The diary entries became increasingly somber. "I feel very sorry for father. He is very much troubled. Had father's office furniture brought home," related one. Other entries read: "Had a long talk with dad and I fear we shall soon be bankrupt. Everything is going wrong. My faith is sorely tried." "Father left for the East, well nigh broken hearted as he is very near financial ruin." Doubtless Bromley's later critiques of capitalism (moderate as they were) sprang from these early observations of the Spencerian jungle in which his father struggled to survive.

Unquestionably, Bromley's father and mother were the two individuals most influential in his development. Contrary to the experiences of most boys raised in nineteenth-century American homes, however, his father's role overshadowed that of his mother. This observation is in line with the conclusions of William R. Hutchison's comparative study of the origins of liberal and conservative Protestants. Hutchison found that the influence of the father exceeded that of the mother in the raising of children who became liberals.

Thomas Oxnam looked like the man he was—a mining engineer who had once himself labored in the pits and wrestled in the ring. His face was rugged but not harsh, his body square and muscular. Bromley inherited his father's commanding appearance. A second inheritance from his father was organizational skills, passion for meticulous attention to detail, methodical record keeping, and "scientific study"—surely his favorite phrase. The mature Bromley spoke sincerely when he stated, "I may be forgiven when I say that I have never met a nobler man [than my father]." The diary Bromley kept as a youth iterates and reiterates this sentiment: "Father grows dearer to me as the days pass. I am beginning to appreciate the life struggle he has made. I see the barriers he has climbed or smashed. I see his love. I would that he could live long enough for me to really show him how I feel." When Bromley graduated from the University of Southern California, Thomas wept through the commencement exercises. The following fall, Thomas, a USC trustee, attended the opening of the school. "Everybody was there but you," he wrote his son. "I did not care to remain." Yet Bromley was kidding himself when, in maturity, he claimed that "my father was more like a brother than a father to me." Bromley was too much in awe of his father to think of him as he did Tom and Willie. And no Cornish man of that era thought of his son as a brother. When the father ordered the son to "jump," he jumped, Bromley recorded.

Thomas was an ardent Republican. He deplored the famous "Social Creed of Methodism" promulgated by the 1908 General Conference. He decried the coming to Los Angeles of a prolabor newspaper. He spied on the after-hours behavior of his mine workers and fired those he caught boozing, womanizing, or gambling. He planted Pinkerton detectives to ferret out union organizers. When his employees threatened a strike, he beat them to the punch with a lockout, thanks to his informants stationed in the mine, saloon, and drug store. Thus he forced the laborers to come back to the mines on his terms. Managers were to manage, and workers to obey the owners and to work. Remembered Bromley: "My father was a large employer of labor and I, as a youngster, sat in Dad's office, and was actually thrilled when I saw him handle industrial disturbances with a firm hand. Strikes were broken and the organization of the working man was destroyed. . . . To me my father was a hero, that was the way I looked at things for a time."

Indeed Bromley did. Early in 1909, he began a speech before a young peoples' church group with the assertion, "Socialism is the biggest idiocy ever presented to the public." Perhaps with his father in mind, he continued, "Now listen, how is the wealth of the world to be divided? Do you think it is fair for a man, who has gone out into the mountains, endured hardships, privations and danger, and has finally discovered a mine or an oil field, tell me, do you think it is fair or right, for him to have to divide this equally with a loafer, who hangs around the saloon and does nothing for the benefit of himself, his family or his country? Of course it is not fair." Then came the peroration: "Vote for the strong old Republican Party . . . the party that stands for strongly organized companies, for advancement, and for the superiority of the United States over the entire world."

The point is not that Bromley remained a lifelong conservative. This third inheritance from his father was much more subtle than that: There remained in the mature Oxnam, as university president and bishop, a strong authoritarian streak. As his father before him, he saw himself as the "chief," and he expected the "Indians" to follow orders.

If Thomas was such an aggressive capitalist, how could Bromley have ended up in the world of religion instead of business? The obvious answer is that there was another half to Thomas's life: Methodism. When Thomas died in 1915, the London *Mining World and Engineering Record* wrote, "He was notable as an engineer, and even more notable as a man. He was a distinguished mining engineer and noted preacher." Bromley observed that the *Record* had the priorities reversed: his father was first a preacher and second an engineer.

Thomas never departed a mining camp without leaving a church behind. In his younger years he built them with his own hands, while later he raised or contributed the money to have them built. A well-worn prayer book testifies to its use at gravesides and sickrooms in mining camps. He supervised the largest Home Department on the Pacific coast, perhaps the largest in the world, numbering 1,030 members. As Thomas explained, "Our work is mostly with the shut-ins, those who are confined to their home through age or infirmity, also mothers that have the care of little children, also a large number go to the shut-outs, whose circumstances interfere with their free action on the Sabbath Day, such as nurses, physicians, drug clerks, telegraph operators, railway men, policemen and soldiers, and many others who are legitimately employed, but who can find the time to study the Word at home." Thomas also led prayer meetings in Los Angeles. The Oxnam home began its day, as well as each meal, with prayer. "I read the Bible, all of it, for a prize," Bromley recalled. "It was not a dusty book in our house." On the trip to Europe in 1906, father and son visited the historic Wesley Chapel, City Road, London. Looking up at the pulpit, Thomas whispered, "My boy, if ever a son of mine should be a minister and stand in that pulpit, I would count my highest ideal realized." Three years later, after meeting Bishop Edwin Holt Hughes as they left church, Thomas remarked to Bromley, "If by any chance you should ever be elected a bishop of the church, all the struggle of life would be abundantly worth while."

Bromley was a student at Boston University School of Theology when Thomas Oxnam's great heart failed in March 1915. After an emergency phone call summoned him from class, Bromley listened as his bride read him the brief telegram from his brother in California: "Father passed away quietly at 2:10 this morning. He spoke and called for you often. Our hearts love to you." Shortly thereafter, Bromley wrote a friend of his father's that Thomas had been "an exemplification of the Christ. When I decided to enter the ministry he was overjoyed." Years later he bitterly recalled that he had been too poor to travel to the burial service: "I could not go when father died, and some speak of no limitations in economic circumstances!"

Year after year Bromley noted in his diary either his father's birthday or the day of his death. He described Easter Sunday, 1915, as "the first my precious father has spent in the glory land. While I rejoice in the thought of father's joy [in heaven], my heart is sad and heavy today. Just when I could have been of service to dear old dad he passed on. He stood alone through all the storms. No guy ropes braced him. I hoped to be one, but the last storm was too great, and the mighty tower crashed to earth." The centennial of his father's birth he noted thusly: "Father seems very, very close today. Surely immortality must involve full understanding of the gratitude that is in the hearts of those who carry on after the loved ones have gone on." Whenever Bromley returned to California, he visited his father's grave.

A further but less apparent inheritance Bromley received from his father was Celtic blood. G. Bromley Oxnam may have been the most methodical, disciplined, and analytical of men, but there was also an intriguing sentimental and aesthetic side to his nature. This Celtic inheritance, if such was the source, manifested itself in a passionate love of painting, sculpture, books, music, drama, and the beauties of nature. It further manifested itself through a sentimentalism verging on the lachrymose.

Saint Augustine anticipated Freud when he cried, "Give me other mothers and I will give you another world." True, but the problem is that Mamie Oxnam remains a more shadowy figure than her husband. The shreds of evidence that survive indicate that Bromley deeply loved her. He dedicated his 1944 volume

Behold Thy Mother "to the memory of MY MOTHER." In it, he recalls how she read aloud and said prayers with the children at bedtime. Occasionally his diary mentions having had "a long talk with mother this evening." In 1914, Bromley wrote inside a book he had purchased as a gift for his mother, "This book was a mighty influence in the life of Wesley, and yet I feel that as in his case so in mine—the holy life of my mother was the real power that presented the serious call and pointed me to the life of service."

Although in later years a continent separated them, Bromley faithfully continued to write, visit, and send money to his mother. In the summer of 1942, they visited together some of the old homesteads in the now deserted mining towns of the West. "How wonderful it was to have those days together," he recorded. "I remember distinctly watching Mother as she walked away from the train [I was boarding]. I thought perhaps it might be the last time I would see her, and it was." Only a few months later in Los Angeles, Bishop Oxnam read from the beautiful Service for the Burial of the Dead; his mother wished that there be no eulogy.

Mamie Jobe Oxnam was laid to rest in the Inglewood cemetery alongside of her husband, Thomas, buried twenty-eight years before. At the gravesite, Bishop Oxnam felt a strange sense of peace steal over him. "For the first time, it seemed to me all was well. I realized that Mother and Father were reunited and she was to remain with him and it seemed that it was right," he explained. "I cannot write further about it now. But memory is precious, and my mind has run back through the thousands of little deeds that revealed her love."

Considering the deep piety of Mamie and Thomas Oxnam, it is unsurprising that Bromley was faithful in attendance at the First Methodist Church. On Monday evening, April 26, 1909, he attended a revival service. The preacher was quietly compelling. The next day the seventeen-year-old recorded what had transpired:

> Hugh Smith was preaching, and at last it was over. He asked for all those to come to the altar who thought themselves called to enter the ministry. I was standing by Ruth [Locke, daughter of the church's senior minister], and I said, "I ought to go, but I won't." She turned and earnestly

> said, "Brom if you think you ought to go, don't be afraid to go on." Now I stood and struggled, and at last decided, I think it was greatly through the effect of her brief words, but not till after he had finished his call for preachers, and missionaries and deaconesses, but down we came, and pressed on. On to congratulate those who had taken the stand. There I saw Ruth Fisher, her face radiant, truly her heart must have been filled with the love of God, and there was Clyde, Clyde Collision and Fred Eno, we pressed on, I saw Dr. Drodbeck, he said, "Bromley, I thought you would be among the first." And I said, "Doctor, I am going." I had reached the altar, and the first to congratulate me was Ruth [Fisher]. Then the entire congregation came forward and shook our hands. Oh! it was great. At last I went home and at the door I said good night to Ruth [Locke]. She pressed my hand and answered, "Bromley, I am so glad." Christianity has changed me, now I have sweet peace, a joy in it, all is just right, Christ has made life worth while to me.

Although the episode contains no burning bushes, blinding flashes on a Damascus road, or hearts strangely warmed at Aldersgate, it nevertheless proved decisive in the life of Bromley Oxnam.

CHAPTER 2

COLLEGE DAYS IN CALIFORNIA

The collegian Brom Oxnam, like his hero Teddy Roosevelt, was a combination of St. Vitus and St. Paul; and like not a few saints in their younger days, he was captivated by the baffling charms of young women. In 1909 he entered as a special student the University of Southern California, then a smallish, staunchly Methodist institution which had opened its doors in 1880. By transferring credits from the Los Angeles Business College, carrying extra hours, and attending summer sessions, he made up the three years of high school he had missed. In June 1913, he graduated from the College of Liberal Arts with a bachelor of arts degree. During these years the youth revealed many of the traits recognizable in the adult churchman, though sometimes in more muted, sometimes more intensified forms. They were good years. "I am thankful," he recorded on commencement day, "that everyone has been royal to me."

Academics consumed no more than a portion of Bromley's time. Occasionally, of course, he growled to his diary, "Grind!" or "Nothing doing! Work! Work! Work!" Or again, "Today has been extremely tedious. I had five straight recitations or lectures and am completely worn out." To be sure, he won As and Bs, making possible his election to Phi Beta Kappa in 1929. Still, it cannot be said that he was a passionate student single-mindedly devoted to study. Completing the minimal math and science requirements his freshman year, he rejoiced (surprisingly, considering his cast of mind), "Never again. Hooray." Unsurprisingly, foreign languages were not his forte.

The professors of history, economics, sociology, philosophy, and religion influenced him most. Tully Cleon Knoles was Bromley's mentor in ancient, medieval, English, and American history—such was the range of teaching in those ancient days. Horseman, minister, lecturer, and later president and chancellor of the College of the Pacific, Knoles closely followed his pupil's career. Rockwell D. Hunt taught Bromley economics, and the student was eternally grateful for the solid grounding received in Hunt's courses. (Years later Hunt laconically remarked to Oxnam, "You held some pretty strong opinions. On occasion it might be a matter of some doubt as to who was the teacher and who the student.") Bromley's primary professor of religion was John G. Hill. By welcoming rather than ridiculing the questions of his students, Hill encouraged free inquiry into Christianity's teachings. Bromley adored his philosophy professor, Harmon Hoose. On the eve of his departure for seminary study, Bromley asked the old professor what advice he would give a young man entering the ministry. "Scholarship, no mannerisms," came the reply. The next day at the train station Hoose amended the advice, "Scholarship, sympathy, no mannerisms."

Unquestionably the teacher who had the greatest impact on Bromley, perhaps because his courses involved field work for the municipality of Los Angeles, was Emory S. Bogardus, professor of sociology. When dedicating a book to Bogardus four decades later, Oxnam described him as an "inspiring teacher, distinguished sociologist and considerate friend." For his part, Bogardus reminisced, "He [Bromley] stood out in class. He always sat in the front row, always took copious notes and always asked many questions. He asked 'why' when others often asked 'what.' He often asked what could be done about a problem. Correct theory was important to him, but he always had the practical approach too." Bogardus introduced Bromley to Walter Rauschenbusch's *Christianity and the Social Crisis*, a volume that had a "profound influence" on him, as it did on so many socially minded Christians.

Bromley recorded the books he read during vacations. The lists are not impressively long nor free of saccharine stuff, such as Stratton-Porter's *The Girl of the Lumberlost* and Alcott's *Rose in Bloom*. Happily, however, scattered among the potboilers are weightier works by Shailer Mathews, John Dewey, and Goethe.

Although not at Eton, Bromley spent about as much time on the playing field as he did in the classroom. The cult of "muscular Christianity," then at its zany zenith in England and America, regarded the dumbbell and the Bible as almost equals in the development of Christian character. Athletically, he had two things going for him: a competitive spirit and a strong body. Weighing in at 190, he stood nearly six feet tall. He played as many as ten sets of tennis, his favorite sport, in a single day. He was a member of USC's team; indeed, one year he was the champion of Southern California and Arizona. He won the school's "gentlemen's" championship three consecutive years. He and another student occasionally played teams of professors, to whom they rarely lost. "The professors were afraid to play us today," he good-naturedly remarked. To his credit, Bromley never gloated when he won or whined when he lost. Yet he was hard on himself when he failed to perform up to his capabilities. "Played tennis this afternoon. Played rotten and felt rotten," he confided. Or again, "Munro and I were beaten. . . . We were both so rotten that I was ashamed of myself." Bromley enjoyed tennis as a social activity as well as a sport. In 1911, he was president of the Gentlemen's Tennis Club. He relished mixed doubles, especially if the girls were pretty. "Miss Marion Smith, incidentally a stunning beauty, and I beat Jack Malcom and Miss Nina Chadwick 6-3, 3-6, 6-2, 6-1. I enjoyed it so much," he wrote.

Bromley's prowess was not confined to the tennis courts; he played on the baseball team as a junior and football squad as a senior. Looking back, he decided his greatest thrill as a college athlete had come as a member of the rugby team: USC almost played an Australian squad to a standstill. His aggressiveness is obvious in a student paper story describing a contest between freshmen and sophomores for control of the colors atop a greased pole:

> Oxnam, sophomore captain, was the bulldog of the day. Time and again he hauled down an aspiring freshman from the pole who essayed to stray a trifle too far from terra firma, and several times, charging with lowered head into three or four freshmen trying to tie up a sophomore, he would bowl them over, rescue his classmate and rush back to scrape off a few barnacles off the pole. The sophomores' downfall began when about a dozen freshies succeeded in tying Oxnam and carrying him off the field.

Bromley was a big man on campus, a status he ran hard to achieve. At USC he exhibited the drive, energy, and responsibility that distinguished him in later life. By harnessing talent and ambition in the service of his school, Bromley was able to slake his thirst for public recognition without upsetting his parents' demand that he be selfless. As a sophomore he was class president. That year he also served as secretary of the YMCA, and for the next two years he supervised the group's religious work. As a junior he was elected class secretary, sergeant at arms, vice-president of the Trojan student body, and a member of the school's executive committee. He acted in dramatic productions. On one occasion, in the opinion of a theater critic, he made "a great success out of a difficult role." He joined the staffs of two student publications, *El Rodeo* and *The University Courier*, becoming associate editor of the latter during his senior year. He also worked as news editor of still a third paper, *The Daily Southern California*. "Considerable talk is going on at school over my article. I hope it accomplished what I am aiming at," he remarked concerning his censure of immorality on campus. As a member of Phi Alpha Theta, the International History Honor Society, he was pleased to report that the new initiates were "clean boys with high ideals." Groups such as the Civic and Aristotelian Clubs benefited from his participation. He was a "Yell" leader his senior year.

When arguing for the varsity debating team, he sometimes won a debate by making the worse appear the better reason, he later confessed. In a debate with Pomona, he literally shredded the opponent's argument in favor of a California state income tax. Said a reporter covering the debate, "Again, Mr. Oxnam came back in the rebuttal and showed the audience a complete chart of the contentions of the affirmative. He had each argument on a separate card and as he took them up showing that they were of no avail, he tore the card to pieces and put it in his pocket." When trying out for the team, he eloquently defended a randomly selected position, quoting many statistics and impressive facts. Upon hearing of the coaching professor's immediate invitation to join the team, he guiltily confessed that he had fabricated all the material and did not deserve a place. "I know," the professor dryly replied, "but anyone who can lie like that belongs on our team."

Bromley may have played the sophist in debates, but it is clear that his support of Teddy Roosevelt and the Progressive party in 1912 was sincere. As early as 1910, his praise of Gifford Pinchot's Insurgency Movement and Roosevelt's battle for control of the GOP indicated that he was breaking with his father's rock-ribbed Republicanism. The "Bull Moose" convention of 1912 filled him with excitement: "Thank God!, rotten politics is going. May Roosevelt win and right prevail," he exploded. In the California state elections in September he cast his first vote: straight Progressive. By the time of the national elections in November, he had become chairman of the campus Progressive League, which carried the party's platform to the students. Of course Roosevelt lost to Woodrow Wilson nationally, but with the help of Bromley's bully efforts, Rossevelt beat Wilson by a two-to-one margin on the USC campus. Yet Bromley's role ought not to be overemphasized. The Progressives won the Sunshine State as a whole, perhaps in part because its governor, Hiram Johnson, was Roosevelt's running mate.

In that year Bromley suffered a defeat of his own in his bid for election to the presidency of the Trojan student body. Vastly disappointed, he bitterly acknowledged that "Frances St. John and her machine worked beautifully," while consoling himself with the fact that he had not tried to "use political methods to win." Within months he was counting his blessings. Freedom from presidential responsibilities left him time for football ("an experience worth more than the presidency"), editing the student newspaper, and above all for expanded religious leadership at the First Methodist Church.

Was all this intense activity both a rational method of attacking anxieties and an irrational method of escaping them, to borrow Walter Houghton's insight into the Victorian mind?

Perhaps. It comes as no surprise that Bromley's crammed agenda caused even his deep reservoirs of energy occasionally to run dry. His diary is dotted with revealing entries: "I felt too tired to go to school this morning so I remained home"; "Never have I been so completely worn out before." Accompanying these periods of physical exhaustion were moments of emotional drain. Again the diaries speak: "I am very, very blue"; "I am worn with worry"; "I have been down in the dumps all day"; "I feel like ———— tonight"; "I have been wondering a great deal of late as to: 'What is the use.'" One August day in 1912 while at Gold Mountain, he mused with spooky prescience: "I am feeling somewhat better. This is a good place to break down nervousness. I must take thinking easier when I go back. *I have fifty years yet* and must be in shape for them. Long walks, sketching, etc.— are the daily programmes" (emphasis added).

Gold Mountain was the mine where Thomas Oxnam's ore was dug and milled into bullion. During his semesters at USC, Bromley continued to work for his father in Los Angeles as an accountant. In the summertime he labored manually at the mine. "I shovelled and carried five tons of ore into 92 sacks. I feel all in this afternoon," he recorded one August day. After a "hard and wearing" July day, he noted "I helped bring down the plates from the mill today. Lifting 24-150# plates five times in fifteen minutes is hard." At Gold Mountain he also hunted, swam, hiked, cut and split wood, and rode a nag named Maud. Little wonder his muscles were as hard as tungsten.

As if he were not already sufficiently challenged during his senior year, Bromley worked as a part-time, unpaid inspector for the Los Angeles City Housing Commission. This labor of love—and it was precisely that—grew out of Professor Bogardus' sociology classes. Bromley's responsibilities were to study slum housing and juvenile delinquency in Mexican-American East Los Angeles. After an inspection of one area east of Alameda, he vowed, "Someday I am going to help lead the church against the slums, their causes, etc. and smash them forever. If our people would talk less and study more, the task would be easy." Taking responsibility for a group of youngsters, he earnestly recorded that while he did not know what he was getting into, "All I know is that it is really service and that, God helping me, I'll make those people better." And after a day with "my boys" he exulted, "I feel good." If there is a tone of mugwumpery in some of his diary entries, others convey a real sense of compassion. For example:

> At the house court, I dropped into the room of a family—the only room—A glass was upon an upturned cracker box and in it were three or four poppies. I admired them and asked the boy where he got them. He told me his teacher had given them to him. We talked about flowers for a little while. I asked him if he loved them. He said "Yes. I love them but no one ever gave me any. This is the first bunch I ever got." There was a boy with an artist's soul. But he was but a Mexican boy—fit for street work and nothing more—at least so some say. I asked the youngster if he knew who made the flowers so pretty. He said "No," I asked him if he had ever heard of God. He replied, "No, what is God?" The child is twelve-years old and in our public schools. What a chance the schools are losing in not training the children in religion. Surely no one can object to teaching a child that God makes the flowers because he loves us and wants us to enjoy them.

Only a cynic would lampoon Bromley for forming an order for slum kids named "King Arthur and His Knights of the Round Table." All boys need heroes, Bromley understood, and what nobler model than Arthur? To be a "knight" the boys pledged to honor the following rules:

1. We will always do right because it is right.
2. We will always be kind to girls and ladies.
3. We will not fight except for what is right but when we fight we will never give up.
4. We will not lie. No man can do right and lie.
5. We will keep our body and our clothes clean.
6. We will try to keep our houses clean. Dirty houses make people sick.
7. We will love each other.

Young Bromley appears a strange amalgam of Jane Addams at Hull House and Frank Merriwell at Yale. A touch of Casanova makes the portrait more curious—providing one can imagine that roguish womanizer in the innocent, pious, Victorian youth. Bromley liked girls and girls liked him. Even in church young ladies flocked to sit next to him, much to his pleasure. He partied: "I cut up something fierce"; "I was too witty I fear"; "I escorted Florence Louise Hurt. We were simply full of college spirit and showed it." Of course, cutting up at USC in those days carried no licentious connotations. Furthermore, "college spirit" had nothing to do with alcohol as far as Bromley was concerned.

To the editors of *Current Opinion*, 1913 was "Sex O'Clock in America," and, especially in the East, boozing on college campuses antedated the Prohibition Era's sheiks and shebas, lounge lizards and flappers with their hip flasks. Nevertheless, it is absolutely certain that G. Bromley Oxnam remained a virgin until marriage and in his entire life never smoked or drank. A "good time" at a beach party under the stars involved singing the grand old hymns: "As the sun set we sang 'Abide with Me.' Later with the waves running high we joined in 'Jesus Savior Pilot Me.'"

Indeed, young Bromley was rather priggish, a characteristic that disappeared with maturity. For example, he reported having an "awful time" on a double date keeping the other couple from spooning. As for his own date's armorous suggestions, "I was good and I hope I said a few things which will help the foolish little girl." On another occasion when a "debauched" pal was "about to go on another tear," Bromley lectured him "on morals and I believe it did him some good." "The sight of girls playing men's parts with their limbs exposed above their knees does not seem quite right to me," was his response to the play *The Maid of Orleans*. After viewing a smartly dressed woman wearing the latest fashions from Paris, he admonished: "Such dressing can only arouse the baser passion in men. I could look at a nude woman, and think of her as an expression of God's beauty, but to look upon a woman who tantalizes you with her charms as this one did can only serve to lower her in my estimation and arouse that which I strive to keep down." When buying a doll for a party, he blushed with embarrassment when the sales girl asked if he wanted the doll dressed or undressed.

Still, the wart of priggishness was never the whole toad. He chuckled when a preacher's warning that the road to hell is lined with women and drink elicited from a reprobate the response, "Where O Death is thy sting?" He laughed too, at the limerick:

There was a young lady of Siam,
Who said to her lover, now Priam,

You may kiss me, of course,
Though you have to use force
But God knows you are stronger than I am.

Girls! First came Ruth Locke, the preacher's daughter, whom Bromley soon found boring and booted. "I shall be friendly and polite [to Ruth] but nothing more," he decided. Next came Celeste, who accompanied him to a concert. "She looked very beautiful and all eyes followed her down the aisle. She looked stunning and Ruth Locke looked stunned." Celeste spent several weeks with Bromley and his family at Gold Mountain. Nature took her course. They held hands, she rested her head on his shoulder, he slipped his arm around her waist, and they talked of love. One evening after Celeste cried, "I love you, I love you!" Bromley confided to his diary, "No pen can describe the love and passion and joy which passed through my body and soul as I held her close. I did not kiss her. I told her I would not till the day she would promise to be my wife." The notes they exchanged revealing their feelings for each other they quickly destroyed because his mother "smelled the smoke." Upon her return to Los Angeles loneliness changed the boy's life from "Heaven to Hell." (Reexamining his "steamy" diary entries a year later, Bromley rather archly rationalized: "After reading over this childish foolishness, I remember definitely the cause of it all. After holding Celeste's hand, etc., paying her attention and being in reality forced into her company, I felt duty bound to speak as I did. There was nothing but a reciprocal passion caused by constant association, actually it was not love." The cad!)

With time, Celeste receded from Bromley's heart, making room for others, in turn, to enter it. Ella: "I have been thinking of Ella all day. I often wonder what power she has over me. I cannot forget her." Alice: "I was forcibly struck by Miss Alice Russell's beauty tonight. She was simply charming, her face radiant with a bewitching smile which I see yet." Blanche: "She is the same care free [sic], witty, pouty and laughing girl. We had a jolly time talking of the old days." Hazel: "I had intended to write a whole page about Hazel, but I won't, just this. She is the most beautiful, most admirable girl I have ever met." Glenna: "Miss Long is a rather charming girl, dark brown hair, blue eyes, and red, red lips. She has a pretty figure." Another Hazel: "Tis hard to express perfect beauty and make it real. One who has a perfect figure, beauty and grace, winning features, seemingly a sweet dispositioned character. . . . She dresses well, her clothes fit her perfect figure like a glove." Ruth Mickod: "Dark complexioned, beautiful, big black eyes, a pretty figure, extremely witty and above all common-sensed." After burning his old love letters, "out of them all Kitty McNickol's, alone, were saved. She has such a glowing style." One shudders to think the fate these girls might have suffered had it been a less innocent age, had Bromley's moral code been less stern, had he dared risk his ministerial career by becoming a breaker of girls' reputations, or had he never met Ruth Fisher. The point to be made is that until his death the scientific realist side to Oxnam's nature was always tempered by an almost moony romanticism.

Bromley had known Ruth Fisher for years, since both the Fisher and Oxnam families were prominent members of the First Methodist Church. On that April day in 1909 when he had pledged his life to Christ she had been the first to congratulate him; on that same day she had given her life to foreign missions. As things turned out, love caused her to break her pledge. That same year, Bromley later reported in *A Testament of Faith,* he fell in love with Ruth Fisher and never fell out again. But she resisted his persistent proposals of marriage. While Bromley momentarily may have lost his heart to some of the other girls whom he dated in the interim, his diary attests that Ruth was never long absent from his thoughts.

On May 1, 1889, Ruth had become the third child of Walter Harrison Fisher and Elizabeth Holmes Fisher. The Fishers had traveled westward from Illinois, settling first in the Dakotas. Mrs. Fisher, the dominant figure in the marriage, was determined to carry on to California whether her husband joined her or not. Rather than to see her strike out on her own, Mr. Fisher followed his wife. At her insistence he also changed his middle name from Harry, which she detested, to Harrison. Mr. Fisher dealt with insurance and real estate, until he made his fortune when oil was discovered on his San Pedro properties. The Fishers' plush home on Wilshire Boulevard boasted a conservatory, palm garden, and tennis court. Mrs. Fisher was a major benefactor of the University of Southern California, to which she presented the Little Chapel of Silence. She also built the Fisher Gallery of Fine Art and filled it with her personal collection of paintings by European and nineteenth-century American artists. A woman of uncommon ability, in 1936 she became the first female to serve on USC's Board of Trustees. Not surprisingly, the politically conservative Fishers supported the GOP.

Aside from the revival reference, Ruth's name first appears in Bromley's diary on January 19, 1910: "Every time I see her I think she is more beautiful than the last time. I wish she were two years younger." By late February he could record, "Ruth and I talked on, and in a joshing way still I said, 'Ruth, I love you.' She replied, 'And I love you, too, Bromley.' After more cutting up about rings and engagements in general, we strolled down to Jakes's and eat [sic] some 'Lovers Delights.' I suppose it was all a josh, although I really meant it. I wonder what will come out of it." Bromley continued to record his "dandy times" with that "noble girl." Unfortunately, Ruth's parents were not keen on the courtship, perhaps because of Bromley's burgeoning Progressivism and limited wealth. Besides, he was two years her junior. After they had expressed their reservations to him, he noted, "Dear Lord: Go to it! Amen. . . . I wish I could write what I think of the Fishers."

By early 1912, the romance had quickened; for the first time the diary speaks of kissing and cuddling. "I love her more and more!" But suddenly Ruth cooled things. "Somehow I feel I am losing her," Bromley groaned. "It is tearing me to pieces. . . . I cannot make it out. . . . Blast girls!" Then Ruth thawed. They made up. "We sat in the big old rocker. I held her on my lap. She laid her head on my shoulder and rested. Once when she kissed me she put her arm around my neck and held my lips to hers and there lip to lip we stayed minute after minute. Oh God, I was happy." Two weeks later the bottom dropped out. "This is a day I wish had never been. I have lost Ruth. . . . I almost hate all women. I would but for Lois and mother. . . . Puzzle! Puzzle! That is all women are." In early November Bromley became resigned that the separation was permanent. "I will never ask her to marry me again. It is finished. My mind is made up." Or was it? On the seventeenth, as they walked home from an Epworth League meeting they stopped by the waterfalls in Westlake Park. Bromley proposed for the umpteenth time. This time Ruth caved in. "I will," she replied. Bromley fairly jumped for joy. "Let's sing the doxology," he wrote. After calming down, he added, "I love Ruth. I thought I should never win her. I did all in my power. I was truly English in it. I never gave up till I was sure it was useless and then I felt I would stay with it. Right then she came to me. She is to be my bride. She has made me a man, she has fitted me for the ministry."

During the engagement, the couple's love deepened. One evening in the Fisher library they talked of their love for one another and of God's love. They knelt in prayer and consecrated their lives to him. Bromley turned to her and said, "From God to you, dearest." Kissing her, he continued, "And not very far, either, sweetheart. Praise God!" Nor were the spiritual and physical aspects of their love distant. Clearly Bromley Oxnam was a young man caught up in the passions of a deep love and longing in these days.

One might think school activities, sports, classes, dating, and working for his father and the city of Los Angeles would have precluded any serious commitment to the church. Hardly! Even before entering USC he had pledged his life to Christ, and his four years there reinforced his resolution. On the evening of September 2, 1912, he was examined by the Quarterly Conference, First Methodist Church, and granted a local preacher's license. Since his father was a conference member, Bromley was not questioned too closely in regard to doctrine. "Thank God," he sighed. "I hate forms and word disputes on belief." Dr. Locke announced that his "great ambition" was one day for Bromley to preach in his church. Five months later, Bromley delivered his first sermon in the Methodist Church of Rancho. His decision to preach on "Jesus Christ and the White Slave Traffic" was unfortunate, inasmuch as 80 percent of the congregation turned out to be women and children. He arranged to take the Annual Conference examinations in June, confidently predicting, "I shall get off very easy." His hunch proved correct: He passed without a hitch on August 16. The following month he entered Boston University School of Theology. On October 3, his home church recommended him to the Southern California Annual Conference, and according to the usual procedure, he was received on trial. Obviously, these formal steps do not reveal the full story of Bromley's spiritual quest.

During the decade misnamed the Gay Nineties, Anglican Bishop Hugh Miller Thompson told a college audience that theirs was "the most serious and sadly earnest age that the earth ever saw. We have none of the frivolous unbelief or frivolous skepticism of the last century," Thompson continued. "Where doubt exists in the nineteenth century it is deeply and profoundly earnest." Thousands of young people of that era struggled with doubts so severe that they led to suicidal depressions. Some retreated to the secure fortress of fundamentalism; some, perhaps sadly but proudly, joined the growing army of nontheistic humanists and scientific naturalists; and some (in William Hutchison's marvelous imagery), "cheered as the relief column of liberal theology, bagpipes skirling, marched to the rescue of the threatened Christian regiment."

Bromley seems to have escaped any shattering crisis of faith. His diary mentions turmoil and struggle, to be sure: "My mind has been on the scene of a revolution," he recorded in August 1913. "Ideas have been warring." But the war was not fought over the presence of God; for him God's reality never dimmed. Rather the conflict in his mind was over how best to serve the Lord: through politics, social work, or foreign missions? In the end, he resolved never to "waver from the social point of view." He would become a minister, a goal requiring "intensive study of the nature of God and the methods, teachings, and life of Jesus Christ." Two matters disturbed his religious idealism. First, he hated fire-and-brimstone sermons of intimidation; he disliked Dr. Locke's sermonic forays into the subject of damnation. "Heard a rotten sermon on 'A Request from Hell.' It sounded like it," he complained. Second, local church politics filled him with disgust: "I attended the preachers meeting and left broken up. There were God's representatives—trifling over petty things, calling each other names, whispering while men were talking, forgetting Christ."

Nevertheless, on Sundays, First Methodist Church became the focal point of Bromley's life. First came morning prayer, then Sunday School, the main service, afternoon activities, and finally evening services and meetings. He was present at the church on weekdays as well. As early as 1909 he was secretary and treasurer of the Intermediate Department of the Epworth League of California. The following year he became its president, with Ruth winning the vice-presidency. He held this position until departing for Boston. He exulted after his farewell address to the hundred members, "God gave me strength and power over them. . . . Oh how they listened. . . . Such beautiful and sincere words. I shall not forget my last league." He remarked of his involvement in the YMCA that it was inspirational "to hear college men pray and testify." Bromley also served as a delegate to such bodies as the Laymen's Missionary Convention.

The Baraca City Union, however, was the object of most of his religious fervor. This group of about 150 young unmarried men met on Sundays in the First Methodist Church. For two years, 1912–13, Bromley provided energetic and stimulating leadership. He reorganized the class, taking pains to make the members "feel they were doing it and the plans were their own." Not surprisingly, his emphasis was on "scientific social study," especially the evils of prostitution, a subject he had studied firsthand in police stations and red-light districts—as did so many other genteel reformers in the Progressive Era. Bromley's pastor, Charles Edward Locke, for instance, inveighed against prostitution in his book *White Slavery in Los Angeles*.

"I will make a success" of the Union, Bromley vowed early in 1912. And he did. In preparing for these meetings, Bromley established the speaking practices he would follow for the rest of his career: intense preparation, thinking the subject through without conscious memorization, delivery without notes. He quickly became aware of his power to move audiences. "I held the men just where I wanted them," he exclaimed on one instance. On another, "Today's lesson on 'Love' was the best I have ever done." Similarly, the Epworth farewell address was a triumph: "As I began to speak, a peculiar power came over me. I was master." When he called for a purer inner life, "the men broke down. Strong men wept. Oh it was wonderful." After the service "men with tears streaming down their faces said good bye." Hubris, of course, takes many forms, but perhaps few as perilous to the soul's salvation as the consciousness of the ability to captivate audiences through the eloquence of one's voice. Throughout his life, even after he no longer needed public speaking fees, even after the onset of Parkinson's, Oxnam drove himself on the lecture circuit. One suspects mixed motives, both conscious and unconscious, impelled him. But then, the same thing might be said of Emerson or William James or Reinhold Niebuhr.

Shortly before Oxnam entered theological training, First Methodist Church purchased property in East Los Angeles on which to establish a Methodist center for the heavily Mexican-American lower class. Bromley had been pressing the project for two years. During the banquet at which the purchase was announced, he recorded, someone shouted, " 'the Church should be for Bromley.' Oh! God may I burn up my life—bringing the gospel to the men and women—the real men and women of America." Thus was the seed of the Church of All Nations planted.

The few additional observations to be made about this USC student are elaborations on aspects of his personality already alluded to. The Celtic lyrical side to his nature manifested itself in a love of music. The singing of Madam Schumann-Heinck, "more like the music of a great organ than a human being," simply enraptured him. He "did not think the angels will sing more beautifully." A singer of Scottish ballads filled him with sweet plaintiveness. After hearing a concert pianist, he confessed, "I have always believed that God is good, but tonight, when I see the great gift which God has given her, and which we are privileged to hear, I know it." Rhapsodies on the glory of nature also lace his diaries. "The view [from Mt. Washington] is very, very beautiful. Far, far away lies the placid Pacific, with her fair Catalina on her bosom. Nearer are the hills of purple, of grey, of brown and of green. Over to the south, a little east, are the smoky offerings of eastern Los Angeles. To the north is California's garden spot, Pasadena. Truly it is a beautiful view." The diaries are illustrated with skillful sketches in pen.

Bromley exhibited other hints of thoughtfulness and sensitivity. He walked the beach and prayed for strength to reach his ideals. He sat on the ocean wharf with three friends talking for hours of the deepest subjects. "I love to do that." He strolled the streets of downtown Los Angeles "just to study faces." He listened to the anarchist Emma Goldman speak and admired her. And however mature Bromley may have been in some respects, when his folks were away he got mighty "tired of batching."

Bromley also exhibited less admirable characteristics, albeit universal and human ones. He thrived on popularity. "With apologies to Tennyson I might say, Friends to the right of me, friends to the left of me." And he flushed with pride when a girlfriend observed on the opening day of school, "Brom, everybody seems to be falling on your neck, they are so glad to see you." Compliments, especially those coming from an adult such as Bishop Hughes, made his day, especially if others overheard them. "When a person makes such a [flattering] statement without a motive," he told himself, "it makes me feel pleased and I do not think it hurts me but rather makes me work hard to live up to my reputation."

All of this is scarcely reprehensible in a young man. A trifle more troubling are the suggestions of self-pity: "It seems that the man who will & can work is worked to death." Less flattering still are the suggestions of a taste for power: "I felt I could make the people follow me if I would. The first factor is to get them to believe in you. Their individualities must be wedded into one great individuality and that must be subservient to your personality." On another occasion he wrote, "I spoke at the banquet tonight. I felt a sweet power. It was great!" "How odd it seems that the plans I evolve in the nighttime, when others sleep, form themselves into words that go into other minds and materialize," he wondered.

Also disquieting are Bromley's manifestations of relentless competitiveness: "I climbed Mt. Wilson tonight. I wanted to see if Nature and her grandeur could bring me closer to God. I found, though, that there is little time to think of deity when you are doing strenuous mountain climbing. My nature makes me always try to be first. I was first up the mountain and was very, very tired." In a flash of introspection he then added, "I wonder if the desire to win is a selfish one." Yet the urge to be best had its beneficial side as well. To achieve his goals in life Bromley made repeated solemn promises to himself and his Maker never to let a bad habit get the better of him; to speak only good; to shut out evil words; to view beauty rather than ugliness; to exalt that which is right; to fight that which is wrong. He reinforced one such renewal of vows by reading the sermons of Savonorola!

At age seventeen, Bromley had his fortune told: "I am to live til I am 76, am strong willed, self-confident, will never lose and some day will be on top." Save for a slight error in the age, the soothsayer was right on target. In truth, many of young Bromley's attributes are clearly discernible in Bishop Oxnam.

CHAPTER 3

SEMINARY DAYS IN MASSACHUSETTS

On August 26, 1913, Bromley boarded a train bound for Boston to enter American Methodism's oldest institution of training for the ministry, Boston University School of Theology. Bromley fought hard to control his emotions as he parted with his mother, father, Lois, Willie, and Ruth. While the train chugged north to Vancouver and east through the Canadian Rockies, he poured his feelings into his diary: "I have gone out into the world. I must be master of what comes to me from now on. God helping me, I shall rule my little kingdom as He would have His ruled." He promptly violated his vow, first by ducking a pullman porter to avoid giving him a tip and second by rather sanctimoniously shining his flashlight on a couple in a darkened corner of the station to put an end to their kissing.

Bromley chose to study at BU School of Theology because he considered it Methodism's premier seminary. He admired the school's contributions to the Church, its emphasis on the social aspects of Christianity, the Old Testament scholarship of Hinckley G. Mitchell, and the tradition of liberalism associated with Borden Parker Bowne's philosophical idealism, Personalism. By 1913, however, Bowne had died and Mitchell had departed.

To attempt a full survey of Bromley's course of study would entail a history of early twentieth-century BU School of Theology. Consequently, only a few observations will be made. It comes as no surprise that Bromley attended classes faithfully, kept copious notes in shorthand, studied hard, earned solid though not superlative grades, and graduated cum laude. His thirty-one-page Bachelor of Sacred Theology (STB) thesis on the life of Father Junipero Serra is neither distinguished nor rigorously graded. Luckily for Bromley, Hebrew was dropped as a requirement in 1913–14. He passed the Greek exam only because he recognized the biblical passage to be translated as one he had memorized. He knew almost no Latin.

Bromley and his classmates found systematic theology under "Uncle Henry" Sheldon so dreary that they sought to overcome their boredom by publishing a newspaper during the class hour. Although uninspiring, former president William Warren's course on non-Christian religions revealed "many unknown treasures," for which Bromley was grateful. Dean Lauress Birney's introduction to the life and teachings of Jesus was rewarding, and in this course he eagerly read the works of the great German church historian Adolf von Harnack. Bromley praised Professor Albert C. Knudsen's Old Testament and philosophy classes for continuing and deepening the Personalistic persuasion of Bowne. "I firmly believe," Oxnam predicted, "that he will soon have as great a reputation as a teacher as did Borden P. Bowne. He lectured on Hosea today, and truly his wonderful scholarship overpowers one." All his students worship him, Bromley observed.

Bromley leaped at the chance to work with Professor Harry F. Ward, who came to BUST in 1914 to head the new Department of Social Service. Thinking to praise Dr. Ward, Bromley noted that he "is absolutely uncompromising with unrighteousness no matter where it is. I think that is why I like him so much."

Later their friendship withered, because, according to Oxnam, Ward became an obdurate Leftist doctrinaire. But in 1913–14 Bromley found Ward not only prophetic, he also served as the professor's part-time secretary and babysitter. Bromley entertained the Ward children by drawing pictures. One fascinated son, Lynd, picked up a pen and began drawing too. In time he became a renowned illustrator.

As a student, Bromley's heart was aflame with Ward's social activism. He resented Methodist bishops protected by tenure and content in their conservatism. "I am coming to believe that our episcopacy is something like a cold-water, Methodist sprinkling pot, putting out the fire of movements that follow the very action of Wesley himself," Bromley brooded.

In contrast to his undergraduate days, Bromley now read many weighty authors outside the classroom, including Adam Smith and Marx. "People seeing me reading *Das Kapital* say to themselves, 'Another rabid socialist,' " he mused. "I smile and think of the thousands of ignorant who will not give everything fair and honest study. Any man who can so influence the world is worthy of study whether you believe his teachings or not." Bromley also began to memorize poetry daily so that in time he would be "quite conversant with the sweet thinkers." And when noted individuals lectured in Boston, he not only attended but took notes. Rauschenbusch's Harvard sermon, the grandest he had ever heard, touched him deeply.

Bromley was not uncritical of his fellow students, particularly those who were slothful, immature, or profligate. But the majority he liked, and he joyfully accepted membership in a "secret, select" fraternity composed of sound scholars of "general ability" as men. Walter John Sherman, a fellow student, became and remained Bromley's dearest friend until his death in 1942. Another seminarian, Henry Hitt Crane, was also a close companion.

The persuasions of Oxnam the seminarian anticipate those of Oxnam the bishop, although not in every respect and emphasis. Dogma he doubted: "I have not said the Apostles' Creed for four years, because I did not believe in it. . . . I am going to take that Creed, sentence by sentence and try to write what I believe under each sentence." Ritual he resented. After attending a communion service at First Methodist Church he grumbled, "I hate ritual, formalism. Were it not for the command of the Master . . . I would be tempted to leave the whole business from my future services." He welcomed the winds of the New Theology: "We want a new theology for the old religion. I hope it comes soon." He admitted to being "pretty much of a heretic these days," but the fact that if he lived "long enough I know I won't have to change to be orthodox," consoled him. Although he was enough of a scholar to consider pursuing a Ph.D. in history to prepare for a teaching career, always the needle of his internal compass swung back in the direction of religion.

On Palm Sunday, 1914, Bromley attended High Mass at the Catholic cathedral. His response suggests that the seed of his later reservations about Rome was already planted. He found the worshipers ignorant in appearance and the service itself "repulsive." Cardinal O'Connell sat upon a throne waving a fat arm, his face "the coarsest of the coarse. He has brutal and debased features and I doubt not that he is a typical booze fighter." In sum, "it seems as if intelligent, twentieth century manhood had stepped back into the middle ages, with all its nonsense and ritual. God was far, oh so far away."

Church services often left Bromley unmoved. A consecration service conducted by Dean Birney he likened to digging a hole in water. "I was not helped, I had no feeling of joy—not until I was going out and shook hands with a man. Oh the personal touch, man to man. God knows I can make men better that way. I think men can be better won on their feet than on their knees." A revival service forced him to admit that he had never experienced a baptism of power such as described by the revivalists. His fervor was of a different sort: "Unless I am out serving my life is not responsive. I must give out, I must. During the days of intense strain, strain of preparing to speak, of making men better, of planning, planning all the time, I am happy and I feel I am God's man. For that matter I feel it always, but somehow I am not at home in the religious atmosphere here." Hearing Episcopal Bishop William Lawrence preach at Old North Church, his thoughts turned from the irrelevant sermon to the window view of the North End tenements which he hoped one day to clean up. Bromley also continued to speculate, as he had as an undergraduate, about the secret of achieving power over people. Probably with himself in mind, he wrote, "The great mysterious character, the character that loves everyone and loves them really, yet always has a quiet, irresistible, unknown way of accomplishing—that is the man who is power."

Only two bits of evidence indicate the nature of Bromley's own student preaching. One is the manuscript of a sermon delivered December 9, 1915, explaining the differences between the major radical movements. It concludes,

> The social servant must know these folk, and knowing I am frank to say that sooner or later he will come to see that within the heart of the socialists, the communists, the anarchists, the syndicalists, all of them will be found a love for our brother man, closely akin to the love that prompted a young man to say "Father forgive them, for they know not what they do." He will see that these men, perhaps within a narrower vision, perhaps not, are impelled by the same love that drove the man of Galilee to the Cross.

The other bit of evidence is his recollection of his last sermon preached in Boston, during which his description of the massacre of miners in Ludlow, Colorado, caused a factory owner in the congregation to cry, "That sermon was a disgrace to any Church of God."

Although his tuition was only $150, Bromley had to scramble to make ends meet. In addition to serving as Dr. Ward's part-time secretary, he worked as a stenographer for Bishop John W. Hamilton and a noted surgeon named Kepler. To earn his board, he donned a white coat and bussed tables at Marston's Restaurant, feeling, he recorded, as self-conscious as an artist's model posing for the first time in the nude. Perhaps because of his commanding presence he quickly became a bouncer. Mr. Marston explained to him that no one would dare leave without paying his bill with him standing at the doorway.

Partly for money, partly for experience, and partly out of altruism, Bromley held other jobs. He worked for the Morgan Memorial Co-operative Industries in Boston, the first of the famous "Goodwill Industries." He led a men's Bible study group at the Roxbury YMCA, whose working class members he held in esteem and affection. He clerked at the Huntington Avenue Y and performed a survey of the homes of young delinquents for the Children's Welfare League of Roxbury. The labor closest to his heart, however, was with a group of Brookline youngsters, aged twelve to fifteen. Most of the boys had been in jail and some were still on parole. Because of their intense group loyalty, he found these Irish youngsters harder to discipline than the Mexican kids in Los Angeles had been. But Bromley devoted his considerable talents to the task. In the end, after expelling a few of the most recalcitrant youths, he had the club well in hand. At the last meeting he expressed the hope that he had helped the boys "to a little higher level in the long march of life to come."

If Bromley had doubts about church affairs in Boston, he had none whatsoever about the city's cultural offerings. The historic sites absorbed him. He reveled in the art museums. After attending his first Boston Symphony he exalted, "Music still sings of God." After seeing the legendary Forbes-Robinson in *Hamlet*, Bromley confessed how dumb he had been in never before permitting himself to attend a play. Art, music, the theater, and even picture shows remained lifelong loves. But this statement does not sound like the adult Oxnam: "Every day I walk through the crowds. I love to do it. I love to be with people, to bump up against them."

Bromley's first year at BU School of Theology was not without its share of loneliness. Boston was a long way from Los Angeles. His moody roommate and the lingering New England snow were no help in buoying his spirits. He worried constantly about the health of his parents and about his family's financial misfortunes, which forced Lois to drop out of USC. "Absence makes the heart grow fonder" may be a banality, but it happens to be true in Bromley's case. His diaries overflow with *Te Deums* to his family (although his older brother Tom is mentioned less frequently and less effusively than the other members). For example, on Thanksgiving Day, 1913, he wrote:

> As I look back and think of what I owe my family, it seems as though I look out over the ocean, as far as I can see is the mighty water, but I know that on and on it extends. My father has sacrificed and lived Christlike. My mother has lived the Christ. No one can write what they have done. I know today and today I can feel it all. Then my Sister. Who has had such a sister. Her mind is brilliant, her love is her very life. And my brothers, Tom who loves me deep down in his soul, and Willie whom I have loved since the day he was born. What a shout of Thanksgiving I should utter.

If Bromley's family was never far from his thoughts, neither was his fiancée. Ruth wrote to him faithfully, once admonishing him to remember that she was not as intelligent as his sister, not as talented as a concert pianist they both knew, not as efficient as Jane Addams, but "just Ruth," a girl who loved God, humanity, her betrothed, and her home. Bromley anticipated with sweet tenderness his future domestic joy. On at least one occasion his imaginings must have become vivid and carnal. He confided to his diary, "As evening came on I sat alone at home. I have never had a harder struggle along passion's lines. Somehow my whole being was craving sexual satisfaction. But I have fought this thing for years now and have always won, so I made up my mind to win again. Truly that part of a man's nature is very strong. However, I decided to go out to church. I did. I returned home a different man."

In mid-May, after having completed the first leg of a two-year course of study, Bromley packed his bags and returned to California. "The year closed well," he recorded. "We left the men as friends, and the school work done. It has been one of the best years of my life."

Back in Los Angeles Bromley picked up some needed cash by working as a director of a municipal playground as he eagerly awaited his wedding day. On August 19, 1914, he and Ruth were married in the bride's home. We know no details of the wedding, honeymoon, or Bromley's reactions to such events as the outbreak of World War I, because the diary entries jump from July 7 to November 1 with only one entry in between. His 1915 diary is also one of vast blanks and torn out pages.

Taking the train to Boston, the couple lived for a brief time in two small rooms on the third floor of the parsonage of Grace Church in Cambridge. Desiring greater space and privacy, they soon moved to an apartment of their own on Westland Avenue. Walter John Sherman and his wife, Lottie, lived next door. In November, Ruth learned she was pregnant; she gave birth to a son on May 31, 1915, whom they named Robert Fisher. She was rushed to the hospital in a wreck of a car by a YMCA friend. Bromley, tied up at the Y, was unable to join them. He only saw his son and proud but weary wife late in the afternoon. That evening Bromley wrote his son a letter, telling him of the joy that was in his heart and asking him to look after his mother. He mailed it special delivery. Robert cherished it forever.

As we know, Bromley had been received on trial by the Southern California Annual Conference, in absentia, on October 3, 1913. At that time he made a prediction: "How happy I am that in a year or two, I will be able to lead people into the bigger land. They will come to me and talk to me. I feel that my biggest work will be the personal contact with people." In June 1915, he won the STB. Four months later, he was elected to deacon's orders and on January 26, 1916, he was ordained deacon in a service in Boston, Bishop William Fraser McDowell officiating.

Bromley chose to be ordained in Boston because he hoped to pursue postgraduate study there. During the winter of 1914–15, he had begun his application to Harvard's Ph.D. program in history, but did not follow through with the plan. Instead he took a class in Sanitary Science and Public Health at MIT with Professor William Thompson Sedgewick, a founder of the public health movement in America. At Harvard he studied statistics and the social sciences, in part under Professor William Bennett Monroe, a leading authority in municipal administration.

Aside from the grief occasioned by the death of his father and the loneliness of the pre-marriage year, the Boston years were happy ones. Until his death Bromley remained a loyal and appreciative son of Boston University School of Theology.

CHAPTER 4

THE FLEDGLING PARSON

In the spring of 1916 the little Oxnam family returned to Los Angeles where Bromley anxiously awaited a ministerial appointment. During the following two months, he assisted Dr. Locke at First Church, helped run a playground, and spoke before civic and religious groups. The bulk of his time, however, was spent working for his father-in-law, whose varied enterprises included a hotel managed by Bromley's brother-in-law, Wayne. In return for $17.50 a week, Wayne exacted more than a pound of flesh. "After working continuously overtime for him, the gratitude is shown by asking more," Oxnam grumbled. "One week I worked 94 hours. I refused further childish demands on their part & loss of self respect on mine & left. Quite a scene!"

Worse yet, the Oxnams had no choice but to live with the Fishers until they found an apartment of their own on June 12. Although Bromley opposed intervention in the Great War as well as the preparedness movement, Mr. Fisher's ardent support of the Kaiser set his teeth on edge. When the newspaper headlined a German naval defeat, Bromley conspicuously placed it on Mr. Fisher's dinner plate. For her part, Mrs. Fisher was as strong-willed as she was intelligent and competent.

Bromley's frustrations were exacerbated by the ill health of his mother, who was taking the loss of her husband very hard, and by the fact that his sister was selflessly commencing what would prove to be a long career of caring for her. Bromley contributed sums ranging from three to twenty-five dollars to help them out, not small amounts in those days and considering his own limited income.

During these months Bromley began to question whether he had made the right career choice. After turning down an offer from a Congregational church, he noted cryptically, "It is a hard thing to walk right when one family pulls one way, the other another, & Ruth another."

On June 30, Bromley boarded the train for Phoenix, Arizona, where for two months he was to replace the vacationing Dr. Ray C. Harker, minister of the First Methodist Church. Although he could certainly use the two hundred dollars plus room and travel expenses and was glad to get away from the Fishers, his heart was heavy at the thought of leaving Ruth and one-year-old Robby behind. "May God grant me what I seek in going," he anguished to his diary. "I certainly have no desire to go. It is an exile." The fairly new church boasted 875 members. But Bromley knew better: "The padded rolls of churches are a living lie." To make matters worse, the membership was splintered by "petty jealousies and rivalries." Dr. Harker opined that the "people are so lethargic during the summer that nothing can be done." Bromley was inclined to agree.

But Oxnam was not one to give up without trying. His efforts to increase attendance at Sunday worship services, the Epworth League, and Sunday School succeeded. Not surprisingly, he had no such luck with prayer meetings. In Phoenix he performed both his first funeral and first wedding services. About the latter he noted, "The groom was a good sport and Ruth gets her first $5 from a wedding." (He did not accept payments for funerals.) All the while he continued to ponder the future:

> This evening has been very lonely, a kind of crisis affair, wherein I have tried to decide about this ministry business. I really wonder if a man can preach today, denounce sin and those who sin, and yet stay in the church. Sometimes I feel like getting a job and earning my living and then on the side study, write and talk. I wonder if I won't come to it sometime. But I'll wait till Sunday and see if the old pull is still there.

In addition to instituting a club to study social problems, Bromley continued to denounce prostitution. At the time, Phoenix was debating the establishment of a legalized, licensed, medically inspected vice district. In lectures and articles he attacked the proposal as unthinkable. Unlike many of the "purity" crusaders, however, he was most concerned with chastising the new kings of capitalism who "beat my people to pieces, and grind the face of the poor." He recalled the words of Walter Rauschenbusch: "The Social Gospel seeks to bring men under repentance for their collective sins. . . . Sin is not a private transaction between the sinner and God." Bromley agreed with the Baptist prophet that "we rarely sin against God alone." Like the sociologist E. A. Ross, he believed that we "sin by syndicate." At no moment in his life was he closer to becoming a socialist, although he stopped short of joining the Socialist party; at no time was he more convinced that reform activity itself embodied a religious experience.

Bromley became deeply involved in the trade union movement. When strikers at Clifton were brutally intimidated, he corresponded with and personally visited Governor George Hunt in their behalf. He read socialist publications avidly. In fact, Floyd Dell, editor of *The Masses*, a radical journal, requested that he contribute an article. Bromley's communication to the *Arizona Labor Journal* brought editorial praise: "Rev. Oxnam does not mince words, and his sentences are clear cut and to the point. His are perhaps the most liberal views ever expressed by a representative of the Church in Arizona." The same editor judged Bromley's Labor Day sermon the best ever heard by a Phoenix congregation, and both the Phoenix Trade Council and the Women's Trade Union League agreed.

Unpersuaded by the considerable efforts of First Church lay leaders to have him remain, Bromley returned to Los Angeles after his two months had ended. Attending the annual meeting of the Southern California Conference in late September, Bromley hoped to receive an appointment to a city church, particularly one in the polyglot Los Angeles East Side. Instead, Bishop Adna Leonard assigned him to Poplar, mispronouncing his name in the process. Poplar! Bromley had never heard of the place. Nor could he locate it on a map. The preacher who had been there the year before gave him the following directions: "Take the Southern Pacific, go over to Tehachapi Pass, and into the San Joaquin Valley. Get off at Porterville and ask for Poplar. Somebody will tell you." Following these instructions, the Oxnams stepped off the train at the designated place. A Model-T then carried them to nearby Poplar, a burg of several hundred. Two days later Bromley groaned, "Were it not for Ruth I would catch tomorrow's train out of here."

His initial despair is understandable. The church was scarcely more than a "hideous" wooden shack. Of the congregation of sixty, only a dozen were adult males. The salary of fifty dollars a month foreclosed hopes of buying a car. The eight-dollar-per-month parsonage, set in a field of towering sunflowers, consisted of one room crudely partitioned to create the illusion of two. It lacked running water, let alone a bathroom. The ceiling dripped so many spiders that they had to cover Robby's crib with a mosquito net to keep them out. Bromley wept for Ruth when he compared their shanty to her palatial home on Wilshire Boulevard. Yet for the Oxnams, as for Robert E. Lee, "duty" was the sublimest word in the English language. Consequently they fixed their heels in tar. Weeks later when the Los Angeles district superintendent invited him to take up work on the East Side, he declined, resolving first to complete the task at hand. This honorable decision to remain in Poplar is a real tribute to the Oxnams. Although Bromley and Ruth longed for Los Angeles, they refused to be bested by hicksville; they would not run away.

The path the Oxnams selected was uphill and rocky. "What I don't know about country life will make the Encyclopedia Britannica look sick," Oxnam confessed. "Ruth will be the star here." Ruth did shine brightly, but he was too modest about being only a pale reflection. Gradually he won the hearts of his taciturn people. Not even the legendary reserve of the Bostonians had prepared him for the rural obstinacy of Poplar. When calling on parishioners he would often pick up a pitchfork or hoe so that his visit would not interrupt work. He may have been as ignorant as dawn about farming, but he was strong and willing to sweat. He married the young and buried the old, finding it emotionally wrenching to perform both services on the same day. He also found it frustrating to restrain his gung ho nature. "This slow-poke method of conservative farmers gets my goat," he growled.

Nevertheless, Oxnam's goal was nothing less than to infuse Jesus' teachings into every heart in Poplar. "I am so full of enthusiasm over this task," he exulted, "that I have not felt for a moment but that it will be done. . . . This morning I am feeling that the bugle sound for the advance of the brigade of our church has sounded, in my mind's eye I picture the charge and I see in the future a strong, well organized, useful, Christian force in this village." When his troops faltered, he rallied them. "We have journeyed quite a way," he admonished. "But we have come to a landslide on the track. We can run along, but not much further. . . . Steam shovels remove the earth of the landslide. I would to God that I might be able to preach with steam shovel power so that every blockade barring evangelistic progress might be removed." On November 16, the Official Board voted to erect a new church suitable to the needs of the community. It would be a fitting monument to Bromley's achievements.

Concurrently, the "saints" agreed to build a new, more spacious parsonage. The entire community, not to mention the Porterville band, attended the fund-raising supper. Ruth carved the turkey, Bromley waited tables, and "everyone went away smiling." Bromley helped with the actual construction of the parsonage: "It was a very hard day and I am all in. I have to work faster than the rest to keep the speed up, and not talking myself stops a lot of time talking nonsense."

Despite this progress, Oxnam continued to experience periods of despondency. Sleepy and stolid congregations, distracting ushers, and tardy pianists upset him. Above all, there was the "everlasting sameness" of the community. Men and women old at forty. Male conversation confined to rain, crops, and cattle, while female discussion consisted of malicious gossip. No one reads; no one has thoughts. After a particularly "blue day," Oxnam mused, "You feel yourself giving out, giving out, never receiving. Is it because a man has not the magnetic power to draw out that which is within? I think not. At first I did, but now I differ."

Bromley fought the "blues" in several ways. He bought and read books, including his "great friends," the *Encyclopedia Britannica* and Hastings's *Dictionary of the Bible*. He joined the Grange, finding the ritual "most nonsensical." He visited the resident socialist and enjoyed "good talk. Most Socialists are intelligent folk." He coached the boys' football team and refereed interscholastic games. He lectured on social iniquities, especially prostitution, "one of the world's greatest problems." And he became involved in politics, favoring California's adoption of prohibition and backing Wilson for President.

Bad as some days were, the majority were good. In retrospect, Bishop Oxnam recalled with nostalgia that the Poplar days had been a wonderful time in his marriage. He and Ruth enjoyed good health, high hopes for the future, their son, and each other's love. Ruth never complained about having so little money. (For some reason her affluent parents did not assist them financially either while they were in Boston or Poplar, perhaps because Bromley refused to accept aid.) The people presented Ruth, whom they adored, with tokens of their affection; for example, a tub filled with kitchen supplies and food, including freshly made sausage upon which the couple gorged to the point of sickness. Ruth may have been a moral woman, but she was not above filching a few eggs for Robby from a nearby henhouse. And when no one claimed a posted twenty-dollar bill Bromley had found in the street, she whooped with delight.

Simultaneous with the dedication of the new church in September 1917, the congregation published a booklet recounting the achievements of the past year. By every statistical measurement Oxnam's ministry had been a success, including attendance, membership, Sunday School, income, and benevolent activities. More important was the intangible boost in morale. The account closes: "The year has seen Poplar take its first step toward the land of unrealized possibilities, confident in the trust that God will continue to bless the work, and that the coming years will see possibility after possibility realized."

Oxnam's farewell sermon to his little Poplar flock is saturated with tender expressions of affection and sweet sadness at the parting. Such sentiments might be dismissed as pure dissimulation were it not for their ring of sincerity. To be sure, Bromley was embarking on greater adventures in Los Angeles. Nevertheless, he did not leave Poplar, with all its austerity, without some sadness.

CHAPTER 5

THE CHURCH OF ALL NATIONS YEARS

The Newman Methodist Episcopal Church located at Agatha Street and Standford Avenue had been struggling for years to survive. Once a flourishing fellowship in a tony residential district, its life ebbed away as industry and industrial workers, often foreign-born, transformed the square mile of Los Angeles between the town business area and the railroad yards. In the face of this "invasion," the middle class Methodist population retreated. By October 1917, Newman's budget had fallen to a mere seven hundred dollars, while its indebtedness had climbed to sixteen thousand dollars. Sundays found about ten worshipers in the sanctuary and only about fifty children in the Sunday School; other activities were at a standstill. Six pastors had served the church in the past seven years. No alternative seemingly remained but to close the doors, demolish the building, and salvage a few hundred dollars from the lumber.

Happily, Los Angeles Methodism was not ready to run up the white flag and surrender the inner city. No Methodist was more determined to fight the good fight than district superintendent Dr. E. P. Ryland. He recalled that as an undergraduate Oxnam had studied the area in question and knew of Oxnam's further training at MIT and Harvard. On October 7, on Ryland's recommendation, Bishop Adna Leonard appointed Oxnam to the moribund Newman Church, a preliminary step in the birth of a Church of All Nations. (Shortly, the noble Ryland was to be stripped of his position by Bishop Leonard; subsequently, he left the ministry because, as a pacifist, he could not support President Wilson's call for war.)

Patience was never one of Oxnam's visible virtues, but he was too much the son of his engineer father to be completely governed by impetuosity. Therefore, his first action was to survey his new domain. Bounded on the north by Third Street, on the east by Alameda, on the south by Washington, and on the west by Main, the district was home for sixty thousand people, ten percent of the city's population. Forty-two nationalities were represented, including native-born white Americans, blacks, Mexicans, Chinese, Japanese, Spanish, Italians, and Greeks—it was truly a polyglot neighborhood. The minority who attended worship services were Roman and Greek Catholics, Protestants, Jews, and Buddhists. These 213 city blocks housed 491 industrial and commercial establishments. Instead of clinics, settlement houses, or playgrounds, there were saloons, pool halls, and "disorderly hotels." Disease, particularly tuberculosis and VD, adult crime, and juvenile delinquency abounded. One of Oxnam's major concerns, the city's labor movement, was centered in the district, including the Labor Temple. In short, the challenges were formidable, but Bromley gloried in them.

Two obstacles threatened to postpone the fulfillment of the Church of All Nations dream. The first was war with Germany in April 1917. Like Dr. Ryland, Oxnam was unenthusiastic about intervention. Unlike his mentor, however, he was not a pacifist. Never one to sit on the sidelines either in sports or when great events were astir, in early January 1918 he obtained Bishop Leonard's enthusiastic consent to go to France, either as a YMCA worker or as a chaplain. He formally applied for both positions on August 7. The call never came, perhaps because Ruth had given birth to a second son the previous November, or perhaps because his applications had not been processed before the guns on the Western Front fell silent in November.

Bromley's diaries and surviving public utterances make clear that he never succumbed to the war hysteria whipped up by the Wilson administration, never repeated the more exaggerated tales of German atrocities, and never joined in denouncing or suppressing opponents of American intervention. On the contrary, he defended men like Ryland. His diaries reveal his personal anguish over his country's plight: "I wish I might get one thought relative to this war that I could feel was absolutely correct. . . . It seems almost impossible for a man to think straight in this crisis." Another entry cries, "This business of putting a halo over our actions and a skull and cross bones over the enemies' is not conducive to removing our own sin nor is it wise and in line with our policy to make war a thing forever of the past. War is certainly the 'devil's trump card.' "

Publicly he asked, "What Shall Be the Attitude of the Christian Toward the War?" While intolerance abounded, he answered, the "liberty loving people of America" should be extremely careful to uphold the rights of those who differ in opinion. He praised the antiwar sentiments of Senator Robert M. LaFollette and Representative Claude Kitchin as "keen" and "heart-breaking." He also called for the virtual socialization of the war effort in order to eliminate profiteering. For example, he advocated an income tax confiscating all personal incomes over twenty-five thousand dollars. Once the profit motive for war was eliminated, he concluded,

> You must decide it upon this basis. If you believe this struggle is for the benefit of the human race, as was the war which freed our world from slavery, if you believe democracy is imperiled, then my brother I believe you should enlist and fight with all the power God has given you. If you believe that this business is murder, that it is contrary to Jesus' teaching, then my brother as a man and as a Christian you should absolutely refuse to be a party to it. There is an honest difference of opinion here, and it is not something the preacher can decide for another . . . . The issue lies in your own hands.

Oxnam asked God's blessing upon the troops departing for the fields of death in Europe. He bid them to go as soldiers worthy of the United States and of Christ, and he prayed that they might not only come back but return as better and stronger men.

Although the war did not ultimately interrupt Oxnam's task in East Los Angeles, a second factor did. On October 28, 1918, he received an invitation to become the personal secretary to the famed Sherwood Eddy on a tour to study postwar conditions covering half the world. Oxnam ached to accept what he considered "the greatest opportunity of my life," but he regretfully and honorably declined. His letter, describing the plans under way for a Church of All Nations, concluded: "Selfishly I would give it all up to go with you, if the way opened, for I believe two years of association and travel would fit me for a larger ministry in the future, and yet I feel it would be a direct breach of duty if I were to leave my work at this critical moment." Oxnam's Methodist superiors, however, understandingly granted him a nine-month leave of absence, enabling him to travel with Eddy from December 1918 to the following August, a tale to be related in the next chapter.

Oxnam's first years as pastor of Newman Church were but a stopgap until he could raise funds and obtain permission to assume greater responsibilities and to build more extensive facilities. By the end of 1921, morning worship still drew fewer than one hundred souls and Sunday School only slightly over one hundred pupils, while the Epworth League grew by but four and the Junior League declined by eight. Nevertheless, Oxnam's evening lectures, or "sermons," as he termed them, attracted as many as two hundred workingmen, especially after he demonstrated his long-standing sympathy for labor by opening the church doors to trade groups during strikes. Moreover, he instituted a host of new settlement house activities for children and factory operatives, especially women. The showing of free movies in the church was the greatest attraction, drawing ten thousand spectators in a seven-month period. Two paid deaconesses, an assistant pastor, and a survey inspector assisted Oxnam with these activities.

As had been anticipated, the Newman Church was sold on December 1, 1921, after property for the Church of All Nations had been purchased at the corner of East Sixth Street and Gladys Avenue. On the property stood a couple of old three-story apartment houses, which were modified to contain a club room, offices, a kitchen, a clinic, a library, and a theater. There was sufficient vacant property adjoining to provide a playground. Later, an old candy store was converted into a church auditorium. Until the necessary renovations were complete, Sunday evening services took place in the Labor Temple. Oxnam continued to give his Sunday evening lectures there too. His talks spanned a variety of economic, political, and cultural topics.

In 1926, the Institute of Social and Religious Research concluded that "relative to the standard church practice of the [Methodist] denomination, one would have to say that" All Nations "had virtually ceased to be a church, and had become rather a Christian social center." A USC student researching an extensive paper for her sociology of religion class agreed: "We can scarcely maintain that the whole institution is a church, not even a purely religious institution." Oxnam admitted to the student that public worship was hardly central to All Nations, and that his own energies were channeled into activities beyond preaching and administering the sacraments. Indeed, in all the church's voluminous records there is no mention of a communion service. Early in the decade Oxnam did hold Sunday morning worship services in the rented candy store, but no more than thirty or forty attended. In 1924, Los Angeles Methodism inaugurated a City Parish Plan, wherein six Methodist churches, including All Nations, joined in one City Parish under Oxnam's leadership. Until 1926, worship services and Sunday School took place at Grace Church, the largest church in City Parish. "It has been almost three years since we had regular church services [at All Nations]" acknowledged Oxnam in 1927. The members really "haven't had a pastor. My time has been largely taken with other things, things that seemed vital and necessary."

And so, at middecade, the Church of All Nations had an official membership of only 111 souls, only a handful of whom lived in the immediate area. Financial support for the enterprise came from many sources: pledges and gifts from affluent nonresident and resident members, from the Los Angeles City Missionary and Church Extension Society, the Women's Home Missionary Society, the Board of Home Missions, and from small fees charged for some of All Nations' services. The Community Chest also contributed, thanks to All Nations' separation of social and humanitarian functions from its religious work. Oxnam prepared a three-volume study for the Centenary Movement of church and community centers across the nation, recommending that sixty thousand dollars be given to the

Church of All Nations. Oxnam believed that the service of man was also the service of God. Thus he considered the myriad activities pursued at All Nations essential Christian imperatives. These activities are fully chronicled in a monthly, four-page journal initiated by Oxnam in January 1922, appropriately titled *The Modern Samaritan*.

Oxnam's dream of a clinic materialized late in 1921 when a group of doctors responded to his call for assistance. Although inadequately housed and equipped until the opening of a new facility in June 1926, the clinic provided desperately needed medical care. Between seven thousand and seventeen thousand annually received free treatment ranging from dental surgery and eye examinations (and, if necessary, free glasses) to minor operations. Unfortunately, the doctors did not represent the pinnacle of their profession. A 1923 document reports that one developed tuberculosis; one was a drunk; one practiced an antiquated and dangerous anesthetic technique; one quit because he was jealous of a colleague; and one received a kickback from an optical firm. Nurses were on duty around the clock and made home visitations. A free "milk station" complemented the clinic, supplying scores of families. Thanks to Oxnam's ties with USC, the paid professional staff enjoyed the help of platoons of college students preparing for social work.

Women workers in the neighboring laundries could lunch for twenty cents at the church, and view the works and hear the words of the city's artists at the same time. The city public library opened a branch at All Nations and circulated over a hundred books each month. Oxnam encouraged youths to discover the fun of reading. A day care center helped working and husbandless mothers. Movies, pageants, plays, musicals, and drama brightened countless lives. Donated clothing was sold to the needy for a few cents, thus avoiding the stigma of charity. A school of international relations held monthly meetings on world affairs. All Nations cooperated closely with the nearby Methodist Deaconess Friendly House and with the city's social agencies, including schools, juvenile courts, and hospitals.

It is important to emphasize that All Nations was not a "rescue mission," where in exchange for a bowl of soup a bum endured an uplifting sermon. Its primary concern was not the pronouncing of last rites over the dying damned but preventing people from becoming damned by hellish social conditions. Hence, no group on the East Side received closer attention than the children.

A church school under the close scrutiny of a paid superintendent provided quality education (save for that period when all services were held at Grace Church). An Epworth League, troops of Girl and Boy Scouts, and athletic teams flourished. Oxnam himself often suited up for sporting events. Additionally, a score or more clubs and classes pursued all sorts of educational, vocational, and recreational activities. Probably nothing was more exciting than All Nations Camp, situated on the West Fork of the San Gabriel River in the heart of the Sierra Madre Mountains, which featured a cabin and swimming pool built entirely by the staff and youths. The camp must have seemed like heaven to East Los Angeles street kids.

While the adult membership of All Nations did not represent a cross section of the neighborhood, the children who came to its doors did: Spanish-speaking Mexican-American Catholics predominated, followed by native-born white Protestants. Orientals, Italians, and Jews constituted strong minorities. Blacks were scarce but present. Ethnic, racial, and religious tensions existed, but All Nations sought to mitigate them. No effort was made to gain converts, however. The leadership wished only that Catholics, Jews, and Buddhists go to their respective houses of worship. Recalled Oxnam in 1948, "There were a thousand boys in our Boys' Club. I think the majority of them must have been Roman Catholic. We never sought to proselyte. Our service to the community was to enrich the lives of the young people, to push back the anti-social forces. I am proud to say that the juvenile delinquency rate, which was the highest in the city when we went there, dropped until it became less than the average for the city as a whole." In fact, when the new chapel at All Nations was opened in 1927, Oxnam gave serious consideration to consecrating it for Catholic as well as Protestant services. In the end, the difficulties of such an arrangement proved insurmountable.

When a black boy sought to join a club, the Mexican lads objected until Oxnam persuaded them to remove the barrier themselves. On another occasion when a group from All Nations went to a Y for a swim, two blacks and three Orientals were forbidden from entering the pool. The other boys announced that if their pals could not swim, they would not either. The groups at All Nations deliberately were not divided along ethnic lines. Although worship services took place in English, Oxnam was no advocate of repressive Americanism. "We believed," he explained, that "Americanization should seek a contributory fusion not annihilating assimilation. . . . Assuming that a foreigner had a contribution to make, we sought to ascertain and receive that gift, and in the process of receiving share in turn our best with him." Oxnam never learned to speak Spanish, but at All Nations, some activities—songfests, for example—were conducted in that language or in Yiddish.

A decade later when Oxnam saw the movie *Boys Town*, Spencer Tracy's portrayal of Father Flanagan brought back memories of his Church of All Nations years. Judging from the letters of gratitude he received on departing from Los Angeles, Oxnam had every reason to believe that he was particularly revered by the people of East Los Angeles for the loving help he had extended to the children of the barrio.

In 1923, the staff of All Nations jointly declared, "G. Bromley Oxnam is too big a man for the Church of All Nations. He refuses to leave, so we must make the Church of All Nations a big enough institution for him." For his part, Oxnam appreciated his colleagues. When one lieutenant was offered a fifty percent increase in salary elsewhere, Oxnam matched it. After a nurse completed her first month at the clinic, Oxnam handed her a check for double her contracted salary, saying, "It is too bad in this civilization of ours that we cannot give our greatest benefactors a living wage." When the cohorts of the notorious Aimee Semple McPherson came to a little Methodist church in the City Parish and started prayer service for the conversion of the student pastor, they retreated when Oxnam gave them something they had not prayed for, to the young pastor's relief. Yet Oxnam was an exacting leader; he never tolerated laxity or imprecision in his subordinates. When one reported a Boy Scout meeting as having 50 in attendance, Oxnam phoned and asked,

"Byron, was that 50, 49, or 51?" In this instance he may have been justified, but he was scarcely being Christ-like when a secretary haltingly said, "I th—think," and he impatiently broke in, "With what?" It is one thing not to suffer fools gladly, quite another to make the slower-tongued feel foolish.

Still, Oxnam was always hardest on himself. For ten frustrating years of delay and disappointment he planned and pleaded, schemed and sweated to create an amply domiciled and funded Church of All Nations. During that period he declined at least five opportunities that would have advanced his personal career. Finally, in 1926, "the dream of a decade" approached realization. In May an All Nations Community House opened its doors. It was dedicated to the "service of men, women, and children of every nation, to the truth that will ultimately free mankind, and to the faith that rests in the fatherhood of God and the brotherhood of man." Ten thousand donors contributed the eighty-five thousand dollars necessary to build the structure. Next came the All Nations Boys' Club building, thanks to a gift of sixty thousand dollars from two prominent businessmen, Charles Vorhees and Royal Bush. The structure was given in the hope "that boys of every nation may grow in wisdom, and in stature, and in favor with God and man, as did the Carpenter Boy of Nazareth." Finally, at the heart of the completed plant, Memorial Chapel was built with a contribution of thirty-five thousand dollars from Ruth's family. It was dedicated on June 12, 1927, in "Loving Memory of Walter Harrison Fisher." One of the chapel's windows was given in memory of Thomas H. Oxnam. At Bromley's urging, the chancel windows were decorated with Christ as King of Kings and Servant of All, and an inscription that reads, "Come unto Me all ye that labor and are heavy laden and I will give you rest."

Concurrent with the All Nations enterprise, Oxnam served as executive secretary of the Los Angeles City Missionary and Church Extension Society of the Methodist Episcopal Church. That organization studied population trends to determine where new churches would be needed, bought the necessary land, built facilities, and financed the fledgling parish till it became self-supporting. During his secretaryship, the society erased its indebtedness and tripled its annual budget. Bromley's most important contribution came in 1926 with the purchase of the property on which the great Westwood Community Methodist Church would be built. While driving out Wilshire Boulevard into the virtually deserted hills with the district superintendent, Oxnam predicted that before long the city would envelop the area; already USC was making plans to move there. Thanks to Oxnam's vision, Methodism obtained for only forty-six thousand dollars property later to be valued in the millions.

By working from dawn to midnight Oxnam fulfilled an assignment in October 1919 from the Interchurch World Movement of North America, liberal Protestantism's grandiose, handsomely supported (by John D. Rockefeller, Jr., among others), ill-starred effort to unite the churches in a program of Christian service. The Movement's investigation of the steel strike of 1919, headed by Methodist Bishop Francis J. McConnell, remains to this day the finest, most searching, and most devastating labor inquiry ever conducted by a religious organization. Bromley's assignment as the IWM's Director of Los Angeles County was to survey the religious situation in the city. His research provided the foundation for his own volume entitled *The Mexican in Los Angeles*, published by the Interchurch Movement in 1920. Oxnam's meticulous attention to detail, mastery of statistics, and past experience in conducting surveys paid off. The study and the articles he based on it are still cited by scholars investigating both the history of Los Angeles and of Mexican-Americans. Modern scholars, such as Ricardo Romo, marvel at the accuracy of Oxnam's pioneering findings. Oxnam turned over to the Church of All Nations his IWM fee. His salary at the time was three thousand dollars.

While "the dream of a decade" was coming to fruition at All Nations, Oxnam taught part-time at USC. His courses included the "Social Application of Biblical Principles," "The Literature of Social Protest," and "The Church and Industrial Relations." Although listed in the school catalog as an assistant professor, he was not a formal faculty member and did not receive compensation. Why, burdened as he was, did he expend his energies in the classroom? His reasons probably included loyalty to his alma mater, love of teaching, a concern to inspire students with a Christian social passion, and his intent to recruit pupils for volunteer work at All Nations. In 1925, his district superintendent suggested that he be appointed dean of the Maclay School of Religion, an idea Oxnam found "audacious." The post never materialized.

To suppose that teaching on top of all else approached the limits of Oxnam's time and energy underestimates the man's incredible drive. A veritable Niagara of words flowed from his pen and lips between 1917 and 1927. He came out with his second book, *The Social Principles of Jesus*, in 1923, and *Russian Impressions* three years later. He had published fifty-three articles by 1924. In September 1922 he founded a monthly magazine entitled *In Days To Come*. *The Modern Samaritan*, too, had been his child. Although he accepted contributions, Oxnam liked to think of *In Days To Come* as a "letter to a friend"; he sent complimentary copies to a select mailing list. The opening issue announced, "This paper is put out for the single purpose of quickening the interest of men and women of influence in the problems growing out of our modern conscience, which is calling for the rule of Christian teachings in all our relationships. We must have better men and we must have a better society." Although other authors contributed, many of the columns were Oxnam's. Religious items appeared infrequently; Oxnam's clear concern being with matters political, social, economic, and diplomatic.

While it is well known that Bishop G. Bromley Oxnam was one of the most sought-after public speakers in America, it is sometimes forgotten that the young minister of All Nations was judged "the most popular lecturer in Los Angeles and the most brilliant lecturer on the Pacific Coast." His sermons at the church may have drawn only a score or so, but his lectures were heard by tens of thousands, especially after his second trip abroad with Sherwood Eddy in 1921. On Armistice Day, 1921, he addressed a public gathering of twenty thousand in Lincoln Park. He wrote Eddy on December 6, "I have been so driven during the last three or four weeks, speaking on the average three times a day and sometimes four. . . . I have been having really a marvelous time since my return home." He delivered his talk on "The Tragedy and Futility of War" to over one hundred thousand in a two-month period. In 1922 he spoke more than five hundred times; his audiences contained forty thousand high school students alone. In 1924, his audiences numbered one hundred twenty thousand. One year a single radio address reached fifty thousand. The groups inviting Oxnam to speak included church organizations, teachers' associations, graduating classes, women's clubs, civic gatherings, and labor unions. Even businessmen were interested, provided the topic was world affairs and not the local labor situation.

Oxnam was unquestionably a forceful, dynamic, earnest, "rattling good" speaker. But by 1922 he began to realize the price of extensive public speaking. While he never came close to intellectual bankruptcy, he did run the risk of intellectual banality. He wondered what "the old time minister would have thought of averaging two or three addresses a day, handling a staff of church workers, interviews, teaching at the University, serving on Civic committees, and countless other matters. Sometimes I think we would be far more effective if we held to our studies throughout every morning, instead of sitting up until one or two in the early morning to catch up." Put another way, public speaking came at the cost of staleness and repetition. After being initiated into Delta Sigma Rho in 1918, he wrote, "Oratory is indeed a key to power when one thinks in terms of its five most necessary factors—thought, conviction, self-control, truth, courage." These are the musings of a public figure, but are they the meditations of a true Servant of the Word? Indeed, audiences seemed drawn to his secular lectures, not his heralding of the Gospel. In 1927 he admitted that "just as soon as I preach a real sermon the attendance drops."

While it would perhaps not be unfair to say that Oxnam was partially motivated by considerations of personal power and popularity, it would be absolutely false to charge that his social concern was spurious or that he muted his prophetic voice to keep from offending California's barons of power.

Oxnam's realism prevented him from becoming a doctrinaire socialist; his pragmatism warned him that labor violence was self-defeating in America. He could never reconcile his religious faith with Marxian materialism. His idealism pointed instead to a Christian cooperative commonwealth to be achieved through rational means: scientific study, social engineering, education, organization, and the ballot box. In the reactionary climate of postwar Los Angeles, these hardly revolutionary views earned him a reputation as a radical.

After the failure of Teddy Roosevelt's Progressive Party, Oxnam became a Democrat. "I am of the opinion that President Wilson is the keenest man who has yet occupied the President's chair," he confided to his diary in 1919. "I feel the capitalists are secretly gnashing their teeth." He passionately supported United States membership in Wilson's League of Nations. The Republican platform of 1920 he dismissed as a "double-meaning, reactionary farce." As far as California was concerned, he publicly asked, "Shall the state government be kept in the hands of the people, or shall Special Privilege through machine politics determine the destiny of this Commonwealth? Will the fat cats be permitted to put special interests before the good of the common interests? Is California for all of us or a few of us?"

Oxnam publicly deplored California's discrimination against its Oriental population. When he and Bishop Leonard presented a petition of Japanese Methodists to build a church, an "unruly" crowd converged on city hall to protest. The revived Ku Klux Klan he found "almost laughable," but "it will die like all negative movements that capitalize on hate." Elsewhere Oxnam made the wise point that in addition to indicting the Klan, one must understand the social forces that gave rise to it.

Oxnam continued his friendship with labor. He made a conscious effort to know Los Angeles's union leaders, hoping that "after a while I may be able to lead a bit, thus drawing the church and labor closer together." Decades later Oxnam recalled, "I had the closest relationship with the labor movement, was intimately acquainted with the president and secretary of the Central Labor Council, with other officers, spoke often, and participated . . . in the settlement of industrial disputes." On one instance when he was mediating an electrical workers' strike, the city bankers pressured the contractors into withdrawing from the negotiations. Oxnam advised the union not to resort to violence but to turn the other cheek and win the goodwill of the public. Unfortunately, the union leader could not keep his people in line. The men destroyed the wiring of the Grauman Theatre construction project. "The newspapers made it appear, of course," Oxnam reported, "that these men were a group of violent personalities associated with the bomb throwing propensities of Russia." Actually the bankers were responsible for the development of violence, he insisted.

Oxnam's counsel of non-violence in this dispute indicates his nonrevolutionary leanings. On one occasion he canceled a scheduled lecture when he discovered that the Workers-Communist Party was sponsoring it. "Pulpit Pounder Fails to Speak," raged a *Daily Worker* editorial. In April 1921, he refused to speak at a meeting supporting general amnesty for political prisoners because of its association with the Industrial Workers of the World. He opposed detaining conscientious objectors but did not support the "freeing of any man who broke the law"—that is, the outrageous wartime Sedition Act. He declined to speak at another meeting because he could not condone the IWW's alleged use of violence or its philosophy. The Wobblies were admittedly both anti-Church and anti-State syndicalists, but they were within the tradition of native American radicalism; they did not owe allegiance to Moscow; and, they embraced the most disinherited and exploited of American workers. Oxnam realized that their key tenets, "One Big Union" and the "General Strike," were unrealistic. Nevertheless, as a group subject to the most brutal and relentless persecution ever endured by an organization of American workers, they deserved more support and sympathy from Oxnam than they received. When in 1923 a branch of the American Civil Liberties Union was formed in Southern California, he remained in it for only a few months. His reasons for withdrawing are cloudy. Even so, Oxnam's moderation did not save him from the wrath of the Los Angeles oligarchy, and his courage and conviction prevented him from running for cover.

In April 1923, three thousand longshoremen, exploited beyond endurance, went out on strike, tightly tying up the San Pedro harbor. The strikers, led and disciplined by several hundred IWW organizers, avoided violence. The Los Angeles Merchants' and Manufacturers' and the Shipyard Owners' Associations, assisted by inflammatory articles in Harry Chandler's labor-baiting *Los Angeles Times*, quickly swung into action. Invoking California's notorious criminal syndicalism law, the authorities smashed the strike, arresting six hundred longshoremen and brutalizing many of them. Into this ugly situation stepped Upton Sinclair, maverick socialist, muckraker, civil libertarian, and gadfly. Determined to test whether the Constitution held sway in Los Angeles, Sinclair began to read the First Amendment publicly. Within minutes he and his three companions were arrested on "suspicion of criminal syndicalism" and held incommunicado for eighteen hours. After a judge threw out the case and released him, Sinclair organized rallies to dramatize the imperiled state of civil liberties in Los Angeles, to win support for his newly formed branch of the ACLU, and to reveal the ruthlessness of the antilabor forces.

Four years earlier Oxnam had invited Sinclair to speak at the Church of All Nations. "I am declining all speaking engagements at present," the socialist replied, "but your letter is a temptation I cannot resist. A clergyman who is standing for social justice in Los Angeles is certainly in a position to demand support. So I will open your forum." On May 8, 1923, Sinclair phoned Oxnam to ask if the minister would preside and offer a prayer at a free-speech rally to be held at Walker Auditorium the following evening. Oxnam believed the wire was tapped, which may have been the case, considering the illegal methods of the "Red Squad" of the Los Angeles police force. In regard to speaking at the rally, Oxnam wrote, "I know the *Times* will lie about it and I am tossing even the remote chance of being elected to the Board [of Education] into the sea, but free speech in trying times is more vital than a short period on the Board. It is amazing the ignorance big business shows. Free speech is the surest guarantee of peace." To his diary he confided, "Oh that reaction could think. I pray God there may be no upheaval in America. We must go on slowly toward a better social order, but these insane holders of power, ignorant, believing only in force, worshipping naught but the dollar, are doing the very thing to bring violence. They know no history, honor no law save for their own selfish desires, and are all the while laying the foundation for trouble." Oxnam presided at the meeting, led the audience in the singing of "America," offered a prayer, and yielded the stage. The supplication called upon his listeners to be both tolerant of diverse opinions and brave enough to stand up for their convictions. He concluded, "Give us the courage today to stand as Americans insisting upon the maintenance of those principles upon which our Republic was founded." Being the careful man that he was, he arranged for a stenographer to record the prayer so that it could be publicized accurately. His hunch that the audience contained enemy spies proved correct.

Oxnam's fears that his presence at the meeting would step up the attacks of the reactionaries and sink his chances of election to the Los Angeles Board of Education proved all too well founded. Probably, however, this one occasion made little difference[1], since the *Times* had already identified Oxnam as a "radical orator," one who favored "sovietizing the schools, the application to our city education system of the principles of radicalism that have been so fatal in Russia." In *I Protest*, Oxnam relates his school board experience; there is no need to repeat the details. Still, a few aspects merit highlighting.

Oxnam was a candidate for the board on the "teacher's ticket," dubbed the "Oxnam ticket" by its foes, after having won nomination in the spring primary elections. The slate was supported by the majority of teachers and by progressive elements in the city (although not by all of the PTAs). The opposite slate, advanced by the Citizens' School Committee, was composed of individuals with blood and money ties to Los Angeles's power elite. While proclaiming the need to protect the children from the virus of socialism, the Citizens' School Committee actually sought to repress all criticism whatsoever of the status quo. It had already banned both *The Nation* and the *New Republic* from the school libraries.

The opposition had strong supporters. They included The Better America Federation (masquerading as the Committee of One Thousand, which magically grew to the Citizens' Committee of ten thousand), the *Times* and *Express* (Hearst's *Examiner* and *Herald* remained strangely silent), and a raft of business, patriotic, and veterans' groups. The *Times*'s criticism proved crucial. One story carried the headline: "Shall Radicals Head Schools? Facts about G. Bromley Oxnam and Associates. His record as a Supporter of Socialist Doctrines." In two special delivery, registered letters dated April 24 and 26, addressed "To the Editor," Oxnam sought to set the record straight, both in regard to the *Times*'s errors of fact and false innuendos. The second note concludes:

> I would have ignored your attacks if others were not involved. Your charges of "radicalism" are false. The suggestion of sympathy for IWW tactics is false and I believe you know it. Your statements relative to my position in educational matters give the people an entirely wrong impression. Hasn't the time come in American life when as citizens we can face issues as sportsmen, play the game like men, state our ideas accurately to the people and let them decide? Must we forever face the problem of misrepresentation? Let us have faith in our institutions, let each candidate state his views and have them correctly reported, then let the people choose whom they wish. This is the American way, I believe.

An individual as critical of Oxnam as Harry Chandler but even more implacable was Colonel Leroy Smith, executive of the smarmy Better America Federation and a Methodist lay leader. He published sweeping allegations branding Oxnam and the Church of All Nations staff as Bolsheviki. Even after Oxnam conclusively refuted the charges, Smith continued to hound him like Javert on the trail of Jean Valjean. On September 22, 1923, Smith preferred charges with Bishop Leonard, claiming that Oxnam "by the character of his conduct of his church and Sunday School is unfit to be a Methodist minister." As a Methodist, Smith had the right to pursue this disciplinary form. Bishop Leonard had no choice but to present the allegations to the Annual Conference in executive session, which authorized a special committee to investigate them. The committee reported back to the conference that the charges did not warrant a trial. In transmitting this finding to Smith, Leonard noted, "Mr. Oxnam was eager to have an open Conference trial and really regretted, if I understood his statement correctly, that the committee did not permit it to come before the Conference. He declared himself willing and able to defend himself at every point." Smith's action against Oxnam may have been legal, but it was not well-intentioned. Even worse was the Better America Federation's circulation of alleged stenographic transcripts of Oxnam's speeches—transcripts that actually had been composed in their own offices. One such doctored speech was sent to the University of Southern California where Oxnam was teaching part-time. Unfortunately for the Federation, a USC stenographer had recorded the speech, thus exposing the doctored account.

Ministers of a variety of denominations rallied to Oxnam's support with resolutions defending him. The support was not universal, however. The pastor of Westlake Presbyterian Church and former president of the Los Angeles Ministerial Association opposed him, as did the respected Baptist J. Whitcomb Brougher. Robert "Fighting Bob" Shuler, a powerful Methodist evangelist, regretfully withdrew his support of Oxnam's campaign, expressing in a letter of June 1 personal affection and esteem but concluding, "I know, however, that you are dreadfully wrong. I have 3 boys and 2 girls to whom I must answer, and I confess your public attitude in an hour of national peril, and your associations with a mighty attack being made by these forces upon our Government, are too much for me." Concurrently, fearful high school principals withdrew invitations for Oxnam to speak at commencement exercises.

The controversy swirling about Oxnam became more surreal. Between February 1922 and November 1924, Special Agent A. A. Hopkins of the Justice Department's Bureau of Investigation (forerunner of the FBI)—Los Angeles office—began sending numerous reports to Washington on Oxnam's "radical activity." Detailing Oxnam's real and alleged speaking engagements and other activities, Hopkins concluded, along with the *Times* and the Better America Federation, that Oxnam was a "local radical who is among the most influential in this section." In the school board election he had "the all out support of the Communists in Los Angeles." He was an "enthusiastic supporter of and worker for the recognition of Russia," often "advocating the Soviet System of Government." Moreover, "he appears to have become even more radical in his views than he used to be." Oxnam's "vituperation" against the Better America Federation ranked among the "most vicious attacks that have ever been made against any institution." (Naturally Oxnam was unaware that he was the subject of Bureau of Investigation surveilance and to the day of his death he praised the Bureau and its leader, J. Edgar Hoover, who over the years compiled a file on him of over four hundred chuckleheaded pages.)

On Election Day the "teacher's ticket" was defeated, its leader placing thirteenth. Oxnam waxed philosophic over the outcome:

> The lines are clearly drawn. A powerful reactionary morning newspaper and an evening satellite used every weapon available. These papers were backed by strong financial interests and were working apparently in harmony with the Better America Federation through its various aliases. It is little wonder they were for the moment victorious. However, the present defeat has done more to force progressive citizens to think and to organize in the interests of wresting from un-American forces the instruments of government than any event that has occurred locally since the days when the Southern Pacific machine was driven from office.

Writing years later he recalled being in a less sanguine mood following his defeat: "I was . . . badly beaten in the election, and, after reading what was written about me, often wondered whether I ought not find some cell in a county jail and take residence there. I never let others know about it, but it did hurt me."

The defeat, however, did not hurt him in the eyes of most of his fellow Methodists. In 1924, the Southern California Annual Conference elected him a delegate to the General Conference meeting at Springfield, Massachusetts, a considerable honor for a young man of thirty-three. At Springfield, Oxnam's most notable contribution was a joint defense of civil liberties and of his then beloved mentor Dr. Harry F. Ward; the eloquence of his address surely owed much to his recent bruising experience in Los Angeles.

Ward was both the secretary of the Methodist Federation for Social Service and chairman of the National Board of Directors of the recently formed American Civil Liberties Union. In 1922 the Communist party held an underground meeting in Bridgman, Michigan, attended both by agents from Moscow and a Justice Department "mole." When authorities raided the meeting, the Communists caught in the dragnet were charged with violating Michigan's criminal syndicalism law. The ACLU and the Federation sprang to the defense of the accused not out of sympathy with communism but out of concern for the United States Constitution. The Federation's *Bulletin* for January 1923 posed the question: "Can a political party constitutionally be outlawed? If so, where will the process stop?" Outraged conservative Methodists sought to have the General Conference rebuke Ward and disavow the coddling of Communists. After investigation, the Committee on the State of the Church recommended that the conference take no action against Ward. During the debate over the report, Oxnam asserted that the Constitution protected the civil liberties even of Communists, quoting Dean Roscoe Pound of the Harvard Law School with telling effect. The point at issue, Oxnam argued, was not communism, but freedom of speech under the Constitution. "There is no man in the country more fundamentally opposed to the central thesis of Communism than Harry F. Ward," Oxnam declared, inspiring a round of applause. "Ward in no sense tried to prejudice anyone in the Michigan case. He seeks to have the right of free speech which the Department of Justice deliberately violates under the guise of the suppression of radical propaganda." A newspaper reporter covering the conference judged Oxnam's address "eloquent and impassioned," while the *Christian Century* found it "very effective." Special Agent Adrian H. Potter thought otherwise, and made sure Oxnam's utterances were added to the growing FBI dossier in Washington.

The General Conference commended the Federation for its "splendid activities" but reminded the Federation that it did not speak officially for the Church since that could only be done by conference action. In 1922 Ward had dominated the notable conference on Christianity and the Economic Order in Evanston, Illinois. Sponsored by the Federation and chaired by Bishop McConnell, the 250 delegates took a searching and exceptionally critical look at the tenets of capitalism and the economic injustices found in America. Throughout the decade Oxnam praised the Federation, even serving as executive secretary of a national committee created to celebrate its anniversary. The event occasioned churchwide discussion of the social imperatives of the Christian faith. Conservative opponents of the Federation sought to undercut it by the creation of an official social service commission. Thanks primarily to Ward, the Federation was looked upon as the executive agency to rally the forces of Methodism in support of social thought and reform since its inception in 1907. The Federation's relationship to the Church remained unofficial, however. Oxnam was appointed to a commission to study the matter and finally, at the 1932 General Conference, joined in recommending the continuation of the Federation and that an official agency not be established in competition. Oxnam supported the decision since he believed that "official commissions seldom pioneer successfully. . . . I fear official commissions for the reason that such commissions in the early decades of the nineteenth century would have failed to face the real implications of the slavery issue."

At the start of the Church of All Nations adventure Oxnam heard Bishop Leonard speak and recorded in his diary, "I have tried to put myself in his position. I have thought of my own love for autocratic power,—given up thank God, since I have learned the principles of Jesus and democracy." Then he wondered how long he would remain in the ministry, speculating about other careers, including politics. "Yet I love the ministry. My heart is in the work in which I am now engaged. . . . I wonder what the future holds in store. I suppose the wise thing is to remain and get control of the blamed thing." On another occasion he reported, "If the next five years bring as much to me as the last five, I'll hardly be able to stand the joy of living."

Beyond question, much of the joy he knew was a gift from the woman he married. Ruth was as devoted to the cause of All Nations as her husband. She led a number of its activities. She made and packed sandwiches for the boys' ball games and hikes. One Halloween she baked 120 little pumpkin pies for the church party. She cooked beans and spaghetti by the ton. One youth wondered if "Mrs. Oxnam ever remotely guessed that her hospitality was a form of the sacrament of life because that was its real character."

In 1917, Ruth gave birth to a second son, Philip Holmes. On her way to the hospital she cast her vote to make Los Angeles dry. In 1922 Bette Ruth was born, completing the family. Oxnam was an adoring husband and father, and nothing marred a good marriage and happy family life during the Los Angeles years. Sports helped keep Oxnam fit; no adjective was employed more frequently to describe him than "dynamic." Not only did he sometimes play on the All Nations athletic teams, he also pitched for the Los Angeles district ball club, captained a USC faculty baseball team, and occasionally played golf and tennis. Vigorous as he was, he could not escape the influenza epidemic in 1919, which may have contributed to his ultimately developing Parkinson's.

Oxnam's decade at All Nations witnessed the Fundamentalist-Modernist war within the churches, which had been smoldering for decades, burst into full flame. The fighting was less furious in Methodism than in some other denominations, but that is not the only reason Oxnam was not sucked into the conflagration. The truth is, he was not passionately interested in matters of a doctrinal and theological nature. But he did do some homework. He gave lectures on "Mr. Bryan's Attack Upon Evolution" and "Fundamentalism" and "What is Evolution?" He read and praised Harry Emerson Fosdick's *The Modern Use of the Bible*, and reread such champions of the "New Theology" as Moffatt, Glover, and Harnack, explaining his reason for doing so: "It is well to be forearmed for the dear fundamentalist brothers. To think of having a final authority at hand, never to worry about the restless search for the truth, but the trouble is 'it ain't possible.' "

Oxnam chose to place his emphasis elsewhere. "Theological abstractions must be subordinated to an insistence upon the Christian way of life," he cried. "The creedal goosestep may be the frozen marching form for the pomp of synodical conclave, but it is the khaki of the Christ way of service that wins battles for the King." Again and again Oxnam roared, "Today the call is for men who are strong enough to fight. No longer do we want the weakling. The world has no place for him today. He is relentlessly pushed aside and the man of strength takes his place in the line of march." It is not dime store psychology to suspect that Oxnam's vision of Christianity was a projection of himself. Witness the typical utterance: "It is a fine thing to be a soldier in the fighting forces of Christianity. Christianity is one of the strangest of warring organizations. It no sooner wins a magnificent victory than it looks about for new fields to conquer. It is never at peace. It never rests. It is ever preparing for battle."

One honors Oxnam's decade of service to the people of Los Angeles. Still, in reviewing that splendid record one inevitably is haunted by the advice of Screwtape, the Devil's apprentice, in the *Screwtape Letters* by C.S. Lewis: "The thing to do is to get a man at first to value social justice as a thing which the Enemy [God] demands, and then to work him on to the stage at which he values Christianity because it may produce social justice."

[1] Upton Sinclair, to the contrary, believes that Oxnam's election was not hopeless from the start, writing in his *The Goslings*, "There is very good reason to believe that the praying of a prayer for the Constitution of the United States not merely cost Mr. Oxnam his election to the school board, but cost his associates their election as well."

CHAPTER 6

TRAVELS WITH SHERWOOD EDDY

Oxnam's All Nations years were interrupted by three enriching trips abroad with Sherwood Eddy, that astonishing amalgam of evangelist, socialist, YMCA leader, itinerant missionary, inveterate world traveler, tireless speaker, prolific author, and self-proclaimed authority on world affairs. An old-stock American of independent wealth, he annually led an entourage of educators, churchmen, and businesspeople abroad, where he seemed to know every foreign leader personally. In all lands the doors of the mighty were open to him. He was constantly on the lookout for bright young men to help usher in a Christian social order. He brought within his orbit many aflame with social righteousness, including Kirby Page, Reinhold Niebuhr—and Bromley Oxnam. In 1955 Oxnam publicly reported, "I owe more to Sherwood Eddy, I think, than to any living Christian." His admiration is obvious in the effusive letters he wrote Eddy over the years. Their friendship he "treasured above all other."

Eddy, it will be remembered, first approached Bromley in October 1918 about accompanying him as his personal secretary on a tour of Japan, China, and India to study missions, social work, and labor movements. Despite his hunger to accept, Bromley regretfully replied that he could not renege on his Los Angeles responsibilities. His new district superintendent wisely thought otherwise. "Of course you must go," he said. "It will mean so much to you." The Los Angeles City Missionary and Church Extension Society granted a leave of absence, adding that "we desire heartily to congratulate him upon the rare opportunities which will be afforded him, and to assure him of our affectionate regard."

Eddy tested the stenographic skills of his prospective secretary by steadily dictating letters to him on a train trip to San Francisco. The next day he ordered Bromley to join him on a round of engagements. At the end of the day, when Eddy asked about the letters, Bromley handed a completed bundle to an astonished Eddy. When had he written the letters, Eddy asked? Bromley explained that he had slipped away in the evening and dictated them to a hotel stenographer for preparation. Eddy was persuaded that Bromley would make a fine secretary. Indeed, in his memoirs, Eddy singled Oxnam out as one of the ablest men to serve him in that capacity.

On December 5, a steamer of the old China Mail line slipped out of San Francisco bound for Yokohama. On board together with the Eddy group were contingents of French, British, and American troops on their way to Siberia and the Philippines, a few missionaries, businessmen, and tourists. No one was allowed ashore in Honolulu because influenza had broken out aboard ship. After their departure from Hawaii, Bromley spent a number of bitterly cold days reading forty books on Russia assigned by Eddy. To help him with preparing a volume on the Soviets, Eddy had instructed Bromley to underline anything important. "Then I'll go through them," he added. (Later, while Bromley was looking out the window on a train in India, Eddy handed him a volume about the country, saying, "You'll find this interesting." Bromley declined the book, replying, "I prefer to look out the window and see for myself what India actually is.") The Eddy group arrived at Yokohama on the twenty-fifth but remained in Japan only a few days before departing for Shanghai. From there they proceeded to Nanking, Soochow, Canton, Hong Kong, Singapore, and thence to Colombo and Madras.

In addition to visiting churches, mission stations, and Ys in both China and India, Oxnam made a point of inspecting hospitals, leper asylums, prisons, factories, and any other place that would enhance his knowledge. In Hong Kong the sight of women and children dragging wagons filled with rocks up the Peak to build the homes of millionaires evoked the bitter cry, "But then a 'Christian civilization' must build its cities!" The terrible scenes of exploitation he witnessed in the textile mills of Shanghai left their mark on him: The prayer Oxnam gave at his first Methodist General Conference in 1924 contained the supplication, "O, our God, as we are worshipping here this morning in this beautiful room, we cannot but think of the little children trudging the roads towards the great factories in China, there to have their little lives dwarfed and ruined."

China afforded numerous interesting experiences. He was denied permission to preach in the Free Christian Church of Shanghai because of his liberalism. Outside a Buddhist temple he observed the hawking of pornography. After attending a Catholic service in Hong Kong he mused, "It seemed to me the Catholic church with its close relation to the great past, possesses something we do not have, and I wondered if the day would ever come when all the glory of the past, its lessons and holding power, its traditions and its proven truth, may not be harnessed to a living democratic church of today, and in wonderful union the forces of Christ work together to build that edifice that shall ever stand, The Kingdom of God." After attending a service at the Anglican Cathedral in Hong Kong he expressed (for the first time, as far as the record shows) a "love" for "solemn ritual" and for "the contemplative mysticism that a man longs for."

Of the lands in the East, India most captured Oxnam's bewildered attention. It was here he spent almost six months, traveling nearly thirty thousand miles by train, car, and boat as far east as Calcutta, as far north as Lahore, west to Bombay, and south to Ernakulam. Part of the travels were on his own, under the auspices of the YMCA of India and Ceylon. Most of the time he was with Eddy, whose indefatigability, even temper, evangelical message, social passion, and daily devotional practices he continued to admire. For his part, Eddy had good reason to appreciate his secretary, whose responsibilities included looking after twenty-eight pieces of personal luggage. It was not a light task, as Bromley explained:

> I went down early, got five coolies together and when the train arrived, football style rushed to a compartment and got two berths for Mr. Eddy and me. I felt quite proud when, lo and behold, a couple of Indians bribed the guard, and while my back was turned he was getting ready to move my stuff. I got back just in time. And I forgot all about being a representative of a church or any organization, for after all the bother to see that half-breed conductor start on that path—well, I said to him to leave those things alone, and he remarked the other men were going in there. Then I shouted at him, "If you move one of those bags, you'll land on the floor so blamed fast that you won't know what hit you." The old boy straightened up and told me to read some rules he had, and I told him to put his doggoned rules in his pocket. The result was that he backed out bowing, and we slept there. Such is life in India.

For Oxnam, life in India also consisted of bedbugs, prickly heat, abominable meals, dreams of ice cream sodas, late trains, lost trunks, "plotting Hindus," and beating "cock-sure-know-it-all Britishers" in tennis. To his credit Bromley was a marvelous traveler: curious, observant, intrepid, adventuresome, game for new experiences. His diaries brim with detailed notes about Indian customs, food, dress, architecture, and countless other facets of native life. Oxnam's distaste for some things Indian extended beyond the diet, hygiene, and late trains. The temple carvings at Benares he found "so vile that they would put the lewd Parisian post cards to shame." The Hindu priests, he believed, "commit every form of immorality . . . upon the women pilgrims who come here, entirely aside from the temple prostitution." His general admiration for the people was not total, once in exasperation spitting out the words, "I am more and more impressed with the deceit of the Indian. He lies about everything." Another frustrated entry reads, "We passed the lunatic asylum on the way and it seemed quite a popular place. From the number of nuts I have met on the streets it is no wonder."

Oxnam's ambivalent feelings about India reveal the conflict within himself between an authentic Christian idealism and true social passion on the one hand, and on the other that side of his nature respecting authority and demanding order. His response to the nationalistic movement and what the *Encyclopedia Britannica* chooses to call "The Punjab Rebellion, 1919" brings this tension into sharp focus. "India is certainly seething," he reported in his diary. "Down underneath is a current of unrest likely to break out any moment. Britain is using force splendidly, but the question is whether force will hold down 300,000,000 people forever. On the other hand, the Indian seems to fail miserably in honesty, capacity for leadership and general management. It is certainly some problem."

On April 8, Oxnam separated from the Eddy group (which now included the famous Methodist admirer and biographer of Gandhi, E. Stanley Jones) to head north alone to observe British troops stationed in the Punjab. He entered a maelstrom. He passed through Amritsar only half an hour before mobs murdered eight Europeans, including three Britishers, and torched the Anglican church and mission, schools, banks, public buildings, and the train station. Arrival in Lahore did not spell safety, for murders, arson, and looting, which were answered by murderous repressive gunfire from the British authorities, reigned there too. "The Indian is very emotional, a mob is like a thunderstorm. Soldiers are everywhere, and it looks like serious difficulty," he observed. On Sunday, April 13, Oxnam wrote a fourteen-page pamphlet to be distributed among the British soldiers, entitled "In Days of Social Reconstruction." At the moment of the writing of this idealistic tract, fifty miles away in Amritsar, Brigadier General Reginald Dyer's troops fired on a defenseless group of protesters, killing 379 and wounding 1,208. On Monday the fourteenth, Oxnam entered this revealing passage in his diary:

> The mob had gotten out of control of its leaders, and I think the only way out is absolute sternness on the part of Britain. I tell you one admires these British, with all their snobbishness. They are cool-headed, fearless and in such matters usually of unimpeachable integrity. I have just read thru the history of the Mutiny of 1857 and it thrills one to have British blood in his veins when he reads of 5,000 men attacking an armed city of 50,000, behind great walls and supplied with superior guns and ammunition. 50,000 soldiers plus the civil population, and yet the British beat them. I do not fear danger for I feel England has the whole affair in hand now. The Indians little realize the power of modern weapons, *but I understand they were taught something of a lesson in Amritsar*. One feels terrible over the whole situation. *It means that mission work will be slowed up for years*. I have not mentioned the deep antagonism between the Indian and the missionary all over India, but it is indeed a serious problem for Christian leadership to meet. (Emphasis added.)

Oxnam frequently praised the "grit and character" of the British army and predicted, "There would be absolute chaos here if the British left, and certainly frightful bloodshed."

It is not an injustice to Oxnam to state that the turmoil in India saw the warrior in his being prevail over the prophet. His own life, to be sure, was perhaps at stake in the restoration of peace and order, as were certainly the lives of Westerners and Indian converts to Christianity. Nevertheless, what happened at Amritsar was not a "lesson," it was brutal massacre. The central issue was not the future of "mission work," it was that of Indian independence from centuries of exploitative British imperial rule. The courage of the outmanned Tommy Atkins was matched by the *unmentioned* courage of Gandhi's unarmed followers who faced the British guns.

On July 21 Oxnam sailed for home to honor the nine-month leave-of-absence agreement, Eddy's party continuing on to the Near East. Back in Los Angeles, Oxnam parlayed his experiences now that he was widely recognized as an "expert" in Indian and Asian affairs into an endless lecture circuit.

Eddy, satisfied with Bromley's secretarial performance, asked his help again for Eddy's American Seminar in the summer of 1921, the first of his famed annual affairs. The group of thirty included many of American Protestantism's current and future leaders: Paul Blanshard, Jerome Davis, Cameron Hall, Alva W. Taylor, Arthur E. Holt, Kirby Page, Henry Pitney Van Dusen, and Episcopal Bishop Charles D. Williams. Arriving in London in mid-July, the group established quarters at the famed Toynbee Hall settlement house. Eddy's prestige made it possible to schedule daily lecture discussions with an astonishing galaxy of personalities. Oxnam's notes and observations, from which he later composed profiles for *In Days to Come*, still exist. The following capsules hardly do justice to the shrewdness of his judgments.

Ramsay MacDonald, soon to be prime minister, favorably impressed him. Although not a member of the Church at the time, his social idealism and cool intelligence made him irresistibly admirable. Over the years Oxnam would commend MacDonald's British Labour party as an example to America of the successful application of Christianity to politics. Bromley found Mr. B. Seebohm Rowntree, the pious, wealthy cocoa manufacturer "altogether the most progressive and thoughtful employer I have ever met." Intellectual Harold J. Laski, whose critics considered him a vain windbag, gave a brilliant talk that left Bromley's head spinning. Statesman-pacifist George Landsbury won Bromley's reverence, while the priest-pacifist W. E. Orchard struck him as a phony. Bishop William Temple he highly praised. Oxnam gave low marks to Sidney Webb, high scores to R. H. Tawney, but deemed socialist G. D. H. Cole the finest of the lot. Lord Robert Cecil and Philip Snowden, among others, also addressed the group. Bromley had long been hungering for precisely this intellectual fare. His own contribution to the seminar consisted of a lecture on "The Mexican in Los Angeles." Between sessions he reveled in London's cultural life, especially enjoying his first visit to the Tate Gallery.

A trip to Berlin followed the four weeks in London. By drawing a king of diamonds, Oxnam became one of a group of five in the Eddy party to interview Friedrich Ebert, president of the German Republic. "Ebert impresses one as a sincere man, a man of conciliatory ability, a man of a good deal of native power," he recorded. Ebert may have stood tall in Oxnam's book, but not as tall as Walther Ratheneau, German minister of reconstruction and later foreign minister. Within a year this great Jewish industrialist and statesman would be slain by an assassin. Judged Oxnam: "I would place him as head and shoulders in sheer ability above any other man we have met in Europe." It is not clear if by "Europe" Oxnam includes Great Britain. Under any circumstances, he stood as much in awe of Ratheneau as he did of MacDonald. As in London, so in Berlin Oxnam devoured the cultural scene, treating himself to an opera on his birthday.

In September, Eddy received a note from Oxnam reading, "As I look back over the summer I feel it must have been a dream. It certainly was the most profitable six weeks of my life." Naturally Oxnam hit the lecture trail with renewed pace now that he was set up as an "expert" on European affairs.

Five years later, in 1926, Eddy again invited Oxnam to join his seminar abroad. Again the group consisted of liberal Protestant leaders, including Charles Clayton Morrison, editor of the *Christian Century*, and William H. Scarlett, sainted Episcopal bishop of Missouri. July was filled with interviews, including ones with Prime Minister Baldwin of England, President Von Hindenburg of Germany, and leaders of the League of Nations. Three weeks in Russia followed. The group reached Moscow by way of Riga on August 3. For years Oxnam had immersed himself in the study of Russian history, economics, culture, and literature in an attempt to understand that strange land. He was now for the first time actually on Russian soil. Oxnam summarized the contingent's itinerary:

> While in Russia . . . various members of our party met about thirty leaders of the present government, among them were Stalin, Chicherin, Lunacharsky, Smidovich, and Smilag. In addition, we met a few people of prominence in the old regime, who are thoroughly opposed to the present government and live in constant fear. We met the heads of the various branches of the Church, were received by the President and Cabinet of the Tartar Republic, travelled from Berlin to Moscow, thence to Nizhni-Novgorod, down the Volga to Kazan, then into the villages, and back to Moscow. Some of the members of the party journeyed into the Ukraine and the Caucasus regions; others into the Donetz Coal Basin; while one member made the trip from Peking to Moscow and return. All of us visited Petrograd. We returned variously, some by way of Poland, others by Latvia, others by Esthonia or Finland.

Upon returning home in September, the Eddy party collectively expressed to President Coolidge their "conviction that the United States Government should not further delay in its formal recognition of the present Government of Russia on terms consistent with the mutual interests and honor of both Governments." Oxnam also prepared a series of lectures on Russia, first given at the Church of All Nations, and then presented to various Los Angeles civic groups. These lectures appeared as chapters in a book published at his own expense in 1927 entitled *Russian Impressions*, and also served as the basis for the section on Russia in his 1928 volume, *Youth and the New America*.

Bromley chose the title "Russian Impressions" carefully. The finest asset of this ninety-six-page work is the absence of dogmatic proclamation. Oxnam insists that no foreign traveler can know the whole truth about such an enormous, convoluted, and convulsive land. "The sincere student seeks to relate his impressions, keep his mind open, continue his research, and endeavor to be in a position to create better understanding between the nations, but that is about all he can do," he believed. He makes distinctions: "The ideal was to abolish exploitation of man by man. The program was communism. The method was dictatorship."

Almost from the outbreak of the Bolshevik Revolution to the day of his death, Oxnam was charged with being pro-Soviet. Later it will be mandatory to examine this allegation closely. Here it is necessary only to insist that neither *Russian Impressions* nor any of his other writings reveal him as an uncritical fellow traveler. Certainly he left some things unsaid. Surely some of his assessments are too gentle, and some predictions were not borne out by history. But just as clearly, the writings do not fantasize a perfectly just and economically successful society. Above all, they do not mask or try to explain away a harsh dictatorship or the absence of liberties. Indeed, compared to a legion of cloud cookoo land accounts written by self-deceiving American and English intellectuals in the 1920s, *Russian Impressions* is a model of objective reporting. Returning from the Soviet Union, Lincoln Steffens made the immortal observation, "I have been over into the future, and it works," adding "the Future is there; Russia will win out and it will save the world." More than a few American churchmen who visited Lenin's and Stalin's New Jerusalem would have agreed with this crackbrained notion. Oxnam had a much better grip on reality.

Oxnam's travels during the twenties strengthened his belief in the evil of international war. As a Methodist it was appropriate for him to become a crusader for peace, because no major denomination was more dedicated to a warless world or more deeply penetrated by the thrust of pacifism—a pacifism scarcely distinguishable from that of the historic peace sects, the Brethren, the Quakers, the Mennonites—than Northern Methodism. To be sure, Oxnam never became an absolutist, but with other peace lovers (a term perhaps sufficiently imprecise to embrace the amorphous nature of the anti-war movement), he supported U.S. entrance into the League of Nations and the World Court, the outlawry of war (specifically the Pact of Paris), the end of colonialism and imperialism, limiting world armaments (such as the Washington, Geneva, and London Naval

Conferences), and the cutting of American military expenditures. He also favored the constitutional protection of conscientious objectors and the abolition of all military training in high schools and compulsory military training in colleges. He argued that Germany alone was not responsible for World War I, and urged the reduction of German reparations and Allied war debts. He advocated the recognition of Soviet Russia, an end to Oriental immigration discrimination, removal of race barriers, and the moderating of nationalism. In sum, Oxnam advocated ending bloodshed by establishing the necessary conditions for peace.

Oxnam expressed these views in sermons, lectures, General Conference addresses, articles, and in a chapter in *Youth and the New America*. In 1924 he became secretary of a subcommittee on international problems of the Committee on the State of the Church, and in 1928 he served as secretary of the World Peace Commission, Northern Methodism's supreme official agency to create a warless world. Time and again he sounded the refrain, "In God's name—I say it reverently—may we not recognize the tragedy and futility of war, and as one united people send America forward in sacrifice to lead the way upon the march that shall eventually end in the abolition of war." "War is worse than hell," he cried. "It must be banished from the face of the earth."

Episcopal Bishop Paul Jones once observed that a pacifist between wars is like a prohibitionist between drinks. The 1930s would tell if this aphorism would apply to Oxnam.

CHAPTER 7

A TEACHING INTERLUDE AT BOSTON UNIVERSITY SCHOOL OF THEOLOGY

By June 1927 all the new buildings at the Church of All Nations had been dedicated, a ranging program instituted, solid financial support insured, and a skilled staff and fresh leader secured. Oxnam's perseverance had triumphed. It was now time to move on. A year earlier he had been approached by Dean Albert C. Knudson of Boston University School of Theology to join the faculty as professor of practical theology and city church. Knudson, who had just assumed the deanship, had been Bromley's respected seminary teacher. Daniel L. Marsh, recently appointed president of Boston University, also knew and admired Oxnam. From California there came to Knudson strong letters of recommendation, none handsomer than one from Bishop Charles Wesley Burns, who also enlisted the endorsement of Bishop McConnell. Bromley accepted in 1927, and September found the five Oxnams in Boston.

The fall semester Oxnam offered three courses: "Homiletical Theory", "Practice in Preaching", and "The City and Its Problems". The spring semester he taught three classes: "Advanced Homiletics and the Pastoral Office", "Advanced Practice in Preaching", and "The City Church". The thin documentary evidence supports the common sense conjecture that he was an effective teacher. He could, after all, draw upon his extensive preaching and speaking experience for the homiletics instruction; and for the city instruction, upon years of interest, training, and experience in urban affairs. Oxnam and Professor C. Edmund Neil jointly recommended and secured faculty approval for the formation of Preaching Clubs in an effort to secure "greater interest in and better training for our students in Public Speaking." Although run by the students, membership in one of the various clubs was mandatory. These clubs gave opportunities, outside the formal homiletics classes, to preach, hear, and critique sermons.

Certainly neither the formation of these clubs nor Oxnam's teaching left a major impress on the school. However, he was the "conceiver of and bringer-to-pass" (as one tribute put it) of a Conference of Preaching, and this annual gathering became a permanent and important event in the school's life. Every October about a dozen of the nation's, indeed, the world's, greatest preachers assembled in Boston without payment of fee. To hear and meet them came ministers, many of them BU School of Theology graduates, from all points of the compass. In 1941 President Marsh judged the preaching conference to be "one of the most approved gatherings for exaltation of the work of the minister anywhere on this continent," and Richard Cameron reported that hearing these preeminent preachers helped "to push back again the horizons which have a way of closing in after listening too long to one's own sermons."

Oxnam not only touched this assembly to life, for several decades he was one of the invited preachers. He also sent generous checks to help defray expenses. Above all, during the initial years he edited the sermons for book publication by the Methodist Publishing House.

Concurrent with his teaching duties, Oxnam preached and lectured in the Boston area. The tone of his addresses remained, alas, as in Los Angeles, martial. Witness this utterance at the 1928 New England Annual Conference:

> The flute suggests the sweet music that lulls to sleep. The trumpet suggests the blast that summons men to battle. The flute calls forth the dance, costly raiment, the ball-room. The trumpet, the fight, khaki, the battlefield. But above all else the flute is associated with the minuet. The trumpet forever a part of the charge, the march. The question I raise is this: Is Methodism in this crucial hour to busy itself with a lovely minuet, or summon the followers of Christ to a march that shall lead to the Promised Land? The ball-room, bishops approach the polished floor, the

orchestra plays the minuet, and the question is Are my episcopal prerogatives on straight? Am I to lead the Grand March? Other bishops are in no-man's land, have heard the trumpet call, and marched against entrenched wrong.

In 1928 Oxnam moved from a professorship at Boston to the presidency of DePauw University, but this physical separation did not mean a total severance of ties. Perhaps because of his continuing involvement in the preaching conference, Boston University in 1930 bestowed an honorary LL.D. degree. When in 1939 Oxnam returned to the East as bishop, President Marsh flashed the greeting: "Welcome! Hearty, genuine, sincere welcome! I am more happy than you can ever know at your appointment to the Boston Area." In that year BU School of Theology celebrated its one hundredth anniversary. At a centennial dinner held at Methodism's Uniting Conference in Kansas City in 1939, Oxnam gave a national radio address in which he extolled the school, adding, "If I had a million dollars to give, I would give that sum to the Boston University School of Theology." (Although never approximating that amount, he did contribute smaller sums to the school's survival.) In 1939, also, Oxnam was elected a trustee of Boston University, and although he offered his resignation in 1944 on departing Boston for New York, the school declined to accept it.

As bishop of the Boston Area, Oxnam was naturally much implicated in the life of the university and seminary, including the preaching conference, ordination of seminary graduates, and even offering a course in 1941–42. After the fall term, Dean Earl Marlatt expressed the wish that the course be made mandatory. "He was embarrassingly enthusiastic," Oxnam recorded, "stating that he had not received such enthusiastic and insistent references to any course since he had been there."

President Marsh had long dreamed of establishing a great central campus for the university on Commonwealth Avenue, and the consummation of this vision required that the School of Theology pull up stakes and move from its historic location on Beacon Hill to join the main colleges along the Charles River. When in 1938 six of the theological school's most distinguished graduates, Bishops Hughes, McConnell, Magee, Baker, Blake, and Oxnam, signed a "petition" opposing the move, Marsh was vastly disturbed. His reasoned rebuttal was so masterful that Oxnam backed off, writing to Marsh words that do both men credit: "When an argument is presented that answers the questions that I have in mind and I am unable to answer the arguments with better ones for the position I formerly held, there is nothing to do but change my mind. This I have done." From that moment, Marsh had no stauncher supporter. In 1950 a splendid seven-story educational building adjacent to the appropriately named Marsh Chapel, at the center of the growing university, became the new home of the School of Theology. To be sure, entrance into World War II impeded progress, and the understandable opposition of other Methodist seminaries to funneling denomination funds to Boston was formidable, but in the end Marsh and Muelder, Oxnam, and John O. Gross, Bishop Paul Kern, and other friends of Boston prevailed.

Oxnam as chairman of the Division of Educational Institutions, General Board of Education, 1939–44, and as one architect of the mighty Methodist Crusade for Christ, played an instrumental role. When in 1944 Oxnam obtained a pledge of $333,333 for BU School of Theology from the Crusade for Christ budget, Marsh wrote him in gratitude, "The new Boston University building will now be a reality and it will be largely a memorial to your vision, your courage, and your devotion." And in another letter Marsh promised that "I shall keep in mind that the one person who deserves more credit than any other for that glorious consummation will be your own good self." Writing to Marsh in 1948, Oxnam acknowledged that "I made the original proposal for $333,333, wrote the asking into the budget and stood by even though at times one was accused of allowing his love for Boston University to result in an action that in effect was special privilege for Boston. I never so regarded it. I made the decision solely upon the merits, in the light of the history of the School of Theology and its future contribution to the post-war world." (The only request Bromley denied the president was one to solicit a contribution from his mother-in-law.)

"I think it is not too much to say that the Boston University of today is your creation," Oxnam wrote Marsh in 1950. "I know something of what the school was when you came, and I know a bit of what it is now. I think this one of the most amazing achievements in the record of American education." Believing this, Oxnam was much concerned over Marsh's impending retirement in 1951. With the University of Southern California and other originally Methodist institutions in mind, he worried that should a non-Methodist educator succeed Marsh, Boston might walk a similar secular path. As he confided to his diary, "Our problem is to be sure that when Dr. Marsh retires we choose a devoted religious leader to take the institution; otherwise we will have built another university for some group secular in spirit to take it over." Moreover, Oxnam argued, a nationwide canvass should be made to secure the best individual, contrary to Marsh's initial position that the appointment be made internally. Oxnam prevailed. Incidentally, Oxnam was pressured to place his own name in the running but categorically declined because of age, the bad precedent leaving the episcopacy would set, and the awareness that "strong men in Boston would not have been eager to have me in that position." He was enormously relieved therefore when Harold C. Case was tapped, and after phoning Case urging him to accept, sighed in relief to his diary: "This means that all of the work we have done has resulted in keeping the Methodist tradition; a Methodist minister will be President, the school will be kept in close touch with the Church."

The passing years did not totally terminate the Boston-Oxnam connection. From time to time he returned to give addresses. His portrait, loaned to the school in 1939, remained for years a noble reminder. A student lounge permanently bears his name. In 1945 a wealthy Jewish Bostonian established a five-thousand-dollar scholarship in the name of Oxnam and Rabbi Joshua Liebman. In 1953 the oldest Oxnam child, Robert, was made the university's vice-president in charge of administrative affairs.

CHAPTER 8

A LIVELY PRESIDENCY AT DEPAUW UNIVERSITY

Originally chartered in 1837 as Indiana Asbury University, DePauw became one of Methodism's premier educational institutions. Of the sixteen hundred students who annually came to Greencastle to attend DePauw in the 1920s, most were Methodists and virtually all were Protestants. DePauw's graduates ascended to heights in every area of American life, while its presidents, including Matthew Simpson, Edwin Holt Hughes, and Francis John McConnell, found that DePauw had provided a steppingstone to episcopal leadership in the Church.

In 1928, ailing President Lemuel Herbert Murlin retired. A group of DePauw graduates who had studied under Oxnam in Boston, led by Charles Kendall, presented his name to the committee charged with finding a replacement. After visitations in Boston by older and more prestigious alumni, Oxnam was invited to stop in Greencastle on his way to the General Conference. The meeting produced mutual admiration. The young candidate liked what he saw, while the venerable dean and vice-president Henry Boyer Longden reported to the influential Bishop Hughes, "I was greatly delighted with him and without going into detail, I think he has the qualities of a great president of DePauw, and I sincerely hope that the trustees and he may come to some satisfactory arrangements." Oxnam's election was announced at the General Conference.

Arriving in Greencastle, Oxnam asked one of his champions, "Well, Charley, you got us here. What do you want us to do?" Roy O. West, president of the Board of Trustees and secretary of the interior under President Coolidge, informed him that "the one test of your work here is whether or not this university prospers. You may think what you like to think, say what you like, move as you like—all we are interested in is the progress of this institution." Whether or not West "shuddered" at Oxnam's inaugural address on October 12, as one witness insisted, he probably had second thoughts about his advice as he listened to Oxnam condemn war and economic injustice instead of outlining his plans for DePauw's future. Perhaps West nodded his approval when Bishop Hughes charged the new president, "This College has not been put together carelessly. If it were really necessary, it could get on without you for a season."

After his elevation to the episcopacy, Oxnam frequently told various DePauw alumni groups that the time he spent in Greencastle from 1928 to 1936 had been the "eight happiest years of our lives." One might discount such public statements as dissimulation were it not for the fact that his diaries confirm them. Time and again he sentimentally relived his presidency, remembering not the tensions and the troubles but only the adoration of the students, the gracious hospitality with which Ruth opened the president's house to dignitaries and students alike, the childhoods of Bob, Phil, and Bette, and DePauw's gallant struggle to survive the nation's worst depression.

Never before had Bromley and Ruth lived in such high style. Nor would they do so after leaving DePauw, since even the amenities of the episcopal office would pale in comparison. The eighteen-room presidential mansion was surrounded by shade trees, shrubs, flowers, a rock garden, water lily pond, bird sanctuary, and summer house. Tennis and squash courts, a playing field, and a rifle range kept the children busy. Gardeners maintained the grounds, though Ruth's touch helped the flowers and Bromley's muscle shaped the rock garden. A cook, three maids, and a butler (who stood behind Oxnam's chair at dinner) took care of the household chores. (Son Philip, then in his teens, was aware that the butler was skylarking with the maids and assumed that his parents were not blind to the sexual shenanigans. Perhaps in the interest of staff morale, however, they failed to issue any ultimatums. Apparently Bromley had rejected the example his father Thomas had set in dealing with moral lapses.) Bromley's salary and speaking fees and Ruth's handsome inheritance enabled them to adorn the house with a fine collection of art. Other works they presented to the school as gifts. They also bought a seven-passenger Buick sedan and a Buick coupe, motorcyles for the boys, and an airplane for Robert, who graduated from DePauw in 1937. Although Bromley and Ruth were skilled drivers, they hired students as part-time chauffeurs. Football games found the Oxnam family in special sideline seats. Almost annually, the Oxnams used their vacations to travel abroad, once accompanied by a student chauffeur and once with a student companion for the boys. Unquestionably one reason why the DePauw years were so happy is that for the first time in his life, Oxnam enjoyed a certain poshness.

Reminiscing several years after leaving DePauw, Oxnam wondered what characteristics would enable a man to be a successful college president while at the same time afford him "a life second to none in satisfactions of the spirit." In response, he composed a list of criteria. The college president must be a Christian with strong faith. He needed scholarly, business, and executive abilities, self-control, poise, and sympathy. He must be cooperative, helpful, cultured, and decisive. He should enjoy domestic felicity with a refined and cultured wife who shared his goals and possessed the abilities to help him reach them. He must be able to relate to young people and win their confidence. In order to promote religious life he needed the ability to incarnate his faith. He should be an effective public speaker. He ought to be "dynamic" enough to prevent any professor, dean, or board member from overshadowing him. Finally, the president could not treat the college as an end in itself. Instead, his duty is to create a campus atmosphere in which "the vast majority of all students who attend the institution will be drawn to the Lord, who in turn has been lifted up by the faculty and president." It is not surprising that this job description is a self-portrait. Nor is it surprising that others did not always see him as he saw himself.

"I feel that I am most at home with students, and am happiest when among them," Oxnam once confided. Young people brought out the best in him and he the finest in them. He repeatedly insisted that a Christian liberal arts college need not be any less intellectually stimulating than a great university. Before the students he held John Mansfield's vision, "O glory of the lighted mind." A truly liberal education rests upon a broad cultural foundation; it is not merely the development of a set of skills to earn one's bread. He challenged the men and women of DePauw to seek a quickened and deepened understanding, breadth of outlook, appreciation of beauty, catholicity of sympathies, refinement of taste, critical habit of mind—of thinking for one's self, modesty of judgment, dispassion in the search for truth, and "a proper and balanced conception of the various uses of life, of its graces as well as its utilities." Moreover, he believed that as a Christian school, DePauw would be untrue to its high purposes if it failed to give every student a full opportunity to examine the grounds upon which his convictions rested, and to appropriate them until his heart and mind were satisfied. On occasion President Oxnam offered a closed meeting only for freshmen to discuss religious questions, and while he could not compel, he did commend attendance at Greencastle's Methodist Church.

Although Oxnam ran a taut ship, he did not isolate himself in a forbidding captain's cabin. He maintained an air of puissance but not unapproachability. Some students were commanded to his presence for disciplinary action, but far more voluntarily sought his counsel as they might have consulted an oracle, confiding in him and sharing their dreams. His quick smile, hearty laugh, witticisms, and his knack for remembering their names set most students at ease. Nor was the president's home inviolate. Every September he invited the entire bunch of lonely freshmen to supper. In 1933, the championship football team came for a banquet at which each player received a gold football. "Boy, take a look at this. It's eighteen-carat gold, honest," exclaimed coach "Gaumy" Neal. Less exceptionally but more importantly, small groups of ten or fifteen students dined with the Oxnams almost weekly, often joining a guest speaker. Every

DePauw student probably enjoyed the president's hospitality at least once.

On some instances only a couple of students were present at the Oxnam table. One evening the president invited over every student planning to enter the ministry. After a scrumptious meal, Oxnam read aloud their grade averages, sternly pointing out the discrepancy between their high calling and their mediocre grades. The next semester found the combined grade average up by a point.

A large number of students also benefited from Oxnam's financial generosity. He made the graduation of some possible by outright grants of money. Others he provided with loans to complete their graduate or professional training elsewhere or to travel abroad. One year Oxnam treated about fifty students to an opera in Indianapolis, and another year he brought as many guests to a play. Both instances were preceded by a dinner at the Columbia Club. When the DePauw football team played West Point, Oxnam paid for the marching band to accompany the players. The imaginative president originated a unique travel contest among the students, offering from his own pocket a cash prize for the best daily logbook of a mythical trip to some foreign country of the student's choice to be based on a study of the country's maps, guide books, histories, and travel brochures.

Unquestionably Oxnam's greatest contribution to the widening of the students' intellectual and cultural horizons was the speakers series, numbering about thirty annually, which he personally funded. The guest lecturers, coming from all over the world, included leading statesmen, writers, artists, scholars, scientists, explorers, philosophers, and churchmen. Thanks to Oxnam, each DePauw student, over the course of his or her college career, received the opportunity to hear over one hundred individuals of some renown. It was quite a privilege, considering the provincial background of most of the students. Moreover, the lucky handful invited to the Oxnam home for a dinner party honoring the guest enjoyed a thrilling experience. Oxnam ranked these affairs among the happiest and richest of his life, and believed the students felt the same. Deep was his gratitude to Ruth, his unfailingly enthusiastic and gracious hostess, who took care of such details as flower arrangements, candles, silver, napery, and Japanese lanterns in the garden. She was fondly remembered by countless students.

Most of the men and women of DePauw felt Oxnam's presence on campus most frequently and powerfully through his chapel talks. The daily chapel services were of the utmost gravity to him. Held at 11:00 A.M. in Meharry Hall, they consisted of an organ prelude, the reading of announcements by the faculty secretary, and a fifteen-minute talk. Faculty members were expected to attend and did so if they were prudent. Student attendance was not compulsory, but throngs showed up for several reasons. For one thing, thanks to President Oxnam's urgings, the faculty members took their rotating speaking assignments seriously. For another, Oxnam abolished gender-segregated seating, allowing male and female students to sit together. For a third, the names of the speakers were not announced in advance, and many students came chancing to hear Oxnam, such was his popularity. Over eight years, Bromley gave 621 chapel addresses. Above all, as Professor Jerome Hixson recalled, the daily chapel service was a clearing house for information, a place of inspiration, and a strong cohesive influence on the university—it was "the DePauw family." Under Oxnam's guidance, one meeting a week became a formal worship service, held in Greencastle's new Gobin Memorial Methodist Church. It was replete with a robed choir, unison prayers and responses, a processional, and a brief sermon.

After one chapel talk in 1929, Oxnam wrote in his diary, "I doubt there is a finer audience on earth than that superb body of students. Its speed of intellectual apprehension and its forms of emotional response call for one's best which brings its own reward." Fortunately, Oxnam's talks were preserved by stenographers, since he did not write them out in advance or use notes. They were compelling, challenging, informative, charged with urgency, laced with humor, and vastly varied in subject matter. Bromley's imposing physical appearance, resonant voice, rapid-fire delivery, and supreme self-confidence captivated the student audience. Decades after graduation, many recalled the spell cast by their Prexy's chapel addresses.

Vividly remembered also was Oxnam's response to the "Mock Chapel," an annual spring jollification at which the seniors mimicked the faculty and staff unmercifully. One year the proceedings were interrupted when the faculty, led by Oxnam, entered the chapel dressed as seniors and deported themselves accordingly—that is, outrageously. Another year the senior show had scarcely begun when the doors of the fire escape suddenly opened and down the aisle came faculty members dressed in the flimsy raiment of a May Day pageant with Oxnam as court jester. They staged a maypole dance and crowned diminutive Professor Thompson the Queen of May. Once Oxnam and Dean Robert Guy McCutchan blackened their faces and staged a minstrel show, assuming the names Oxcutch and McNam. When they left the hall to serenade the dorms, an uncomprehending student poured a bucket of water on the Prexy's head.

Although a former varsity athlete and a lifelong sports fan, President Oxnam, to his credit, did not permit intercollegiate athletics to consume him or DePauw. To be sure, during his tenure DePauw continued to field competitive teams, but it no longer attempted to take on the Big Ten powerhouses and Notre Dame. The Oxnam years also witnessed the construction of a new field house and the addition of playing fields. Bromley attended most home football games and even some practice sessions. He certainly rejoiced in the school's unbeaten (indeed, unscored upon) football team in 1933. Nevertheless he kept athletics in perspective. Aside from football, he attended few sporting events. DePauw permitted no freshmen to play varsity ball and granted no athletic scholarships. But as Oxnam explained to Coach Neal, if a boy deserved a scholarship academically, it certainly would not hurt his chances of getting one if he played sports. In 1929, he publicly stated:

> We must recognize that insofar as an institution allows its athletic program to become the dominant force and thereby subordinates educational activities to public interest, that institution becomes a "quack" educational institution and should be treated in educational circles with the same scorn that the medical profession treats a "quack" doctor; "quack" colleges are a menace to the educational health of the state. If we are to graduate athletes with no other attainments, let us create a new degree, namely attainments in scientific sports, and let the three initial letters, A.S.S., indicate the intellectual capacity of that individual.

Four years later he recommended to the Board of Trustees that DePauw seek "a health and physical education service that will keep students fit and provide recreation essential to wholesome living and the development of an intra-mural program in athletics with a consequent reduction of inter-collegiate athletics to that place where they offer opportunity for the superior men in athletic ability to compete in wholesome contest with their equals from other schools."

Oxnam considered good sportsmanship more important than victories. Toward the end of a football game played in Greencastle against Wabash College, the male DePauw students began to sing a bawdy song insulting their arch-rival. An outraged Oxnam rose from his chair alongside the playing field and departed. The following Monday he convened the male students in the chapel and dressed them down, warning that any student again heard singing that song would be expelled. Anyone who could not resist singing it should "go out into the woods and sing it to his own filthy soul." In 1934 Oxnam announced that students who crashed the movie theater to celebrate athletic victories would be expelled. Under President Oxnam, in short, the athletic tail never wagged the academic dog.

Fraternities and sororities were central to the social lives of an overwhelming majority of the male and a large majority of the female students, although all freshman girls were required to live in dorms. As a frat man himself, Oxnam made no attempt to dismantle the Greek system. He did, however, abolish freshman hazing in 1933, warned against "social snobbishness," and, as he reported to the Trustees, encouraged "the gradual transformation of the fraternity and sorority from a center of social interest to a center of intellectual interest." Occasionally the Oxnams accepted invitations to teas and dinners in Greek houses, but that was the extent of their social involvement. Inasmuch as the DePauw student body was almost entirely white and Protestant, racial and religious exclusiveness was not a burning issue. Oxnam's 1932 public communication to the DEKE fraternity, however, reveals a curiously disturbing lack of sensitivity—curious, that is, for a man reputed to be a champion of the oppressed and persecuted: "The first word that rhymes with Deke is the word beak. That word brought to mind the far-famed proboscis of the people who once inhabited Palestine, but now control New York City. I am not at all sure the Dekes admit the Hebrew. I cannot say so much upon the subject of the Home-brew." Surely at a time when anti-Semitism raged, young Methodists did not need this heavy-handed "humor."

In accordance with Methodist tradition, DePauw students had never been permitted to dance on campus. This stern prohibition, which had started to crack under his predecessor, completely crumbled during Oxnam's presidency. When initially petitioned for permission to dance at a campus party, Oxnam replied, "On a university campus there ought to be fifty-seven things to do at a party besides dance." "Would you please suggest a few?" asked the student representative. "Well, one could discuss the peace movement, slum clearance, scientific developments. . . ." Unable to suggest fifty-four more things, the president gave in, decreeing that henceforth the university would allow a limited amount of dancing at certain times during parties, along with skits and other forms of entertainment. But initially such events could not be referred to as "dances." In 1930 the first junior prom took place. By the time Oxnam departed, residence hall, sorority, and fraternity dances had become a favorite way for students to socialize. The playing of cards also advanced relentlessly, although Oxnam refused to alter the ban on Sunday evening deck-shuffling, perhaps hoping to encourage students to attend the vespers service instead.

George B. Manhart, a professor of history during Oxnam's presidency, dedicated the second volume of his two-volume history of DePauw University to the memory of Oxnam's two successors, Presidents Clyde Everett Wildman and Russell Jay Humbert. The exclusion of Oxnam is, perhaps, revealing. It has been observed already that while Oxnam was approachable and indeed encouraged student contacts, he ran a taut ship. In fact, there was an element of Captain Bligh in his command. The plight of DePauw's impotent student government is illustrative.

During Oxnam's years the student government lacked the one thing all true governments must possess—power. John D. Millett, a student who later became president of Miami University and a nationally renowned educator, recalled, "President

Oxnam was a great liberal in his discourses; he was considerably less than liberal in his personal relationships with many of the people around him." Millett added that "there was no such thing as a Student Union. I know, because I was 'president' of this organization in 1931–32, and I was simply informed by President Oxnam that I had been selected for this position." In 1932 Oxnam recorded in his diary, "The Student Affairs Committee was called to order, but there was no work to do and it adjourned immediately." In that year he characterized the president of the student body (*not* Millett) as a "liar," a "cry-baby," and "altogether poor stuff." He described campus politics as "rotten." When presented with a petition signed by 338 male students requesting the reinstatement of a professor whom he had dismissed, Oxnam told the student representative that he "could not receive a petition from him, since there was one principle that one must act upon—namely that the student body had nothing whatever to say relative to the employment, dismissal, or continuance of a professor."

Consumption of alcoholic beverages on or off the campus by students was grounds for suspension. Annually a handful of scofflaws met this fate. In 1932, however, a drinking hysteria swept the campus. As a result, a hundred suspected offenders were ordered to the president's office for interrogation. Oxnam adhered to clear-cut rules. Regardless of changing national and state liquor laws, he reminded the students, university law remained fixed: the ban on drinking was absolute.

The investigation resulted in the outright expulsion or the placing on probation of about a score of students, with the consequent loss of their scholarships, student offices, honorary positions, and social privileges. Eight members of the Phi Delta Theta fraternity, the chapter's entire class of seniors, not only drank, but did so in a Terre Haute bawdy house. Although they explained to Oxnam that they had been too broke to visit with the ladies in the back rooms, they were doomed. All were suspended, had their pictures expunged from the yearbook, and were forbidden to participate in the commencement exercises (although they were not denied their diplomas). One sympathizes with Oxnam. As the president of a Methodist institution in that age of strict official morality his duty appeared clear. "There is nothing to do but dismiss them," he told himself in his diary. "It will take every Senior out of the Phi Delta House and bring no end of suffering to parents. However, I take it we've done our best in the matter of meeting the students on the basis of fair play. The law must now take its course."

A disquieting aspect of the 1932 drinking dragnet was its dependence on snooping and squealing. Dean of Women Katharine Alvord and Dean of Men Louis Dirks compiled lists of suspects to be interrogated by Oxnam. Individual professors gratuitously presented their own lists to the concerned president. Even the students lengthened the rolls by snitching on their peers. In the winter and spring of 1932 a miasma of suspicion blanketed the campus. Equally disturbing is the questionable accuracy of the verdicts Oxnam reached after interviewing the suspects. If, in Oxnam's formidable presence, a student appeared "exceedingly pale" or "does not look one squarely in the eye," Oxnam assumed the frightened youth was lying. The assumption, of course, does not necessarily follow.

The First Amendment did not protect DePauw's student publications during Oxnam's tenure. In November 1931, *The DePauw* carried an article critical of the venerable Dean Alvord. Oxnam was then in Japan. Acting President Dr. Henry B. Longden placed both the offending author and his editor on probation, removed them from the paper's staff, forbade the criticism in print of the faculty without prior approval, and appointed the head of the journalism department to censor future editions. Oxnam, ever sensitive to student criticism of the faculty or administration, later approved this disciplinary action. He did, however, sympathize with the students' impression of the dean of women and "her petty little legalism." Witness this diary entry: "Her worry about improper thoughts upon the part of the girls is but the reflection, I think, of a morbid mind. She refused to let one girl wear pajamas since her roommate did not, because pajamas might be 'suggestive.' Oh Lord." Subsequently *The DePauw*'s drama critic was removed because of his critical review of a play presented by the Drama Department.

On another occasion trouble arose over an issue of the *Yellow Crab*, a campus humor magazine, which published an issue containing putatively risqué jokes (lifted from other college humor magazines) and an article critical of G. Herbert Smith, whom Oxnam had recently appointed dean of freshmen. John D. Millett was then president of Sigma Delta Chi, the honorary journalism fraternity, an editor of *The DePauw,* and a member of the *Yellow Crab* staff. He later recalled that cause célèbre:

> The *Yellow Crab* appeared just before Thanksgiving recess in 1932. Almost at once the Administration reacted by declaring that the magazine was a disgrace to DePauw University. All the copies quickly disappeared; it was said that the officers of the University bought them. The members of Sigma Delta Chi were given a summary hearing by a board of administrative officers headed by President Oxnam. We quickly discovered that the question was not whether or not the issue was of dubious taste; the Administration had obviously already decided that question. We were simply asked individually who was responsible for the publication, and we all acknowledged our collective responsibility. The decision was swift and certain. The chapter of Sigma Delta Chi was suspended; the *Yellow Crab* was abolished; and each of us was placed on conduct probation. As a consequence we lost all of our positions in campus organizations other than our fraternities. I always thought that President Oxnam over-reacted to the publication. I continue to this day to believe our real offense was criticizing G. Herbert Smith.

Millett learned then and there that a university president "had better learn how to absorb criticism without over-reaction."

The sexual situation on the DePauw campus was probably assessed accurately in a report the president of the student body made to Oxnam: "He tells me that very few DePauw women are mixed up in intimate relationships with men here, but that necking is everything but the limit. He has been to Indianapolis on several parties and the girls, some from DePauw, have been along." Oxnam had no choice but to be stern with malefactors, but he humanely wondered to himself whether counseling by a trained psychiatrist might not be a better answer than punishment. He also mused: "I fancy many of these so-called 'problem cases' will be laughed at in days to come when newer and I think saner ideals govern in the matter of sexual relationships."

In 1936, a small group of DePauw students formed a chapter of the American Student Union and made plans for a "peace strike" on Armistice Day. Oxnam went to New York and ferreted out the information that the ASU was a Communist front organization. Returning to Greencastle, he announced that any student who struck on Armistice Day would strike himself out—out, that is, of the university. Instead of striking, the Student Union held a little meeting of their own off campus. On campus, a school-sanctioned event honored the fallen dead, and the students pledged themselves to constructive efforts to develop a peaceful world. Although investigated, the members of the ASU were not dismissed from school. While Oxnam was correct in believing that the group was Communist-dominated and that it did not espouse nonviolence in the class struggle, a diary passage reveals that his real concern rested elsewhere: "A strike has no place upon a college campus. If a strike be legitimate in the interests of peace, some will think it *equally legitimate in efforts to effect curriculum changes and changes in staff. It is so used in some foreign universities. It has no place in democratic American institutions*" (emphasis added).

If Oxnam's authoritarianism is beyond debate, so was the sincerity of his devotion to and concern for his students. For their part, the overwhelming majority of the student body respected and honored their Prexy, regarding him with a mixture of awe and love. Student societies awarded him medals. *The Mirage* (1931) editors judged that "DePauw is proud and fortunate to have him." The official student farewells in June 1936 were fulsome. Above all, countless graduates, many of them who later became leaders in their chosen fields, continued to seek Oxnam's counsel over the years. Their admiration for their old leader is transparent.

While a few DePauw students found Oxnam's authoritarianism irritating, a large segment, perhaps a majority, of the faculty found it intolerable, although in that era administrative power in academic life was more total and faculty rights more fragile than it would be a generation later. Moreover, dwindling school enrollment and income, especially after 1929, put Oxnam in a difficult position. He had no alternative but financial retrenchment. Perhaps Oxnam recalled the words of St. Augustine, "the misery of these necessities," when he lamented to his diary in 1933: "How to cut $75,000 from a budget of half a million, protect the educational standards of the school, be just to the teaching staff, and remember the ethics I have been preaching, is more than I know." While one can sympathize with Oxnam's dilemma, however, one can also understand the faculty's rebellious mood. Oxnam's noble words about "democracy" ring hollow in light of his less-than-democratic leadership.

On many instances during and after his presidency, Oxnam tried to help the nonacademic public understand the teaching profession, pointing out that the hours actually spent in the classroom represented only a fraction of the total work week. He favored sabbaticals, adequate library and laboratory resources, and decent salaries for the faculty. He lauded the competency, vitality, industry, and devotion of those faithful souls who "gladly teach," citing by name particularly noteworthy past and present staff members. His diaries reveal a compassionate concern for professors who suffered sickness or the loss of loved ones. He visited the bereaved and ill in their homes. When great DePauw teachers died, Oxnam gave eloquent eulogies, as in the case of Edwin Post. There are hints that Oxnam personally financed the research trips of a few professors. Moreover, both the public and private record show a mutual admiration—even a warm friendship—between Oxnam and the linchpin DePauw faculty, including esteemed Vice-president Henry Boyer Longden, faithful workhorse Dean William M. Blanchard, talented and colorful Dean of Music Robert Guy McCutchan, organist Van Denman Thompson, English professor Raymond W. Pence, political scientist W. Wallace Carson, and not a few others. No fair assessment of Oxnam's relationship with the faculty can ignore these favorable relationships.

Yet Bromley held reservations about professors in general, as exemplified by the recommendation he gave to a new college president:

> You will also find little people, interested in professional chairs, whose ego increases as, through the years, they confront immature persons. Unlike the lawyer, who must meet his equal in the courtroom, the surgeon who must make decisions on which his reputation rests, the businessman whose very future depends upon his course of action, this individual can put off until tomorrow. Inferiority can be covered. He becomes petulant, this person, he feels he has full right to academic freedom, unlimited tenure, and the equal right to be disloyal to his president, to his board, to his institution. He wishes his pay check regularly, but he wants to destroy the institution through criticism with the same regularity.

As the Depression deepened, student enrollment declined, the endowment fund (heavily invested in Chicago's plunging real estate) shrank, as did gifts from alumni, causing deficits to mount. Economies *had* to be effected. The first thing to be cut was funds allowing faculty members to attend professional meetings and for the university to send representatives to the inaugurations of college presidents. In the academic year 1932–33, faculty salaries were slashed by 53 percent. (An American Association of University Professors report found that during the Depression, 84 percent of the schools studied cut professors' salaries, but usually only by about 15 percent.) The clerical staff and maintenance workers suffered comparable losses, leaving some with incomes as little as fifteen dollars a week or less. Given that Oxnam had no alternative but to pare employee salaries to the subsistence level, several critical points remain. First, he seemed oblivious to the cruel contrast between his own high style of living and the near destitution of the faculty and staff; such insensitivity aroused much bitterness. Second, as a famed champion of social justice and the rights of labor, the disparity between what he preached and practiced seemed especially striking. Third, when, according to Professor Hixson, he commented that if faculty salaries were inadequate, the employees could nevertheless "live on their incomes," curses, not loud but deep, were muttered. Fourth, Oxnam's diaries do not reveal *many* cries of anguish over the fate of the professors. On the contrary, his entries chide them for chanting the same old "less work and more pay" litany.

Economics also dictated a reduction in the length of the payroll. Again, the question is not one of necessity but of scope and manner. During the period 1928–34, sixty faculty members either resigned, failed to secure reappointment, or were dismissed, including seventeen in 1933 alone. DePauw historian Manhart charitably notes, "In view of the normal turnover and the fact that decreasing enrollments seemed to justify cut-backs in the staff, this figure was perhaps not excessive." An American Association of University Professors investigating committee, however, found the number "alarming," since twenty-six of the sixty were in professorial grades, and the dismissals, in effect, had been made by Oxnam alone with no protection afforded by tenure, peer, or Trustee review. As a result, an atmosphere of faculty unease pervaded the campus. Independent evidence supports the AAUP's conclusion that in matters of firing, hiring, and promotion, Oxnam's word, if not absolute law, was certainly inordinately commanding. A professor who could not perform in the classroom, Oxnam said publicly, "must seek work elsewhere," but at the same time he would not grant the students a voice in rating the professors.[1] His diaries reveal the subjectivity, not to say idiosyncrasy, of his faculty evaluations. Individual after individual simply "will have to go." Of one who told "vulgar stories" in class "to the embarrassment of the girls," Oxnam wrote that he "will have to go." Of one who was a gossip, the president felt he had little leeway: "There is nothing to do but let him go." An outspoken malcontent "will have to go." A teacher who imbibed would of course have to go. As president of a Methodist institution, Oxnam had a right to expect a teacher not to be irreligious. Still, it is unpleasant to find that he asked the students to report to him the names of faculty they deemed "unduly hostile to religion or discouraging to a religious profession." Oxnam's lack of empathy for the faculty is illustrated by an excerpt from an address he gave to it: "It would appear that one of two actions should be taken: either get a new president or get a new faculty. I scarcely need remind you that in the present conditions of the man market, it would be easier to get a new faculty."

One stiff-kneed individual unintimidated by his president's commanding manner was Ralph W. Hufferd, a professor of chemistry who had served DePauw since 1920. For refusing to march briskly to the beat of Oxnam's drum, he was accused of being uncooperative, disloyal to the new administration, and destructive of DePauw's weal, and was warned to that effect in 1930 by Oxnam. When his contract was not renewed in 1933, he took his case to the AAUP. The investigating committee report, based on over a hundred pages of evidence, appeared in the AAUP *Bulletin* in May 1934. At the annual meeting of the AAUP in Chicago the following November, DePauw was removed from the "eligible list," formerly known as the "recommended list," of colleges and universities. According to more accurate terminology later used by the AAUP, DePauw would have been placed on its list of "Censured Administrations." The report is devastating. While acknowledging Hufferd to be "blunt and tactless," it found Oxnam to be "impatient of opposition, debate, and delay." The report concluded:

1. That as to procedure, Professor Hufferd's dismissal is to be condemned without qualification. The evidence was not properly collected or used, and no hearing was accorded. Further, that the causes assigned for dismissal are not established by the evidence. Finally, that Professor Hufferd is thoroughly competent, has been loyal to DePauw University, and has been victimized because of his fearless stand for faculty control of academic questions.
2. That the general tenure situation at DePauw is very uncertain because of the power and disposition of President Oxnam and of the policy of annual appointments. While insecurity is not universally felt, it is the prevailing impression among the faculty.
3. That the delegation of such wide powers to President Oxnam under the circumstances herein stated and the manner of their exercise have been detrimental to the interests of DePauw University.

Hacking through a jungle of detail, only a few points need to be made. On the one hand, Oxnam was defended in public statements issued by the Student Senate, by nine senior professors, and by the Board of Trustees. On the other hand, conservative and patriotic groups, long critical of Oxnam, delighted in the AAUP's indictment of his leadership. More revealingly, liberal voices also condemned him. An editorial entitled "Fascist DePauw" in the progressive Madison (Wisconsin) *Capital-Times* charged that Oxnam "has inaugurated the rule of annual appointments and applied it like a whip-lash to keep faculty members in an ordered goosestep." The report's "findings show Pres. Oxnam as an academic Mussolini whose word is law and who is always sure of being backed up by the trustees."

Most revealing of all are two remarks by Oxnam himself. Asked to comment on being dropped from the AAUP's "eligible list," he insouciantly replied, "It means nothing in the educational world." Considering his national reputation as a champion of labor unions, his comment on the report induces vertigo: "Business men will understand the nature of this report when it is pointed out that an investigation of this kind is similar to an investigation that a business agent of a labor union would make of a business establishment. . . . The report in large measure represented the view of a single individual who became exceedingly angry when he found it impossible to dictate policies for a university that is quite capable of directing its own affairs." The AAUP censure of DePauw was not lifted during Oxnam's administration.

Beginning in 1930, Oxnam undertook a complete reshuffling of the educational administration, abolishing department organization and eliminating department heads. He did this in the interests of efficiency, economy, rationality, and order. The details need not concern us. The consequence was a further concentration of authority in the hands of the president and a few close administrators. The faculty was left virtually powerless. By 1935, acknowledging that the "reforms" had not produced the prized results, Oxnam restored a degree of authority to the faculty. Perhaps Oxnam had this failure in mind years later when he sighed to a companion, "Oh, how I wish I could come back and do it all over again! There are so many things I would have done differently." And in a letter to Chancellor Charles W. Flint of Syracuse University he ruefully remarked, "I am of the opinion that a Board of Trustees ought to insist that a man have at least ten years experience in the office of college president before it elects him to such an office."

If faculty criticism of Oxnam ran deep, it also ran largely silent; the criticism of outsiders, however, was both ocean deep and louder than sound. The myriad chapters in this stormy story must be summarized in a few paragraphs.

To begin with, Oxnam's old nemesis in California, the trufflehound-nosed Colonel Leroy F. Smith of the Better America Federation continued to sniff out Oxnam's "un-Americanism," submitting reams of "documentation" to the members of the Board of Trustees and to Indiana newspapers. Stung beyond endurance, Oxnam traveled to California to seek redress and finally decided to press a libel suit, which Smith's death prevented from coming to trial.

For another thing, conservatives and patriots charged that Oxnam "regularly and repeatedly" brought to the campus speakers who infected the student body with the twin poisons of socialism and pacifism. (Truth to tell, Oxnam's invitations were extended overwhelmingly to individuals of liberal persuasion.) This particular pot boiled over in 1931 when Sherwood Eddy spoke on the subject "Sex and Youth" and proceeded to sell his book of the same title at a discount in the school bookstore. Although *The Hoosier Legionnaire* primly informed its readers that the book's content could not "with propriety" be detailed in its columns, the matter was blown out of proportion: the bookstore only sold fourteen copies including one to that intrepid dean of women, Miss Alvord. Incidentally, it says something about Oxnam's surveillance system that he quickly found out the names of all fourteen purchasers. Following Eddy's visit, an influential DePauw graduate, W. P. Evans, informed an alumni group that "there are things in this highly immoral book that no one should know," and denounced Oxnam for exposing innocent youngsters to "Sex, Sovietism, and Socialism." Naturally the Indiana press headlined the story—the alliteration of the charge was almost as tripping as "Rum, Romanism, and Rebellion." Happily the Board of Trustees, the faculty, the students, the Northwest Indiana Methodist Annual Conference, and even the Greencastle chapter of the American Legion (in contrast to other Indiana chapters), issued public statements in Oxnam's defense.

Naturally Oxnam's public utterances got him into trouble with certain groups. For example, he opposed the bonus demands of the World War I veterans and the jailing of Earl Browder, Communist party candidate for president of the United States, by the mayor of Terre Haute. An address before the inmates of Pendleton Reformatory in 1930, one he had previously delivered to other groups, including Rotary International, without incident, put a hornet in the bonnets of the Daughters of the American Revolution. In it he said, "If we mean by 'America First,' America first in world service, it is a sublime slogan, but if we mean America first, and because our oil reserves may some day be depleted we will allow certain groups to stir up public opinion that we will enter Mexico and steal her oil reserves because we need them, then that slogan will do for us just what it did for Germany a short time ago." Headlined the newspapers of Indiana: "D.A.R. Brands Oxnam's Speech an 'outrage.' " and "D.A.R. After Scalp of

Depauw Prexy." Once again DePauw groups rallied around their president and the storm subsided, although individuals such as Felix McWhirter, treasurer of the DePauw Alumni Fund, put forty-three questions to Oxnam concerning his past and present record of supporting radical causes. Fantastic question 6 read, "Is it a fact that you have consistently opposed the Boy Scout movement?" Of course, he had not.

The status of DePauw's Reserve Officers' Training Corps was unquestionably the issue calling forth the heaviest criticism of Oxnam. In 1928, the General Conference of the Methodist Episcopal Church adopted a resolution opposing military training in high school and all compulsory military training in colleges and universities, the exact position of the Methodist World Peace Commission, of which Oxnam was secretary. DePauw was the only Methodist college in which military training was still mandatory. All male students were required to join ROTC during their first two years. If they so chose, they could continue the program as upperclassmen. In 1928, the unit enrolled 548, and its summer camp was ranked the highest in the United States despite persistent efforts to eliminate the compulsory feature during Dr. Murlin's presidency. Shortly after arriving in Greencastle, Oxnam announced his decision to make military training optional starting in 1929. Unlike his predecessor, Oxnam made no effort to consult with the faculty or students, since "this is an administrative, not an academic problem. It is administrative for the reason that the administration enters into agreement with the government relative to the establishment of a military unit at the university. The faculty did not vote upon the question as to whether there should or should not be a unit at the school." As the friends of ROTC predicted (including Professor Ralph Hufferd, an American Legionnaire), enrollment in the program sharply declined to only 106 in 1933–34 as a result both of its voluntary status and the conscious harassment (it was alleged) of the Department of Military Science and Tactics by the Oxnam administration. The second shoe dropped on January 23, 1934, when on Oxnam's recommendation the Board of Trustees voted overwhelmingly to request the War Department to withdraw the unit entirely. Naturally ROTC students felt abandoned and patriotic groups across the state were outraged. Oxnam's son Phil recalled that the football coach benched him for an entire game attended by his father to show his displeasure at the decision. A DePauw graduate recalled being thrown out of the office of a prospective employer (a former army officer) in Indianapolis because she came armed with a recommendation from Oxnam; she never used the letter again in Indiana.

Running a medium-sized school scarcely commanded all the attention of a man of Oxnam's energies and ambitions. Starting in September 1935, he wrote a weekly newspaper column entitled "Facing Facts," which was carried by over sixty Indiana newspapers. The column ended in June 1936 but was revived in 1937 and renamed "Facing Facts with Bishop G. Bromley Oxnam." The column commented on current events, domestic and foreign, and occasionally on cultural matters, but not religious subjects. In September 1934 Oxnam began a fifteen-minute Monday evening radio broadcast from station WFHM, Indianapolis, called "The Significance of the Week's News." "It is not enough to hear the news," he explained to his audience. "We must interpret it, evaluate it, and as Americans consider its possible effect upon our interests and ideals." About half of the program, as in the case of the newspaper columns, consisted of excerpts from books and articles he had read. This job took some doing. "Worked on the radio material in the afternoon," he lamented to his diary. "Who ever dreamed of being a scholar and an 'executive' at the same time. One must fight for his study hours, and winning them is often too fatigued to use them."

He may not have been so fatigued if he had not served concurrently as an arbitrator charged with settling the disputes that arose between the United Mine Workers of America and the Indiana Coal Operators' Association. "I have forgotten the number of disputes," he later recorded, "but there were many which involved very careful study and written decisions. I think that generally the decisions were well received and were indicative of the interest of churchmen in good industrial relations."

He may not have been so fatigued, above all, if he had not accepted so many off-campus speaking assignments. While profitable, this business was surely grueling. Between 1928 and 1936, he delivered over eight hundred lectures and sermons to audiences of businessmen, educators, civic clubs, church groups, women's societies, and students. His speaking journey carried him to every corner of Indiana. Thanks to his student chauffeur, he could read during the long drives en route to the engagement and nap during the return trip late at night. As his fame spread, he became in ever greater demand throughout the Midwest and even on both coasts, requiring travel by train, and increasingly, by plane. A measure of Oxnam's widening reputation during this period is suggested by the honorary degrees he received from Boston University, USC, Wabash College, and Ohio Wesleyan. He was also invited to a Washington dinner in 1929 to honor President and Mrs. Coolidge. Later he was a dinner guest of the Roosevelts at the White House.

In 1929 alone, Oxnam accepted 175 speaking engagements. Considering that his summers were spent abroad, this means that during the academic year he was lecturing approximately every other day. This total does not include his talks at DePauw. He used over three hundred different speeches, although fifteen were given ten times or more and accounted for about half of his appearances. He delivered a single commencement address sixty times. He gave speeches on public affairs far more frequently than on religion. Before visiting a town in Indiana, he would memorize the names of all the DePauw students who lived there and some fact about each one. When a doting parent asked about his child, Oxnam could then mention the child by his first name and make some flattering reference to his prowess as a football player, scholar, debater, fraternity president, or the like.

Clearly Oxnam coveted the fees he received for speaking and relished his popularity and the acclaim of clapping hands. Nevertheless, there were moments when the cream curdled, moments of bone-tiredness, moments of boredom, perhaps, when delivering a talk for the thirtieth or sixtieth time, and moments of exasperation. After a high school commencement address in Clay City, Indiana, he wrote self-pityingly in his diary:

> How under the skies Indiana carries on with the frightful work done in some of these high schools is more than I can understand. As dumb a lot of people as I have ever met assembled for this affair. It was poorly done

from start to finish, the youngsters graduating were most unpromising in looks, and the whole evening stupid. It took more energy to hold that crowd in line, with its crying babies, restless people, and atrocious music than it does to speak to ten times the number of intelligent people.

A final question must be raised about Oxnam's extracurricular activities—the newspaper column, radio program, labor mediation, foreign travel (in addition to the summers, he was absent from the DePauw campus the entire fall semester in 1931), and peripatetic speaking engagements. Did he spread himself so thin as to leave his faculty feeling neglected? Professor Hixson suggested as much when he wrote, "In fact, he [Oxnam] was so wrapped up in world problems that he may at times have overlooked the needs of individual faculty members, particularly during the depression years." That this feeling may have been widespread is hinted at in a diary passage. In 1937 Oxnam returned to Greencastle for the inauguration of his successor, President Clyde E. Wildman. Oxnam judged Wildman's presidential address long and dull. "In fact," he wrote, "I fear that the faculty desire to have somebody who cannot talk has been fulfilled."

In 1932 Oxnam was elected a delegate to the General Conference for the third time. Defeated by Daniel Marsh for the chairmanship of the key Committee on the State of the Church, he served as vice-chairman. In that capacity he was charged with drafting the social pronouncements. Although the *Christian Century* correspondent termed the conference "negative, unadventurous, even timorous" and feared for its "flickering out in futility," the pronouncemnts drafted by Oxnam and his committee and adopted by the conference hit hard. The Depression was interpreted as a "rebuke and spur" to the Christian churches. The committee condemned the industrial order as "unchristian, unethical and anti-social, because it is largely based on the profit motive, which is a direct appeal to selfishness." The presence of poverty amidst plenty necessitated the replacement of "our present policy of unplanned competitive industrialism with a planned industrial economy, which aims definitely at economic security for all." While horrifying to conservatives, this position was too mild for Professor Harry F. Ward, who unsuccessfully sought to have the delegates adopt a statement submitted by the Methodist Federation for Social Service instead. The gulf between Oxnam and his old mentor was widening.

Oxnam was on the winning side of a debate to liberalize the Church's position on divorce but vainly opposed reducing Methodism's monetary contribution to the Federal Council of Churches. He also spoke in favor of higher education requirements for entrance into the Methodist ministry.

In the weeks preceding the conference, various individuals had urged him to permit his name to be advanced for the episcopacy. "The whole matter seems funnier and funnier to me," he noted in his diary after one solicitation. "It is utterly beyond belief to me and I am not sure even now that if it were to come I would accept," he noted after another. At the conference his name was advanced, and although a dark horse, he gained strength steadily with each ballot. The fourteenth found him in fifth place with 206 votes. At this point he came to the platform and requested his supporters to cast their votes for someone else: "I came to the Conference with no thought at all that I would be so considered. I would have withdrawn at the beginning, had I not thought it would be disregarding proprieties."

At the 1936 General Conference, however, Oxnam was made bishop, ending his presidency of DePauw. Thereafter he closely followed developments at the school, served on the Board of Trustees, and always enjoyed his return trips to the campus. His diaries contain repeated references to "my friends of yesterday," "many happy memories," and wonderings "about the wisdom of having left a place so filled with life and opportunity. But what's done is done." In appreciation, the Oxnams gave to DePauw Daniel Chester French's *Lincoln* and a valuable collection of original manuscripts and first editions by Bret Harte which they had lovingly collected over the years. In turn, DePauw awarded Oxnam a Doctor of Humane Letters Degree in 1938.

Oxnam thought little of his immediate successor, Clyde E. Wildman, considering him to be henpecked, dreary, pompous, slovenly, a poor speaker, "everlastingly in the slough of indecision," and so crude "that he simply does not know how to be courteous." Oxnam occasionally acknowledged that Wildman was "doing his very best and desires to be kind." But ultimately Oxnam concluded, "Wildman is proving himself a stupid ass. An ass is bad, but a stupid one is worse." (This assessment is poles apart from that of DePauw historian Manhart and others.) President Russell Jay Humbert Oxnam regarded more favorably: "President Humbert has brought new life to the institution. Wildman's inability to lead well-nigh destroyed DePauw. Humbert is bringing it back."

In sum, from 1928 to 1936, Oxnam brought many improvements to DePauw. Asbury Hall, a maintenance building, a heating plant, a field house, and a publications building were all built under his leadership at a cost of more than $315,000. Other structures were renovated. Some additional land was added to the campus. DePauw's gift of $50,000 made possible the completion of Gobin Memorial Church. The office of comptroller was created. Student health and library services were enlarged. Gifts to the university included the large Harrison and Hill estates. This list by no means completes the gamut of Oxnam's achievements.

Nevertheless, the Oxnam record is open to a more mixed evaluation. Such an evaluation must include three major (though admittedly subjective) points:

First, his relationship with the students, with some exceptions, was splendid. He knew, liked, and respected them and they knew, liked, and respected him. In short, he possessed the qualities necessary to win the admiration and affection of most of the men and women of DePauw.

Second, his relationship with the faculty, with some exceptions, was unfortunate. He was too insensitive to both their financial insecurity and their fearfulness of being discharged without due academic process. Moreover, any professor with pride in his calling would be ashamed to have his school censored by peers, the AAUP. Oxnam's authoritariansm and his stripping of the faculty of any real power in academic affairs left the faculty sullen.

Third, and most debatable, there are knowledgeable individuals who assert that President Oxnam was not an effective fund raiser; that he gratuitously alienated too many alumni; that he was involved in so many activities other than DePauw concerns that the result was the advancement of his personal weal at the expense of the school's woe.

In 1960 President Humbert issued the following statement about Oxnam's tenure: "He was a students' president. They admired and truly loved him. He gave great leadership to the staff and faculty, and for this he was respected by all. The trustees speak of him with an admiration and affection. Bishop Oxnam set a pace on this campus that has left those of us who followed him almost breathless." The opening and closing sentences in that statement are most certainly true.

[1] Years later, in 1944, Oxnam favored tape recording every class meeting, explaining, "This means supervisors can check every word that a professor says and all the discussion elicited from the students. It might be tough on college teachers, but if some such plan were adopted, ridiculously poor instructional methods of so many professors would be improved radically." I must say that the first day that idea was put into practice in one of my classrooms would be my last day at the school.

CHAPTER 9

WITNESSING EUROPE AND ASIA ON THE EDGE OF FLAMES

Oxnam confidently, perhaps too confidently, embraced the adage "Travel is broadening." Thanks to his wealth he was able to make five trips overseas during the swirling 1930s. In the summer of 1931, the Oxnams had their seven-passenger Buick modified to carry large amounts of luggage and then shipped it to England to use on their two-month, chauffeured tour of the British Isles. Next they moved on to France, Belgium, Holland, Czechoslovakia, Austria, Hungary, and Switzerland before returning to England.

In the fall of 1931, DePauw granted President Oxnam a leave of absence for him to join a commission to study educational institutions in Japan. The trip was funded by the Rockefeller Foundation and headed by John R. Mott, chairman of the International Missionary Council. Ruth's company brightened the trip. On their departure the men and women of DePauw gave them a heartfelt send-off. As if that were not enough, the Oxnams found 234 expressions of bon voyage from the students waiting for them in the stateroom of their San Francisco–berthed ship. The Mott Commission traveled throughout Japan, visiting not only schools but Christian churches, Ys, and hospitals as well. Oxnam occasionally spoke and preached. Of the educational institutions he visited in Japan, he was most impressed with a girls' school run by Catholic sisters. About the nuns he wrote, "I shall never forget these sweet-faced, devoted servants—

no wonder Catholic missions appeal to the native people." An evening with American missionaries was dull: "A fool parrot talked through most of the meal and ruined conversation. Didn't have sense enough to swear and enliven things." The Oxnams experienced their first Kabuki play, *The 47 Ronin*. Bromley and Ruth made it home in time to spend Christmas with the children, having survived fearful Pacific storms and boring traveling companions on the ship.

The summer of 1933 once again found the Oxnam family in Europe. Their travels by boat and hired motor car carried them to Spain, Italy, Palestine, Egypt, Istanbul, the Black Sea, Odessa, Yalta, Greece, and the French Riviera. As always, Oxnam kept complete notes in his diary, on which he would base his later talks and writings. Like so many other Americans visiting Italy at this time, he was astonished by the putative progress, both materially and in terms of national morale, made by Mussolini's Italy. This is not to say that Oxnam ever remotely flirted with fascism. He did not. It is to say that he was amazed by the improvements he saw: swamps drained, sanitation advances, masterfully engineered roads and bridges, and punctual trains. Moreover, the people went "about their business with a new spirit, most of which is a great pride in the fact that they are Italians." As for Mussolini personally, Oxnam judged him "the greatest orator I have ever heard." In fact, he was "a man far abler than Hitler, a man of action and extraordinary power." Clearly, foreign travel is not without its perils.

The following summer held another adventure. Bromley, Ruth, and son Bob joined Sherwood Eddy's fourteenth annual American Seminar, which included about fifty ministers, teachers, and a sprinkling of others. In England, Eddy arranged meetings with the high and mighty, including Ramsay MacDonald, Clement Atlee, Lord and Lady Astor, and the American ambassador. Revealingly, Oxnam was much taken by the Very Reverend Hewlett Johnson, dean of Canterbury, "a glorious ecclesiastic of social vision, physical vigor, penetrating mind, and wholesome soul," a "giant in stature, a saint in soul, a crusader in spirit!" At least it cannot be denied that Johnson was a "giant in stature." The Oxnams basked in London's cultural life, judging the theater superior to Broadway. They found treasures in the art shops and second-hand bookstores.

On July 7 the group traveled to Berlin. Oxnam temporarily took over as the seminar's leader, a prudent move, since Eddy had earlier made statements offensive to the Nazis. The Americans met with many German politicians, professors, labor leaders, and U.S. Ambassador William E. Dodd, but the climax of Oxnam's visit came on July 13. That evening Hitler was cheered by multitudes as he drove in his open car to the Tiergarten. Before the Reichstag, he then defended the murderous killings of his opponents two weeks earlier. Oxnam was present, standing just behind the first row of inner guards. He witnessed the Führer, Göring, Goebbels, black-uniformed storm troopers, Reichstag members, and mesmerized throngs. What he heard shocked him and forced him to change his mind about Hitler, as he both recorded in his diary and reported to the American people: "Cartoonists who portray him as a clown strutting the stage, cast as a ruler, are in error. He appears, rather, a modest person of awful dignity and compelling magnetism; a mystic, a man of purpose, a personality in respose, yet ready to deliver devastating blows for a cause, a man tender at heart but willing to become ruthless in his messianic mission." Oxnam was now convinced that Germany was on the road to dictatorship and that anyone who opposed Hitler "lives in terror. The concentration camp, the firing squad and exile loom like specters of the night in his mind." Oxnam was also convinced that while Hitler did not want war immediately, his vision for a greater Germany made it ultimately inevitable. He also discerned the mounting persecution of Germany's Jews and alerted Americans to the terror. In response to the warnings of Oxnam and others, the Board of Bishops of the Methodist Episcopal Church adopted in November 1938 a resolution protesting "the cruel and destructive anti-Semitic riots throughout the German Reich."

With Eddy back in charge, the American Seminar crossed the Baltic by steamer and entered Russia on July 17, after infuriating delays occasioned by both Finnish and Soviet border officials. The group visited Leningrad, Moscow, and Kirzanov, where they spent three days in a primitive commune. As always, Eddy had arranged meetings with Russian leaders (though not with

Stalin) and with Americans living there, including Ambassador William C. Bullitt. As in 1926, Oxnam found many cultural achievements to admire, such as the paintings in the Hermitage, the ballet, and the theater. Most of what impressed him antedated the Communist triumph. The works produced under the new regime he found generally drab and dispiriting. The general filth of the USSR was unspeakable, and the economic conditions disappointing. Inefficiency and shoddiness reigned, which was hardly calculated to impress a man of his exacting nature.

Oxnam did not avert his gaze from Stalin's tyranny or attempt to rationalize it. The point is important in light of the pro-Soviet charges leveled against him then and later. His private diaries and letters attest to his belief in what he was later to say publicly in the United States. The intellectual isolation of the Russian people was total. Various classes and groups were gagged, starved, killed, or purged of dissenters. "I knew the autocracy of czardom was among the cruelest in the world," he informed the readers of the *Indianapolis Star*, "but I know that the dictatorship of Russia has been as ruthless and cruel in stamping out its enemies, and that for an opposition group at least autocracy has not been shaken off, and I fear that the day of civil liberty is still in the distant future." Oxnam bluntly warned the American people not to be beguiled by the Communist party's invitation to join hands in a "United Front" against fascism. The fundamental purpose of the Communists was not to fight fascism but to win control of the American labor and progressive movements. "The United Front is a dangerous Gift Horse," he concluded.

The integrity and independence of Oxnam's views are underscored by his questioning of Eddy's judgment while in Russia: "I feel Mr. Eddy has lost his grip," he confided to his diary. "He wears blinders to avoid seeing the sordid and rose colored glasses to give a happy tint to the grim sights." When Eddy hailed the enlightened rehabilitation of prostitutes, Oxnam noted that this observation was based on faith in the official word, not objective fact. When Eddy spoke of Soviet justice, Oxnam asked, "What does Eddy mean by this abstract something called justice? Is it just to 'liquidate kulaks' when under the law they had through greater energy gotten ahead?" Ultimately, Oxnam concluded that "Mr. Eddy is fundamentally an evangelist, out to save. First it was individual souls, that was on our India trip. Now it is society. He is a man who must have a cause."

The American Seminar departed for Poland, where, in contrast with the USSR, Oxnam found much to admire. Vienna was the next stop, where they had interviews with key individuals, including Chancellor Kurt von Schuschnigg and U.S. Ambassador George Messersmith. After a stop in Munich, Bromley, Ruth, and Bob left the American Seminar and made their way via Freiburg, Geneva, and Paris back to London, where they joined Phil.

Oxnam's election to the episcopacy in 1936 caused him to cancel that year's summer travel plans, but in 1937 he and Ruth crossed the Atlantic again. During June they journeyed by sea and land to Norway, Sweden, Denmark, and the North Cape. July and the opening weeks of August found the Oxnams back in England.

From July 15 to July 26, over four hundred delegates and as many more associate and youth participants from forty countries and a hundred Protestant bodies assembled to attend the momentous Oxford Conference on Church, Community, and State, the sequel to the first Life and Work Conference held at Stockholm in 1925. Oxnam attended as an associate delegate. As such, his official responsibilities were nil. He played no role in the planning or preparation of this great gathering; his presence at Oxford was virtually invisible. He and Ruth took the train from London to attend a session or two, but that was it. He was simply not interested, either officially or personally, in the drama hailed by some as the most significant gathering of Christians since the Council of Nicea in 325 A.D. Even more puzzling than Oxnam's conscious absence from the deliberations at Oxford is his lack of any retrospective regret at missing this exciting moment in the history of modern Christianity. Instead of attending the conference, Oxnam busied himself visiting the Albert Museum, the National Gallery, Wesley's house, the theater, Davis Cup matches at Wimbledon, cathedrals, and second-hand art and bookshops. He also sat several times for the famous portraitist Frank Salisbury. Clearly Oxnam loved England—save for the heavy bodies and unpleasant body odor ("British Odor," as he termed it) of the English women. "No wonder there is little nude art in British statuary," he remarked. Oxnam was also bothered by "the dirtiest lot of waiters among the Nordics," the general snobbishness of the upper classes, and the inefficiency of the functionaries.

Between August 3 and 18, there convened at Edinburgh the second World Conference on Faith and Order, the sequel to the first meeting held at Lausanne in 1927. Present were 414 delegates, many of whom had been at Oxford, representing 122 church bodies in 43 countries. Oxnam was a delegate, not merely an associate delegate. In the end that distinction did not make much difference.

In a United Worship Service at St. Paul's in London between the Oxford and Edinburgh conferences all the delegates assembled. Oxnam judged the service to be "as significant as the Councils of the Ancient Church," and thanks to his being a bishop he "was up front with the big babies." Oxnam considered the importance of the sessions at Edinburgh another matter entirely. Though Oxnam respected his erstwhile travel colleague, John R. Mott, a Methodist layman and Protestantism's greatest ecumenical statesmen, Oxnam found his prayers rather like "a great man dictating to a secretary." Mott's stentorian manner led Bromley to muse, "I'd like to see him in pajamas and snoring to see if he carries on with dignity." He debunked other church officials in a refreshingly candid fashion. His rapid disenchantment with the whole Edinburgh enterprise, however, is disturbing. His attitude was not simply one of boredom with theological discussion; it verged on actual disgust. His diary entries grow increasingly biting. On August 4, he wrote,

> I sat with Dean Knudsen. I listened resolving to understand what it was all about if possible. I simply cannot believe that so many intelligent men can regard these questions as serious, without something of a serious nature being involved. But great heavens, if after two thousand years of disputation, we are still to hear "the nature of the sacrament must go back to the nature of grace, but that is dependent upon the nature of God" and on and on, trinitarian distinctions, "Holy Ghost," "the church, the body of Christ." Latin phrases, and on and on. . . . It seemed like the chatter of

> monkeys at a zoo. One monkey with a mirror flashing it in the eyes of another. One Bishop with a doctrine blinding a fellow Christian.

Less than a week into the conference he growled, "I am finally and completely fed up. Endless and pointless discussions; words, propositions and syllogisms—none of which Jesus ever heard, and most of which I doubt he would understand. But we must have unity that rests in agreed faith and accepted order. Sure,—we cannot love one another, we cannot give a cup of cold water, we cannot forgive,—unless we have a clear understanding of such supremely vital matters as (1) What is the meaning of a sacrament? (2) What is a true eucharist? (3) With whom are we in communion? Good-night!" Two days later he "threw in the sponge, bought my ticket for London, wished all the sweet blessings upon the great word-fest." He was relieved to escape the disputations: "In order to get Faith and Order out of our systems we went to see the Marx Brothers 'At the Races.' I shall recommend their names as delegates to future Conferences. We would get somewhere, I don't know where, but somewhere with them along."

In 1942, Oxnam contributed an article on "Intercommunion" to *Christendom.* In it he recalls Edinburgh and reaffirms his original reaction, though in far more chaste language:

> The arguments at Edinburgh were often revelatory of the pride that should go before a fall, pride of scholarship and phrase, some men speaking interminably with much reference to Latin and Greek phrases, burdened by their erudition—burdensome, too. . . . Does any serious man really believe that world law and order depend upon the theories associated with the Sacrament? Is economic justice to be won by revising the Ritual? Is racial brotherhood to come by way of a Communion administered solely by men who are "properly" ordained? Is not the road to unity along the highway of service to our fellows and in the complete gift of self to others, coming at last to respect one another through the spirit and significance of the service rendered, and recognizing finally that exhausting discussions of the eucharist are less important than the breaking of our bodies and the shedding of our blood in the interest of others?

Not all "serious" men who attended Edinburgh agreed with Oxnam on the irrelevancy of doctoral and theological disputation. Instead of sharing his understanding of the Lord's Supper as merely a reverent and solemn memorial, they held rather that Holy Communion was the supreme and divinely ordained means of communicating the life of the incarnate Lord through his body, the Church, to its members. The words of Richard Roberts, penned shortly after Edinburgh, encapsulate the position of those who took the conference seriously:

> A good deal of the comparative impotence of contemporary Protestantism in the Western world has been due to the fact that it did not know where it stood in its theology; and Edinburgh in particular, by its preparatory publications and its conclusions, will do a very great deal to correct this defect. After all, the business of the Church is with "the faith once delivered to the saints" and preserved in the great classical formulations East and West; and it is the business of theology to interpret and reinterpret these documents from age to age. It is only, I believe, by restoring to theology its proper importance in the life of the church that the witness of the church can regain its power. Great theology is a requisite of great preaching; and one consequence of Edinburgh should be to set this theological renaissance afoot.

The Oxnams returned home aboard the *Queen Mary*. They brought with them pleasant memories of Scandinavia and the glories of England, as well as lovely old books, works of art, and the portrait by Salisbury. Doubtless Oxnam had no premonition that one day he would be a major leader in the World Council of Churches. The irony, of course, is that it was the very disdained conferences at Oxford and Edinburgh that brought the Council into being.

Oxnam's trips heightened his reputation as an expert on world affairs. His proclamations were heard and read throughout Indiana and beyond. A typical newspaper headline read, "OXNAM WHO WILL TALK HERE MONDAY IS AUTHORITY ON JAPS." Tens of thousands of avuncular words tumbled from his pen and lips, enlightening tens of thousands of troubled American citizens—plain citizens, for the most part, since his talks were not delivered before foreign affairs experts. Nor did his articles at that time appear in such opinion-shaping national journals as *Atlantic*, *Harper's*, *The Nation*, and *The New Republic*, let alone professional journals. Unquestionably, Oxnam influenced the thinking of Methodists everywhere, especially students and teachers, but it cannot be said he was a mover-and-shaker of the stature of a Walter Lippmann or a Reinhold Niebuhr.

Beginning with the Manchurian Incident in 1931, Asia and then Europe cascaded sickeningly into war: Italy's conquest of Ethiopia, the civil war in Spain, the undeclared Sino-Japanese War after the Marco Polo bridge clash in 1937, German reoccupation of the Rhineland, Hitler's absorption of Austria, Munich, and the Berlin-Moscow pact. Finally, inexorably, general European war erupted with Germany's invasion of Poland on September 1, 1939.

Oxnam had never been an absolute pacifist, though he honored and sought legal protection for those who were; he could never quite repeat the furious litany of Walt Whitman: "I say God damn the wars—all wars: God damn every war: God damn 'em! God damn 'em!" He repeatedly reported that in the event of an actual invasion of the United States he would take up arms in defense of his beloved country. Nevertheless, anguish as he did over the fate of those conquered peoples pinioned on Japanese bayonets or broken on Nazi swastikas, and chastise as he did those isolationists who were quite prepared to permit the world to hang itself, at no time prior to Pearl Harbor did Oxnam advocate America's use of armed force to resist the aggressors. Most Americans were equally desirous of keeping their nation out of war. "Ninety-nine Americans out of a hundred," estimated the *Christian Century* in 1935, "would today regard as an imbecile anyone who might suggest that, in the event of another European war, the United States should again participate in it." A year later a poll conducted by the American Institute of Public Opinion set the exact figure at 95 percent. Methodists were among the antiwar Americans. The famous 1934 Kirby Page questionnaire showed that Methodists led all other clergymen in holding that the church should go on record as refusing to sanction or support any future war or participate in it. The Methodist World Peace Commission was dominated by such absolute pacifists as Ralph Sockman and Ernest Fremont Tittle. The 1932 General Conference confirmed the strong antiwar stand of 1928, and in 1936 it edged Northern Methodism even closer to a position of outright pacifism, declaring "that the Methodist Episcopal Church as an institution does not endorse, support or propose to participate in war," condemning it as destructive, a denial of the ideals of Christ, a violation of human support or propose to participate in war," condemning it as destructive, a denial of the ideals of Christ, a violation of human personal liberty, a threat to civilization, a sin. The great Uniting Conference of 1939 adopted this position: "We believe that war is utterly destructive and is our greatest collective sin and a denial of the ideal of Christ. We stand upon this ground, that the Methodist Church as an Institution cannot endorse war or participate in it."

Although not an uncompromising pacifist, Oxnam was not far out of step with these Methodist positions. Indeed, he helped to formulate them. He was nevertheless more aware than most of the terrible ambiguity confronting the Christian. If it became necessary to repel an invasion, he would fight, but "I want no preacher telling me Christ is in khaki; no ecclesiastic picturing Christ driving a bayonet into the breast of some lad. I want to know that I live in a day that is yet pagan, that I use pagan means. I want my church out of it. I want one institution clear of it. I want to come back, to kneel before an altar that is still an altar and not a recruiting table, there to ask God to forgive me and mankind, and to give us strength to try again, believing that some day we may banish this curse of war and approach the Kingdom ideal of brotherhood for the world."

Of course the agonizing question confronting America in the 1930s was not one of actual invasion, but of how the nation should respond to the swirling events in Asia and Europe. "Europe is headed for another great conflict. We must not be drawn into it. Never again must we send our boys overseas to fight a war that settles nothing," Oxnam publicly counseled in 1935. When Italy's invasion of Ethiopia threatened a general European conflict, Oxnam called for a tidal wave of neutrality sweeping all before it: "We must not be rushed off our feet by sordid interests of armament makers, money-lenders and others who profit by war. The profiteer profanes patriotism. Our patriotic societies may well turn their attention to those interests that, for Judas-like profits, would betray the nation and involve it in European war. This is a red-menace of significance. Blood is red. And the blood will be that of American boys." "Why not a New Year's resolution, No foreign war," he suggested in 1937. "Such a New Year's resolution would save us from a New Year's

Revolution." His warnings mounted in 1938: "American soldiers should never be sent to foreign soil"; "I think we ought to stay out absolutely"; "I am certain that I would refuse to bear arms to invade the territory of another country"; "As an immediate policy we cannot help a thing by going into Asia or foreign conflict. We must keep out absolutely." "Let every Methodist . . . develop a public opinion based upon the slogan NO FOREIGN WAR. Let him repeat that slogan again and again, until the leaders of the nation hear it—NO FOREIGN WAR. Let us say it as one person, until NO FOREIGN WAR becomes a command—NO FOREIGN WAR." Believing as he did, Oxnam logically found himself opposing Roosevelt's efforts to increase the size of the U.S. Navy. Instead, he endorsed the isolationist Neutrality Acts passed by Congress, prohibiting the sale of armaments to belligerents, including the Spanish Loyalists in Spain's civil war.

Oxnam's diaries prove that his publicly expressed fear of America's involvement in war was authentic, as was his publicly expressed loathing of totalitarianism. As a pundit on public affairs, he counseled the American people to support isolationist policies that may have kept America out of war, but they did nothing to deter the aggression. Because he was not an absolute pacifist, Hitler's invasion of Poland caused his antiwar position to crumble. This is not shameful. Millions of Americans were equally bewildered by complex events abroad. Even other respected commentators, not excluding Lippmann and Niebuhr, called wrong shots, too. Circumstances, especially Hitler's mounting might and ambition, made a foolish consistency the hobgoblin of little minds.

Still, there is something terribly disconcerting about Oxnam's behavior. Acknowledging his wide travels and extensive readings, was he in fact competent to offer so much advice on world affairs through newspaper columns, radio broadcasts, articles, and books to the American people? In the 1930s, his primary duties were those of college president and later Methodist bishop. Did he spread himself too thin, thereby making his pronouncements superficial? Also, one wonders about his intellectual honesty when, even as he predicted war in Asia and Europe, he sought to assure his audiences that "internationally, selfish nationalism with its warring imperialism retreats before the advance of sensible internationalism." Above all, one wonders about Oxnam's later marvelous ability to condemn others while absolving himself. For example, in 1948, in an address at the Conference of Young Churchmen in Ohio, he stated that "appeasers, who at Munich put class interest above national interest, plunged mankind into war. In their selfish stupidity they held aloft a pitiful piece of paper and proclaimed, 'Peace in our time.' Statesmen wise enough and brave enough, could have suffocated fascism in its swaddling clothes; but, behind the realities, they preferred the compromises of ignorance, until at last their sons had to face the ruthless Nazi giant almost with bare fists." Oxnam blocked from his memory the fact that in 1938, after the Munich agreement, he had counseled that "we ought to stay out completely" since "we can make no constructive solution in terms of force." In 1938, he warned against the dangers of Roosevelt's naval program, informing his congressman of his "fundamental opposition to such unprecedented naval expansion." In 1936, he would have neither American arms nor American volunteers aiding the Spanish loyalists against fascist Franco. In a word, one may sympathize if not agree with his 1930s broadsides yet wish that he had not been retrospectively so self-righteous in his judgments on the other bewildered souls of that decade.

The fine shadings of the term "isolationist" must be left to the Talmudic scholars; it would be unfair to hang that tag on Oxnam, much less the epithet "appeaser." Nonetheless, the public policies he advocated in the 1920s and 1930s required the United States to possess only minimal military force and placed an absolute veto on the use of it, unilaterally or in conjunction with other nations, save only in the event of outright invasion of its territory. Bluntly put, the policies Oxnam commended and recommended prior to 1940 were not ones to cause the slightest concern to the ambitions of Hitler's Germany, Mussolini's Italy, or Imperial Japan. Oxnam never admitted either publicly or privately that his position may have been wrong or contradictory.

CHAPTER 10

"IF GOLD RUST, WHAT THEN WILL IRON DO?": HUSBAND, FATHER, FRIEND

G. Bromley Oxnam's life was one of a truly staggering number of accomplishments, and while one may debate the enduring significance of these achievements, one can scarcely question their breadth or their import for Methodism in the era in which he lived. The biographer's task is not to assert this or that about his subject's life but to reveal that life as it unfolds in the subject's thought and deeds. This I have attempted to do for the first forty-five years of Oxnam's existence and this I will continue to do for the remaining increasingly momentous years. Nevertheless, perhaps it is appropriate to pause on the eve of Oxnam's election to the episcopacy to look more closely not at what he did but at who he was. The more intimately we are able to know the private man, the more fully we may understand the motivations propelling his public actions. "We have the dead at our mercy" is a charitable adage wise for the living to remember, all the more because Oxnam was the most paradoxical of souls. But paradoxes, after all, can be resolved, and perhaps in our attempts at resolution the humanity of the man will be more fully revealed. Because by Christian definition no individual is free of imperfection, this will entail some less than merciful observations. Every individual is doomed to be seen through the subjective lenses of those who view him, or who study the record about him, and like the witnesses to that terrible scene in the Japanese movie *Rashomon*, the observations, and judgments, reveal as much about the interpreter as about the subject. This truism may be taken as the text for what follows.

On hearing the news of Germany's invasion of Russia, June 1941, Oxnam speculated as to the eventful consequences for the world, adding, "I have always wanted to live in one of the great crises of history. That wish, at least, has been granted." His old and dear mentor, Bishop Herbert Welch, said of him after his death, "Bromley Oxnam's ambitions were high and strong. I think he had a sense of destiny—a feeling he was intended for big tasks and heavy responsibilities; and as he was impatient of laziness and of mediocrity, in himself or others, he felt the urge to prepare himself by unflagging diligence for whatever lay ahead." Oxnam did live in a time of destiny, he did have a sense of his own great destiny, and contemporaries inside and outside Methodism believed that in his company they stood in the presence of greatness. Bishop Gerald Kennedy, an adoring protégé and friend, averred that "Bishop Oxnam was one of the three or four great men I have known in my life"; he was a "magnificent and great bishop of The Methodist Church." "Now and then," Kennedy added, "there appears on the scene a man so great that when he dies, it seems as if we shall never be able to find one man or 10 or 100 to do for the world what he has done." (Privately Kennedy wrote Oxnam confessing that you are "the man I adore most in all the world.") To Bishop John Wesley Lord, Oxnam was "one of the summit souls with whom God on occasion blesses mankind"; to Bishop Earl Ledden he was a "truly great man"; to Bishop James C. Baker, who wept on learning of Oxnam's death, his services to the world were "extraordinary and illustrious"—he was "one of the most creative persons in our Methodist history"; to Bishop Gerald Ensley he was "something elemental in the life of the Church and the nation. . . . his vitality was so great that it kindled the fire of life in other men"; to a southern Methodist bishop he was "the best known and most influential churchman in Christendom"; to a northern Methodist bishop he "was by far the best-known American Protestant churchman around the world"; and Methodism's powerful layman, Charles C. Parlin, noted that "nowhere in the Christian world—Protestant, Anglican, Orthodox or Roman Catholic—and be it in North America,

South America, Europe, Africa, Australia or Asia would you ever hear from a responsible churchman: 'Bishop Oxnam—who he?' "

Bishop William C. Martin judged Oxnam a "really great man," adding "My personal indebtedness to Bromley is greater than I can ever hope to express." Bishop Frederick Buckley Newell stated: "I think he was the greatest churchman I ever knew. I loved him with an affection deeper than you will ever know and he did more for me than any man in the Church." Said Bishop Lloyd C. Wicke: "Bishop G. Bromley Oxnam was a man of . . . majesty and wide-sweeping proportions." Believed Bishop Fred G. Holloway: "No man in our generation has made a greater impact for good, and all of us shall treasure the memory of a truly great Christian leader." "What a magnificent career Bishop Oxnam had," opined Bishop Roy Short, "and what an unusual contribution he was able to make to the Kingdom and to the Church!" Concluded Bishop James Straughan, "He was simply a magnificent human being."

It will not do to discount totally these expressions of admiration and adoration from the lips of fellow Methodist leaders—and the list could be immeasurably extended—because they are echoed by individuals not biased by denominational loyalty. Louie D. Newton, a Baptist leader with whom Oxnam worked closely on church-state matters, judged Oxnam to be "one of the truly great men of our day and generation—a man of surpassing intellectual ability, and Christian conviction and courage rarely found in our times." Episcopal Bishop Henry Knox Sherrill, whose co-labors with Oxnam were close and extensive, expressed the heartfelt words, "I am grateful for every remembrance of him." Sherrill in his autobiography recalled: "I came to have a deep affection for Bromley Oxnam. I found him a charming, unselfish companion, a dynamic leader in the Methodist Church. A strong leader in the Ecumenic Movement as a president of the World Council of Churches, he has made a great contribution to the whole Christian Church." Lutheran Bishop Franklin Clark Fry, another intimate in ecumenical matters, deemed Oxnam a "towering leader" and to have known him "one of the signal honors of life." A raft of world church leaders—Barnes, Cavert, Mott, Visser 't Hooft, Fisher, and

Niemöller—and again the list could be extended—both publicly and in their correspondence "thanked God for a Glorious life carried through to Victory" and termed Oxnam "a great servant of the Church." At the time of Oxnam's death, Reinhold Niebuhr wrote Episcopal Bishop Will Scarlett: "Too bad about Bromley Oxnam. He was a good warrior for the cause of Christian justice. Did you know him? Methodists are too sentimental for me but Bromley was an exception."

As might perhaps be anticipated, Oxnam won the praise of famed Methodist associates Sockman and Crane, Marsh and Case, Knowles and Diffendorfer, and John O. Gross for openers[1]—but praise, again public and private, was forthcoming from such public figures as Arthur Flemming, Glenn Archer, Bernard Kilgore, Walter Reuther, John Foster Dulles, David Sarnoff, Charles Taft, and David Lilienthal, the last writing: "How is it possible in mere words to express to you those deep emotions of respect, gratitude and affection which I feel toward you, for the light you have been on my path these many years, and for the inspiring example of courage and manhood you have provided for our generation?"

Oxnam received twenty-two honorary degrees, including ones bestowed by America's leading universities; other prestigious awards fell about his shoulders like autumn leaves in a breeze. *Time* magazine featured him as a cover story. When son Phil congratulated him on his picture on the cover of *Time*, the father asked pointedly, "Phil, do you even remember whose picture was on the cover of last week's issue?" It may come to pass, as Andy Warhol mordantly predicted, that in modern American society every individual will be able to be a "celebrity" for fifteen minutes. It may come to pass, such is the historical amnesia of the American people, that the name of G. Bromley Oxnam will fade from the public memory. Perhaps all that need be observed here is that a lot of individuals who knew Oxnam, and who were not fools, believed in his greatness.

The first thing observed about Oxnam was his commanding physical presence. Asked to describe him, a woman church worker replied, "Well, he was a 'bishopery' bishop, if you know what I mean." Yes, one senses what she meant. Countless individuals testified that if Oxnam were placed in a room of ten persons—ten powerful, dynamic individuals—an hour later he would emerge as their leader. This is a tribute to his puissant personality, eloquence, mastery of facts, but it is also a statement about his imposing appearance. Once in Chicago, a sizable cab driver refused to take Oxnam to a certain location, ordered him out of the taxi, and when the bishop refused to budge threatened to throw him out bodily. Warned Oxnam, "My brother, you may attempt that, but please remember that before you step in here, whatever happens to you after you come in, you asked for it." The cabbie sized up his passenger and thought better of his threat.

In mid-life Oxnam stood 5 feet 10 1/2 inches. His weight fluctuated between 200 and 220 muscular pounds. The adjective "burly" rather than "portly" more fittingly describes him. When Oxnam admonished a colleague for violating the Methodist rule against smoking, the colleague reminded him of the Methodist injunction to fast, and Oxnam struck a bargain saying, "I won't mention again your smoking if you won't again mention my weight." Methodist minister Harold Bosley's young son, on being introduced to the bishop, pointed at his stomach and blurted, "You eat potatoes, don't you?" There was about the cut of his jib more than a suggestion of strength: square face, wide brow, penetrating dark eyes, blunt nose, bulldog jaw, thick neck, deep voice. With a ready grin and prominent teeth reminiscent of Teddy Roosevelt, he laughed with a hearty roar, not a giggle. And like Roosevelt, since youth his eyes had required the assistance of spectacles—in time, bifocals. Age drastically thinned his dark hair to the point he ruefully confessed he could afford to send only one lock to son Phil overseas to accompany the generous cuttings from Phil's mother and wife.

While perhaps not a clotheshorse, Oxnam attended to his appearance carefully. The conservative, double-breasted suits were tailored to perfection, not purchased from a rack. When traveling, even for only a day's trip, he carried an extra suit, to avoid the discomfiture early in his career of split trousers. DePauw's Dean McCutchan recalled that the only time he saw Oxnam embarrassed was when he pointed out a gravy stain on Oxnam's tie. Son Phil reported that his father, dining at the

Russian Tea Room in New York and then suffering from the tremors of Parkinson's, dribbled food on his vest; acutely humiliated, Oxnam never again ate in public. After World War II Oxnam began wearing clerical garb on some public occasions; during the war itself on overseas inspection tours he gloried in his tailor-made army officer uniform. Carefully garbed, Oxnam took pains to be cleanly shaven at all times, lugging an electric razor in his briefcase to do the job when shadows on his face appeared.

Judged as he was by others, and not inaccurately, by his physical presence, Oxnam tended to judge others, and not always accurately, by their physical presence. The scrawny and overweight alike were conned and found wanting. Telltale signs of dissipation were noted critically. Shifty eyes and trembling voices manifested character weaknesses. Slovenliness of dress was but an outer sign of inner slough. The weak of chin and limp of wrist were suspect. Oxnam seems excessively susceptible to first appearances; excessively confident that phenotype is destiny.

This unfortunate trait was especially salient when it came to sizing up women, compounded because few could measure up to his wife in loveliness of face and figure and quiet elegance of grooming. He once interviewed six candidates for the position of his secretary. All fell short, being either too blatantly sexy or too big-eared and nosed ("somewhat Jewish"), or too "dried up," or too typically "old maid," or lame "due to some dislocation." The wives of fellow bishops in their new evening gowns elicited the cutting comment: "Why some of these ladies worry about evening gowns I do not know. Nature seems to demand payment, and there is no use trying to hide the nature of the payment by putting on a silk dress." Methodism's leading female theologian, Georgia Harkness, received this description: "Harkness, brilliant mind, old maid, big stomach, lacking in humor, extremely practical in recommendations." The wife of shipping magnate Henry J. Kaiser he found "a person of much fat, and most of it in the wrong place." After addressing a Methodist women's society and being mobbed by several hundred of the gushing delegates, he gruffly noted, "Not a good looking one in the whole blessed outfit." The wife of one preacher he dubbed "Queen Dominance"; of another, he jotted down the facts of her bad grammar, big mouth, big stomach, and hideous collection of paintings.

After a church service during which a local female preacher, gowned, read the announcements, he grumbled, "She was a positive, possessive type, affecting a preacher tone. The Lord help us. Maybe the phrase 'God Save the King' arose under similar circumstances." A woman who addressed the World Council of Churches received the left-handed compliment, "brainy but bulky—a sort of two-ton truck," followed by the crafty suggestion: "We would do well to find a beautiful woman, equally brainy, for such a task. A heavy old-maid, who discusses 'men-women' relationships, feminism, ordination, etc., doesn't quite do, since the case could be made so much better by a woman of charm." Oxnam held the invincible axiom that unmarried female intellectuals, unrequited in their natural longings, must bear the stigmata of their virginal estate. "Pregnancy never mars the figure of a woman," he observed of the Wellesley faculty, "as does the celibate residency of an intellectual female upon a woman's campus." About the only extenuating thing that can be said about Oxnam's notions is that he discerned the same baleful consequences of repressed sexuality in unmarried males—priests, monks, celibate Episcopal clergy, and bachelors in general—all of whom must burn with frustration and consequently must bear psychic scars. (Parenthetically, Oxnam took care never to be placed in a compromising position. For example, he refused to accept a ride or give a lift in his car to a woman he did not know, especially after the adjournment of an evening meeting.) [2]

Lord Morley remarked that Teddy Roosevelt was a great wonder of nature, like Niagara Falls, and a similar observation might be made of Oxnam. Energy emanating from seemingly inexhaustible reserves cascaded from his being. His awesome record of activity was made possible by a prodigious physical vigor in the service of cherished causes. He never debilitated his body with liquor or tobacco, and never quieted his nervous pace with tranquilizers until 1959 when doctors prescribed Seconal during an overseas trip. Neither did he breakfast in bed nor nap afternoons. Episcopal Bishop Sherrill recalled that he and

Oxnam, flying together to England, were grounded by bad weather in the Azores. After lunch, Oxnam paced up and down their hotel room frustrated with the loss of time. Finally Sherrill suggested, "Why don't you take a nap? Who wants to fly in this weather?" So Oxnam did—perhaps for the first time in his adult life, and maybe the last.

When stricken with minor ailments, he drove his suffering body: "Flu says bed, and I hate bed"—and off he flew to a meeting; "One must keep going even though you feel mean enough to slug everybody nearby"; "It is no fun to keep going when you would like to kick everybody in the shins."

His one near-phobia concerned catching germs from the shaking of hands in a reception line or drinking from a common communion cup. ("I refuse," he reported after a "beautiful" service at Canterbury, "even in such sacred moments to violate the simple laws of health and drink from a cup scores have touched.") [3] Still, he betrayed no fastidiousness about germs in the bosom of his family, and this concern never assumed neurotic proportions.

Strong though his constitution was, it was not quite ox-like even in his prime. Sinus headaches wrought their agony, as did stomach aches, perhaps due to his penchant for fiery food and perhaps to endless lethal banquets. His eyes were a source of trouble and by 1954–55 the trouble was serious, though its precise nature unknown from the record. (His diaries report visiting a distinguished oculist accompanied by such cryptic notations as "the less said about this news the better," and Dr. Simpson confirmed "some of the fears that had been expressed by Dr. du Prey"; and, "His diagnosis . . . was most disconcerting, but it is good to deal with a man who is completely frank, tells you what the facts are, then rocks you back on your heels by telling you there is absolutely nothing that can be done about it"; "This eye difficulty is coming back with a vengeance.") Throughout his adult life Oxnam suffered from rotten teeth. He spent hundreds of hours in the dentist chair including major oral surgery in 1938 involving the removal of diseased teeth, roots, and jaw bones which had distributed poison to his entire system and slowed him up for months.

Oxnam's doctors were forever advising him to slow down, take a complete rest (and lose weight); and on very rare occasions he did. In 1942, for example, he spent seven weeks at the noted Sansum Clinic in Santa Barbara. Usually, of course, he ignored the advice. One year, he passed a physical exam with high marks, commenting "even the Wasserman was negative, pretty good for a bishop." But when the doctor told him to take it easy, Oxnam noted, "He did not say how to do it, so I paid my bill and left."

As Oxnam approached age sixty his thoughts turned increasingly to retirement, perhaps at sixty, certainly no later than sixty-five, he predicted, and these thoughts were fueled by increasing spells of bone weariness. In 1949 he entered Boston's famed Lahey Clinic for the first time for a complete check up. In the summer of 1950 he ruled out an arduous trip to India, holding "the strain has been too heavy this year, and I must go at a very different pace next year, if I am to go at all." Oxnam being Oxnam, if anything the pace quickened. In 1951 he reported, "I've had little sleep and find myself staggering about" and three days later "I have been so dead tired it's been like a person staggering out for the eighth round when he's been battered all through the seventh." In the fall of that year, receiving "some rather unwelcome warnings that I must go a bit slower," he canceled several speaking engagements and again entered the Lahey Clinic for further examinations.

Leaving the New York Area in 1952 and assuming the leadership of the Washington Area hardly lessened his responsibilities, and the diaries continue to record feelings of physical exhaustion and nervous strain. In February 1956, during an address in Australia, his renowned memory betrayed him; he became momentarily incoherent, and almost blacked out. Though he managed to finish the speech, he knew he was in trouble. Still, he flogged himself for seven weeks to complete the Pacific assignment. However, even quiet days of rest in June at a lake in New Hampshire failed to restore vitality or calm tortured nerves. Troubled by these symptoms and also by an inability to concentrate and "some tremor in my right arm," in July Oxnam entered Methodism's noted Deaconess Hospital in Boston. There doctors removed a small tumor from under the arm and an abdominal tumor as large as a brick. Luckily, both were benign and the abdominal one caught before abscessing. Nevertheless, in the immediate aftermath of the operation Oxnam found any physical exertion exhausting and even a game of Scrabble too much of a nervous strain. He canceled a projected denominational trip to Africa and recuperated at his summer cottage until October 1.

December 1956 found Oxnam ailing again. Returning from Los Angeles to Washington by plane, he experienced intense pain across the lower chest and vomited at least fifteen times. The following week on a train he reported having "another one of those confounded spells, but of briefer duration, about two and a half hours." Examinations proved inconclusive, one Washington specialist diagnosing serious heart trouble, another a "non-functionary gall bladder." In January 1957, he underwent major gall bladder surgery in the Deaconess Hospital after further tests at the Lahey Clinic.

Despite two back-to-back operations, Oxnam continued to perform his manifold duties, including a heavy speaking schedule, foolishly rationalizing that he could not afford to cancel "some $1500 worth of lectures." Whipped by an implacable will, Oxnam's body cried for mercy. By noon each day his former seemingly inexhaustible energy was depleted, his famed powers of concentration dissipated. "There must be a physical reason for such nonsense," he recorded in March. "The Clinic advises me that it takes much longer to reach normal health than the patient anticipates, and there is nothing to do but to adjust to that fact, and be sensible . . . , but, as they say in French or is it Sanskrit, 'What the hell?' " Nevertheless, he was forced to admit to himself that "yesterday was a bit too much and possibly it was yesterday and the yesterdays before that." Physical exhaustion and a persistent feeling of nervous strain continued to haunt him, as did a developing painful condition of bursitis.

By 1958 Oxnam was facing a fate unrelated to the adominable operations of 1957 and January 1958 and more dangerous—Parkinson's. At no point in the diaries prior to 1959 does he specifically employ that dreaded term, but he does relate seeing concerned neurologists at the Lahey Clinic. On June 23 he commented stoically that "the news from [Dr.] Hurxthal isn't at all good and I suppose there is nothing one can do about a fact other than face it. I shall not go into that." And in July he reflected that Dr. Hurxthal "is one of the great diagnosticians of the world. He certainly does not kid you. He laid the facts on the table to me about as cold bloodedly as one could do it, and I thought he might be lacking in some sympathy. Then when I left the room and saw him standing there in the doorway, watching me walk away with apparent concern on his face, I understood this was part of the treatment. You've got to tell a man the truth."

Because Parkinson's is central to Oxnam's final years, this cruel yet gallant story will be reserved for a later chapter.

Oxnam surely knew the biblical injunction, "Be still and know that I am God"—and just as certainly ignored it. Rather, as Bishop Welch observed, Oxnam was a true Methodist, a people of whom it is said, "They always want to do something about it." And American Methodism seemed to raise to the nth degree that "*Aktivisimus*" (as charged by European critics) characteristic of American Protestantism in general. Yet the sobriquet "steam engine in britches" is applicable to Oxnam for reasons deeper than his Methodist and American background. The compulsion to act was at the very core of his psyche.

A clue to an individual's character is provided by the quotations he cherishes. Witness a few of Oxnam's: "Life is an affair of cavalry . . . a thing to be dashingly used and cheerfully hazarded" (Robert Louis Stevenson); "May God deny you peace, but give you glory" (Miguel de Unamuno); "The attacker is always spiritually superior to the defender" (Marshal Ferdinand Foch); "Victory is will" (again, Foch). And when caricaturing monasticism, Oxnam quoted approvingly Sabatier's description of monks, "deserters from life."

His early penchant for martial terminology scarcely moderated in the years of maturity. In selling to Methodism the mighty Crusade for a New World Order, he opened the appeal with the passage: "OBJECTIVE! MASS! IMPULSION! These words were used by Marshal Foch a generation ago when he delivered his famous lectures on 'The Principles of War.' Every move of a company or of an army must have an objective, and that objective must be in harmony with the objective of the

Commander-in-Chief." In persuading Protestantism to support the World Council of Churches, Oxnam argued, "We cannot win the world for Christ with the tactics of guerrilla warfare. We are not a resistance movement. We hold that Christ is to conquer, and that before his name every knee shall bow. This calls for general staff, grand strategy, an army." The noun "crusade" laces his talks and articles, and one book is given the title *By This Sign Conquer: A Study in Contemporary Crucifixion and Crusade.* In 1948 he coined the slogan "Advance for Christ and His Church: From Crusade to Conquest." Military terminology dominates his prose: "Men may kneel in repentance, but they must stand upon their feet to march. The day of the march is upon us." Foes, he asserted, must be met with "spiritual ammunition." Little wonder he was described by the press as "a warrior of the Lord."

Always on the march, Oxnam "marched" fast. It is ludicrous to think he wore a St. Christopher medal, but it is also miraculous that he was never involved in a serious automobile accident while he was behind the wheel. (Several times he was in crashes but as a passenger.) He drove with a heavy foot on the gas pedal and a heavy hand on the horn, speeding at seventy and eighty miles an hour, even in the 1930s before superhighways. He kept compulsive records not only of miles traveled but also of time traveled, taking pride in breaking his own speed records. Quite conscious of his fast driving, nevertheless he never repented and never slowed down. Occasionally flagged by patrol cars, apparently he was never ticketed, being let off with warnings when the officer learned of his clerical status.

In 1950 Bishop Martin, in introducing Oxnam, reported a story that has been retold a thousand times. Immediately following the adjournment of an Annual Conference, Oxnam rushed to the street where Ruth waited behind the wheel of their car. She noted the stern expression upon his face. "What is it, dear? Am I not in the right place?" "Yes," said Bromley. "Well, isn't the car heading in the right direction?" "Yes," was the reply. "Well, darling, what is it?" Snapped Bromley, "The motor isn't running!" Oxnam observed, "Of course it never happened, but it was an awfully good story." And revealing, too.

Setting aside the possible hazard to others by driving at such high speeds, one ponders an incident that took place in a driving rain in Maryland in 1956. A terrible two-car accident occurred, barely missing the Oxnams' car. Recorded Oxnam: "Rather than stop to see what had happened since a crowd would be there in a moment and many cars, we made our turn and went on up the road with somewhat heightened breath." Of course, to have stopped might have further clogged traffic and hindered the arrival of an ambulance and of course some who did stop were doubtless motivated by ghoulish voyeurism. Still, if one of the accident victims had been dying (and who knows?), would not the presence of a minister of Christ have been comforting? One thinks of the biting observation that the priest and Levite passing on the other side of the beaten man were probably hurrying on their way to a social reform meeting in Jerusalem.

A person reveals himself in the sports he does and does not pursue. Oxnam was not a hunter and cannot be accused of blood lust (though this reputation is unfair to many avid hunters). Nor was he a fisherman, doubtless because he lacked the requisite patience. With his sons and friends he played ping pong and pitched horseshoes. A champion at tennis in his youth, advancing age, added weight, and the pressures of time forced a gradual abandonment of the game in the 1930s. He continued into the 1950s shooting an occasional round of golf, but though a fair player, the game was unsatisfying. As he tellingly explained, "There is no opponent to maneuver into poor position, no bodily contact. One must beat himself and who likes that." Even more tellingly, he confided to his diary that "golf is a great game, but I prefer an opponent who is met in actual physical contact as in football, or beaten by outplaying as in tennis. In this game you must sit still, politely watch someone make a birdie, and refrain from tackling him, hitting him in the shins, or knocking his club aside." About 1955 age and ill-health wrecked his game, and one day in the middle of a round after making a bad shot, he broke the club, walked off the course and that was that. Oxnam did not put on boxing gloves after the Church of All Nations days, but he followed professional boxing and delighted in being told of a new version of turning the other cheek: "Simply turn it and allow the shoulder and fist to come through with it."

Bishop Ledden termed Oxnam a "moral bulldozer." "What is the point of decision?" was a question Oxnam often asked. "Get to the point," he often ordered. "Deliberation is a virtue but hesitancy a vice in getting things done," he often barked. He was decisive and he did act. Nevertheless, the Celtic impetuosity in his blood never completely overwhelmed the painstaking calculation of the engineer in his heritage.

Oxnam's compulsive record keeping belongs in the *Guinness Book of World Records.* He kept track of every mile traveled by means of air, bus, train, electric, ship, and car. He recorded every book read and many of the journals as well. Six leather-bound volumes contain his speaking engagements arranged alphabetically by state and then by city within the state and also by name of the foreign country when given abroad. Smaller books noted facts about and impressions of ministers in the Areas he served. Date books kept him on schedule. Just about every extant photograph shows him with a date book in hand. Observed Bishop Kennedy, "He had a form for every activity which he made sure was filled out so that he knew exactly where he was at any moment and where he ought to be." Time was precious. When abroad, he wore two watches, one set for local time and the other for New York/Washington time. Some individuals report that even in the States he carried an extra watch—just in case. To his credit, he was faithful in keeping appointments, even at the risk of traveling in dangerous weather, and this faithfulness extended to minor as well as major meetings. He stood up no one, however humble. He was prompt. Meals were to be served on the minute. Woe to those who were late for meals or appointments: they did not eat or they were not seen. It was his custom to arrive at train, bus, and air terminals well in advance of departure; his grandson Robert speculates that this was a conscious design to obtain a little more free time for himself. On only one recorded instance did his vaunted systematizing break down. "Of all the stupid things I have done," he gruffed in 1940, "this is the stupidest. For the first time in years of dates and literally hundreds of thousands of miles of travel, I have arrived on the tenth for an eleventh date. So here I am [in Topeka] until tomorrow." Of course, as all mortals he was at the mercy of air and train lines, and sulphurous diary entries lash these lines for misinformation, incompetency, delays. (The Pennsylvania Railroad, in particular, might wish these diaries permanently sealed.)

When traveling by train, plane, or ship, or while being chauffeured, he read or dictated to a machine or typed on a portable. In the Boston Area he thought up a scheme for hooking a dictation machine to his car battery so that he could park at spare moments and dash off a few letters. After finding himself stalled with a dead battery several times, he reluctantly abandoned the experiment.

Oxnam's mastery of shorthand saved time in note taking, but it was the dictating machine that he most treasured for correspondence and diary entries. For twenty-nine years Miss Christine Knudsen transcribed these dictaphone recordings. No individual was ever more faithfully and efficiently and, indeed, adoringly served by a secretary than was Oxnam. When in 1956 Miss Knudsen married Methodist minister Marion Creeger, Bromley and Ruth rejoiced in her new happiness.[4]

Oxnam's attention to detail is perhaps best illustrated in the area of financial accounting, an expertise and carefulness of great significance in his official duties as bishop and officer of the Federal Council, National Council, and World Council of Churches. He ruined one "lovely evening" searching for a missing fifty cents in an account, though his children chided, "The money is gone, they are your books, put in fifty cents and quit." On another instance, he sweated for two hours to locate a ten-cent error, though Ruth chided, "Put in a dime you silly." Replied Bromley, "That is sensible everywhere except in accounting."

All this excruciatingly detailed record keeping unquestionably increased the efficient performance of his duties, made possible his astonishing defense before the House Un-American Activities Committee, and is a boon to his biographers. One hopes that at the last Oxnam found comfort in reviewing the exact number of places he had been, the exact number of speeches he had delivered, and on and on. There is a heartbreaking poignancy in a story recalled by J. Edward Carothers (and confirmed by the Oxnams' daughter). When Oxnam, nearing death, was a patient at the Burke Foundation in White Plains, New York, he had his wheelchair stationed in the area by the elevator. Though he had no place to go and no schedule to keep, watch in hand he timed the elevator operation, once grumbling to his visiting friend, "Carothers, that elevator operator is wasting everybody's time. It takes him twice too long to let people out and get people in."

Nature does not abhor a vacuum more than Oxnam abhorred inefficiency, incompetency, slothfulness. He did not suffer fools gladly, but because of his position there were times when he had to suffer them nonetheless—or if not fools, the dull, the boring, the long-winded. It is altogether possible that he paid a high emotional price for restraining himself and it is equally possible that, like Harry S Truman and Cotton Mather, he released his frustrations by pouring them on pages of his diary at the end of the day. After one conference he stormed, "I take it that courtesy is a wise thing, when a swift kick is the proper thing." After another, he sighed, "One does his best with these situations to send them out feeling reasonably decent, keeping what you think to yourself becomes an art." A "dreary" meeting brought the thought, "Men who must hunt for words, and enliven the pause while hunting with ah, ah, ah, should be drawn and quartered." An "officious negro attendant on the stream-liner train" touched off the tart thought, "Felt like kicking his shins. Christianity is a nuisance." Returning from a banquet he complained, "Had a boresome talk with a dumb dowager next to me." Recalling a reception line experience, he lamented: "They came and came, coughed in my face, said nothings by the score, thanked me for writing John Oxenham's poetry." He concurred with the wife of Bishop Frank Smith who whispered to him, "It takes me two hours to get this smile off my face." Older folks at an inn in Pennsylvania, bent, hobbling about, depending on canes, gossiping in their creaking rocking chairs drove him crazy and he packed up.

Oxnam confided that he had developed a habit of tuning out the words of a tiresome individual in conference until the words were no more distracting than the background noise of a radio. When bored at a meeting, he would stand up and pace the room to the discomfort of the individual speaking and, when presiding, sometimes read a book during reports and debates. A masterful presiding officer and invariably on top of the situation, Oxnam was capable of being both attentive to what was transpiring and reading, but a few others naturally found this practice discourteous. Reinhold Niebuhr said of him, "He gets through a meeting faster and better than anyone I know." In personal consultation, when the individual's allotted time had elapsed, Oxnam would rise from his chair causing the visitor to rise also; then the visitor would find the bishop's hand on his shoulder gently but firmly guiding him to the door. Oxnam instructed his secretaries in handling phone calls to take the caller's name, not put the call directly through, and only if the call was judged important would he return it. This saved him time, but patently cost the caller time. Oxnam's legions of admirers might protest, and deem the judgment unfair, but the record is clear that at least a few individuals, including Methodist theologian Albert C. Outler, experienced Oxnam's brusqueness as downright rudeness.

Not even the whisper of a hint of such criticism shadows the name of Ruth Fisher Oxnam. Oxnam was the sort of man who desperately required the intimate companionship and nurturing care of a wife, the union with another of heart, mind, and body. In Ruth he found the perfect partner. As it is inconceivable to imagine Oxnam as a lifelong bachelor, so it is inconceivable to wish for him a more splendid wife. One knows experientially, observationally, and statistically that many marriages are disasters and that most marriages perhaps are only marginally and sporadically happy. Yet one knows, too, that a very few marriages must be pronounced "good"—for the Kingdom of God, it was said a long time ago, is like a man who gives a marriage feast.[5]

Testimony to her perfection is unanimous; she was a rose without thorns. "If understanding, devotion, patience, wisdom and sweetness of spirit were to be personified, they could well be named—'Ruth Oxnam,' " resolved the Baltimore Annual Conference. Similar resolutions were passed by *every* Annual Conference served by Bishop Oxnam. Only half-jokingly, Bromley's friends reminded him that he "undoubtedly would have been a miserable failure without the help, encouragement and inspiration of your wife, Ruth." "I admire your energy, your industry, and your sagacity," wrote Bishop Welch to him, "but I still think the greatest display of wisdom in your career was getting Ruth!" Publicly Welch extolled Ruth's "rare combination of beauty, intelligence, and charm . . . ," adding, "It must be admitted that she did him [Bromley] one ill turn by damaging his eyesight. The glow of her loveliness so bedimmed his eyes that he was never able to give more than a casual glance at any other woman! He has been a man's man, everywhere, except in his own home. How happy they have been!" Bishop Kennedy noted, "One of the secrets of Bishop Oxnam's strengths was the calm loveliness of Mrs. Oxnam. He never would have been what he was without her, and their mutual devotion was a very great inspiration to us." Individuals close to Bromley never tired of reminding him of what a lucky guy he was, kidding that Ruth's decision to marry him was "for reasons which none of us could understand."

"Ruthie," as her closest friends called her, was a handsome woman, always beautifully, but unostentatiously, groomed. There was about her an aura of dignity, culture, and refinement commanding respect. Yet her graciousness, warmth, concern, and consideration won love as well as admiration. She possessed that ineffable quality known in the vernacular as "class." Mrs. Oxnam held her fair share of offices in church and civic societies, more so in earlier than in later years, but generally she had little interest in becoming a powerful figure in the Methodist Establishment and she held no high office in the Church at large. (The honorary degree Doctor of Letters awarded her in 1946 by Willamette University is not explicable without reference to her husband's status.) Ruth was neither a "social climber" nor recluse. She entertained graciously—usually at luncheons and teas—bishops, district superintendents, ministers, and their wives, and attended with her husband proscriptive social occasions. "If there is anyone who loves people more and enjoys them as much, I do not know the person," her husband said. She was adored alike by the wives of Bishop Welch and Bishop James Mathews, one old enough to be her mother the other young enough to be her daughter. Occasionally she would stop by her husband's office and invite the secretaries to lunch. Ruth made all ages and classes of people feel at ease.

Music, art, the theater, meant much to her, but not, perhaps, more than the beauties of nature, whether European vistas of grandeur or rose gardens or the fall foliage of trees. In the early years of marriage she hiked, camped, and golfed with her husband. To the end, she often traveled abroad with him, and some of these trips—to Russia and the Orient—were not without their physical rigors. Unlike some spouses, she refrained from red-penciling Bromley's manuscripts, and while she certainly participated in his career decisions, there is not much evidence that they spent long evenings in heavy discussions political and doctrinal. Evenings alone together found them playing canasta or listening to the radio and records or watching television; that is, those rare evenings when Bromley was not on the road speaking or at his study desk. When watching sporting events, to make things interesting, Ruth cheered for the team Bromley opposed.

She did endeavor, unsuccessfully, to moderate the pace of his public speaking, once quoting the adage, "When the tongue makes one thousand revolutions a minute, the brain is usually in neutral." Also, she watched his health like a hawk, but failed in getting him to slow down. One service she performed was of great help. When driving with Bromley she was often behind the wheel, permitting him to read or rest. He had total confidence in her driving skill, though she, too, raced at high speeds, and she continued to be his chauffeur even in her early seventies.

Save for an acute appendicitis operation in 1930 and a prolonged winter illness in 1938, Ruth knew good health until she entered her fifties. In 1941 persistent fatigue was attributed to a heart ailment. She underwent two serious operations in 1943 and 1944; blessedly, no malignancy was discovered. Within a decade she was being treated for painful spinal and bursitis conditions, which perhaps accounts for the fact that the Oxnams slept in twin beds, and on trips in separate rooms if twins were unavailable. (His weight may have been a factor, too.) There followed continued periods of pain for unnamed troubles and unnamed severe hospital treatments. In 1959 she underwent a mastectomy, sighing to son Phil, "Might as well cut them both off." Ruth survived her husband by more than a decade, dying a lingering death of bone cancer in 1975. Toward the end she asked of her child, "Phil, if I become senile don't pay attention to what I might say about the naughty things I've done in my life." Phil knew of no "naughty" deeds and no one else has intimated what they might be for the good reason that there were none.

In truth, Ruth Fisher Oxnam was a marvelous human being and Bromley was smart enough to recognize how lucky he was to have her. When separated by his frequent travels or her prolonged visits with her mother in California or to soak up the winter California sun, his diaries ache with her absence. "I am so desperately lonely when the week-end comes that I hardly know where to turn," one passage reads. "A lonely apartment. The very rooms resent Ruth's absence, they seem to miss her too," reads another. "It was so blessedly lonely here today that I phoned Ruth. Her voice does things, somehow . . . and the day is not so bad now. . . . The loneliness vanished, and there was really a song in the air," reads a third. As for Ruth's letters, "I look for them with the eagerness of a child," and on reading them he felt as though he had swallowed sunshine.

What husband would not glory in the letters, telegrams, and birthday and anniversary cards (to say nothing of exquisitely chosen gifts) that Bromley received from Ruth: "Lots of love my precious—I've missed you so very much. Am living in the memory of our wonderful trip. Thank you for taking me"; "The birds are singing, calling you back to the wilds. My heart is singing too. I *love you* darling. I'm *proud* to be the wife of the Bishop of Washington." Ruth's gift on their fortieth anniversary was accompanied by the words, "The most perfect life any girl could have had. My love always, dear." On Oxnam's departure from the New York Area a farewell banquet was given, attended by seven hundred. Bromley burst with pride when Ruth rose and in the course of her remarks sang in the cadence of Mary Martin (in *South Pacific*): "I'm in love, I'm in love, I'm in love, I'm in love, I'm in love with a wonderful guy." And these lyrics she added to his sixty-sixth birthday card.

Oxnam overflows with admiration and appreciation for Ruth in his diaries. He rejoices in how she is universally beloved by others. He marvels at how even the flowers seem "to know she loves them so. They respond to her touch, and seem to delight when she shakes them a bit to get just the right arrangement. I can enter a room and tell at a glance whether Ruth has touched a bowl of lilies or a vase of roses." On their thirtieth anniversary he pronounced the benediction: "Ruth is one of those rare souls who carry into middle age all the beauty of spring, the warmth of summer, and early autumn is glorious, fall comes without fear, and winter promises all the gladness of the 'Snow-bound' she read so often to the children." On her seventieth birthday he recorded, "To me she is lovelier and our life is richer together than in anytime in all of these years." Perhaps no expression is more revealing of his devotion than this: "Never have I known one whose disposition was so even, whose love was so constant, whose sense of just what to do was so accurate—words fail when I try to write about her. I could easily make her my religion, and honestly worship."

Bromley was totally devoted to Ruth, but, as one daughter-in-law, Dalys, pointed out, Ruth never would have blossomed into the sophisticated and charming woman she became if married to a lesser man. This is not to suggest a Pygmalion relationship but simply to honor Oxnam for fructifying rather than diminishing the woman he married.

Scarcely less an adoring father than husband, Oxnam once expressed the thought that he would rather see his two sons and daughter become liberally educated, Christian in spirit and in action, equipped to earn their living, loyal to the best interests of America, and responsive to the needs of mankind, than anything else in all the world. Such are the mysteries of parenting (that odious term), he and Ruth pulled off that wish. Two things emerge from the record with crystal clarity: he was a loving father, and, if he erred at all, it was in being excessively indulgent rather than forbiddingly domineering. In turn, his children idolized him. A third point, subjective in nature and impossible to document fully, is that the two sons could never fully escape the formidable physical and psychological presence of their father. It is not a question of the father's imposition of articulated demands and high expectations but of the sons' internalized pressures.

Robert Fisher Oxnam entered maturity taller, leaner, and handsomer than his father and with every bit as much physical vigor. (The father may have been projecting his own bellicosity when he recorded with pride young "Bobs" clearing the way for his parents through a crowded English sidewalk: "Damn them all," raged the son. "Some were bumped and some got away from six foot three of incensed Americanism on the warpath.") Graduating from Greencastle High School and DePauw University (by transferring senior year credits from the University of Washington), Robert was a high-spirited and perhaps spoiled young man. On one instance (Oxnam recorded rather more in pride than dismay), "Bob drove an automobile around the public square using the sidewalks to suit his convenience and spirit. That's a story that will never die in Greencastle." On another occasion, he was injured while bravely rescuing possessions from a burning girls' dorm. When reports reached Oxnam that Robert was driving his motorcycle over one hundred miles an hour the father counseled the son. "Now look here, Bob, I would far rather have you fly than ride a motorcycle like that." A few weeks later Robert reported, "Dad, I soloed today." "You soloed what?" "Well, you said you had rather have me fly than ride a motorcycle, so I have been taking flying lessons recently, and I soloed for the first time today." Robert proceeded to win a pilot's license, log hundreds of hours, and even fly the movie actor Brian Aherne across the continent. Later in life he became an expert skier, sailor, fencer, scuba-diving enthusiast, champion archer, and crack shot with rifle and pistol. He truly excelled in every sport and this perhaps explains why as an adult he was deeply involved in both the Boy Scouts and U. S. Olympic Committee.

Initially thinking to enter law school, a path favored by his father, Robert abandoned the plan to embark upon an acting career. It is significant that Bishop Oxnam acquiesced in the decision, philosophizing, "Forcing young people to enter professions they are disinclined to master is not wise." For three years Robert gave it his best shot: studying drama and all aspects of the theater abroad; enrolling in Mary Pickford's El

Capitan school of drama in Los Angeles; unsuccessfully trying out with MGM; performing professionally on the stage in Los Angeles and San Francisco. Seeing Robert in the role of the missionary in *White Cargo*, the father exalted, "And now the long hard trail to Broadway and a name in lights." In October 1939 Robert married Dalys Houts, a beautiful aspiring actress, Oxnam officiating. When *White Cargo* closed and the company folded, the young couple tried their voices in radio for Tucson stations and teaching communications at the University of Arizona. Chucking radio as they had been bumped off the rocky road to acting, Robert and Dalys enrolled in USC, she completing two years of undergraduate work magna cum laude and he earning in 1942 the M.A. in political science. Concurrently, Robert was employed as the university's assistant director of public relations.

By then the United States was at war. Robert volunteered for the Army Air Corps but was rejected because of less than perfect vision, though actually his eyes had been only temporarily strained by heavy reading and writing. Drafted into the Army, he served four long years. Knowing no glory, for he escaped serious combat, Robert did win honor, rising from buck private to captain. He bore first heavy training responsibilities stateside and then in defeated Germany was in charge of POW camps. A lieutenant who served under Robert reported: "His leadership was superb . . . . He demanded high standards and got them. He could speak German and get away with it, and when the Russians came in, believe it or not, he knew how to talk with the Russians too." When in the spring of 1945 Bishop Oxnam toured the armed forces in Europe, General John C. H. Lee assigned Robert to accompany his father, holding Robert personally responsible for his father's safety. Recalled Oxnam: "There were times when we were not too far from the German lines but when I threw myself down on the bed and I saw him [Robert] unstrap that holster and a .45 automatic was placed on the chair, I knew that he was responsible for my safety and went right to sleep."

Mustered out of the service, Robert returned to USC to win the M.S. and Ph.D. degrees. He now began to climb the road of academic administration, being called to Syracuse University in

1948 as an assistant dean and rising to the dean of the School of Speech and Dramatic Art and assistant to Chancellor William P. Tolley. A few boulders on the upward road were nudged aside by Bishop Oxnam, who predicted that Robert would one day be president of a fine Methodist institution. Tolley cooperated, pledging Bromley, "We will make any adjustment here necessary so that he may receive the fullest training and enter the college presidency in the near future." In 1953 Robert was called to Boston University to the newly created post of vice-president in charge of administrative affairs, President Harold C. Case expressing to Bishop Oxnam his personal delight and the bishop predicting, "A little later there must be some splendid presidency awaiting him [Robert] and that will be his career." (Later Bishop Oxnam received communications wondering if Robert would be interested in the presidencies of Ohio Wesleyan and Illinois Wesleyan.) In 1957 Robert was tapped to be president of a non-Methodist school, Pratt Institute in Brooklyn.

In 1960 Robert left Pratt to become Drew University's eighth president and the first who was not an ordained Methodist minister. By then he had won a fine reputation for service on a number of committees and commissions of The Methodist Church and for his leadership in higher education and civic affairs. "I have had much exposure to a central fact," observed an academic leader about Robert's career, "the Methodists do take care of their own, preferring and advancing them in the academic leadership spots, and really as devotedly as do the Jesuits!" Perhaps it was justifiable pride as well as Parkinson's that caused Bishop Oxnam to tremble visibly as he gave the benediction at the inauguration ceremony. It was Robert's bad joss, as it was that of every university president, to be at the helm during the turbulent 1960s, when student unrest was pandemic. A ferocious battle involving the Theological School endowment compounded his woes, leaving that component of the university with a gutted faculty, mutinous students, and angry alumni and friends. This is a fearfully convoluted story that cannot and need not be retold. There are those who see Robert as a puppet of Charles C. Parlin, Bishop Oxnam's powerful layman friend and Drew trustee. This charge is unfair.

While controversy continues to surround Robert's presidency, time has tempered the anger of many champions of the Theological School. And one has only to read the record and the words of high praise of his leadership, including those of Prince A. Taylor, Jr., then bishop of the New Jersey Area, to reach the conclusion that Drew was a far finer school in every respect—enrollment, buildings, budget, programs, and redefinition of its mission—when cancer suddenly, quickly, cut down Robert at age fifty-nine, in 1974.

Robert's achievements are beside the point, for the true point is that Bromley loved his oldest son and articulated that love, as extant letters document. Robert and Dalyss' three children, Robert Bromley, Philip Linton, and Mary Elizabeth were to their grandfather pure joy, and he baptized all of them. "I found 'Dad,' " vouched the children's mother, "to be so genuine, warm, loving and caring. With it all he possessed the most delightful sense of humor. He was a wonderful husband and father. 'Mommie,' as we called her, was beauty, charm and grace combined with intelligence. They were a rare couple."

If in Robert one discerns the Oxnam attributes of drive, intensity, and methodical precision, in Philip Holmes, born in 1917, there are suggestions of the Oxnam Celtic heritage. Termed by his mother "Smiling Eyes," Phil was a good looking, freckle-faced, friendly, outgoing youth whose room was always a study in chaos and whose shirttail was eternally hanging out. Yet even as the father unavailingly read the riot act he rejoiced in Phil's being "the very incarnation of affection, generosity, friendliness," Oxnam often shouting, "Hey, Phil, let's go for a walk"—or pitch horseshoes or play a game of ping pong. Phil's college career was as directionless as a leaky hose as he skipped from school to school, finally graduating in 1939 from the University of Missouri with a B.A. in speech.

While still a junior at Nebraska, Phil tumbled into love with the lovely Louise Magee, "sweetheart of the university," and within weeks the nineteen-year-olds eloped. Although a small wedding service was later held, Oxnam officiating, the fact of elopement indicates Phil's independent and uncowed spirit. Oxnam's response was not that of a parental tyrant. "I do not know of anyone in the world that I would rather have for Phil's wife than Louise," reads a diary entry. "As I told him when there, I could not figure out how he ever got her any more than I could figure out how I got Mother." Over the passing years Bromley and Ruth continued to think of the daughter-in-law as being "as close to us as though she had been one of our own children from the beginning."

Although Phil at age fourteen announced his intention to become a minister, the calling was scarcely carried on divine winds and only after much wafting about did he find himself at his father's old school, Boston University School of Theology, in 1939. Applying himself, doing sound academic work, he won the S.T.D. while serving a Cherry Valley church as student minister and then was appointed to his own charge at Oxford. (During this time Oxnam was bishop of the Boston Area and officially involved in Phil's ordination and appointments. The diaries overflow with pride at Phil's advancements.)

When General Sherman said "war is hell" he must have been talking to the ladies, as Phil was to learn existentially. Volunteering to become a chaplain, after seven months' stateside training and service, he was shipped overseas in February 1943. For the next thirty-two months not once was he furloughed to permit the embrace of Louise and their two young daughters. The loneliness was crushing. Yet he endured the unendurable without complaint. He witnessed and risked death in North Africa, Sicily, and Italy. The campaigning in this theater of the war was as exhausting and grim and deadly as any experienced by American fighting men. Phil's ship at the Anzio beachhead was bracketed by bombs, barely escaping destruction, and the fierce concussion he suffered forced his hospitalization. At the bloody Volturno River crossing he was wounded by shrapnel fire. For an eternity he saw members of his "flock" fall all about him, some dying in fox holes only feet from his own. Twice he joined Ranger and O.S.S. teams on perilous raids against German forces in Yugoslavia. He received the Purple Heart, five overseas stripes, four battle stars, and the Bronze Arrowhead, and also the highest ratings possible for a chaplain. Bishop Oxnam's diaries reveal his fears for Phil's safety and his pride in Phil's service. But no father's diary can fully disclose what the ordeal meant to the son. That he was a brave and true chaplain beloved by his men is beyond peradventure. That the war took its toll later from his tortured body and nerves is equally certain. That the war drained some of the joie de vivre from his spirit is a conjecture made by his younger sister.

The cruel war at last over, Phil initially elected to remain a chaplain, but changing his mind, in October 1945 he left the service to become an assistant minister at Minneapolis's great Hennepin Avenue Church, only to return to the Army in 1946. Two years later he again returned to civilian life and took up a series of smaller pastorates in New York State. His father, now bishop of the New York Area, joyously recorded what he deemed his son's splendid ministries. Phil was fully capable of making it on his own, although he bore savage headaches and a duodenal ulcer as wartime legacies. In 1952 Phil left the ministry for personal reasons to embark upon a highly successful career with Mutual of New York. Perhaps it is as well that he finally turned from the saving of souls to the selling of life insurance, for it saved him from running an internalized race to catch up with his father, the prestigious bishop, and, possibly, his brother, the university president. It is bootless to speculate on this point. With his genuinely warm and outgoing personality, he succeeded in the life insurance business; his health held reasonably enough; his love for Louise deepened; his daughters grew to womanhood and married happily, presenting him with grandchildren.

Oxnam's fondness for Phil jumps from the record, perhaps because he recognized in the son those qualities of spontaneity, dash, and vulnerability he so severely repressed in himself. Oxnam's fondness for Phil's wife is equally clear. During the war, with Phil overseas and Louise living with her parents in Nebraska, Oxnam wrote her the sweetest letter imaginable. The opening sentence reads: "I want to send just a word of love upon your Anniversary, and to say that in all the world I do not think Phil could have found another girl so wonderful."

For his part, Phil flatly stated that his father was the greatest man he had ever known. His letters attest to this conviction—and more. When in 1956 Oxnam entered the hospital for an operation, Phil flashed the message: "It takes something like this to remind me how deeply I am tied in affection to my Dad.

You will never know my deep feeling, love, and respect and admiration for you. In times of crises you have been with me. In times of happiness you have congratulated me. In times of bewilderment and lonesomeness you have consoled me. All in all you have been a father, friend and advisor—what more could a man wish for." Phil and Louise had two daughters, Judith Louise and Elizabeth Catherine, both baptized by their grandfather.

Bromley and Ruth's wish for a daughter to complete the family was fulfilled with the birth of Bette Ruth in 1922. It is trite but simply true to say that she was eternally the apple of his eye. Time and again he reported that "Betts" has "brought nothing but joy to me" and "she has been a wonderful child . . . not once in seventeen years has she given me a single ground for worry. She is so steady, so thoughtful, and possesses organizing ability of a very high order." In 1943 she graduated in only three years from USC, president of her sorority and elected to Phi Beta Kappa. Sentimentally she wore her father's graduation gown and on her finger a little sapphire ring given her by her father when as a child she had entered the hospital for a minor operation. Perhaps in a later era she would have become a successful professional or business woman, such was her ability, intelligence, appearance, and character. Instead she married Robert McCormack, a highly successful corporate lawyer, an ardent and active Methodist layman, and splendid human being. Performing the wedding ceremony, Bromley struggled to control his emotions, confessing that "inwardly it was the most difficult fifteen minutes I think I ever experienced." The McCormacks' three children, Ruthie, Robert, and Thomas, brought to eight the number of adored grandchildren.

Save only when Bette Ruth was ill as a child or suffered miscarriages as a woman did she cause her parents a moment of concern or grief. She was the sort of daughter every father might hope to claim; for her part, she remembers her father with love and admiration and appreciation for being such a grand granddaddy.

As an adult, Bromley saw little of his older brother Tom, who as a mining engineer spent four years in Russia developing copper mines and then time in the Philippines as chief engineer of Royal Paracale Mines, Inc. Perhaps it is just as well that the brothers' paths crossed only twice, in 1932 and 1935, for after both meetings Bromley entered angry, cutting remarks about Tom in his diary. Tom was fatally stricken by illness in 1939.

Quite in contrast to his feelings about his older brother, Bromley cherished his younger sister, Lois. Gentle, poetic, physically frail, and devoted to caring for their mother until her death in 1942, Lois was perhaps too tender a soul for this tough world. Bromley invariably visited her on his frequent trips to California (though she seems never to have come East), remembered her with thoughtful gifts, and tendered her small amounts of money. Lois's few surviving letters to Bromley reveal a lovely, sweet spirit who worshiped her older brother.

Oxnam loved little brother Billy, who knew only middling and contingent success as an actor whose stage career was interrupted by twenty-six months in the Pacific as a Chief Petty Officer during the war. Bromley felt protective toward Billy, as he did toward Lois, and liked being in his congenial company, perhaps at supper after one of Billy's shows. Though of sunny disposition, Billy led a rough life, and Bromley worried when a show closed or when Billy's first marriage ended in divorce and the second in death. (After the death of Eva, Billy remarried his first wife, Ann, and Bromley gave his heartfelt approval.) Almost providentially, Billy died while at the piano singing light lyrics.

As for Ruth's family, Oxnam got along well enough with Ruth's sister, Rachael, and her brother, Wayne. Ruth's formidable mother lived until age eighty-eight. Oxnam clearly respected her abilities and drive and liked her company provided the conversation steered clear of political topics—and religious ones, too. "I think of the vulture-like propagandists who have plagued her from the day Mr. Fisher died," he bitterly recorded in 1955. "Had she remained in the Church and exercised the extraordinary leadership which had been revealed in the days gone by at First Church, she might well have headed all our women's work." But "crackpot religionists," anti-Semites, Negrophobes, and Communist-hunters filled her with great fears. "It is really very, very sad."

Oxnam also sought to be a loving grandfather and in turn won the love of his eight grandchildren. Robbey and Judy were treated to a grand if forced-march tour of Europe and England. (After being introduced by their grandfather to the Archbishop of Canterbury, Judy observed that he was a "living doll," and on learning of this compliment Geoffrey Fisher was delighted.) When grandchildren visited New York or Washington their grandfather personally showed them the sights. (At the National Gallery Oxnam thoughtfully limited the number of pictures to his favorite five so as not to tire or bore the kids.) Above all, he relished the presence of grandchildren at the summer home on Pine Island, Lake Winnepesaukee in New Hampshire. There with the littler ones he rolled on the floor and taught them to jump into his arms from the mantle, and with the older ones played charades, reminisced and submitted to practical jokes. However, even beloved grandchildren were expected to be at meals on the minute, and at meals conversation was to be about serious, not silly, subjects.

Oxnam's family satisfied much of his need for human fellowship. To be sure, Bromley was not a dour recluse, and he would have agreed with John Wesley that "a sour godliness is the devil's religion." To be sure, his speaking engagements involved endless rounds of banquets and forced conversation. To be sure, he and Ruth did host social affairs, although almost invariably of an "official" nature. Nevertheless, it cannot be said that he was what Samuel Johnson termed a "clubable" man. At conferences, if Ruth were with him, generally they elected to dine alone and between sessions set off alone to sight-see. Hearty backslaps and hollow smiles in hotel lobbies, feckless jokes and fey gossip in hotel rooms left him bored. Even wholesome camaraderie could not ease his urge to be "up and doing." When an Annual Conference closed, looking neither to the left nor to the right, he bolted for the door to his waiting automobile, though this was a matter of episcopal strategy (he believed) as well as personal preference. "He was no easy man to know," admitted Bishop Kennedy, who *did* know him, "for, like John Wesley, he could hardly ever fold his legs for just a visit. . . . This did not leave him any extra time for the friendly, gentle gossiping about work and men so apparent whenever two or three Methodist ministers gather together." Another episcopal colleague, Bishop Roy Short, recalled that Oxnam was "all business" and that on those few occasions when he dined with other bishops, "it was often to convert the meal into a committee or a conversation on a problem." No visitors other than family were ever invited to the summer vacation home, and Oxnam could not comprehend why his summer neighbor, Henry Hitt Crane, seemed to be running a hotel.

Cocktail parties in particular Oxnam considered abominations, not simply because alcoholic beverages were served but because the necessary small talk was "a frightful waste of time when one might become acquainted with people who do have ideas." Invitations to have cocktails were about as welcome as would have been invitations to dine with the Borgias. To his credit, even a swank champagne affair at the British Embassy in honor of the Queen Mother, attended by Washington's power elite, did not change his low opinion of such functions. Also, when Methodist hosts served imitation nonalcoholic pre-dinner drinks he still held the "social hour" a waste of precious time. Visiting Phillips Academy, he loathed a cocktail party given in his honor but liked a small luncheon because "there were interesting subjects to be discussed. The small talk that one has to endure in so many places was absent."

Although Oxnam possessed that quality the Romans called *gravitas*, and although no one could charge him with being a frivolous fellow, he was not totally unconvivial. Both Crane and McCutchan delighted him with their jokes. He marveled at and appreciated the storytelling ability of the southern Methodist bishops. Like most highly intelligent individuals he was capable of a spontaneous witty remark. However, he admitted an inability to tell jokes, revealingly adding that by telling them badly he would find his listeners laughing *at* him, which he could not bear. On at least one instance he did not object to a laugh at his expense, and that was when at Annual Conference he requested Albert E. Day to lead in singing hymn number 44. Day shouted, "I will not!" An angry Oxnam glanced at the hymn title, "Day Is Dying in the West," and then roared.

Intolerant of inefficiency, he was not considered an ogre by those secretaries and office workers and servants whose testimony we have. For instance, at the time of his death, Ruth received a note from the Pine Island caretaker reading: "This is to let you know that it was with a deep sense of sorrow, as I read of the passing of Mr. Oxnam. He was to me a friend, many a time, and in my thoughts, I shall miss him likewise." The night watchman at the Methodist Building in Washington recalled, "Mrs. Oxnam—and the Old Man, too—was mighty fine people." Little children, and not simply his own, brought out in this bear of a man a real tenderness. On occasion, Oxnam presented gifts of money making it possible for an impecunious parson to purchase a book or travel to a conference. Literally countless individuals received from him thoughtful notes of appreciation or congratulations or condolence.

A sentimentality tempered Oxnam's renowned tough-mindedness. On extraordinarily special occasions he always wore, like a talisman, a pair of gold cuff-links given to him in 1905 by his father. His children on their graduations wore his USC commencement gown. He revered family traditions and his children carried them on, such as writing notes to a newborn baby to be forever cherished. He favored the Cavaliers, not Cromwell, in the English civil war. Edward VIII's abdication speech when he declared his love for Wallis Warfield Simpson he considered "the most moving words I have ever heard." He endlessly played on the Victrola "The Happy Wanderer" with its emotive lyrics. Bishop Welch once wrote Oxnam not to praise him again for his leadership but to thank him for the qualities of tender-heartedness, gentleness, and compassion. Welch recalled in gratitude "the hour when you stood beside the casket of my beloved and spoke words that comforted and blessed us all. Let others admire the champion of great causes; we will love the man." Bishop Ledden also spoke of Oxnam's "exquisite tenderness"; he too remembered that when his wife died, Oxnam broke a prestigious social engagement in Washington to be at Ledden's side.

Unusual and lucky is the adult American male who can count as many friends as there are fingers on his hands—and maybe for a bishop, by the very nature of his authority, the number would merely equal the fingers on one hand. From time to time Oxnam names individuals whom he terms among "my dearest friends," usually dating from California days. Certainly he counted many fellow bishops as friends. Nevertheless, a few individuals appear especially close to his heart.

Jack Sherman was, Bromley repeatedly reported, "the dearest friend I ever had" from the moment of their meeting as students at BU School of Theology, although Jack's major pastorates were in California even as Oxnam moved east. One summer the Shermans were the guests of the Oxnams on a wonderful Mediterranean cruise. In 1939 Sherman suffered a severe stroke, death releasing him from the imprisonment of his hospital bed in 1942. During those long months Oxnam supplied him with a copy of his diary entries. After a visit with his paralyzed friend, Oxnam in anguish reported, "Isn't it strange that this once most eloquent preacher in all Methodism can now only utter one word, 'Damn, damn, damn.' " After Sherman's death, his wife, Lottie, wrote Oxnam: "He loved you so devotedly, Bromley—you will never know how much your kindness in sharing your diary with us meant to him. . . . Jack and I have both loved you and Ruth so much, I feel I'm going to take over his share and go on loving you even more." And Bromley wrote Lottie that while at first rebellious at losing Jack, he came to the understanding that "It would have been selfish to have desired him to continue, suffering as he did, limited as he was. Now, if our faith means anything—and it must mean everything—Jack will speak again, and he will be with those who will understand his rare talent best."

From the DePauw days, Robert Guy McCutchan remained closest to Bromley. Distinguished musician, hymnologist, and editor of *The Methodist Hymnal* (1935), McCutchan set "Rise Up, O Men of God" to a new tune and named it for Oxnam. For his part, Bromley reveled in McCutchan's company and considered him one of his "dearest and most treasured friends." In the Omaha, the Boston, and the New York Areas the two men spent weeks traveling together, conducting great Festivals of Song in dozens of towns, Oxnam being responsible for the preaching. McCutchan was a grand story and joke teller, one of which particularly appealed to Bromley's fighting nature: An old man reported to his minister that he did not have an enemy in the world. Impressed, the minister asked for an explanation. "I outlived the sonsabitches!" came the salty reply.

If it were possible for a person to exceed McCutchan in exuberance, that individual was Henry Hitt Crane. Henry and his wife, Helen, were seminary neighbors of the Oxnams in Boston and later summer neighbors at Lake Winnepesaukee, and Oxnam hoped they would be neighbors in heaven too. The adage "opposites attract" may be generally questionable, but in the case of the Oxnam-Crane relationship it is true. One of Methodism's most popular preachers and for two decades minister of Detroit's large Central Church, Crane was charming, dashing, convivial, dramatic, eloquent, spontaneous, unprogrammed —like a handsome ship with full sails and modest keel. Once when Henry appeared late for a meeting Bromley in loving exasperation recorded, "Bless his heart, if he weren't the dearest friend I have I would explode." On another instance, Bromley noted with insight, "Henry is an actor, must be center stage, preaches absolute sacrifice and utter loyalty to the Master, but is fundamentally selfish." Still, Bromley adored him. Together the two men would go at each other playing golf, ping pong, bowling, pool, badminton, horseshoes, and race about Lake Winnepesaukee in Henry's Chris-Craft. Together they would sit up until 2:30 jawing. Henry unbuttoned "Brom" as few persons were able to do. Publicly Crane (with typical hyperbole) praised Oxnam as "the grandest thing we have got in Protestantism" and as "the Martin Luther of the modern Protestant Church," and privately he told him, "The great fact is that I love you with a deeper affection and more abiding loyalty than even you yourself, I think, can realize."

Another Methodist minister who had a place on Lake Winnepesaukee and whose association with Oxnam went back many years was Ralph Davis, of whom Oxnam once exalted, "Our friendship deeper than ever if possible."

Among Methodist laymen, no association was more important to Oxnam than that with Charles C. Parlin. They first met in 1946, when Parlin was only just emerging as a figure of monumental power in the councils of Methodism, American Protestantism, and world Christianity. While the two men were never truly intimate, perhaps because neither was a Henry Hitt

Crane, they did work intimately together in matters of extreme significance as later chapters will relate; and they showered fulsome praise on each other. They meant the praise, too, because the positive qualities they found in each other were the very qualities they saw in themselves.

Among non-Methodists, no association was more important to Oxnam than that with Episcopal Bishop Henry Knox Sherrill. They traveled together, labored together, and both their public utterances and private letters show that mutual admiration was joined with real affection, as one will see in later chapters. Many, many other individuals were termed by Oxnam "friends," and such they were if one means working smoothly together. But with only a handful of souls—Sherman, McCutchan, Crane, and Davis, especially—did he enjoy a truly relaxed social intercourse.

Such a statement is unexceptional, and while revealing of Oxnam's personality, it might also be said of many who possessed the power and bore the responsibilities of high church office. What *is* truly unusual is the range of his interests and the time given to these interests. Oxnam is often described as a "workaholic." As we know, he did labor long and hard, and he did moan to his diaries about the burdens he carried, one entry being, "Everybody has his work to do and there is nothing to do but to do it, but once in a while you feel like chucking the whole business. There are so many wonderful books to read, so many places to see, so many people to hear, and not too many days." Nevertheless, there was another side to this protean man known, perhaps, to only a few outside the family. When Bishop Welch said that Oxnam took too seriously John Wesley's rule, "Never be unemployed; never be triflingly employed," even Welch was misled—or at least even Welch was apparently unaware of Oxnam's off-the-job pursuits.

Bromley and Ruth dined out a lot together and with the grown children if they were in town. The favored restaurants were those serving adventuresome food, especially Chinese, Indian, and Russian and also (particularly in London) Spanish and Italian.

Oxnam found movies relaxing. He spent hundreds of hours in darkened theaters. Apparently in them he could escape from both people and his own relentless thoughts. While publicly indicting Hollywood for falsely depicting Americans as "gangster-minded, over-sexed, and luxury-mad," he was no prig, for privately he praised Mae West's open, honest "sex appeal without apology" and Heddy Lamar's charms, fortunately quite fully revealed in *Ecstasy*. He also had the critical taste to discern the cant in de Mille's *Quo Vadis*. Oxnam became a home movie buff, in 1941 taking a course at the School of Modern Photography in order to develop and print his own hundreds of feet of color films.

Oxnam was much attracted to the legitimate theater and the not-so-"legitimate" stage, and he saw just about every major play and renowned actor of the era. "I seldom give way emotionally to a play," he said of *Sunrise at Campobello*, "but found myself broken up again and again." Katharine Cornell in *The Wingless Victory* and Gertrude Lawrence in *Susan and God* gave matchless performances, as did Maurice Evans in many roles, judged Oxnam, and Noel Coward was "the most versatile sinner writing plays." He found *A Streetcar Named Desire* well-written and acted but its moral message deeply disturbing. The controversial *The Moon Is Blue* he deemed delightful. Musicals enchanted him, including *Guys and Dolls*, *The Music Man*, *Artists and Models*, *South Pacific*, *Pajama Game*, and *Kismet* with "the lovely ladies half-clothed in the alluring garments of the Orient." He liked Gracie Fields and adored Ethel Merman who, he observed, "could read the Lord's Prayer and give it a double meaning." One evening he saw *Hellsapoppin* and found it a "scream"; another evening Mae West; another evening Gypsy Rose Lee who "is all they say she is, and during such a performance everyone has full opportunity to be certain as to what she is." He also took in alone less chic "bump-and-grind" shows, such as Chicago's burlesque house Rialto. In Paris Bromley and Ruth attended the Folies Bergère and the Casino de Paree, recording little enthusiasm for either vaunted French contribution to the "visual arts."

Because of his California background, Oxnam personally knew several actors and actresses. After seeing *South Pacific* he joined members of the cast at a supper party, returning to his hotel at 3:00 A.M., "which isn't quite the best hour for a minister!"

After seeing Glenda Farrell in *Separate Rooms* he reported: "I married her to a sailor twenty years ago. Thought I would send a card back stage and meet her, but the play was so filled with filthy lines that I wasn't sure she would get me straight if, as a bishop, I told her I enjoyed it."

Among Oxnam's favorite radio programs were the Jack Benny and Charlie McCarthy hours, the latter he dubbed his "Sunday evening devotions." He and Ruth came to enjoy television "immensely." As for long-playing musical records, "They beat radio, they beat television, they beat everything."

After visiting the marvelous holdings in New York's Metropolitan Museum of Art, Oxnam growled, "Life is too damned short." He gloried in painting and sculpture, although as an adult he abandoned his own quite talented drawing skills. In whatever city he found himself, in America or abroad, inevitably Oxnam was drawn to the museums and galleries. His enthusiasm for art was overflowing, his admiration for artists boundless, his knowledgeability nearly that of a professional critic. Over the decades Bromley and Ruth assembled with careful discrimination and wise judgment a notable collection of paintings and sculptures by English, French, Italian, Russian, and American artists. To describe this collection would require a small book. Son Phil estimated the collection's value in 1963 at at least $500,000 and the figure surely would have soared to several million as the years passed. What is significant, of course, is not the value but the fact that Bromley and Ruth surrounded themselves with beauty, loved their treasures, daily feasted their eyes upon them, did not part with them for profit. They took deep satisfaction in showing their objects to visiting bishops and ministers and students. However capable individuals might be, if they were ignorant and unappreciative of art, or of music and literature, they were in Oxnam's book seriously flawed.

Some critics assert that Oxnam himself is open to the charge of ignorance in that he had no appreciation of "modern" art. His descriptions of such art employ terms like "utterly grotesque" and "downright ugly." "I honestly think if they had taken hamburger steak and had flung it into a picture frame it would have done just as well," he grumbled after viewing an exhibition of surrealism. On the other hand, he did admire modern architecture and sought to educate Methodism to break away from tired traditional forms in church structures.

Oxnam collected books almost as avidly as paintings, and he haunted secondhand bookstores in America, England, and Europe. His superb corpus of Wesleyan and rare Methodist hymnals he willed to Wesley Theological Seminary and to DePauw went his Bret Harte first editions. He collected the autographs and letters of authors—Emerson, Dickens, Hardy, Shaw, for example—as well as rare editions of their works. He also owned a collection of the signatures of every president beginning with Washington and of the gold medallions that were struck at the inauguration of each. Only Yale University possesses another such collection.

Oxnam was somewhat of a joiner as well as a collector, having membership in the following organizations: Kappa Alpha, Phi Beta Kappa, Delta Sigma Rho, Alpha Kappa Delta, Phi Eta Sigma, American Historical Association, American Academy of Political and Social Science, National Geographic Society, National Economic League, American Geographical Society. Made a Master Mason in 1929, exactly twenty years later he was elected a Thirty-Third Degree Mason. He found parts of the initiation service beautiful, other parts comical; still, he respected the honor, not the least because his revered father had been a loyal Mason.

Henry Hitt Crane called Lake Winnepesaukee, New Hampshire, "a God blessed place," and he persuaded Oxnam to purchase in 1946 a summer home on Pine Island, adjacent to his. Tall Pines, as Oxnam named his property, nine acres, was heavily wooded with white pine, Norway pine, hemlock, ash, birch, beech, oak, and studded with giant granite boulders. The two-thousand-foot shoreline permitted an unobstructed view of the lake and in the distance the White Mountains of New Hampshire. Oxnam believed the vistas were more beautiful than any he had seen around the globe and his diary descriptions are rapturous. The summer months at the lake possibly prolonged his life by years for, he observed, "There is a peace here that I find nowhere else." He and Ruth reveled in the visits of children and grandchildren, but they also found joy in being alone together.

At Tall Pines Oxnam divided his time between reading and writing in a study separated from the main house and hard physical labor: cutting and trimming trees, chopping wood, moving boulders, making house repairs, tending flowers. At the end of sweating hours he would gulp down ice-cold Cokes. Curiously, he was not adept with machinery and utilized manual tools—always clean and sharp and two of each kind. Although the property came with a power boat, Oxnam rarely took it out. Nor did he sail or fish. Early each morning he would go for a swim in his B.V.D.s. The only recorded negative aspect about Tall Pines was that Oxnam could never quite establish the back property line, and to a man of his temperament this was intolerable; and so he wasted a lot of time (and the time of his grandchildren) attempting to plot it definitely.

The Oxnams' many possessions were made possible by money and they enjoyed a sizeable sum. Precisely how sizeable is unclear. Bromley completed his own income tax returns, explaining: "I suppose I ought to pay someone who is an expert in this matter to prepare the reports, but I hesitate to turn over such confidential information here in the city to people I do not know, and hesitate almost as much in the matter of persons I do know. One's income, whatever it is, ought to be a personal and private matter." Rumors circulated at the time that the Oxnams were millionaires and one writer flatly stated, "Bishop and Mrs. Oxnam had great wealth, even millions, due to inheritance." This seems an exaggeration. One piece of concrete information is a letter from a California investment banker to Oxnam dated November 13, 1934. He reminded Oxnam that at the death of Ruth's father in 1930 Ruth "acquired through inheritance one-sixth of the ten thousand shares of the Walter H. Fisher Corporation stock held by Walter H. Fisher. For your information this Stock was appraised at $3,319,755,62. Ruth's share amounted to one-sixth, or 1666-2/3 shares, and I have always used the above figure in accounting for both Mrs. Fisher and for Wayne." Son Phil reported that at Mr. Fisher's death he left an estate worth $3 million to his wife, and the estate, in an ironclad trust, was passed on to the three Fisher children, including Ruth. Whatever the amount that came to Ruth through inheritance, that sum coupled with Bromley's salary and speaking fees made possible a more than comfortable living. Sometimes Bromley complained because as bishop he received only half his DePauw wage, and sometimes he wondered about refusing handsome offers that came from business. Other times he expressed guilt over his wealth: "I was at the bank early, clipping the coupons due in March. What a strange procedure this! To think that a few sheets of paper with certain promises attached bring income, which, after all, one does not earn, and yet which gives the freedom that others cannot have." And on many occasions he indulged in pious hypocrisy. "There are tastes that require wealth to satisfy," he informed audiences. "The mistaken fools who see true value in the latest gowns, the burdened dinner table, the palatial habitation, the luxurious liner, are mastered by tastes that only money can satisfy. When money is gone, their lives are in ruin"—as if Ruth's gowns were not fashionable, their meals meager, their DePauw house and later episcopal apartments modest, their ocean crossings in steerage.

After hearing a sermon by Bishop Ralph Cushman, Oxnam commented, "It was pious, unctuous, filled with personal anecdote, at times compelling, but generally nauseating to me. I cannot stand religion on a clergyman's gown any more than a heart upon a sleeve." Three cheers that Oxnam was not a canting Tartufe, though this is not to say Cushman was. Yet disquieting questions intrude concerning G. Bromley Oxnam. Here is a revered Methodist bishop who was disinterested in theology, largely unread in theology, and unimpressed by theologians. The disquietude does not end there. Here is a powerful Methodist bishop who apparently had a minimal contemplative life. When Albert E. Day spoke of his mystical experiences, he left Oxnam cold. "I do not respond to the mysticism that underlies Day's address," Oxnam remarked. Nor was he compelled by "the abstract arguments that grow out of contemplating deity in the hours of meditation and separation from the world." Oxnam budgeted his time to the minute, but his total devotion to the gospel of salvation through good works left little time for private devotions. There is not the slightest hint in the record that he ever quietly sat still and practiced the presence of God;

he could not have had the slightest understanding of the meaning of "the grace of doing nothing." At his death, *World Outlook* paid him the compliment: "The phrase 'rest in peace' is an incongruous one to apply to Bishop Oxnam. To his eternal glory, he never did. Even now, we suspect that they had better be sure everything is all right in heaven and that none of the saints are being mistreated for, otherwise, they will hear about it." Fair enough. But if he never rested in peace on this earth, where is the evidence that he sought peace in the solitude of prayer? Like a shark, he felt he had to keep moving or he would die. This question may be unjust and is prompted only by the fact that the diaries are totally silent regarding any periods set aside for prayer. To be sure, Oxnam declared, "I know prayer changes one." This is an assertion, but where is the demonstration? He declared, "Prayer must be continuous, that is, a daily practice." Again, when did he do so? He states, "Prayer takes time." In his carefully crafted calendars, not one indicates a period of time set aside for prayer. Still, one likes to think, even in the absence of evidence, that at daybreak Oxnam lifted up the words of Sir Philip Warwick on the eve of the battle of Edgehill, "Oh Lord! Thou knowest how busy I must be this day: if I forget thee, do not forget me."

Here is a leader of world Christianity who, flying from Asia back to America, concluded that the West "has more downright spirituality in it, I think, than all the talk of spirituality that you find in the filthy East. A good clean meal is a darn sight more spiritual, from my point of view, than a dirty one with flies about in the name of mysticism." (The lunch he devoured on the plane consisted of smoked Danish salmon, creamed spinach, potatoes chateau, tournedos, stuffed tomatoes, green salad, Scandinavian cheese, petits fours, coffee.) Here is a famous churchman who, on occasion, had to flog himself to attend church as a matter of duty and appearance. This is human and understandable and surely the experience of most ministers at one time or another. Nevertheless, if his official duties did not dictate otherwise, simply a lot of Sunday mornings and evenings found him at home reading, listening to the radio, watching television. Not a few of these Sundays were Easter. In fact, the forty days of Lent, and certainly the practices of penitence, self-denial, fasting, held little meaning for him. This fact he frankly stated to a Methodist audience. He makes no mention in his diaries in regard to such holy days as Ash Wednesday, Palm Sunday, Good Friday. It must be added that such was Ruth's devotion to her husband, she hoped he would remain at home on his free Sundays, even Easter.

In 1933 Oxnam's utilitarianism and authoritarianism led him to this curious position: "I know that monasticism is impossible today, first of all because the state will not allow individuals to separate themselves from the world, and secondly because oncoming social movements will insist that if a man does not work he shall not eat." Patently Oxnam's New Jerusalem is a technocrat's heaven from which the Thomas Mertons would be exiled.

A final observation. An individual reported hearing Oxnam say, "Modesty is a virtue without which you get much further in life." It would be unfair to charge him with arrogance. Further, self-confidence *is* a virtue. Yet Oxnam's infinite capacity for self-illusion is disturbing. Only rarely could he bring himself to admit being motivated by other than altruistic considerations. Only infrequently could he confess to being mistaken. His bulldog tenacity in pursuing courses of action is legendary and admirable, but he also could be gripped by fixations. An idea once lodged in his mind was immune to countervailing evidence. His mind was powerful but not subtle. He tended to see things in a Manichean fashion. Paradoxes he found disturbing which, of course, is ironic because he himself was such a bundle of paradoxes.

---

[1] Sockman exalted: "Our greatest Methodist leader no longer moves among us, but his spirit and work will go on forever. All Christendom has been advanced by his mighty deeds." Wrote John O. Gross: "Bishop Oxnam became Methodism's foremost leader after unification."

[2] It does not necessarily follow from this discussion that Oxnam was an absolute foe of female liberation in or out of the church. This matter will be touched on later. The point here is simply that all individuals, female or male, had to pass a rigorous, but surely on occasion inaccurate, physical inspection.

[3] In *A Testament of Faith* he wrote, "I have received Communion at Canterbury." Presumably he received the wafer but not the wine.

[4] As bishop, Oxnam had the services of several secretaries, including Mrs. Mary Anderson whom he singled out for praise, but Miss Knudsen was clearly his mainstay.

[5] Readers of my biographies of Ernest Fremont Tittle and Harry Emerson Fosdick must think me either hopelessly innocent or guilty of masking unpleasant truths because I found the marriages of these ministers, as the marriage of Oxnam, good. Would that I had uncovered tales of passionate infidelities, dangerous liaisons, secret affairs for such revelations might have boomed sales. Alas, I did not.

CHAPTER 11

BISHOP OF THE CHURCH: THE OMAHA AREA, 1936-1939

When Oxnam withdrew his name at the 1932 General Conference as a candidate for the episcopacy, this scarcely ended the matter. During the quadrennium Indiana newspapers speculated that "Dr. Oxnam Soon To Quit" and "Report Oxnam To Be Bishop" and "Oxnam May Resign As Head Of DePauw University To Accept Methodist Bishopric." The rumors mounted as the date of the 1936 General Conference at Columbus, Ohio, approached—and not without reason. Three of the four presidents of DePauw preceding him had become bishops, and it was generally assumed that the DePauw presidency was a stepping-stone to the position of bishop. (Actually Oxnam was the last president to be elevated to the episcopacy.) Further, he had been elected as a delegate to every General Conference since 1924 and at every meeting he had been an influential, articulate spokesman. Finally, liberal Methodists increasingly viewed him as their paladin, and it was predicted he would be the Elisha of aging Bishop McConnell.

Oxnam's ambition was an engine that gave him little rest, but it is by no means certain that he was a moth irresistibly drawn to the flame of the episcopacy. Bromley and Ruth were not unhappy in Greencastle. And he feared that, if elected, as a junior bishop his initial assignment might be to an unrewarding overseas area. Above all, he sensed with Dean McCutchan, who in 1934 advised Oxnam on the matter, "that the position is no longer one of major importance. To be a leader in a retreat never has given opportunity for attack and victory"—or so he expressed to his diary in 1934.

Nonetheless, at the opening of the Columbus meeting in May 1936, Bishop McConnell came up to him and whispered, "Thane of Cawdor, Thou shall be king hereafter!" Oxnam received the highest number of votes after both the first and second days of balloting, virtually assuring him of swift victory. At this juncture he demurred saying, "After serious consideration I ask that my name be withdrawn from the list of candidates. I was out of the city yesterday when the first balloting was announced and could not as a result decline to remain a candidate." Wilbur Hammaker, Charles Wesley Flint, and Alexander P. Shaw proceeded to win election. However, a fourth and final vacancy remained unfilled due to a deadlock between Harry W. McPherson and Oscar T. Olson. Oxnam's name reappeared in the voting on the twelfth balloting. Olson then dropped out and on the final vote Oxnam easily defeated McPherson, becoming at age forty-four the youngest bishop of the Church. At the consecration ceremony of high solemnity, he was presented by President Knowles of the College of the Pacific and President Marsh of Boston University, Marsh privately informing him that he had lobbied on his behalf because "you are my ideal of what a Bishop ought to be."

Oxnam never personally disclosed the reason for his volte-face; only later accounts by his friends and colleagues reveal the probable cause. The diary is absolutely silent about the events surrounding the election, and Oxnam's public statement scarcely illuminates: "The conditions which had existed at the time I withdrew my name changed in the meantime, and I felt this was an opportunity, a duty and a privilege to have my name put before the conference again."

What were those changed conditions? A retired Methodist minister, Charles H. Jack, then an assistant to Dr. Olson of Cleveland's renowned Epworth-Euclid Church, vividly recalls being given the following explanation by Olson. Methodist liberals pressured Oxnam to accept election. Oxnam was reluctant to leave DePauw. At this point, Dean McCutchan, devoted though he was to Oxnam, felt compelled to tell the blunt truth as the two friends walked the streets of Columbus together. The majority of the DePauw faculty by 1936 did not wish Oxnam to remain, confided McCutchan. It would be better to accept election to the episcopacy (despite McCutchan's earlier reservations about the office) than return to Greencastle to face a continuing faculty revolt. Henry Hitt Crane, who served as a friendly mediator, then explained the matter to Dr. Olson, whereupon Olson withdrew his name and the way was cleared for Oxnam's election. This explanation, although based entirely on subsequent testimony, not contemporary written documentation, has the ring of truth.

Oxnam made his presence at Columbus felt in other ways. As a member of the Committee on Foreign Missions he presented the report entitled "Next Steps in Foreign Missions." More significantly, he led the debate to defeat a resolution to establish a tractable official social service commission, a conservative move to undercut the loathed Methodist Federation for Social Service, termed by the Reverend Rembert Gilman Smith, author of *Moscow Over Methodism* and *Methodist Reds*, the "Marxist Federation for Social Strife." Oxnam's stance took courage, for it chanced the hope of conservative support in the balloting for bishop. Of greatest importance was his chairmanship of the subcommittee of the committee on the State of the Church charged with preparing a "Statement on Social and Economic Questions" to be adopted by the conference, a declaration actually coming from his pen.

Methodist lay and clerical leaders had anticipated that there would be a showdown between conservatives and liberals at the conference, likening it to a gladiatorial contest from which only one combatant would emerge alive. A black quartet opened a session with the song "Keep in the Middle of the Road." The selection was, if not providential, certainly appropriate. Oxnam's report, deliberately designed to be "The Peace Pact of Methodism," reviewed the terrible suffering caused by the Depression, listing fourteen specific evils ranging from unemployment to tenant farming, and suggested such palliatives as cooperatives and "enlightened" capitalism. But whatever the solution, Oxnam emphasized, Methodists were pledged to work within the democratic form and to resist the totalitarianism of both communism and fascism. Thus, though the 1936 conference did retreat from its 1932 utterances, it was hardly pushed back as far as the conservative trenches. Said Oxnam in defending his report, "It is better to have a united church studying social issues scientifically in a Christian spirit than a divided church fighting over it."

Being a bishop carried its costs, as Oxnam learned when he assumed the leadership of the Omaha Area embracing the entire states of Nebraska and Iowa. The episcopal office in downtown Omaha was satisfactory enough, but the modest apartment into which Bromley and Ruth moved, lacking even a single guest room, seemed shabby compared to DePauw's presidential mansion. Though independently wealthy, Oxnam grated at receiving as bishop only half his former presidential salary. His predecessor, Bishop Frederick Deland Leete, had "left the situation in desperate straits," a lament Oxnam was to make of his predecessors in three later areas. Son Bob was now gone and much missed, as was son Phil part of the time; and during the school year 1938–39 Ruth and Bette lived in Los Angeles and Bromley almost drowned in a well of loneliness compounded by the growing realization that as bishop it was, as he confided to his diary, "impossible to have close friends in an organization wherein the future of men depends upon your decisions." A year after arriving in Omaha, he expressed the hope of a visit from some old DePauw friends, the invitation closing, "We would be happy to show you all the dust, the heat, and the burnt corn of this glorious part of America."

The Omaha Area embraced 1,680 churches with 326,000 members, five higher education institutions (Cornell, Iowa Wesleyan, Morningside, Simpson, and Nebraska Wesleyan), and six hospitals. Exclusive of schools and hospitals, Methodist property value in the two states approximated $30 million. Oxnam took up his responsibilities in a time of the locust. The minutes of the four Annual Conferences speak of bone-dry drought, hot winds, grasshopper invasions, hail storms, crop failures. And they also chronicle straitened finances, paralyzed building programs, reduced institutional budgets, slashed ministerial salaries. "Pastors and their families on the whole have exemplified an heroic spirit of self-sacrifice. Some have uncomplainedly borne almost unbelievable hardships," declared the 1936 Nebraska Annual Conference.

Despite the inauspicious timing of the appointment and the relatively unprestigious standing of the Omaha Area, Oxnam brought his inexhaustible energies and innovative ideas to the task at hand. Because an hour's conversation a year with each pastor would demand 150 ten-hour days, a patent impossibility, Oxnam published a little monthly paper called "Today and Tomorrow in the Omaha Area." Mailed without charge to every pastor, almost all the editorials and articles and book reviews, dealing with national and international affairs as well as church topics, came from the bishop's pen. (Concurrently Oxnam wrote a weekly syndicated news column, as he had done in Indiana, carried by Nebraska and Iowa newspapers.)

To establish channels of communication with the Methodist laity of the area, Oxnam contracted with station WOW, Omaha, for fifty-two Sunday afternoon half-hour sessions at regular commercial rates to be known as "The Methodist Radio Hour." The program consisted of transcribed music, an opening prayer, and an address by the bishop. Small contributions from listeners helped defray expenses; the printed addresses sold for ten cents. (Some of the addresses were prerecorded so that it was not necessary for him to be in Omaha every Sunday.) Oxnam emphasized that the program was intended to complement, not replace, the Sunday morning worship service. Some of the talks dealt with religious subjects, many others with national and international questions. At that time Oxnam supported the New Deal (even President Roosevelt's attempt to "pack" the Supreme Court) and was a strong opponent of war. He prepared the addresses carefully (and attorneys for the broadcasting company reviewed them closely), because, he believed, his words were reaching "tens of thousands, and perhaps hundreds of thousands, rather than just a few hundred."

Unquestionably, the high moment of his radio ministry came on Sunday, May 24, 1938, at a time when Methodists worldwide were honoring the bicentennial of John Wesley's heartwarming Aldersgate experience. Fifty thousand Methodists met in 1,500 midwestern churches to kneel, hear Oxnam read the Communion Ritual, and then receive the sacraments from their own ministers, many of whom were unordained "supply pastors" and therefore unable to administer Communion save as acting as the bishop's assistants.

Like every bishop, the bishop of Omaha received a heavy volume of mail. Even during the first year Oxnam was dictating one hundred letters daily; with the radio broadcasts, the correspondence mounted.

Hungering for more personal contact, Oxnam undertook to visit every church and parsonage in the two states, in the process becoming, he observed, a kind of "God's traveling salesman." It was a grueling business, each district superintendent being held responsible for charting the map of his district and maintaining the schedule to the minute. In the Holdrege District of Nebraska, for example, the bishop visited eighty-three towns and villages over a three-day period covering 945 miles. "Doctor Lyle had a watch on me all the time and refused to allow me to sit down once in three days," he reported in mock dismay. In true dismay, he lamented the architectural atrocities passing as Methodist churches and parsonages.

Authentic perils and indubitable trials dogged these peregrinations. Narrow roads, blind curves, mud- and insect-splattered windshields, ice storms, snow storms, dust storms, cyclonic winds, all were true hazards. Oxnam himself roared those rural roads at sixty and seventy and ordered his part-time chauffeur to drive with a heavy foot. To keep on schedule, the district superintendents were forced to race. Tires blew. Wheels fell off. Car hoods sailed over fences. Generators weakened, which meant driving in the dark without horn or lights. Gas tanks ran dry necessitating long hikes. And at least one nonfatal accident occurred. After one near traffic mishap Oxnam commented aphoristically, "Dying at fifty does put an end to work, but I have other desires on that subject."

Endless exasperating but not dangerous tribulations also tried Oxnam's equanimity: district superintendents and parsons hoping to talk nonstop from breakfast to midnight; heatless railroad stations; crowded, smoke-filled trains; inaccurate travel schedules; dingy hotels awash with drunken conventioneers boozing to dawn; leaden and lethal banquet food. Oxnam did his share of complaining to his diary and in his letters, but he never broke a commitment or failed to honor an engagement, however minor, even though it meant literally risking his neck to reach an appointed place on time. To his vast credit he heeded John Wesley's admonishment: "Be sure never to disappoint a congregation unless it is a case of life and death. Begin precisely at the time appointed. Let your whole deportment before the congregation be serious, weighty, and solemn. . . . Beware of clownishness. Be courteous to all."

The Omaha Area consisted of twenty-two districts and four Annual Conferences. As every bishop must, Oxnam depended heavily upon his district superintendents and met regularly with his Cabinet. While surely opinions of him varied, the minutes of the Annual Conferences record only expressions of esteem and gratitude. Moreover, several superintendents recalled that for the first time they and their wives were entertained socially by the new bishop and his wife.

Oxnam was absolutely superb when he presided at Annual Conference: informed, fair, firm, decisive, and a master of church law and parliamentary procedure (although he did sometimes read from a book while reports were being made). The thoughts he recorded in his diary after the 1937 Nebraska Annual Conference attest to his Solomon-like qualities:

> A person who has not conducted a Conference has no conception of the nervous strain involved. It is not only necessary to work at high pressure from early morning until late at night but to do so under constant interruption of individuals who feel that their own case is the most important matter in the entire world and must be considered at length. It is the truth in the individual's case; but when you multiply it by more than four hundred and seek to find time for adequate consideration, it is extremely difficult. As a rule a man adds very little to the facts that one knows about him. Only careful preparation for conference after long consultation with the Cabinet really gives a man a far better opportunity of a just appointment than for him to come in and state his case, which as a rule he does in overdone terms or under nervous tension. A person who sits in the Conference and participates from time to time cannot realize the mental strain involved in keeping every motion in mind, grasping the significance that is involved from the standpoint of future policy, recalling the facts of personality evident in the different moves, and all the while to be certain to enforce the law of the Church and be in accord with parliamentary procedure. Numerous addresses are demanded, of course, including a devotional address each morning, usually several other civic addresses, and in this case as in all Conferences a Sunday morning

> sermon, and an occasional Ordination Service in the afternoon. At Nebraska there was a funeral service also, that left the great Youth Rally on Sunday evening. The District Superintendents leave our Conference for a two weeks' "vacation," the Bishop must go on to the next one, which convened in Waterloo, Iowa.

Oxnam perhaps best revealed his innovative leadership in his plans for the celebration of the Aldersgate anniversary in the spring of 1938. He held a conference in each of the twenty-two districts to which all the preachers and key lay leaders were invited. At the postsupper service the bishop preached on the life of Wesley. On display were his valuable personal possessions of Wesleyana, and on hand to add inspiration to the occasion were DePauw's Dean Robert Guy McCutchan and a quartet of singers and a pianist who instructed the gathering in the great hymns of the two Wesleys.

While the Depression presented Oxnam with continuous financial difficulties, other problems would have cropped up even in boom economic times. A student protest at Nebraska Wesleyan over the discharge of two popular professors brought the bishop to the campus to calm the scene. Pressure from one church caused Bromley to ask his Cabinet the sardonic question, "Do any of you have Harry Emerson Fosdick for $800.00?" After hearing a tale of woe from a preacher he groaned, "Some day when I meet a man who realizes that he himself may be partially responsible for the trouble into which he gets, I shall be willing to retire." Another preacher drowning in self-pity Oxnam deemed best helped not by cheap sympathy but by "the trouser-kick method." And after working out a system of careful reporting from each minister, he discovered to his anger that many had not won a single new member to his church in six months; the explanation, he believed, was ministerial laziness. To his credit, Oxnam ordered all churches to prune from their rolls "dead wood." While this meant a paper reduction in membership size, it surely was a more honest accounting. Time and again he moaned that a bishop's heavy administrative duties were making him "a good real estate agent, a good promoter, eventually a good-for-nothing." After a stormy session with the Scottsbluff Hospital staff where he was informed that he was "a terrible dictator," Oxnam captured his troubles most trenchantly in this late-evening rumination: "Perhaps some of the things these fellows said did get to me after all. It's too bad that a man has to be in a profession wherein you can't tell a fellow to go to hell or poke him in the chin."

As a member of the Board of Bishops of the Methodist Episcopal Church, Oxnam had responsibilities transcending the Omaha Area. From 1936 to 1938 he served on the Committee on Plan, Committee on Agenda, Committee of General Reference, Committee on Law and Administration, Commission on Central Conferences. As chairman of a committee on The Freedom of the Protestant Pulpit he largely wrote a forceful statement, adopted by the Board of Bishops, containing these words: "Reactionary forces strive to discredit ministers by labelling them 'red' and revolutionaries rise to seek to destroy honest conservatives by labelling them 'fascists.' In some states the totalitarian philosophy incarnate in forces of law and order have silenced some preachers. Methodism refuses to sacrifice its freedom of preaching." Further, Oxnam was elected as the bishops' representative to the press, and in 1936 he presented to the bishops a report on the Million Unit Fellowship. In 1938 he presided at the Southern California Annual Conference, at which time the old-home folks threw a banquet attended by seven hundred.

As the Board of Bishops' representative on the Continuation Committee of the World Council on Faith and Order, Oxnam gave a "thrilling" address in Chicago at a conference, attended by four thousand, judged by the press to be "probably the most significant Methodist gathering in years." In November of the following year, 1938, the Boards of Bishops of Northern Methodism and Southern Methodism met together for the first time since 1848, anticipating formal union in 1939, Oxnam delivering the final address. The spirit of the meeting he found "excellent" and the atmosphere "electric."

Thanks to the airplane, Oxnam could accept speaking engagements in ever more distant places. Annually he continued to address tens of thousands beyond strictly Methodist audiences. What this meant to him, aside from the speaking fees, is revealed in the April 7, 1938, diary entry. Joining Rabbi Stephen S. Wise and Catholic liberal Dorothy Day in a morning round-table discussion before a large audience in Chicago's Palmer House, he averred, "I never had a finer time." That afternoon he spoke at the University of Chicago on a radio program also featuring the distinguished scientist Professor Arthur Compton. Finally there came an evening radio broadcast, again accompanied by Wise, over station WGN. Exalted the diary: "Altogether it was a day that I shall never forget. I could not help but think, and perhaps it may sound strange to write it down, that the Reverend Bromley Oxnam of Poplar found himself broadcasting with the famous Arthur Compton and Rabbi Wise. That was a day."

For Oxnam's three years in Omaha to have been free of a little controversy would have run counter to his entire public life. In 1937 Omaha's triple-chinned mayor, Dan B. Butler, forced the deletion of five pages of script from the play *Tobacco Road* and absolutely banned the film *Ecstasy*. Butler then proceeded to censor lines of Robert Sherwood's play *Idiot's Delight* whereupon the actors Lynn Fontanne and Alfred Lunt refused to open the show in Omaha. Oxnam suggested that should His Honor continue in politics he take as his theme song for his next campaign, "Every little damma must be taken from our drama." The play opened without bowdlerization and Oxnam received cheers across theater-going America. About that time he bumped into his old acquaintance Channing Pollock and the playwright cried in surprise, "My God, Bishop, I am glad to see you." Replied Oxnam dryly, "My dear Pollock, you may know all about the theater, but the proper way to address a bishop is 'My Lord' not 'My God.' "

Another episode in which Oxnam figured prominently involved Mrs. Elizabeth Dilling, who blew into town like a cyclone in May 1938. Attractive and charismatic, Mrs. Dilling was a sort of antiradical Carrie Nation whose notorious 1934 book, *The Red Network,* had cited Oxnam among the nation's noxious "Reds." Oxnam took the occasion of Mrs. Dilling's visit to say of *The Red Network* over radio station WOW: "If there is any book elsewhere that contains more robust and athletic falsifiers than that volume, I do not know it. It is not taken seriously by anyone who is worthy of the name of student. In addition to the fully developed lies, there are a number of little dwarfs running about, more than seven, and not a Snow White among them—half lies, crooked statements, undernourished allusions, hideous little monstrosities with over-developed heads and scrawny little legs. They belong to the lie family."

Blocked from speaking over WOW by the station's lawyers, who considered her script libelous, Mrs. Dilling rented the civic auditorium and before an audience of eleven hundred she delivered a slam-bang, rip-snorter, two-hour tirade, laced with frequent references to "my great, big handsome bishop"; "my boy friend here in Omaha"; "the schoolmaster from DePauw who wants to spank my hand." She then had copies of her suppressed radio address distributed by messenger boys at the doors of Omaha's Methodist churches.

In April-May 1939, after decades of prayer, planning, and debate, a Uniting Conference was held in Kansas City to bring together the Methodist Episcopal Church, the Methodist Episcopal Church, South, and the Methodist Protestant Church to form The Methodist Church, the largest Protestant church in the nation. Because of his relative youth, Oxnam was not a prime mover in this devoutly-to-be-desired consummation. Nevertheless, on the eve of union he, together with Bishops Hughes and Flint and speaking for all northern bishops, issued the extraordinary statement: "The followers of Christ, representing the three major divisions of the Wesleyan movement, are now ready to achieve the greatest reunion of Christian people ever accomplished in all the history of the church." He also served as cochairman of the Committee on Education of the Methodist Unification Commission. At Kansas City he presided at one session, introduced Governor Alfred Landon, whose radio address was broadcast around the world, and preached a devotional sermon, "He Came Too Soon—This Christ." Praising the addresses of Bishops Hughes, Moore, Flint, and McConnell, Oxnam's diary overflows with descriptions of the various beautiful services.[1]

During the course of the conference several individuals expressed to Oxnam their hope that he would be assigned to the Washington, D. C., Area, Frederick Brown Harris of Foundry Church whispering, "We would like to have Mrs. Oxnam represent Methodism socially at the Capital." Washington would have to wait for the presence of the Oxnams for they were assigned to the Boston Area, a prospect not at all displeasing. Once again President Marsh of Boston University figured in Oxnam's life, for Marsh had sounded him out about the appeal of the Boston Area and lobbied for the appointment. The Boston Area delegation to the General Conference resolved unanimously in favor of the appointment. Bromley's successor at Omaha was Bishop William C. Martin, whom he liked a lot. After counseling Martin and turning over those records Martin desired and the usual round of farewell affairs, the Oxnams were off to Boston.

[1] He could not resist noting, however, that a woman speaker in charge of cultivating the missionary giving of women began her report by observing that when she took the position "she looked over the field and found it virgin territory."

CHAPTER 12

BISHOP OF THE BOSTON AREA, 1939-1944

Although Oxnam had studied and taught in Boston, it was not quite like returning home, for California with its warm memories continued to lay major claim to his heart. Nevertheless, Boston beat Omaha both in terms of prestige and cultural opportunities. Never one to shun a challenge, Oxnam was not really dismayed to find the Boston "situation needing a rather strong hand." Bishop Charles Wesley Burns had died in 1938 and Bishop Welch, nearly 80, had been called from retirement to fill the vacancy temporarily under difficult circumstances. In 1940 the Northeastern Jurisdictional Conference was to return Oxnam to the Boston Area at the Area's request (a follow-up to his appointment in 1939), although he reported the Washington Area was his for the asking but only at the price of bitter politicking.

The Oxnams slipped into town quietly on May 22. The bishop proceeded to establish friendly relations with the press, square away his office in the Wesleyan Building, on Copley Square, and preside at two Annual Conferences. Early in June he convened a two-day meeting of his district superintendents where plans were laid for the major emphases to be pursued. This ambitious program embraced quickening interest in the world mission of the Church, an aggressive evangelistic endeavor, the development of a youth movement, broadening the base of financial support—looking toward a debt-free Area, and a closer system of record keeping.

Oxnam's enterprise and energy led him to undertake a visitation of all the 1,032 churches in the Area, an arduous task never attempted, perhaps understandably, by any of his predecessors. This meant covering the thirteen districts in the five Annual Conferences located in the states, or parts of them, of Massachusetts, Connecticut, Rhode Island, Maine, New Hampshire, and Vermont. For this grueling business Oxnam set aside forty-two days between June 26 and November 28. They were long days, too, often necessitating arising at 5:15 in order to reach the first destination at 7:30 and not concluding until midnight after the last visitation at 9:45. Meals consisted of sandwiches prepared by Ruth, who often accompanied her husband. One district superintendent reported that the bishop would not accept even a glass of water from his hosts.

Because Oxnam continued this practice in New York and Washington (as he had begun it in Omaha) and because he found the game worth the candle and because younger admiring bishops emulated him, a further word is in order. For one thing, the trips provided a marvelous opportunity to take the measure of the district superintendents who accompanied him, sometimes as chauffeurs, always as navigators. How well informed were they about their districts? Were they respected by the ministers under them? A Methodist bishop is mightily dependent upon the judgments of his district superintendents, not the least in the matter of pastoral appointments, and being in the close company of a man for many hours, even in some cases days, enabled Oxnam to know that individual in a way not possible in any other setting.

Equally important, the inspection of a church "from basement to belfrey," and of a parsonage, and the meeting of a minister and his family, transformed names and places, statistics and reports, into concrete realities. Little escaped Oxnam's hawklike eyes: the geographical setting of the church in the community; the church's architecture; the neatness of the parsonage and yard; the books (or absence of them) in the pastor's study; the minister's appearance and conversation and those of his wife as well; the manners of the children. Oxnam augmented his powerful memory by keeping careful notes of his observations and when, weeks or months later, a decision needed to be made about a church or a minister, he drew heavily on what he had learned during these personal visitations. And what he learned often meant unlearning prior erroneous impressions and assumptions, as he confessed.

Important also was the impact of his presence on the ministers' morale. Many pastors wistfully observed that no bishop had ever before been in their homes. Wives were naturally flattered to have the bishop and perhaps his wife as guests. Children were excited by the presence of the big man with the impressive title, although not necessarily awed, one shouting to his parents, "G. Bromley is here!" and another saying on his departure, "Good-by, Old Boy!"

The affirmative aspects, then, of these visitations cannot be denied. Oxnam himself swore by them. Many individual ministers and their wives expressed their gratitude. District superintendents formally recorded their appreciation in Annual Conference reports. And Bishop James Mathews, who viewed Oxnam as his mentor, followed the practice with enthusiasm. Nevertheless, the expression of a doubt or two may not be out of order. Because of Oxnam's meticulous record keeping we know that the tentative allocation of twenty minutes per church was more theory than fact. On occasion only one minute was given to a church and one minute to a parsonage. Often only two or three minutes could be spared. The twenty-six churches and ten parsonages in the Vermont Conference on September 9, 1939, received an average of six minutes each. No church in all Vermont merited twenty minutes, and in the entire Area only large urban parishes received the full theoretical time. Could a one- or three- or six-minute inspection leave an indelible memory, especially when followed by a score or more inspections in the same day? A diary entry lets the cat out of the sack: "Milton Keene . . . was in next. All of these men assume that the little visit I had at the beginning of the work here means that I remember them, their homes, their families, and all. I wish I could."

Then there is the question of "first impressions." Dean Walter G. Muelder of BU School of Theology is not the only individual to marvel at the apparent "instant clairvoyance" of Oxnam and other bishops in sizing up people. One has only to read Oxnam's visitation notes to be suspicious of some of his judgments. One minister's wife passed muster because she wore "stockings with seams straight"; another did not pass because of dirty dishes in the sink in midafternoon. Oxnam was good with children—he liked them and they instinctively liked him, but are well behaved or ill behaved children a sure clue to a father's ministerial competency? To be sure, Oxnam depended on Ruth's keen eye and ear, and when a minister attempted to sell himself in hope of promotion, she would quietly say as they drove away, "The Death of a Salesman." Oxnam himself said of his candid notes, "If these sheets of paper ever got back to the ministers, it would be well for me to pack and keep going forever and forever, since they say Methodist ministers are everywhere." One minister recalled that when Oxnam announced his intention to visit every church, "It was greeted with derision because the visits could only be token ones." And a famed Methodist theologian dismissed the vaunted visitations as largely "showboating." This charge Oxnam would naturally deny and indeed the record on balance seems to support him.

Not long after Oxnam had made his presence felt in New England, he received a note from William L. Stidger, BU School of Theology's exuberant professor of homiletics written in Stidger's inimitable style: "I got copies of The Area Calendar. That is the most intriguing and inspiring programme for an Area we have ever had in these parts and it almost makes me want to be a pastor to put it to work . . . . I feel that there is something alive and kicking in New England at 'long last.' Hurrah for Hell! It heartens me and the Lord knows we need heartening in this part of the Universe." Oxnam understood the point for earlier he had pledged, "Somebody has to build a fire under New England. . . . There is much dead wood here. Maybe the bishop is supposed to supply the spark. We will have a try at it." Time and again he grumbled about the coldness of the people matching the frigidity of the climate, the hammerlock hold of stodgy tradition, the prideful confusion of the antique with culture, the poverty of imagination. After one unpleasantness, he signed, "Boston was forever thus." Reluctantly he concluded in 1940:

"Industries leaving New England, the population growing old, the Brahmins proud but poorer, Vermont in poverty, inbreeding evident, the foreigners politically in saddle. New blood, new ideas, new strength—needed everywhere."

Oxnam gave the Area his best effort and by every measurement New England Methodism did quicken under his leadership, in part, to be sure, because the coming of the war gave the region's economy a measureable shot in the arm. The pages of *Zion's Herald*, an independent Methodist publication strongly supported by Oxnam, relate this quickening of activity and morale, as do the pages of a monthly newsletter instituted by the new bishop, "The Boston Area of The Methodist Church: A Publication from the Bishop's Office." The minutes of the five Annual Conferences are replete with reports on membership and financial growth, heightened enthusiasm, and expressions of praise for Bishop and Mrs. Oxnam. The 1940 churchwide "Forward Movement" received considerable support in New England, Oxnam serving on the committee of direction. The even more mighty "Crusade for a New World Order," Oxnam's brainchild, was naturally accorded massive support. Methodist institutions, particularly Boston University and the famed New England Deaconess Hospital, were accorded loving attention by the bishop. Oxnam's diary entries become increasingly enthusiastic with the passing of each year. The 1941 New England Conference, for example, he found "altogether the most satisfying I have ever attended." New England Methodism is on the move, he rejoiced.

Of course, trials accompanied the triumphs. "Finding a Methodist minister in Boston in the summer is like finding an Episcopalian talking about church union and meaning it," he observed. At one point the New England Southern Conference caused him "extreme difficulty." Slugabed ministers were a disgrace as were the loutish in manners. Worse were those who attempted to renege on an understanding, Oxnam once exploding, "I told that brother off, informing him that I was willing always to hear all facts, to proceed slowly, but that when after full consideration policy was agreed upon, I would not tolerate last minute changes of an emotional nature that jeopardized the greater work of the Kingdom in the Area." A continuing problem was the senior preachers who remained at the same prestigious church for twenty years or longer, thus destroying the Methodist system and the virtues of itineracy.

These minor scratches must not mar the general picture. As bishop of the Boston Area, Oxnam's leadership was imaginative, energetic, and wise, and New England Methodism had reason to be grateful. On June 27, 1944, five hundred individuals gathered to bid the Oxnams farewell, the celebrants including leaders from all faiths and all walks of life. The tributes were lavish, echoing those tendered since their arrival in Boston in 1939. (Privately, Oxnam acknowledged that it was really Ruth who had unthawed the supposedly cold New Englanders and that she was worth a half dozen Bromleys.) Rather than quote pages of tributes taken from the minutes of the various Annual Conferences, the statement made by a New Hampshire district superintendent will serve to illustrate the general tone: "Bishop Oxnam is more than an Area Bishop, he seems to belong to the whole Church. We are exceedingly proud of him in the counsels of the Church at large, and in the confidence of our government at Washington in affairs of such vast importance. He is loved and regarded in his own Area as being among the first Bishops of the Methodist Church."

Surely the superintendent had in mind Oxnam's involvement during the Boston Area years in large matters embracing the city of Boston, Methodism, the Federal Council of Churches, and the nation at war. Moreover, during these five years he traveled 304,871 miles lecturing, including the famed Lyman Beecher Lectures at Yale, the Enoch Pond Lectures at Bangor Seminary, the Fondren Lectures at Southern Methodist, the Merrick Lectures at Ohio Wesleyan. Additionally, articles and books flowed from his fecund pen. In 1941 Northeastern University bestowed an honorary degree. More about these matters later.

Here, however, it is appropriate to examine Oxnam's role as secretary of the Council of Bishops. The 1939 Plan of Union established a Council of Bishops as a constitutional entity giving it a standing which neither the Board of Bishops in the former Methodist Episcopal Church, nor the College of Bishops in the former Methodist Episcopal Church, South, had. The new Council was charged with "the general oversight and promotion of the temporal and spiritual interests of the entire church." In May 1940 Oxnam succeeded Bishop H. Lester Smith as secretary, a post he was to hold for sixteen years. His fellow bishops later honored him by election to the presidency of the Council, but truth to tell it was as secretary that he moved this body of strong-willed men in the directions he desired.

It would be an exaggeration to say that the meetings of the Council prior to Oxnam had been "chaos without an index"—to borrow Justice Holmes's description of the common law. Nevertheless, there had been no Agenda; "We had simply met," confessed Bishop Welch. The minutes of the meetings were fragmentary. Then came Oxnam and order. He was really an executive secretary. It was he who set the Agenda for each meeting, which meant the power to highlight business he judged important and screen out matters he deemed inconsequential. The president of the Council did not even see the order of business until after Oxnam had submitted it. Because of his knowledge of shorthand, his meticulous record keeping, and methodological nature, the minutes became awesomely detailed. (Oxnam was also responsible for persuading his colleagues to adopt a rule that retired bishops could not vote.)

One bishop who had profound respect for Oxnam's efficiency, while heartily disagreeing with his policies, declared, "The Pope is no more the superior of his Cardinals than is Oxnam the dictator of the activities of the Bishops of Methodism." Bishops in agreement with his policies ungrudgingly acknowledged his suzerainty. Said Welch, "He believed that the Bishops should give to the Church a real leadership, and he undoubtedly led the Bishops." "You are THE SECRETARY nonpareil!" Welch informed Oxnam. "The Lord has given you . . . an analytical, constructive, creative mind. You have far more than one man needs! Why don't you share with some brothers who are obviously suffering from a shortage?" And again, "Bromley, you have utterly ruined the Council of Bishops. You have made us so dependent upon you now that whenever anything comes up the customary statement is, 'What does Brother Oxnam think about this?' And when we know what Brother Oxnam thinks then like meek little boys we just trudge down the road and do exactly what he thinks." Recalled Bishop

Charles W. Brashares, "He could be so courteous and gentle while he held the meeting all together 'til it did exactly what he wanted it to do." Bishops T. Otto Nall, Wicke, and Mathews all gratefully testified to Oxnam's masterful secretaryship, while Bishop Ledden observed, "For all the power and brilliance of his eloquence in Council discussion and debate, we have never heard him utter a discourteous or unkind word. He manifested an unfailing affection for all his brethren here." Bishop Kennedy reported he had never known such an efficient secretary: "We had our agenda properly before us, and all the issues which were to be faced were brought to us in sharp and concise form. I always had the feeling that with him as secretary, we could never lose ourselves in useless meandering but would always face the real questions." Bishop Roy H. Short judged that as secretary, Oxnam, "more than any other person, was to determine the character of the operation of the council." He "was really the pilot of the ship." When Bishop F. Gerald Ensley thanked Oxnam for his skill as secretary, Ensley also expressed "how very appreciative some of us are for the splendid way that you halt the threat of social conservatism in the Council of Bishops. You are a kind of safety man for the rest of us when our Southern brethren get loose in a broken field. And you haven't missed a tackle yet!"

During his first years as bishop, Oxnam had been dismayed by what he termed the "extremely disorderly" nature of the bishops' meetings. He chaffed at the absence of planning, sloppy parliamentary procedure, rampant individualism, time wasted on nonessentials, too little care given to major considerations, and the "brothers who possess no terminal facilities." He fully comprehended when accepting election as secretary the latent authority of the office, an authority he correctly believed more significant than that of the president of the Council who, after all, served only one year. He knew the power adherent in the preparation of an Agenda. And once when asked why he continued such an arduous task year after year, he replied, "You'd be amazed at what you can do with a set of minutes."

Oxnam realized also the job would be no sinecure. He lugged records in suitcases weighing ninety pounds to the meetings because he knew some "slovenly brethren" would forget to bring their files. It was needful to listen alertly to every word and then stay up until 2 A.M. to complete the minutes, often rephrasing motions and legal queries unclearly stated. It meant answering hundreds of questions and advising an unprepared president on proper procedure. It meant carefully checking records. It involved assisting colleagues who had not done their homework. The year before his resignation he made this diary entry: "It becomes an increasingly difficult task to act as secretary. The Council relies altogether too much upon the research that I do. I have been foolish to do it. Committee after committee will be appointed. No one will do any of the documentary studies necessary for opinion. I have read all of the documents and thus have been able to present the facts when committees fail but this has developed a kind of reliance that is quite unwholesome."

Nor was this all. After months of preliminary preparation by Oxnam he arranged for the entire Council of Bishops to meet in February 1943 in Washington with President Roosevelt, Vice-president Wallace, Secretary of State Hull and other members of the president's cabinet and members of Congress, and foreign dignitaries Madame Chiang of China and President Quezon of the Philippines. These meetings were to be the springboard for Methodism's mighty Crusade for a New World Order. Oxnam ramrodded the show and in his judgment the "Bishops were deeply impressed and the officials equally so," a dubious belief for which, of course, he may be forgiven considering the letters of praise he received from Roosevelt and leading members of the cabinet. Oxnam feared the alienation of Methodism from the Roosevelt Administration and he hoped that personal contacts with government leaders might heighten Methodist influence. On the eve of the Washington conference he made this revealing diary entry: "For five years I have been working to establish close and cordial relationships with the government. But our old men, who dream no dreams and whose only visions are nightmares caused by stomachs too filled with reactionary economics and politics, and heads too empty; well, the old men have blocked the way. Bishop Hughes spoke of the President as the 'beer president' and questioned his veracity. And others similarly, Cannon and the like. But now they have adopted the proposal I made that we spend a week in Washington to visit, to know, and to draft policies of significance."

Heartened by this week in Washington with government leaders, in 1945 Oxnam proposed to the Council that the bishops meet for a week in New York with leaders of business (such as John D. Rockefeller, Jr. and Eric Johnson, president of the United States Chamber of Commerce) and labor (Walter Reuther, David Dubinsky) and religious commentators (Reinhold Niebuhr, Monsignor Fulton J. Sheen). As he explained, "seeking to ascertain their views relative to the post-war world, the information gained might be of great worth to the Council in planning its post-war program; and I am confident would make a considerable impression upon business and labor leaders who will be making major decisions in the next decade." Oxnam volunteered to issue the invitations and make all the New York arrangements. This he did with marvelous efficiency and the subsequent meetings he also judged highly successful. In 1949 he arranged for the bishops a seminar in New York on "Communism" embracing eleven authorities.

In 1954 Oxnam again sought the edification of his fellow bishops by setting up a three-day conference with the "big guns" of the United Nations, including Dag Hammarskjöld, Ralph Bunche, and Ambassador James Wadsworth; and once again the Council passed a resolution of appreciation to their indefatigable secretary. The meeting was intregal to the Crusade for World Order authorized by the 1952 Council of Churches.

Oxnam's final service of this nature came in April 1959, after he had stepped down as secretary, when the fifty-one members of the Council spent a week in Washington conferring with President Eisenhower (the bishops' wives met with the First Lady), Vice-president Nixon,[1] Chief Justice Warren, the secretary of defense, the chairman of the Joint Chiefs of Staff, Senators Humphrey and Kennedy,[2] and other movers and shakers. Oxnam, always foresighted, set things in motion with a letter to Secretary of State John Foster Dulles, an old associate and friend from Federal Council of Churches days, in May 1957, requesting an April 1959 meeting with the president. Dulles in a memorandum for the president, supported the idea, advising Eisenhower:

"I would recommend that, in principle, we should try to give them [the bishops] the opportunity they seek. The Methodists are the largest Protestant denomination and also the religious group which concerns itself most actively with public affairs. They are, I think, very sympathetic to the point of view which you stand for internationally." Eisenhower acquiesced: "Dear Foster: I have no objection to meeting the Methodist Council of Bishops, particularly since the date is as far off as the spring of 1959. By that time I hope I may be doing a bit of 'coasting.' " Subsequently there followed a raft of letters and phone calls between Oxnam and Thomas E. Stephens, secretary to the president, and between Oxnam and President and Mrs. Eisenhower to nail down the day and hour—to say nothing of the mountain of correspondence involving the other Washington officials.

The April 14 meeting with the president in the White House was cordial but brief. When Eisenhower finally entered the room, Oxnam presented each bishop in turn. He then quoted the letter that Francis Asbury had once read to President Washington. Eisenhower responded by noting the simplicity, spirituality, and loyalty of those earlier times, attributes much needed today. Although Oxnam wrote the president an effusive letter of thanks, privately he groused that the meeting was so brief because "down underneath the President was eager to take the helicopter and get back to Augusta, Georgia, for some more golf."

The record does not disclose any Methodist bishop questioning either the wisdom or effectiveness of these meetings set up by Oxnam. Indeed, periodic consultation with the movers and shakers of the nation was continued by the Council after Oxnam's retirement. Setting aside for the moment the issue of how Protestants might view delegations of Jewish leaders and members of the Catholic hierarchy requesting and receiving audiences with high government officials, several thoughts intrude. For one thing, how tempting it must have been for the bishops to exaggerate in their own minds Methodism's influence in the formation of public policy simply because their photographs with the president appeared in the *New York Times* or a story about their meeting with the secretary of state appeared in the *Washington Post*. For a second thing, and on the other hand, how tempting it must have been for the men of political power to use these briefings to win support for and blunt criticism of their policies. The warning is in order not to exaggerate these meetings as revelations of Methodism's muscle or to imagine that policy in the White House or in the Pentagon or on Capitol Hill or at Foggy Bottom was fundamentally affected as a consequence. One might dream otherwise, but the reality as revealed in the biographies of Roosevelt, Truman, and Eisenhower—the presidents personally known to Oxnam—does not suggest governmental policies being much informed by the Christian ideals of Oxnam or all the Methodist bishops combined. Not to mince words, when the clerics met with the wielders of secular power, the greater influence seems to be that of the profane on the sacred rather than the re-sacralization of the secular.

The Plan of Foreign Visitation was an idea that sprang from Oxnam's fertile brain about which there should be no demur, although some ministers and laymen criticized this gallivanting far from the bishops' home responsibilities. Before the reunion of Methodism in 1939, it was a common practice to assign newly elected bishops to a tour of duty overseas, but with the coming of the jurisdictional system, bishops were assigned to the Jurisdictions in which they were elected. Oxnam rightly feared this new organization would make episcopal leadership sharply sectional and much more provincial in outlook. The retirement calendar made it clear that within a few years no bishop serving the United States would have had experience abroad, but these were the very individuals who were called upon to make decisions that vitally affected the work overseas. "The general oversight" of "temporal and spiritual interests" could not be exercised effectively by men unacquainted with the "general" work of the Church. Oxnam proposed the Plan of Foreign Visitation, which was adopted by the Council in 1943 and unanimously approved by the General Conference in 1948. It provided that each bishop serving in the United States should visit a foreign field once a quadrennium. No visit was to involve more than three months, and with the development of overseas air travel, the difference between the time of the ocean voyage and the air flight was saved. This meant that at no given time would there be more than two American bishops out of the country; but it also meant that within a quadrennium each bishop would have had some acquaintance with the work overseas. The visits were in no sense junkets. The purpose of the visitation was to give episcopal leadership first-hand knowledge upon which to act in determining policies affecting the world mission of the Church. It is a basic requirement of the episcopacy that bishops be able to think in world terms. Such knowledge involves not only acquaintance with the organization and activities of the Church in evangelism, education, and social service, but also an understanding of the cultures in which the Church serves. It calls for an apprehension of the basic trends that characterize the major areas of missionary interest and some acquaintance with the underlying forces transforming the world. The visitation enabled bishops to see churches, schools, hospitals and to come to know the dedicated men and women who serve the Church in its world-wide mission. Equally important, it made it possible for the bishops to meet with the leaders and the people of the land. The visiting bishop had no administrative function; he was not sent to the field to conduct surveys. He certainly was not sent to preach or lecture or throw his weight around. He was there to observe, listen, study, learn, and in the process become a better informed and wiser leader in a worldwide enterprise. World Methodism may well be grateful for Oxnam's inspirational formulation of this program.

Oxnam first considered laying down the burden of the secretaryship in 1949, after ten years of service, but his fellow bishops persuaded him to reconsider. In 1955, on his sixty-fourth birthday, he noted in his diary: "I have decided to reduce as many outside activities as possible. I shall resign as secretary of the Council of Bishops. This is a very hard decision to make, since this office has been and is the most influential position in the Church. Many have no idea of how influential it is." The following April his resignation was accepted, his successor named (Bishop Short), and at the same meeting the Council elected him president-designate. A resolution recorded the bishops' "deep appreciation of the magnificent and painstaking service" Oxnam had rendered. "With untiring industry, amazing insight into all phases of the complex problems of the church, and with brotherly fairness, he has brought to his office high business-like efficiency. He has exalted what under some might have been a routine task into a place of glorious service and honor. He has given his rich resources of mind and spirit without reserve. Through his knowledge of world problems and in social and political fields, as well as in areas of religion and theology, he has been able to guide his brethren through the uncertainties of a changing order."

Only days before his election as Council secretary Oxnam had groused to his diary about the disorderly nature of the meetings, the strong-willed not to say bull-headed individualism of the bishops and their penchant for pressing their own pet projects to the detriment of the general weal. Yet, he concluded this lament with the observation, "Generally, our men bring superior talent to their tasks and very great devotion. On the whole, I think the Council is probably one of the finest bodies of men that it is possible to know." Although criticisms of the Council continued to crop up, far more frequent are the affirmative comments. "This is a remarkable fellowship here. I do not know of one richer upon the earth," Oxnam noted after one meeting. After another, he sang, "This is a wonderful body of men, each one an individualist accustomed to leading, and yet perfectly willing to come to common agreement in the larger interests of the Church and the Kingdom." Other meetings were characterized by "generous evidences of friendship," "rollicking good humor," "exquisite devotional addresses." Oxnam cherished the good reputation of the Council, believed the bishops' leadership stronger than at the time of his election in 1936, and, recalling the wave of antiepiscopal sentiment which swept the 1932 General Conference of northern Methodism, held, "If it should ever be that we would hear again what we heard back in '32, I know one bishop who will walk straight out."

As early as 1943 Oxnam's name was being discussed for both the New York Area and the Washington Area. Individuals high in Methodism counseled him, some insisting New York was the more powerful post, others making the case for Washington. He professed that personally either assignment would be welcomed: "They are very different and call for radically different but equally important programs. We will wait and see." In 1944 the second Northeastern Jurisdictional Conference named him to New York. "A dream has come true," he sang. "Ruth and I are to serve in New York and I am to succeed Bishop Francis J. McConnell." He now convinced himself that "while Washington is very important during the war, it is neither national nor local, and that New York is a much more powerful center for America as a whole, more cosmopolitan and more influential."

[1] Oxnam found Nixon in complete command of himself when the vice-president reviewed the world situation. "Altogether it was an outline of world affairs that was most illuminating and indicated the extraordinary strength of this man. I gained the impression, however, I was dealing with a man who might be very able as an attorney is able, an attorney who sells his abilities to the highest bidder and will do a first rate job. This is not to discount his ability at all but you wonder a little bit about the fundamental interest of the man. Is it purely selfish? Others had the same impression, I felt."

[2] The debated propriety of Methodist bishops' interrogating Senator Kennedy on church-state questions because of his Catholicism will be discussed in chapter 21.

CHAPTER 13

SERVING THE NATION IN TIME OF WAR AND WAR'S AFTERMATH

At three o'clock on Friday morning, September 1, 1939, President Roosevelt was awakened by a phone call from Ambassador William C. Bullitt in Paris informing him that Germany had invaded Poland. At ten-thirty in the morning the president held a special press conference at which he stated his belief that the United States should and could and would remain at peace.[1] He then conferred with Secretary of State Hull and, with Hull's concurrence, decided to call Congress into special session within a short time to revise America's neutrality legislation in order to permit supplies to flow to England and France. The tension thereby established on September 1 between the objectives of keeping the peace and aiding the Allies was to heighten for the next twenty-seven months.

The outbreak of war in Europe following by only two years Japan's cruel invasion of China found Oxnam pondering, as did all thoughtful Americans, the role to be played by the United States as the world's fate hung in the balance. During the opening months of the European conflict he counseled against involvement, "not because we are afraid to die for an ideal, but because the ideal cannot be realized by the method of war." We must not again throw a million Americans into France. "Our task is to preserve our political liberty and use it to win economic justice." Time and again in urging a policy of nonintervention he insisted that such was the policy of the Roosevelt Administration, and for any critic to suggest otherwise was "malicious." "I have had the honor of meeting the President of the United States and am convinced that the President wants peace. He knows war. He hates war. Such unfounded rumors are not only unpatriotic; they divide our people in an hour that demands unity." Of course, a Republican isolationist or a Democratic pacifist might well interpret Oxnam's position as a call for the end of all debate on the wisdom of Roosevelt's foreign policies and a sheeplike endorsement of these policies on the grounds that dissent was divisive and un-American. Anyhow, Oxnam's admiration for F.D.R. blinded him to the fact that the president consciously engaged in dissimulation in statements about his measures "short of war."

In February 1940, Oxnam, as Enoch Pond Lecturer at Bangor Theological Seminary, spoke on "The Preacher and World Order." He urged the United States to cooperate with the coming of the peace in the establishment of a world legislative assembly, a world court, a world executive, a "United States of the World." "But just as certainly," he continued, "we must keep the United States out of the present conflict." He then advanced a most curious argument. "It has begun as a conflict between vertical sections, that is nations, with rich, middle class and poor of each nation fighting the rich, middle class and poor of another nation. It may shift the alignment. Loyalties may leap over national line. The vertical columns may end. We may see a horizontal alignment with classes at war. If so we make no contribution to democracy by entering a class war. Our fundamental contribution may be made in forming the terms of peace and by willingness to lead the way in those adjustments necessary to world order." How in the world did such a strange notion lodge in Oxnam's brain?[2] What evidence was there that the poor in England and France and Germany and Italy and China and Japan were about to unite in a class war against the elites in those nations? And why, if this incredible scenario materialized, should Oxnam, a professed champion of the oppressed, consider it worse than warring nations? In April, even as Hitler's armies were storming into Denmark and Norway, Oxnam continued to inform the American public: "I am convinced that we should stay completely out of the European conflict. If the latter develops into a class revolution, we then will be outside of it, and free to evolve our own destiny."

The 1940 General Conference, meeting in April and May, adopted after spirited debate a statement on the war coming from the pen of pacifist Ernest Fremont Tittle. To the extent that it called for the participation of America in many areas of international life, it was not isolationist. Nevertheless it firmly held that the United States "should remain out of the present conflicts in Europe and the Far East." The heart of the report reads: "Therefore, we stand upon this ground: The Methodist Church, although making no attempt to bind the consciences of its individual members, will not officially endorse, support, or participate in war. We insist the agencies of the Church shall not be used in preparation for war, but in the promulgation of peace. We insist that the buildings of the Church dedicated to the worship of God shall be used for that holy purpose, and not by any agency for the promotion of war." Observed Oxnam: "Ernest Tittle in presenting the reports from the Committee on the State of the Church did as fine a piece of work as has ever been seen in the General Conference. Tittle was masterful. He won a body, I think, that had no intention of adopting the report he presented. He did so by calm argument, clear statement of fact, and the maintenance of a beautiful spirit." Oxnam, of course, placed his signature to the Episcopal Address presented to the conference. "We must not yield to the fallacy that the United States must get into the war if it is to serve in establishing a new peace basis," the bishops proclaimed. "We can serve best by staying out. The mood of either victor or vanquished in war cannot aid peace. Only those who have escaped the blood-lust of actual fighting can see a world situation steadily and see it whole. Meantime we protest against the shipping of war-supplies from the United States to any aggressor nation." At that very moment Oxnam was writing in his diary: "I am still of the opinion that we will make our fullest contribution to the preservation of Democracy by remaining out of the European conflict, but I am equally convinced that the forces of the hour are moving in such fashion as to make our participation almost inevitable." The 1940 General Conference also set up an important

Committee on the War Emergency and Overseas Relief, Oxnam being named a member.

In the terrible spring of 1940 the countries of Denmark, Norway, Belgium, the Netherlands, Luxemburg, and France suffered invasion, defeat, and Nazi occupation, while soon in central and southern Europe Rumania, Hungary, and Bulgaria became Axis satellites and Yugoslavia and Greece Axis victims. Mussolini, of course, sniffing Hitler's ultimate triumph, had plunged an Italian dagger into France's back. Britain, after the miracle of Dunkirk, gallantly resisted Göring's Luftwaffe with "blood, toil, tears, and sweat"—and Spitfires and Hurricanes—but it seemed incredible that Churchill's England alone could long endure. Concurrently, Japan continued to apply the flame to China's already blistered flesh, and then aggressively pressed southwestward into Indochina. "What a majority of the American people want," wrote Freda Kirchway in *The Nation*, "is to be as unneutral as possible without getting into war." Increasing numbers of Americans, especially after the terrifying fall of France in June, supported their president's determination that the United States become "the great arsenal of democracy." The ranks of pacifism and isolationism thinned as the administration's posture toward Japan and Germany hardened, both because fewer and fewer citizens could remain morally neutral toward Japan and China, Germany and England, and because fewer and fewer continued to believe that the Western Hemisphere would be impregnable from attack should Hitler win control of the Atlantic and Africa and should Japan conquer China, Southeast Asia, and the western Pacific.

Oxnam flowed with this general tide of public opinion. "I believe we should send every aid to the Allies," he concluded in June. "I know the danger that lies in this belief; but it would appear to me the least that can be done if our statement that democracy is of value means anything." He now supported (as earlier he had not) an immediate and massive build-up of America's armed forces. Although (as we shall see) much involved in securing protection for conscientious objectors, he urged these young men who were "almost arrogant in their assumption of being the only true Christians" to register for military service on October 16; to refuse even to register would be to "flout the generous and wise action of the government" in providing legal status for them.

By December of that fateful year 1940 Oxnam had joined William Allen White's newly formed powerful nonpartisan Committee to Defend America by Aiding the Allies. "I see no other course than to give Britain every aid possible," he informed Colorado's Governor William E. Sweet. He further opposed the pacifist dream of a negotiated peace, holding that Hitler could not be trusted and agreeing with Reinhold Niebuhr that Europe's neutral nations were shivering little mice waiting for the cat to pounce. And he successfully secured the elimination of that section from a statement of the Methodist World Peace Commission, dominated by pacifists, calling for a ban on the sale of munitions to all belligerents—in effect ending aid to Britain and China. Nevertheless, when the new year, 1941, opened, he traveled to the Florida Southern College School of Religion to repeat his fantastic Bangor address: the United States, while aiding the democracies, must keep out of the present conflict for it might become an even more dangerous class conflict.

Mounting tensions with Japan caused The Methodist Church to withdraw its missionaries from Japan, Korea, and North Central China in early 1941, a wrenching decision concurred in by Oxnam for he believed war between the United States and Japan more imminent than involvement in the European war. In March Congress passed Lend-Lease, artfully designated H. R. 1776, the transcendent measure committing the United States to aiding the Allies. Characterized by Churchill as "the most unsordid act," isolationist Senator Burton K. Wheeler dubbed it "the New Deal's triple A foreign policy; it will plow under every fourth American boy." (An angry Roosevelt termed Wheeler's remark "the most untruthful . . . dastardly, unpatriotic thing that has ever been said." Yet when queried by a reporter whether the bill would not lead to war, the president replied emphatically, "No, not a bit of it." That really is one of the most disingenuous things said in public life in Roosevelt's generation.) Oxnam supported the Lend-Lease Act, continuing to believe that Roosevelt sought to avoid all-out war. "We live in a world and cannot avoid the impact of world revolution,"

Oxnam thoughtfully asserted. "There is as much danger in inaction as action. To refuse aid to Britain is to aid Germany. There is grave danger of becoming involved in war, either by giving aid and incurring the eventual attack by the axis powers, or by refusing aid, witnessing the defeat of Britain and later experiencing the attack of victorious totalitarian powers."

Germany's invasion of Russia on June 22 Oxnam saw as "a final evidence of the utter duplicity and insatiable greed of the Nazis." The invasion may postpone America's entry into the European war, he pondered, but "I do not see how, even then, the United States can let China down." By autumn the United States and Germany were engaged in a deadly undeclared naval war in the North Atlantic, and Japan was preparing to strike at Pearl Harbor should a final diplomatic effort fail to gain her ends. Oxnam was certain his country would be at war within a few weeks, at best a few months. Therefore, the Japanese attack on December 7 did not surprise him; only the place, Pearl Harbor, did. "If it had to come, it is better that the issue is clear-cut," he consoled.

The most striking thing about Oxnam's pre–Pearl Harbor position—or rather, positions—is the unexceptionality. Renowned as a pundit on world affairs, he was as much the victim of the momentous events uprooting Asia and Europe as the man-on-the-street. He may have "hated war," but he was not an absolute pacifist and consequently could not stand fast on the unshakeable rock of New Testament absolutism. (This is not a critical observation, for only a tiny minority of Christians have ever felt compelled by their reading of Scripture to be pacifists.) He was not an isolationist (although prior to 1939 he embraced isolationist positions) and therefore could not stand fast on the unbudgeable foundations of "continentalism," "exceptionalism," and "unilateralism." Just like John Doe, when the European war broke out, Oxnam favored nonintervention. When Russia invaded Finland, he was outraged but not to the point of succoring militarily the Finns. When Hitler's legions overran France, he supported increased aid to beleaguered Britain but not America's entry into the war. As the menace mounted, he endorsed peacetime conscription (though with legal protection for conscientious objectors). When Hitler's U-boats threatened

Britain's very life, he defended the administration's measures: the destroyers-for-bases exchange by executive agreement, the order to American forces to occupy Iceland, the order to extend Lend-Lease to Russia, the order that American warships should convoy British as well as American vessels in the North Atlantic, and later to "shoot on sight"—and to seek out—German submarines. In the Far East, he defended aid to China and the imposition of economic sanctions against Japan.

Like the majority of Americans (as revealed by polls at the time and in the judgment of historians), Oxnam hoped for peace but became increasingly moved by events to accept the risk of involvement by aiding England and China and Russia and thwarting Germany, Italy, and Japan. Pacifists and isolationists might censure Oxnam, as they did rebuke the Roosevelt administration, but in effect this is to censure the majority of the American citizenry who came to feel in their bones that Nazism and Japanese imperialism had to be checked, even at the risk of war.

This does not quite let Oxnam off the hook. For one thing, after September 1939, one searches in vain for a single criticism from his lips or pen of any decision made by the Roosevelt administration; he bestowed carte blanche on a president he loved not wisely but too well—a president quite capable of duplicity in winning the people to his policies. Worse, Oxnam seemed to deem any questioning of Roosevelt as subversive; those who did were selfish, sinister, "saboteurs, who would scuttle the ship of state to preserve their privileges . . . and discredit our President and national leaders." For a third thing—and this point has been made earlier, Oxnam later excoriated the "isolationists" of the 1920s and 1930s, conveniently forgetting his own befuddled record. Finally, one suspects that Oxnam's fervid determination to influence the outcome of the war and shape the postwar world, motivated by an authentic Christian idealism to be sure, was also driven by a passion that Methodism—and by extension, G. Bromley Oxnam—not be excluded from the great historic movements of the century.

On hearing the news of Japan's attack at Pearl Harbor, Oxnam mused, "I feel the nation is not likely to hate as before, but will be the more terrible because of cold determination." America's "cold determination" was nowhere demonstrated with sterner implacability than in the death her pilots (and those of Britain) rained from the skies upon her enemies.

Early in 1944 Dr. Cosmo Gordon Lang, former archbishop of Canterbury, and the Right Reverend George K. A. Bell, bishop of Chichester, protested in the House of Lords against the indiscriminate bombing of German cities by the Allies. On February 20, fifteen American and Canadian churchmen, including Methodist pacifist Tittle, cabled Lang stating their agreement that "obliteration of historic cities and incineration of masses of civilian victims does violence to professed war aims and standards of Christian faith." *Fellowship*, the journal of the pacifist Fellowship of Reconciliation, published as a supplement to its regular March issue an article by Vera Brittain entitled "Massacre by Bombing," an eloquent indictment of Allied bombing strategy, a jeremiad especially forceful because it was penned by a sensitive English woman who had witnessed the horrors of the Great War and who had herself endured German bombing in the second conflict. As a foreword to the article there was an appeal to end obliteration bombing by twenty-eight American clergymen. The appeal read in part: "Christian people should be moved to examine themselves concerning their participation in this carnival of death—even though they be thousands of miles away. Here, surely, there is a call for repentance; that we have not acquainted ourselves with the verities and realities of what is being done in our name in Europe; and surely Christian obligation calls upon us to pray incessantly to God that He in His own way may bid the winds and waves of war be still." [3]

The appeal touched off what Harry Emerson Fosdick, a signer, termed "an outburst of vitriolic denunciation." Vera Brittain estimated she was condemned in two hundred articles. The *New York Times*'s story stimulated a heavy reader response, the letters running fifty to one in opposition to the protest. Among those who challenged the bombing critics was Oxnam. Because his words were free of character assassination, they carried all the more restrained force. And because his statement was part of a nationwide "March of Time" radio broadcast, March 9, it was heard by millions, viewed in theaters by additional numbers, and when picked up by the press read by tens of millions. He began by honoring the character and loyalty of the signers. He observed that his son and comrades in the bloody Italian campaign were being bombed and strafed by planes manufactured in German cities. He expressed his conviction that Hitler intended to conquer and that "subjection to Fascism is more degrading and destructive in the long run than war, hideous as war is." The statement closed: "I hate war, and like other fathers, never open a telegram these days without hesitation. But I want a world free from Fascism. I want to be certain that my sons' sons do not march a generation hence. I believe victory is essential to that end, and these bombings a revolting necessity. . . . We are in it. To call for a lessening of applied force, either in bombing, blockade, or battle is but to prolong this awful thing."

And so the bombs continued to fall with ever increasing frequency and fury and with ever decreasing concern for even the pretense of sparing civilians. In the end, Allied bombs killed 600,000 German civilians. Additional tens of thousands in the occupied countries were slain; almost as many French civilians died (58,000) from Allied bombs as Britains died (60,000) from German bombs and missiles. Only a handful of Christians in all America withheld their sanction of this form of warfare. Oxnam was not one of them.

Even as Russian and Anglo-American armies closed in on Germany and bombers blasted the vaunted Third Reich, Japan's wooden cities and paper homes and the mortal flesh of her citizens were subjected to the hell of General Curtis LeMay's armadas of low-flying B-29s. Nagoya, Kobe, Osaha, Yokohama, and other human habitations were left in screaming flames. A single air attack on Tokyo on the night of March 9–10 incinerated, broiled, asphyxiated, crushed, over one hundred thousand men, women, and children. Before the war's end the number of Japanese civilians killed in the air raids approached 500,000.

By June, the Japanese were suing for peace via their ambassador in Moscow, asking only that before surrendering they be accorded the right to keep their emperor. Oxnam sternly sanctioned the continued bombings; he severely rejected the idea of a negotiated peace—Japan's surrender must be unconditional. In a word, as he had proved to be the perfect patriot in upholding the government's conduct of the war in Europe, so he was in the Pacific war.

"I take great comfort in God," smiled James Russell Lowell, a favorite poet of Victorian America. "I think he is considerably amused with us sometimes, but that he likes us on the whole, and would not let us get to the match-box as carelessly as he does, unless he knew the frame of his universe was fireproof." These comforting nineteenth-century words could not have been written after August 6, 1945. On that date a uranium atomic bomb, "Little Boy," was dropped over the inhabitants of Hiroshima. Three days later the people of Nagasaki received the visit of "Fat Man," a plutonium atomic bomb. On hearing the shattering announcement of Hiroshima, Oxnam recalled an earlier visit to the doomed city, adding "we could do no other, I know."

The next day, the seventh, John Foster Dulles, chairman of the Federal Council of Churches' Commission on a Just and Durable Peace, conferred with Federal Council officer Richard Fagley, and then telephoned Oxnam, president of the FCC. The three men agreed on a statement to be released over the signatures of Dulles and Oxnam. Dulles telegrammed the statement to Oxnam, who was then vacationing in New Hampshire, for confirmation. On the ninth (before news of the Nagasaki bombing was released) the statement was given to the press. At no point does the utterance condemn explicitly either the atomic bomb itself or America's use of it; indeed, it opens with the staggering sentence, "Americans can be proud that under their auspices a scientific miracle has been performed." Nevertheless, while eschewing the biblical language of "sin," "repentance," and "judgment," Dulles and Oxnam urged "a temporary suspension or alteration of our program of air attack on the Japanese homeland to give the Japanese people an adequate opportunity to react to the new situation through leaders who will accept the surrender terms we and our allies have offered." The two men further declared in the most profoundly concerned words in the entire document: "One choice open to us is immediately to wreak upon our enemy mass destruction such as men have never before imagined. That will inevitably obliterate men and women, young and aged, innocent and guilty alike because they are a part of a nation which has attacked us and whose conduct has stirred our deep wrath. If we, a professedly Christian nation, feel morally free to use atomic energy in that way, men elsewhere will accept that verdict. Atomic weapons will be looked upon as a normal part of the arsenal of war and the stage will be set for the sudden and final destruction of mankind." The initiative for this statement clearly came from Dulles and the wording was largely his. Still, Oxnam gave his approval and placed his signature to it.

Oxnam's diary contains no mention of the Nagasaki bombing, the entry for the tenth merely noting that Japan's surrender was imminent. The next entry is confined to a long, loving description of the beauties of Lake Winnipesaukee, not to anguished reflections on the fate of the bombs' victims.

On August 21 Oxnam and Dulles sent a letter to President Truman. Whether it came primarily from the pen of Oxnam or Dulles or was truly a collaborative effort is unknown, though one senses it was Oxnam's handiwork. The letter read in its entirety:

> We express profound.thankfulness, which we know is felt by millions of our fellow citizens, that the Japanese Government was brought to accept the Allied surrender terms without our continuing to the end to release the wholesale destructive force of atomic energy. As indicated by our statement of August ninth, it seemed to us that the way of Christian statesmanship was to use our newly discovered and awesome power as a potential for peace rather than an actuality of war. To the extent that our nation followed that way, it showed a capacity for self-restraint which greatly increases our moral authority in the world. Also, we have given a practical demonstration of the possibility of atomic energy bringing war to an end. If that precedent is constructively followed up, it may be of incalculable value to posterity.

Truman must have been pleased to receive such soothing, canting, self-righteous words from an honored Methodist bishop and a peerless Presbyterian layman.[4]

On September 13 Oxnam and Roswell P. Barnes, an FCC officer, met with President Truman to discuss conditions in postwar Germany and in the course of the conversation, they invited the president to address a meeting of the Federal Council, to which Truman replied he would consider it but observed that he was not a preacher and must not attempt to be one. Oxnam broke in with the observation, "Mr. President, you preached a remarkedly fine sermon recently." A puzzled president inquired as to the bishop's meaning. "On the atomic bomb," came Oxnam's reply. One is curious to know when Truman ever spoke words about Hiroshima and Nagasaki that could be interpreted in any Christian understanding as a "sermon." In fact, Truman's reaction to the Dulles-Oxnam statement of August 9 was defensive: "When you have to deal with a beast [Japan] you have to treat him as a beast." From the first, Truman rejected any suggestion that the decision to use the bomb may have had a tragic or morally ambiguous dimension. When Robert Oppenheimer suggested to him that some atomic scientists felt they had blood on their hands, Truman contemptuously offered a handkerchief and said: "Well, here, would you like to wipe off your hands?" After Oppenheimer left the Oval Office, Truman turned to Dean Acheson, who was also present, and said: "I don't want to see that son of a bitch in this office ever again." Near the end of his life, when the producers of a television series on his career suggested a pilgrimage to Hiroshima, Truman replied, "I'll go to Japan if that's what you want. But I won't kiss their ass." [5]

Oxnam's determination that the West be saved from fascist tyranny and that the East be released from Japanese conquest led him to support closer wartime cooperation with the Soviet Union. He comprehended, as did Roosevelt and Churchill and Eisenhower, that it would be the massive Red Army that would ultimately chew up Hitler's feared *Wehrmacht*. The "strange alliance" between the democracies and Stalin came on June 22, 1941, when Germany invaded Russia, an insane but integral element in Hitler's grand design for the Third Reich. In the 1920s and 1930s, as we have seen, Oxnam was far more critical of the Soviet Union than many self-deceived American liberals. The August 1939 Berlin-Moscow nonaggression pact, Russia's rape of eastern Poland following Germany's invasion of Poland and in accordance with the cynical pact, Russia's defeat of Finland and seizure of Latvia, Lithuania, and Estonia—all of these events wrung from Oxnam bitter condemnations. Time and again he excoriated Stalin's tyrannical dictatorship, the cruel crushing of freedom in Russia itself, the "liquidation of the kulaks, the destruction of the capitalist class, the purges, and the filling of the concentration camp or labor gang with those who dared oppose." Even during the war itself, Oxnam never pretended that Stalin was other than a ruthless ruler.

Nevertheless, he did involve himself in seeking a wartime United States–Russian rapproachment. These activities were duly reported by FBI agents in Boston to the Washington office and later became the partial basis for the House Un-American Activities Committee's false charge that he was a fellow traveler.

On November 8, 1942, while bishop of the Boston Area, Oxnam participated in a "Salute to Our Russian Ally" rally held in Symphony Hall, Boston, an occasion endorsed by the Massachusetts governor, the U.S. secretary of state, and other luminaries, American and British. "The hour has struck," Oxnam proclaimed, "when American and Russian, now allies in war, must become collaborators in peace to the end that liberty and equality may live in both lands, and thus mankind's march toward fraternity." He praised Russia's efforts to seek economic and social equality. The address closed: "Americans, who cannot accept a philosophy of materialism nor agree to dictatorship regardless of the end for which it may be established, must be wise enough to see in the basic objectives of the Russian government a fundamental interest in human beings, a clear recognition of the real worth of persons. These objectives are of the essence of Christianity and democracy." Oxnam was then approached in a series of letters to join in the formation of a national and a state organization, both with the aim of furthering American-Soviet Friendship. The letters came from Professor Dirk J. Struik of MIT, a Dutch-born mathematician and in truth an individual clearly within the Communist orbit, a fact unknown to Oxnam at the time. Then on April 13, 1943, Struik notified Oxnam that he had been elected chairman of the Massachusetts Council of American-Soviet Relations (later American-Soviet Friendship), and on the twenty-second Oxnam accepted. Oxnam later made this observation to Struik: "It is unfortunate that we cannot have accurate pictures of Russia presented. . . . The friends overdo their praise and completely disregard the fact of dictatorship that does exist, while the enemies give a picture ignoring the real achievements." On August 31 Oxnam offered his resignation as chairman because of his embarrassment at being unable to attend the executive committee meetings, but assented to staying on the job, noting in his diary, September 14: "I agreed to remain as Chairman of the Boston group, giving limited time. It was agreed that the Boston group is autonomous, that no statements or commitments can be made except by vote of the body, and that the sole purpose of the movement is to deepen friendship and make collaboration possible. I hope the Communists will have sense enough to see that friendship can be based only upon honesty, fair-play, and full recognition of American democracy and equal understanding that it is our freedom we are going to preserve, learning from them in matters of equality and teaching in matters of liberty. It will not be easy to collaborate with Russia, unless there is a swing from dictatorship there, and a willingness to live and let live."

In May 1944 Oxnam stepped down as chairman, agreeing happily to be continued as honorary chairman. Finally, on December 20, 1946, he requested his name be dropped as honorary chairman inasmuch as he was no longer a citizen of Massachusetts, adding: "I do not wish this to indicate a change of attitude in the matter of peaceful relations with Russia."

Concurrently, Oxnam was involved in the national Council of American-Soviet Friendship, informing Struik in November 1942 that he supported the formation of such a group and giving the assurance that he would "be delighted to cooperate insofar as I can." In the spring of 1943 he stated his delight in having his name included in the list of sponsors, but he declined an invitation to become a member of the board of directors on the grounds of an inability to attend the meetings. To his credit, Oxnam refused to give his name to several of the more extreme pro-Soviet statements of the council. However, he did offer the opening prayer at a meeting sponsored by the council in Madison Square Garden, November 16, 1944. The audience *applauded* the supplication he lifted to the Lord for the thousandth time: "Grant us, O God, the wisdom to translate the ethical ideals of religion into the realities of economic justice and racial brotherhood." When the House Un-American Activities Committee later called Oxnam to account for his participation in this love feast, he devastatingly observed that the affair had received the blessing of scores of America's leaders, either by their presence or their messages, from President Roosevelt on down. In January 1947 Oxnam severed all relationships with the council, William Howard Melish, then chairman, accepting the severance with great regret, believing it was a case of Oxnam's misunderstanding the council's criticism of America's Cold War diplomacy.

Surely Oxnam's enemies were being unfair in chastizing him for seeking warmer relations with Russia at a time when the Russian people were dying by the millions in the defense of Mother Russia and the Red Army was gutting the most terrifyingly efficient war machine the world had yet witnessed—and in doing so, sparing the lives of hundreds of thousands of British and Americans grappling with the Nazis in North Africa, Italy, France, and western Germany. Nevertheless, there were perils in Oxnam's instant pronouncements on the great wartime events. What, for example, is one to say about his assessment of the fateful Yalta Conference? "The agreement reached at Yalta is 'applied idealism' of a high order," his widely read judgment begins. "The religious forces of the world will regard the decisions of the Crimean Conference as marking substantial and significant advance toward world law and order," the statement continues. "Those who object to the present proposal concerning Poland are obligated to present a better solution rather than to reject the plans for an ordered world because the solution proposed in the case of Poland does not suit them," is the nonchalant comment on the fate of the doomed Polish people. The final paragraph reads: "I believe religious leaders are rejoicing in the fact that the leadership of the great nations has been sufficiently far-visioned to take all presently practical steps necessary to defeat the common enemy, but, more, to establish the organization essential to the control of power and the further extension of justice. They have been equally far-seeing in renewing their pledge to principles. It is principle that summons men to further advance. . . . Crimea is indeed 'applied idealism' deserving the support of idealists and realists alike."

In justice to Oxnam, the initial reaction to Yalta in America was one of widespread hope; only later did bitter disenchantment became widespread.

Early in the war, Oxnam was made a member of the newly formed Methodist Commission on Chaplains, and after Bishop Leonard crashed to his death in Iceland, Oxnam was elected vice-chairman.[6] He took the responsibilities associated with the post seriously. The commission procured, maintained contact with, furnished supplies to, and, to a degree at least, supervised the work of 1,747 Methodist chaplains, twenty-eight of whom sacrificed their lives. No other Protestant denomination matched the number of Methodist chaplains. Oxnam devoted hours to the examination of candidates. These close interviews left him bone tired, but he knew the work was "very necessary if good men are to enter and poor men be kept out." One minister who ran the gauntlet and won the review committee's approval, chaired by Oxnam, was named Philip Holmes Oxnam. Harvard University hosted an Army Chaplain School, and, while bishop of the Boston Area, Oxnam entertained at a dinner the Methodist men in each class, the dinner being followed by a devotional service. Moreover, at his own expense he sent to each Methodist chaplain copies of two of his books, *Behold Thy Mother* and *Facing the Future Unafraid*.

Oxnam also served on the General Commission on Army and Navy Chaplains, recognized by the government as the official cooperative agency of the major Protestant denominations. In 1941 he used his influence to secure the election of Methodist Bishop Leonard as chairman. Oxnam made a point to call on a major general chief chaplain to alert that feckless fellow that The Methodist Church was observing carefully his performance to the end that Methodist chaplains not be shortchanged. From time to time Oxnam was designated by the general commission as its representative in visiting Protestant chaplains throughout all New England. "I am extremely happy to be upon this Commission," he rejoiced.

Oxnam's admiration for President Roosevelt's wartime leadership was total. He rejoiced in Roosevelt's fourth-term victory and excoriated the Republican candidate, Thomas E. Dewey, and the gutter campaign, in his judgment, conducted by the GOP.

The Oxnams were invited to attend the inaugural buffet at the White House, January 20, 1945. News of Roosevelt's death caused him to record: "Never before has the death of a public official come as such a personal shock. It was like losing a member of the family." Phoned by the Columbia Broadcasting System, Oxnam was raced by Ruth to the studio while he composed a tribute to be read over the air. "The American people have lost a leader who takes his place in history with Washington, Jefferson, Lincoln and Wilson," the tribute began. The message concluded: "The world is now ready, if it follows on in his spirit and wisdom, to possess the promised land of Four Freedoms. We bow in grief, and in silence dedicate ourselves to establish world law and order, economic justice and racial brotherhood. May God comfort and sustain his bereaved loved ones, guide the leaders who take up his task and strengthen the people everywhere."

Only two days later, April 14, Oxnam flew to England, the beginning of a six weeks' adventure. As president of the Federal Council of Churches he was selected to represent that body at the enthronement of the archbishop of Canterbury. He was also the authorized representative of the General Commission on Army and Navy Chaplains, the Federal Council, the Methodist Commission on Chaplains, and the Service Men's Christian League to visit the chaplains in the Mediterranean theater of operations. He was armed with a letter from President Roosevelt dated April 9, perhaps one of the last things to come from the pen of the dying leader: "I wish you Godspeed as you take off on a dual mission, in some respects of unique interest." When the invitation to go to the Mediterranean was initially extended, Oxnam rejoiced to his diary, "It will be an opportunity for service that I really covet, since I have been most restive through this entire conflict to be at a desk or upon a platform when others are facing danger." He further recorded that the Protestant chaplains had caucused and specifically requested his coming. Oxnam's flying companion was his friend Episcopal Bishop Sherrill, the only other American churchman to be invited officially to the enthronement ceremony.

A British flying boat carried the men to London via Bermuda and Lisbon. The day after their arrival they attended a memorial service in honor of President Roosevelt held in St. Paul's Cathedral. Deeply moved by the experience, Oxnam noted that Prime Minister Churchill, too, reached for his handkerchief to dry away the tears. Then came the enthronement of Geoffrey Fisher, another mightily stirring experience. Before the pageantry Oxnam had dined with Fisher and remarked, "Your Grace, did you choose April 19th for your enthronement as another tribute to the Americans?" Fisher looked puzzled until Sherrill reminded him, "You know, your Grace, April 19th is the date of the battle of Lexington." Responded the archbishop in his high-pitched British falsetto, "You know, it's quite all right. Just suppose we were still responsible for people like you!"

After six days in England, Oxnam flew to Paris where he preached in both the Protestant Episcopal Cathedral and the American Church on the Quai d'Orsay. Then on to Reims where he was joined by son Robert, assigned by General Lee to be his father's personal protector in the perilous journeys ahead. Throughout these journeys Oxnam was also escorted by Colonel Milton O. Beebe, chief of chaplains of the Mediterranean theater, and Major A. Stanley Trickett, deputy chief of chaplains. Traveling through Luxembourg and Belgium, the group reached Germany and proceeded to meet with chaplains, generals, G.I.'s, and political and religious leaders in Bonn, Koblenz, Wiesbaden, Weimar, Leipzig, Bayreuth, Erlangen, Nuremberg, Stuttgart, and then back across the Rhine to Strasbourg, Colmar, Lyon, and Marseilles.

Midway in the visitation Germany surrendered, May 7. Oxnam noted little exhaltation among the Americans—a dirty job was done, another remained in the Pacific, no "crowing" over the defeated foe, respect for the fighting efficiency of the German soldiers. Oxnam's prayer upon the occasion of the defeat of Germany, cabled to America and sent out over the air waves by CBS, opened with the moving petition:

> Almighty God, our Heavenly Father, God of all the nations, Lord of all worlds, hear us, we beseech Thee. The words come haltingly to our lips, our hearts are too full for speech. We were summoned to the terrible duty of war; but all the while we yearned for peace. We gave our sons and our daughters that the children of tomorrow might be free. Thou dost understand, for Thou didst give Thy Son that the world might be saved from

> sin. But, O, our Father, we have hated the very work of our hands. We were not created to burn and bomb and kill. Thou didst give us minds and freedom to bring truth and goodness and beauty to the earth. We would have found another way, but that was denied us. And so we have fought; and now victory has come. We are grateful. We would wash the blood from our hands and purge our souls of hatred. God of all knowledge, give us the wisdom to be just. Keep us from the foolishness of a false pity. We would not be filled with revenge; we would not be blinded by hate. But we would be strong in the resolve that righteousness shall endure.

Peace in Europe did not end the perils facing Oxnam and his companions for there remained the real dangers in Germany and then in Italy of fatal car or plane crashes, and as both chauffeurs and pilots informed him, there was more than one close shave. Still, he made his appointed rounds faithfully, proud in his officer's uniform. The sight of Germany's bombed cities elicited the solemn observation, "I left the ruined cities with a strange feeling of having heard some awful voice breathe the lines of the committal service: 'Ashes to ashes, dust to dust.' " He learned the falsity of the reassuring saying "There are no atheists in fox holes," noting instead: "All the chaplains here say no deepened interest because of war, no striking return to the church. You help a man, but that does not mean he feels obligation to attend services." The inspired cursing a stalled car received from a GI chauffeur brought a rebuke from Col. Beebe, but Oxnam informed the soldier that "I regretted that he knew I was a Bishop, since I hesitated to limit the creative talent of a literary artist." And Oxnam roared with laughter when a GI at chow time formally presented him with a spanking clean towel with the marking Hotel Waldorf-Astoria. However, he was not amused when General George Patton, an Episcopalian, said of a Methodist chaplain, "That God-damn chaplain can neither pray nor preach. Get rid of him." Investigating the removal, a junior officer explained to Oxnam: "A CO has the right to get rid of a chaplain if he wants to. A CO has the right to do anything to you he wants to, except get you in a family way, and that is physically impossible."

A few miles north of the lovely town of Weimar lies a beech forest, beloved by Goethe and Schiller, whose spirits were uplifted and poetry inspired by the natural beauty. Here the Nazis built a concentration camp they named Buchenwald, or beech wood, at the precise spot of an ancient oak tree often sought out by Goethe. American troops entered the camp on April 11. Shortly, Oxnam and Robert and three Methodist chaplains did so. They returned again the next day. Oxnam's diary entries for these two dates, while certainly factual descriptions of this inner circle of hell, fall short of conveying the full, awful enormity. Perhaps he could not find the words to express his emotions. Perhaps, as other witnesses, he saw death reduced to such a state of ordinariness that it left him numb and feeling nothing, not even sickness at his stomach. Perhaps simply to carry on he had to unconsciously repress the sights and sounds and smells his senses carried to his brain. Later he was to write, "I looked on bestiality revelatory of inhumanity at once incredible and indescribable. The mind refused the evidence the senses rushed from eye and ear and nose. Reason rejected fact. Such brutality could not exist. But the evidence was overwhelming." And later he was to describe in many utterances the torture chambers, the medical experimentation room, the ovens, the lampshades made from tattooed human pelts, the dead stacked like cordwood, and the living apparitions. "When an artist sketches a human face, he begins by drawing an oval. . . . But at Buchenwald the faces were not oval. They were triangles. Starvation had changed the contour of the faces. The sunken cheeks, the fleshless heads, were triangles. As I looked upon these hundreds upon hundreds of prisoners, it seemed I was walking about in some mad nightmare." In justifying taking and publishing photographs of Buchenwald, Oxnam said only documentary, visual evidence could persuade the world to believe the unbelievable. "It seems essential that the world fully understand that such pagan disregard for human life is the logical outcome of the Nazi doctrine of 'the nothingness of the individual.' " He carried away from that place of death hordes of lice, the torment ending only with an Army DDT fumigation.

A camp survivor was asked, "Where was God at Buchenwald?" There came the reply, "Where was man at Buchenwald?"

Leaving Germany meant saying "adios" to Captain Bob, but after several days in France Oxnam was flown from Marseilles to Naples where he was greeted by Chaplain Phil. Together they visited the Anzio beachhead and Phil's foxhole, which sheltered him for two and a half months from the fury of German eighty-eights. They visited the cemetery at Nettuno with its nine thousand crosses and Stars of David where Oxnam said a prayer at the grave of Phil's best friend whose head had been blown off while advancing on the beach only a few yards from Phil; and at the grave of a Jewish lad from Brooklyn Oxnam thought it fitting to recite the Twenty-Third Psalm.

On May 2 Oxnam was summoned to the stockade at Naples. Private McGhee, a black soldier and a Methodist, was waiting to be hanged. He had fatally shot a fellow GI in a poker game argument. He had asked that the bishop come to his cell. Oxnam did. They talked about sports and McGhee's mother and son (his wife had divorced him). "I would appreciate it if you would see my mother some day. Just call and she will come," petitioned the doomed young man. "No," replied Oxnam, "I will go see her," and on returning to the States he did. Oxnam read the Words of Assurance from the Ritual. McGhee asked that Oxnam return on the day of his execution. Oxnam desperately wanted to beg off, pleading other engagements. But he did not. Oxnam returned, again consoling the condemned with prayer and words of comfort. Then an ambulance carried McGhee, Oxnam, a black chaplain, and MP's to the gallows site. Major Neiswanger read the sentence and the trap was sprung. The major then acknowledged his was tough duty. "Yes, sir, it is very tough. I've had sixteen of these to do. His neck was broken, sir, no suffering I am sure." Recorded Oxnam in his diary: "Strange, I have passed through fields where thousands died, and spoke of war and death, but here one boy, who according to our custom deserves to die, he had killed a fellow soldier, rocks me back on my heels."

Departing Naples, Oxnam conferred with General Mark Clark in Florence and then he and Phil, Beebe and Trickett, traveled to Bolonga, Verona, Vincenza, Venice, Innsbruck, Milan, Genoa, Leghorn, and back to Naples. On landing in Naples, the pilot of the A-26 bomber confessed, "That's the closest shave I have ever had; she stalled just as I came in." In Naples Oxnam met for the first time Pastor Martin Niemöller, recently freed from a Nazi prison. Unwell and desperately worried about the fate of his seven children and the fact that he had been unable to inform his wife in Munich that he was alive, the German Protestant leader turned to Oxnam for succor. Oxnam picked up the phone, directly contacted an American general to cut through the red tape, and the following day Oxnam learned that British General Sir Harold Alexander had ordered that Mrs. Niemöller be reached and that full information concerning her and the children be made immediately to the pastor. When Oxnam informed Niemöller of Alexander's telegram the German cried, "That is wonderful, wonderful. I shall rest so much easier. I thank you. I thank you." In the years ahead Oxnam was again and again to befriend Niemöller and the German's gratitude mounted.

The next day a B-17 carried the bishop's party to Greece on the invitation of Archbishop Damaskinos, recently selected and British-approved regent of Greece, who had courageously resisted the Nazis. Dignitaries in waiting limousines escorted the guests to a palatial residence in Athens. United States Ambassador Lincoln MacVeagh presented the guests to the six-foot-seven-inch regent in the government palace. There followed two days of formal luncheons, state dinners, escorted tours, conferences, exchange of gifts. Subsequently Oxnam praised his host—"Damaskinos, a Christian statesman, unafraid." And he secured $25,000 from the Methodist Crusade for Christ fund for the regent, to be used to feed the hungry children of Greece. Neither in his public statements nor private diary jottings did Oxnam say a word about the Damaskinos government's savage repression of the Greek Left, a repression encouraged by Churchill and cynically not discouraged by Stalin. Perhaps Oxnam was unaware of this tangled political situation. (On March 5, 1948, at a ceremony at the Greek Embassy in Washington, Oxnam received, on order of the King of Greece, the Cross of the Grand Commander of the Royal Order of Phoenix in recognition of his service to Greece.)

Oxnam's group flew from Athens to Cairo for several days. Additional days followed in Jerusalem. On May 28 Oxnam hugged Phil goodbye, boarded an army transport command plane, and returned to New York by way of Casablanca and Bermuda. During those six weeks he had traveled 18,000 rugged miles, counseled with five hundred chaplains, comforted hundreds of GI's in camps and hospitals, conferred with generals and officials, witnessed the ruins of bombed cities and the horrors of Buchenwald, cherished joyous reunions with Bob and Phil, experienced the excitement of being in a war area, and the relief at Germany's defeat.

Oxnam's reports on returning home to the American people contained some hard truths: the reality of the bombed cities, the reality of Buchenwald, the reality that "there is a singular lack of regret among the German people. There appears little acceptance of responsibility for the war, or a recognition of the pagan nature of the Nazi philosophy." The reports contained inspiring words about the sacrifices of the chaplains and medics and the bravery of the soldiers, the unwhimpering stoicism of the American wounded. The reports also contained some dubious propositions: "In my contact with at least 25 Generals, there was not a war-monger among them. Each one resented the fact of war and shrank from the necessity of it." And they contained some bromides: "The resistance of the churches to the Nazi doctrine has resulted in a development in the realm of faith that I think is significant. The people of Europe feel that the ethical ideals for which religion stands must be translated into justice and brotherhood."

Shortly after the coming of peace, Secretary of the Navy James Forrestal appointed Oxnam to the newly created Civilian Advisory Committee and he served as chairman of the subcommittee on religion and morals, for which he received on February 11, 1947, a letter of commendation from Forrestal. From General Mark Clark he received a letter of appreciation stating: "Your presence in Italy was an inspiration to me and to my troops and we still draw inspiration from your patriotic efforts in behalf of the perpetuation of American ideals and world freedom." In 1947 Rear Admiral Kelly hosted a ceremony at which Oxnam was awarded the Navy's Certificate of Appreciation.

The war caught up Oxnam in still other endeavors. He served on the executive committee of the World Alliance for International Friendship Through the Churches, a venerable organization. In July 1943 he presided at the International Round Table at Princeton University, a conference bringing sixty world figures together to consider the postwar world. The Mutual Broadcasting System invited him to join a priest and rabbi in a nationwide broadcast on Armistice Day, 1942. His V-J Day prayer, as earlier his V-E Day prayer, reached millions over the air waves.

Because of his long experience as a labor mediator, the National War Labor Board requested his services in arbitrating several "highly explosive" management-labor disputes. In 1942 President Roosevelt requested him to write a monthly report on the state of the nation based on the observations made during his incessant travels. The director of the Office of War Information found Oxnam's reports "highly constructive."

Although Franco had been the beneficiary of Italy's and Germany's support during Spain's savage Civil War and although Franco might have joined the Axis early in the Second World War had Hitler been willing to meet Franco's asking price, in the end Spain remained neutral, despite Hitler's enticement and coercion, and Gibraltar was saved. Spain's nonbelligerency in the war did not save Franco from Oxnam's wrath. On January 2, 1945, a rally was held in Madison Square Garden to support a Republican Spain and in opposition to Franco's dictatorship. Known for his long-standing condemnation of Franco, Oxnam was invited to speak. "I desire the severance of all diplomatic relations with Franco Spain," Oxnam began, "because I want to keep my faith, in myself, and in what men are and may be. I do not want the hand of democracy made foul by clasping the hand of fascism." The plea continued: "I would not be true to myself if I did not add that whenever the Church, in a blind endeavor to preserve its privileges and its property, makes common cause with fascism, allies itself with the great landlords and the military, it not only repudiates its Christ but deserves the wrath of the masses it has betrayed. In making this statement I do not mean to attack a particular church. It so happens it was the Roman Catholic Church in Spain." Acknowledging that Franco ordered the imprisonment, exile, and execution of thousands of defeated Loyalists, Oxnam somehow failed to note that the righteous "wrath of the masses" had resulted in the massacre of thousands of Catholic bishops, priests, nuns, and seminarians. More to the point, even as Oxnam's conscience would not permit him clasping the foul hand of fascism, he was calling for the American people to cooperate with Stalin, that "pock-marked Caligula," as Pasternak spit out. Concurrently also, Oxnam was extolling Generalissimo and Madame Chiang Kai-shek, those "devout Methodists" (as they were described) who ruled China with corruption, chicanery, and cruelty. Early in 1943 Madame Chiang Kai-shek made her triumphal American tour, receiving a tremendous ovation during her appearance before Congress and bringing an audience of seventeen thousand in Madison Square Garden to their feet in admiration. Oxnam was in that audience, and he and the Methodist bishops were granted a private interview with Madame Chiang Kai-shek. Oxnam could scarcely contain his praise. He characterized the Dragon Lady as "the foremost woman of China, perhaps of the world." "I've often wondered what Joan of Arc was like; and now I know." "Yes, she was more than a little wonderful. . . . I cannot find words to describe her, personality, dress, power, charm. . . ." "I bow to Madame Chaing Kai-shek in her greatness that summons her people not to hate."

Oxnam's total devotion to the war effort led him to take several questionable positions on civil liberties. For example, when in March 1942 the Reverend Edward Lodge Curran, president of the International Catholic Truth Society, was selected as speaker for Evacuation Day (to commemorate the evacuation of the British from Boston in the Revolutionary War), Oxnam protested. Father Curran, accused the Methodist bishop of Boston, was anti-British, anti-Semitic, anti-Russian, and anti-Roosevelt, and had been pro-isolationism. Therefore, the invitation should be withdrawn in the interests of unifying the nation behind the war effort. "The United States is predominantly a Protestant country, and Protestantism has been active in securing for all Christians [sic] the liberty it demands for itself," Oxnam observed. "It is to be hoped that the Roman Catholic Church will repudiate fascism and fascist sympathizers, to the end that men of religion may co-operate to preserve democracy, win the war, and build a just and enduring peace." Oxnam also supported the government's dumb and dangerous prosecution in *United States v. McWilliams* of neo-Nazis (including Elizabeth Dilling!), a wartime "Brown Scare" anticipating the postwar "Red Scare." And his diary entries make clear that newspapers critical of the government, such as Col. McCormick's *Chicago Tribune*, deserved censoring.

In August 1945 Oxnam, still president of the Federal Council of Churches, conferred with Samuel McCrea Cavert, general secretary, and other council officers about the religious situation in postwar Germany. Agreement was unanimous that it was wiser to send a united Protestant review group rather than a cluster of individual denominational delegations. Two logical individuals to join Oxnam in the mission were Franklin Clark Fry, president of the United Lutheran Church, and Bishop Sherrill, chairman, it will be remembered, of the General Commission on Army and Navy Chaplains. Both men were approached and accepted the assignment. The next step was to secure the authorization and support of President Truman. This the president gave verbally to Oxnam at a meeting in the White House on September 13 followed by an official written order dated October 15, a document naturally carrying weight with the army and civilian brass in Germany.

Oxnam and Sherrill arrived in Paris on November 26 and then took a night troop train to Frankfurt, where they were joined by Fry. Stewart W. Herman, Jr., deputy director of the Department of Relief and Reconstruction of the embryo World Council of Churches, who had been in and out of Germany for months and who before the war had been pastor of the American Church in Berlin, became a fourth member as a translator (Oxnam believed) and *interpreter of German conditions* (as Herman understood his assignment). Happily, Captain Robert Oxnam was present throughout, having received the "request" from General Lee, "I want you to look after your father and the party as a personal favor to me." Prior to departure from the United States, Cavert had prepared a memorandum to remind the group of their purpose: One, make contact with German church leaders; two, encourage the American Military Government to strongly support the new church in Germany arising from the ashes; three, seek to secure relief supplies from America with the cooperation of the United States Army in transporting the supplies and of the German churches in distributing them ("We have no doubt whatever that relief will be desperately needed this winter if starvation, epidemic, and even revolt are to be escaped"); four, bear in mind the ten million refugees pouring into Germany and their most desperate need because UNRRA (the United Nations Relief and Rehabilitation Administration) aid is limited to non-German displaced persons; and five, endeavor to see what if anything can be done for the starving in the Russian zone.

For two weeks the Oxnam party (as chairman it was called for the chairman) visited Frankfurt, Baden, Stuttgart, Munich, Nuremberg, Hof, Berlin, and other places carrying them, thus, to the American and British zones and through the Russian zone; Berlin was not yet divided so the entire city was open to view. To be sure, they received VIP treatment, staying in the finest accommodations available, traveling in GI-chauffeured sedans, conferring with Generals Lee, Joseph T. McNarney, Lucius D. Clay, O. P. Nichols, and B. L. Milburn. Still, the dangers of driving the ice-and-snow-covered roads were real, the pace exhausting. Above all, there was the challenge of making sense—and therefore sound recommendations—out of the myriad swirling, conflicting sights and words that assailed them. On returning to the States, Oxnam, Sherrill, and Fry published their widely distributed and controversial report and then on January 16, 1946, reported in person to Truman.

Here are some of Oxnam's observations as recorded in his diaries, embedded in the official report, and stated in subsequent utterances. Oxnam found few Germans, other than churchmen, who displayed any sense of guilt for the crimes of Nazism; Germany's only guilt was in losing the war. Almost never was the fate of the Jews mentioned. Indeed, one German made the monstrous charge that America's "harsh" occupation policy was "developing anti-Semitism" in the German people! Thanks to General Lee, who had made possible Oxnam's earlier inspection of Buchenwald, Oxnam attended one day of the Nuremberg trials. He viewed with loathing the "whole dirty, dangerous lot" of defendants and justified the conduct of the trials and the principle behind them.

Repeatedly he commented on the unbelievable damage suffered by Germany's cities by bombing. On the other hand, there were other areas where the scars of war were less visible. The official report contains this paragraph:

> Generalizations concerning hunger, disease, lack of clothing, inadequate housing and widespread suffering are apt to be misleading. There is more than one Germany; the Germany of the bombed cities; the Germany of the rural areas largely unscathed by war; the Germany of the refugees composed of perhaps ten million persons evacuated from territory once German and now moving into the communities of the present Germany. Then, too, there are the Russian, French, British and American zones. Living conditions differ radically in these different areas.

General Clay, deputy military governor for the American zone, wrote in his memoirs: "For three years the problem of food was to color every administrative action, and to keep the German people alive and able to work was our main concern." The problem was vastly complicated not simply by the war's devastation but above all by the fact that in the last months of the war and with the coming of the peace, Germany was to receive the most gigantic population movement in European history. "All the refugees," as Churchill dryly put it, "bring their mouths with them." In they poured from the East, fleeing the rapacious wrath of the Red Army—from East Prussia, Silesia, Pomerania, Rumania, Yugoslavia. Moreover, the Big Three at the Potsdam Conference agreed to formalize the expulsion of populations of German origin still remaining in Poland, Czechoslovakia, and Hungary. By the month of Oxnam's visit, 1 million of these wretched souls had reached the Western zones; soon the number mounted to 7 million, swelling the population of the American and British zones to 43 million, compared with a prewar population of 34 million. By 1950 the forceable transfer of Germans eventually involved over 12 million people, 4 million of these *Vertiebene* living in the Soviet zone, and over 8 million in western Germany. Excluding the civilians deliberately slaughtered by Soviet soldiers, an estimated 2 million refugees died from hunger, disease, exposure in flight. Postwar Germany was concurrently the scene of the mass movement of myriad Allied prisoners of war and civilian slave laborers being expatriated to their homelands, and, alas, the most despised and doomed of all, the freed death-camp Jews, huddling in their barbed-wire–surrounded displaced persons' camps.

What judgments could Oxnam, or any mortal, make in two weeks about these interrelated issues of hunger and refugees?

On the flight to Paris Oxnam was informed by a French general in the plane that the coming winter there would be no starvation in France and therefore France would not need food from America. At dinner in Paris Professor Joseph Hromadka stated of his country: "The people of Czechoslovakia will not starve. We are agriculture and there will be enough food. Of course, there will be undernourishment." In Baden a German pastor gave the judgment: "There is hunger, not alone in refugees but here. I have eight grandchildren. I see them growing paler daily. Many will die this winter. Baden people will starve." In Stuttgart in the railroad station Stewart Herman pointed out the frayed clothes. "I disagree," noted Oxnam. "Most coats were in good shape and reasonably heavy." Elsewhere another German pastor said the food allowance was inadequate, especially the shortage of milk, sugar, and fats, but at least the allowance was back up to 1550 calories. In Munich a bishop judged that Bavaria could feed her own and no Bavarian would starve, but the flood of refugees could not be cared for. In Munich, also, a Roman Catholic cardinal made much the same observation: "There is need, but no one will starve save those who pour in from the East, millions upon millions."

Refugees from the Sudetenland were flooding across the border into the town of Hof when the Oxnam party arrived. There, growing hostile feelings between Herman and Oxnam boiled over. Oxnam recorded in his diary what his eyes saw: "It was harrowing, people trying to sleep in bunks with a bit of straw for a mattress, insufficient food. But I must say what we saw was far less terrible than it had been pictured by Herman and others who talked of naked people crossing, soldiers walking on stumps of legs without crutches, wasted bodies, etc. Yes, they die, some of them, it is frightful and the evacuation could have been planned to take place in spring when weather is warm." As twilight approached, they departed. Recorded Oxnam: "Herman was furious because I refused to stay longer to see a room in which 30 orphans were being cared for. He seems to be on fire to show us that Germany is suffering unjustly, that starvation is about. 'See those shoes are cracked.

That man looks hungry.' His interpretations were not accurate and included much of his own interpolations. I had to request him to express his own opinion separately so we could know who was saying what." The next morning Herman offered to resign from the mission and return to Geneva, but Sherrill graciously poured Episcopalian oil on the troubled waters and Herman remained.

Years later Herman gave his side of the story. Recalled Herman: Oxnam ran the show, and the final report came from his pen, Sherrill and Fry (very reluctantly) signing it. Herman did not wish his name linked with it and said so. Oxnam's mind could not register what his eyes saw. Herman had witnessed east of Berlin terrible scenes of dead, dying, crippled refugees. In the refugee camp at Hof, Oxnam seemed to shrink from the horror, wiping everything he touched with his handkerchief and cutting the visit short in order to return to VIP quarters.[7] Oxnam treated Herman as a mere interpreter and ignored Herman's experience gained from months in postwar Germany.

In his memoirs Sherrill gently alludes to "some tension even within our own group" and lets it go at that. Oxnam's diary entries praise Sherrill as a splendid traveling companion but characterize Fry as "a very difficult brother, highly opinionated, emotional" with unattractive traits. In fairness to Oxnam, the final report did contain this stark description:

> . . . in Germany as a whole, the expulsion of millions from their homes in territory once German is causing unspeakable hardship. These millions have been torn from their homes, their personal property taken from them, and forced to migrate to Germany under conditions that result in starvation and the unnecessary death of tens of thousands. They are without food, medical supplies, adequate clothing, shelter. Children and old people die enroute, many diseases are becoming epidemic, and the cruelty accompanying this evacuation will affect all of Europe and manifest itself in widespread disease in the present and in hatred tomorrow.

Moreover, after returning to America Oxnam reported, "I have seen the long lines of refugees moving from Poland and Czechoslovakia into Germany, emaciated men and women and starved children." [8]

As the Oxnam group continued its rounds the members continued to listen as well as witness. Frightful tales were reported about the refugees in the Russian zone. After hearing Niemöller preach in a packed church, Oxnam recorded that both Fry and Herman made disparaging remarks. (Herman flatly denies this, writing that "I have consistently placed Martin Niemöller in the select company of the most courageous Christians I have had the honor of knowing from Albert Schweitzer to Bishops Berggrave and Bell and Martin Luther King, Jr. Niemöller baptized our twin sons in Geneva in 1946. Faults he had, but I thought *very much* of him.") After the sermon, Niemöller informed Oxnam regarding the food situation: "In the American zone there is no great need. Bavaria is best. But it will be much worse when the refugees come." In Berlin when informed that 4,000 were dying daily, Oxnam did a little figuring and calculated that half of Berlin's population would be dead in a year. This raised real doubts in Oxnam's mind about the informant's testimony.

On December 5 the Oxnam group met with General Clay, the most crucial interview of the entire mission because of Clay's commanding position and because Oxnam recorded that the "interview will change our report in several important particulars, I am certain." Here are the diary notes of the meeting, quoting Clay:

> We do not want to starve the Germans and will not. Five hundred tons of food are on the way. This will give a 1550 calorie standard to all Germans living in our zone including 3,000,000 refugees. There is no need for private relief to send food, it would be a pittance. Of course, there will be suffering, we cannot provide heat, and some will die as a result, but not from starvation. It is necessary to get clothing and the churches would do well to start collecting it. The very fact of collection might bring the decision to open the way for its transportation the earlier.

Clay then stated his opposition to the sending of individual packages from Americans to individual Germans, explaining, "I don't want one German eating and fat next to a German on a 1550 calorie basis and thin. They must be treated alike."

After a hazardous drive from Berlin to Frankfurt, Oxnam recorded: "Then a long session revising the report, agreement was reached and I sat up until midnight, typed it, to make sure I got Fry's signature to it. These Lutherans are a strange lot." Back in New York, Oxnam met with a Lutheran leader and an officer of the World Council of Churches. The two shredded the report and denounced Fry (in his absence) for signing it. Oxnam asked the inquisitors if they were interested in telling the truth to the American people or misinforming them. He then faced thirty members of the press, overwhelmingly hostile, who grilled him about the food question, asserting that people could not live on 1550 calories per day. "The fact that they are living and are on the streets and apparently in good health doesn't seem to bother her," Oxnam said of one reporter, "because she knows people can't live on 1550."

The Oxnam-Sherrill-Fry official report dated December 10 contained a paragraph noting that the devastation widely varied in different areas of Germany and a paragraph graphically depicting the intense suffering among the refugees. It also reported General Clay's announcement of the arrival of 500,000 tons of food and the assurance of a standard in the American zone of 1550 calories per day. The report then expressed the judgment: "*Under these circumstances, there will be no need or opportunity for the churches or individuals to contribute food or money to purchase food;* but on account of the inevitable lack of heat, there is a serious need of clothing. We appeal to the government to grant permits for churches and relief agencies in the United States to provide this" (emphasis added). Although the judgment was based precisely on information given by Clay, the report came under immediate attack.[9] A Quaker journal, citing eyewitness accounts, asserted thousands of Germans were dying outright as the consequence of malnutrition. The journal condemned the Oxnam group for forgetting the clear Christian law: "If thine enemy hunger, feed him." The *Christian Century*, normally Oxnam's defender, termed the report "inaccurate and misleading." From the headquarters of the World Council of Churches in Geneva, J. H. Cockburn, S. C. Michelfelder, and Methodist Bishop Paul Garber, then assigned to the Geneva Area (embracing nine European countries and North Africa) cabled their dismay with the report. The ration of 1550 calories was not available in much of Germany and even if met in the American zone was still insufficient for the hundreds of thousands living in unheated ruins and shelters. Garber elsewhere declared, "I can say with absolute confidence that many shiploads more of food must go to Germany if her children are not to be stunted, warped and lost to religion and good will. This assuredly is a job for the churches." Vainly Dr. Robbins W. Barstrow, director of the Commission for World Council Service, a united Protestant group concerned with relief, explained to the protestors that the objectionable sentence in the report was taken out of context and that "the government allows us to send both food and clothing to other countries in Europe, and we have been sending it right along, but it will not allow us to send even clothing to Germany because it has not worked out a policy concerning relief to former enemy countries. The State Department and our military government officials keep putting us off."

On January 16 Oxnam and Fry met with President Truman in the White House. A request was made, among other items of business, that the churches be permitted to send clothing to the American zone. The president replied that he generally favored the idea and was working on it, but could not give a definite time as to when this might be done. Afterward, Oxnam informed reporters of the request by the churches to send clothing, opined there would be no mass starvation in the American and British zones, but acknowledged that elsewhere thousands of refugees did face starvation.

On January 26 General Clay announced that private groups, including, of course, the churches, would now be permitted to send clothing and food and medical supplies to relieve German civilians. The situation remained stark, Clay reporting on March 16: "Failure to receive food shipments as scheduled has resulted in making it impossible to maintain present ration. We are disturbed by rumors that this ration is in excess of German needs. While it is true that it has prevented starvation, our health authorities are convinced that it is insufficient to prevent serious mass deterioration of health over a long period of time."

In February Truman had created a Famine Emergency Committee with Herbert Hoover as honorary chairman, Chester Davis as actual leader, and on March 12 Oxnam received a telegram from the president asking him to serve on the committee. Of course he accepted. Although the Truman administration could not bring itself to reinstitute wartime rationing, as

Oxnam publicly favored, between June 1946 and June 1947 the United States performed the feat of shipping one-sixth of its food supply abroad. "It is no exaggeration," judged an informed historian, "to say that American relief shipments in 1945 and 1946 were the salvation of Europe." Concurrently, Oxnam gave his energies to the Emergency Food Collection campaign on behalf of UNRRA and in September 1946 received a letter of appreciation from Henry A. Wallace, national chairman of the campaign.

The Oxnam delegation's primary purpose was, as the official report stated, "to seek to establish fellowship with and to ascertain the present status of the churches in Germany; to discuss with church leaders there the matter of reestablishing relationships with the churches in the United States and the possibility of cooperation between the American churches and the German churches as the latter seek to rehabilitate the spiritual life of their nation. . . ." To this end, the Oxnam group met with a number of church leaders including the towering Protestants Bishop Theophil Wurm, Bishop Hans Meisser, and Pastor Hans Asmussen, all of whom had resisted Hitler during the *Kirchenkampf*.

In Munich Oxnam interviewed Michael Cardinal von Faulhaber, finding the Catholic prelate a "brotherly, mellow spirit" radiating beautifully "love and fellowship." "It was," Oxnam concluded, "a delightful and inspiring visit with a wise old man, a German 'tis true, but what is more important, a Christian." Apparently Oxnam was impressed by the fact that he was the first American churchman to be received by Faulhaber, not even Francis Cardinal Spellman being accorded that honor. Apparently, too, Oxnam was unaware that the German cardinal had not protested Hitler's Jewish persecutions and, indeed, after meeting the Führer in 1936 had reported that "without doubt the Chancellor lives in faith in God. He recognizes Christianity as the foundation of western culture"; and after the attempt on Hitler's life he denounced *"das himmelschreiende Verbrechen des 20. Juli."*

Bishop Otto Dibelius, courageous Confessing church leader who suffered arrest because of his resistance to Hitler, won Oxnam's admiration as a man of decision and bravery. Another staunch pastor, who had survived years in a concentration camp, viewed with Oxnam the ruins of Berlin and with a rueful laugh quoted Hitler's boast, "Give me ten years and you won't know Berlin."

On two occasions Oxnam dined with F. Otto Melle, bishop of the Germany Central Conference, formed by German Methodists in 1934 and approved by the 1936 General Conference in America. Oxnam recorded that the meetings were "very friendly," although Melle resisted any suggestion that he should resign. (Melle had achieved peace with the Nazis by praising Hitler's leadership, sending Hitler a telegram of congratulations after the failed assassination attempt, and never questioning the Reich's genocide policies.) Melle retired in 1946 and died in 1947.

On returning home and at the meeting with President Truman, Oxnam petitioned that the Protestant churches of America be permitted to appoint an American churchman to serve as a liaison between the German church leaders and General Clay in order to bypass junior occupation officers, cut red tape, and permit immediate and direct access to the deputy military governor. Truman deemed this wise and in March Oxnam learned from Secretary of War Robert Patterson that the permission was official, with the additional information that American Catholics and American Jews would be able to tap their own liaison officers. Shortly Oxnam received from General Clay a letter of thanks, closing, "I have been most grateful for your cooperation and for the understanding of our problems which you developed on your previous trip to Germany."

No German Oxnam met during his spring and fall visits to Germany inspired more admiration than Pastor Niemöller. World War I U-boat commander, critic of the democratic Weimar Republic, German nationalist who patriotically volunteered in 1939 to serve in Hitler's Navy, father of three sons who did serve, one dying on the Russian front, Niemöller was an ambiguous hero. A man of contradictions and authoritarian temperament, he was a flawed great man, but still a great man. He came to see Nazism as a pagan excrescence on the German nation, defied Hitler, and though acquitted in the courts of sedition, he was imprisoned for eight brutal years at Hitler's personal insistence. He was one of the few German Christians to accept a personal share of the German collective responsibility for the crimes of Nazism, including the Holocaust, and to assert that the members of the churches, and the Christian Church itself, were guilty. Oxnam praised Niemöller in the pages of the *Christian Century* in June 1945 and then when the German came under orchestrated attack by liberal Americans, including Eleanor Roosevelt, Oxnam answered in the *Christian Century* in August in one of the finest articles to come from his pen. Thanks measurably to Oxnam's efforts, the Federal Council of Churches invited Niemöller to deliver a series of addresses in America, Oxnam introducing him. Again liberal voices, including Mrs. Roosevelt's, denounced the invitation. As outgoing president of the FCC, Oxnam requested permission from the council to reply. His telegram, released to the press, read: "We urge you to correct erroneous impression created by your column and to give recognition to the fact that Niemöller took a courageous stand against nazi policies long before our own country alerted to the danger." Unpersuaded, Mrs. Roosevelt in a telegram and two letters let Oxnam know how strongly she felt: "I want us to be vividly aware of the fact that the German people are to blame [for Hitler and the war], that they committed horrible crimes. Therefore, I think you are doing something which is stupid beyond words in bringing this gentleman here and having him touring the country, much as you like him." In his reply Oxnam could only say that he was fully aware of the Nazi crimes and the guilt of the Germans, however, the letter closed, "I find it difficult . . . to justify a policy that refuses constructive cooperation with those in Germany who fought the Nazi philosophy . . . , particularly when the individuals involved are those who know the German people are to blame and are seeking at heavy odds to bring their own people to repentance and works, as the Bible put it, 'meet for repentance.' "

In subsequent years Bromley and Ruth and Pastor and Mrs. Niemöller became friends and the two men continued to labor together in church matters. When Bishop Gerald Kennedy first met Niemöller, the German told the American Methodist that if he were not a minister in his own communion he would prefer to be a Methodist. When asked why, the reply came: "Because of Bishop G. Bromley Oxnam."

---

[1] In September 1939, also, Senator Harry S Truman declared, "The role of this great Republic is to save civilization; we must keep out of war."

[2] Oxnam was so enamored of this idea that he repeated it in two later lecture series.

[3] Among the signers were the following Methodists, all well known to and respected by Oxnam: Henry Hitt Crane, Georgia Harkness, E. Stanley Jones, Ralph Sockman, and Ernest Fremont Tittle.

[4] These are severe words. Perhaps an explanation is in order. My personal belief is that Japan would have surrendered without the necessity of using the atomic bombs and without the necessity of the invasion of her home island if only the United States had exercised greater patience and wiser diplomacy. This, of course, cannot be proven; historians will continue to debate the question without reaching a consensus. But this question is not the issue here. If the bombs had not been dropped and if the home islands had been invaded, I might not now be at my typewriter. In August 1945 I was a young Marine officer with the Sixth Marine Division stationed on Guam. This division was assigned to invade the major southern island of Kyushu. Everyone knew the casualties would be ferocious. This point, too, is not the issue here. The Dulles-Oxnam statement is. How can Christians express "profound thankfulness" for America's exercise of "self-restraint" when in fact the United States did release all the "wholesale destructive force of atomic energy" she then possessed—two bombs, the second only three days after the first, scarcely time for the Japanese leadership to respond to Hiroshima? The deeds may arguably have been inevitable, but one gags at the hypocrisy in their description as "the way of Christian statesmanship." If, as Dulles and Oxnam assert, Hiroshima and Nagasaki "increases our moral authority in the world," then one must only ask what a nation must do to diminish its moral authority in the world. Finally, one wonders if the souls of the 340,000 victims in the two cities found comfort in knowing that they served as "a practical demonstration of the possibility of atomic energy bringing war to an end." (The figure 340,000 includes those who died instantly and those who suffered lingering deaths within a period of five years.)

[5] Still, in fairness to Truman, it must be remembered that while over fifty-four thousand American men were dying in Korea, he refrained from employing atomic bombs against either North Korea or China, later explaining, "I could not bring myself to order the slaughter of 25,000,000 noncombatants. . . . I know I was *right*."

[6] Later, during the Korean War, he was elected chairman of the commission.

[7] One remembers Oxnam's experience with lice at Buchenwald and his general fastidiousness, including his refusal to drink from a common Communion cup.

[8] Further, in December 1945 he wrote a public letter, in his capacity as president of the Federal Council, urging expediency in admitting Europe's displaced persons into the United States.

[9] Apparently Oxnam expressed his views privately to Mrs. Eleanor Roosevelt, for she wrote him a brief note on December 21 reading: "I very much appreciate your letter and I am glad that you agree with my views. I too, feel strongly that our Allies should have any extra food, and that the Germans be given enough, but no more."

CHAPTER 14

SERVING THE FEDERAL COUNCIL OF CHURCHES IN TIME OF WAR AND THE WAR'S AFTERMATH

During the war and the war's aftermath the government in many instances had called on Oxnam's services because he was visibly associated with the Federal Council of the Churches of Christ in America, a federated union formed in 1908 and embracing most of the nation's largest denominations; and while it did not challenge denominational sovereignty, it did give a semblance of unity to American Protestantism's voice when addressing public issues. (In 1941 conservative Protestants formed the American Council of Christian Churches in protest against the Federal Council's liberalism in matters both doctrinal and social, but this new organization never matched in number the Federal Council's twenty-five constituent bodies with a total membership of twenty-seven million and consequently never rivaled it in influence on public affairs.) Oxnam's diary contains this late 1942 entry: "The Biennial of the Federal Council was satisfying and significant. I have refrained from participating actively in the Biennial until I had won my way in the Executive Committee and other directing groups of the Federal Council. This time the policy proved wise, and I cherish a letter from Samuel McCrea Cavert, very generously suggesting my influence had been perhaps the most influential during the meeting." American Methodism from the inception had provided the council with support and leadership, and Oxnam's ecumenical interests were of long standing; these factors coupled with his ambition led him to ever-increasing involvement.

In August 1940, on the eve of the passage of the first peacetime conscription act in America's history, Oxnam was named chairman of the council's newly formed Committee on the Conscientious Objector. After Pearl Harbor he also headed a committee coordinating the council's war services activities and chaired the committee charged with drafting the council's labor messages. His voice was heard as a member of the executive committee and then in January 1943 he was elected chairman of the advisory committee of the executive committee, the body that actually planned policy and program, the council's most important position, save only the presidency. In November 1944 he was invited to become president. "This I regard as the highest honor that can come to an American churchman and to say that I am very proud and very happy is to put it mildly," he recorded. "I had resolved to say nothing about it to anybody in advance. If it comes, it must come because they deserved it and now it appears they have." The delegates to the biennial meeting in late November in formal election ratified the executive committee's nomination. (Benjamin E. Mays, president of Morehouse College, was concurrently installed as vice-president, the first black to hold such a high post.) Perhaps no letter of congratulations pleased Oxnam more than the one from John Foster Dulles, for the two men had worked together on council affairs since 1940 and were to remain in close association until Dulles's death.

Oxnam's involvement in the fate of America's conscientious objectors—those youth who could not bring themselves to kill another human being even though that person marched under the brutal banners of the swastika or Rising Sun—was manifested as a member of the Methodist Commission on World Peace and as a trustee of the National Service Board for Religious Objectors, a coordinating agency, and as chairman of the Federal Council's Committee on the Conscientious Objector. Although a million young lions who answered their country's call to the colors came from Methodist homes, about one thousand Methodist lads refused to shoulder arms. Their absolutist stance was firmly supported by the Methodist General Conferences of 1939, 1940, and 1944. Considering the pacifist passion of Methodism in the interwar era, the ratio of one thousand resisters to war to one million warriors suggests a whiff of asymmetry; nevertheless, The Methodist Church supplied more CO's than any denomination other than the Historic Peace Churches—the Quakers, Mennonites, and Brethren. The total number of conscientious objectors in the nation is a matter of speculation, perhaps approaching 100,000. Before the war's end over 25,000 CO's served as noncombatants, especially in the Army Medical Corps. Close to 6,000 went to prison, either because they refused to register or because their objection was based on grounds inadmissible under the law, and of these many were Jehovah's Witnesses. Some 11,887 reported for alternative service under the Civilian Public Service (CPS), a program proposed by the Historic Peace Churches and rather warmly accepted (though not without wrangling) by the Selective Service Administration, "glad to have the churches shoulder the responsibility for the conduct of persons who could, with infinite firmness, say 'No' to every military demand." In the CPS camps or on detached service these individuals toiled more than 8 million man-days of work for the United States, tilling the soil, building roads, fighting forest fires, caring for the mentally ill, acting as "guinea pigs" for medical research. If the government had paid for this labor at the same rate as for its Army, it would have spent over $18 million. As it was, the CO's were obliged to work for nothing, while they, their families, and the churches paid for their maintenance.

Oxnam's responsibilities compelled correspondence and conference with government officials, including Attorneys General Frank Murphy, Robert Jackson, and Francis Biddle, and Selective Service Directors Clarence Dykstra and then Brigadier General Lewis Hershey. Oxnam much liked Hershey, who was not unsympathetic to the CO's.

When the Burke-Wadsworth Bill was originally presented to Congress in the early summer of 1940, exemption for conscientious objectors was limited to persons holding membership in a "well-recognized religious sect whose creed or principles forbid members to participate in war." This was virtually the same formula used by draft boards in World War I. Pacifist and nonpacifist churchmen, including Oxnam, and church bodies, including the Federal Council, were not satisfied with this narrow formula and placed intense pressure on Congress to broaden the basis for exemption from combatant duty. The final bill contained the following provision:

> Nothing contained in this act shall be construed to require any person to be subject to combatant training and service in the land or naval forces of the United States who, by reason of religious training and belief, is conscientiously opposed to participation in war in any form. Any such person claiming such exemption from combatant training and service because of such conscientious objections whose claim is sustained by the local draft board shall, if he is inducted into the land or naval forces under this act, be assigned to non-combatant service as defined by the President, or shall, if he is found to be conscientiously opposed to participation in such non-combatant service, in lieu of such induction, *be assigned to work of national importance under civilian direction*. (Emphasis added.)

In Oxnam's judgment, this law was wiser and fairer and provided broader protection for the CO than the World War I statute. Nevertheless, he further held that conscientious objection to war need not be based upon religious training and belief alone, explaining: "If a man of conscience is opposed to participation in war upon intellectual grounds, or humanitarian ideals, or even on grounds of philosophical anarchism, I believe we should respect his conscience. To single out religious belief as the sole basis is to penalize a sincere unbeliever whose conscience is nonetheless his guide." (Years later the government tardily arrived at Oxnam's position.)

Although the law was not perfect, although the dangers of placing the youth of America under state control were real, Oxnam concluded that it was democratically enacted and should be obeyed. Therefore, those CO's who refused even to register were dangerously misguided. As he publicly declared: "We can co-operate with our Government, follow the procedures established in giving conscientious objectors legal status, or we can raise absolutist issues and in all probability create a situation that will make it increasingly difficult to protect the conscientious objector." Privately Oxnam's expressions were stronger: "The brother who will not register, who courts martyrdom, and who may be as sincere as the early apostles (though some I fear like headlines) will have to take the consequences, and a few poor devils are doing just that."

The tangled origins of the Civilian Public Service camps must be sketched in broad strokes. The initiative came from the Historic Peace Churches, fearful as they were that if run by the government, even under civilian authority rather than military direction, the pacifists assigned to these camps would be placed in harm's way. The larger Protestant denominations acquiesced in the Quaker/Mennonite/Brethren proposal, with reservations, to be sure, and only after President Roosevelt advocated putting all the CO's to work under Army direction. The Historic Peace Churches underwrote the cost of feeding the Civilian Public Servicemen, providing medical care and educational materials, and employing a camp director and a nurse for each project. The major denominations also made contributions.[1] Unlike men who elected noncombatant military service, those in the CPS camps received no pay, no dependency allowances, and no insurance. Moreover, in actuality the Selective Service controlled major policy decisions; General Hershey retained final authority over work projects and assignments. The government (not the churches) provided the cost of transportation, furnished certain equipment, some sites, technical supervision. In fact, often the CO's were not assigned "to work of national importance under civilian direction," as the law stated, but in trivial labor. In fact, as the CO's lamented, the camps, though technically under civilian control, did resemble military camps with military regimes. In fact, the men entering the camps were conscripts under the ultimate authority of General Hershey. Commented a Selective Service subaltern of Hershey's, "There is no obligation to provide an assignee with work for which he has been particularly prepared, wishes to do, or regards as socially significant. . . . The impression that camps are democracies to be run by the assignees is entirely erroneous." Senator Mon Wallgren of Washington, when the situation was explained to him by Hershey, gasped, "You are treating these fellows worse than the Japs." Increasingly the angry young men in the camps believed that the churches had sold them into bondage to the warmaking State.

Oxnam from the onset questioned the arrangement pushed by the Historic Peace Churches. He met with their delegates and argued: "It is essential that Government, having recognized the right of Conscientious Objection, should do more than that. The right must be recognized by support. If men are assigned by Government to the Army, they are supported. If they are assigned to non-combatant service under the military, they are supported. By the same token, if the law recognizes a third category, namely work of national importance under civilian auspices, those assigned should be supported." Oxnam pressed home this argument in meetings with Hershey and other officials in Washington. All to no avail.

Inevitably rebellion brewed in many of the CPS camps as the realization dawned on the inmates of their "slave labor" status (as the more radical and defiant resisters termed it) and their growing conviction that they had been betrayed by the old "Pacifist Establishment." Hunger strikes, slowdowns, sabotage, mounted; some walked out of their camps knowing that in so doing they were in effect walking into prison.

Oxnam felt little sympathy for these CO militants. After all, he was not a pacifist; his sons were facing death in the service of their country; and temperamentally he loathed disorderly questioning of authority. "My boys are in an army fighting to preserve a society that recognizes the right of conscience," he growled. "Let the CO's pull off a nation-wide demonstration and the camps will go, and the CO's too. They are so blessed cock-sure in their assumption of being the only Christians in the nation." Repeatedly he compared the hardships and dangers endured by America's fighting men with the selfish demands of the soft CO's for a forty-hour work week, evenings free, week-ends at home. One day in October 1945, Oxnam met with almost one hundred CO's on leave from CPS camps. "I have yet to address any group," he recorded, "who have been less respectful, whose spirits have been more combative, and who reveal less of the very preachment which, according to their theory, is the one answer to international strife." As the papers of the veteran pacifists Ernest Fremont Tittle, John Haynes Holmes, and Harry Emerson Fosdick reveal, they too wondered with nonpacifist Oxnam if the radical CO's were not at heart anarchists against all government.

Oxnam's anger at some of the CO's did not blind him to real injustice. On November 20, 1945, he petitioned General Hershey: "The war is now over and the demobilization of the men in all branches of the armed forces is going forward rapidly. Further to postpone the issuance of a directive covering the progressive demobilization of CPS would in my opinion be a grave miscarriage of justice." Later President Truman was urged to proclaim "a general amnesty for conscientious objectors now in federal prison and for those who, although released, bear continued civil disabilities." During the war, every sixth male in the federal prisons was a CO, mostly Jehovah's Witnesses who refused any classification other than ministerial exemption. (In Germany, they also bravely dared Hitler to do his worst to them—and he did.)

Save for the remnant of conscientious objectors, Japan's attack on Pearl Harbor united Americans in the common cause of winning the war. Until that day that will live in infamy, however, the Federal Council was sharply divided over the Roosevelt Administration's interventionist policies—as indeed was all American Protestantism. In December 1940 the Federal Council created a Commission to Study the Bases of a Just and Durable Peace (soon shortened to simply Commission on a Just and Durable Peace). Designed to "clarify the mind of our churches regarding the moral, political and economic foundations of an enduring peace," all could rally around this new commission as interventionists and noninterventionist churchmen alike labored together in the creation of a more just and peaceful postwar world. The commission was an extraordinary enterprise and for six years its chairman, John Foster Dulles, provided extraordinary leadership. In truth, the media often referred to the body not by its formal name but by simply the "Dulles Commission." All Dulles biographers, critical and sympathetic alike, acknowledge his domination of the commission. Praise of his strong leadership came from a whole synod of respected Protestant associates, including Reinhold Niebuhr, John C. Bennett, Henry Pitney Van Dusen, Samuel McCrea Cavert, Richard Fagley, Roswell P. Barnes, Frederick Nolde,

John Mackay, Henry Smith Leiper, John R. Mott, for openers. Dulles's most judgmental biographers charge that he cynically used the Federal Council as a vehicle to advance on his road to political power, but surely this is unjust. One may conclude that Dulles later made a dangerous secretary of state, but one may not assume that his Christian faith was feigned and spurious. It was not.

On March 19, 1943, Oxnam, not yet president of the Federal Council, wrote Dulles: "From the beginning, I have regarded the work of the Commission on the Bases of a Just and Durable Peace as of major importance. Under your leadership the work has gone forward far beyond our highest hopes." He was in a position to know. Not only a member of the commission (one of fourteen Methodists), he was also a member of the smaller, inner Committee of Direction of the commission.

Significantly, the first Exploratory Conference on the Bases of a Just and Durable Peace was convened and chaired by Oxnam and conducted under the auspices of the Methodist Peace Commission. Held in Chicago over a period of four days in late May 1941 and receiving the active cooperation of the Federal Council, the several hundred participants heard addresses by distinguished authorities, American, British, European, and Asian, including ones by Dulles and Oxnam. "The fundamental purpose of this Conference is to unite Christian people to the end that the bases of a just and enduring peace may be discovered," Oxnam explained. "Its further purpose is to win such support that the social structure of tomorrow may be erected upon these bases." Inasmuch as the conference represented the cooperative effort of The Methodist Church and the Federal Council, it is an "expression of what is believed to be a nation-wide movement upon the part of the Protestant forces of the United States." Seven months before Pearl Harbor Oxnam was intoning: "The Communion Table must precede the Conference Table"; "After the bomber comes the builder!"; we must affirm "our faith that will summon mankind first to its knees and then to crusade"; "competitive struggle is to be succeeded by cooperative enterprise"; "International anarchy must go. World law and order must come. This means the setting up of world government in fact." The report of the conference, *When Hostilities*

Cease, representing the thought of both Methodism and the Federal Council, was widely circulated. Unsurprisingly, Oxnam considered the conference highly significant for both Methodism and the Federal Council. "Our central idea was to unite our people upon ultimate objectives, rather than allow the Church to become divided upon discussion of immediate issues," he explained. "This Pacifist-Interventionist fight is likely to split many a church. If we can center all of them upon a discussion of what are the bases of a just peace when at last the war is over we will do something constructive. All of the speakers held fast to the assignment."

The success of the Chicago conference gave impetus to a great National Study Conference on the Churches and Just and Durable Peace convened by the Dulles Commission in early March 1942. Significantly, the 377 representatives assembled at Methodism's Ohio Wesleyan University. The conference was chaired by Dulles. "It is probably as fine a gathering of Christian leaders as we have had in this century," believed Oxnam, who was present as a member of the Economic Section. The conference received a "Statement of Guiding Principles," drafted by the Dulles group, including Oxnam, which affirmed: "We believe that moral law, no less than physical law, undergirds our world. There is a moral law which is fundamental and eternal, and which is relevant to the corporate life of men and the ordering of human society. If mankind is to escape chaos and recurrent wars, social and political institutions must be brought into conformity with this moral order." This goal mandated the end of economic and racial injustice and the curbing of "the sovereign power of the nation-state." Bishop McConnell, who edited for publication the major conference addresses, Oxnam, and other leaders of Methodism were justly gratified at the nationwide generally favorable publicity accorded the meeting.

In early 1943, as the Commission on a Just and Durable Peace continued its labors, a major statement was formulated and given the name "The Six Pillars of Peace." The statement called for continued United Nations collaboration after the war and in due course of neutral and enemy nations; international economic and financial cooperation; treaty structures that would be adaptable to changing conditions; assurances of autonomy for subject peoples; control of military establishments; and the right of individuals everywhere to religious and intellectual liberty. The document was given massive publicity: sixty thousand copies were mailed to ministers, including every Protestant chaplain at home and abroad; hundreds of newspapers carried the brief text; local study groups were supplied with a seventy-page study guide; radio time was purchased; the message was spread across the oceans. Even President Roosevelt, that consummate politician, was impressed by the public relations campaign and summoned Dulles to the White House to discuss the "Six Pillars." Dulles always believed (as did Oxnam) that the "Six Pillars" campaign helped break the hold of isolationism, educated the American people to the necessity of accepting responsibility for shaping the postwar world, and made possible the formation of the United Nations and U.S. membership in it.

In July 1943, the Commission on a Just and Durable Peace convened at Princeton University an "International Round Table" composed of sixty-eight Christian churchmen and laymen from twelve countries. Oxnam chaired the three-day affair, a considerable honor. It was widely hailed as another major step toward the goal of a better postwar world.

Further evidence of Oxnam's standing in Federal Council affairs was manifested on February 15, 1944, when he was asked to join the council's president and secretary and Dulles in a meeting with President Roosevelt. The purpose of the visitation was to impress upon the president the need for a world organization that would be "curative and creative, not merely regressive." The delegation handed him a council statement expressing concern over the potential big-power domination of the postwar world which would perpetuate the status quo, disenchant idealistic Americans, and stampede the nation back to isolationism. Naturally Roosevelt radiated friendliness, as Oxnam reported, and naturally the president's charm masked his conviction that postwar affairs would operate under a system of Great Power control—not under idealistic universalist arrangements.

Even as Oxnam and his Federal Council colleagues planned for a righteous world after the dogs of war had been leashed, there remained the immediate question as to the righteous or unrighteous conduct of the war by the belligerents. In November 1944 a Federal Council commission, under the chairmanship of Yale theologian Robert C. Calhoun, submitted a report entitled "The Relation of the Church to the War in the Light of the Christian Faith." This controversial report reflected the fact that some members of the commission were pacifists, including Methodists Tittle and Harkness, while others were certain that the Allied cause was just. The report condemned the killing of prisoners or hostages and "the massacre of civilian populations." Total war is suited only for a totalitarian society. "No matter what the provocation, however great the extremity of military peril—even to the imminence of defeat—the Church dare not approve a supposition that military expediency or necessity can ever rightly become the supreme principle of human conduct." However, the majority of the commission also endorsed "all needful measures" necessary to defeat the Axis powers, and for some this meant acceptance of the obliteration bombings of cities. Oxnam was present when Professor Calhoun submitted the document to the executive committee. "I was very much disappointed," Oxnam reported. "When the theologians speak in profound terms, they deal with little more than is dealt with in the simple discussion of people who face realities. They make the evidence confused and then discuss their own confusion, coming to conclusions often times that a child would reach in a moment's reflection." Of course, eight months earlier Oxnam had given endorsement to the terrible necessity of obliteration bombing.

A Second National Study Conference on the Churches and a Just and Durable Peace was held in Cleveland, Ohio, January 16–19, 1945, and although Dulles served as chairman, Oxnam, because of his recent installation as president of the Federal Council, also played a commanding role. On the shores of Lake Erie the 481 delegates, representing thirty-four communions, assembled to consider the peace settlements with Germany and Japan, relief and reconstruction, human rights, and the Dumbarton Oaks proposals concerning the United Nations, the

Federal Council having earlier proclaimed that the world organization proposed by the United States, Britain, Russia, and China at Dumbarton Oaks "can be developed into one that will commend itself to the Christian conscience." As Oxnam viewed the assembly he judged the delegates to be the ablest leaders in all American Protestantism and predicted their labors would prove to be of historic significance.

Oxnam was chairman of the Findings Committee of the entire conference and also chairman of the Findings Committee of the subgroup dealing with Dumbarton Oaks. His responsibilities entailed constant committee meetings, presiding at the Dumbarton Oaks session, presenting the report known as "The Message to the Churches," engaging in debate, and giving the closing address.

The structure of the future United Nations was at the heart of the conference. Dulles and Oxnam led an effort to secure unconditional approval for the Dumbarton Oaks proposals. They acknowledged that the proposed world organization was based on power politics, but they urged Christians to be realistic. "All politics deal with power," Oxnam enlightened the delegates. "The primary issue is to bring power under control. . . . Dumbarton Oaks brings that power under the control of solemn agreement." Pacifists such as A. J. Muste, E. Stanley Jones, Holmes, Tittle, and the influential editor of the *Christian Century*, Charles Clayton Morrison, challenged this view, offering nine changes.

The pacifists urged that the United Nations Charter provide for commissions on human rights and trusteeships for colonial peoples, denial of the veto to a country involved in a dispute, increased development of international laws, armaments reduction, eventual universal membership, and more clear protection of smaller nations from the possible arbitrary power of great nations. After bitter debate, the conference adopted this position: "Accordingly, we recommend that the churches support the Dumbarton Oaks Proposals as an important step in the direction of world cooperation, but because we do not approve of them in their entirety as they now stand we urge the following measures for their improvement." In a word, Dulles and Oxnam secured eventually what they sought: the churches' unconditional support of the Dumbarton Oaks general plan, while striving for its improvement.

Oxnam's leadership at Cleveland received favorable comment, *The Churchman*, an Episcopal journal, editorializing:

> Constantly in the foreground of the conference was the new president of the Federal Council. . . . Keenly intelligent, markedly experienced, forthright in speech and one of the best presiding officers we have ever seen in action, Bishop Oxnam demonstrates some of the same characteristics that are identified with the late Archbishop Temple. . . . There is something most heartening in the emergence on this side of the water of a personality of similar potential stature. Here is a new leader from whom Protestant churches and the ecumenical movement may expect very much indeed.

Among the personal letters of gratitude and congratulations was one from Dulles opening: "As I look back over the Cleveland Conference I realize more and more what a tremendous contribution you made to producing a Message which I believe will be a powerful influence for good. Your presentation of the findings, with reference to Dumbarton Oaks, was masterly and contributed decisively to the action taken." For his part, Oxnam expressed this thought about his pacifist opponents: "It is very interesting to note that the absolute pacifists have no constructive answer to make to the question of the postwar world. All they can do is to damn Dumbarton Oaks, claiming that it is a new method of the balance of power. They are certain that they know what is perfect, but when you ask them to translate perfect into practical, then they are stumped."

Immediately following adjournment, Oxnam as Federal Council president asked all Protestant congregations to observe "United Nations Sunday" on April 22 by holding special services as a fitting climax to Dumbarton Oaks Week. On that Sunday millions of men and women gathered in their churches to pray for the success of the San Francisco United Nations Conference. Surely Dulles and Oxnam were not wrong in pressing American Protestants to abandon their prewar isolationism, endorse the United Nations, and embrace responsibility for creating a just and durable peace. Nevertheless, Oxnam, the realist, was not immune from idealistic self-deception. After characterizing the Cleveland Conference "as the most significant meeting of churchmen perhaps in the history of the country," he added: "Its profound influence upon Washington has, I think, expressed itself somewhat in the agreements that have come from Yalta." It is interesting to speculate on the commentary that statement might have elicited from Roosevelt, Churchill, and Stalin—to say nothing of the peoples of China and Poland and Eastern and Central Europe in general.

While Dulles was unquestionably the commanding figure in the Federal Council's Commission on a Just and Durable Peace, just as certainly was he a senior partner in the Wall Street law firm of Sullivan & Cromwell with a powerful, lucrative international clientele. Equally clear was his life-long Republicanism. In 1940 when Thomas E. Dewey made his first bid for the Republican nomination for the presidency he had turned to Dulles for consultation; Dulles responded with advice and twenty thousand dollars. Four years later Dewey won the Republican nomination and predicted victory over Roosevelt in November. Dulles gave Dewey close advice, wrote his speeches, shaped the party's foreign policy plank in the direction of a greater internationalism, brokered Dewey's relationships with such Republican power brokers as Senators Vandenberg and Robert Taft and with the incumbent Secretary of State Cordell Hull (even as Dulles Red-baited the Roosevelt administration). As Dewey's senior advisor, certainly he would have been decreed secretary of state had the voters decided differently. Naturally, Dulles's legal and political activities caused the Federal Council's leadership concern.

In September 1944 Dulles offered to resign as chairman of the commission if the executive committee deemed either his legal work or political involvement threatened the commission's weal. He assured the executive committee that, contrary to the charges, Sullivan & Cromwell had not continued to do legal work for Germany's banks and businesses after Hitler's rise to power. The executive committee refused to accept his tendered resignation. At the meeting of the executive committee Dulles found a champion in Oxnam, who voted with the majority to retain the services of this "devoted and talented layman." (Actually Oxnam had defended Dulles from critics as early as the April meeting of the executive committee.) Further, Oxnam met personally with Dulles to assure the Presbyterian that he was "a very great Christian layman." Oxnam followed the meeting with a letter consoling Dulles for the "unfair" attacks on him "from individuals to whom good sportsmanship, to say nothing of the word 'gentleman' or 'Christian' is unknown." Then in October Oxnam joined John C. Bennett, Reinhold Niebuhr, and Justin Wroe Nixon in an open letter to the editor of the *Christian Century* in which Dulles was exonerated of all charges of partisan politics and all allegations of collaboration with legal clients in Germany, Italy, or Japan. (Presumably Oxnam did not know of the depth of Dulles's involvement in shaping the Republican foreign policy plank or in guiding Dewey's campaign because Oxnam found the plank impossible and the campaign disgusting. And Niebuhr could have had no premonition that he would later find Secretary of State Dulles to be dangerous and stupid.)

On the eve of his death, President Roosevelt invited Dulles to be advisor to the American delegation at the San Francisco Conference which brought the United Nations into being. Loathing Dulles, the president had reluctantly tapped him to give an aura of bipartisanship to the proceedings and only after being pressured to do so by Senator Vandenberg and Bernard Baruch. Dulles eagerly accepted the assignment, despite his mistrust of the dying president, because the formation of a world organization had been close to his heart since his vocal presence at Versailles in 1919 when President Wilson advanced his League of Nations; further, a world organization was then at the heart of Dulles's vision of a postwar world of justice and peace. In order to avoid potential criticism of his official appointment to the American United Nations delegation, Dulles on April 5 temporarily resigned from his responsibilities with the Federal Council, stating that at San Francisco he would be a government, not a church, representative, because, "I am, and always have been, strongly opposed to representation of the churches at any peace conference." Before doing so, Dulles phoned Oxnam on April 2 seeking advice. Oxnam urged the acceptance of the assignment and resignation from the council because Dulles would now be in a position actually to influence the shape of the United Nations Charter as an official insider.

On hearing this, Dulles said: "Bishop, this is good for my soul. If you had indicated a negative reaction, I would not have accepted official appointment. In the light of your judgment, it is my present intention to accept official appointment and to sit officially as an advisor."

After completing his labors at San Francisco, Dulles reported to the council's executive committee. "The Charter . . . fulfills our hopes even beyond our expectations," he exulted; its "new and lofty conceptions" could turn it into "a Magna Carta for the world." The council proceeded to adopt an eloquent endorsement of the United Nations, including the warning: "In many respects the Charter will need continued improvement after it has been ratified and has become operative. To these improvements the churches and all men of good will must dedicate themselves in the coming years. . . . The road to a better world is long. The journey is arduous. Only God can assure its achievement. As we move forward we humbly seek His help." After sending this message to the churches, the council proceeded to threaten that if the Senate procrastinated, it planned to have the Charter read from the pulpits of the Protestant churches across the land.

Even as the Federal Council expressed its hopes for the United Nations, it was haunted by the fear of nuclear war, adopting in September a statement prepared by the Department of International Justice and Goodwill: "Used destructively . . . atomic energy can mean the end of our civilization or even the end of man on earth. The bombing of two cities, which shocked the consciences of men, foreshadows the peril of the future." "Consequently," the statement continued, "the establishment of a single world control of destructive atomic power is an urgent necessity. . . . We urge our government to state now its intention to place the new discovery under a world-wide authority as soon as all states will submit to effective controls."

Oxnam's proudest moment as president of the Federal Council came at a special meeting of the council, March 5–7, 1946, in Columbus, Ohio. Earlier, in November, he had persuaded the executive committee to convene a special meeting in advance of the next scheduled Biennial in December 1946, because (as the enabling resolution declared) "the desperate needs of the world and of our own nation in this post-war era press upon our churches so urgently for new spiritual and moral leadership and for the building of Christian community where tensions are now deepening to conflict" that early attention must be paid. Meeting with President Truman in the White House on January 16, Oxnam extended an invitation to address the assembly and received a tentatively affirmative answer. Oxnam believed the Columbus meeting the most significant "in the history of cooperative Christianity in our country" and the *Christian Century* concurred: "This assembly brought together the largest and most distinguished company of its kind yet to convene in this country. Over 500 leaders of the major non-Roman churches of this nation and Canada gathered in extraordinary session."

In addition to presiding at the three-day sessions, Oxnam challenged the arriving delegates with what some described as "eloquence." After citing the fear that the dominant instrument in the orchestra of organized Christianity is the flute, he continued:

> The flute speaks of costly raiment, of the ball-room, and of the minuet. The trumpet summons to khaki, to battle-field, and to the march. If I sense the spirit of contemporary Christianity, we are done with genuflections and pageantry, the pretty parades of peace, the sorry spectacle of pomp and privilege. We weary of the minuet, and are no longer interested in full length mirrors before which episcopal leaders may be assured their prerogatives are on straight before they attempt the highly polished floor. We no longer see talent in the ability to dance with a lovely little creature called Mademoiselle Tactfulness and evade all the issues of contemporary society. No, we hear the clear call of the trumpet. It summons men to take Christ with seriousness and to follow Him into the uttermost parts of the earth resolved that His will shall rule in all the activities of men. I believe men are ready to wear the fatigue uniform of service, to stand unflinchingly upon battlefields where the issues of economic justice are determined and the victories that mean racial brotherhood are won, to advance if need be by the way of the Cross.

Almost at the moment Oxnam was delivering his exhortation in Columbus, in Fulton, Missouri, there came rumbling from the throat of Winston Churchill the fateful words, "From Stettin in the Baltic to Trieste in the Adriatic, an Iron Curtain has descended across the continent." The next day a train carried Churchill and President Truman to Columbus where they were greeted by Oxnam and Governor Frank Lausche. Ohio's governor, the president, and the bishop then traveled in open car to the conference hotel (Churchill electing to remain on the train with his books and bottle) where Truman, presented by Oxnam, made a major address winged nationwide by radio. Oxnam closed the session with prayer. In the evening he introduced to the delegates David Sarnoff, president of RCA, who spoke on "Science and Peace."

Among the many additional significant aspects of the Columbus meeting perhaps several may be singled out. Dulles, returning to the chairmanship of the Commission on a Just and Durable Peace, in grave tones reviewed the world situation, especially the hardening of the Soviet position. Secondly, the council adopted its strongest report to date on race relations, a report firmly rejecting the continuation of segregation in the nation and specifically in the churches. This report was hailed by a black historian as a "great landmark" in Establishment Protestanism's position on race.[2] Thirdly, the council urged Christian Americans to curb their food consumption in order that surpluses might be sent to the starving world. Fourthly, the council resolved that the control of the atomic bomb and of atomic energy generally be placed in civilian hands. It further received a second report from the famed Calhoun Commission entitled "Atomic Warfare and the Christian Faith." Although some members of the commission, including Reinhold Niebuhr, dissented from the confession, the report opened with a mea culpa: "We would begin with an act of contrition. As American Christians, we are deeply penitent for the irresponsible use already made of the atomic bomb. We are agreed that, whatever . . . one's judgement of the ethics of war in principle, the surprise bombings of Hiroshima and Nagasaki are morally indefensible. We have sinned grievously against the laws of God and the people of Japan."

If Oxnam opened the Columbus meeting with an excess of dubious "eloquence", his remarks closing the assembly were thoughtful. The Church must not be mobilized to lead in a "Holy War" against Communism, he warned. "We refuse to identify the Christian gospel with an economic order, whether it be capitalist, communist, or socialist. There may be more of Christianity in a synthesis in which the creative initiative that has flowed from individualism is conserved and the benefits that lie in collective action are appropriated than in either of them." His final words carried a good Methodist ring: "Let the Church be the Church, and let its dynamic teaching so transform the social order that brotherhood comes alive and justice reigns. It must proclaim its own program, mobilize its forces to enthrone it. It is the Kingdom of God on earth it would establish."

On March 8 and 16 Oxnam wrote Truman letters of appreciation for the president's presence in Columbus, both understandably a little forelock-tugging in tone. He also mailed Truman an inscribed copy of his recently penned inspirational trifle, *Behold Thy Mother*, explaining, "You have brought greatness to your mother and, because of that, I thought I might feel free to send you this little volume."

In May Dulles informed the members of the Commission on a Just and Durable Peace of his feeling that the commission had "been derelict in not facing up to the Russian problem" and in June Dulles published an alarming two-part article in *Life* warning of Russia's plan for world domination. Clearly he was moving with increasing rapidity toward his ultimate Cold War posture as a "high priest of American nationalism," to borrow a biographer's term. Oxnam's diary entries disclose that he and some other members of the commission resisted Dulles's hardening line. In Oxnam's judgment, Dulles's position "leads to but one conclusion, namely, that war is inevitable." In meeting after meeting Oxnam contested the Dulles posture that any criticism of American policy or economic system provided grist for the Soviet propaganda mill. Contrary to the impression given by Dulles's biographers, he did *not* have an absolutely free hand in drafting Federal Council statements and his tough stance was moderated, at least on occasion, by the commission members. For example, in the same month that *Life* carried the Dulles article, the press carried these words of Federal Council President Oxnam: "Energy expended in fighting Communism, if devoted to preserving democracy, would make totalitarianism undesirable, and democracy impregnable. Men who summon us to a holy war against Communism are not only declaring war on Russia, but are diverting our attention from the primary obligation to democratize our own economic, political, ecclesiastical and social life." Dr. Channing Tobias, who was black, reminded the commission that even as the commission decried the absence of free elections behind the Iron Curtain, his people were scarcely the beneficiaries of American democracy. Half the population of South Carolina, the home of Secretary of State Byrnes, could not vote; similarly Texas, the home of the chairman of the Senate Foreign Relations Committee, Tom Connally, denied blacks the ballot, Tobias observed.

In mid-October the Federal Council issued a major statement on U.S.-Soviet relations, the last such document during Oxnam's presidency. It represented four months of reflection, and although Oxnam chaired the drafting committee, Dulles's input was significant, suggesting that at even this late date Dulles the church spokesman was more moderate than Dulles the government representative. "War with Russia can be avoided and it must be avoided without compromise of basic convictions," the statement opened. True, real differences and tensions existed. However, it did not follow that war was inevitable. "There is no excuse for the American people to fall into this death trap. They should know, from their own experience, that it is possible for irreconcilable and dynamic beliefs to subsist side by side in peace." Moreover, neither socialism nor free enterprise is unflawed as an economic system; each can learn from the other. "Only blind fanaticism looks upon either system as perfect." The arms race should be bridled. "The United States should set an example by renouncing the acquisition of new military bases so far distant from the continental United States and so close to the Soviet Union that the offensive threat is both disproportionate to the defense value to the United States and also incompatible with a policy designed to dissipate distrust and to increase good-will." This major statement cannot be fairly categorized as either sword-rattling or appeasing. (Incidentally, Oxnam supported the admission into membership of the Federal Council the American branch of the Russian Orthodox Church with its 300,000 members.)

In early December at the Biennial Meeting of the Federal Council, Oxnam stepped down as president. "The honor of serving in this great organization is one that has meant more than any other privilege that has ever come to me," he informed the delegates. The resolutions praising his leadership were fulsome and numerous, more so General Secretary Cavert told him than any in the history of the organization. Read one resolution:

> To his high office he has brought not only the scholarship of a great mind but also the spiritual insight of a great Christian and a devoted churchman.

Read another:

> In Bishop G. Bromley Oxnam as President the Federal Council has had during this crucial period in world life a great leader. He has truly been a master of assemblies; with statesmanship, confidence, saneness, high merit, he has discharged the duties of the high office of president. His outstanding leadership has placed us here assembled, the successors chosen and the Federal Council all in the debt of Bishop Oxnam and we are happy in the leadership he has given. For this leadership we record our deepest gratitude.

Especially praised during this era, embracing both the years 1944–46 and the earlier wartime years, was the work of the Commission on a Just and Durable Peace. Accolades were bestowed by Presidents Roosevelt and Truman and lesser public officials; by churchmen; and by later historians.

Oxnam's successor as president was Charles P. Taft, a layman, brother of the senator and son of the American president. Unsurprisingly, the Taft Papers reveal a somewhat different perspective. Conservative lay members of the council thanked Taft for turning back "the obviously socialistic and, at times, communistic bent given to the policies enunciated by recent leaders of the Federal Council"—and Oxnam was singled out by name. Dulles, too, was disturbed by (as he wrote) the "Left Wing and Socialist tendencies" of the council, though he did *not* specify Oxnam. When Taft retired in 1948 the incoming president, John S. Stramm, thanked him for lifting the work of the council in many ways, especially in the matter of lay enlistment and participation. At that time, General Secretary Cavert informed Taft: "I cannot even begin to tell you how much I value the leadership which you have given to the Federal Council in the last two years. It simply has been grand. Unless I am a much poorer judge of a situation than I believe I am, the Council is in a much stronger position today than it was when you took the helm two years ago. The thing which pleases me most is the prospect that for the first time we are headed in the direction of a much greater lay participation."

Perhaps a fair evaluation of Oxnam's presidency, in light of the conflicting evidence, is that his vigorous leadership increased the council's power and influence; but precisely because the council took strong positions on public questions, the attacks from conservative quarters mounted. To which liberals might add, "We love him for the enemies he has made."

[1] The "moral obligation" of the Methodists amounted to about $490,000, of which some $425,000 was forthcoming.

[2] However, council vice-president Mays recalls in his autobiography that "some of the Council leadership" thought it improper for a black to sit on the platform with the president of the United States, and until the last moment he was relegated to a special chair on the floor with the audience. Oxnam's position on the matter is not revealed by the record, though as council president he could not have been unaware of the original segregated arrangement. We do know it was an individual other than Oxnam who interceded to place Mays on the platform.

CHAPTER 15

SERVING METHODISM IN TIME OF WAR AND WAR'S AFTERMATH

However full a measure of time and energy Oxnam gave to the Federal Council of Churches during the war and the war's aftermath, however great his labors on behalf of conscientious objectors and chaplains, however exhausting his travels to wartime and postwar Europe, however manifold his services to the government, and however draining his normal duties as bishop of Boston and then New York, he could not escape further involvement in Methodism's relationship to the war. Oxnam being the man he was, sought of course not escape but added responsibility for himself and his Church in furthering the war effort and creating a new world order.

Throughout the war the Council of Bishops sought to provide guidance to the people called Methodists. Only days after the Japanese strike at Pearl Harbor, the bishops flashed a message that most certainly expressed Oxnam's convictions:

> Our country has stood, always and unequivocally, for the democratic way, and therefore the clash was inevitable. . . . There can be no peace in the world until the totalitarian threat against the liberties of all freedom-loving people is thoroughly eradicated. Our duty as American citizens is clear. The enemy leaves us no alternative. In this crisis, as in all previous crises, the Methodists of America will loyally support our President and our nation.

The bishops' message continued to assert that there were values more precious than physical survival, concluding: "We roundly condemn the processes of war even while accepting the awful alternative, not of our making, forced upon us by the selfishness and perversity of men. From a measure of the guilt of this, none of us is free."

Other proclamations from the Council of Bishops beat the theme of support of America's just war against totalitarian aggression. These statements certainly represented a withdrawal from the pre–Pearl Harbor antiwar position of the episcopal leadership. Just as clearly, however, the bishops' utterances were free of the bombastic jingoism and merciless hatred that had characterized so many Protestant pronouncements during the First World War against the Hun. In World War II the bishops did not forget, even as they stressed Methodism's patriotism, the unique nature of the Church as the body of Christ and as a worldwide, supranational fellowship. They were determined "to keep the church, as a church, free from participation or entanglement in the clashing activities of war. . . . The church recognizes the immediate duty of the Christian citizen, but the church must ever transcend the mere immediacies." Moreover, the episcopacy never faltered in the purpose to create out of all the wartime suffering "a just and righteous postwar world." Nor for the bishops did this terrible war crush the good Methodist hope that the Kingdom of God "has not been defeated; it has only been delayed."

Oxnam's individual statements on the war are in line with the collective ones of the bishops. The record reveals only occasional disagreement with his colleagues. For example, when in 1942 Bishop James Cannon, Jr., moved that the council alert the president and Congress to Methodism's concern that the boys in service be protected from the liquor and vice traffic, Oxnam suggested that the communication be broadened to include more basic wartime and postwar issues confronting the nation. Oxnam carried on a more continuing clash with Bishop Wilbur Hammaker, whom he considered an isolationist and obstructionist. In 1944 Hammaker was the only council dissenter to Oxnam's resolution praising the Dumbarton Oaks conference, causing Oxnam to grouse: "Discussion is always upon a friendly plane, but none the less direct and forceful, and it was necessary to bring the documents and fair interpretation of them with full power to silence him." Pacifist minister Tittle corresponded with Hammaker about Oxnam's determination to poll the Methodist clergy by mail about the Dumbarton Oaks proposals, writing, "I whole-heartedly support your stand. It would be a tragedy for the Church to give moral and religious sanction to this document as it now stands. Let the Church demand a better plan."

Tittle was a key member of the Methodist Commission on World Peace. Oxnam continued to serve as one of the two episcopal representatives on the commission as he had prior to the war. Oxnam honored the sincerity of the pacifist members while attempting to check their domination of the body. "They are philosophical anarchists and don't know it," he believed. On one instance he insisted that the commission file a minority report representing the view of the nonpacifists. Consistently he supported the pacifists' desire to protect conscientious objectors. Nor did he object to the peace education efforts of the commission. But his major concern was to have the commission share his vision of planning for the postwar world, and the commission did indeed throw itself into the crusade for a new world order. On balance, the commission adopted positions perhaps less "patriotic" than the Council of Bishops, but at no time did it declare immoral America's drawing the sword after Pearl Harbor.

As we know, Oxnam did not hold in dishonor COs, but he was insistent that those young Methodists who had volunteered to wear the uniform of their country be accorded the honor their sacrifice merited, and forcefully argued that point in the debate over the creation of a Methodist Commission on Veterans' Affairs. Before the guns fell silent, he ordered the ministers of the Boston and New York Areas to inform him of the wounding or death of any combatant in their churches in order that he might write a note of sympathy to the bereaved families.

The only wartime General Conference of The Methodist Church was held in 1944, and what transpired at this Kansas City meeting is the clearest revelation of American Methodism's wartime witness—a divided witness, to be sure, but not a division that sullies the Church.

On May 3 Tittle, as chairman of the Committee on the State of the Church, presented Report No. 8 on "The Church in Time of War." It was a reaffirmation of the 1940 General Conference position: The Methodist Church will not officially endorse, support, or participate in war, nor shall the buildings of the church be used for the promotion of war. Two additional paragraphs recognized that the United States was now, unlike in 1940, at war. The final sentence reads: "Believing that God has a stake in the victory of peace with justice in the present conflict, we commend our case to Him, praying 'Thy Kingdom come, Thy Will be done.' "

The report presented by Tittle voiced the position of the majority of the Committee on the State of the Church. A determined minority of the members of this committee led by Charles C. Parlin, however, had caucused, drafted a minority report, and come to the session hoping to win conference endorsement of their substitute. The stage was set for what observers agree to be one of the most brilliant debates in the annals of American Methodism.

On that fateful Wednesday when the two reports were submitted to the governing body of Methodism, it was agreed, by suspension of rules, to permit one leader and five supporting speakers for each report. There was to be no applause. Tittle spoke first for the majority, followed by Henry Hitt Crane, Albert E. Day, Glenn James, Edmund Heinsohn, and Mrs. Frank Wright, the mother of a conscientious objector, a 4-F, and a sailor. Parlin presented the minority report with Lynn Harold Hough and Nolan Harmon giving the most stirring of the five supporting addresses. Amendments were proposed and accepted by both sides permitting the use of church buildings by "agencies of mercy and healing such as the Red Cross" and endorsing the provision of chaplains for the "ministering in the Name of Christ to those engaged in military service."

After an agonizing delay because of adjournment, by separate vote of the clergy and lay delegates, the minority report was adopted by a margin of one ministerial vote. The General Conference now officially declared:

> In this country we are sending over a million young men from Methodist homes to participate in the conflict. God himself has a stake in the

> struggle, and he will uphold them as they fight forces destructive of the moral life of men. In Christ's name we ask for the blessing of God upon the men in the armed forces, and we pray for victory. We repudiate the theory that a state, even though imperfect in itself, must not fight against intolerable wrongs. While we respect the individual conscience of those who believe that they cannot condone the use of force, and staunchly will defend them on this issue, we cannot accept their position as the defining position of the Christian Church. We are well within the Christian position when we assert the necessity of the use of military forces to resist aggression which would overthrow every right which is held sacred by civilized men.

A point must be made clear. The minority report adopted is not a jingoistic statement; it does not glorify war; it does not call for the damnation of the enemy. Not a single speaker for the Parlin group may be fairly characterized as a war hawk. In the debate there was no spread-eagleism. The most significant thing is not the narrow repudiation of Tittle's report, but rather that the statement adopted was itself far different from the frenzied denominational proclamations of 1917–18.

A second point must remain shadowed. Oxnam fails to mention this great debate in his diary or in his correspondence or in his public statements. This is inexplicable considering how strongly he felt about the issue. Nevertheless, it is as positive as any conclusion can be in the absence of documentation that he fervently favored the minority report, and it is certainly possible that he counseled his friend Parlin and had a hand in shaping the adopted minority position.

The forcible uprooting and relocating in concentration centers of over 100,000 Japanese-Americans, the great majority being native born United States citizens, is a shameful chapter in the story of America's war effort. The Methodist Church sought in various ways to succor these hapless victims of fear, racism, and greed, although not all Methodists were united in believing the government's action unjust; and even if united, government policy would not have been changed. Even so, individual Methodists, individual congregations, individual Annual Conferences (especially the crucial Southern California-Arizona Conference), the Peace Commission, the Methodist Youth Conference, and the 1944 General Conference (rather weakly) questioned the government's action, expressed sympathy for the victims, and aided financially and spiritually Japanese-Americans in and out of camps.

Oxnam appears not to have anguished deeply over their fate. Still, he did show a friendly (if patronizing) concern for a Methodist Japanese congregation in New York City. Further, at a 1944 meeting of the Board of Missions and Church Extension, he presented a resolution of the Committee on General Reference calling for just and compassionate treatment of Japanese-American citizens. Although Bishop Straughn and others protested that such a resolution endangered the safety of America, the resolution was ultimately passed, thanks especially to its support by California delegates.

The Bishops' Crusade for a New World Order was Methodism's parallel to the Federal Council's Commission on a Just and Durable Peace, and although, as we have seen, the two movements cooperated closely, the Methodist Crusade was independent and by no means merely a shadow of the council's commission. This mighty endeavor far exceeded in magnitude that of any other denomination. At its conclusion, the *Atlanta Constitution* expressed the widespread judgment: "No more important movement for the establishment of an international brotherhood of nations, for the end of selfish, blind isolationism, has been undertaken than this by the Methodists of the United States." Methodist historians, understandably, have hailed the Crusade as a "tremendous and brilliant" success and a "phenomenal experiment." Non-Methodist historians, free of denominational pride, agree that the "Methodist crusade achieved spectacular results." Judged Oxnam: "This was probably as significant a piece of church support of an ethical principle in international affairs that I know"—and he proceeded to buttress that judgment by citing what President Roosevelt told him in person and in letters. Oxnam had good reason to be knowledgeable about the Crusade and to be proud of it. While called the "Bishops' Crusade" it might with justice be named "Oxnam's Crusade." The idea originated with him, was given its initial impetus by him, was largely planned by him, and more than by any other single individual, was implemented by him. If G. Bromley Oxnam had never lived, Methodism's massive Crusade for a New World Order would never have come into existence—at least not in the form it took. This is the simple truth of the matter.

It will be remembered that even before America's entry into the war, the Methodist Peace Commission held an Exploratory Conference on the Bases of a Just and Durable Peace, convened and chaired by Oxnam, and its findings, published under the title *When Hostilities Cease*, were widely distributed by The Methodist Church and the cooperating Federal Council. Then in July 1942 at a joint meeting of the Council of Bishops and the Commission on World Service and Finance, Oxnam proposed that a commission be established to "plan for a really significant church-wide appeal for post-war reconstruction." Although the opposition to the idea was heated and the debate prolonged, Oxnam prevailed; and thus the seeds of the Crusade for a New World Order and the broader Crusade for Christ were planted. In August the Council of Bishops convened the members of the Commission on World Service and Finance, the executive committee of the Woman's Division of Christian Service, and the Council of Secretaries to discuss the idea further. It will be recalled also that in December 1942 the Council of Bishops at Oxnam's suggestion voted to spend a week in late February in Washington with the leaders of government to make inquiry concerning plans for the postwar world and that Oxnam was the ramrod. On February 18, 1943, just prior to the Washington visitation, Oxnam said to his fellow bishops: "We have had our Methodist Advance, our Day of Compassion, our Week of Dedication. Can we not unite the Church under some worthy slogan and make it effective in this, one of the most important issues of our generation? The following suggestion is too long for such a purpose, but suggests the idea: In the Name of a World Savior, Methodists Mobilize for World Order and World Justice." The Methodist Church, he pointedly observed, because of its numbers and organization, might be the balance of power in determining whether the United States would withdraw into sullen isolationism as it did after World War I or follow the path of "full participation in and continuing cooperation with the world organization necessary to world law and order and economic justice." Oxnam's eloquence brought the bishops to their feet in applause and they voted to accept his motion to appoint a commission of twelve bishops to consider the proposal, to draft plans for its execution, and upon approval by the council to organize and direct the movement. And so the Crusade for a New World Order came into being, with Oxnam as chairman.

Four days later the bishops began their meetings in Washington with government leaders, the leaders having been alerted by Oxnam in advance as to the bishops' concern: "The Council of Bishops is alarmed by evidences of growing isolationism in the United States. There is grave danger that the war may be won, but the moral objectives for which it has been waged may be lost. The Council believes that our Government seeks to establish world law and order and recognizes the necessity of translating the ethical ideals of religion into the realities of economic justice and racial brotherhood. It is the desire of the Council to be effective in mobilizing the public opinion that will support those measures that are essential to an ordered and just world. If this is to be done, the Council believes its members must become thoroughly informed relative to the major proposals, both international and domestic, now under consideration for the post-war world." Oxnam then proceeded to a description of Methodism's size and strength, calming the possible fears of the politicos with the reassuring concluding words: "The Methodist Church does not wish to cross the line that properly separates church and state, nor does it wish to enter the political field as a political force. Its desire in this matter is to be of service in creating support for proposals that look toward an ordered and just world. This service is regarded as properly within the function of the church because it is believed the objectives sought are moral in nature, and rest ultimately in the basic doctrine of religion, namely, the fatherhood of God and the brotherhood of man."

Under the slogan "The Coming Peace and the Prince of Peace," the Crusade for a New World Order marched on with Oxnam exhorting: "United Methodism may prove a determining factor in the world-wide movement for a United World. This is a Crusade for citizen and churchman. In international cooperation Old Glory will win New Glory. In discovering the techniques whereby the ethical ideals of our faith may be translated into the realities of the common life, Jesus Christ will become the ruler of the earth." In another explanatory article entitled "Objective! Mass! Impulsion!" Oxnam intoned: "The world is one. It calls for government. We must take the next step up in the evolution of government and do for the world what our forefathers did for us. They united thirteen warring colonies to form the United States of America. We must build the United States of the World. Of course, the task is more difficult; but with the contemporary means of communication and the yearning of millions everywhere for an ordered world, it is not an insurmountable task."

He then urged Methodists to flood Washington with a million individual letters, continuing: "It may be that the weight of Methodist opinion may be decisive." The article concludes: "Multiply Methodist Mass by the principle of Impulsion. Concentrate our full strength upon the single issue, the basic objective. International collaboration—yes! Isolationism, with power politics—no! Make every letter an expression of individual opinion. Send the letter to each of your senators and congressman. *Objective*—World Order, World Justice, World Brotherhood. *Mass*—The ministers, membership, and institutions of the Church. *Impulsion*—Concentrate upon the single task of becoming influential at the place decision is made before it is made, by exercising the democratic right and duty of expressing opinion—Give us an ordered world."

At this time The Methodist Church had 8,000,000 members, 41,000 churches, 114 Annual Conferences, 578 district superintendents, more than 25,000 preachers, and a vast array of general boards and agencies and publication outlets to spread the message. As the old saying goes, the Greeks have a word for it and the Methodists have a pamphlet for it. As the Crusade moved into high gear in the fall of 1943 and early 1944, Oxnam understandably anguished to his diary, "This Crusade business is driving me nuts. In addition to organization, direction, conferences, I have"—and he then proceeded to list an awesome burden of Crusade obligations. In April 1944 Oxnam wrote a sixty-four-page booklet entitled, *The Crusade for a New World Order: A Report of the Chairman*. Because that report is available and because the Crusade has been described in detail in published histories dealing with American Methodism (and unpublished dissertations as well) and because the Crusade has also been the subject of diplomatic historians, a brief summary here may suffice.

The central ideas undergirding the Crusade were Doric in their simplicity. Methodists are and have always been since Wesley world-minded. In isolationism lies the certainty of continuing war; in international collaboration lies the possibility of enduring peace. Methodists, as citizens, have the right and duty to inform their government of their will that the United States cooperate with such international organization in the political, economic, and other fields as may be necessary to end war, to establish world law and order, economic and racial justice, and to guarantee the freedom of the individual. Methodists, as Christians, reject isolationism which subordinates the well-being of the world to national self-interest and denies the Christian doctrine that all men are children of one Father and members of one family. The Crusade's slogans are revealing: "JESUS CHRIST is the Saviour of the WORLD" and "He [Jesus Christ] saves the Individual. We must save the World."

From Oxnam's pen came many thousands of words of explanation about the Crusade and of exhortation to support it appearing in Methodist publications, Methodist adult church school lessons, and such secular magazines as *Look*. He wrote personal letters to President Roosevelt, every cabinet member, every member of Congress, and officials of the State Department, enclosing a copy of "The Crusade for a New World Order" pamphlet. The many acknowledgments expressed high appreciation of the Methodist endeavor. He addressed mass meetings; a Brooklyn audience numbered over one thousand, a Worcester audience exceeded five thousand. He personally approached Howard Chandler Christy (famed for his World War I propaganda posters and cavorting nudes) to design a poster with a picture of Christ over the caption "The Coming Peace and The Prince of Peace." Oxnam then sent copies to every Methodist church in the country and distributed thousands of postcards displaying the Christy picture for Methodists to send to loved ones in the service. He also had a hand in having Marlatt and Stidger of BUST write the Crusade hymns, one to the tune of the Russian Hymn, the other using Finlandia.

One of the Crusade slogans was "The Peace May Be Won with a Three-Cent Stamp." Ministers and lay people, adults and school children, were urged to write the president and their congressman and senators expressive of their concerns for world order, justice, and brotherhood. Petitions and form letters were expressly discouraged. Oxnam hoped Methodists, writing at least one letter each month, would dispatch a million communications. That goal was probably reached. "Washington received one of the largest outpourings of mail in history," judged a noted diplomatic historian. Folks who never in their lives had written Washington sent their penciled postcards and handwritten letters. One congressman received the simple petition, "Please, may we have Christ at the peace table?" Senator Truman was implored, "As one of your fellow Christians, I beseech you to line up your influence with those who plan an international cooperation which is unselfish and casts aside hatred and revenge, opening up the way to brotherhood of all mankind."

In January 1944 inspirational mass meetings were held in 76 cities from coast to coast. An estimated 200,000 Methodists turned out to hear 25 teams of speakers composed of 30 bishops, 12 ministers, 9 laymen, assisted by over 400 workers from Methodist boards and commissions. Following the meetings, teams of two visited every Methodist home distributing literature. Other traveling teams visited churches to hold Crusade seminars. The literature was extensive: 2,000,000 copies of the leaflet "Your Part"; 600,000 copies of the leaflet "Christian Citizens' Opinion on World Order"; 75,000 copies of the pamphlet *The Primer of Action* (designed for church leaders rather than all lay people); special pamphlets prepared by Oxnam and Bishop Arthur J. Moore and a torrent of material emanating from the Commission on World Peace and other Methodist agencies and from the Federal Council. For a Methodist, there was no place to hide from the Crusade's zealous message. It filled the pages of *motive* and *Power*, thereby reaching young people. *The Methodist Woman* devoted two issues to it, thereby reaching the 1,300,000 organized women of the church. *World*

Outlook, Methodism's missionary journal with a circulation of 200,000, carried letters by President Roosevelt, Vice-president Wallace, Secretary Hull, Wendell Wilkie, and Alfred M. Landon commending the Crusade. *Pastors Journal* gave wide publicity as did *The Christian Advocate* and the *Conference Advocate* and other journals such as *Zion's Herald*. *The Upper Room*, with a circulation of 2,000,000 (200,000 sent to the armed forces) devoted an issue to the Crusade theme. The curriculum of the church school was revised for the 80,000 adult classes and the 40,000 youth divisions so that for one entire quarter nearly 3,500,000 individuals studied lessons especially designed to create (as Oxnam phrased it) "international understanding." The secular press, such as the *New York Times* and *Time* magazine, carried the word.

Reports on the Crusade were contained in cinema news specials and in nationwide broadcasts over CBS, NBC, and Mutual Radio networks. Thirteen fifteen-minute transcriptions were carried by some 240 radio stations, free of charge to the Church, and the Office of War Information delivered three worldwide broadcasts on the Crusade and its objective.

March 26, 1944, was set aside as the Day of Consecration. In services throughout the United States and England, Methodists rededicated themselves to sacrifice and service on behalf of world peace, order, and brotherhood. In May the Methodist General Conference continued the Crusade for a New World Order as part of a larger quadrennial Crusade for Christ.

As 1944 deepened and 1945 opened, the Crusade concentrated its efforts on winning support for the United Nations. The Methodist Church launched a massive propaganda campaign in support of the Bretton Woods, Dumbarton Oaks, and climaxing San Francisco conferences. When in the White House Oxnam informed President Roosevelt that Methodists had written a million letters supporting the creation of the United Nations and American membership in it, F.D.R. replied, "Bishop, I believe the influence of the churches was decisive in this matter." Earlier the president had written Oxnam: "I am grateful to you for sending me the report showing the truly extraordinary response to the Crusade for a New World Order conducted under the leadership of the Methodist Church.

Before it arrived, I was already aware of the impact of your great denomination on the minds and hearts of Americans." Shortly, a new president, Truman, was to express to Oxnam his awareness of and appreciation for the churches' support of the United Nations.

On July 28 the U.S. Senate voted to ratify the U.N. Charter, 89-2. "The faith of Woodrow Wilson has been vindicated," exalted an elder statesman to his diary. "The record of the United States of 1920 has been expunged. Civilization has a better chance to survive." Nine days later the people of Hiroshima received their baptism by atomic fire. *New Yorker*'s E. B. White wrote how the shape of the brave new world now appeared to him: "The preparations made at San Francisco for a security league of sovereign nations to prevent aggression now seems like the preparations some little girls might make for a lawn party as a thunderhead gathers just beyond the garden gate. The lemonade will be spiked by lightning."

The United Nations was born. The United States became a founding member. The Methodist Church made a significant contribution to both achievements. Need anything more be said save to praise (once again) the people called Methodists and their most notable leader in this mighty enterprise, Bishop G. Bromley Oxnam? The answer, churlish and cruel though it may be, is "yes."

Individuals of goodwill may be grateful for the existence of the United Nations. As in the past, it continues to serve usefully the peoples and nations of the world. It is a blessing to mankind. One may truly pray that the future will see its enhancement in scope and authority and respect. It would be a monstrous libel to sneer that the mountain, the Crusade for a New World Order, labored and brought forth a mouse—the United Nations. Nevertheless, wise individuals, who were not necessarily cynics, saw that Oxnam's great expectations ("Tomorrow there must be the United States of the world") were about as accurate as Salvador Dali's watch. What world leaders present at the United Nations' creation—Roosevelt, Truman, Churchill, Stalin, De Gaulle, Chiang Kai-shek—believed it had or desired it to possess an authority higher than their nation's? What world power has subsequently even remotely accorded the U.N. absolute deference? What nation, including the U.S.—in Korea, Vietnam, Dominican Republic, Grenada, Panama, for openers, has requested the U.N.'s permission *before* taking military action against another nation? Oxnam was not wrong to crusade for the United Nations, but one does question his Kahil Gibran–like dithyrambs.

Consider how Oxnam's cries, "Jesus Christ will become the ruler of the earth" and "JESUS CHRIST is the Saviour of the WORLD" might have fallen on the ears of the world's billions of other faiths or of no faith at all, not excluding Marxist materialists? After all, only one citizen of the world in three was then Christian. The point of this is not to challenge the Christian conviction that Christ *is* the Hope of the World, but to question Oxnam's linking the New World Order and its political instrument the United Nations with the universal triumph of Christianity.

Oxnam's incantations, "We demand a world of law and order" and "Give us an ordered world" and "Law and order must supplant international anarchy," are projections of his own personality. Orderly and legalistic himself, the world *must* (surely his favorite word) be shaped in his image. Oxnam might have paused in his breathless cheerleading to ask, "Whose law?"; "Whose order?" Surely the colonial peoples of the world and the peoples in China, the Middle East, and Latin America and the Third World in general dreamed of something other than a tightening of the *prevailing* law and order.

Oxnam identified isolationism with "power politics" and the "certainty of continuing war." The dubiety of this coupling should be self-evident. On the other hand, he identified internationalism with the absence of "power politics" and the "possibility of enduring peace." What he could not bring himself to consider was that as the United States moved from "a sordid and selfish isolationism" and strode the world stage, she might become more deeply enmeshed in "power politics," gripped by what Dennis Brogan at the time termed the "illusion of omnipotence," mesmerized by what Senator William Fulbright later named the "arrogance of power," and dangerously overcommitted to fighting wars to defend her newly self-assumed global

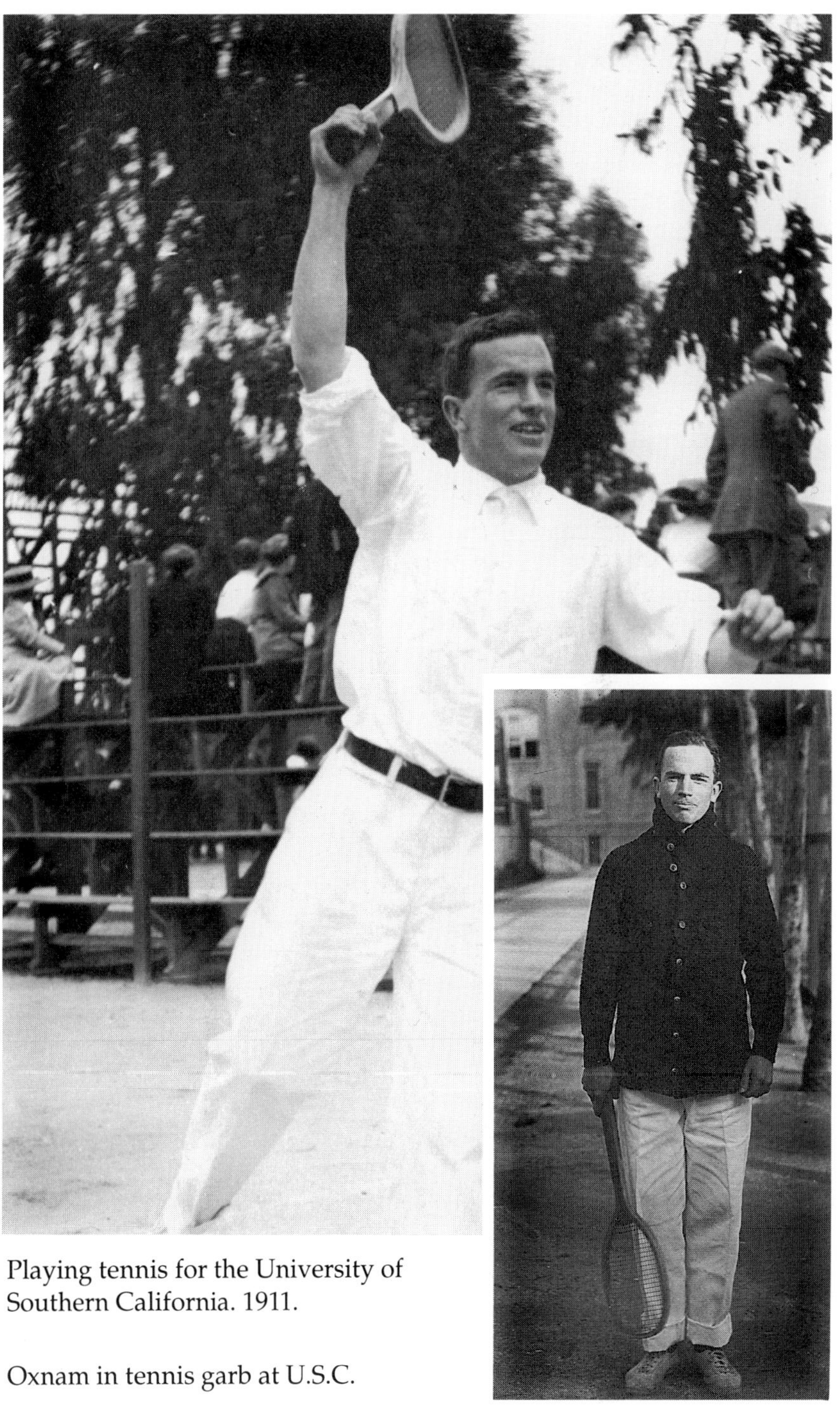

Playing tennis for the University of Southern California. 1911.

Oxnam in tennis garb at U.S.C.

Bromley Oxnam and Ruth Fisher on their wedding day. August 1914.

Bromley and Ruth Oxnam on their honeymoon. 1914.

Oxnam lecturing at Boston University School of Theology. 1927.

The Oxnam family in Greencastle, Indiana, DePauw University days. *Seated*: Bette, Bob. *Standing*: Phil, Bromley, Ruth. 1933. *photo: Cammack's Studio*

Bromley and Ruth Oxnam. 1937.

Bishop G. Bromley Oxnam. 1938.
photo: Townsend

Ruth Fisher Oxnam.
Los Angeles. 1941.

Bishop Oxnam kneels at the grave of an American soldier. Anzio, Italy, cemetery. 1945.

President Harry S Truman, Governor Frank J. Lausche of Ohio, and Oxnam in Columbus, where Truman addressed the meeting of the Federal Council of Churches. 1946. *Acme Photo.*

Bishop Oxnam with Archbishop Athenogoras of the Greek Orthodox Church as Oxnam received the Cross of the Royal Order of the Phoenix. 1948.

Oxnam as vice-president and president-designate of the Council of Bishops, The Methodist Church.

Ruth and Bromley Oxnam at Pine Island. 1961.

interests and to the intervention in the internal affairs of countries worldwide.

An observation made earlier bears repeating. Oxnam's nature was to be a leader. He desired and became the imposing leader of the Crusade for a New World Order (at the very moment he was president of the Federal Council and a leader in the Commission on a Just and Durable Peace). He desired for The Methodist Church leadership in the movement to shape public opinion and influence public policy away from isolationism, and no other denominational campaign to that end remotely matched that of Methodism. He desired for his country leadership in building the "United States of the World" modeled on the thirteen colonies forming the United States of America.

In the end the result of this herculean effort was the elfish U.N. and the giant of United States globalism, including a determination by the U.S. to bend the U.N. to its will.[1]

It will be recalled that as early as 1942 plans were initiated by The Methodist Church for a mighty program for postwar relief and reconstruction. The road was bumpy. Some bishops were unenthusiastic. When the district superintendents met in St. Louis, there was such fundamental difference of opinion, many thought the idea would die. As the various denominational interests and agencies entered the act, the sums sought by these groups totaled an impossible $114,000,000. It was necessary to review the proposed items and pare the total money to be raised for the program to a realistic but still staggering $25,000,000. Small wonder that Oxnam would recall in 1948, "Men who said today that we do not have the unity we had in the Crusade for Christ know nothing of the diversity that lay in the early meetings."

At the 1944 General Conference, advocates advanced an emphasis on relief and reconstruction; others championed the priority of evangelism; still others sought a stress on stewardship; and a final group favored the cause of increasing church school enrollment. There was also the question of continuing the Crusade for a New World Order. One day in a room in the President Hotel where a small group debated the matter, Ralph E. Diffendorfer, executive secretary of the Division of Foreign Missions of the Board of Missions, wondered why these competing interests could not be brought together into five interlocking sections. Suddenly there flashed in Oxnam's mind: Why not have one great quadrennial objective under the name Crusade for Christ instead of five different movements—"all of us, together, through the whole quadrennium, moving under the banner of our Lord." For three years Oxnam had been laboring with the planning Committee of 21 and then the Committee of 7 and was convinced that action taken by the General Conference would "affect the future of the church for a century."

Oxnam's Crusade for Christ idea struck fire. He was asked to prepare the proposal and present the enabling resolution to the General Conference. "Never before has so much sorrow, desolation, and utter destruction come to so many people," Oxnam informed the delegates. "The world awaits the healing touch of Christ upon its misery and desolation."

A committee of two hundred was set up to manage the Crusade, from which an executive committee was formed, Oxnam serving on both. Ultimately Bishop J. Ralph Magee served as the devoted director of the Crusade. Oxnam's New York Area churches raised for the Crusade the significant sum of $1,145,000 and brought into their doors 34,000 new members.

In addition to continuing the World Order movement, the Crusade had four facets, one for each of the years of the quadrennium: World Relief and Reconstruction; Evangelism; Stewardship; and Church School Enrollment and Attendance. In the opening fourteen months alone, Methodists gave $27,000,000 to the Crusade's support. At its conclusion, Oxnam judged, "This has been one of the truly great achievements in the history of Protestant Christianity. The Crusade for Christ proved conclusively that when the total organization of the Church is concentrated upon a high and worthy objective, Methodism is well-nigh irresistible." The Crusade dollar, Oxnam continued, "became bread for the hungry, clothing for the destitute, shelter for the dispossessed; it became scholarships that brought brilliant youth to our universities who will return to native lands as Christian leaders; it became 'the glory of the lighted mind' in our educational institutions; the healing of broken bodies and of distressed minds in our hospital; and expression of love in hate-ruled areas, but, above all, the dollar became the Gospel, as minister and missionary, devoted layman and laywoman, went to the far corners of the earth to serve in the name of Christ." During the Year of Evangelism, 578,317 new members were received on profession of faith, and 485,417 were received by transfer. "This is the largest number of people to be received by any church in any similar period in the history of the United States," Oxnam calculated. Church school enrollment gained 566,275. Twelve thousand men and women made a commitment to full-time Christian service and 925 new churches were built. Methodist historians understandably pay high tribute to this postwar Crusade for Christ in which Oxnam played such a central role.

As all bishops, Oxnam had a number of duties and served on a raft of commissions in addition to his normal Area responsibilities. Only two of special significance may be mentioned. Upon the formation in 1940 of the Commission on Public Relations and Methodist Information, he was made its first chairman and held the post for eight years. He much admired the commission's gifted general secretary, Ralph W. Stoody, and praised him to the heavens. Under their combined energetic leadership the commission became a real force in the life of the Church.

Education was a second area of exceptional activity. The unification of Methodism in 1939 saw the creation of a General Board of Education with three divisions: Educational Institutions, Local Church, and Editorial. Oxnam was named president of the Division of Educational Institutions and concurrently was a vice-president of the general board. Dr. Harry W. McPherson served as the division's executive secretary. (Oxnam found McPherson to be "utterly inadequate in this job" and in 1948 maneuvered for his replacement by the able Dr. John O. Gross. "There has been a complete transformation of the whole Division since he came," Oxnam rejoiced.)

At that time there were 131 educational institutions related to The Methodist Church: 9 universities, 69 colleges, 9 schools of theology, 25 junior colleges, 14 secondary schools, and 5 other institutions of miscellaneous classification. Collectively they enrolled 117,000 students taught by a faculty of 6,000. The annual budget was $42,000,000. Methodism had invested more than $400,000,000 in campus, buildings, and equipment to make these schools possible. This was fitting for the first Methodist institution was not a church, nor a chapel for preaching, but a school.

Except for doubts about the wisdom of the Church's remaining in the business of secondary education, Oxnam was a champion of Methodism's educational institutions, and for the five years of his division presidency he labored successfully on their behalf. He sought and won a more definitely structured relationship between the Church and its schools and he sought and won greater financial support from the Church for its schools and students.

The secularization of American higher education had been a clear and present danger to all church-related schools since the opening of the century. Increasingly as the century deepened, a profane worldview edged out a sacred worldview; professionalism and scientism rendered piety anachronistic; cosmopolitanism challenged solidarity; and, schools Christian in their origins suffered an identity crisis. Seeking institutional survival in an increasingly godless academic world, these schools ran the risk of losing their own souls. Indeed, by mid-century the religious souls of a host of church-related schools were in fact irredeemably lost, including Oxnam's beloved University of Southern California. Oxnam's convictions about the matter were strong and honorable. They also led him down a perilous path. In 1941 he was requested by the Board of Education to chair a commission to study objectives and goals for the Division of Educational Institutions. The completed report, coming from his pen and unanimously adopted by the board in 1942, contained much that was wise, but also a central recommendation with fateful implications. The key passage reads:

> If the Church is to be called upon for greater support of its institutions, the Church must be convinced that these institutions stand deliberately for something in the field of religion and the practices that religion demands. There is a Christian world view, a Christian way of life, a Christian commitment to the Christian Leader. The educational institutions related to the Church in addition to their educational service, must be evangelistic, in the proper sense of that term. Without apology, the Methodist institution must seek to win its students to the Christ. Our schools must be Christian without apology and Methodist with pride.

> Our faculties must be Christian in fact. Our efforts must be to make the students Christian just as truly as we try to teach them to think. We must seek to graduate Christians as certainly as we must graduate doctors, lawyers, musicians. There must be an end to the negative liberalism that glories in non-sectarianism that too often is non-everything in religion and that, in the long run, destroys the reason that justifies the Church's maintaining educational institutions.[2]

Oxnam then broadened his recommendation in an address before the 1944 General Conference entitled "Christian Without Apology, Methodist With Pride." The key passage reads:

> When a teacher is selected, he may be a Christian. It is possible for a man to lose his Christian experience; and some men have remained upon some of our campuses who have developed the attitude of the cynic and have ceased to be Christian leaders. The whole question of academic freedom and tenure arises, when a Board of Trustees or an executive takes the action necessary to remove from its faculty one who has ceased to be in harmony with the essential spirit of the school. I am of the opinion that we ought to write into our original Contracts with professors a clear understanding of the fact that the institution is Christian, and when a professor ceases to be Christian, he is done no harm if he is removed from the faculty and requested to seek work elsewhere. . . . The great and devoted teachers in our institutions across the nation deserve our highest commendation and our fullest support, and one way to support them is to see that their colleagues who cease to be Christian in philosophy and spirit find opportunity to work elsewhere and the Christian campus maintain a faculty that is Christian.

Oxnam's concern that Methodist schools not lose their Christian character is laudable. Indeed, in 1957 the General Conference Commission on Higher Education echoed his position when it proclaimed, "Every institution of learning identified with the Church should rededicate itself openly to its historic mission as a Christian school." At that time the Commission Chairman Bishop Paul Garber issued the reminder that the Methodist schools owed their existence to the conviction that religion and education are inseparable and that Methodist educational institutions were to be centers of vital religion. Certainly a Methodist institution of higher learning has every right to cherish its origins and identity. Certainly it is imperative that a *critical mass* of the student body and faculty remain committed Christians. Certainly today Baptists, Lutherans, Presbyterians, Episcopalians, Friends can be proud of such firmly denominational schools as Baylor, Augustana, Davidson, University of the South, Earlham. Certainly no Christian should be ashamed of the flourishing existence of such respected colleges as Wheaton, Geneva, Calvin, to cite only a few loyal to evangelical Christianity.

Having ungrudgingly acknowledged all of this, one is forced to ponder the logical consequences of the strict implementation of Oxnam's recommendations. For one thing, non-Christian students would be subject to proselytization or nonadmission in the first instance. How impoverished intellectually, culturally, and socially Methodist schools would be bereft of Jewish students, students of diverse faiths from foreign lands, students, for that matter, who proclaimed with Nietzeche the death of God. If admitted, how intolerable life would be for those Jews, Muslims, Hindus, agnostics, as their Christian professors sought to win them "to the Christ."

For a second thing, attempt to imagine Methodism's great universities with their law schools and medical schools and science and history and English departments gutted of all those faculty unable to profess or sustain the Christian faith. Under Oxnam's iron law, thousands of the nation's (and the world's) most brilliant scholars and distinguished teachers would be barred from Methodist institutions. Moreover, would even the most devout Christian university professor, if he or she were a self-respecting scholar as well, wish to be associated with a faculty from which respected fellow scholars were excluded because of wrong or no religious belief?

Then there is the question of the contract clause outlined by Oxnam. If implemented, his proposal would require a campus inquisition to ascertain if and when a faculty member lost "his Christian experience." Lawsuits and censure by the AAUP would follow as the night the day. Phi Beta Kappa chapters would be withheld or withdrawn. Faculty morale would plummet. Hypocrisy would rage as professors masked a possible loss of faith in order to escape firing.

Finally, Oxnam would have Methodism's universities denied government support. The 1971 case of *Tilton v. Richardson* was the first time the Supreme Court ruled on a suit challenging the constitutionality of federal aid to private higher education. The Court decided that federal aid programs could benefit only such church-related schools as were not "pervasively religious" in nature. Under *Tilton*, church colleges qualifying for aid included those that did not discriminate on religious grounds in faculty hiring and student admissions, did not maintain compulsory religious activities, did not "proselytize" religious doctrine in their courses, and met the generally acceptable standards for academic freedom.[3]

While one honors Oxnam's authentic concern for the integrity of Methodism's institutions of higher learning, one can also imagine the possible consequences if his Draconian measures had been put into effect: Syracuse University becoming an Oral Roberts University, Southern Methodist University becoming a Bob Jones University, Boston University becoming a Jerry Falwell Liberty University, Emory University becoming a Moody Bible Institute.

Ironically, in light of Oxnam's condemnation of Roman Catholic authoritarianism, his design for Methodist schools curiously foreshadows the plans of Pope John Paul II in the 1980s for Catholic institutions of higher learning in America. Not incidentally, Oxnam as a trustee of a number of Methodist schools habitually would grill a school president on the piety of the faculty.

Insofar as the record discloses, no one of Oxnam's associates raised questions about his recommendations. The fellow commission members gave their names to the 1942 report which was unanimously adopted by the Board of Education. Oxnam's 1944 General Conference address was hailed. The bishops reviewed his 1948 Episcopal Address without dissent. Did Methodism's leadership really and unanimously believe that Methodist institutions of higher learning should be open only to Christian students and Christian faculty; that these institutions must seek "to make the students Christians just as truly as we try to teach them to think"; that professors who found their faith failing must be fired? How can this be?[4]

A final point, minor but revealing of Oxnam's good sense. The Division of Educational Institutions was responsible for the publication of *motive*, a new magazine for Methodist youth edited by young Harold Ehrensperger. A 1942 issue was devoted to a frank (for that era) and witty discussion of the subject of sex. Bishop Leonard, president of the general board, and other conservatives, mostly in the South, were outraged. Ehrensperger must go!; *motive* must be muzzled! Oxnam took command of the situation. He appointed a committee to investigate and named himself committee chairman. Hearings were held. The committee then issued a report which, while regretting some mistakes in editorial judgment, recommended the continuation of the magazine and of its editor. Oxnam, supported by Bishop McConnell, defended the report and it was adopted. An explosive situation was defused thanks to Oxnam. In puzzlement he noted in his diary that in the South where religion prospered and sexual prudery reigned, "prostitution flourishes as no where else in the nation." [5]

---

[1] The political, psychological, and financial power of the United States over the United Nations was acknowledged in 1972 by Senator Fulbright, chairman of the Senate Foreign Relations Committee, when he said, "Having controlled the United Nations for many years as tightly and as easily as a big-city boss controls his party machine, we had got used to the idea that the United Nations was a place where we could work our will."

[2] Oxnam incorporated these recommendations in his 1948 Episcopal Address.

[3] The Supreme Court generally followed *Tilton* in the cases of *Hunt v. McNair* (1975) and *Roemer v. Board of Public Works* (1976).

[4] This curmudgeonish critique of Oxnam's position, I must confess, carries less validity (if indeed it carries any at all) regarding Methodist *colleges* than it does with respect to Methodist *universities*. What a tough nut this is to crack! Oxnam had every reason to be concerned. Because I do not agree with his recommendations, it does not follow that I am confident that I have the answers. Oxnam would scorn rightfully such a limp confession. To his credit he at least faced the issue I am ducking.

[5] Oxnam was honored by being asked to serve on the significant President's Commission on Higher Education, surely indicative of some stature in the field. The commission submitted its six-volume report to Truman, after two years of deliberation, in 1948. This subject is more appropriate for examination in chapter 21.

CHAPTER 16

BISHOP OF THE CHURCH: THE NEW YORK AREA, 1944-1952

Oxnam's assignment in 1944 to the New York Area, where he remained for two quadrenniums, brought responsibilities even heavier than those he had known in the Boston Area. On arriving in Gotham he informed the press, "There is an intellectual atmosphere here that is easy to breathe. My predecessor, Bishop Francis J. McConnell, is a great churchman and a great liberal. It's good to work after a fellow like that." Privately he rejoiced in McConnell's legacy of openness to the winds of change. Nevertheless, Oxnam found that his predecessor had done little in the field of church extension and had ignored major administrative problems crying for resolution. (Oxnam also noted with rueful admiration McConnell's reputed solution to the stack of mail daily piling up on his desk: he simply swept the unanswered letters into the wastebasket and called them "filed.")

In the early summer Bromley and Ruth settled into a handsome apartment at 1165 Fifth Avenue overlooking Central Park, and he occupied the spacious episcopal office at 150 Fifth Avenue. As at Omaha and Boston, he embarked upon a visitation program of the Area churches; eight years later he estimated that he had succeeded in actually visiting "only" 70 percent of them.

The New York Area embraced New York City, Long Island, eastern New York State, western Massachusetts, western Connecticut, Vermont, northern New Jersey, and a piece of Pennsylvania. The 350,000 Methodists in this crucial region worshiped in 1438 churches valued at over $100,000,000. Fourteen district superintendents provided essential assistance in the assignment of about 1,200 ministers. This task was Oxnam's (and every bishop's) most important and emotionally draining responsibility, for it meant transferring annually about one-quarter of the clergy. (Oxnam wisely made no attempt to move Ralph W. Sockman from the pulpit of Christ Church, Methodism's leading church in Manhattan. The largest Methodist congregation in New York worshiped at St. Mark's in Harlem.)

It scarcely need be added that in addition to the churches, Methodism in the New York Area was responsible for an imposing array of schools, hospitals, missions, camps, homes for the aged, children, and young women, denominational offices, training centers, and rental property—the last including the Paul Laurence Dunbar Apartments built for blacks by John D. Rockefeller, Jr., at a cost of $3,000,000 and sold to The Methodist Church for $1,000,000. In this connection, Oxnam praised the invaluable services of Frederick B. Newell, executive director of the New York City Society of Methodist Churches, who in 1952 was to follow Oxnam as bishop of the Area. Oxnam believed that the New York Area provided church extension opportunities unequaled in the nation, with the possible exception of California, and he threw himself into this work, including raising $500,000 for Drew University.[1]

A volume would be required to detail Oxnam's services to the Area. By every measurable indicia Methodism advanced during the eight years, 1944–1952. Memberships mounted; stewardship increased; clergy morale quickened; new churches opened; indebtedness reduced.[2] It is true that a postwar surge of piety bathed the entire nation, and New York Methodism was not the only denomination or section to prosper. Nevertheless, tribute must be paid to Oxnam's dedication. A month after arriving in Manhattan, he lamented to his diary: "There is no point to setting down the details. Up each morning early, and seldom to bed before one or two in the morning; sessions, committees, individual conferences!" Shortly he was to confess: "I find I am so weary that I can sit across the table from someone who presents some matter with care, or without it, and the presentation makes utterly no impression upon me at all. I do hope that I do not appear outwardly as dumb to others as I am certain I am to myself." February 1946 he reported being the heaviest scheduled month he could recall. After the 1948 General Conference he sighed, "I find myself extremely weary. It has been, I think, the hardest year I can remember with no opportunity for entertainment—just a steady and consistent use of every hour to meet the assignments."

Commingled with these cries of exhaustion were even more frequent expressions of appreciation of conscientious district superintendents, able preachers, skilled agency administrators, and loyal Annual Conferences. He rejoiced that the Fifth Avenue apartment was sufficiently spacious to permit inviting to lunch his Cabinet and other groups and having in students to whom sodas and cookies were served. In the late afternoon after district meetings, the Oxnams began the practice of meeting with the pastors and their wives in "intimate and informal talk." "As I look back," he judged in 1947, "I think I have done nothing since coming to the Area that has been more valuable. It has deepened our fellowship and understanding, and I hope has been helpful to the ministers.[3]

If it would require a book to detail the history of the New York Area under Oxnam's leadership, it would necessitate at least a booklet to quote in full the paeans to him found in the minutes of the Annual Conferences of New York, New York East, Newark, and Troy. Certain it is that all four conferences expressed the wish that the 1948 Northeastern Jurisdictional Conference reassign him to the New York Area and rejoiced when that hope was honored. When in 1948 the Area hosted a tribute banquet, attended by a thousand, Oxnam hurrahed, "The whole affair was so evidently sincere and spontaneous that we were quite on the mountain-top." He was equally elated by a second honorary occasion tendered in 1952.

Maybe some of the conference tributes have an inauthentic ring, such as the trilling resolution, "May God bless you and help us to reflect all over the Troy Conference the sweet, brotherly, humble Christian spirit, which you have manifested among us." Still, the feeling is inescapable that New York Methodists were proud of their leader and stood in awe of him. Declared the New York East Conference in 1952: "Not only the Methodist Church but also the National Council of Churches and the World Council feel the constant impact of Bishop Oxnam's insight, vision and courage, and recognize him as the outstanding leader of the Protestant forces the world around. His tireless energy and his many and varied accomplishments arouse our respect and admiration. We rejoice and are glad that the greatest area in Methodism (we say it humbly) has for its Episcopal Leader (we say it proudly) the greatest bishop in Methodism." Dr. Harry N. Holmes, respected layman whom Oxnam admired, also spoke the heart of New York East: "To us in his intimate home circle he is not only our Bishop but one of the most notable living Americans and one of the greatest Christian leaders of our generation."

Oxnam's New York years coincided exactly with the period of his presidency of the Division of Foreign Missions of the Board of Missions and Church Extension, headquartered in the same building as the episcopal office.

He brought to this leadership all of his renowned qualities. Luckily for him, the executive secretary of the Division of Foreign Missions was Dr. Ralph E. Diffendorfer. Experienced, able, respected, "Dr. Diff" rivaled Oxnam as a human dynamo. True, Oxnam was not the only individual to find Diffendorfer's torrential monologues, dogmatism, and bludgeoning tactics "exceedingly trying." Nevertheless, at Diffendorfer's retirement ceremony Oxnam praised him as the "greatest missionary leader of our day," and he repeated that judgment when the great missionary statesman died. Oxnam meant these public tributes as both his letters and diary entries attest. After one division meeting, Oxnam glowed, "Diffendorfer is head and shoulders above any one here, in possession of facts, mastery of principle, acquaintance with major trends and real executive ability."

In 1948 Eugene L. Smith assumed the post of executive secretary. If Oxnam admired Diffendorfer, he both respected and loved Gene Smith, discerning in him not only impressive administrative talent but also a profound, quiet spiritual power and scholarly prowess. When Smith confessed to Oxnam his persistent fear of failure (he was repeatedly beaten as a boy), Oxnam shored up his confidence. Smith served Methodism in many capacities with true distinction.

One of Oxnam's efforts was to attempt to unfreeze millions of dollars the Board of Missions had squirreled away in investments, bluntly asking, "Are we in the banking business or are we in the church extension business?" Instead of doling out sums, he informed the board's executive committee, we should be pouring out aid, doing for our new age of expansion what our forefathers did for theirs. However, Bishop A. Frank Smith, president of the Division of Home Missions, was determined to defend the autonomy of his division, and he successfully headed off the raid. Recalled an insider, "Now Bishop Oxnam was accustomed to winning every battle he fought, but he sure got snowed under in that one." To Oxnam's credit, such was his admiration for Smith, in defeat he wrote the Texas bishop a letter of apology and explanation.

Regarding foreign missions alone, by the end of Oxnam's tenure in 1952 Methodism was expending $21,000,000, a stunning increase over 1944. The missionary outreach of The Methodist Church was worldwide and Oxnam believed the meetings he chaired, where decisions were reached involving millions of dollars and millions of lives, to be analogous to those of the United States Department of State. The analogy is hyperbolic, but Bishop Nolan Harmon was not inaccurate when he referred to the Church's "farflung missionary empire upon which the sun never sets."

Of course, in a central respect the sun was setting on the older Western missionary "empire" in the postwar era. In Asia and Africa, formerly subjected peoples were throwing off the bonds of colonialism in a burst of rising nationalism. In some lands these movements were tied to a resurgence of non-Christian faiths, notably the renewed dynamism of Islam and Buddhism and Hinduism. In other lands where communism rode the tiger of nationalism, as in the People's Republic of China after 1949, Christianity was crushed. Every land penetrated by Western Christian missions witnessed powerful movements to raise up an indigenous leadership and to create churches independent of Western hegemony. Increasingly the responsibility for Methodist work in non-Western lands was assumed by the peoples of those areas; increasingly the Methodist churches became autonomous though affiliated with the American church; increasingly indigenization challenged the traditional crusading "foreign missions movement" with its assumption of Western cultural superiority.

At no time did Oxnam speak with more intense passion than in that section of his 1948 Episcopal Address entitled, "Our World-Wide Church and Mission," opening with the burning words:

> Methodism has never been parochial, save in the sense that the world is our parish. Our mission is a world mission. In His blessed name, and in response to His irresistible call, the people called Methodists have crossed the seas, and in His spirit have sought to teach the nations and to baptize them in the name of the Father, and of the Son, and of the Holy Spirit. We speak of them as missionaries, preachers, teachers, physicians, and social workers, and they are; but before the formal commissioning they had heard the Great Commission. . . .

The words became edged with martial terminology:

> It is that Jesus may become the ruler of the kings of the earth that we send our talented and our dedicated to the remote corners of the earth. To the common people of the world, they have brought the unsearchable riches of the Christ. These outposts of the Gospel now take on major significance in a world of warring ideologies. The lines of communication must be kept open. Reinforcements must reach them in increasing numbers. These our brethren who maintain the far-flung lines of the Kingdom must know that the Church has resolved at last to pledge its all in the grand attack that means victory. Nations, winning their independence, and taking their place at last in the United Nations, are about to make fundamental choices concerning their ways of life. Are these ways to be the ways of materialism, or the way of Christ?

He then acknowledged the relative handful of Christians in Japan, China, India, Pakistan, Africa, and the peoples of Latin America who were only nominally Roman Catholic. "In many lands, we are not yet an occupying force. We hold a few bridgeheads. We must become not only an occupying force, a liberating force, but a Christianizing force." The address continued with the wise words:

> The natural and normal national self-consciousness of many peoples of the so-called mission fields means new emphasis on the development of

> national leadership, national responsibility, and support on the part of the younger churches in every land. To this end, missionary policy should be increasingly directed. . . . Missionary policy should be directed toward the strengthening of the younger churches, toward the education and training of Christian leaders with a definite program of increasing self-government, along with more responsibility for the financial support of the churches and institutions. These policies are not now a question of simply being desirable. They are imperative. Nationals must come definitely into real leadership.

The appeal closed with a plea to "win the world for Christ."

In these sentences there are words of wisdom and sincerity. Taken as a whole, however, there is an excess of martial prose and a tone of triumphalism quite reminiscent of the evangelicals who at that moment were moving in force into the missionary enterprise.[4]

In May 1947 Oxnam's episcopal colleagues elected him to prepare and deliver the Episcopal Address at the 1948 General Conference meeting in Boston. This address is intended to convey the positions of the episcopal leadership, indicate the Church's thought on matters of moment, and suggest the direction of the Church's march. It is a kind of party platform. Although prepared by one individual, the other bishops serve as an editorial board, suggesting changes, offering dissenting opinions, altering emphases. The final version, perhaps markedly revised, carries the initials of every bishop and to that extent it can be said to represent the mind of the Council of Bishops. Oxnam presented his handiwork to the council on April 15 and that evening sang to his diary: "The Council was never more generous, never more brotherly, never more helpful. To my utter amazement, the Episcopal Address was adopted almost as written."

Despite Oxnam's legendary rapid-fire delivery, the address to the General Conference consumed two hours. Afterward, friends such as Crane gushed to him that it was "the most important Episcopal Address in the history of the Church." (Because of the address's sweep, the many subjects covered are taken up elsewhere in the appropriate chapters.)

Later at the conference Oxnam was granted permission to urge that the Church join the National Council of Churches then in the process of forming, and the conference so voted. The conference also brought into being the Methodist Commission on Church Union, strongly favored by Oxnam. He then served on it under the chairmanship of Bishop Holt. Oxnam's reputation as a champion of church union is suggested by the fact that he was tapped to represent The Methodist Church at the first General Conference of the recently formed Evangelical United Brethren Church, and in his fraternal message he stressed the naturalness and possibility of the two denominations coming together. He said that he had a letter in his pocket inviting the Evangelical United Brethren Church to explore the possibility of organic union with The Methodist Church, but considered the presentation of the invitation inappropriate at that time. Sadly, he did not live to rejoice in the consummation in 1968.

The General Conference's most significant action was to give sanction to a second, new quadrennial emphasis known as "The Advance for Christ and His Church: From Crusade to Conquest." It is really quite extraordinary that the idea struck fire in Oxnam's imagination as had the Crusade for Christ just then coming to its amazing conclusion, an idea he had sold to the Council of Bishops, the General Commission on World Service and Finance, the Council of Secretaries, and the Woman's Division of Christian Service. The name, as one might guess, was his and was first presented to the New York Area conferences. The Advance, Oxnam predicted, "will do more for the mind of the Church than anything we have undertaken in many decades." Faith would be deepened; understanding of the Church broadened; recruiting for the ministry and missions quickened; and a world hungry for spiritual and material assistance succored.

Oxnam spent countless committee hours attempting to hammer the Advance into shape. The initial resistance was sometimes sharp. Fortunately, the bishops, especially Harrell, Kern, and Martin, provided crucial support and leadership. After the final meeting in January 1952 of the Advance committee, Oxnam exalted: "This whole movement has been such an extraordinary success that it's almost beyond belief that only a few short years ago, it was but an idea. . . . It is seldom we have come to the close of a great movement in such complete harmony. It was a love feast indeed."

In addition to conceptualizing the general thrust of The Advance for Christ and working with Bishop Martin's committee in guiding the movement, Oxnam headed the "Our Faith" phase. This involved the preparation, editing, and distribution of eight booklets examining and explaining Methodist belief: "Our Faith in God," "Our Faith in Christ," "Our Faith in Love," "Our Faith in the Bible," "Our Faith in Prayer," "Our Faith in Immortality," "Our Faith in the Holy Spirit," and "Our Faith in the Kingdom of God" (coauthored by Oxnam and Martin).

Oxnam was concerned that multitudes of lay people were ignorant of Methodism's fundamental beliefs. The Advance's mission was to remedy that lamentable condition. Methodists thoroughly grounded in their faith, Oxnam hoped, would be inspired to heightened evangelistic and missionary action. He rejected the objection that the booklets would either be so bland as to be meaningless or so dogmatic as to alienate either conservatives or liberals or both.

Oxnam approached seven Methodist scholars to prepare the booklets. The authors were given forty-five days to write their ten-thousand-word essays for a "modest honorarium" of $250. Their names were not to appear in the booklets, explained Oxnam as editor, in order that the manuscripts might be revised by him to achieve a common prose style. Each author was instructed: "The purpose is to deepen understanding of the faith and to evoke also a commitment to the faith. It would be unfortunate if our emphasis upon the faith should result in divisive argument concerning the content of the faith. We wish the faith stated affirmatively, so that what a layman ought to know . . . is there before him, and put in such a fashion that it is convincing and commanding." Over four million of the booklets were sold the first year and an additional million were ordered printed. They served as the basis for discussion groups throughout Methodism. As part of the Advance, Oxnam also arranged for every Methodist minister to receive the massive report of the First Assembly of the World Council of Churches and for every district superintendent to receive a special set of five volumes on the Church. Halford Luccock's *Endless Line of Splendor* sold by the hundreds of thousands; Oxnam's own address of the same title exceeded fifty thousand in distribution.

Is it possible to raise any valid reservations about these "Our Faith" booklets? Perhaps not and one hopes not. Nevertheless, one consideration comes to mind. Oxnam selected the authors. Their names are unknown, save only that the Edgar Sheffield Brightman Papers disclose that this BU School of Theology professor was the author of "Our Faith in God." Unknown, too, is the extent of the editing done by Oxnam. Considering Oxnam's authoritarian character, considering his loathing of fundamentalism and American neo-orthodoxy and Continental Crisis theology, is it not at least conceivable that Methodist lay people received what Oxnam judged to be the Methodist faith—that is, the Boston University School of Theology personalism "party line"? [5]

The 1952 General Conference, the second while Oxnam was bishop of the New York Area, assembled in San Francisco. He had been a member of the Committee of Twenty-eight charged with presenting to the conference a new quadrennial program for its approval. He had also served on a committee chaired by Bishop Harrell established to study and report upon the local church and to make recommendations with regard to its disciplinary structure. This duty consumed much time. The conference adopted almost all the report's recommendations, though only after much questioning from the floor.

Nothing caused Oxnam greater concern prior to and at the General Conference than the Church Survey Report. The 1948 General Conference had authorized and funded a study of the entire structure of the Church. A management consulting firm was employed to undertake the analysis. The report, exhaustive and exhausting, brought 104 specific recommendations to the conference for consideration. On reading an advance copy of the report in December 1951, alarm bells rang in Oxnam's mind, especially regarding the projected "undue concentration of power" in the Council (formerly Commission) on World Service and Finance. In March he informed the New York Area delegates to the conference that "we have to organize the opposition to this thing or we are going to face disaster." Oxnam then conferred with Parlin, who had assumed the leadership of the report's opponents. (Incidentally, on Oxnam's arrival in New York as bishop, Parlin had arranged a series of luncheons at his club in order that Oxnam might come to know the city's leading movers and shakers.) After two days of impassioned debate, the conference created a Committee of Six, cochaired by Parlin and Harold C. Case, another of Oxnam's friends, to consider the findings of the Church Survey Report. Oxnam rejoiced, knowing that Parlin and Case would emasculate the report, however in "such fashion that the Survey people can save their face." In the end, while some structural reforms were instituted, the grand design of the Survey was found unacceptable.

At the conclusion of the opening day of the General Conference, Oxnam rejoiced: "There is something thrilling in this great body of more than 700 delegates from all over the world. Every man and woman who sits upon this floor as a delegate, has been elected by the free franchise of his fellow members in the Annual Conference. Everyone who sits here is the equal of everyone else as far as all rights are concerned. It is democracy in action." When his turn came to preside, he did so with customary consummate skill. Faced with a knotty question, he untangled it thusly: "The Chair does not believe the point of order is well taken because the original motion of reference had to do solely with the amendment. The present motion of reference included the entire paragraph, plus the amendment now before us and the substitution, all to be referred. The point of order, therefore I think, is not well taken." Faced with a complaint from a delegate in a far corner who had not been recognized, he apologized, "I shall do my best to turn to the left, though I usually try to avoid that." That evening Oxnam made a diary observation: "Presiding over a General Conference is like a big league baseball game. When you are out there you have to field the ball fast and to the right place. It is no good to try to pull a rule book out of your pocket and find out what to do with a fast grounder when a man is on first base. I think I had a very happy time. If one knows parliamentary law, is courteous, and yet firm and is all the time ahead of the group, in a word has the debating body off balance, it is a very simple thing to move forward without tension to keep the spirit right and get the business done with dispatch."

For Oxnam the highlight of the conference was "California Night," held in a packed civic auditorium and featuring the singer John Charles Thomas and Oxnam's talk "Wesleyans in Wonderland." When the conference adjourned Oxnam found himself chairing the Crusade for World Order, authorized by the conference; a member of the committee charged with drafting the Quadrennial Plan for 1956–60; vice-chairman of the powerful Council on World Service and Finance, becoming chairman in 1956; and chairman of the Commission on Chaplains.

Oxnam's growing visibility in the Protestant Establishment brought him invitations to President Roosevelt's inauguration in January 1945 and President Truman's inauguration in January 1949. It also brought him in 1948 the Churchman Award from *The Churchman* and in 1949 the Churchman of the Year Award from *Zions Herald*. Further, during the New York years the following honorary degrees were bestowed: D.D. from Wesleyan University; S.T.D. from Yale University; and LL.D. from Allegheny and Dickinson.

On the eve of the 1952 Northeastern Jurisdictional Conference, Oxnam expressed the hope that he would be returned to the New York Area for an additional four years. The Area, he reasoned, was the center of great interdenominational and ecumenical movements as well as the center of national life. All four Annual Conferences had recorded their wish that he remain and he could continue to build on the foundation of eight years of friendship. The opportunities for church extension remained challenging. Moreover, he and Ruth had agreed that he would retire after one more quadrennium. Why not go out with a substantial twelve-year record of achievement rather than starting out anew elsewhere? Finally, as he wrote Henry Hitt Crane, "May I say to you and confidentially that I simply cannot be a party to what is going on at the moment. I want to be completely clear of attempts which seem to me vulgar and almost cheap to move into important positions in our church."

The accusation was a reference to Bishop Fred Pierce Corson of the Philadelphia Area. Oxnam's diaries are laced with passages accusing Corson of outrageous political maneuvering to win appointment to the Washington Area. The charges need not be explicated, save to make the central point that although Oxnam may have been sincere in denying that he coveted Washington, he felt just as strongly that Washington not be awarded to Corson.[6]

If indeed Corson courted Washington Area Methodists, Oxnam was being wooed by key Area leaders including Albert E. Day, minister of Mt. Vernon Place, Baltimore, and Frederick Brown Harris, pastor of historic Foundry Church, D.C. Concurrently, Parlin, chairman of the Jurisdictional Episcopacy Committee, and other New Yorkers leaned on Oxnam to remain with them. On Friday, June 13, Ralph Sockman, representing the Episcopacy Committee, informed Oxnam to start packing. Despite the date, this was not really bad news, for Oxnam had already been formulating grand plans for the Washington Area should marching orders take him there.

---

[1] Oxnam gave all-out support to Boston University earlier, and later as bishop of the Washington Area, pressed successfully the claims of American University, and this is understandable. On occasion, however, this loyalty to the Area he served at the moment influenced his good judgment. For example, while serving New York he unsuccessfully lobbied to have the headquarters of the World Methodist Council located there rather than the site selected at Lake Junaluska, North Carolina.

[2] Oxnam believed that the clearing up of the Broadway Tabernacle's debt in excess of $3,000,000 was an "achievement perhaps unequaled in the history of the church."

[3] Dr. Dorothy McConnell, daughter of the bishop and editor of *World Outlook*, lived in New York during Oxnam's entire tenure there. It must be recorded that she did not find Oxnam particularly approachable or hospitable; certainly she was never entertained by the Oxnams, a curious fact considering Bromley's indebtedness to her father and her own distinction in Methodist circles. It is also a curious fact that in 1948–49 the Oxnams moved from their Fifth Avenue apartment to a smaller place at 29 Washington Square where they stayed only briefly. Dr. McConnell suspects that the Oxnams were lonely, the reason being that his authoritarian streak prevented him from meeting his district superintendents and ministers on equal terms. This is Dr. McConnell's speculation, but it is worth noting that the 1952 Newark Annual Conference district superintendents' report contained the revealing question, "Can you imagine any one of us presuming or daring to call him Bromley?" Happily, it is possible to close this note affirmatively. In 1953 when Dr. McConnell was under fire for her alleged radicalism, she received from Oxnam a magnificently supportive letter.

[4] In 1952, some 18,000 North American missionaries were serving overseas, of whom approximately 8,000 were supported by evangelical organizations. By 1960, the total number of foreign missionaries had grown to more than 29,000, and the proportion sponsored by evangelical organizations had risen from 44 percent to 65 percent. Promised Jerry Falwell, "We have the people and the resources to evangelize the world in our generation." Of course these words were first cried by John R. Mott. In all of this, however, it is important not to forget William R. Hutchison's observation that mainline denominations were sending in large numbers their church people to serve in a manner hard to distinguish from the work of earlier mainline missionaries.

[5] As will be noted later, Oxnam's own *A Testament of Faith* appeared in 1958, and this winsome volume is straight BUST theology.

[6] In November 1984 I informed by mail Bishop Corson of my efforts to write a biography of Oxnam. His reply was most cordial and encouraging. He did not state his opinion of Oxnam save to say that Oxnam merited "a real first-class biography." We planned to meet on his return from Florida in the spring. Alas, he died while in Florida. Therefore, I do not have from Bishop Corson's pen or lips his memories of Oxnam.

CHAPTER 17

BISHOP OF THE CHURCH: THE WASHINGTON AREA, 1952-1960

After making certain the New York Area was in shipshape for incoming Bishop Newell and after briefly casing Washington, the Oxnams spent a restorative summer at Lake Winnepesaukee, although Bromley could be found at his desk much of every day. In September they arrived in Washington, Oxnam saying to the press, "Wherever a bishop is assigned, he goes like a good soldier." Ailing Bishop Flint had done little (Oxnam moaned) to make the Methodist Building habitable as either an office or a home. Located adjacent to the Supreme Court Building and with a view through the trees of the Capitol, the structure itself was imposing. The Oxnams proceeded to knock out some walls and make other alterations to provide spacious offices on the second floor and a handsome, art-filled apartment on the fourth floor.

The Washington Area was composed of the Baltimore, the Central Pennsylvania, and the Peninsula Conferences embracing the states of Delaware and Maryland and part of Pennsylvania and West Virginia and, of course, the District of Columbia. The Methodist Church membership of 371,421 was served by 988 regular ministers and 207 approved supply pastors. Church property, including an array of schools, hospitals, and other institutions, approached one billion dollars in value. (At that time the Washington, D.C. Annual Conference was composed of black churches and members.)

In September, October, and November, Bromley and Ruth, with district superintendents sometimes serving as navigators, visited every one of the 1691 churches in the Area, averaging between twenty and twenty-five per day. Oxnam continued to find the game worth the candle, and ministers and their families continued to express their appreciation at the honor of having for the first time, perhaps, a bishop in their church and parsonage. "No matter how carefully the statistical records of the Area are kept," Oxnam reported to the Northeastern Jurisdictional Conference, "it is impossible to visualize the coal town in which the mines have been worked out, an oyster town upon the Eastern Shore, or the new communities developing near Baltimore as a result of industrial expansion and amazing population advance, unless one sees these communities with his own eyes. Some of the most beautiful and religiously significant services of worship are being held in some of our smallest churches in rural and industrial communities."

As we have seen, while bishop of the New York Area Oxnam had had some association with President Truman (and earlier F.D.R.) regarding foreign affairs, and as we shall see in chapter 21, his visits to the Truman White House concerning church-state matters numbered four and his correspondence with the Missourian was brisk. Now he was stationed in the nation's capital within shouting distance of the halls of Congress and within long walking distance of the White House. His eight years of service in Washington were to coincide quite closely with the two terms of the Eisenhower presidency. As a servant of The Methodist Church, what were his dreams of Methodism in the service of the nation? How could Methodism serve the nation's public servants? For Oxnam these questions were particularly salient because (in his opinion) Flint had been politically invisible and Flint's predecessors, Leonard and Hughes, had been too conservative to have influenced the Roosevelt administration.

Within less than a year after serving in Washington Oxnam reported to the ministers of the Area:

> *And the big question of relations with leaders of government!* I am sure the Church expects the Bishop in Washington to know our leaders. We as a Church want nothing for ourselves, and believe in the separation of

> Church and State. But we do have great moral convictions that ought to be conveyed to our leadership, not by way of demand but as a cooperative service to the representatives of the people. We ought, as we did in the Crusade for a New World Order a few years ago, to be influential at the place decisions are made before they are made. We do not, and ought not, lobby. We do not engage in politics. But we do have an obligation as Christians to create public opinion in support of great moral measures upon which the Church has spoken. How can this be done? First, there must be a personal relationship established. This takes time. I had lunch with the Secretary of State last week. Mr. Dulles is a great Christian layman, who needs the understanding, the support, and the prayers of Christians as he faces critical and complex problems upon which hang the peace of the world. I have met others; but it, too, takes time.

In his 1956 report to the Northeastern Jurisdictional Conference Oxnam noted that within the bounds of the Washington Area there were three state capitals and the nation's capital, cited the number of Methodists in Congress, and sighed that "Methodism has yet to develop a strategy by which the Christian spirit becomes regnant in the halls of political decision." The report continued:

> Sooner or later, the Church must take decision concerning the service it expects the Bishop in Washington Area to render. There ought to be a suitable Episcopal Residence in Washington where distinguished Methodists coming from different parts of the nation and the world may be entertained by the representative of The Methodist Church who resides in Washington. This will take time and be expensive; but the true influence of the Church in the nation's capital must be an influence in terms of the character, intelligence, and friendship of its representative here. It is not a lobbying influence that will make the Church effective in the heart of the nation; it is a pastoral relationship with men and women charged with national responsibility that is essential. It must be of such a nature that a man of religion may speak a friendly word to a heavily burdened political leader when he is charged with decision or may communicate to him the thought of the Church upon some great moral issues confronting the nation. It is from a home, not an office, not a platform, not a chancel, that such influence at once proper, patriotic, and religious may radiate.

In assessing Oxnam's political presence in Washington one might as well begin by noting when and why he found himself in the presence of President Eisenhower. The Oxnams were pleased to accept an invitation to Eisenhower's inauguration. Perhaps the bishop's attendance was requested by virtue of his position or perhaps it resulted from the suggestion of Methodist layman Howard W. Selby to Sherman Adams. In any case,

Oxnam was thrilled to be at the occasion and seated next to the actress Irene Dunne. (When Miss Dunne expressed the pleasantry that she hoped one day the bishop might visit her in California, Oxnam replied that he *often* was in California. Her face blanched and she changed the subject.)

Over a year passed without a neighborly word from the White House, compelling Oxnam to remind Eisenhower of his existence: "It was my honor to sit but a few feet from you at the inauguration. I was deeply moved by the reverent prayer that you offered. I feel, therefore, you may pardon me if I communicate the opinion of our people throughout the nation, and add the personal word that if there is ever any way in which The Methodist Church or its members can be of service to you in the furtherance of the great moral ideals which you have enunciated in your speeches and revealed in your life, we trust you will feel free to command us." Finally, on April 2, 1953, thanks to Secretary of State Dulles's intercession, Oxnam, Dulles, and three World Council officers conferred in the White House with the president about the projected Assembly of the World Council of Churches in Evanston, Illinois. Lasting only a few minutes, the meeting was long enough for Eisenhower to say, "Gosh, you don't have to convince me about the churches." A few days later Oxnam telegrammed Eisenhower praising a recent presidential address as among "the noblest of historic American pronouncements on international relations." The following month Oxnam joined a delegation of churchmen in presenting the president with the new Revised Standard Version of the Bible. Shortly, Eisenhower spoke at a meeting of the National Council and Oxnam judged he made a "grand impression. It is all very wonderful." The next day, November 19, 1953, Oxnam and a World Council official again met with the president about the Evanston Assembly. Although Eisenhower was cordial, Oxnam pouted because no photographs were permitted and because it was intimated that the White House preferred that the archbishop of Canterbury, not Oxnam, introduce Eisenhower in Evanston. Increasingly Oxnam's letters and diary entries bemoan the administration's indifference to, even hostility toward, American Protestantism.

Still, Oxnam persisted in wooing the president. He continued to send the White House ingratiating missives. When scheduled to preach at Methodism's Foundry Church, he suggested to the pastor that Eisenhower be invited to be present. The invitation was declined. When a testimonial dinner was to be given in Oxnam's honor, Crane suggested to Eisenhower that the White House send a message. The suggestion was ignored. It does not seem to have occurred to Oxnam that the Republican White House had understandable political reasons for wishing to distance itself from a Methodist bishop known to be a Democrat, renowned as a liberal, reviled as a "Red," and judged by American Catholics to be their most implacable critic.

In August 1954 Oxnam *did* introduce Eisenhower at the Evanston Assembly of the World Council. In October the Oxnams were privileged to shake the hands of the Eisenhowers at a reception hosted by the president of Liberia. This scarcely mollified the bishop; for in that month he growled to his diary "that it is about time to throw the so-called business administration out with its bird dogs and kennel dogs, with its giveaway of natural resources, and its utter stupidity in public relations." Again and again the diary flays the administration for ignoring the existence of the Protestant churches and, indeed, for being blatantly hostile to them. "It is not enough to tell us that the Cabinet meetings are opened with prayer," Oxnam noted. Moreover, his sources informed him that liquor was served in the White House, although the Methodist temperance leader in Washington had been assured otherwise. Little wonder that Oxnam rejoiced in the Democratic congressional gains in November. "It is quite apparent there is to be no opportunity to be influential in government here during a Republican administration. . . . It is stupid politically, and then, of course, after the relationship with both President Truman and President Roosevelt, it is a little disappointing." Oxnam took what solace he could from the fact that Episcopal bishops Angus Dun and Sherrill reported they too were virtually invisible to the eyes of the White House.

Eisenhower accepted *from* Oxnam an invitation to be at a ground-breaking ceremony at American University on June 9, 1957. Then in March 1958 at an International Trade Policy banquet, Oxnam was seated between Eisenhower and Dulles. Oxnam's invocation carried the petition "Save us from mere repetition of religious platitude" followed, as it happens, by the platitudinous words that had tripped from his tongue a thousand times: "Grant us the wisdom to discover the concrete means whereby the ethical ideals of religion may be translated into the realities of world law and order, economic justice and racial brotherhood."

Oxnam's elation at being included in this rather minor occasion occupies twenty-two diary pages: photographs, newspaper clippings, and self-congratulatory musings. Any American citizen would rejoice, of course, at being seated on the president's right hand in the presence of fourteen hundred guests, but why should a Methodist bishop feel the subjective need to blow up the event out of all objective proportion? The final meeting came in April 1959 when, as we have learned, Eisenhower greeted the Council of Bishops.

From time to time Oxnam attended affairs where the vice-president was present. Although the bishop found something about Nixon's face unappealing and although he speculated as to Nixon's sincerity, the diary references are actually surprisingly positive: the vice-president appeared informed, articulate, and personally pleasant.

Oxnam's continuing relationship with Dulles will be examined later. Here it need only be noted that the churchman's hopes of influencing the policies of the new secretary of state were mostly fanciful. For example, Oxnam suggested that Dulles meet monthly with a select group of church leaders (including two Methodist bishops) to brief them on world affairs. Oxnam might as well have dropped a rose petal to the bottom of the Grand Canyon and awaited the echo.[1]

Oxnam's hunger to be recognized by Washington's power elite would be risible if it were not so poignant. In mid-June 1954 he shared in commencement exercises at American University with Attorney General Herbert Brownell, traveled to Princeton University where he and Adlai Stevenson received honorary degrees, and attended a dinner hosted by the ambassador of India at which Allen Dulles, director of the CIA and brother of Foster, was present. The diary fairly jumps with joy: "We left the dinner party about eleven o'clock, and came to the conclusion we had a wonderful week-end, Herbert Brownell, Adlai Stevenson, Allen Dulles, and people of this kind. The doors seem to be opening at last." Following another party at the Indian Embassy attended by such notables as Chief Justice Earl Warren, Oxnam sang, "It was a good evening and I was happy to be included in this group because when meeting some of these people socially in this fashion, doors are opened for later conferences if desired."

An observation made earlier still stands. Oxnam was not by nature either a party thrower or a party goer. Social affairs were not for him occasions of conviviality but opportunities to meet individuals of influence. Furthermore, he may be taken at his repeated word that he sought the friendship of these persons not for personal aggrandizement but in order to further the concerns of The Methodist Church and the idealistic causes of Christianity. Nevertheless, it is possible to wish that he had preened less on those fairly rare instances when he was thrown socially with Washington's powerful and rapped the high chair with his spoon less when he was not.

This is not to suggest that Oxnam's days were spent seated by the phone or standing at the mail box in hopes of hearing from "official" Washington. The thought is an absurdity. During these Washington years he continued to serve the National and World Council of Churches in the highest capacities and to lecture and write extensively. Nor did he neglect his responsibilities to The Methodist Church at large, not excluding his continuing secretaryship of the Council of Bishops. He chaired the Methodist Commission on Chaplains and as a continuing member of the General Commission on Army and Navy Chaplains he kept a weather eye on Methodism's interests. For example, he used his influence to secure a Methodist minister, Marion J. Creeger, as director of the latter commission. Oxnam investigated and protested the lock that Episcopalians had on the West Point chaplaincy and also the exclusive use by the Naval Academy of the Episcopal Book of Common Prayer. Needless to say he was not flim-flammed by attempted usurpations of Armed Forces chapels by the Roman Catholic Church. When it came to protecting the rights of Methodism, Oxnam, unlike Admiral Nelson, never placed the spy glass to his blind eye.

The 1952 General Conference created the Council on World Service and Finance. Oxnam served on it from the onset and then in 1956 was elected its president. This powerful body administers the huge sums which are entrusted to its keeping and prepares and presents the reports concerning the church-wide budget and assessments. It works out an equitable schedule of apportionment by which the total World Service budget is distributed and apportioned to the Annual Conferences. The General Conference, as final authority, takes these reports for its "action and determination." Oxnam did not consider the job a sinecure; nor was it. After chairing one meeting of the executive committee, he recorded: "It was a very heavy schedule and trying. There are a few men who can come and make an effective financial appeal. Usually they have to rush into oratory, deliver set speeches, and tire everybody out. I had to call the speakers and tell them that we are not interested in oratory, we were interested in budgets and would like to have come immediately to a consideration of their askings. One or two got it." No council member was eligible for membership on any other general agency in the Church. This provision knocked Oxnam out of the presidency of the Division of Foreign Missions, a beneficiary of World Service Funds. He considered the rule unwise, for it cut bishops off from the great missionary and educational endeavors of Methodism.

Oxnam further chaired the committee charged with directing the Crusade for World Order authorized by the 1952 General Conference. Compared to the 1944 and 1948 great crusades, it was of very limited success; the world was too messy to be tidied up.

The 1956 General Conference authorized a new quadrennial program with a twin emphasis upon higher education and the development of the local church. Oxnam was a member of the Committee of Twenty charged with presenting this quadrennial emphasis to the conference and he, together with Bishop Harrell, had drafted the wording. Oxnam was then involved with the implementation, 1956–60, although the key leaders were Bishop Garber and Bishop Short, respectively.

Oxnam was a bishop of the Church for twenty-four years. What was his understanding of the episcopal office in Methodism? Speaking for the Council of Bishops in his 1948 Episcopal Address, Oxnam uttered the grateful words, "It has been a joyful privilege to be your servants in the work of the Church." An Annual Conference praiseful resolution said of him, "Worthy to be called great because like the Lord he chooses to be servant of all." Oxnam would have agreed with the statement of Bishop James Mathews: "We are an office, not an order. We are not prelates on the one hand, nor diocesan officers on the other. We exist for the connection and are a kind of cement uniting the whole denomination." In Methodism the Council of Bishops is the chief executive arm to carry out the mandates of the General Conferences; Methodism is not so much governed *by* bishops as it is governed *with* bishops. Therefore, Oxnam was in accord with the historic Methodist position: bishops are elected and consecrated to an "office" to be "servants in the work of the Church"; they are not ordained to a separate order as in the Protestant Episcopal, Anglican, and Roman Catholic traditions.

The paradox is that even as bishops were to serve they were concurrently to lead, Oxnam's last utterance before the Council of Bishops being a passionate plea for his colleagues to *be* the Council of Bishops. After all, the council has the constitutional charge to direct the spiritual and temporal activities of the entire Church. And as he observed, many of the mighty movements since unification in 1939, such as the Crusade for Christ and The Advance for Christ, emerged from the collective thinking of the council. Especially did Oxnam urge younger bishops not to permit the episcopacy to be ensmalled, and, as we shall see momentarily, this was a major basis for his critique of the jurisdictional system that had been established with reunion.

To lead, a bishop must be a leader and the most requisite quality was decisiveness, a gift, Oxnam believed, that could not be learned; it was a matter of genes. "You have it or you do not." He, happily, had it. Of all the tributes by those ministers who served under his leadership, perhaps the following most closely captures the essence:

> The title "Bishop" was to me the equivalent of the name "G. Bromley Oxnam." In my young eyes, he was a strong and virile leader of the Church . . . and I never lost this impression. Bishop Oxnam was a strong leader. His presence radiated courage. And yet at the same time it radiated personal concern. Men who have had military service will understand what I say. For a soldier to have a commanding officer with both brains and guts, who demands discipline, and yet who knows and cares about his men—this is to experience a freedom and a courage beyond one's own. For a sailor to know that the Old Man is a great sea captain, that he is unafraid either of the enemy or of the desk-jockeys in the Navy Department, and that he believes in and will go to bat for his men—this is to have a Ship. And this is precisely how one felt about Bishop Oxnam. A leader draws strength from the loyalty of those who follow him. But those who follow draw strength and courage from him who is at the helm. And one knew that there was this strength, this support, from his bishop, if that Bishop was G. Bromley Oxnam.

On more than one occasion Oxnam expressed this thought to his diary: "I am more and more convinced that the greatest contribution that an individual makes to an organization of the magnitude of The Methodist Church is to see that men of competence are put in the responsible posts." The written record and oral testimony are in absolute agreement that Oxnam gave careful consideration to the appointments he made or the appointments he supported. If the individual tapped performed conscientiously and well, Oxnam backed him or her to the hilt. Many souls have testified that when under attack, from within or without the Church, and most especially if the attack came from conservative quarters, Oxnam was an ever-present help in their time of troubles. One minister under fire and saved by Oxnam added: "He demonstrated the genius of the . . . Methodist system of appointments, for it is the greatest invention for the support of freedom in the pulpit the Christian movement has ever seen." Moreover, he was generous in his praise and made no attempt to steal credit from another and assign it to himself. In a word, if you were selected by Oxnam for a job and measured up to his stern standards, you could count on being supported and applauded.

Oxnam merits additional praise for his understanding of the parable of the talents. He comprehended that not every individual, however industrious, was big enough to fill every job. Great expectations must be restrained by realistic assessments of talent: "We do not demand that every college boy run a hundred yards in ten seconds. He knows he can't, and does not blame the track, poor shoes, the weather. But we do ask preachers to do more than they are cut out to do. We have too many twelve second men in ten second races."

Inevitably in making appointments Oxnam ran into the question of God's will in the matter. When one preacher declined to become a district superintendent because he did not feel the Lord was calling him to this type of ministry, the bishop shot back, "Strange thing about the call of the Lord, Ross. I am certain that I have been directed by the Lord to issue this call to you." One wonders, however, if Oxnam often solicited the Lord's assistance in appointment matters, as this diary entry suggests: "But Stewart is not sure it is God's will, must have some inner voice. What did God give us minds for, and how does a man know that it is God's voice, or his own fear, or self-interest, or a bad stomach? I do not mean to be irreverent, nor to discount divine guidance; but these brothers who want some light to be turned on by a heavenly operator—Go, Slow, Stop. I do not understand it."

In Methodism the concept of an itinerant general superintendency is central and unique; a bishop is a general officer, not a diocesan one, related to the whole Church with a duty "to travel through the connection at large." As surely these pages have suggested, Oxnam, following the examples of Wesley, Coke, and Asbury, was the very model of an itinerant general superintendent. But what about the pastoral responsibilities of the episcopal office? Was Oxnam a real pastor to the pastors and people of the Areas he served? Many individuals have answered with a ringing affirmative, recalling a thoughtful note or call or conference when personal tragedy struck or ministerial problems became snarled. And as we have seen, Oxnam certainly gave rock solid support to preachers under reactionary attack. We have also noted his morale-building practice of Area visitations. Still, one wonders how available Oxnam made himself to troubled souls seeking counseling or to those simply hungry for a personal chat with their leader.

Oxnam's conscious custom of racing away from Annual Conference and other meetings precluded any friendly exchange between bishop and parson. Why did he not tarry a moment to listen to an individual boast about a child's accomplishment or lament a spouse's illness? Surely a word, a smile, an arm around a shoulder—any gesture of recognition—would have been more symbolic of a Good Shepherd's concern than the sight of a rapidly disappearing back. Oxnam boasted that his disappearing act saved between thirty and sixty minutes after each meeting; nevertheless, it is possible to question his priorities, especially since he chose solitude during coffee and luncheon breaks unless business dictated companionship. Maybe he might have sacrificed a few of his innumerable speaking engagements.

If Oxnam did not permit himself to be nickel and dimed to death in casual encounters, did he open his office for pastoral consultation? Of course he did but rather grudgingly it seems. "Do we want a bishop sitting in his office with the door open to anybody who wants to come in and engage in small talk for an hour or two because he has nothing else to do, or do we wish a bishop who plans his time, as Wesley ordered him to do?" he asked of the Northeastern Jurisdictional Conference. He also explained to the Washington Area ministers why he could not "sit in the office in Washington and be available when callers drop in for a friendly chat." Anyhow, Oxnam *did* set aside time for *scheduled* appointments. Woe to the secretary (when Miss Knudsen was on vacation) who permitted a caller to enter his office without an appointment. Woe to the individual who arrived after the appointed time. To Oxnam's credit, he understood the wisdom of simply sitting back and listening as an individual poured out his feelings. And he did listen and strove to give the impression of doing so sympathetically. But as his diaries attest, he found these office appointment days "trying," even vexing, for "you cannot say 'Go to hell' " to a fool droning on.

Surely Oxnam was a pastor to the pastors in the Areas he served, but one cannot honestly conclude that counseling his flock was the focal point of his episcopal leadership. This conclusion is buttressed by a telling diary entry following a meeting with a group of seminarians. "Perhaps I enjoyed the hour," he admitted, "because I talked most of it. Giving is so much more satisfying than sitting hour after hour, listening to problems." [2]

Although Oxnam was often absent from his office and although when present his door was often closed, at least he was the soul of conscientiousness in answering correspondence. Early each morning he dictated at "high speed" to a machine between fifty and one hundred and fifty letters. He likened the process to a horse eating oats: "I bury my head in a stack of letters and eat my way through." He was a "clean desk" man, never permitting correspondence to pile up, saying "the only reason for a piece of paper to enter your office is in order for it to go out of your office." Even when on extended trips or vacationing at the lake his secretaries daily forwarded mail and daily phoned in messages which he promptly answered rather than postpone doing so until returning to the office.

While in Washington Oxnam conceived the idea of an annual Area pastors' retreat at Buck Hill Falls. These gatherings were really postgraduate seminars led by authorities in such fields as homilectics, liturgy, biblical studies, church management, world affairs—and many ministers were grateful for these opportunities.

Declared Oxnam in 1956, "I regard the District Superintendency as the key administrative office in the church." Believing as he did, he took painstaking care to appoint capable individuals to these linchpin posts. He also held strong conviction that a bishop should not attempt to usurp the responsibilities and labors of the district superintendents. To do so was an impossibility in terms of physical strength and time, and even if feasible the result would be ruinous. "When a bishop tries to do the work of the District Superintendency, the laity will quickly bypass the District Superintendent and in effect end the Superintendent's effectiveness," Oxnam explained. "The Superintendent meets the leadership of the local church and he must through persuasion and skillful education—and I know of no harder spiritual and no more fatiguing task—carry the policies and programs of the whole church to the very place where the policies and programs come alive if they are to have any effect." For a bishop to step in and try to administer the district "is to destroy the Superintendency and Samson-like to push out the key stones and to bring the entire edifice down upon us." Privately he compared a bishop to a military general planning strategy and a district superintendent to a company commander entrusted with tactics. As in the case of other appointments, if Oxnam believed a district superintendent was performing competently, that individual would be given elbow room, support, and praise.

As regularly as a whippoorwill's call at dusk, Oxnam bemoaned the absence of a staff to whom authority might be delegated. He felt himself drowning in minutiae because, unlike in business, universities, the military, there was no one in his office to whom he might delegate real responsibility. At one point, in 1944, his exasperation reached the point where he seriously proposed that the district superintendency be abolished and replaced by a diocesan episcopate while retaining the general superintendency. For example, in the New York Area there would be the bishop of the New York Area, a general superintendent, under whom there would be four diocesan bishops, one for each of the four Annual Conferences of the Area. Although spelled out in detail, nothing came of the proposal. Oxnam insisted the reform was designed to enhance the district superintendency and elevate the status of the district superintendent by conferring the term "diocesan bishop."

Unification of the three major branches of American Methodism brought into existence a jurisdictional structure. Five of the newly created jurisdictions had a geographical basis and one, the Central Jurisdiction, composed of blacks, had a racial basis. As shall be noted in chapter 23, Oxnam favored ending the segregated Central Jurisdiction, but he also sought the dismantling of the entire jurisdictional system for reasons other than race. The Southeastern Jurisdiction, and to somewhat less degree the South Central, poured effort and money into creating a jurisdictional structure that really worked—or so it was passionately claimed. On the other hand, in much of the North and West, beyond meeting quadrennially for the sole reason of electing and consecrating bishops, the jurisdictions, including Oxnam's Northeastern, scarcely created more than a structural scaffolding. In 1955 Oxnam suggested that a commission be formed to study the matter. Just such a commission was authorized by the 1956 General Conference with instructions to report its recommendations to the 1960 General Conference. This commission was chaired by Parlin, who received from Oxnam the information: "Personally, I should very much like to serve upon a committee that would be charged with working out a system for the Church based upon the end of the whole jurisdictional idea." As a member, Oxnam found the meetings of the commission aggravating. The southern "brothers" who had made, in their judgment, the jurisdictional system work wonderfully well, inevitably peeved him. The diaries characterize them as "emotional," "childish," "utterly impossible," "stubborn." After one tense meeting, Oxnam recorded: "Our southern brethren are becoming adamant. They are emotionally so wrought up they cease to think. I found when speaking to them that I was talking to a blank wall." After another: "I think we have made some progress though it is very, very dreary and very aggravating to have men of the south speak in terms of morality when doing a distinctly immoral thing. They are stubborn, vote agreements and then insist that because the Commission is still in session that they don't have to stay by their agreements." Nevertheless, in the end compromises were effected, especially after Bishop Arthur J. Moore, chairman of the powerful Southeastern Jurisdictional Council, and Oxnam reached agreement on key recommendations. The report submitted by the Parlin Commission to the 1960 General Conference was designed to conserve the jurisdictional system (though the end of the Central Jurisdiction was foreseen in the future), but at the same time to discourage the development of five or six separate regional churches within the United States. Accepted by the conference, the report was defeated by a narrow margin when it was submitted to the Annual Conferences.

Concurrently, the jurisdictional system was the subject of much discussion in the Council of Bishops. Generally the southern bishops defended its merits, the northern bishops stressed its flaws, and the black bishops (if Oxnam's reports are accurate) lamented the racial basis of the Central Jurisdiction but wavered in demanding its immediate demise.

By far Oxnam's most vigorous indictment was a twenty-nine-page address before the 1956 Northeastern Jurisdictional Conference. "It is regionalism, and can become regionalism gone mad," he charged. "Jurisdictional promotional agencies are an unnecessary, costly, and ineffective interposition of potential bureaucracy and constitute a danger of deepening provincialism in outlook as well as of separating our people from the fuller riches of the whole Church." The danger is real that the jurisdiction may become a church within a church, or six churches within a church. The Jurisdictional Conferences undermine the whole Church's General Conference. The regional Colleges of Bishops undercut the whole Church's Council of Bishops. Historically Methodist bishops have been world leaders; under the jurisdictional system they are shriveling to a parochial, diocesan stature, marching to the boundary lines of their Areas, about-facing and marching back again like a sentry on duty. Oxnam spoke his heart when he cried: "There is so much fair play in the American spirit and so much more in the downright righteousness of a Christian democratic body that I see no reason at all why we should not return to the General Conference for the election of our Bishops and the election of our general boards and get done, once and for all, with this divisive, expensive, cumbersome crank that long since served its purpose." The "crank," believed Oxnam, had been designed in 1939 to protect the minority interests of the South in the united Church. If such protection was initially needed, that time had long since passed.

After the address, the audience of northeastern Methodists rose to give thunderous applause. When read by southern Methodists, the enthusiasm was more muted.

While Oxnam was bishop of the Washington Area, his colleagues elected him president of the Council of Bishops to serve in 1958, an honor that might have come earlier if he had not been secretary. Honorary degrees were bestowed by Princeton, Northwestern, Monmouth, Alfred, American, Western Maryland, Pratt Institute, Wesley Theological Seminary, and Budapest Reformed Theological Seminary. In 1953 Oxnam was runner-up (to Catholic Bishop Fulton Sheen) as the outstanding man in religion in the annual poll of news and radio editors conducted by the Associated Press. In 1955 he was elected honorary fellow (along with Sir Lewis Namier!) of the Consular Law Society and also received an Award of Merit. In 1959 he received The Upper Room Citation, an award given annually for outstanding contribution to world Christian fellowship. There were other recognitions as well.

[1] Earlier, in July 1948 when Dewey seemed certain of victory over Truman in November, Oxnam had written Dulles: "Sometime before the Governor becomes President, I think it would be of great value to him to meet four or five of our Bishops in a quiet and off the record conference. The Methodist Church seeks nothing for itself in terms of power or property or prestige. It does have an interest in certain moral objectives, and is eager to be of help to all those who are seeking to realize such objectives." Dulles replied that Dewey was agreeable, but would prefer to postpone the meeting until after the election. However, earlier still, in 1947, when Oxnam learned that Dewey had referred to him as a "communist," Oxnam asked Dulles to straighten the governor out and Dulles *did* set up a private meeting between Oxnam and Dewey at the Hotel Roosevelt, June 10, 1947.

[2] Judging from the list of books in Oxnam's personal library, pastoral counseling held little interest for him as almost none of the outstanding works in the field were in his possession. Alas, that seminal figure Freud apparently escaped his attention entirely. He could have had no comprehension of Auden's observation that "Freud is a whole climate of opinion."

CHAPTER 18

BISHOP OF THE CHURCH: THE WASHINGTON AREA, 1952-1960: THREE SPECIAL CONCERNS

"Surely the Lord will remember that Bishop Oxnam came to Washington," praised the grateful Methodist leader Norman L. Trott on the eve of Oxnam's retirement. Only secondarily was this a reference to matters already related or to advances under Oxnam's leadership at Dickinson College, Lycoming College, Western Maryland College, Wesley Junior College, the future splendid Methodist retirement village in Gaithersburg, and elsewhere. Rather, the institutions Trott had in mind were Wesley Theological Seminary, American University, and Sibley Hospital. The intensity of Oxnam's concern for the fate of these institutions compelled him to remain at the Washington helm a quadrennium beyond the eagerly planned retirement in 1956; he was determined to see his goals through to successful conclusions. In his mind the three institutions were intertwined and a part of a larger dream to bring them together in a great Methodist center buttressed by the existing Metropolitan Memorial "cathedral" and projected new headquarters buildings; Methodism would now become a vital presence and force in the life of the nation's capital.

Because there exists a splendid history of Westminster/Wesley Theological Seminary[1] there is no need to narrate again the story of those transforming years, 1952–1960. Rather, attention will center on only those aspects most revealing of Oxnam's leadership.

Westminster Theological Seminary, a Methodist Protestant institution founded in 1882, operated for its first seventy-five years on a campus adjacent to Western Maryland College in Westminster, Maryland. After the 1939 unification of the three major branches of American Methodism it was the only theological school in The Methodist Church bearing the Methodist Protestant heritage. Therefore, prior to 1939 it had had no experience with episcopal leadership, as there were no bishops in that branch of Methodism. Upon Oxnam's arrival in Washington, the school was to know the meaning of episcopal leadership in its full force.

However, even before Oxnam entered the picture, Westminster's future had been adumbrated when in 1947 an external review authorized by the denomination's Board of Education presented its findings. The report exposed with devastating clarity Westminster's many weaknesses, above all its geographic location, distant from a major university or city. Moreover, in 1949 in an editorial entitled "Let's Go to Washington!" *Zion's Herald* asked, "Why not combine Westminster with The American University and develop a complete and well-rounded university in Washington!" By 1952 this idea was becoming a brisk breeze in the Methodist air, not the least because American University's new president, the able and energetic Hurst Anderson, championed it.

Oxnam first attended the school's Board of Governors meeting in September as an ex officio member due to his episcopal office. Although he had heard good reports about President Welliver, he was not impressed with the president's handling of the meeting and found Dr. and Mrs. Welliver lacking in those social graces in which he put so much store. On February 12, 1953, Oxnam returned to Westminster. The board proceeded to elect him chairman. Commented historians Chandler and Goen: "This was irregular, to say the least, since the charter stated that board members were to be elected by the General Conference. But it was a simple matter to change the charter later and retroactively to legalize the board's action." After his election Oxnam immediately turned to the subject of the school's moving to Washington; a Committee of Seven was promptly authorized to study the matter; and now, he rejoiced to his diary, "we shall be on the way." (Naturally Oxnam was one of the seven, and chairman at that!)

Oxnam spelled out his dreams on many occasions, perhaps most fully in a five-page, single-space typed letter to the Kresge Foundation dated April 24, 1953. As we shall see, he had met with the Kresge people earlier; in this letter he was now making a formal petition for a grant of two million dollars to make possible the seminary's transfer from rural Maryland to D.C. The letter's forceful flavor is suggested by a few extracts:

> The location of The Westminster Theological Seminary upon the campus of The American University in Washington is the first major project in the plan to develop The American University as a national university under Christian auspices in the nation's capital.
>
> It is the conviction of those responsible for this development that the first step should be to place a great School of Religion or Theology upon the campus. We wish to affirm to the nation that The American University is an institution of the church, that religion is to be at its heart, and that the free society cannot be maintained unless the individual citizen and the nation accept and practice the moral principles that lie at the heart of the Christian faith.
>
> *The first reason, therefore, to move the Seminary to Washington is of national and world-wide significance. It is to make certain that religion will dominate the life of the national university.*
>
> The Seminary, located on the American University campus, would enable The Methodist Church to lead in the preparation of American Protestant clergymen in the nation's capital. *No Protestant Seminary is now located in Washington.* It is apparent that the nation's capital likewise needs the wholesome influence of a dynamic Protestant School of Religion. [Oxnam forgot about the existence of the Howard University School of Religion that had long been training black ministers and the Episcopal Virginia Theological Seminary in Alexandria.]
>
> This matter is of such vital importance to the church at large, to the plans for a national university in the nation's capital, and to the Seminary itself, that we present it for favorable consideration, after long and careful study and prayer. (Emphasis added.)

Elsewhere Oxnam beat these themes, informing the press that "the School will be moved, because we want to put religion at the center of a great national university"; adding, "No other Protestant seminary is in Washington." In a promotional blurb he asserted: "This seminary is the only Protestant theological seminary in the nation's capital. . . . Methodism proudly assumes its obligation to theological education in the most important city in the world."

Two points merit mentioning here, although both will be taken up in detail later. Oxnam's utterances implied that if the seminary moved it would somehow become attached to American University. But no structural connections were ever established—or for that matter, considered; they both continued under separate administrations. Second, in his incessant references to Catholic schools in Washington, Catholic University and Georgetown University, he was playing on Methodist nightmares even as he legitimately appealed to their dreams.

The seminary's transfer to Washington would have been unthinkable without the enthusiastic cooperation of American University President Anderson who in his inaugural address again advanced the plan. Between Oxnam and Anderson there was mutual admiration as well as a shared vision of the future. And so American University deeded, for the sum of one dollar, nine acres on the northwest corner of its campus to the seminary.[2] On first viewing the property Oxnam exalted, "I have never seen a finer location. It is easily worth a half million dollars." In the inspection group was Westminster's President Welliver and the bishop's cup of anger ran over when he noted "this long faced Welliver striding about unable to see buildings on that site." The diary fairly explodes:

> I finally had to say, "Now Dr. Welliver let us get something straight. I happen to be the Bishop here and you are the President of the institution. It is your duty to lead this institution, to raise these funds, and to see it out. It is the duty of a Bishop to drop in occasionally and offer prayer upon some event. I personally am perfectly willing to forget this school and turn my attention to more rewarding educational opportunities. We simply cannot go along with the President himself dragging his feet. He has got to be out and leading." Then he jumps in, "Oh, Bishop, I am enthusiastically for it." Bishop Straughn said, "I have not heard a word of enthusiasm out of you all day." He will come along, but he will never lead anything. What to do? It is the question. But we are on the way, at least, and we drafted a report in which we are recommending, that subject to certain conditions, we will recommend to the Board that the School be moved.

One of the conditions was the sale of the seminary's property in Westminster to Western Maryland College, whose president,

Lowell Ensor, Oxnam respected. Oxnam engineered the deal for $175,000, less than the seminary hoped to receive but more than the college initially hoped to pay. (Welliver wanted to hold out for $200,000 but did not stand a chance.)

The Westminster faculty scarcely represented a stumbling block to Oxnam's plans. Those who expressed an opinion were judged to have a "disregard for proprieties." As Oxnam informed the Committee of Seven, "the faculty has not been invited to participate in this matter, and at the present stage it was frankly not its privilege to enter the discussion." When Oxnam did assemble the faculty for a confidential meeting in his office, it was to solicit their opinions of their president. Oxnam found it appalling that some reported Welliver to be authoritarian!

Another bump or two on the road from Westminster to Washington barely slowed Oxnam down. The presidents of several Methodist theological schools complained to the denominational Commission on Theological Education that Oxnam was acting independently of the commission's higher authority. He soon set the commission straight. At an Area Cabinet meeting some of the district superintendents—graduates of Drew, Boston, Garrett—grumbled that Westminster was receiving favored treatment at the expense of their alma maters. "The opposition began to mount," recorded the bishop. "I had to step in and make as strong a speech as I have ever made to any of the leaders here concerning the necessity of this campaign."

Nevertheless, two obstacles of extreme seriousness *did* exist, one involving an individual and the other money. That individual was President Welliver, who had served with deep dedication at Westminster's helm since 1943. He loved the school, gave totally of his talents to save it in the 1940s, and was confident that the school was on the march and would celebrate its Diamond Jubilee Program on schedule in 1956 with new buildings, increased enrollments, expanded programs, and fattened finances. The problem, of course, was that this march of progress would be at the school's historic location while Oxnam's plan called for a literal march to Washington. Welliver was not a fool, but Oxnam still did not suffer him gladly. The diaries depict the president "whining," "weeping," "not thinking clearly." They describe him as "indecisive," a "snoop," "hopeless," "very arbitrary," "all of his work is slovenly," "quite impossible," "not cut out for the great task." By May 1953, Oxnam feared Welliver was cracking up mentally under the strain of fighting a battle he knew he would lose to an irresistible force. On June 2 Oxnam visited the president in his home, reporting, "He is completely broken, and I fear will have to have long psychiatric treatment." The bishop then suggested that the president take a six-month leave of absence at full salary. Oxnam sought the concurrence of Welliver's doctor, wife, and a son who was then a third-year medical student. Yes, they agreed, the sick man they loved had to lay his burdens down and seek healing. "They at least understood my sympathetic attitude," Oxnam dubiously opined. The next day the Executive Board of Governors voted to adopt Oxnam's recommendation that Welliver be granted a sick leave and then proceeded to elect Dr. Norman Trott acting president, a splendid choice and a man whom Oxnam considered one of his ablest district superintendents.

In December Welliver returned from his furlough feeling fully recovered and fully expecting to continue as president. His optimism was shattered at a meeting of the Board of Governors. He was informed by Oxnam that the majority of the board and of the faculty wanted him out and that if he remained "there might be a rebellion in the student body." Reported Oxnam: "I told him that while he was there for the rest of the year, because this was the understanding, no man had a position of perpetuity and that I thought he ought to give serious consideration to the whole question. I think he got the idea."

The months passed, Welliver defending his presidential leadership and refusing to tender his resignation. At the same time Oxnam's conviction that the seminary's future would be crippled under Welliver became Carborundum hard. Although Oxnam spoke of proceeding "in the most brotherly fashion," in his more honest moments he knew that the decision to force Welliver out was a "hard" one, "but that is what a bishop is paid for." The showdown came at a meeting between the two men in October 1954. They were alone. The bishop requested the president's resignation in writing. The president demurred. The bishop then informed the president that not only did the faculty and students desire his departure, not a dime would be forthcoming from the Kresge Foundation if he remained. Oxnam proceeded to make a proposition that the shaken Welliver could not refuse: if the president agreed in writing to resign effective June 1, 1955, Oxnam would promise to appoint him superintendent of the Williamsport (Pennsylvania) District. Oxnam further pledged that he would not inform the Board of Governors of the deal until May. Both men kept their words.

Happily, Welliver proved not to be a butterfly broken (in spirit) on the Iron Wheel of Methodism. After leaving the seminary, he served The Methodist Church faithfully and with distinction, including the presidency of the powerful Judicial Council. Oxnam spilled his own feelings after the May 2 Board of Governors meeting at which Welliver formally resigned: "It has been a long and difficult journey to bring this impossible situation to a conclusion. . . . I hope we have handled this matter amicably. I am sure that the decision that was taken was a wise one."

When in April 1953 the decision had been formally reached to move the seminary to Washington, an elated Oxnam wrote in mock dismay that now "we have the little job of finding two million dollars. That's all!" Even earlier he had decided that the Kresge Foundation was the best bet as the source of such a vast sum of money—and in 1953 that was a real bundle.[3] Sebastian Kresge, founder of the famous chain of five-and ten-cent stores, established in 1924 a charitable and educational foundation, of which his son Stanley S. was president. Both men were warmly evangelical and staunchly Methodist. Oxnam was quite capable of employing bulldozer tactics, if necessary in a situation, but if required he could be a master of finesse. His approach to the Kresge Foundation was a model of subtlety, exquisite planning, and patience. President Trott deserves similar praise. The bishop and the president worked as a team in an operation as smooth as silk. A couple of illustrations only about this detailed story.

Oxnam first met Sebastian Kresge in 1950 when they both were awarded honorary degrees by Dickinson College, a meeting Oxnam carefully noted in his diary. On January 28, 1953, he flew to Detroit to meet privately with Howard Baldwin, vice-president of the foundation and a Methodist, to seek confidential advice on how best to approach the Kresges. Baldwin supplied him with certain tips about the senior Kresge's philanthropic eccentricities. Before making formal written application, Oxnam secured promises of endorsement from the Kresges' pastor in Detroit, Chester McPheeters, and the bishop of the Michigan area, Marshall Reed. Subsequently Oxnam added to his cheering section Dr. John Seaton who for ten years had been the educational counselor for the foundation. Since directing the damaging 1947 survey of Westminster, Seaton had favored the seminary's transfer to Washington. In 1956 Oxnam and Trott shrewdly reduced the petition from two million dollars to a million and a half; moreover, the grant need not be in a lump sum for installment payments were perfectly acceptable. In January 1957 after almost four years of negotiations, the Kresge Foundation flashed the good news to Oxnam and Trott that the sum of one and a half million would be available in four annual grants provided the Methodists raised a matching amount. Trott must be credited with the central role in the seminary's successful denominational fund-raising drive, but we may be certain—as Trott was certain—that the Washington Area bishop was using all of his resources in the Area and at the national denominational level to see that the goal was reached. (Incidentally, the seminary received in 1958 a $760,000 loan from the federal government to build two dormitories.)

After the announcement of the Kresge gift, the seminarians could be heard singing, "I Found a Million-Dollar Baby in a Five-and-Ten-Cent Store." Oxnam's heart sang also. Oxnam was a principal participant at the various occasions of Wesley Seminary's growth (for such was the new Oxnam-approved name): ground breakings, cornerstone laying, the opening of classes, the dedication of buildings, and all the rest. He also was passionately involved in the architectural planning, including the striking figure of Christ on the exterior wall of the chapel overlooking Massachusetts Avenue and the admired equestrian statue of John Wesley. Interesting as these matters are, they cannot be explicated here, nor need they be.

What must not be forgotten is that the lovely chapel bears his name and it is there he wished his ashes interred. In the library are four thousand (perhaps five or six thousand) [4] books presented by Oxnam from his personal holdings. Happily, he instructed that they not be placed in a separate room but rather that they be intermingled on the shelves with other volumes as working tools for students. A "Precious Materials Room" does house separately Methodist historical materials of great value bestowed by Oxnam during his final years and by Mrs. Oxnam after his death, including John Wesley's Bible, personal seal, and original letters by him and many rare first editions of his books, and tracts and letters written by Bishops Coke and Asbury. In the president's office there is permanently a prie-dieu presented by Oxnam.

As the Wesley Seminary rose, Oxnam publicly declared, "Before our very eyes, one of the great institutions of the church is being built, and what we do is not for this quadrennium but for the centuries." Elsewhere Oxnam publicly asserted, "In an hour when the world is engaged in ideological struggle, the erection of the buildings to house a theological seminary at the very heart of the great development upon the American University campus is historically significant." On the completion of the major campus building program, a spokesman for the Board of Governors, the faculty, and student body declaimed, "I dare say that there is no one in this room who would take exception to the statement that had it not been for the vision and the courage of our Bishop this consummation could hardly have been achieved."

From the perspective of time, what can be said of Oxnam's dream and its consummation? In attempting an assessment one thinks immediately of Browning's question, "Ah, but a man's reach should exceed his grasp, Or what's a heaven for?" Without Oxnam's leadership the Westminster Theological Seminary would not have been transferred physically to Washington and transformed into the Wesley Theological Seminary—at least not until additional years had passed. Without the move it is at least possible that Westminster would have withered and died. Unrelenting in his determination to oust Welliver, the stern deed had to be done. Welliver's religious faith and strength of character permitted him to survive in other important capacities and he did so with Oxnam's support. Trott was Oxnam's choice to be the new president and Trott brilliantly confirmed the wisdom of Oxnam's judgment. Today Wesley splendidly fulfills its mission of preparing men and women of all races for the pastoral and educational ministries of the Christian church. Surely Wesley will endure and continue to make its sound, valuable contributions. In these respects Oxnam's grasp matched his reach.

Nevertheless, it is honesty, not cynicism, that compels the further observations. The presence of Wesley adjacent to American University did not make, as Oxnam predicted, "religion central to this great institution of higher learning"; Wesley is not today "at the very heart" of American University. Moreover, how realistic was this public prediction made in 1960: "Wesley Seminary is destined to become one of the really great theological schools of the future." Oxnam willed Wesley into existence. It was beyond his grasp to will either its centrality to American University or its ultimate destiny as a *great* seminary. As in so many areas of his career, Oxnam's great expectations, valid and valuable as they were, did not jibe with reality. He was fond of quoting Marshall Foch's "Victory is will." Curiously, Oxnam, who prided himself on his realism, could not see that Foch was mistaken.

Upon the occasion of the dedication of The Greater American University Center in 1960, Albert P. Shirkey, pastor of Mount Vernon Place Methodist Church and American University trustee, observed: "It is a fact of history—God is forever looking for a man in whose heart He can put a dream, and through whose life He can work to bring it to pass. God found His man in the person of G. Bromley Oxnam. If every institution is the lengthened shadow of great men, then let it be said that The Greater American University Center is the lengthened shadow of Bishops John Fletcher Hurst and G. Bromley Oxnam. Today, they stand clasping hands across these intervening years—'founder and developer'—in a togetherness that is both beautiful and inspiring!" Upon Oxnam's death, Guy Snavely, respected higher education leader and American University trustee, wrote Robert Oxnam: "Your father was the person most responsible for the continuing and increasing support from The Methodist Church which has changed American University from a moribund to an outstanding institution. . . . He ever showed wisdom and discretion in this service."

Upon Oxnam's arrival in Washington he informed newspaper reporters of his intention to endeavor to make American University "one of the finest in the world." His initial written appeal to the Kresge Foundation outlined his plan "to develop The American University as a national university under Christian auspices in the nation's capital." To every Area minister he sent the message, "I am convinced The Methodist Church must mobilize its full strength in support of The American University. There must be a great university under Protestant auspices in the national capital." To other audiences he appealed for "the development of a great national university which may shape the thinking of the nation in its international affairs . . . by pouring into the national and foreign services graduates so committed to Christianity, to the Protestant faith, that we may count upon them as bulwarks indeed." Soon the Baltimore Annual Conference was referring to American as "Methodism's National University."

Oxnam's manifold contributions to American's weal may only be sketched, and these contributions are in addition to his service on the school's Board of Trustees and Executive and Honorary Degree Committees and in addition to giving President Anderson, whom he vastly admired, wise advice and moral support. More than any single other individual (though of course American had other friends in Methodism's leadership), Oxnam was responsible for securing from The Methodist Church supporting appropriations of $100,000 annually from 1952 to 1960 when the sum was increased at his insistence to $250,000. Naturally there was resistance, for not all Areas, bishops, and presidents of Methodist schools were pleased to see American favored as "the especial responsibility of The Methodist Church and . . . worthy of our support on a national level."

Oxnam had a voice in the selection in 1952 of Anderson as president, succeeding Paul Douglass whom he considered an ineffectual prima donna. Anderson, it goes without saying, was a Methodist. Oxnam was almost as concerned that the president of the Board of Trustees also be a Methodist. When eighty-nine-year-old Judge Robert Fletcher retired as board president, another Methodist succeeded him. But that was insufficient to protect the school's integrity, for the then vice-president was an individual named Laskey—a non-Methodist; Charles Parlin was elected to replace him. As Oxnam explained, "We must watch situations of this kind to be assured of Methodist leadership in the important posts. If anything should happen to Mr. Reeves it would mean in all probability Mr. Laskey would succeed him. He is an excellent person but of another church, and there is a world of difference in the cooperation one gets under these circumstances. Charles Parlin will be superb." Oxnam further sought to protect Methodism by having the title to the university vested in The Methodist Church through action of the General Conference; by giving the Board of Education confirming powers over all new members of the Board of Trustees; and, by prohibiting changes in the charter without the consent of the Board of Education.

Unquestionably American University is today a far, far finer school than it was in 1952 and for this fact Oxnam deserves much of the credit. However, as in the case of Wesley Theological Seminary, American falls short of the original dream of its becoming a "great national university" and "one of the finest in the world." In the 1980s under President Richard Berendzen, American was on the march. But it is not today and in the nature of things probably can never be a *great* university of international top ranking. This is not intended as a disparaging statement. It is meant only to suggest again that while Oxnam unquestionably was a major factor in raising American University from a mediocre to a very good school, he deluded himself in denying what it takes to build a great university.[5]

At the inauguration of President Anderson in 1953 Oxnam delivered the charge:

> This is a university of the Christian Church. Because we are convinced of the truth of the Christian revelation; because we repeat "I believe in God, the Father Almighty" with complete intellectual honesty; because we reverently declare, "I believe in Jesus Christ; His only Son, our Lord," we believe it the privilege and the duty of a university to reveal the faith that

> Jesus revealed in His person, not alone in catalogue pronouncements but in the conduct of the affairs of the university. . . . Knowing you as I do, I look to the future with complete assurance, confident that this institution will be worthy of Christian support and loyal to its splendid name, The American University.

What in fact did the future bring? To be sure, even today three-fifths of the members of the Board of Trustees must be Methodists and all elected trustees must meet the approval of the Board of Education of The United Methodist Church. To be sure, The United Methodist Church continues to contribute annually to the university's budget. (The sum varies; it is not insignificant, but still only a fraction of the total budget. The support given by the Baltimore Annual Conference is trifling.) Yet not even P. T. Barnum could sell the fiction that American University is today "Methodism's National University."

The influence of Wesley Theological Seminary on American University has been minimal. In 1986 Richard Berendzen wrote a book about his experiences as American's president. (In April 1990 he was to resign from the office.) Absent from the book's index are such expected words as "Methodist," "Protestant," "Religion"—and "Oxnam." Indeed, the preface, written by Harvard's David Riesman, mentions this "once-Methodist" institution. The school's 1984-85 catalog lists the school as being "independent," not Methodist-related. The school's combined Department of Philosophy and Religion is small; its offerings limited. In 1984 President Berendzen announced the creation of the Interfaith Garden (near the Adnan Khashoggi Center) "dedicated to the world's major religious faiths." As Berendzen explained, "This university has a long and rich religious heritage. The Center and the Garden will stand as permanent testaments to the institution's dedication to pluralism, diversity and faith." This is not quite what Oxnam said in his charge to President Anderson in 1953.

On the campus of American University there is a School of International Service and prominently displayed in the school is Oxnam's portrait by Salisbury (having been "lifted" from Boston University School of Theology). The place of the portrait is appropriate for without Oxnam there would be no School of International Service.

For four years Oxnam labored to secure funding for this dream. The diaries fairly scream with the emotional tension and physical exhaustion wrought by the tortuous maneuverings necessary to swing the Church back of the plan. Finally, the 1956 General Conference gave its approval to the appropriation of one million to bring the School of International Service into existence, then the largest gift in Methodism's history to a single institution. Even as Oxnam rejoiced, he came "to see that a million dollars from the Church will only do part of this, that we are going to be involved in a two or three million dollars, perhaps more, proposition as we get the School of International Service on its feet." He arranged for funds to be tapped from the Crusade for New World Order. He and President Anderson made repeated visits to Masonic leaders. And both men solicited funds from the federal government.

All honor, then, to Oxnam, save only in the reasoning he advanced to justify a new School of International Service at American University. Annually for years there had been pouring into the United States diplomatic corps individuals "trained in the Jesuit tradition and conditioned to a Vatican foreign policy," claimed Oxnam. Their indoctrination, of course, had been received at Georgetown University's School of Foreign Service headed by the brilliant power broker Jesuit Edmund A. Walsh. Georgetown could not be expected to close its doors; therefore, as Oxnam informed John Foster Dulles, "in the freedom of the Protestant campus we hope to prepare our proper proportion of those who may go into the service of our government overseas in days to come." In one appeal before a Methodist body he said: "I regard this enterprise as vital. It should be apparent to any thoughtful person that students trained at Georgetown under Jesuit auspices moving into key positions in the State Department will of necessity, whether Protestant or Catholic, be conditioned favorable to Vatican world policy. Georgetown has been training people now since 1930 and perhaps 1500 to 2000 individuals are now in positions of influence in our foreign service. We must establish a similar school where people may be trained for this service in the freedom that characterizes the Protestant campus. The question of religious liberty, the necessary freedom for missionary enterprise, and related matters are involved." The warnings became darker: "If the officers of the United States Army, of the United States Navy, and of the United States Air Force were trained in a private military academy controlled by a foreign state, rather than at West Point, Annapolis and the Air Force Academy, we would expect the graduates to be so conditioned as to be sympathetic to the views of the foreign state. A substantial number of men holding key positions in the foreign service, both Protestant and Roman Catholic, are trained under Jesuit instruction at Georgetown University, an institution controlled by a Church which is also a temporal state, headed by the same person. It is difficult at times to distinguish between the policies of Pacelli, the pontiff, and Pacelli, the politician." Oxnam continued to charge that "the hierarchy is determined to exercise controlling influence in our political life, and therefore has sought to infiltrate the foreign services of the government so as to apply its principles to that service. This is done by training these servants of the government in Roman Catholic schools." Therefore, "We must build a School of International Service in the capital of the United States, which is today the chief center of world power. We must establish the school, guarantee its future, staff it with distinguished teachers, recruit a brilliant student body, train candidates for degrees and for effective service in the Protestant atmosphere of freedom and with full understanding of religious liberty, and thereby start a chain reaction that will explode the tyrannies of economic, political and ecclesiastical demagogues. Clericalism can be stopped in its tracks."

Then came the climax when the entire nation learned of his address at the combined commencement exercise and ground breaking for the new School of International Service, June 9, 1957. Speaking some words of conciliation, Oxnam nonetheless felt compelled to continue gently the mugging of Georgetown. Witness this passage:

> It is in no sense a matter of anti-Catholic spirit to be pro-Protestant. We are fearful of the authoritarian principle and of the totalitarian spirit, whether the principle and the spirit be manifest in the political, the economic, or the ecclesiastical life of the nation. It is natural, perhaps even proper, that students trained by Jesuits in a Jesuit institution should graduate conditioned favorably to Vatican world policy. For us, this

> conditioning raises serious questions from the standpoint of the maintenance of democracy. We, therefore, affirmatively seek to offer training upon a campus where the unhampered pursuit of truth is not only possible but a matter of principle, where religious liberty, together with the basic civil liberties of the democratic order, may be examined and espoused, and where men and women of tolerant spirit, abhorrence of bigotry, and commitment to the free way of life may become equipped to serve the new world, the one world, in the spirit that will preserve and extend liberty to all men everywhere.

An unwell President Eisenhower appeared after Oxnam to turn the sod, accept an honorary degree, and say: "It seems to me most significant that this great university should join her sister institution in the Capital, Georgetown, to carry on this kind of work, because in the great foreign service of the United States we do not recognize race, color or creed—only merit." [6]

Today the School of International Service enjoys a respectable reputation. However, other than the presence of Oxnam's portrait, does not find the school's atmosphere particularly "Protestant."

A final major interrelated matter confronted Oxnam upon his arrival in Washington and this was the move of Methodism's sixty-five-year-old Sibley Memorial Hospital from one of the now worst sections of D.C. to the American University campus (or adjacent to it, as events turned out). The decision to do this had already been made as had the decision to accept $3-4 million of assistance in a dollar-matching grant from the federal government. But in the spring of 1952 nothing had been nailed down. No contracts had been signed. No formal legislation had sanctioned the government's tentative offer of assistance. No property deeds had been tendered. No negotiations had been undertaken with the District Zoning Commission. No courts at any level had rendered verdicts. No plans had been laid to raise the matching dollars from either Methodist or non-Methodist private sources. No professional fund-raising firms had been consulted. No architects or building contractors had been approached. Beyond a rather ethereal understanding that a move was wise, there was nothing concrete. Moaned Oxnam in November 1955, six months after he had been elected chairman of the Sibley Board of Trustees, "This hospital here is driving me crazy. It is a project I cannot support enthusiastically and yet must do so." In July 1952 he had explained his less than total enthusiasm:

> I favor the move of the Sibley Hospital to the American University campus. This involves accepting perhaps 3.5 million dollars from the Federal Government, which will match a similar 3.5 million that we will put in. I have personally been fundamentally opposed to the acceptance of such funds from government for private institutions. However, this is not under the Hill-Burton Act, but is a matter involving the District of Columbia solely. It is precisely as though Los Angeles, or some other local community, needing hospitals called upon the private hospitals of the city to take over the obligation, provided there would be a subsidy equal to one-half of what the private institutions put in. Since the decision had been taken before I came, it seemed to me there was nothing to do but concur and to cooperate.

Having satisfied his conscience, Oxnam sought to sail swiftly and directly, but repeatedly he found himself becalmed or "caught in irons." He may have felt less passionate about Sibley than he did about Wesley or the School of International Service, but that does not mean the hospital worried him less. In fact, if the diaries are indicative, if anything might have driven him to drink (of course, unthinkable), it was Sibley. "This is the most difficult situation I have ever faced"; "This is one of the most trying situations I have confronted anywhere"; "This is the most unsatisfactory situation I have ever faced"; "The situation is absolutely impossible as to the caliber of the Board and the competence of our leadership." (The last lament was primarily about Dr. John Orem, Sibley's director, and a man whose supposed vagueness, vacuousness, and evasion drove the master of precision Oxnam mad. Of course, it is possible that this was a protective strategy consciously employed by Orem to preserve his independence of Oxnam's domination.)

The vicissitudes encountered, the complex maneuverings before victory was achieved, would fill a book and must not long detain us. American University deeded to Sibley 7.5 precious acres of its limited campus, but only over the opposition of powerful Board of Trustees members including chairman Judge Fletcher. Property owners in the neighborhood protested the projected hospital. Two angry hearings were held before the D.C. Zoning Commission; the commissioners upheld the property owners' position. To reverse the commission's adverse decision, American University turned to the courts; the case moved up from Federal Court to Appellate Court and finally to the Supreme Court where the university won. It did not matter.

At that juncture in April 1957 the government offered Sibley twelve acres of prime land about 1.5 miles from the American University campus, the site of the old National Training School for Girls, in exchange for the site of Hahnemann Hospital, 135 New York Avenue, which had merged with Sibley in 1956. The proposition was more than acceptable because twelve acres would allow room for both a 350-bed hospital and the Lucy Webb Hayes School of Nursing. Moreover, the 7.5 precious acres deeded by American University would be returned.

In September 1958 a bill passed Congress authorizing a dollar-matching grant of $4,374,000. In April 1959 ground was broken by gold shovels for the $9-million hospital and nursing school, the school to be affiliated with American University. Oxnam prepared and read the ground-breaking liturgy: "In proud recollection of John Wesley, scholar, evangelist, and founder of The Methodist Church, whose little book 'Primitive Physick' was an endeavor to carry the remedies of medicine to the poor of 18th century England, and marked the beginning of hundreds of great hospitals and the investment of hundreds of millions of dollars in the healing ministry of Christ."

To Oxnam's credit, however critical he had been over the course of six tortuous years of Dr. John Orem, in the end he bestowed on him high public praise, saying Orem did not know the meaning of the word "defeat." Oxnam reserved his highest praise, however, for Methodist minister "Abe" Shirkey, who, on becoming vice-chairman of the Sibley Board of Trustees, rescued an enterprise that was foundering and brought it safely into port. Maybe in the whole matter Oxnam's only regret was his inability to change Sibley's name to The Methodist Hospital.

There is an amusing footnote to the hospital tale. Among those present at the ground-breaking ceremony, gold shovel in hand, was Representative John McCormack of Massachusetts who had (together with Senator Everett Dirksen) introduced the enabling legislation in Congress. When Oxnam wrote still another article laying the cat to the Roman Catholic back, McCormack sent a blistering letter to the journal pointing out that Protestant and Jewish as well as Catholic institutions received federal aid, Oxnam's insinuation to the contrary. Referring specifically to Sibley, McCormack boasted, "As an American, I was proud to introduce the bill and getting it through Congress. As a Catholic, it showed an understanding mind." McCormack also set the bishop straight in a personal letter. Rather lamely, Oxnam replied that the decision to move the hospital and accept federal assistance was made before his arrival in D.C. "I felt myself bound by any commitments made by my predecessor." When Oxnam was joshed for his inconsistency, Dean Muelder recalls the response, "Anyone who is absolutely consistent doesn't have the qualifications to be a Methodist bishop."

John Wesley Lord succeeded Oxnam as bishop of the Washington Area, and in a memorial tribute, Lord observed that "in Washington, all one needs to do is to look around him in order to see and extol G. Bromley Oxnam's achievements." That is a fair statement provided only that it is further noted that time and circumstances, perhaps inevitable ones, placed limits on Oxnam's achievements, splendid as they were.

---

[1] *Pilgrimage of Faith: A Centennial History of Wesley Theological Seminary*, 1882–1982 by Douglas R. Chandler and edited by C. C. Goen. Some admirers of Oxnam believe that he is treated too harshly in the book. I found the study to be scholarly, balanced, and fair to both Oxnam and President Lester A. Welliver. In response to my inquiry, L. Allyn Welliver, himself a Methodist minister, replied: "It is my opinion that the history of the Seminary by Professors Chandler and Goen presents an eminently fair assessment of my father's work at the seminary and the circumstances of the move to Washington." The letter is silent concerning any opinion of Oxnam. Incidentally, discerning readers will note slight discrepancies in some of the quotations found in the book and those found in these pages. I have elected to follow my own research notes. Incidentally, also, although Chandler and Goen have written in great detail, I have included a few points they either did not encounter in their researches or chose not to include. This is not a criticism, for their study is excellent.

[2] When Oxnam discovered a "reverter clause" in the deed he arranged its withdrawal, thus protecting the seminary's future.

[3] In 1955-56 the Rockefeller Foundation made it known that if Wesley Theological Seminary and Howard University's School of Religion merged it would provide generous support to make the union possible. Oxnam met on several occasions with the presidents of Wesley, American University, and Howard and Rockefeller representatives. Both Wesley and Howard were willing to institute a cooperative program, but both balked at a merger; and so the Rockefeller Foundation lost interest.

[4] In addition to the original gift of four thousand volumes, on March 30, 1961, Oxnam offered President Trott one or two thousand more.

[5] In 1957 The Methodist Church bought from Wire Properties, Inc., a valuable nineteen-acre tract at Massachusetts and Nebraska Avenues across from the American University campus. The land was to be the site of buildings of a greater Methodism in Washington. Oxnam, of course, was involved in the purchase and in the dreams of the

property's development. The dream never materialized. The Methodist Church sold the land to American University for several million dollars—a reasonable price. However, American University officials wonder why the property was not given as a gift if the Church truly believed in the school's future as a Methodist institution.

[6] I am indebted to Peter F. Krogh, present dean of the Edmund A. Walsh School of Foreign Service (and a non-Catholic, incidentally), and Walter I. Giles, secretary to Walsh, 1944-45, 1946-50, for the following observations relating to the Walsh era of Georgetown's SFS: 1. Thirty-five to 45 percent of the students were non-Catholics. 2. The great majority of them entered commerce and business, not the Foreign Service. 3. Perhaps only 10 percent of the Foreign Service Corps were Georgetown graduates and if anything its graduates were underrepresented not overrepresented. 4. About 40 percent of the SFS faculty were non-Catholics including some of the most prominent; perhaps a majority of the part-time lecturers (adjuncts) were non-Catholics. 5. Other than Walsh, there were no Jesuits on the SFS faculty (save for one who taught only the required religion course) until Walsh handpicked Frank Fadner to be his successor. 6. Religion never figured in Walsh's scheme of things in the curriculum and teaching and for this he was persistently criticized by other Jesuits who referred to SFS as "the pagan school." 7. Only Catholic students were required to take the one-year religion course. 8. Perhaps more than 50 percent of the students never took a course with Walsh. 9. Walsh was numero uno and didn't want any other Jesuits messing in his garden patch. 10. To learn there was a Vatican party line to be followed would have puzzled SFS faculty and students alike. These observations were made to me by Krogh in an interview and in a seven-page, typed, single-spaced, memorandum prepared by Giles at the dean's request and shared by Dean Krogh with me. Incidentally, in 1986 a senior in the School of Foreign Service observed: "It's really possible for a senior to go four years here and never feel a significant Catholic influence." Incidentally, on learning of Methodism's plans, Georgetown's president, the Reverend Edward Bunn, S.J., made the mild public statement: "We welcome the advent of American University into the field of foreign service. There is a great demand for more institutions to prepare more candidates to meet the needs consequent upon our nation's role of international leadership in the world."

CHAPTER 19

A FLOW OF WORDS

If there is any Protestant minister of his generation who addressed in person more people than Oxnam, that individual's name does not easily come to mind. It is true that Billy Graham's crusades attracted their audiences of thousands, but they were not daily happenings. Certainly Reinhold Niebuhr was much coveted as a speaker, but generally he spoke before selected groups of limited size; and besides, he could not be away perpetually from his teaching responsibilities at Union. Surely the radio carried Fosdick's and Sockman's voices to millions, and then came the battalion of television evangelists with their legions of viewers. But who could match Oxnam's record of fulfilling *in person* speaking engagements numbering hundreds annually over a period of over four decades? We recall the incessant wagging of his tongue during the Church of All Nations and DePauw presidency eras. The assumption of episcopal responsibilities scarcely silenced him. To the contrary, in the 1940s and 1950s he reported averaging ten talks a week and increasingly they were before audiences numbering many thousands; and for a period he also enjoyed a regular worldwide radio audience and from time to time television viewers as well.

When Oxnam reported averaging ten talks a week, this figure was not far off target if one excludes from the tally the summer vacation weeks and those periods that found him traveling abroad, although some of these foreign excursions involved the business of lecturing. Even if the total is pared to 250 talks annually the number remains staggering. Little wonder he sighed in 1940, "Six addresses in one day are too many, and I was weary." And one cannot help but wonder if the growing availability of travel by air was not, in terms of his mental and physical well being, more of a bane than a blessing. (He, of course, could not admit that it was anything but a blessing.) The one consideration that makes Oxnam's speaking schedule imaginable is to recall that a lot of sweated professors in colleges lecture twelve or fifteen or eighteen hours a week, and this on top of other advising and administrative responsibilities. These burdened souls manage to pull it off, at least after the sleepless preparatory years, by relying on a backlog of old lectures. Oxnam, too, opened his files and lugged out old lectures to repeat scores and scores of times, a luxury that most parish preachers do not have and many would not want. (The Alkahest Celebrity Bureau of Atlanta, Georgia, a booking agency, has a list of Oxnam's most popular talks late in his career. Apparently he had other agencies earlier.)

It is manifestly impossible to list here all the wide variety of audiences addressed by Oxnam. A few generalizations must suffice. Obviously he spoke before Methodist groups of all sorts and sizes ranging from small congregations at the dedication or anniversary services of rural churches to vast General Conference audiences and thousands assembled at denominational city-wide or Area-wide rallies. Clearly, also, as a Federal Council, National Council, and World Council officer he was often a speaker at large meetings convened by these bodies.

Between 1940 and 1955 Oxnam was honored by invitations from twelve prestigious established lecture series: The Enoch Pond Lectures at Bangor Seminary (twice); The Merrick Lectures at Ohio Wesleyan University; The Lectures at the Florida Southern College School of Religion; The Fondren Lectures at Southern Methodist University; The Lyman Beecher Lectures at Yale University; The Earl Lectures at the Pacific School of Religion; The Alden-Tuthill Lectures and the Hoover Lectures, both at the University of Chicago; The Quillian Lectureship at Emory University; The James Bowdoin Day Speaker at Bowdoin College. Seven of these lecture series were subsequently published in book form.

The above accounted for only a fraction of his campus visits. Early in his episcopal career, Oxnam had received from the revered Bishop McDowell the advice, "Bromley, keep in touch with the colleges and universities of the nation. Few bishops can or do. There is the great evangelistic opportunity of the future." For Oxnam, speaking to college students was a joy as well as an evangelistic obligation; they were certainly his favorite audiences. He held annual appointments to speak at Harvard, Yale, Cornell, and elsewhere. Across the land he traveled to give chapel talks, commencement addresses, baccalaureate sermons, and other utterances. As an illustration, the three-year period 1955–1957 found him declaiming on the campuses of Harvard, Yale, Vassar, Bowdoin, Carnegie Tech, Wisconsin, Dickinson, Bryn Mawr, Cornell, Duke, Tuskegee, Monmouth, Kansas, Berea, Rutgers, Randolph-Macon, Princeton, Michigan, Oregon, Washington, Lycoming, Southwestern, College of the Pacific, Bucknell, Delaware, Ohio Wesleyan, Pennsylvania, North Carolina A.T.&T., and Andover and Choate.[1] Some of these campuses, such as Harvard's,[2] were visited six times in these three years. Off campus, he also addressed thousands of Methodist youth at conferences and retreats.

If students were Oxnam's favorite audiences, public school teachers came in a close second. He was the darling of a raft of State Teachers Associations. As an example, in 1954 at the Iowa State Educational Association Centennial Convention, over thirteen thousand turned out to hear him. While it was not unknown for Oxnam to knock college professors, he had nothing but praise for public school teachers. They in turn idolized him, not the least because he defended them from the attacks of jingoists and Red-baiters and because he was a leader in the fight against state funds for parochial schools.

On Reformation Sunday, October 28, 1945, Oxnam addressed a St. Louis audience of nineteen thousand. This occasion marked his emergence as American Protestantism's premier proponent of the perils of the Roman Catholic hierarchy to the nation's weal. He delivered this message on subsequent Reformation Sundays, at Protestant Festivals of Faith, at POAU (Protestants and Other Americans United for the Separation of Church and State) rallies, in Masonic temples—everywhere. Over a sixteen-year period literally hundreds of thousands of Protestants heard him proclaim the glories of the Protestant principle of religious freedom and totalitarian Catholicism's threat to it.

On June 21, 1953, Oxnam at his own request appeared before the House Un-American Activities Committee. This ten-hour ordeal and his book about it, *I Protest*, made him a hero in the eyes of citizens concerned with the imperiled fate of civil liberties during the mistermed McCarthy Era. Immediately he began to receive numerous invitations to speak about his experiences with HUAC.

There was, of course, a continuing stream of invitations to speak on subjects unrelated to either Catholicism or communism, such as from the Chicago Sunday Evening Club and similar organizations. In 1954 he spoke before the twenty-five hundred delegates to the National Council of Congregational Christian Churches and in 1958 he addressed the International Convention of the Disciples of Christ. In 1955 he gave the annual Charles P. Steinmetz Memorial Lecture, the only Protestant churchman to join the honored ranks of such individuals as Michael Pupin, Robert Millikan, Karl Compton, and Arthur Compton. All things considered, it is not surprising that Tau Kappa Alpha, national college honor society in speech, should cite him in 1954 as the outstanding religious speaker of the year.

In 1946 Harry Emerson Fosdick retired as the principal preacher of "National Vespers," then the flagship of Protestant radio religious broadcasting. Oxnam and Dr. John Sutherland Bonnell shared the signal honor of being invited to fill Fosdick's larger-than-life shoes. "It is a unique opportunity to reach millions," rejoiced Oxnam, "instead of tens of thousands." Although the program's sponsoring agency was the Federal Council, the American Broadcasting Company as a public service freely provided several million dollars worth of radio facilities. Weekly for four months in 1946–47 and for four months in 1947–48 Oxnam's voice was heard across the land and by shortwave across the oceans by perhaps three million listeners. Mimeographed copies of the sermons were mailed to listeners on request. In 1948 twelve of Oxnam's radio efforts were published under the title *The Stimulus of Christ*. As the letters of appreciation for his radio ministry poured in, Oxnam exhalted, "Radio is the way to reach out." This is why as bishop of the Washington Area he arranged to broadcast thirty-three "Radio Meditations" consisting of the National Vespers sermons reduced in length. (It will be recalled that as early as the Omaha years he had turned to the radio to broadcast his messages.) From time to time Oxnam could also be heard on radio town meetings, and forums, and talk shows.

Oxnam's popularity as a public speaker is beyond peradventure. Why should this be? One explanation is his impressive physical presence. Standing erectly with penetrating gaze, he carried the authority of a sea captain scanning the ocean from high in the quarterdeck. Another is his clear, deep voice. He spoke without those phony affectations that plague sensational preachers, but the words did come with explosive velocity—like bullets from a machine gun. Accompanying the rat-tat-tat of the words was the pound of a clenched fist into a palm. Rarely did he read from a manuscript before him. His astonishing memory permitted him to fix securely in mind even the longest addresses after only a few prior readings. In 1940 he apologized to Bill Stidger: "I am sorry you had to sit through the dreary paper I read. That's the last time I shall ever attempt to read anything in public. I worked hard on that address, but find that when one does his best in a public speech, he is foolish to attempt reading." The Boston professor agreed: "It is always foolish to tame a Tornado or a whirlwind." When Oxnam understood that it was a *requirement* that his Yale Beecher Lectures be read he regretted the instruction because he felt much of the power was drained from them. Oxnam may have been correct, but one doubts the universal truth of his opinion that "no man can read a paper and hold the attention of a group of scholarly minds. They are so often in front of the reading speed."

Oxnam's rhetoric was staccato, not legato. It was vibrant and virile and martial, more masculine than feminine. He favored short words over long and eschewed theological terminology. Wit was present but rarely jokes. The illustrations employed were often drawn from his own experiences, giving them a personal touch. Oxnam radiated an intense impression of disciplined power, restrained force, reined emotion. Audiences were convinced that they were in the presence of a speaker who fervently believed that what he was saying was of supreme urgency. Sincerity was a hallmark of his rhetoric.[3]

Quite humanly, Oxnam shamelessly congratulated himself when he sensed a talk went well and captured the audience. Yet he was also capable of shame and would confess that he had given a "perfectly rotten talk." Once after addressing a large but unresponsive and inspirationless group, he admitted, "The speech deserved it. When I go back to the Sunday Evening Club again I will be older, and I'll bet they'll be older before they invite me back."

Oxnam roared around the lecture circuit as though he were Barney Oldfield on a race track. What compelled him to seek out and accept such an endless round of speaking engagements? One puzzling answer is "money." Returning bone tired from an engagement he pondered, "I wonder what value lies in these addresses. One takes them, I'm a little ashamed to say, as much for the fee as for the privilege." In 1953 he vowed, "Anyone who gets me for a date in the next four years . . . unless it is in the service of the Church is going to pay for it. Maybe this is mercenary and maybe it is just common sense." After a poorly attended campus lecture he gruffed, "If it weren't for the honorarium, I would write that day off as one of the very worst. The honorarium was not so much either." On occasion apparently his conscience bothered him: "One wonders about these very large fees, but after all if others receive them and they are willing to pay them, I suppose it is quite all right." However, he groused when he considered the payment stingy as when a Methodist church in Akron coughed up only one hundred bucks and the pastor presented the sum "as though he was bestowing an honorary degree." Nonetheless, all in all Oxnam deemed public speaking more remunerative than writing magazine articles.

Surely, however, money could not have been the prime consideration. He had plenty of it without the speaking fees. He drove himself to the podium even as late as 1960 when Parkinson's was taking its terrible toll, and he did so out of the conviction that what he had to say was important to the Church and the nation. This motivation is not discreditable and, indeed, is honorable. But was there also an element of personal fame involved? After addressing two thousand ministers in Columbus, Ohio, he thought that things had not gone too well, and then added the revealing consolation, "but I think the press release will be satisfactory, anyhow, and after all, that's where the real influence seems to be these days."

Although public speaking was more profitable than writing, the written word had its appeal, and in 1945, as he pondered the future, Oxnam vowed to devote more time to writing. The major impact of speaking, he reasoned, "is in the realm of the emotion regardless of what the material may be." Moreover, the written word reaches a larger audience, and its effect is more lasting. And so articles and books continued to flow from his pen. In truth, as Oxnam spoke too often so he wrote too much. In addition to thousands of articles and news columns, he edited five books and wrote seventeen. To be sure, the contents of eight of these books were originally delivered as lectures or sermons: *The Ethical Ideals of Jesus in a Changing World* (1941); *By This Sign Conquer* (1942); *Preaching in a Revolutionary Age* (1944); *Labor and Tomorrow's World* (1945); *The Stimulus of Christ* (1948); *The Church and Contemporary Change* (1950); *Personalities in Social Reform* (1950); and *On This Rock* (1951). It is difficult to imagine that any of these books will continue to be read into the twenty-first century.

In point of fact, of the seventeen volumes, only several hold interest today. Historians of Los Angeles and of Hispanics will continue to consult Oxnam's 1920 study, *The Mexican in Los Angeles*. Historians of U. S.-Russian relations may still find value in *Russian Impressions* (1927). *I Protest*, relating his encounter with HUAC, remains a source for students of the Second Red Scare. *A Testament of Faith* is Oxnam's last book, published in 1958, and one he anguished over. It is a sincere, winsome, even moving statement of his beliefs about God, Jesus Christ, life everlasting, prayer, the Church, the forgiveness of sins, and man. It is good Methodist doctrine—that is, it is good BU School of Theology. Personalism. Certainly many readers found Oxnam's hortatory, hopeful, faith-inspired words helpful and will continue to do so. It was as though, praised a friend, "you had pushed aside all reference works and had simply spoken out of your mind and heart."

Lest this judgment on Oxnam's writings appear too harsh, one hastens to add that only a tiny fraction of authors—historians and biographers definitely included—write stuff that does not prove to be ephemeral. The suggestion has been made that there is nothing more inimical to writing than talking. The two indeed are rooted in the same impulse—to express, to explain—but one mode of communication disables the mind for the other. Maybe the case of G. Bromley Oxnam supports this suggestion.

A deservedly famous stump speaker once advised, "Fill yourself with your subject, then knock out the bung and let nature caper." Was Oxnam able to fill himself with a subject? Well, he certainly was in agreement with J. H. Jowett's warning, "If the study is a lounge, the pulpit is an impertinence." He fought desperately to salvage hours for intense study. When unable to succeed, the diaries roar with frustration. Invariably on board a train, plane, or ship or in a station waiting he could be found with a book in hand; and in a car, too, if being chauffeured. Entire summer months were set aside for reading and writing. His personal library contained between five and six thousand volumes. He subscribed to a slew of newspapers, magazines, and scholarly journals. In 1956 he reported: "A bishop must set aside and sacredly hold at least eighteen hours a week for careful study and preparation of sermons, addresses and articles, if his utterances are to be significant and represent the Church in a profitable way." The revealing point about this statement is that the eighteen hours embraced *both* reading *and* writing. This could mean, perhaps, only nine hours filling himself with a subject.

Everything Oxnam did he did at breakneck speed and this includes reading. In one day, between phone calls, conferences, and dictation, he reported, "I went through about six weeks of magazines, The Nation, the Survey, Current History, The Atlantic, World's Work, The Forum, our church papers, The Manchester Guardian, Foreign Affairs, and several others." Indeed! Is there any more point to setting speed reading records than to setting speed driving records? Even with his remarkable memory, how could he possibly have absorbed the contents of these publications? Apparently he conned books with comparable rapidity. One gasps at the number of meaty works he records as having devoured on a train trip or over a weekend or other short periods of time. A sampling of the books from his personal library willed to Wesley Seminary reveals that he marked them up only rarely and slightly. This statement does not imply that the books were left unread, but simply that he rarely paused to make a marginal note of agreement or disagreement with the author or other reflections.

As we know, when it came to writing, Oxnam was as fecund as a shad. This truly prodigious outpouring could have been possible only if he composed rapidly, and so he did. It is true that not *all* of his manuscripts came easily. He did sweat his share of blood. Yet on balance the judgment stands that his pen can be described as facile. One unhappy consequence was the repetition of the same (increasingly stale) ideas, illustrations, and phrases decade after decade.

A rather close glance at Oxnam's writings discloses how heavily he drew upon his personal experiences and ideas picked up in personal conversations. Because his experiences were wide and interesting and because he knew many of the world's movers and shakers this gave a vividness and immediacy to his writings. Bishop Welch said of Oxnam, "His mind was even more rapid than his speech, and worked not so much by logic as by insight and flashes of brilliance." This is a fascinating observation. So much emphasis has been placed on Oxnam the master of facts and his vaunted objective, scientific approach to issues that the intuitive, Celtic side to his nature is forgotten. And so Oxnam's writings are based not exclusively on books studied; they are also informed by a sight observed, a remark heard, an event experienced.

For a final point we take as our text a 1955 Oxnam statement: "I have been through the courses, have read somewhat extensively in theology, and have listened relentlessly to the long discussions and have witnessed the parades of erudition at ecumenical conferences; I bow in respect but confess I am not an active member of the lodge or of the fraternity. I know the grip, have been instructed concerning the password, and might possibly be able to work my way into the meeting, but I am not a theologian." Of course not every Methodist bishop can be expected to be the theologian that Bishop McConnell was. But should Methodist bishops echo Oxnam's growl, "theologians get me down at best"? Should they dismiss biblical scholars, as did Oxnam, as academic theorists speaking in strange jargons who take themselves all too seriously? Here is one of his critiques of biblical scholarship: "I read through one or two of the Commentaries, that is, the sections dealing with some of these verses, and I was astonished by how little *The Interpreter's Bible* really brings to an individual in the comment. Shakespeare's 'words, words, words' would describe a lot of it, page after page of surmise. . . . One of the disillusioning features of a lot of this stuff . . . is that what scholars do is pile up a bunch of books upon a table written by other scholars and then go through all and try to say something different. . . ." [4]

Oxnam's personal library contains four books by Shailer Mathews, six by Bowne, and six by Knudson. This is not surprising. He found the neo-orthodox theology of Americans impossible and that of the European "Crisis" theologians even worse. It is therefore not surprising but it is nonetheless disconcerting to find in the careful lists of books he owned not a single title by Karl Barth, Emil Brunner, Dietrich Bonhoeffer, Paul Tillich, Rudolf Bultmann, Martin Buber, H. Richard Niebuhr, Reinhold Niebuhr (save for *Leaves from the Notebook of a Tamed Cynic*), Nels Ferré, Robert Calhoun, Albert C. Outler, William Temple, C. S. Lewis, Edwin Lewis, Hans Kung, Karl Rahner, Søren Kiekegaard. It is true that in *A Testament of Faith* he refers to Reinhold Niebuhr and Walter M. Horton and Robert Calhoun as "my friends." True, in *Testament* he quotes Barth and John Baillie and mentions finding Tillich tough going. True, in *Testament* he states that he had listened with respect to theologians lecture and "labored through their heavy volumes." Unfortunately, these assertions are not supported by a mountain of countervailing evidence. Oxnam was simply not interested in theology or biblical studies and was much too busy with other putatively more important matters to give theology and biblical studies serious and sustained thought.

[1] Eleanor Roosevelt, after hearing Oxnam at Choate, wrote in her "My Day" newspaper column: "His was a most interesting sermon and so challenging that I did not see a single head nod, which is a fine tribute to anyone addressing a group of boys just after lunch."

[2] Oxnam was on the Board of Preachers of Harvard and was tapped in 1952 to be on the Board of Electors, charged by President Pusey with revitalizing and restaffing the Harvard Divinity School.

[3] As must be clear from comments throughout this biography, I do not totally share this high estimate of Oxnam's speaking. Maybe this is because I never had the privilege of hearing him in person. Mark Twain once said of Richard Wagner's music that it is better than it sounds. My personal feeling is that just the opposite might be said of Oxnam's rhetoric.

[4] Of course, these widely acclaimed twelve volumes are one of the glories of The United Methodist Publishing House.

CHAPTER 20

"THE WORLD IS MY PARISH": LABORS AT HOME AND ABROAD IN THE INTERESTS OF METHODISM AND THE FEDERAL, NATIONAL, AND WORLD COUNCILS OF CHURCHES, 1947-1960

When in December 1946 Oxnam stepped down as president of the Federal Council of Churches, this did not put a period to his labors on behalf of the ecumenical movement. Because it was not in his nature to give any undertaking less than total intensity, he grappled this cause—Laocoon-like, and it squeezed from his heavy schedule many thousands of precious hours. As in so many areas of Oxnam's life, in the realm of action he brought to the ecumenical enterprise energy, dedication, pragmatism, and an attention to detail; in the realm of rhetoric, however, he envisioned Celtic dreams impossible of fulfillment.

The final four years of the Federal Council's existence found Oxnam serving on the executive committee and the advisory committee. Oxnam's role in helping shape the council's position on public affairs was ranging. When in 1947 and again in 1950 the council convened a National Study Conference on the

Church and Economic Life, he helped draft the statements of principles.

Concurrently, Charles P. Taft, lay president of the Federal Council, 1946–1948, was writing America's foremost Protestant businessmen urging their attendance at the council-sponsored conferences. "I think it is extremely important to get a good business representation for the [Pittsburgh] meeting," Taft cautioned General Electric's Charles Wilson. "The trouble with the church pronouncements in the past has been that they come from a one-sided and badly informed group." Taft also issued invitations to business people to become members of the new Department of Church and Economic Life, explaining to a Standard Oil executive, "The preachers and the teachers, a decent and open-minded bunch, get only the left wing viewpoint of Hansen or Gilbert, as interpreted in the New Republic or the Nation, or the cockeyed and fallacious economics of the CIO News or its economic monthly, all presented by people who lay appealing emphasis on the human factor." In fairness to Taft, he specifically stated he was not calling for "a hysterical anti-communist witch hunt" and described his own economic philosophy as being "pretty close to the middle of the road." Taft and Oxnam liked and respected each other. "I have never met a finer Christian layman," said the bishop of Taft; and on the eve of Oxnam's appearance before HUAC he received from Taft a supporting note: "More power to you when you put your head in the Lion's Den." Nevertheless, Taft's sincerely motivated wooing of business lay persons was in time to cause Oxnam a lot of woe.

Foreign affairs was a second area of Federal Council concern implicating Oxnam. He persuaded, as we know, the advisory committee of the wisdom of having Dulles continue as chairman of the Commission on a Just and Durable Peace, arguing, "The mere fact he has powerful political responsibilities does not mean that he cannot serve as a Christian layman. If we say we cannot have a man of his strength in the Council because he has other responsibilities, then we are saying to all laymen of ability, 'We cannot use you.' " One piece of information Dulles brought from the political world of Washington to the church world is of vast interest. On *June 6, 1947*, Dulles informed Oxnam: "Confidentially, we now know that the Russians will have an atomic bomb, we think within a year." Certainly, the Truman administration failed to share this prediction with the American people! In March 1949, the council sponsored a third National Study Conference on the Churches and World Order. Oxnam helped in the arrangements, presided at one session, gave an address, and helped draft, together with Dulles and Niebuhr and others, a statement on Soviet-American relations.

Even as Oxnam gave unstintingly of himself to the Federal Council, he advised the planning committee for the proposed National Council of the Churches of Christ in the United States of America. The idea of bringing together the Federal Council with other interdenominational cooperative agencies concerned with home and foreign missions, education, and other matters, had been germinating since December 1941, and by the end of the decade a time of blossoming had come. The Constituting Convention of the National Council of Churches, held in Cleveland in late November 1950, witnessed the representatives of twenty-nine denominations with a combined membership of thirty-three million affix their signatures to the constitution of this new body and twelve interdenominational agencies certify the transfer of their several assets and responsibilities to it. Needless to say, Oxnam was present, one of four presiding officers.

The National Council was not an organic union of denominations; it was not a super-Church; it was always responsible to the member churches. It was, said its first president, Bishop Sherrill, "just what our name implies, a *council* of churches." The council was a vehicle wherein the varied constituents—ranging from Episcopalians to Quakers and from Methodists to Old Catholics—might give expression to their common faith and witness. It was not even a "pan-Protestant" organization for four charter families came from non-Protestant Eastern traditions and in 1952 the large Greek Orthodox Archdiocese of North and South America joined. (As early as 1946 Archbishop Athenogoras had informed Oxnam that his church was ready to do so.) Finally, it was a council of *some* of the Churches of Christ in the U.S.A. Major denominations such as the Southern Baptist Convention and the Missouri Synod Lutherans and American

Lutherans elected to walk separate paths. For differing reasons such groups as the Christian Scientists, Mormons, and Unitarian/Universalists remained out, either voluntarily or by council mandate. Conservative Christians patently found more comfortable homes in the American Council of Christian Churches or the National Association of Evangelicals.

Henry Pitney Van Dusen characterized the council's highly complicated administrative structure as "the most complex and intricate piece of ecclesiastical machinery this planet has ever witnessed." It is not mandatory to attempt a description here. It is important to note how deeply Oxnam plunged into the council's life and work.

He was present at the General Assemblies meeting biennially and then triennially. Throughout the decade he was a member of the powerful General Board meeting bimonthly. He chaired the Committee on Appraisal of Programs and Budgets which in 1952 submitted a twenty-four-page document charting the future organizational course for the council. He then chaired a new Committee on Study and Adjustment to carry on the organizational self-examination. He was a member of the Department of the Church and Economic Life, headed first by his Methodist friend Arthur S. Flemming and then Taft. In 1957 he was elected a council vice-president to head the Division of Christian Life and Work with its departments dealing with economic life, social welfare, international affairs, race relations, and others. At one time or another he was a member or chairman of the Department of Religious Liberty, the Department of International Justice, the General Policy and Strategy Committee, the Committee on Reference and Counsel, and the Committee on Study and Program. He spoke at the 1953 Fourth National Study Conference and gave the keynote address at the 1958 Fifth National Study Conference with its theme "Christian Responsibility on a Changing Planet." In 1954 he joined with William A. Brown, Jr., Howard Bowen, and John Bennett in writing for the council (under a grant from the Rockefeller Foundation) a volume entitled *Christian Values and Economic Life*. He threw his weight behind the debated decision to establish the council's headquarters at the new, massive Interchurch Center in New York. The fact that Methodist Bishop William Martin followed Sherrill as council president surely did not diminish Oxnam's influence in council affairs; nor did the subsequent election of Presbyterian Eugene Carson Blake. Not surprisingly, Oxnam sometimes wondered if he could afford permitting council business to consume a day or two each week.

Shortly after the National Council's formation, a conservative Protestant paper warned its readers not to assume that Oxnam would become less visible than he was in the old Federal Council: "Bishop Oxnam is simply in a more powerful place to promote his kingdom-of-God program. . . . We believe he realizes this also. And any who question it are just deceiving themselves." The warning was in order. It may well be that Oxnam's finest service to the National Council was in standing up to a group known as the National Lay Committee.

The National Council was not intended to be cleric-ridden. In truth, it was universally held that lay support and participation would determine its fate. From the onset, increased lay involvement was sought, continuing Taft's efforts in that direction as president of the old Federal Council. The delegates to the 1950 Constituting Convention elected Charles E. Wilson as treasurer, James L. Kraft as associate treasurer, and Harvey S. Firestone, Jr., as chairman of the standing committee on business and finance. Among other committed laymen active in council affairs were Chester Bernard, president of New Jersey Bell, Paul Hoffman, president of Studebaker, J. Irwin Miller, chairman of Cummins Engine, Noel Sargent, secretary of the National Association of Manufacturers (N.A.M.), Charles Hook, chairman of Armco, and John Holmes of Swift.

Oxnam could work in harness with these individuals—or most of them—just as he teamed with such moderate conservatives as Taft and Parlin. But the National Lay Committee was another matter altogether. Composed mostly of Episcopalians and United Presbyterians, few of whom were active leaders in their denominations, its spearheads were banker B. E. Hutchison, Du Pont's Jasper Crane, and above all J. Howard Pew of Sun Oil Company, whose family was perhaps the fifth richest in the nation. The genesis of the National Lay Committee stemmed not only from the desire to increase lay participation but also from the need to secure the financial support of individuals of large means, the fear being that denominational contributions could not alone underwrite the council's projected expanded program. This was playing a dangerous game as Oxnam warned as early as the first meeting of the newly elected General Board on December 2, 1950.

The Lay Committee was an anomaly in that it had no formal place in the constitutional structure of the council; it was never made a regular standing committee of the General Board. Members of the committee, of course, could be and were elected to the General Board, and as a concession, an additional ten committee members could sit on the General Board as consultants without voting privileges. Unsurprisingly, Pew and his associates were not content with an "overarching advisory" status. They sought virtual empowerment to countermand decisions of the General Board, censor council public policy statements, suppress such reports as "Basic Christian Principles and Assumptions for Economic Life" and substitute their own "Manifesto," a document that Herbert Spencer would have found heartwarming. Concurrently, Oxnam was receiving reports that representatives of labor were being elbowed out of council affairs. He also learned that a gift of two hundred thousand dollars from the CIO might be rejected. He put a stop to that nonsense. "I shall see this through," he pledged to Victor Reuther. "We are not going to take money from big business and turn it down from labor."

The greatest danger was that if Pew prevailed, the council would become Sphinx-silent on public questions. Bishop Sherrill put the issue plainly: "The National Association of Manufacturers, the Chambers of Commerce, the labor unions, the American Bar Association, the Daughters of the American Revolution, and the Pope express opinions on matters of public concern. Apparently in the mind of some only the National Council should remain silent. This point of view would cause the churches of the United States to lose their prophetic function and to approximate the situation of the churches in Russia where public worship is allowed, but where no expression of opinion is allowed unless it coincides with that of the State."

President Sherrill was not an activist liberal; nor were Martin and Blake, his successors. Nevertheless, these individuals, joined by concerned clergy and lay people, including some of conservative persuasion, finally prevailed when on June 30, 1955, the Lay Committee was forced to disband. Some coins ceased to flow into the council coffers as Pew, despairing of dominating it, founded with his fortune *Christianity Today*, a journal severely critical of the council and one with an enormous circulation.

For five years Oxnam resisted the Lay Committee's ambitions —in meetings of the General Board and various committees, in correspondence, and in private sessions with Pew and associates. As the Lay Committee pressed the attack, the morale of liberal council workers plummeted, and in word and letter they thanked Oxnam for coming to their rescue. Oxnam did save, though certainly not single-handedly, the integrity of the NCC.

It has been widely charged that the liberal leadership of the National Council was bent on purging all conservative evangelicals from its ranks.[1] While constantly maintained, the indictment cannot be sustained. Oxnam's quarrel was not with evangelicals or even with moderate economic conservatives, for he could and did work with them, including the NCC's first layman president, industrialist J. Irwin Miller who, after all, believed that "our society has intrusted business with the present opportunity to lead America." What concerned Oxnam was not so much that Pew was attempting to blunt the council's moderately liberal social witness but Pew's insistence on having a major voice on public policy independent of the member churches, thereby endangering the council's internal stability. Oxnam was an economic liberal and Pew was not. Fair enough. Both men sought to shape the NCC's public positions. Again, fair enough. The difference is that the bishop carried his cause within the democratic constitutional structure of the council and the oil magnate did not.

As Oxnam's leadership in the Federal Council led to his involvement in the National Council, just so did it intimately implicate him in the affairs of the World Council of Churches. In one sense, this is surprising because we recall his yawning indifference to the great 1937 Oxford Life and Work Conference and flat-out hostility to the momentous 1937 Edinburgh Faith and Order Conference. On reflection, however, for Oxnam to have remained aloof from the powerful ecumenical stirrings of the era would have been unthinkable, such was his need to be in on mighty undertakings.

Following Oxford and Edinburgh, representatives of the churches and ecumenical organizations met in Utrecht, Holland, in May 1938 where they established a Provisional Committee of the World Council of Churches to oversee the work of the merging bodies until such time as the proposed WCC should be officially constituted. In the United States a Joint Executive Committee consisting of the American members of the Provisional Committee and representatives of the Universal Christian Council for Life and Work and the Continuation Committee on Faith and Order was formed for promotional work. It functioned until 1944, when it was succeeded by the American Committee for the World Council of Churches, the members of which were appointed by the denominations which had signified their intention to join the World Council. Oxnam was not at Utrecht and was not a member of the original Provisional Committee, but in 1941 he delivered by short-wave around the globe a Communion Sunday message in the name of the embryonic World Council, and in 1944 he became a member of the American Committee, regarding it "as one of the significant developments of the day, and am happy to be a member, so I can understand its policy from the inside."

The storm unleashed by World War II washed out the timetable of the ecumenical planners, but though the conflict consumed the lives of millions, it could not kill the dream of Christians drawing closer together. In February 1946 the Provisional Committee met in Geneva—the first fully attended meeting in seven years. Representatives from the churches of both the victorious and the vanquished nations turned to the business of naming five presidents to serve until the World Council of Churches should be constituted, set a time, 1948, and a place, Amsterdam, for the constituting assembly, and elected four individuals to fill vacancies in the Provisional Committee, Oxnam being one of two Americans tapped. This honor did not place him at the top of the WCC ladder, but it did mean an upward advance of several rungs.

In August 1946 a conference was convened at Cambridge, England, by the Provisional Committee of the World Council of

Churches and the International Missionary Council in order to set up a Commission of the Churches on International Affairs, which would act on their behalf in the field of international relations. Delegates from seventeen nations were present, Oxnam being a member of the American group. Dulles may have been the most visible American, chairing the assemblage. (He and Oxnam conferred nightly after the formal meetings.) Niebuhr may have been the most electrifying American speaker. Still, Oxnam may have been the individual most responsible for the actual creation of the commission. He cut through the obfuscating debate of the Continentals concerning the nature of the Church's ecumenical task in the realm of international affairs. He cut down the "cautionary words" of Britain's revered ecumenical leader J. H. Oldham by reviewing for the non-American delegates the mighty achievements (as Oxnam believed) of the Federal Council's Commission on a Just and Durable Peace and The Methodist Church's Crusade for a New World Order. "We had never dreamed that any such work had been done by churches anywhere," cried the Swiss theologian Emil Brunner. Maybe Oxnam's words really were the turning point. Anyhow, two days later the charter was adopted and the Commission of the Churches on International Affairs was authorized and charged with making a formal report at Amsterdam in 1948. The four Americans elected to membership on the commission were Dulles, Niebuhr, Episcopal Bishop G. A. Oldham—and Oxnam. He was now up the WCC ladder another rung or two.

Between Cambridge and Amsterdam Oxnam met periodically with the American Committee of the WCC, presided at a WCC occasion honoring the visiting archbishop of Canterbury, saw to it that Methodism's financial responsibilities to the WCC were honored, and made the case for the WCC before various Methodist assemblies. When the Provisional Committee met for the first time in America in April 1947, Oxnam of course was present, terming it "one of the most significant experiences of my life, a meeting from which may come an organization that will change the course of the Church, perhaps of the world." Perhaps he was not totally surprised when Ralph Diffendorfer informed him in January 1948 on the eve of Amsterdam that his name was being widely mentioned as a first president of the body soon to be formally constituted. Perhaps Oxnam was not totally dissimulating when he replied that he really hungered for more time to be with his family, not the assumption of new church burdens. Then again, perhaps such was his sense of duty and so great was the possible honor that the issue was never in doubt in his mind.

The Assembly called to organize the World Council of Churches convened at Amsterdam in August 1948. There were 351 official delegates and nearly as many alternates registered from 135 denominations in 44 countries. Consultants, fraternal representatives of various ecumenical and confessional organizations, accredited visitors, staff members, 242 press and radio reporters, and observers brought the total of those who had come for the meeting to approximately 1,500. It was the most representative gathering of Christian churches in history, embracing every major branch of Christianity except Roman Catholicism and the Russian Orthodox Church. (For reasons of their own, the Southern Baptist Convention and Missouri Synod Lutherans declined the invitation, not surprisingly, for they had elected to remain out of the Federal Council of Churches.) What transpired during those fateful late August days in the Dutch capital—a city in a festive mood to celebrate the jubilee of Queen Wilhelmina and the investiture of Princess Juliana and rejoicing to be free of Nazi occupation—is the subject of hundreds of reports, articles, and books. In these accounts the names of many ecumenical leaders figure more prominently than Oxnam's—and properly so.

Nevertheless, Oxnam was not an invisible presence at Amsterdam. *Time* magazine saw fit to place Oxnam's picture on the cover of its issue featuring Amsterdam, and almost half the story was devoted to his career, accompanied by photographs of him and quotations from him. In *Time*'s judgment, Oxnam showed himself to be "a master of organization" as chairman of the Planning Committee; he was in the "top flight" of the "new leadership rising in the new World Council." Daniel A. Poling, editor of the influential *Christian Herald*, covered Amsterdam, and his description of Oxnam's role contained the praise: "This story of the World Council of Churches would be incomplete without comment concerning Bishop G. Bromley Oxnam. Not since the revered Archbishop of Canterbury, William Temple, became the almost universally recognized voice of Protestant Christianity in the world, has any man grown to the intellectual and executive proportions of this bishop of the American Methodist Church." Charles C. Parlin was admittedly close to Oxnam; nevertheless, his opinion deserves respect because he was chairman of the American Committee responsible for raising the money for the Assembly, was present at Amsterdam and worked with Oxnam on financial matters, and later became a president of the World Council. Parlin recalled how his heart sank at the opening sessions when delegates argued that because of financial limitations only a skeleton, paper council could be hoped for so soon after the devastating war. And then Oxnam expressed the conviction that the churches of America would be willing temporarily to carry more than their fair share of the burden and promised personally to present the cause in America. In so doing, Oxnam pledged, Americans would never attempt to dominate council affairs. Argument ceased. "Except for Bishop Oxnam," Parlin confirmed in 1960, "the great World Council of Churches, a living and functioning organization as we know it today, would not exist."

When the venerable Dr. Mott declined because of advancing age to accept nomination as one of the World Council presidents, such now was Oxnam's stature that he was an obvious choice to be the only American member of the Presidium and to represent the Free Churches. The other presidents were Archbishop Geoffrey Fisher of Canterbury (for the Anglican communion); Pastor Marc Boegner, president of the French Protestant Federation (for the Reformed churches); Archbishop Germanos of Thyateira (for the Orthodox churches); Archbishop Erling Eidem, Primate of the Church of Sweden (for the Lutherans); and Professor T. C. Chao of China (for the "younger" non-Western churches).[2] The Assembly could do no other than name Dr. Mott honorary president out of respect for this magnificent Methodist layman who for almost three score years and ten served the ecumenical cause.

Oxnam was naturally elated at his election. However, he did find it strange that there was no installation service. "A beautiful service might well have been planned for this occasion, properly photographed, and sent to the far corners of the earth," he groused. Privately he found his fellow presidents, except for Fisher, too old, looking "like cadavers suddenly come to life" and "casting gruesome shadows." Moreover, as presiding officers, "Eidem and Germanos are impossible, and Boegner poses." (However, when Germanos died in 1951 Oxnam attended the service and recalled the Greek's sweet, kindly spirit.) Thanks to Oxnam's insistence and over Fisher's objections, New York Methodist Sockman preached at the final service, clearly outshining (Oxnam believed) both Bishop Dibelius of Berlin and Pierre Maury of Paris.

The fact is that practical finance and organizational matters, not theological ones, were Oxnam's primary contribution to the birth of the WCC. He was chairman of Committee III on Program and Administration. The responsibility was heavy. A council without funding to sustain it would be stillborn. Oxnam and his committee sweated blood and shed some, too. The brilliant WCC general secretary, Dutch theologiean W. A. Visser 't Hooft, thought a budget of general totals would suffice; Oxnam held that budgets are not made that way and insisted on detailed itemization. The American ecumenicist Henry Smith Leiper thought that the old method of appealing to private benefactors would suffice; Oxnam held that if the council was truly to be one of churches, then denominations, not individuals, should be principal supporters. The British leader Dr. Oldham and the archbishop of Canterbury thought that the British churches, gutted by the war, could not possibly increase their support; Oxnam held that these churches *collectively* might reasonably be expected to contribute more than their present \$5,000. When Oxnam reported his committee's recommendations to the Assembly, they were adopted without debate and unanimously. "I was amazed," he recorded. "I had memorized the figures, anticipating a severe barrage of questioning, but they appeared satisfied with the presentation and were kind." The adopted budget for 1949 totaled \$363,000, excluding the Department of Inter-Church Aid and Service to Refugees. (John D. Rockefeller, Jr., added a gift of \$60,000 for an Ecumenical Institute.) The member churches were to provide \$300,000; and of this sum,

$240,000, or 80 percent, was assigned to American churches, with The Methodist Church being the most generous of all council benefactors.[3]

The authority of the Assembly of the Council passed upon adjournment at Amsterdam to nearby Woudscotten where the Central Committee and smaller Executive Committee held their first meetings. Oxnam by virtue of being a president was automatically a member of both; and almost automatically he was elected chairman of the Finance Committee. The night before returning to the States he assessed his feelings: "It is a dazed mind, but a happy heart. I think I am leaving the World Council with many friends, I trust with respect, and certainly with opportunity at the key posts to be influential in this very great enterprise, which may some day take its place among the first events of church history."

During his six-year term as a member of the Presidium Oxnam estimated that his WCC duties cut into his schedule "terrifically," chewing up thirty or forty days annually, but, he quickly added, "they are worth it." He was on the Executive Committee of the Commission of the Churches on International Affairs, formed to be the world affairs agency of the WCC and the International Missionary Council. He also served as chairman of the United States Conference for the World Council of Churches. Its responsibilities included interpreting the WCC to the member denominations in the United States; administering in America the programs of the different departments of the WCC; and securing financial support for the WCC. "I feel somehow that this setup is kind of fifth wheel but don't know what to do about it," he mused.

It was as finance chairman perhaps even more than as a president that Oxnam most helpfully served the World Council, and for this he received tribute after tribute. Being the conscientious and precise man that he was, he did not lollygag at this labor. He was guided by the following principles. Support should be sought from the member churches to give them a stake in *their* council; while contributions from concerned individuals were welcome, private gifts must not become primary. Second, support should be sought from all and not only from the largest and most affluent churches. This meant reducing the contribution to the budget from U.S. churches to 70 percent by 1953. Third, a deficit must be avoided and a reserve fund established.

Normally in the inevitable debates at the meetings of the Central Committee and the Executive Committee, Oxnam's voice was heard in matters relating to finances, administration, and public policy, but at Toronto in 1950 his convictions compelled him to criticize a report entitled "The Ecclesiological Significance of the World Council of Churches." The linchpin sentence that sparked intense debate read: "There is a place in the World Council both for those churches which recognize other churches as churches in the full and true sense and for those who do not." Finally Oxnam's patience slipped from his hands. He arose and proposed to amend the report to read that the World Council is a fellowship of some true, healthy, and complete churches in cooperation with some untrue, unhealthy, and incomplete churches. He then suggested it would be necessary to go further and strike out the word "fellowship" because the council under such circumstances would have ceased to be a fellowship; and if this were true, it would be wise to strike out all reference to our blessed Lord, because the members would have long since departed his spirit. Oxnam lost the debate. The document adopted by the Central Committee and commended to the member churches for study contained the statement: "The member Churches of the World Council consider the relationship of other Churches to the Holy Catholic Church which the Creed professes as a subject for mutual consideration. Nevertheless, membership does not imply that each Church must regard the other member Churches as Churches in the true and full sense of the word." Oxnam of course believed the statement un-Christlike. Visser 't Hooft in his *Memoirs* held to the contrary that "the very originality of the World Council was precisely that it sought to create fellowship between churches who were not yet able to give full recognition to each other." In his judgment, the Toronto statement allayed fears that the council would become a "Super-Church" and, moreover, opened the doors to the Russian Orthodox Church and to closer fellowship with the Roman Catholic Church.

The Toronto exchange is a concrete illustration of a larger generalization. On balance, Oxnam exasperated many WCC theologians and ecclesiologists, especially those across the seas. At the same time and for the same reasons he was admired for his leadership by WCC pragmatists, especially Americans, and also by theologians such as Muelder and Van Dusen who resisted the domination of the WCC by Continental Barthians.

The Central Committee met in Lucknow, India, December 31, 1952 to January 8, 1953, as guests of Isabella Thoburn College, a school bearing the name of its Methodist missionary founder. Its principal was Sarah Chakko, who in 1951 had been elected a president of the WCC, the first woman and the first lay person so honored. Oxnam revered her. Together the American bishop and the Indian principal were primarily responsible for the Central Committee's first meeting in Asia.

This was a matter of great moment in the life of the WCC. The Amsterdam Assembly had been dominated by North Americans and Britishers and Continentals and its central themes and concerns were Western. To be sure, from the beginning there was a small and growing interest in the "younger churches" of Asia and Latin America, and later of Africa, but delegates from these churches filled only two-thirds of the mere fifty seats reserved for them at Amsterdam. In the minds of many Westerners, Asia, Latin America, and Africa were still "mission fields." The WCC leadership was not unaware of this unfortunate orientation. The issue was fully confronted by the Executive Committee at a meeting in Bièvres, France, in January 1951. Principal Chakko informed the group that it would be disastrous for the Second Assembly to convene as scheduled in the United States in 1953 before the Executive Committee or Central Committee ever had met on Asian soil. Oxnam sensed that she was expressing not merely the East's irritation but that area's deep hostility to the West's arrogance. Alerted, the chairman of the Central Committee, G. K. A. Bell, bishop of Chichester, appointed Oxnam to chair a committee to bring in a revised schedule of meeting places and dates. The committee recommended that the Second Assembly in America be postponed to 1954 in order that the Central Committee might first convene in

India. Oxnam was convinced of the wisdom of the recommendation and so was the WCC.

Despite an epidemic of influenza which decimated the delegates and the infernal howling of the ubiquitous monkeys, Oxnam considered the Lucknow meeting the best in the brief history of the WCC. Principal Chakko was a marvelous host. The Asian delegates were informed and informing, and a clear advance was made in East-West understanding. Oxnam's finance report was accepted without modification. Nehru's address to the Central Committee was profound. Moreover, in New Dehli Oxnam was entertained at the Government House and was granted an interview with Nehru. "I had wondered what Nehru would be like," he recorded. "There is always the danger that such a person had been idealized. I have read all of his books, I think, that are in English and had come to regard him as one of the truly great men of our day. There is always that moment of actual meeting when dreams are dissipated and a man stands before you with the limitations of humanity. Nehru measured up in every sense."

Oxnam performed another service at Lucknow. Three theologians had drafted a New Year's message. A correspondent for the International News Service complained to Oxnam that it was incomprehensible. Oxnam agreed it was "terrible stuff." The bishop of Chichester and Visser 't Hooft asked him to rewrite the message. "I do not know whether my low tastes are in keeping with the demands of I.N.S. or not, but in any case they used it," he reported.

Oxnam's sagacity and powers of persuasion resulted in another action taken at Lucknow of unestimable significance for the WCC's future. At an earlier meeting of the Central Committee he had advanced the thought that the WCC constitution be changed to read, "A President shall be ineligible for re-election when his term of office ends." The proposition now came before the Lucknow delegates. The debate was heated, the amendment being opposed by such formidable individuals as Dr. Boegner, Archbishop Brillioth, and the bishop of Malmesbury. Oxnam was permitted the privilege of closing the debate. The possible reelection of one or two presidents and the defeat of the other members of the six-person Presidium would result in hurt personal feelings and perhaps embittered communions, he maintained. Secondly, there was a danger in thinking that the holder of a particular office must be, or remain, a president. (Privately Oxnam feared that the Anglicans assumed that the archbishop of Canterbury had a permanent lock on one of the presidencies.) Finally, he was certain that no individual was indispensable and that in such a great body as the WCC surely there was a reservoir of talented souls from all corners of the globe. Oxnam won by a vote of thirty-six to eleven. In advancing this amendment Oxnam was of course unselfishly foreclosing the possibility of his own reelection.[4]

In a letter to the Washington Area ministers Oxnam sketched his busy schedule, writing in passing, "As a rule, World Council meetings are like a trip to Chicago. Ordinarily, I would leave New York on a Tuesday night plane, attend sessions at London, Paris, or Geneva on Wednesday, Thursday, and Friday, and be back home on Saturday morning." The operative word in that sentence is "ordinarily." But not "always." Considering his conscientiousness as a council officer, it may be unsporting to note that on occasion he crossed the ocean wrapped in the luxury of the liners *Mauritania, Queen Mary,* and *United States.* On occasion, too, for every business day abroad he spent a week vacationing. On these trips Ruth often joined him. This observation is in no sense a rebuke, save only to wonder if the ministers of the Areas he served had any idea that their absent bishop's waking hours were not totally spent in the service of the Church.

Almost from the day of the adjournment of the Amsterdam Assembly Oxnam was heavily involved in planning for the Second Assembly originally scheduled to be held in 1953 but postponed until 1954, as we have seen, at his recommendation in order that the Central Committee might first meet in Asia. Oxnam was chairman of the Committee on Arrangements for the Second Assembly and according to Sam Cavert, who was in a position to know, "carried the heavy end of all the practical planning." Robert S. Bilheimer gave yeoman's service as executive secretary. Oxnam was largely responsible for the selection of Evanston, Illinois, as the place of meeting. The home of Northwestern University on the shores of Lake Michigan, this verdant, affluent suburb just north of Chicago Oxnam considered ideal. Other communities and other schools (including Yale and Cornell) sought unavailingly the honor of housing the gathering. Midcontinent Evanston was tapped because delegates would be coming from across the Atlantic and from across the Pacific. Even for United States delegates the Midwest represented a compromise. Moreover, Oxnam explained, he desired that visitors from abroad "see us the way I think we are," and that meant Middle America, not New York City. Northwestern University offered to house and feed the delegates for a mere $3.50 per day (Cornell's bid was $4.50) and contribute $25,000 to the Assembly travel budget. Garrett Biblical Institute (Methodist), Seabury-Western Theological Seminary (Episcopal), and the First Methodist Church placed their full facilities at the disposal of the Assembly. Finally, consciously or unconsciously Oxnam may have been influenced by the fact that Evanston in its origins was a Methodist community and evidence of this was everywhere, including the "Cathedral of American Methodism," First Church. Northwestern University was Methodist in its origins and as late as 1954 retained Methodist ties. Methodist layman Dean James Alton James had long been a leader in the world ecumenical movement, and in 1949 First Church had hosted the very first meeting of the American Conference of Member Churches of the WCC, Oxnam being present. In March 1950 Oxnam traveled to Evanston, conferred with Northwestern's president, Dr. J. Roscoe Miller, the mayor of Evanston, and other officials. What he saw and heard was favorable, and in July he moved that the Central Committee agree on Evanston, and it did. Oxnam proudly made the announcement "as a member of the great American free church tradition, whose roots are so firmly embedded in the Midwest." [5]

In addition to playing a pivotal role in selecting the site of the Second Assembly, Oxnam was instrumental in having President Eisenhower address the gathering. Thanks to Dulles's intercession, Oxnam and three WCC officials—Fry, Nolde, and Bilheimer—went to the White House on April 2, 1953 to extend an invitation. The meeting was brief but cordial, Eisenhower expressing a warm interest but unwilling to make a firm commitment. On November 4 Oxnam saw the president's appointment secretary, Thomas E. Stephens, repeated the invitation, and requested permission to present Visser 't Hooft to the president on November 19. Oxnam then wrote a follow-up letter and the meeting took place on schedule. The invitation was again repeated and on returning to his office Oxnam put in writing what had been said to the president orally. To Eisenhower, August seemed a long way off and he remained unable to firmly say yea or nay. With time running out, Oxnam wrote Stephens on March 16, 1954, and April 7 pleading for a decision. Meanwhile, the White House was receiving numerous communications protesting the possible presence in Evanston of churchmen from behind the Iron Curtain, and it is clear that some of Eisenhower's advisors were warning him not to risk political contamination by addressing the WCC. In fact, on May 12, Stephens flatly informed Oxnam that Eisenhower would not be present. However, in late May the president changed his mind and so informed Sam Cavert, and finally on July 23 Oxnam received an affirming letter from Stephens. Naturally Oxnam found Eisenhower's indecision worrisome, but in the end the bishop's tenacity prevailed.

The absence of the American president would have wounded the Second Assembly; the absence of Christians from Communist countries would have killed its being held in the United States. More than any single other individual, Oxnam saved the day for the WCC—and America.

On March 3, 1953, Fredrick Nolde, WCC associate general secretary, asked Secretary of State Dulles if there would be any difficulty in obtaining from the government visas for WCC delegates from behind the Iron Curtain in light of the restrictions imposed by the 1952 McCarran-Walter Act, a dangerous measure passed over Truman's veto at the height of the Great Red Scare. Dulles replied "that there would be very great difficulty under present law and the present state of public opinion." On the morning of April 2, before Dulles met with Oxnam, Nolde, Fry, and Bilheimer, and before the group met with Eisenhower, Dulles had called Attorney General Herbert Brownell to seek his judgment; the tentative answer was not reassuring. Four days later Oxnam wrote Dulles: "You have done all that any man could do, and more than we had a right to expect, in helping us solve a very difficult situation. If it be we must cancel the Assembly . . . , I believe the action will be misunderstood in influential quarters in the major nations of the earth. I believe there will be a critical reaction throughout our own country." Nevertheless, Oxnam absolved Dulles of all responsibility should the WCC be forced to meet in Toronto rather than Evanston. At this juncture the United States was close to being disgraced in the eyes of the world by forcing the Second Assembly to meet outside its borders. On October 30 Oxnam, Fry, Nolde, and Bilheimer again saw Dulles. The secretary of state wanted the WCC officers to pledge that the Communist country delegates were worthy of entering the United States; that is, assume the responsibility for their thought and behavior. Oxnam responded that the member churches had full right to select their own representatives and that the WCC officers had no veto authority. Senator McCarran now announced that the "Red" churchmen might enter "as long as they mind their own business, leave when they are supposed to, and don't participate in sabotage or propaganda against this country." Oxnam continued to correspond with Dulles. Dulles continued to confer with Brownell—and presumably the two cabinet officers continued to counsel with the White House. Finally on November 9 Dulles informed Oxnam that "I have . . . spoken to the Attorney General and he had indicated that he would be sympathetic to granting visas upon my recommendation where there is discretion to do so under the law."

Ultimately twenty delegates came to Evanston from Czechoslovakia, Hungary, and East Germany.[6] The most famous of these individuals was the eloquent Dr. Joseph L. Hromadka, dean of the John Hus Theological Faculty, Prague, who was to be honored at Evanston by election to the Executive Committee. The most suspected was Bishop Janos Peter of the Reformed Church of Hungary who was a member of the Hungarian Parliament, although Bishop Albert Berecky of the same church also was known as a critic of the West in the Cold War. Among these twenty delegates, fifteen had no restrictions upon their activities while in the United States and were thus in the same position as all other delegates from any part of the world. Four were limited merely by the requirement that they should accept speaking engagements only on religious subjects and only under the auspices of religious organizations. One delegate, Bishop Peter, was granted full freedom of expression and participation only at Assembly sessions.

Naturally the presence of these "Iron Curtain churchmen" brought a howl of outrage from conservative Protestants and Catholics and from patriotic and ethnic societies; indeed, Representative Bentley demanded that the Hungarian delegates appear for questioning before his House Subcommittee. Of course they were advised not to do so, and the WCC leadership reprimanded Bentley for his "impropriety."

"Christ—the Hope of the World"—this was the theme that drew many thousands to Evanston. At 11:00 A.M., Sunday, August 15, the organ of the First Methodist Church rang forth the stirring Reformation chorale "A Mighty Fortress Is Our God" as a great procession of church leaders garbed in stunning variety moved through the doors. After the opening order of service conducted in English, French, Greek, and German, Oxnam rose to preach the sermon. For one of the few times in his life he confessed that while waiting, "nervousness just about got me down." The sanctuary was hot and his robe heavy. His mouth was dry. His words were to be heard by millions via radio and television—and only moments earlier he had been ordered by the television people to cut the sermon by five minutes. Above all, he knew the council had been racked by theological disputation over eschatology—that is, what is the true meaning of "Christ—the Hope of the World"? Would the division widen at Evanston and split the council asunder?

After many false starts in preparing the sermon, Oxnam had decided to take as his text the message and pledge of the Amsterdam Assembly: *"We intend to stay together."* Recalling the familiar, reassuring words of St. Paul, Oxnam beat the refrain "There can be no separation from the Eternal nor from each other when we stand in His love." The sermon closed: "Nothing can separate us from the love of God. Let the Redeemed of the Lord say so. Jesus Christ is to become the Ruler of the kings of the earth. King of Kings and Lord of Lords. In this faith, *we intend to stay together."* The sermon contained many good things. Oxnam spoke of the kindling fellowship he had experienced working and worshiping with his council colleagues: "I was unaware of the fact that my brother was Scotch or Russian or German or American; I did not think of the communion he represented; I knew we were brothers, united in love, loyal to our Blessed Lord, children of one Father. We were together. *We intend to stay together*." He spoke at length of his own father, the Cornish miner. He humbly admitted that his faith had been cost-free: "I have read of faggots and of lash and of the goodly company of martyrs. But for me, it has been too much a matter of appropriating the benefits of Calvary rather than of sharing in Calvary that the world might be redeemed." He summoned Christ's followers to seek the end of economic exploitation and war: "It must be made clear that we dare not identify the Gospel of Jesus with any historically conditioned political, social, or economic system. The Gospel stands in judgment of all of them. . . . The Christian Gospel is not to be found in Adam Smith's 'Wealth of Nations' nor in Karl Marx's 'Das Kapital.' It is to be found in Matthew, Mark, Luke, and John, in the Acts of the Apostles, the Epistles of the New Testament, and in the vision of John in the Revelation. It is to be found in the Hebrew prophets, in the lives of saints and martyrs, in the service of the faithful followers of Christ, and in the continued revelation of God."

It was a compelling sermon. Writing to Henry Pitney Van Dusen on the eve of Evanston, Oxnam set forth his intent: "I have sought to ground the sermon in the fact that nothing can separate us from the love of God, which is in Christ Jesus our Lord. Frankly, that is where my hope lies." The sincerity of Oxnam's hope illuminates and gives conviction to his words at that solemn opening worship service of the Second Assembly.

That evening, following the afternoon opening plenary session, the Assembly delegates traveled to Chicago's Soldier Field to join 125,000 fellow Christians in a Festival of Faith. (Possibly 40,000 gathered outside the stadium's packed confines, for the festival drew the faithful from hundreds of miles away.) The assembled sang for an hour hymns of faith; heard the Chicago Symphony Orchestra and a choir of 5,000 voices; witnessed the procession of delegates eight abreast and then a pageant portraying mighty biblical themes. Even hard-bitten Chicago newspaper reporters were strangely moved when under the darkening vault of the heavens France's venerable Pastor Boegner rose to give the "interrogation." The assembled fell silent with a vast sigh. "Who are you to have come here?" rang out the solitary voice with its Gallic inflection. "We are Christians. We have come from many different traditions," responded the congregation in a rising roll of voices. "What is it to be a Christian?" The reply came back like the sound of the sea, "It is to believe in God the Father and in Jesus Christ his only Son, our Lord, the hope of the world, and in the Holy Spirit." "From where have you come?" And the response, "From 163 churches, 48 nations, and 5 continents." "Why have you come?" "We have come to worship God."

As the festival drew to a close, Oxnam left the platform where he had been seated with the other members of the Presidium. Charged with pronouncing the benediction, he climbed a forty-foot pylon with orders not to say a word until a green light came on. The final chords of music ended. He waited. And waited. No flash of green light. Finally a voice shouted, "Let her rip up there!" The benediction uttered, he climbed down and was told, "Sorry, those blamed lights went out of commission." He then rushed to a waiting car and commanded the young minister-chauffeur to beat the traffic by driving in the bus lane. When the poor driver protested, Oxnam shouted, "For the love of Pete, pull out. I'll pay for a new fender." Back at his Evanston hotel he awaited hours for "poor Ruth," stuck in the impossible traffic. "It was a wonderful evening, overwhelming, and is vital testimony to the place of faith in our life," reads the last diary entry for the day.

As an outgoing president Oxnam presided at assigned Assembly sessions with his usual consummate skill and grace, but the fifth day was one of exceptional importance to him and the twenty-three thousand gathered at Northwestern's lovely Deering Meadow to hear President Eisenhower. Oxnam was asked to greet the American president on his arrival at Deering and introduce him to the council presidents. Oxnam then offered prayer, the closing words anticipating the theme of Eisenhower's address: "Grant us peace, O God, not only in our time but forever and forever, and speak again to us 'Blessed are the peace-makers, for they shall be called the children of God.' Amen."

The cordiality of Eisenhower's accompanying party was especially pleasing to Oxnam. "I was surprised," he admitted, "because it has been clear the little coterie around the President has not wanted me prominent in this visit—frightened, little people, who do not know the church and its power." As Oxnam watched Eisenhower receive the honorary LL.D., surely his memory returned to Monday evening when Northwestern had conferred on him and the other council presidents honorary S.T.D.'s.

The opening plenary session had been a far different and less pleasant occasion. There the delegates received a report on the racking eschatological question. For four years a committee of theologians had sought to define the council's position on the relation of the Kingdom of God to human history and the Ultimate Hope to proximate hopes. Understandably, the question was one of intense feelings, dividing purely futurists and purely realized eschatologists, quietists and activists, "pessimists" and "optimists," fundamentalists and liberals and Barthians, Continentals and Americans.

The report, simply being commended to the member churches for study and such action as they chose to take concerning it, was reviewed by Professor Edmund Schlink of the University of Heidelberg and Calhoun of Yale. McGaw Memorial Hall was hot and crowded and the acoustics wretched, but even if the physical conditions had not been irritating, Oxnam would still have found Schlink's interminable address exasperating, stressing as it did the hope found in the promise of Christ's Second Coming. "He took more than an hour," Oxnam grumbled. "If this is scholarship, then I'm a bumble bee, or whatever gets stung." As the German droned on, Oxnam whispered to Norway's Bishop Berggrav, "Bishop, Jesus could tell a simple story and everyone understood. This man gets lost in his own erudition, becomes increasingly involved, and finally confused." Berggrav whispered back, "Third rate, third rate. The Word became theology and did not dwell among us." Later another individual remarked to Oxnam, "Schlink seemed to think we do not have much time before the end of the world, but that rotter used one hour of it." Later, also, a reporter asked, "Bishop, what about this Second Coming business?" Replied Oxnam, "To me it is a contradiction in terms. If Jesus is present now, and I believe He is, why discuss a second coming? I believe He is here in all His power now. It's a terrible thing to admit, but I don't understand what they are arguing about." (Oxnam gave the American Calhoun higher marks, but then lowered the ranking by adding, "but theologians get me down at best.")

Perhaps Oxnam was wise not to be sucked into the dark whirlpool of theological confusion. Certainly he may properly have disputed Schlink's emphasis. Still, reading today the German's report one must say in honesty: Right or wrong, here is a Christian struggling to come to an existential understanding of a question central to the Christian faith. Further, the division was not strictly between Americans and Continentals, Methodists and Barthians, for American Methodist theologian Albert C. Outler gave this judgment on the eschatology debates at Evanston: "The Assembly's wrestling with its high theme was something less than a resounding triumph. And yet, no single event in the Council's history has done so much to demonstrate the common footing beneath the swirling tides of theological confusion. Evanston helped us all to realize, more vividly than we had done before, that our hope is in Jesus Christ, that He is the hope of the world."

It must not be assumed that Oxnam was critical of all those who addressed the Assembly. To the contrary, to cite only a few names receiving praise, he employed such superlatives as "great," "magnificent," "really superb," "very good," to describe the utterances of Dag Hammarskjöld (secretary general of the United Nations), Visser 't Hooft, Nolde, Benjamin Mays, Bishop Berggrav, Bishop Dibelius, and Reinhold Niebuhr (read by Bishop Dun). Expecting political fireworks from Professor Hromadka, Oxnam heard instead "a scholarly and Biblical discourse."

A full account of the Evanston Assembly must be found elsewhere, although some reference in later chapters will be made to positions taken relative to economic, racial, and international questions. Even Oxnam's full involvement cannot be sketched, such as the meetings of the Executive Committee,

Steering Committee, Finance Committee, and the celebration of Holy Communion according to the rite of The Methodist Church in the First Methodist Church on Sunday, August 22.

On the evening of August 30 Oxnam wrote in his diary: "The days are beginning to tell on my nerves, and I shall be glad when the final adjournment is pronounced. So far the spirit has been excellent. There has been no harsh word, and I think we have demonstrated there is something here far more significant than discussion. It is the fact of love within the faith." The following morning he took the chair as retiring American president at the last plenary session. Others spoke of course. It was he, however, who thanked by name those who had made the convocation possible, including unknown aides and stewards, interpreters and translators. Because some of the delegates, he observed, would be returning to tasks of great difficulty and others to posts of grave danger, he thought it fitting that the audience read together the Twenty-third Psalm—as previously they had sung "O God Our Help in Ages Past." The plenary session ended with an act of worship as the six incoming presidents were recognized, individuals commended by Oxnam as members of "an endless line of splendor, those troops with heaven for a home." He offered prayer, the Assembly sang "Love Divine, All Loves Excelling," and the proceedings were brought to an end with the Aaronic Blessing. That night Oxnam entered in his diary the words, "Anyone who thinks the Church of Jesus Christ is defeated had better think again." [7]

The adjournment of the Second Assembly found Oxnam no longer a president or chairman of the Finance Committee. Nonetheless, The Methodist Church elected him as one of its representatives on the Central Committee, and the Central Committee in turn tapped him as one of its representatives on the smaller, more powerful Executive Committee. He remained on the Finance Committee and continued as a member of the Commission of the Churches and International Affairs. These responsibilities meant continued travels within the States and across the seas.

The diaries are replete with descriptions of those individuals with whom he worked in the World Council. With only a couple of exceptions, he admired his colleagues. Some of the vignettes are lovely. Once when Oxnam was presiding at a meeting in Chichester, Fisher arrived late (as was his habit), disrupting the proceedings as the delegates rose to greet him. Visser 't Hooft whispered to Oxnam to honor Fisher by asking him to say a few words. Oxnam refused, simply announcing instead: "I am very happy to note present a distinguished gentleman *who has come all the way from England* to be with us, the archbishop of Canterbury." Traveling by train with Bishop Berggrav, the Primate of Norway who had courageously resisted the Nazis, Oxnam described him bundled in a great coat, a great bottle of cognac in one pocket, puffing on a great meerschaum pipe, and remarking, "Isn't it wonderful to have a bad heart so one can have a good excuse for cognac?"

For their part, the WCC leadership appreciated Oxnam. "We are terribly sorry to hear that we are not likely to see you again in the meetings of the World Council," wrote Visser 't Hooft in 1961, "and we find it difficult to imagine those meetings without you. Ever since 1948 you have played such a very important role in our deliberations and given so much of your time and energy to ecumenical affairs that you have become a seemingly indispensable part of the fellowship." Mott, in resolutions and handwritten notes, expressed gratitude for Oxnam's providential leadership. Fisher told him that "I have always enjoyed immensely your clarity of mind and decisiveness of judgment and wisdom." The bishop of Chichester, Bell, chairman of the Central Committee, and Fry, Bell's successor, both honored Oxnam's contributions. Wrote Bishop Sherrill: "You have been such a tower of strength . . . to the ecumenical movement, wise, indefatigable and courageous. I think that the magnitude of your work will only be fully realized when an attempt is made to fill your place. My guess is that a small army will be required." Future council presidents Parlin and Niemöller gave statements whose tenors can easily be guessed. Roswell Barnes said, "He certainly found life—abundant life—by losing it, giving it, for Christ's sake and the Gospel."

As has been suggested, perhaps some theologians, especially Europeans, might have been more reserved in their judgments. A letter from Liston Pope to Sherrill in 1958 indicated that a second group had less than positive thoughts about Oxnam.

Pope explained that there was not much hope in securing WCC support from the Lilly Foundation because the "Lilly trustees think of Bishop Oxnam whenever they think of the World Council of Churches, and they do not like Bishop Oxnam very much!"

Oxnam's journeys were not confined to WCC business. In the summer of 1951, the Greek Orthodox Church issued invitations to a two-week celebration of the nineteen hundredth anniversary of the visit of Paul to Greece. Oxnam (joined by Phil) was named to represent the NCC and The Methodist Church. Phil recounted the journey in a charming, moving inspirational article for the readers of the *Christian Advocate*. The tale unfolded in his father's diary, however, is quite different in tone: Greek mismanagement, awful rooms and food, dysentery, sea sickness, delayed schedules, endless lectures, excessive ceremony.

In early 1955 and again late in that year, Oxnam conducted retreats for Methodist chaplains and their wives stationed in Europe, North Africa, and the Near East in his capacity as chairman of the Methodist Commission on Chaplains. Doubtless the Army generals whom he met were pleased to read his statement given to the press on his return. The Army leadership, he opined, were deeply concerned with the moral and spiritual welfare of the troops. To picture American soldiers as participating in "sin orgies" is "unforgivable false witness" and turns attention away from the "great rank and file of clean living, patriotic, and decent American youth in uniform."

From Germany Bromley and Ruth traveled to Budapest. The occasion was the centennial of the Budapest Reformed Theological Academy of the Reformed Church of Hungary. Oxnam was one of eleven churchmen selected to receive honorary degrees; among the others were Barth, Niemöller, John Baille of Scotland, and John Mackay of America. On landing at the Budapest airport the Oxnams were certain they were placed under immediate surveillance. The atmosphere was stifling. Nevertheless, the people were "very, very kind" and the congregational singing magnificent. "I wonder what it means," Bromley mused. "Is it possible to express the yearning for something else in song that you cannot express in speech?"

Oxnam's known presence in Hungary prompted Representative Francis E. Walter to send him a radiogram in care of the U.S. embassy in Vienna requesting that while he was in Budapest to receive an honorary degree from "communist governmental clergy" that he "please ascertain the possibility of the speedy release of fellow man of the cloth Cardinal Mindszenty." [8] Oxnam was tempted to reply (but did not) that unfortunately Cardinal Mindszenty could not be admitted into the United States under the McCarran-Walter Act. Oxnam did make inquiries of his Reformed Church hosts as to the Catholic prelate's fate and was informed that it was their understanding that he had been released. "I do not know on what they base their information," Oxnam subsequently told the press, "but they are honorable men and I am satisfied they told me all they knew. It is possible they may have got their information from the newspapers and of course what appears in the newspapers is put there by the government." At dinner one night he was seated next to an American-born Hungarian woman whose parents had been deported in 1934. Even Representative Walter would have been proud of the American bishop's reply to her criticism of U.S. foreign policy: "You call us imperialists, but the truth of the matter is the only time we ever moved out in any war and took over territory involved the Philippines and we promised to give them freedom and they have it. Consequently, when you talk about the sincerity of our purpose, it is our entire history which evidences our sincerity." And this from a man then widely being accused of "un-Americanism"!

Departing Hungary for Austria, Oxnam noted, "What a world of difference there is! Maybe it was our imagination but I thought I could really breathe better when we got across that blessed border." Back in the States, Oxnam, at the request of the United States Information Service, issued a challenge over the Voice of America: "If Krushchev will guarantee the civil liberties essential to the proclamation of the Christian faith, we face the future with complete confidence. Theism is not afraid to meet atheism in the free market of ideas. The superstitions of the Communist faith will vanish before the realities of the Christian faith in any fair competition for the minds of men." He also informed Visser 't Hooft that in his judgment the WCC was making a bad mistake in having the Central Committee meet in Budapest in 1956 and that he did not intend to be present. And he shared with Bishop Sherrill this assessment of the Hungarian situation: "It was apparent . . . that the Church was under the leadership of men who were too largely tools of the present regime, but it was equally apparent that there was creative courage in the Church itself and that sooner or later that spirit would manifest itself as it did."

Oxnam may have ducked the 1956 WCC session in Hungary, but earlier in that year a meeting of the Executive Committee commanded his being in Australia, and Methodist matters extended the trip to other areas of the Pacific and Asia. He and Ruth departed on January 25 and returned on April 5. Most of the month of February was spent in Australia and New Zealand; March was devoted to a review of Methodism elsewhere. No other journey in a lifetime of travels so heavily taxed Oxnam's now ebbing energies.

Oxnam's first stop, save for touching down at Honolulu, was the island of Tonga where Queen Salote headed The Methodist Church and where Methodism most nearly approached the position of a state church in the world. His addresses impressed the queen and she, rightly, impressed him. Australia followed. Flattered at hosting the first major ecumenical meeting ever to be held in the southern hemisphere, the Aussies were determined to accord the twenty-three World Council leaders a reception they would never forget. The New Zealanders shared that conviction, although Oxnam found them slightly less relentless in their "hospitality" than their northern neighbors. What followed for Oxnam (and the other visitors) were almost four weeks of speaking engagements; broadcasts; press interviews; conferences; receptions; banquets (church- and goverment-sponsored); greetings by a crowd of forty thousand on the Royal Sydney Show Ground; a mammoth Festival of Faith attended by seventy-five thousand; tours by car, bus, and plane to Queensland, South Australia, and Tasmania—and then an uncomfortable night flight to New Zealand and a round of the same. Recorded Oxnam: "I hope I do not give the wrong impression of the visit to Australia, but as I look back on it now while dictating here in Manila, we were really exploited. The Australians seem to think they own their guests, arrange the program as suits them, announce topics without consultation and seem to assume a round of speaking three, four or five times a day. . . ." Doubtless this mordancy reflected his physical exhaustion. The ferocious schedule had left little time for sleeping and while in bed sleep had refused to come. He had suffered sharp pains around the heart and down the left arm and side. On February 20, while speaking, his memory had failed him and in his dizziness he almost blacked out. To be sure, both before and after that scare he reported having happy times speaking and meeting many gracious and friendly people, but mostly Down Under was an ordeal.

The second half of the long journey was spent visiting Methodist enterprises on authorization of the Council of Bishops. Things brightened but not to high noon. A day in Jakarta convinced Oxnam that Indonesia was "utterly impossible." Bali was "most disappointing." Staying at the Raffles Hotel in Singapore gave him the false assurance that the "British really intend to hold this place. There is no question about that." Bangkok revealed U.S. Air Force planes at the airport and the conclusion, "It is perfectly evident that millions of American dollars are being spent here, and there is a determination to hold this area." Leaving an unpleasant Thailand with no regrets, the Oxnams flew to Manila where Bromley visited Methodist churches, schools, and hospitals. Thence by *S.S. President Wilson* to Hong Kong for a round of shopping and a banquet arranged by Ruth—"a wonderful many-course affair." (Only two days earlier, just before sailing, Oxnam had summoned a doctor because of intense chest, arm, and side pains!) From Hong Kong to Japan, where Oxnam continued his Methodist inspection tour. Then the return home aboard the *Wilson*, Oxnam conducting two shipboard religious services. The first diary entry after docking reads: "There is no point in recording from April 6 to the 16th. These days have been bewildering from early morning until very late at night."

In 1958 Bishop Gerald Kennedy wrote an article entitled "Around the World in Thirty Days." The subject was a trip he and his wife Mary and the Oxnams took, October 28–November 28, 1957. The little group first flew to Japan where the bishops conducted a Methodist chaplains' retreat outside of Tokyo. Ambassador MacArthur (nephew of the legendary general) hosted a cocktail party in the Americans' honor, rather a waste of wine since the Kennedys, like the Oxnams, did not imbibe, but the bishops were flattered by the honor. In Seoul, Korea, the bishops inspected Methodist institutions, preached, and met with the U.S. ambassador and General George Decker and Syngman Rhee, a Methodist. Oxnam publicly agreed with the president of the Republic of South Korea that recognition should not be extended to "Red China" until her conduct was worthy of the term "peace loving nation." The four Americans then flew to Taiwan by way of Okinawa where Methodist institutions were cased. Madame Chiang granted an interview, Oxnam publicly gushing, "Madame Chiang is the same captivating, brilliant, beautiful personality we had met in the United States." (And this in 1957, when the scales surely should have dropped from Oxnam's eyes!) There followed a relaxing stay at the superlative Peninsular Hotel in Hong Kong, and then on to New Delhi via Bangkok and interviews with President Prasad and Prime Minister Nehru, Oxnam's admiration for the prime minister remaining undimmed. The bishops also met with the U.S. ambassador and Christian leaders. On to Istanbul via Teheran to conduct some church business with Orthodox leaders; then to London and then home. The Kennedys and Oxnams came to like each other a lot, happily, for their thirty days together were intense.

Oxnam had prophesied in 1947 before the delegates to the Seventh Ecumenical Methodist Conference: "I believe union must be established. I believe that the union of the larger Protestant churches could be consummated within a decade. I believe our laity and our clergy desire union. I believe our Lord is calling upon us to unite." "I believe," he opined elsewhere, "the reunion [sic] of American Protestantism a far easier task than is generally thought. . . . It is really a problem of will and heart, rather than of intellect. We simply do not want it enough. We do not love enough." In 1959 Oxnam received *The Churchman's* Upper Room Citation for his "lifetime of service to the building of the ecumenical church and its ministry to all the world." We know the leadership he gave to the Federal Council,

National Council, and World Council of Churches. Before closing this chapter, it is imperative to note his convictions concerning organic church union, for they were the subject of an entire book, *On This Rock* (the Hoover Lectures); the subjects of chapters in other books; the theme of numerous addresses and articles; and a key section in the 1948 Episcopal Address. What motivations fueled this crusade for church union? What assumptions informed it? What goals guided it? Were Oxnam's great expectations grounded in reality? Is it possible to be critical of his positions without being guilty of twenty-twenty hindsight since the decades following his death have not witnessed the fulfillment of his dreams?

Oxnam was widely considered one of Methodism's point men in the advance toward church union. There are a few individuals, however, including Albert C. Outler, who were gripped by the uneasy suspicion that Oxnam was less a True Believer in the movement than a determined believer that The Methodist Church not find itself relegated to the fringes of the movement.[9] An event took place shortly after Amsterdam that might have puzzling implications. Oxnam was then a member of the Board of Trustees of Union Theological Seminary in New York. As was his thoughtful custom, he invited all the Methodist seminarians at Union to his apartment for dessert and coffee. He then requested the students to fire questions at him concerning the ecumenical movement, fielding them with customary eloquence and passion. One student, Tom F. Driver, subsequently a Union professor, has recalled what then transpired. After the final query, Oxnam looked the group over and said he had a question: "I would like to know," his tone accusatory, "why you gentlemen have chosen to go to an interdenominational seminary instead of to one of our fine Methodist seminaries?" "We were flabbergasted," reported Driver. "In spite of his being a member of the Board of our chosen seminary, it appeared that his ecumenicity stopped when it came to training for the ministry." Oxnam's 1948 Episcopal Address touched this concern when he noted the possible dangers of Methodists training for the ministry in non-Methodist schools, and the need for supervision "to the end that the education received does prepare him for the ministry of the [Methodist] Church he is to serve."

Perhaps parenthetically, while Oxnam publicly extolled interdenominational brotherly love, privately he raged at denominations, especially the Congregationalists, who raided the Methodist ministry. "Stealing our men irritates me no end," he gruffed more than once. "Without any sense of bad conscience, they offer our ministers enough to buy them. Why don't they produce their own?" And so repeatedly he poured his powers of persuasion upon tempted Methodist parsons, but, he sighed, "money has a subtle voice." Perhaps parenthetically also, Oxnam was so persuaded of the superiority of the Methodist appointment system that in 1951 he sent to the Cincinnati Conference on Church Union a rather vehement letter protesting that the draft plan of union did not include anything like the Methodist system. One further wonders if anything could convince him of the superiority of the diocesan over the Methodist episcopal system, for repeatedly he said it was clearly not.

The Christian churches must become the Church Universal, trumpeted Oxnam. "I believe that the Christian churches should, *must,* and *can* unite into a world-wide Church of Christ." He envisioned the following scenario:

> First steps toward union must be taken by the Protestant communions. The Protestant churches must continue the present brotherly and inspiring co-operation with the Eastern Orthodox churches until such time as Protestantism is itself reunited. They may then consider union with Eastern Orthodoxy, which it is prayerfully hoped may be consummated. When the full union of Protestantism and of Eastern Orthodoxy is accomplished and the Christians of the world belong to but two great churches, the leadership of that day may be Christian enough and creative enough to kneel before a common altar, beg forgiveness of the Christ for disunity, and, sharing in the bread and wine of Holy Communion, rise in His spirit to form the Holy Catholic Church to which all Christians may belong.

An interesting point in this scenario is the assumption that the organic union of global Protestantism with Eastern Orthodoxy (including the Russian Orthodox Church) would precede union with the Roman Catholic Church. Plainly Oxnam's ecumenical zeal was not unconnected to his fears of Rome. Oxnam understandably found "blasphemous" the Catholic assumption that one individual is the Vicar of Christ upon earth. He correctly found intolerable the Catholic presumption that one day all Christians must return to Rome. He dubiously discerned a common democracy present in the Protestant and Orthodox churches. "The union of Christendom can never be achieved by one part of the Holy Catholic Church insisting that all other parts shall deny their Christian connections and shall discard their creative contributions in order to return to a part of the church universal," he declared. Inasmuch as Roman Catholic exclusiveness is "both a denial of true catholicity and of the spirit of Christ," the first steps must be taken without Rome's participation. Publicly he proclaimed, "It is only a united non-Roman Christianity that can hope to save Roman Christianity from its exclusiveness and its ecclesiastical totalitarianism, and thereby enable non-Roman Christianity and Roman Christianity to work together for the eventual unity of all Christendom and the building of Christ's Holy Church." Privately he confided the hope that a united Protestantism and Orthodoxy would be "a force that will counter-balance the hierarchy's weight which is so often thrown around these days." In 1947 Oxnam received an Episcopal Church appeal for funds to help with the completion of the National Cathedral in Washington. He declined to contribute, but in doing so he expressed the hope that soon the Protestant Episcopal Church and The Methodist Church might unite, which would bring into one church, Oxnam asserted, "a quarter of all Protestants of the nation." In the exchange of letters between Oxnam and George Wharton Pepper, renowned Philadelphia lawyer and Episcopal layman, the fears of Catholicism surfaced, Pepper making the dire prediction: "When all is said . . . , one fact stands out with startling clearness: that unless non-Roman Catholics can within fifty years wholeheartedly unite, there will either be no Christian Church at all or the Roman Church will have survived all the others." After Oxnam's sermon opening the WCC Assembly in Evanston, a Catholic journal observed, "It is unfortunate that Bishop Oxnam was the man chosen to keynote the Evanston session on 'unity.' He has perhaps done more to bring discord and division into Christian American circles than anyone else among his conferees." This is an uncharitable statement. It is also a revealing one.

Oxnam may be believed when he said: "Personally, I would be proud to kneel at any altar and to have the hands of Harry Emerson Fosdick placed upon my head, symbolizing the passing of the freedom and the independence of the Baptist tradition to the new Church; similarly, I would rejoice in receiving from Henry Sloane Coffin and from Rufus Jones the treasures of their traditions. I would count it an honor to have the hands of my dear friend Bishop Henry Knox Sherrill laid upon my head, symbolizing the unbroken traditions of the centuries, and so through the other communions, as we in turn participate, thus all becoming new ministers in Jesus Christ." Of course, Fosdick was a liberal northern Baptist; Coffin a liberal northern Presbyterian; Jones a liberal northern Quaker; Sherrill a mildly liberal northern Episcopalian. Congenial fellow Christians all! To be sure, Oxnam adds "and so through the other communions." Yet nowhere in his vast outpourings condemning the scandal of disunity and demanding a united Protestant Church in America (to say nothing of his pleas for a united Christian World Church) does he embrace by name in his love feast Southern Baptists, Missouri Synod Lutherans, Seventh-Day Adventists, Jehovah's Witnesses, Assemblies of God and Church of the Nazarene and Church of God and Pentecostal Holiness Church adherents, Primitive Baptists, Mennonites and Amish and Moravians. Presumably in Oxnam's New Jerusalem there would be no need to continue such Protestant cooperative agencies as the Federal or National Council of Churches, but could he reasonably be confident that the American Council of Churches and the National Association of Evangelicals would cooperatively close their doors? Oxnam envisioned a cluster of superior "united theological seminaries." Would Fuller and Wheaton and Moody be subsumed in them? And in this new Church, democratic in structure, naturally, according to his organizational model, what would happen if there were elected to positions of power the likes of Carl McIntire, Frank Norris, Gerald Winrod, Gerald L. K. Smith, William Dudley Pelley, Jerry Falwell, Pat Robertson, Jimmy Bakker, Jimmy Swaggart, Oral Roberts & Co.? Oxnam's All-American Protestant Church was chummy and neat and tidy, but then he never could abide messiness.

In 1950, Methodists assembled at the Newark Annual Conference pondered Oxnam's call for the consolidation of all Protestant churches on a community level. "The all-over plan," said their bishop, "would involve, for instance, Methodists becoming

Presbyterians in a community in which the Presbyterians outnumber the Methodists and, concurrently, the Presbyterians in another community becoming Methodists where the Methodists are in a majority." Such a plan would "eliminate harmful competition, thus leaving in each small community a strong denominational church and releasing funds and personnel for services in communities at present unchurched." The plan, explained Oxnam, would pave the way for ultimate worldwide union. The holes in this scheme would put a proud Swiss cheese to shame. Do or should Christians give up their distinctive beliefs and forms and traditions simply because they find themselves in a minority? Do not demographic changes alter a community's religious population, making minorities majorities and majorities minorities? Presumably the conversions would be carried up each step of the geographic ladder from village to town to city to state. For instance, all Protestants in New Jersey would affiliate ultimately with the denomination having the largest numbers. After the pattern was followed in all fifty states, logically the entire Protestant population of the nation would belong to the largest *existing* denomination. One hesitates to speculate how Oxnam might have responded to finding himself a member of the Southern Baptist Convention.

On countless instances Oxnam cried, "We can no longer call upon God to bless us in wasting wealth and talent in useless duplication, not to say downright competition. Such inefficiency is wasteful." Inefficiency! There was the enemy! Whatever other considerations motivated Oxnam, a rage for order was one of them. Witness this lyrical depiction of what would follow the union of American Protestantism:

> United action in many fields would follow rapidly. Our foreign or overseas missions could become one within the world organization and fellowship. We could have a common hymnal! There could be a Protestant daily paper. With what strength we could take up the modern media of radio and television, and use them both for the glory of God! Visual education would cease to be the sorry attempt of amateurs who enter a field calling for the highest art. A united Protestantism could summon the talents of the greatest artists of the earth, and from the screen would come the message of our Lord. There could be a united system of higher education, unitedly supported, in which we would train the lay leadership of our Church, the teachers for our colleges and universities, and, in

united theological seminaries, the ministers of the Church. The union of American Christianity [sic] would electrify the world and accelerate the trends toward union in every continent. . . . Let the Methodists take the lead in a great affirmative decision, stating that we desire union. . . . Our sons sleep beneath the crosses because we have not brought all men to the cross. 'And I, if I be lifted up, will draw all men unto me.' When a United Church of Christ is established, He will be lifted up!

The trouble with this vision is less its utopianism than its chilling bureaucratic implications. Anyhow, it is based on a profound misreading of the religious history of the American people and what their churches meant and continue to mean to them.

---

[1] "Then and now," wrote John Richard Neuhaus in 1983, "the putatively ecumenical Christians claimed that the evangelicals and others had 'dropped out of the dialogue.' In truth they were never included. The history of the National Council of Churches (NCC) is one of attempted consolidation of liberal, mainline Protestant hegemony in American life. To this extent it was and is anti-ecumenical in originating impulse and continuing practice."

[2] Bishop Sherrill, a member of the nominating committee, recalls sounding out Anglican Bishop Y. Y. Tsu of China about non-Western candidates for the Presidium. When Sherrill intimated that a woman would be preferable, the Chinese protested, "I am not antifeminist, but if the Council wishes a woman president, why begin with the Far East? Why not elect Mrs. Roosevelt in place of Bishop Oxnam?" That closed Sherrill out. In 1951 President Chao resigned in protest of the Council's condemnation of the North Korean invasion of South Korea.

[3] In actuality, the sums forthcoming were only $220,000 from U.S. churches and only $45,000 from member churches in all other countries. That is, churches in six countries actually met their suggested allocations to the budget, while churches in twenty-two lands failed to do so.

[4] This decision by the Central Committee was confirmed by the Second Assembly meeting in 1954. The opposition was led by the bishop of London and other delegates from the Church of England, but the archbishop of Canterbury did not vocally oppose the proposal. Again, the debate was hot and again Oxnam's closing argument was decisive.

[5] Duke University, like Northwestern originally a staunchly Methodist school, had also been favored by Oxnam. Benjamin E. Mays, president of Morehouse College, protested to Oxnam that the segregation practices of Durham, North Carolina, would be offensive to many delegates and embarrassing to the Americans. Oxnam remained unpersuaded that Duke was an unacceptable site, but Mays took his case to Henry Pitney Van Dusen (and possibly other leaders) and Duke was ultimately scrapped. The university authorities pledged that there would be no discrimination on the Duke campus but could not guarantee that there would not be any in Durham. At that time, Duke's doors had not yet been opened to blacks.

[6] Two additional visas were granted, but one individual became ill and the other was denied an exit permit. The only reason that Polish delegates were not admitted was that their visa applications were received in mid-July, too late for normal processing.

[7] Midway in the Assembly, Bromley and Ruth had celebrated their fortieth wedding anniversary by co-hosting with the Sam Caverts a dinner at the Westmoreland Country Club attended by the Council presidents and other officials. He told Ruth that his anniversary message was identical with the theme of his sermon opening the Assembly:

"We intend to stay together." A concert at Ravinia followed. In passing it might be noted that Charles Parlin performed a marvelous job as chairman of the Press and Broadcasting Committee. In advance of the Assembly he called on the big guns in the media world to assure wide coverage, and the coverage proved to be astonishing. He also buttered up the media people by inviting them to be his personal guests at a filet mignon dinner at the swank Edgewater Beach Hotel. About five hundred showed up!

[8] In America, conservative spokesmen censored those Americans who disgraced themselves and their country by accepting honorary degrees. And in case the FBI might be napping, alert citizens informed the bureau of Oxnam's travel to Hungary.

[9] Dean Walter G. Muelder had the same uneasy feelings about Charles C. Parlin. Muelder respected the Methodist lawyer's impressive abilities, but questioned Parlin's worship of bigness, rationalization, efficiency. Parlin sought for his beloved Methodist Church, surely an authentic devotion, a paramount position in the affairs of the World Council. Muelder recalled hearing Parlin make this Freudian slip at the New Delhi meeting of the WCC: "We want to greet our Methodists and all our overseas affiliates."

CHAPTER 21

MOUNTING PROTESTANT-CATHOLIC TENSIONS

One might reasonably suppose that the ecumenical movement absorbed the bulk of Oxnam's extra-Methodist (if they were indeed extra-Methodist) energies and concerns, but in fact there arose a question of comparable intensity to him—namely, the place of an authoritarian Roman Catholic Church in a politically democratic United States and the status of a burgeoning Roman Catholic population in an America where Protestants historically had considered themselves the senior partners.

As we examine mounting Protestant-Catholic tensions in the postwar years, a tale as tragic as it is intense, several points might be kept in mind.

First, Oxnam retired in 1960, the year of Kennedy's election and on the eve of Vatican II. In 1963 death claimed him, as it did America's first Catholic president and Pope John XXIII, both of whom so moderated Protestant anxieties. If Oxnam had remained at the height of his powers after 1960, perhaps he might have joined, even led, in the great reconciliation the decade witnessed. If he had, what follows would be less grim. But he lived in a pre-1960 era when, despite liberalizing signs of the times, there were honest, objective, substantive differences separating Catholics from their non-Roman Christian brethren. Or so both groups authentically believed.

Second, although on occasion Oxnam trotted around the paddock such old dobbins as the Inquisition, the 1864 Syllabus of Errors, Pope Leo III's 1899 apostolic letter *Testem Benevolentiae* with its condemnation of "Americanism," and Pope Pius X's 1907 sharp action against Modernism, the fact is that as late as 1960, Rome affirmed that the state (and not only individuals) must worship God and is bound to maintain the Roman Catholic Church as the only true church and that the idea of religious freedom is a grave error (though the state may tolerate non-Catholic religions for the sake of civil peace). The fact is that these were also the official positions set forth in works sanctioned by the Roman Catholic hierarchy in America, and written by American Catholics. To be sure, liberalizing fissures were appearing and they deepened in 1958 with the election of Pope John XXIII. Still, Oxnam's position must be placed in the context of his times. Officially, the Roman Catholic Church claimed to be the only true Church; officially, "error has no rights that Truth is bound to respect." For Oxnam, it was Cardinal Francis J. Spellman, not Father John Courtney Murray, who symbolized American Catholicism's true colors: authoritarian, intolerant, arrogant, and in conflict with true Americanism.

Third, it will not do to suppose that the keelhauling of Catholicism was a monopoly of benighted fundamentalistic bigots bogged down in the Bible Belt. To the contrary, as these pages will demonstrate, it was "enlightened" liberal Protestantism that was in the forefront of the war with Rome.

Fourth, Oxnam sought (successfully or not) to draw a distinction between the hierarchy of the Roman Catholic Church and the rank-and-file priests and nuns and lay persons.

Fifth, although Oxnam considered himself a champion of the separation of church and state, one cannot fail to note how perilously close he came to absolutizing democracy, granting to the secular state an almost autonomous status, elevating the "American Way" to an almost religious icon and investing it with the aura of the sacred.

Sixth, although Oxnam was judged by Catholics to be their most relentless critic, attention must first be paid to his record of words and deeds upholding the affirmative side of the Catholic Church. As a boy he revered the founders of California missions, saying of them, "Some people feel that these men because they were Catholics did not know God. Oh they did—may I serve as truly as they served." And recall that his S.T.B. thesis was on Father Junipero Serra. He showered youthful idealism on Mexican-American kids in Los Angeles and Irish-American lads in Boston. As leader of the Church of All Nations he betrayed no trace of anti-Catholicism save only in regard to the Church's opposition to family planning. He treasured the Catholic traditions in San Francisco and admired the work of the Paulist fathers in Chinatown. In the 1920s he condemned the Ku-Klux Klan. The record does not disclose how he voted in the election of 1928, but at least the silence of the record indicates that he did not join the Protestant furor surrounding Al Smith's Catholicism.

When Oxnam departed the Omaha Area for Boston, a Nebraska Catholic woman mailed a warning to Boston's Cardinal William O'Connell: "There's a 'wolf in sheep's clothing' in your midst. He hails from Omaha. He is Methodist Bishop G. Bromley Oxnam. He is tied up with communist-supporting organizations. He is the new bishop in the Boston territory. Watch him!" As a matter of fact, the only meeting between the two men took place on November 29, 1943. At that time an ugly anti-Semitism was blanketing the Boston area including vicious street beatings of Jews by gangs of black-shirted youths. Oxnam, in his capacity as president of the Massachusetts Council of Churches and as chairman of the Massachusetts Civil Liberties Union, called on the eighty-four-year-old cardinal to ask that he join in a public appeal to end the violence directed at Jews. O'Connell hesitated, suggesting that "the way of Christ was the quiet way." Oxnam replied that the Council of Churches would prepare a statement, submit it to the cardinal for his criticism, and would be grateful for his signature. After the meeting Oxnam recorded: "I am impressed by the Cardinal. He is a wise man, knows how to handle the affairs of life. I think he can be several personalities, hard and intelligent as well as kind and understanding. We have much to learn from Catholics—their certainty, their sense of history, their insistence on the primacy of religion. But they could learn, and oh so much." On December 27, Oxnam submitted the council's statement. O'Connell found the tone "rather more compulsory than persuasive." Oxnam agreed to accept the Catholic's substitute. On January 24, 1944, there was made public an appeal carrying the signature of the two men. Rather more vague than the council's draft, at least the final statement did witness a Methodist bishop and a Catholic prelate coming together to condemn bigotry.

There are additional good things in the record. Upon the death of Pope Pius XI, Oxnam made the radio statement: "The Catholic world sorrows this day. A great leader is dead. Briefly, but in deepest sympathy and the utmost sincerity, I would extend to all the members of the great world church who may hear my voice the love of the people called Methodists and express the hope that the man chosen to succeed the Pope will be qualified not only to lead a great church, but to lead all mankind toward peace, justice, the love of Christ and the Kingdom of God." Upon the death of Pope Pius XII, Oxnam said to the press: "A great spiritual leader is dead. Pope Pius XII was a courageous, devoted and talented man who will take his place among the most significant personalities in the history of the papacy. Methodists throughout the world join Christians everywhere in love and sympathy to Roman Catholics in every land."

Perhaps not surprisingly considering his liberalism, Oxnam expressed in his diary or in public or both high regard for such socially concerned individuals as Father John A. Ryan, Auxiliary Bishop Bernard Sheil, Monsignor George Higgins, Dorothy Day, and Father George Barry Ford, although the tales told him by Ford about Spellman made the few hairs on Oxnam's head stand like the fretful porcupine's. A number of members of the National Catholic Welfare Council impressed him personally, as did such members on the Secretary of the Navy's Civilian Advisory Board as Fathers O'Hara and Cavanaugh of Notre Dame and Father Flanagan of Boys Town. Then there were a raft of nameless priests, often chaplains, he admired for their ability or captivating wit, including the one who informed him, "Bishop, I'm comin' over to hear ye tonight. I may have to say five Hail Mary's in the mornin' for doing it, but I'll sure be there!"

Oxnam made it a habit to drop into Catholic churches, often expressing admiration for what he observed, after one such visit confessing, "This great institution is not built on a lie, even if liars are at times harbored by it. And I think there is perhaps one in Protestantism."

As to the question of the Oxnam children, Philip recalls that his father hoped he would attend Creighton University in Omaha, and though Philip for reasons of his own declined to do so, the point is Oxnam's high regard for a Catholic school. Bette Ruth believes that had she chosen to marry a Catholic and convert, her parents would have honored her decision as they raised her to be independent in her thinking and life decisions.

There is, alas, a darker side to Oxnam's understanding of Roman Catholicism and his encounters with the Catholic hierarchy. To this somber story we must now turn. On February 4, 1947, Oxnam called on Cardinal Spellman. (Father Cavanaugh of Notre Dame earlier had suggested to Oxnam that a personal meeting between the two leaders might be more profitable than angry public exchanges.) The cardinal answered the bell himself, greeted the Methodist warmly, took the coat and umbrella, and invited him into a parlor. "He almost fluttered about," Oxnam recalled, "yet fluttering is not a word you associate with this man, who possesses very great influence." Oxnam then raised the question of Catholic-Protestant tensions and five times suggested a conference between Catholic and Protestant leaders at the highest levels. Naturally Spellman did not agree with the Methodist on the church-state issues discussed and was evasive about a conference. "When I rose to go," Oxnam's diary continues, "he was most solicitous, went out to get my coat for me, insisted that I do not go out in the rain until my car was there. As a matter of fact, he said that he had arranged for his car to be present to take me anywhere I wished to go, and the driver was there. I told him Mrs. Oxnam was coming, so he said he would stand by the window and wait until she arrived. He couldn't have been nicer in all these matters." The diary entry concludes: "Spellman gave no real indication of his awareness of what Protestantism is, the nature of the services, or our spirit. There was a certain arrogance about it all that was hidden beneath an outer courtesy that left nothing to be desired. There are assumptions here, however, that I think we can never overcome, but we will keep at it."

The two men did not meet again until December 10, 1952, and during the long interval they had exchanged bitter words. Oxnam, returning from India, and Spellman, returning from Korea, found themselves on the same flight out of Delhi. When they encountered, the cardinal blinked his eyes and said, "Well, Bishop, what under the sun are you doing out here? You are certainly looking fit. I am getting old and flabby. What do you do to keep in shape?" They chatted quite a long time about church-state matters. "He is a very friendly person," Oxnam admitted to his diary, "who makes the most of all such opportunities [chance meetings]. His cordiality quite surprised me and was really enjoyable." When Spellman left the plane at Beirut, Oxnam noted the entourage to greet the Catholic and how skillfully he played the photographers and movie people, sighing, "There is a lot to learn in the field of public relations." (Incidentally, in fact it may not be so incidental at that, Protestant leaders in their travels abroad felt like second-class citizens when they compared the receptions they received to the red carpets rolled out for Spellman by top civilian and military brass. Objectively these Protestants may have been accorded quite handsome treatment; nonetheless, subjectively they felt like cockboats coming in the wake of a man-of-war. For example, when in 1945 Bishop Sherrill and Oxnam encountered exasperating red tape in preparing to be present at the enthronement of the archbishop of Canterbury and then undertake an inspection of the war zone, the Episcopal bishop fired off an angry letter to the director of the General Commission on Army and Navy chaplains: "Certainly if Archbishop Spellman wished to go to Rome, you can just guarantee that everything would be done to facilitate his movements. . . . Far more than any personal consideration is my desire to see the non-Roman Catholic churches have a fair representation and real consideration, so if we do not obtain this immediately, I think we will have to put up more of a holler.")

Much earlier, in Omaha in one radio broadcast, Oxnam addressed the subject of public funds for church schools, saying that such a course of action "menaces the future of democracy and . . . endangers religious liberty." In another broadcast, he noted Rome's opposition to communism, adding "It is hard, however, to understand the prostitution of the Church to fascism." Oxnam also made a strong defense of a child labor amendment then before Congress and which was opposed by the Catholic hierarchy.

Moving to Boston, Oxnam's moment of amity with Cardinal O'Connell did not foreclose his questioning of public policies advocated by the hierarchy. Oxnam supported, over O'Connell's opposition, a proposed referendum in Massachusetts that would permit doctors to advise married women who needed contraceptive information for health reasons. He supported, again over Catholic opposition, a petition to repeal a 1936 Massachusetts statute that provided compulsory free transportation to all private school children in towns and cities where such services were operated out of public funds for public schools. In addresses, he called for the Catholic Church to extend the principle of religious liberty to Spain and Latin America. In articles he asked, "Why does the Catholic Church exert an influence far beyond what which its numbers justify?" His language was not restrained: "Dictatorship is repugnant to free men, whether it be that of a state or of a church. It makes little difference whether it be a brown shirt, a black shirt, or a shirt with a collar on backwards. Let the church remember that the political shirtmakers are sewing at once with a double thread, 'a shroud as well as a shirt.' If religionists march the road of dictatorship it will become the march of death." Privately he mused, why does the Catholic Church come up on the reactionary side with such consistency unless it be part of a long-range Vatican plan? On visiting army bases he complained that "neutral" chapels were in fact transformed into Catholic chapels.

The political presence of the Catholic Church in New England was palpable, but the disquietude of Protestants was not confined to Beantown and its neighbors. In 1942 John R. Mott convened in New York a group ultimately to form the Committee for Religious Toleration, Inc., which combined with the Joint Committee for Religious Liberty of the FCC, which in turn became the Department of Religious Liberty of the NCC—all three agencies implicating Oxnam as secretary-treasurer or otherwise. The individuals summoned by Mott in 1942 were distinguished in Protestant circles: Episcopal Bishops Sherrill and Endicott Peabody, the presidents of Union and Princeton Theological Seminaries, Coffin and Mackay, Dr. Luther Weigle of

Yale, Lutheran leader Adbel Ross Wentz, and Methodist Bishops McConnell[1] and Oxnam. In fact, Coffin wrote sometime later advising that their group avoid even the appearance of bigotry and therefore, "We must dissociate ourselves from 'Protestants United.' "

Coffin's reference was of course to the organization, officially formed January 12, 1948, Protestants and Other Americans United for the Separation of Church and State, commonly known as POAU. (In 1972, over protests of several of the founders, the opening three words in the cumbersome title were lopped and today the popular rendering is simply "Americans United.")

Oxnam was one of the founding fathers of POAU. Alarmed in particular by President Truman's continuation of the Myron C. Taylor mission to the Vatican and by mounting Catholic pressure for public funds for parochial schools and in general by what Oxnam termed a "cultural offensive" by the Catholic Church in America, sixty concerned Protestant leaders assembled in Washington in October 1947, Oxnam chairing the meeting. The group reassembled in Chicago in November to hear a four-thousand-word "Manifesto" written by Charles Clayton Morrison, retiring editor of the *Christian Century*, with the assistance of five individuals including Oxnam, who was elected first president of the new organization. Because of pressure of other duties, Oxnam left the leadership in 1948 but remained as a vice-president. In 1954 he sought to be released from that responsibility, but stayed on when Executive Director Glenn Archer, the very heart and soul of POAU, told him that his name alone was worth ten thousand dollars annually in contributions.[2]

POAU drew into its ranks a variety of concerned citizens. Northern Protestant leaders remained prominent, but they were joined by such noted Southern Baptists as Louie Newton and J. M. Dawson. Edwin McNeill Poteat, a North Carolina Baptist who became president of Colgate-Rochester, succeeded Oxnam as president of POAU. As a generalization it might be said that liberal Protestants feared that the use of public funds for private schooling would strengthen Catholic schools, while conservative Protestants feared such use would end with the federal government controlling the public school system. As Glenn Archer, who was himself a Kansas Republican and former law school dean, explained, the latter fear was the reason Sovereign Grand Commander John H. Cowles of the Scottish Rite Masons' Southern Jurisdiction tendered a check of fifty thousand dollars to get the organization off the ground. Also, a number of Jews contributed support not only because they did not wish state aid for Catholic schools but because they feared a growth of religious influence, that is, Christian influence primarily and inevitably, in the public schools. As Poteat wrote to a friendly rabbi, "You will also be glad to know that we have some very substantial and competent members of the Jewish community on our National Advisory Board and are making every effort to make our organization rest on as broad a base of patriotic and public interest as possible." Indeed, when Poteat received critical letters from Catholics, he could only reply that POAU had Catholic friends who shared its concern about the separation of church and state and that "our interest does not touch even by implication any of the religious practices or doctrines of the Roman Church."

The Protestant element seemingly least supportive of POAU was that identified with neo-orthodoxy and Niebuhr's leadership. By 1957, Protestant theologian Robert McAfee Brown could dismiss the organization as "Protestantism reduced to anti-Catholicism."

From its birth, POAU came under violent Catholic attack. From the perspective of most Catholics, it appeared an assault on the True Church, and for them to reply is understandable. What is less understandable, or rather, less defensible, is the uniting of this charge with the allegation of pro-communism, Poteat and Oxnam in particular being fingered for their "Red" associations. On February 1, 1948, Archbishop Richard J. Cushing of Boston addressed the Knights of Columbus in Manchester, New Hampshire, the address being broadcast over station WMUR. Cushing referred to Oxnam personally, designated the POAU's "Manifesto" as "anti-Catholic pronouncements," and spoke of its leaders as "fomenters of bigotry" and "architects of antagonism." He also linked anti-Catholicism with communism. The Protestant ministers of Manchester invited Oxnam to reply and he was granted forty-five minutes to do so by station WMUR. The reply was printed and *widely* distributed. Catholics might take issue with everything Oxnam said, but it also must be suggested that he spoke with restraint, in an ironic tone, and directly faced the Vatican representation and school issues. It was not one of Oxnam's more intemperate blasts.

A year later, on January 27, 1949, at a POAU rally in Constitution Hall, Washington, D.C., Oxnam brought an audience of thirty-six hundred to its cheering feet. Among his provocative utterances: "Americans who have learned to breathe freely are forever done with manacled minds and shackled souls. Here, Roman Catholic, Protestant and Jew have enjoyed the blessings of liberty. Wise men of all faiths will refuse to follow mistaken men whose training has conditioned them to subjugation and whose principles compel them to seek mastery." And: "When will the hierarchy learn that there is no return to the darkness of the Middle Ages, during which a totalitarian church ruled the minds of men?"

Oxnam never recanted his support of POAU, despite the growing coolness toward it in some Protestant circles, including the NCC; and as late as 1960 the General Conference of The Methodist Church endorsed the organization and urged its financial support. When three years later Glenn Archer learned of Oxnam's death he walked into the woods alone and wept, for, he recalled, "I loved him so much."

On Reformation Day, October 28, 1945, Oxnam addressed a St. Louis audience of nineteen thousand. His words were broadcast and then printed, possibly reaching a total of millions of Protestants and surely not a few interested Catholics as well. He noted the Roman Catholic Church's intimidation of a cowed media. He observed its grabbing of public funds for sectarian education. He protested the repression of Protestant missionaries in Catholic lands and the Church's favored relationship with the fascist regime of Franco. The Taylor mission to the Vatican was decried. "It is not intolerance," he insisted, "to point out the fundamental contradiction that lies in the Roman Catholic position on religious liberty that, in effect, means a demand for religious liberty where the Roman Catholic is in the minority but denies it in practice where the Roman Catholic is in the majority."

Oxnam again made national news with an address delivered March 27, 1946, before the largest audience ever to assemble in Boston's historic Trinity Church, the occasion being an ecumenical service sponsored by the Massachusetts Council of Churches. He repeated the concerns set forth in the St. Louis talk. Sang one Boston newspaper: "CATHOLIC CHURCH IS ATTACKED. BISHOP OXNAM HITS ALLUDED INTOLERANCE OF OTHER-FAITHS. SAYS PROTESTANTS ARE PERSECUTED." Praised a Quaker paper: "This is a well-balanced, wise, and statesman-like call to American Protestantism to be on the alert." Lamented *The Pilot*, organ of the archdiocese of Boston: "In sincerest fraternal charity, can't Bishop Oxnam understand what we're driving at? Heresy is a sin! It is a mortal sin! Is 'one religion as good as another'? If that's true, then one religion is as false as another and the death of Christ is made void." *The Pilot* concluded, "At the heart of Bishop Oxnam's objection to the Catholic Church is his unwillingness to acknowledge the divinity of Christ." Sighed one proper Bostonian to Dean Muelder of BU School of Theology, "It's all very well for Bishop Oxnam to come to Boston, raise the roof, and depart, but what about those of us here who have to live with the aftermath?" To that question Oxnam *might* have replied: "When the Catholic Church states that a Methodist bishop is in a heretical sect and denies the divinity of Christ, then the roof *should* be raised in Boston."

In the following months and years literally hundreds of thousands of American Protestants heard from Oxnam's lips and literally millions read from his pen disturbing questions relative to the Roman Catholic Church and American democracy. He compared the totalitarianism of the Church to that of the Communist Party. He suggested that the individual who takes his "religious thought from an authoritarian hierarch is likely to be so conditioned that he may be willing to take his political thought from a dictator or his economic thought from a party." He drew the invidious parallel: "The American Catholic hierarchy, as well as the American Communist Party, is bound by directives from a foreign capital. Directives from Rome, like directives from Moscow, are based on principle." He explained the essential un-Americanism of the Church: "A hierarchy never understands democracy. It does understand dictatorship. It is one. Faithful priests in the United States, men who know the meaning of democracy, are restive under the dictatorial leadership of a hierarchy that plays the political line of Rome." And of course he raised the century-old question: "The Roman Catholic Church insists upon being a church and a state. How can an American citizen be at once loyal to his own country and his President and also loyal to another political state and its political ruler, if the two states differ in international policy?"

American Catholics were not amused. The laconic contented themselves with sending Oxnam unsigned postcards bearing the single word "BIGOT!" Other Catholic communicants were more fulsome: "Bigotry such as yours should be wiped off the face of the earth. Your stupid comments show you to be jealous, small, ignorant, womanish, narrow-minded and completely unfit to head a church—even a Protestant church. You are certainly undeserving and unfit to have the title Bishop. It should be Bastard." Both Edward Cardinal Mooney and Bishop Francis J. Schenk wrote Oxnam long letters, chaste in prose, polite in tone, yet frank in pointing out what the prelates deemed Oxnam's fantastical misrepresentations. The Methodist's replies were as gracious as they were obdurate.

On December 19, 1949, Oxnam heard from an occasional luncheon companion, Henry R. Luce of the *Life* and *Time* empire. "I am bound to tell you," the tycoon wrote the bishop, "that one factor in the American scene which is very disconcerting to me is an attitude to which you have again given expression and which is mainly associated with your name. That attitude could be summarized by saying: 'Communism is a menace but Catholicism is equally a menace.' " Oxnam of course denied the assertion, adding, "If any of us are misrepresenting our Roman Catholic friends in a fashion similar to that which the diocesan press which is clerically controlled misrepresents me, I would find myself as a Protestant not only embarrassed but humiliated."

Oxnam's lament was not without a factual basis. The Catholic press did not remain humbly or ingloriously mute. As Auxiliary Bishop John J. Wright, speaking as well for Archbishop Cushing, explained to a perplexed inquirer, "The scandal to our young people would be increased, I am afraid, if their spiritual leaders kept silent in the face of charges so fundamental and so compromising as those which these Protestant leaders are renewing."

Not only did the Catholic press not deem silence was golden, some Catholic responses to Oxnam's cuts and thrusts were nutty or casuistic or jejune or slanderous or all of these at once, and on reading them one is tempted to mutter something about the mote and the beam. In any case, an author in *The Sign* expressed a widespread sentiment when in 1950 he termed Oxnam "the leading spokesman in America today of organized, militantly anti-Catholic Protestantism."

If Oxnam was angered by what he judged misrepresentation, he must have been miffed by the patronizing tone of Catholic commentators. "Bishop G. Bromley Oxnam cuts a pathetic figure in his bigoted blasts against the Catholic Church," yawned the *Catholic Mirror*. "His accusations are illogical, confused and false. Answering them is like replying to an anonymous letter." Editorialized *America:* "It is hard to hit his pitches because they are so wide of home-plate. In fact, his pitches are so wide that they endanger the safety of the spectators." Opined a San Francisco Catholic paper: "Poor Oxnam! He is at it again, and this time, more vapid than ever. It is difficult to be disturbed with a poor soul like G. Bromley Oxnam. He should be the object of our pity and prayers rather than our anger." Oxnam was warned that "you are not only placing your person in jeopardy of your eternal salvation, but even worse than that, being responsible for the souls of other innocent human beings whom you may be influencing."

In all of this the vast pity is that apparently Oxnam never corresponded with or talked with John Courtney Murray, S. J., and never, perhaps, read his words. Murray and like-minded Catholic liberals were courageously attempting—and with success, as events in the 1960s proved—to lead the Church in America in new and less dogmatic directions. Maybe, however, it would have made no difference. Monsignor George G. Higgins, who liked Oxnam personally and teamed with him on labor matters, recalled that regarding Catholicism Oxnam could not be reached in intellectual discourse. With a man like noted critic of Catholics Paul Blanshard one could talk and disagree about the Church, Higgins believed; with Oxnam one could not even talk.

It is past time to move from the general to the particular, the first particularity being the Myron C. Taylor mission and its aftermath. President Roosevelt considered seeking a closer relationship with the Holy See as early as 1936. When Oxnam whiffed the possibility of a United States–Vatican diplomatic tie, he successfully moved on April 21, 1939, that the Council of Bishops establish a watchdog committee, he, naturally, becoming a member. His suspicions proved well founded. At Christmastime, Roosevelt wrote Pope Pius XII that "it would give me great satisfaction to send to you my personal representative in order that our parallel endeavors for peace and the alleviation of suffering may be assisted." The individual named was Mr. Myron C. Taylor, an Episcopalian and former board chairman of United States Steel. Roosevelt then announced that Taylor would remain in Rome for the duration of the war, hold the title of "extraordinary ambassador," and serve without salary. The president subsequently explained that he was sending Taylor to the pope "as head of the Roman Catholic Church, not as the sovereign of Vatican City State" and that the appointment "did not constitute the inauguration of formal diplomatic relations with the Vatican." Therefore, the appointment did not require Senate confirmation—after all he was merely a personal representative of a president to the head of a church. (Of course the Vatican did not view or treat Taylor in quite that casual light; nor did the United States State Department which assigned Harold H. Tittmann to be "Assistant to the Personal Representative of the President of the United States to His Holiness the Pope.")[3] Among those who viewed Roosevelt's decision as a Christmas present were Pius, Spellman, Joseph Kennedy, Secretary of State Hull and all those who sought closer ties between America and the Vatican and all those who hoped the pope and the president together might restore peace to Europe and all those pragmatists (including Roosevelt himself) who believed Rome possessed sources of information invaluable to the United States.

Simultaneously with the sending of the letter to the pope, the president sent letters to Dr. George A. Buttrick, president of the Federal Council of Churches, and Dr. Cyrus Alder, president of the Jewish Theological Seminary of America, expressing the hope that each would, "from time to time, come to Washington to discuss the problems which all of us have on our minds, in order that our parallel endeavors for peace and the alleviation of suffering may be assisted."

Buttrick, suspecting that he was being flimflammed (as he was, for those "from time to time" discussions in the White House never took place), twice wrote Roosevelt for clarification of Taylor's status (receiving from the president the bland assurance that the mission was neither formal nor permanent[4]), and in early 1940 the Federal Council's executive committee thrice resolved (in the wording of the January 26 statement): "If the appointment should unfortunately prove a stepping stone to a permanent diplomatic relationship, we should feel obliged in good conscience to oppose it, as a violation of the principle of the separation of governmental function and religious function, which is a basic American policy and which both history and conscience approve, and as an ultimate injury to all faiths."

Concurrently, outside the FCC, other Protestant voices were raised in protest, including those of the Methodist Council of Bishops and of the delegates to the 1940 General Conference.

As the end of the war in Europe drew into sight, concern over the Taylor mission mounted. In November 1944 Oxnam's resolution of opposition to U.S.–Vatican diplomatic relations was adopted by the FCC. His thinking on the question is revealed in a diary passage: "One wishes to avoid an anti-Catholic movement and yet, unless proper force is brought to bear, the same political control that has developed in other nations may develop here. There is no question but that the Vatican anticipates recognition by our government and is bringing very heavy pressure upon each of the candidates at the moment to get a commitment in advance of the election upon the issue. I fancy this can be blocked. It must be. There is no more reason for the Roman Catholic Church to be regarded a state than for The Methodist Church. We might just as well purchase some section of the world, set up a little church of our own, and then insist upon recognition of the Council of Bishops. How utterly absurd it seems when we put it that way!"

Roosevelt died, the war ended, and Taylor's mission remained intact. Therefore, in early 1946 the FCC authorized Oxnam, still president, to confront President Truman personally. This Oxnam, together with Roswell Barnes and Franklin Clark Fry, did on January 16. Recorded Oxnam: "The President said that as long as he was President we need have no fear concerning the appointment of an ambassador to the Vatican, that he thought as deeply about this as anybody, but he said, 'You know, we face a fact, not a theory, here.' " Oxnam then explained the Protestant position. The diary entry concludes: "When we left, Fry was very much upset, exploded when we got outside and stated that the man—referring to the President—was proud of his incompetence. Of course, this could be heard by one of the secretaries there. We tried to quiet the brother, but didn't get too far." Even as Protestant denominational bodies, the Protestant press, and individual leaders mounted criticism of the mission, Truman in May returned Taylor to Rome, explaining, "I feel he can continue to render helpful service to the cause of Christian civilization if, at my insistence, from time to time, he resumes his duties in Italy."

On June 5 a delegation of eleven Protestant leaders waited on the President, the group, led by Oxnam, representing nine major denominations, among them the conservative Southern Baptists and the Missouri Synod Lutherans. Let Oxnam's diary relate the encounter. The president's greeting was cordial. As spokesman, Oxnam reviewed the initial appointment by F.D.R. and then continued: "May I say, Mr. President, that we were not only surprised, but shocked when the reappointment of Mr. Taylor was announced?" Truman broke in to point out that Taylor had not been reappointed, that he, Truman, was simply continuing an inherited situation. Then Newton, president of the Southern Baptist Convention, "unfortunately" began to lecture Truman on the unconstitutionality of the appointment. "The President interrupted him and spoke somewhat sharply, saying 'It is constitutional. I am sworn to uphold the Constitution.' Of course, there was a certain non-sequitur in that kind of statement, but one could see the President was somewhat irritated." As the meeting continued, Truman made clear that he stood for a complete separation of church and state; that he regarded this appointment as a temporary expedient, and that he looked for its early termination. He said that he was fundamentally opposed to any diplomatic relations as such with the Vatican or with any church anywhere. He stressed the fact, however, that there were certain values in this matter which were of great significance and that he needed Mr. Taylor there at the moment. After a while Oxnam asked the president if the group could carry to their people the following message: "We were given assurance that the appointment of Mr. Taylor was a temporary expedient to give the President the fullest opportunity to make his contribution to the peace, that it might terminate at an early date but would certainly terminate with the signing of the peace treaties." Truman gave his approval of the statement.

Cardinal Spellman took the occasion of his June 12 Fordham University commencement address to express his displeasure. Fixing Oxnam and Co. with a basilisk stare, employing such terms as "bigotry" and "ignorance," the prelate declared that the demand for the recall of Taylor represented "the anti-Catholicism of unhooded klansmen sowing seeds of disunion within our treasured nation." Commented the *Christian Century* on the address, "It is a declaration of war." Oxnam publicly replied and privately mused, "I am of the opinion that Cardinal Spellman must have made certain promises to the Vatican, and that President Truman's announcement that what he told us was a fact has so disturbed the Cardinal that he is now speaking emotionally rather than thoughtfully."

The situation continued to bubble, though not yet, perhaps, to the boiling point. Much of the Protestant leadership fretted and countless national, regional, and local Protestant bodies made resolutions of one kind and another, Oxnam declaring in 1947 that the issue has "done more to unite the religious groups of the nation than any single act in recent years." Oxnam's friend Dulles saw Truman and reported back the president's puzzlement as to why Protestants were so exercised. Concurrently, if historian Fogarty is correct, the Vatican was growing concerned about the imprecise status of Taylor's mission, and according to Fogarty, Taylor himself wished to see the mission substantially changed or abolished. On August 6, 1947, Truman wrote Pius XII saying he was again sending Taylor back to Rome. Spellman immediately wrote the president of his pleasure at the announcement, Truman replying, "Ever so many thanks for your kind note." In late August and early September Truman received additional letters of gratitude and support from such members of the hierarchy as Stritch, Cantwell, Howard, McNicholas, Ritter, and O'Hara—among other cheering letters in the Truman Library.

On November 14, 1947, four Protestant leaders joined Oxnam again in seeing the president. Again we have Oxnam's diary for the record. Oxnam reminded Truman of his earlier pledge of the temporary, expedient nature of Taylor's continuation. Truman replied that the situation had changed; the Russians had broken every agreement; "it is a case now of morality versus immorality." Moreover, the Taylor situation "is simply a straw man which you folks have put up to knock down." Oxnam demurred: "I am sorry, Mr. President, the truth of the matter is, we never set up any straw man. Mr. Taylor was appointed. We were not consulted. The fact is someone else set up the situation and now we are accused of bigotry because we do not wish a fundamental principle violated." Seeing Truman was becoming disturbed ("and he is apt to be petulant if one is not careful"), Oxnam then advanced the proposal: "Change the designation of Mr. Taylor from the Personal Representative of the President, with the rank of Ambassador, to His Holiness the Pope, to the Personal Representative of the President to Religious Leaders of the World." Oxnam explained: "This will end the ambassadorial rank. It will mean he is not appointed to a church or to a religious organization, but he is appointed by you in an hour when you need advice around the world as your personal representative to individuals, namely leaders. This means that all he is getting from the Pope could be gotten and he similarly could meet the Archbishop of Canterbury, other Protestant religious leaders, Jewish leaders, leaders of the Eastern Orthodox Church as well as other religions. This is in strict keeping with our principle of treating all religions with equal favor and it is in accord with our principle of the separation of Church and

State." Said Truman: "I believe that this is a constructive suggestion. It appeals to me very much. I cannot give you a definite answer upon it until I have had opportunity to analyse it, but I will invite you back to talk it over."

The following day Oxnam wrote the president repeating the proposal that Truman change the designation of Taylor's mission from "the personal representative of the President, to His Holiness the Pope" to "the personal representative of the President to the religious leaders of the world." The White House on November 20 acknowledged the communication. There followed a long silence. On February 11, 1948, the bishop inquired as to Truman's inaction. On March 26 came a reply. The president thanked Oxnam for his counsel, but after careful consideration he concluded that he could not bring himself either to terminate the mission or to change its essential character.

Lutheran leader Fry then informed Oxnam that he had never had much faith in Truman's word that he would "disavow this obnoxious excrescence on the face of American diplomacy." "Like you," Oxnam replied, "I had little confidence in any real action from the very beginning, but I thought it wise to press the matter diplomatically as long as there was any hope of action." However, Truman continued his policy of holding out hope—at best a policy of stalling; at worst, one of dissimulation. For example, Truman's secretaries, first Charles G. Ross and then Matthew J. Connelly, assured Protestant leaders that the mission of Taylor would be terminated "when peace is made."

Methodism's Council of Bishops and the 1948 General Conference, to say nothing of other denominations, continued to question the denouement of this strange mission of (as one Disciples of Christ leader put it) "the ambassador-who-was-not-quite-an-ambassador [who] was listed in the Vatican calendar as the American ambassador." Ironically, the Vatican was wondering the same thing. It the spring of 1949 the rumor spread that Truman was to give Taylor full diplomatic rank as the accredited ambassador of the United States to the Holy See. Oxnam shot an inquiry to Truman, June 13, 1949, adding his doubts about Taylor's competency based upon the unfortunate experiences of World Council of Churches leaders, including Oxnam himself, with Taylor. (More about this in a moment.)

Secretary of State Dean Acheson, in a "memorandum for the President," July 5, 1949, stated that "the Department of State is unaware of any such proposal as that reported by the columnist to be under consideration. However, it is recommended that you reply to Bishop Oxnam so that he may have no doubts in this respect." This Truman did, July 7: "My dear Bishop: I have your letter of June thirteenth. As you surmise, there is no basis in fact for the statement in the press to which you refer. At the present time no change is contemplated in the mission of Mr. Myron C. Taylor." Maybe, after reading the reassurance, the Methodist muttered to himself the motto of Missouri naturally known to Truman: "Show me!"

Mr. Taylor tendered his resignation as personal representative to the pope on January 18, 1950. Would Truman now seek to establish formal diplomatic relations with the Holy See, as Oxnam and Co. had long feared? Oxnam by a letter to the president and then by telegrams to the president and secretary of state repeated his opposition. He sent a telegram to each of the six hundred Methodist district superintendents, urging that they have each pastor and church send immediate protests to the White House and State Department. "The issue may be decided shortly," warned the telegram. "It is a Roman Catholic bid for power that should be defeated." His colleagues on the Council of Bishops poured in their protests also, including one from Bishop Fred P. Corson, soon to be apotheosized by Pope Paul VI and the Catholic University of America for his ecumenical spirit, who headed Methodist observers at the Second Vatican Council and had private audiences with the pope on three occasions. The White House increasingly bulged with thousands of individual and group protests.

On September 11, 1950, Oxnam convened a meeting of Protestant and Orthodox leaders to prepare a document bearing the title "A Brief in Support of Maintaining a Valuable American Tradition," subsequently approved by the Federal Council's executive committee and the new National Council. Plans were laid for every individual denomination to bring pressure to bear on Washington to block appointment of another more formal representative. Oxnam petitioned the president to receive a delegation of thirty or thirty-five leaders of the Protestant and

Eastern Orthodox churches of the nation. After some backing-and-filling, Truman agreed to see Oxnam and one other man, Edward H. Pruden, pastor of Truman's Washington church, the First Baptist Church.[5]

At this fourth and final meeting, October 31, 1950, when Truman was presented with the brief on the separation of church and state, "A Valuable American Tradition," he broke in, "You don't have to convince me of that! I am a Baptist, and no one believes more in the separation of Church and State than I do." When the subject turned to Spain and Latin America, Truman growled in regard to Franco, "I don't intend to have a damn thing to do with him. Forgive me, that profanity." (Oxnam forgave him.) The president continued: "I know the situation in Latin American countries, and I know what is going on in Spain. The Protestant is buried like a pauper; there are no rights. Masonry is restricted.[6] I've already told representatives of the Vatican to convey to the Pope the necessity of cleaning up that situation in Spain, so that the Cardinal who is responsible will know that we never will have any dealing with Franco until they do clean the matter up." Truman then again stressed the necessity of the moral forces of the world standing together against those deceitful "fellows" in the Kremlin, adding, "Of course, the Vatican is the greatest listening post in the world." Oxnam sallied, "If the Pope has anything to tell us, and he's really interested in fighting Communism, is there any reason he can't send that information to you, just as any other Church can do it? We do not see the necessity of that recognition." After Oxnam and Pruden warned of the united American Protestant opposition to an appointment of an ambassador, they departed; and although the president made no promise not to seek Senate confirmation should he decide in favor of such an appointment, the spirit of the meeting was friendly, or so Oxnam believed, and in his diary he wrote words of praise of Truman.

Nevertheless, after writing a bread-and-butter note on November 6, Oxnam sent still another stern letter to the president on November 14, opening, "I have just received disturbing news, perhaps I should say alarming news." Can the reports possibly be true that an ambassador is about to be nominated? Why is the Roman Catholic Church pressing such an "unpatriotic demand?" "I sincerely trust that no decision will be made that will force the Protestant churches of this nation to take the necessary steps to maintain our tradition of the separation of church and state and to protect our liberties." And so the issue remained unresolved as 1950 closed.

Sometime between the meeting with Oxnam and Pruden on October 31, 1950, and January 4, 1951, Truman definitely made up his mind to nominate an ambassador extraordinary and plenipentiary of the United States of America to the State of Vatican City, for on January 4, Charles P. Taft was called to the White House and offered the post. He declined, and in doing so advised Truman that the idea be scrapped "because it would cause a very bitter fight." The Taft Papers record the interesting fact that Truman had not consulted either Secretary of State Dean Acheson or the White House secretariat before offering the post. Interestingly, also, earlier, in 1948, Taft had suggested that, with the termination of the Taylor mission, a minister be appointed to the Rome Embassy and assigned to the Vatican. "Dean [Acheson] told me, however," reported Taft, "that they had tried out my proposal . . . and that the Vatican had refused to receive anybody not directly accredited to them." A final fascinating point about Taft's understanding of the matter is found in a letter to Sam Cavert of the Federal Council dated October 5, 1949: "Appendix C leads me to say to you in confidence and with no indication of the source of my information, that the working officers of the State Department have made a careful study of all of Mr. Taylor's reports from the Vatican, and their final conclusion is that, with perhaps one or two minor exceptions, they added nothing to our information. They do not feel that the experiment was worth it, from that standpoint." Consequently, on March 10, 1950, Taft sent the following telegram to Acheson: "Informed that careful official review of Myron Taylor dispatches over entire period shows that little of value was added to State Department knowledge of operations. Appointment of successor can therefore only be placed on political grounds and urge strongly that it is not justified." [7]

During the next ten months a restive American Protestantism (as well as the Jewish and secular), a disturbed Vatican, and a divided Roman Catholic population wondered what the president's ultimate decision would be.[8]

Finally, on October 20, 1951, Truman nominated General Mark Clark as the first United States ambassador to the Vatican. The deed was done—but done in such a seemingly maladroit fashion as to ensure defeat. Why nominate a general hated for his bloody generalship in the Italian campaign and do so without informing Acheson or smoothing the way on Capitol Hill, especially with Senator Tom Connolly, the chairman of the Senate Foreign Relations Committee—and from Texas to boot, where Clark was especially hated? Why nominate a general, which would involve changing the law in order that Clark might still receive his military benefits? Why submit his name on the eve of the adjournment of Congress when action by both the Senate and House would be required?

Some pundits speculated that Truman named Clark in order to woo the Catholic vote, knowing that the Protestants would then be placated when the Senate denied confirmation. Asked how the bill was received, one senator, understandably, replied, "Like a deck of heroin." For his part, Oxnam was convinced that "the President fully intends to go through with this thing. When he makes up his mind on this he is as stubborn as a mule." In any event, editor Harold E. Fey of the *Christian Century* immediately expressed to Oxnam the view that the "nomination offers Protestants the first opportunity we have had in a generation to speak with one united voice." [9] Bishop Sherrill informed Oxnam that it "is perfectly clear that we had to face this as a cold-blooded political maneuver, and that there was no possibility of any appeal to conscience in the matter; that we simply had to make it perfectly clear to the President and to others that this is politically unwise." This touched the neuralgic point.

With the Clark nomination, a situation that had long been briskly bubbling now boiled over. Oxnam addressed the issue in numerous sermons and lectures, in articles, over the radio, and on television. He worked closely with POAU and the National Council. He convened and planned with Methodism's Council of Bishops and with leaders of other denominations. He counseled with shapers of public opinion, notably Freda Kirchway of *The Nation* and Mrs. Agnes Meyer, wife of the owner of the *Washington Post*. (Meyer personally opposed the nomination, but editorially the *Post* supported it, as did most major newspapers, including the *New York Times*.) Here are part of Oxnam's instructions mailed to every Methodist minister on December 10, 1951:

> 1. Write each of your Senators protesting this appointment, and be certain to send a second letter on January 10, 1952, just after Congress reassembles. It is a matter of first importance that we indicate a continuing determination in this matter. 2. Write the President a similar letter. 3. Organize a committee in each local church to call upon the members of the church and bring this issue to the personal attention of as many members as possible. Order from The National Council . . . a sufficient number of the pamphlet entitled "Diplomatic Relations With The Vatican" so that each member may receive a copy. . . . 4. And this is very important! Write letters to your local papers, express your views respectfully but with determination. Write Time, Life and other great publications. 5. If Area mass meetings are held, be sure to have a large delegation.

In his concern, Oxnam delivered up such public statements as the following:

> Casuistical camouflage cannot conceal the fact that when the United States government sends an ambassador to the Vatican, it is actually sending a representative to the Roman Catholic Church. The fact that the present Pope is up to his ears in politics, that it was he who negotiated the concordats with Hitler and Mussolini and whose heart is warmed when he thinks of Franco, and that he finally got a bit of land and absolute sovereignty for a price, does not change the real fact that he is the Pope, and it is with him we deal.
>
> . . . the American people must consider the implications of the act. Does this mean that priests are spies and report secret information to their superiors, and through channels finally reach Rome? If the Vatican sells the United States such information as it is ready to sell, what does the Vatican sell Peron, Franco, and Adenauer? What was sold to Hitler and Mussolini?
>
> It is alleged that the military wants the information the Vatican is supposed to possess. It would appear that a Pope really interested in fighting communism would offer all the resources at his command without exacting a price. In this case it is alleged that the information was refused unless the price were paid, namely, the appointment of an ambassador.
>
> The road to Rome is also a road to Washington. The appointment of an ambassador to the Vatican gives the Roman Catholic Church a privileged status in the United States, since the papal nuncio from the Vatican who would travel from Rome to Washington would, after a time, become the

senior member of the diplomatic corps. He would have access to the officials of the United States government denied the church leaders of the nation. His sacerdotal robes would grace the affairs of state.

Apparently the only Methodist bishop to question the tactics employed by Oxnam in the anti-Clark crusade was Charles W. Brashares. "I hesitate to think that with all the needy causes of the world," he wrote Oxnam on October 26, 1951, "the one thing which would rouse Protestantism to stand as a man is not the issue of the world's need, or wheat to India, or war, or anything except a matter so easily interpreted as a defense of our own Protestant advantage." The then bishop of the Des Moines Area noted that even "if we can arouse every man, woman, and child in Protestantism to attend all of these [protest] meetings, we have not at all proven they resent an appointment to the Vatican. We have only proven that there is a central authority in Protestantism that can either scare or conjole our Protestants to do what the central authority wants them to do. Out this way where we believe so much in freedom and democracy, we wonder if that is the kind of Protestantism we are building. Even if we should enter into a race with the Catholic Church as to who can have the larger mass meetings and get their people to do what the central authority demands, surely the Catholics would have us beat at that. They can excommunicate anyone who does not follow their orders, and we neither have that authority nor want it. Let's not play their game!"

Brashares's letter touches on Catholic historian F. William O'Brien's thoughtful speculation that Clark's nomination "was an issue not nearly so deep nor so wide as some have presumed it to be. If at times the question does seem to have set the country ablaze, there are strong grounds for suspecting that it might have been due more to incendiarism than to any spontaneous combustion." Perhaps O'Brien is not incorrect to suggest that the leaders of the Protestant Establishment, not the least Oxnam, lit up the skies with flares of warning alerting the rank-and-file to an otherwise mostly unperceived danger. Perhaps a comparison to the prohibition issue with the issue of U.S.-Vatican diplomatic ties is misleading. Prohibitionists knew existentially the perils of booze—alcohol was a clear and present danger objectively proven and subjectively known—whereas one suspects that to most Protestants, until alerted by their leaders, Vatican representation was a murky and remote danger. Oxnam, of course, might reply that the issue was only one of many threats by the Catholic Church to the separation of church and state and to the American "way of life" in general.

General Clark must have felt the skies had fallen on him, and on January 13, 1952, he withdrew his name. Truman's reaction was the bitter observation, "I think the United States does have a monopoly on bigotry." A relieved Oxnam nonetheless remained vigilant, feeling the continuing issue could "well determine the 1952 election." And so he continued to work with the National Council's Committee on Diplomatic Relations with the Vatican and joined the other Methodist bishops in proclaiming: "This is an issue of principle, not of persons. It is but to compound a blunder to name a substitute for General Clark." Truman half-heartedly announced he would search for a substitute for Clark, but dropped the idea as the fall election neared. Adlai Stevenson said he would not make an appointment and Eisenhower evaded a stand and in the end the issue was (Oxnam to the contrary) a nonissue.[10]

Two sidelights to the story. Shortly after Clark announced the withdrawal of his name, Oxnam was called on by Morris Ernst. The visitor boasted about his friendships with F.D.R. and Truman, relating that only recently he had spent ninety minutes with the president. He then implied he was on marching orders from Truman and put to Oxnam the question: How would Oxnam respond to the appointment of a liberal Jew as ambassador to the Vatican? The president was now considering the appointment of such an individual on the theory that Protestants could not attack two minorities at once—Catholics and Jews. Barked Oxnam: "Mr. Ernst, don't make a mistake. The true friends of the Jews are in the Protestant communions, but this is a matter of principle, and we shall attack it no matter who is appointed, whether it be a Methodist, a Presbyterian, a Baptist, or a Roman Catholic, or a Jew. All you are asking for in such a matter is the release of all the anti-Semitism that is present in this country upon an issue that will give that anti-Semitism a standing that it does not now have."

A second sidelight. Senator John F. Kennedy at the Gridiron Dinner in 1958 announced that one of his first acts, should he become president of the United States, would be to appoint Bishop G. Bromley Oxnam as his representative to the Vatican. When informed of Kennedy's tongue-in-cheek tease, Oxnam observed, "He must have a rollicking sense of humor and be much of a human being."

A tangential matter, but not an inconsequential one, concerns a misunderstanding between Oxnam and Myron C. Taylor relating, primarily, to the World Council of Churches. (The Taylor Papers and the Truman Papers disclose that both men exchanged copies of Oxnam's communications with each man. In a word, Taylor kept the president informed of Oxnam's activities and Truman kept his personal ambassador alerted to what Oxnam was up to.)

Oxnam and Taylor first met in Florence in early May 1945, the bishop being on assignment to visit the chaplains in the Mediterranean theater. Oxnam orally and then in follow-up letters petitioned Taylor to suggest to the pope that he issue a statement on religious liberty; namely, the following: "The Roman Catholic Church, in the Name of Our Blessed Lord, desires the same religious freedom from the State for all Christian bodies that it desires for itself; and as a Church will manifest the same spirit towards all Christians and Christian churches that it desires expressed toward itself." It is a simple formula, Oxnam patiently explained. "It is but Our Lord's command: Do unto others as ye would be done by." Taylor orally and then in follow-up letters patiently explained "that I was not authorized to act in a general diplomatic capacity to deal with the internal affairs of the Roman Catholic Church, nor have I done so." Taylor insisted that he had never taken up any questions with the pope that were strictly religious questions "so far as they might affect the conduct of the Catholic Church or other churches." Taylor's last letter in 1945 closed somewhat sharply: "As you have the opportunity to present your ideas to the President directly, it would seem wise that you pursue that course rather than through me."

A further exchange of letters followed, and finally on October 20, 1947, Oxnam and Taylor met at the Union Club in New

York. Present also were Fry, Cavert, Edwin T. Dahlberg, president of the Northern Baptist Convention, and Presbyterian layman William B. Pugh. (Bishop Sherrill was unable to attend.) The meeting lasted almost three hours, Taylor doing almost all of the talking. (Taylor's minutes of the meeting and Oxnam's diary are in accord as to what transpired.) The Protestant delegation listened in fascination as Taylor informed them that "I had the most secret code to the President that existed. This is the main reason why you have never seen anything published about these activities." And: "This is all very secret material. It is not even on file in the State Department. But President Truman has said I might tell you the story in general outline." For his part, Oxnam recorded: "I am quite convinced that Mr. Taylor believes he has been and is doing patriotic service in the interests of peace. He said that all of his correspondence has been direct with the President, that he had a secret code and that it did not flow through the State Department.[11] Nevertheless, Oxnam lamented despite the interesting information, "it was in no sense a satisfactory answer to the real issue."

Oxnam and five colleagues next met with Taylor, at his request, on May 3, 1949. Cavert prepared the following "Memorandum on Conference with Myron C. Taylor":

> At the invitation of Mr. Myron C. Taylor, a consultation was held with him at the Union Club, Park Avenue and 69th Street, New York, on May 3, 1949, in which the following participated: Bishop G. Bromley Oxnam, Rt. Rev. John B. Bentley, Dr. Edwin T. Dahlberg, Dr. William B. Pugh, Dr. F. Eppling Reinartz and Dr. Samuel McCrea Cavert.
>
> Mr. Taylor made a rather detailed report of his conversations with representatives of the World Council of Churches in April-May, 1948, with special reference to the attitude which he felt he had found in World Council circles toward the representation of the Roman Catholic Church at Amsterdam. Mr. Taylor read reports of his conversations with Dr. Visser 't Hooft and Pastor Boegner and correspondence which he had had on the subject with Pastor Boegner and the Archbishop of Canterbury.
>
> Several members of the group pointed out that at certain points Mr. Taylor apparently had inaccurate information—for example, in saying that there were "300 denominations" in the World Council and that the World Council's constitution "estops the Catholic Church from participating."

In his presentation Mr. Taylor reported that the letter addressed to him by Pastor Boegner had "shut the door" to the pope's designating two observers to attend the Amsterdam Assembly. Mr. Taylor believed that, if the pope had been invited to do so, he would have named two observers. It was suggested to Mr. Taylor that he had misunderstood Pastor Boegner's letter, for the Provisional Committee of the World Council had always desired that there should be Roman Catholic observers in attendance on some basis.

Members of the group were especially troubled by Mr. Taylor's remarks that Pastor Boegner had said that "official observers were not desired," that "American Protestantism would fight a proposal that two observers be named by the pope," and that "American Protestantism wanted no Catholic representation at Amsterdam." Members of the group assured Mr. Taylor that the remarks as quoted did not represent the point of view of either the Provisional Committee or the American members of it.

In response to a question, Mr. Taylor said that he would be very glad to receive from the World Council a statement concerning its contacts with the Roman Catholic Church and the pope during the various states of development of the ecumenical movement, together with official information about the World Council's constitution and structure.

When Mr. Taylor referred in informal conversation to his feeling that Amsterdam should have included representatives of "all moral and spiritual forces"—specifically referring to the Moslems—it was pointed out to him that the meeting at Amsterdam was not an *ad hoc* conference of people interested in world peace or international affairs, but an official assembly of delegated representatives of Christian churches which were forming a permanent council.

Mr. Taylor read a letter from Cyrus Sulzberger, correspondent of *The New York Times*, expressing the judgment that the Russian Church is a "tool of the Kremlin." Mr. Taylor emphasized the importance of a common front on the part of all the forces of religion and freedom in opposition to atheistic Communism. It was suggested to him that there were also dangers to freedom from ecclesiastical totalitarianism.

In response to a question, Mr. Taylor stated that he had no intimation that President Truman contemplated submitting Mr. Taylor's name to the Senate for ratification as an ambassador to the Vatican.

Samuel McCrea Cavert

Taylor's own minutes of the meeting confirm Cavert's record; most salient are the points that Taylor understood—and so had informed Truman—that the pope *definitely* would have sent two observers to Amsterdam if an invitation to do so had been extended, and secondly, that American Protestants had blocked the idea. Mr. Taylor was mistaken. We have the testimony given at the time by such individuals as Willem Adolf Visser 't Hooft (and also his *Memoirs*) and Pastor Marc Boegner. We have the most authoritative histories of the World Council of Churches. And we have Oxnam's records.

The meeting of May 3 left Oxnam, head of the delegation, furious. Taylor, Oxnam recorded, revealed a "complete lack of knowledge of the World Council"; "an ignorance that is inexcusable and with a naiveté that was almost laughable"; "an impropriety of . . . breaking into a situation which was none of his business." "It was really as pitiful a presentation as I have ever listened to, a man utterly incapable, by way of preparation, of understanding what is going on, a man who seems to have no understanding of the relation of church and state, who seemed to think (he used the word 'corral') that it might be possible to corrall the religious groups of the world in our present fight against communism." "I finally suggested to him that we request him to file with the President a research document which would cite all of the correspondence and resolutions, so that the President might know that Mr. Taylor's report was directly contrary to fact."

During the meeting, Lutheran Reinartz reminded Taylor that the World Council was not an organization formed to stop communism or block atheism, as Taylor and Truman appeared to think, but an association of those who have very essential oneness in their religious outlook. Presbyterian Pugh confirmed the reminder: "I think one thing that should be conveyed to the President and the Pope is that the Council of Churches was still at this time in process of formation, and that our primary interest as a world conference of churches was not necessarily world peace or the fight of religions against communism, but that we were really coming together as a family of churches for the purpose of organizing the ecumenical movement."

The crucial point is that both Taylor and Truman seemed to view the World Council of Churches as an instrument in the Cold War—a corporation to embrace not only Christians but Hindus, Buddhists, and Muslims united in resistance to atheistic communism. Taylor had pouted when his suggestion was declined that he should be invited to attend Amsterdam as the representative of the president of the United States. When Pastor Boegner pointed out that it would be inappropriate for any representative of a temporal power to be present, Taylor retorted that John Foster Dulles would be there, and Boegner explained that Dulles was a Presbyterian *church* delegate. Visser 't Hooft recalls that later he "received a discreet inquiry whether we would be interested in having an ambassador from the U.S.A. accredited to the World Council of Churches." When he replied he had no idea what to do with such an ambassador, Washington dropped the matter. It would be like asking the manager of a china shop, explained the Dutchman, after he had had a visit from a bull, whether he would like to have the bull as a permanent guest. Truman's simple mind-set is revealed in a letter to "Dear Bess": "Had Myron Taylor in too. Looks as if he and I may get the morals of the world on our side. We are talking to the Archbishop of Canterbury, the bishop at the head of the Lutheran Church, the Metropolitan of the Greek Church at Istanbul, and the Pope. I may send him to see the top Buddhist and the Grand Lama of Tibet. If I can mobilize the people who believe in a moral world against the Bolshevik materialists who believe as Henry Wallace does—'that the end justifies the means'—we can win this fight. Treaties, agreements, or the moral code mean nothing to Communists. So we've got to organize the people who believe in honor and the Golden Rule to win the world back to peace and Christianity. Ain't it hell!" (One wonders what "the top Buddhist and the Grand Lama of Tibet" thought about that!)

Increasingly Oxnam lost all confidence in Taylor, reporting to the Council of Bishops that he was a "poor old man" who "has been bowled over by the fawning of the Roman Church. He makes his reports, and the President, in turn, is misinformed." When Oxnam suggested to him that he become the president's representative to the religious leaders of the world, without the formal rank of ambassador, Taylor replied, "But where would I sit at banquets and similar functions in Europe if I were not an Ambassador?" The bishop allowed how the hosts of Harry Hopkins did not insist that he dine alone!

Although exasperated, Oxnam wrote Taylor in September about the Amsterdam misunderstanding. Taylor in turn reported to Truman advising a stalling strategy: "I have thought to tide this subject over until after the advent of the new year, when I am confident it will not be of further significance to him [Oxnam]. . . . I believe it would be a mistake to give him any reply or to submit to him any documentation at this time." Meanwhile, Henry Smith Leiper, general secretary of the World Council of Churches, was preparing a document, "Relations Between the Ecumenical Movement and the Vatican in the Twentieth Century," to be presented to Truman for his edification. On October 25 Taylor phoned Oxnam to protest an article critical of him written by Oxnam and Fry, suggest that Amsterdam was water over the dam, and request that the "Relations" document not be sent to the president. Oxnam agreed to hold up the document until the new year. Taylor resigned January 18, 1950. On the twenty-ninth of January Oxnam wrote Truman, "Since . . . Mr. Taylor has now submitted his resignation we are not now inclined to present this memorandum, provided we may assume that no successor to Mr. Taylor is to be appointed." Later, Taylor again called Oxnam and the bishop again agreed to hold up the document. Taylor again protested, "I did not like the item you gave the newspapers last year. The tone was very unfortunate. I was not happy about it." "I am very sorry for it," said Oxnam. Two months later, when it was clear that Truman was considering nominating a successor to Taylor, Oxnam forwarded the document. Secretary Hassett promised Oxnam that the president would give it "very careful study." If he did, he obviously did not share the document's conclusions.

The response of the Roman Catholic Church to the truly historic 1954 Evanston Assembly of the World Council of Churches hardly muted Protestant-Catholic tensions. The pope forbade Catholic participation. Cardinal Samuel Stritch issued a pastoral letter echoing His Holiness. Chicago-area Catholics recall that they hesitated even to *pass through* Evanston, so severe were the warnings of their superiors. Catholics, or some of them (as well as some fearful Protestants, of course), made it clear that they did not wish to see the land of the free polluted by Iron Curtain commies even though they professed to be Christians. Among the peaceful picketers at the Assembly, one lone soul carried a sign reading, "All roads lead to Rome. Come home brothers."

A clear expression of American Catholicism's coming of age was the postwar push for public aid for parochial schools, Catholics declaring it their right as American citizens to receive government support for the education of their children just as did people with children in the public schools. The issue was a financially acute one because of the vast expansion of the Catholic school system, bearing heavily on Catholic parents, and because of the possible increase in availability of federal funds for educational purposes. Although billions of dollars were at stake, the issue went deeper than dollars. It raised up enduring church-state constitutional questions. It symbolized to Protestants the Catholic Church's insatiable grasp for power; and to Catholics, it spotlighted Protestantism's bigoted denial to American Catholics of their full citizenship rights.

Would G. Bromley Oxnam become involved in this vexing controversy is about as innocent a question as asking if a cow would lick Lot's wife. Upon his motion, the Methodist Council of Bishops sent a letter to all Methodist ministers urging them to voice their position to their congressmen and to call upon their parishioners to do likewise. "Roman Catholic attitudes toward our basic civil liberties," counseled the bishops, "are of such a nature that if an increasing percentage of our people is to be trained in such schools, fundamental changes will occur in American culture. The catechisms used in some parochial schools condemn and reject the basic civil liberties of free speech, free press, free assembly, and freedom of conscience." The General Conference passed a resolution, as did, probably, every Annual Conference. Oxnam took the lead in placing the Federal Council firmly in opposition. He of course was up to his hips in the POAU's campaign. He met with the officers of the National Education, Association in strategy planning sessions. As a member of the President's Commission on Higher Education, he blocked efforts of the Catholic representatives to have the commission endorse federal aid to nonpublic schools.[12] Chirping like a canary in a coal mine, he endlessly addressed the subject, especially before groups of teachers. Articles from his pen appeared in journals as diverse as *The Nation* and *The Nation's Schools,* some being reprinted in pamphlet form and widely distributed.

Oxnam's arguments were penetrating. "Secularism is a smoke screen," he maintained. "Behind it the Roman Catholic hierarchy mobilizes to secure public funds for the support of parochial education. The ultimate objective is the destruction of the American principle of the separation of church and state." "Personally," he said, "I do not want public monies to be used to support Communist schools, Fascist schools, Roman Catholic schools or Protestant schools. Public money should be used to support public schools." Appealing to Jewish Americans, he asked, "Is a Jew to pay taxes for the support of Roman Catholic parochial education when he believes in some quarters the emphasis is of such a nature as to contribute to anti-Semitism?"

The Supreme Court was taken to the woodshed by Oxnam and the Council of Bishops for upholding a New Jersey law providing for bus transportation to parochial schools in the famous decision in *Everson v. Board of Education.* However, the following year, 1948, the Court received from Oxnam a pat on the back for deciding in *McCullom v. Board of Education* that it was unconstitutional for voluntary religious instruction to be given on public school premises. Revealingly, twenty-one Protestant leaders, including Bishops McConnell and Baker, questioned the Court's wisdom, fearing that "whatever its intention may be, this hardening of the idea of 'separation' by the court will greatly accelerate the trend toward the secularization of our culture."

On February 6, 1947, Oxnam spent an hour with Senator Robert Taft. Oxnam reviewed what he had told the senator about his position regarding federal aid to education:

> Namely, that it be administered without discrimination as to race, secondly that federal support should not mean control of educational policy or personnel in the state, third that public funds should go to states, but should be used only in institutions which the state itself decided should receive public support. The reason for this position is, of course, that while we are opposed to any public funds going to private institutions, particularly parochial institutions, we recognize the value of upholding the doctrine of states' rights in this matter. We can oppose the matter in

> the states, and will. The best way to keep it down, however, federally, is to keep the state situation in the forefront. Once it is established federally that the public funds may go to parochial schools, then it is policy everywhere. When we keep it in the states, only a few states will so allow at present, and we can win the battle there. It gives all the Senators who are opposed to public funds for parochial schools a chance to insist that it only be given to the state where the states themselves have made the decision. I told him we should also affirm our position about the separation of church and state. He agreed thoroughly with this proposal and said that he intended to see it through.

Taft proceeded to introduce such a bill in the Senate. It was supported by the National Education Association, and the *NEA Journal* carried Oxnam's long endorsement. (POAU, unsurprisingly, opposed it, believing it conceded too much.) Passing the Senate, the measure died in the House.

The issue flared up again in 1949 with the introduction of a bill, H.R. 4643, by Democratic Congressman Graham A. Barden of North Carolina, specifically limiting federal aid to "tax-supported grade schools and high schools which are under public supervision and control," an amendment to a Senate measure, S. 246. Many Catholics were outraged at the prospects of having $300 million of tax moneys barred from supporting their parochial schools. After all, they reasoned, Catholic tax dollars had contributed to that sum. Cardinal Spellman led the resistance movement, delivering a Fordham University address on "The Barden Bill—Brewer of Bigotry." In the address the prelate characterized the supporters of the measure as "unhooded Klansmen" and Barden as a "new apostle of bigotry" busy "venting his venom upon children" and used other language hardly conducive to civil discourse.[13] Mrs. Eleanor Roosevelt in her newspaper column, "My Day," took moderate exception to the cardinal, and Spellman in turn immoderately made reply, his letter closing, "For, whatever you may say in the future, your record of anti-Catholicism stands for all to see—a record which you yourself wrote on the pages of history which cannot be recalled—documents of discrimination unworthy of an American mother!" The late president's wife replied that she had no sense of being an unworthy American mother. "The final judgment, my dear Cardinal Spellman," her riposte calmly but cuttingly closed, "of the unworthiness of all human beings is in the hands of God."

In the end, the Barden bill died because of Catholic opposition and that of civil rights advocates who believed segregated black schools in the South would not be beneficiaries, Catholic John Lesinski, chairman of the House Education and Labor Committee, finding it reeking of "bigotry and racial prejudice." In the end, Spellman (under marching orders from the Vatican, according to his biographer John Cooney) wrote a letter of conciliation to Mrs. Roosevelt and when traveling up the Hudson he "happened" to find himself in the vicinity of Hyde Park and found it "convenient" to pay her a social visit.[14]

Before the Barden-Spellman-Roosevelt brouhaha was over, Oxnam's growl was heard. He praised the Barden bill: "It is the preservation of American public education and its protection from a prelate with a prehensile hand." Spellman was a "little man with big ideas" whose "ineptitude and ignorance were revealed in his vicious attack upon . . . Mrs. Roosevelt." However, it is easy to understand "why the Cardinal lost his head with more than two hundred million dollars at stake. Perhaps the apology trip up the Hudson kept him from losing his red cap." Spellman in his Fordham speech bore "false witness," indeed, what he said "is to lie." [15]

In early August Oxnam kicked out the bung and let his anger flow undammed. The occasion was a recorded interview for commentator Ed Hart's radio program. The interview took place in New Hampshire, near Oxnam's summer home. Hart desired a firm answer to Spellman. (Hart later invited Spellman to answer Oxnam, but the cardinal declined.) Hart and Oxnam talked for several days before the actual interview was recorded. The disk that was cut was distributed nationally to interested radio stations in addition to Hart's WWDC, Washington. The interview was picked up by both the Associated Press and the United Press International. Therefore, it is possible that tens of thousands of Americans, including Catholics, heard or read Oxnam's intense and provocative words. A few passages to capture their flavor:

> The attack upon Mrs. Roosevelt reveals the methods that we may expect from men determined to master American life.

> Thus Roman Catholic political parties in European nations follow the Vatican political line just as Communist parties follow the Moscow line. We want neither the Vatican political line nor the Moscow political line in America. We do not appreciate the interference of Pacelli, the head of the Vatican state, nor of Stalin, the head of the Communist state, in our affairs.
>
> Roman Catholicism in conditioning the mind to authoritarianism in religion, conditions the mind to authoritarianism in politics and economics. How do you account for Communist strength in Italy itself, where we are told 90% of the people are Roman Catholic?
>
> Note the striking parallel between the organizational structure and method of the World-Wide Communist political party and the World-Wide Roman Catholic political party. Both are totalitarian. Both seek control of the minds of men everywhere. Both practice excommunication, character assassination, and economic reprisals. Neither Rome nor Moscow knows what tolerance means. Both demand blind, unthinking loyalty. Neither Moscow nor Rome believes in the separation of church and state. Both Moscow and Rome interfere in the affairs of other states. Both Moscow and Rome seek to shackle the minds of those they control by telling them what they can read, what movies they can see, what newspapers they must take. Neither Rome nor Moscow can brook opposition. And both Moscow and Rome have perfected the Hitler technique of repeating prevarications often enough and big enough to insure their acceptance. Both seek to divide and rule, they create separatism.

Small wonder that the *St. Louis Post-Dispatch* could observe of the Spellman-Oxnam donnybrook, "If there has ever been so sharp an exchange at so high a level in American church circles, it does not come to mind." That observation is right on the money. The slugfest was not between two flyweights but between the most powerful figure in the American Catholic hierarchy and certainly one of the most powerful individuals in the American Protestant Establishment. The tragedy is that surely some Catholics believed that their champion hit below the belt and that surely some thoughtful Protestants believed (or should have believed) that their leader did so also. If Oxnam was attempting to persuade his fellow American coreligionists of the errors of the hierarchy's leadership, surely the disingenuous analogy he drew between Rome and Moscow—in effect, that Catholicism was as un-American as communism—was counterproductive.

A hero of the public school teachers, Oxnam was not less so of family-planning advocates. His message was broadcast by lecture, article, and radio. He championed Margaret Sanger, godmother of the birth control movement in America and abroad.[16] And in 1947 he accepted the chairmanship of the National Sponsoring Committee for the First National Planned Parenthood Campaign. Oxnam's sincerity is unquestioned. Musing over the deaths of the infant children of Samuel and Susanna Wesley, he wrote in his diary: "No, no we have made no advance in caring for children, and restriction of family is a sin. In the almost vulgar lines of 'Women,' the New York play, 'Are you Catholic or careless?', the celibates might do well to abandon the sacred name of 'father,' wake up to the fact that a small family well-raised, well-educated, and physically fit is a better line-up than indiscriminate breeding with ignorant masses. But Catholicism has never worried too much about ignorant masses, and the rulers never too much about cannon-fodder." In his zeal, Oxnam gave public support to the dangerous eugenics movement, informing Methodist seminarians: "The State, of course, owes it to the future to disallow the marriage of the physically and mentally unfit. Sterilization of the feeble minded has already proved to be worthy of the most careful consideration." At that time thirty-one states had compulsory sterilization laws dooming thousands of hopeless souls to childless existences.

The essential correctness of Oxnam's position on family planning would be acknowledged by a majority of Americans today, even by a majority of Catholics in the United States and the West. One can be appalled, even outraged, at the continuing official dogma of Rome regarding contraception. The global population explosion threatens humanity, and all living creatures, as does no other peril except only that of thermonuclear war itself. Rome's blindness to this is reprehensible. Therefore, one questions not the justice of Oxnam's case, but the unloving language which he employed to defend it. Once again no paraphrase will do; his exact words must be quoted for their full import:

> Religious leaders who declare that sexual intercourse in the married state shall be solely for the purpose of procreation, and who dare designate all other sexual intercourse as lust, seek to defile one of the most sacred of human relationships, to besmirch the beautiful, and, in effect, to blas-

> pheme. The men who forced Galileo to recant spoke the same dogmatic assurance that characterizes the men who attack planned parenthood. It is as sinful to identify ignorance with God's will in the twentieth century as it was in the seventeenth. It must never be forgotten that the same so-called authority that condemns planned parenthood is the authority that justified and practiced the inquisition. The obscurantism that tortured human beings in the name of religion is kin to the obtuseness that once denied a mother anesthesia in childbirth and now would bar the doors of the planned parenthood clinic.
>
> When a priest condemns a refined and devout Protestant mother as sinful because she uses the means medical research has made available for the proper spacing of her children, that priest not only insults American womanhood, he commits sin.
>
> When rituals declare that a child is conceived in sin and born in iniquity, I say such declarations are themselves sinful and iniquitous.
>
> The attack upon planned parenthood is often phrased in patriotic or religious terms. It is well to note that dictators called for large families and the appeal was couched in the noble diction of love for country. The truth is that these madmen wanted cannon-fodder. They desired the insurance that lies in vast numbers. They coveted the earth. . . . No group, whether political, social or ecclesiastic, should be allowed to hide its true purpose in moral platitude, when the real objective is to breed itself into a majority.

Who would gainsay the right of a *secularist* to employ such accusatory words to destroy a hated position of a powerful church? Still, can liberal Protestant *Christians* read these words of a Methodist bishop living in the mid–twentieth century without wincing?

The emerging Cold War abroad after 1945 exacerbated Catholic-Protestant tensions at home, or rather, more precisely, Catholic–liberal Protestant tensions, for many Protestants were as fervent Cold War warriors as the most militant Catholics. Oxnam's enemies charged him with the appeasement of the Soviet Union and with being "soft on communism." The allegation is absolutely false. Nevertheless, while absolutely not an appeaser or fellow traveler or pacifist, Oxnam's angle of vision was scarcely that of the Vatican's or Spellman's or, indeed, American Catholicism's in general. After all, the editors of *America* in fact *did* call for the nation to wage "holy war" if necessary to keep communism at bay. After all, it was not Oxnam but the liberal Catholic editors of *Commonweal* who in 1951 observed: "But for many people, sterile anti-Communism has become the hall-mark of Catholicism; it is the one characteristic note of our periodicals, sermons, academic addresses, speeches at Communion breakfasts. In many minds anti-Communism is actually a synonym for Catholic Action. It should give us pause that as men in their desperate need have stretched out their hands for life-giving bread, we Christians have been offering them the dead stone of anti-Communism."

By early 1946 Oxnam was convinced "that the Roman Catholic Church has declared war on Russia by announcing a worldwide war on Communism." He warned against having United States foreign policy determined by the will of Rome. He wondered why, if the Catholic Church was so willing to risk war with the dictator in the Kremlin, it was so silent about dictatorships in Catholic hands. He challenged (as did even Reinhold Niebuhr) the pope's hubristic proclamation, "Everyone knows that the Catholic Church never acts from worldly motives." Above all, perhaps, Oxnam denied that the Catholic Church stood as an impregnable bulwark against communism's spread; to the contrary, he asserted, it was Protestantism that provided the true shield. Oxnam gave fullest expression to this argument in a 1949 article for *Look* magazine entitled "How Protestants Fight Communism" which was reprinted and distributed by the Federal Council and The Methodist Church, an estimated several million reading it. The article opens:

> It is a striking and significant fact that communism has been unable to take root in Protestant countries. No Protestant land is seriously infiltrated by communism. Why?
>
> The answer is found in soil and atmosphere. The soil is enriched by liberty and the atmosphere cleansed by truth wherever Protestantism prevails.
>
> Protestant teaching fertilizes the good earth with freedom and democracy. Protestant insistence upon "the right of private judgment" develops the scientific attitude of mind, and penetrates the fog of ignorance and superstition.
>
> Protestant countries are characterized by the free man in the free society, who discovers and declares the truth that frees, and who in co-operation with free fellow men seeks to apply that truth for the common good. In such freedom-loving Protestant lands lies the real barrier to Communist expansion.
>
> Recently the State Department issued a map indicating the religious affiliation of the people of Europe. The countries predominantly Roman

> Catholic are shown in purple. The countries predominantly Protestant are shown in orange. A distinguished diplomat looked at this map and said, "This purple section from Poland right across Europe, including southern Germany and on to Spain, is Roman Catholic and constitutes a formidable barrier to Communist expansion."
>
> He was challenged immediately by one better acquainted with social fact. The real barrier to Communist imperialism is the orange area, the Protestant lands. Communism has not made headway in Protestant Finland, Protestant Sweden, Protestant Norway, Protestant Denmark, Protestant Holland, or Protestant Great Britain.
>
> On the other hand, Italy, which is 99 percent Roman Catholic, was but recently in danger of Communist revolution. Poland, Czechoslovakia, Hungary and Austria are in the Moscow orbit. Catholic Spain is free from communism, but only at the cost of a bloody civil war and a Fascist dictatorship.
>
> Today, Protestant Australia and Protestant New Zealand are not threatened by communism. Protestant United States is in no serious danger of accepting communism—certainly not in the great rural areas which are overwhelmingly Protestant, nor in the Protestant West with its heritage of the individualistic pioneer and the itinerant preacher, nor in the Protestant South.
>
> It is high time that Protestant strength and Protestant strategy·be understood.

The problem here, of course, is that the logic is not grounded in historical fact or historic perspective—or geography. Russia in 1917 was not a Roman Catholic country. How does it happen that in 1949 China fell to the Communists when its peoples were scarcely Roman Catholics and its government's leaders were Methodists? Protestant Finland was defeated by Soviet Russia and Protestant Latvia and Protestant Estonia absorbed. What is one to make of Protestant East Germany? (Or of Catholic West Germany and Catholic Belgium?) Roman Catholics were a minority in Yugoslavia and a tiny minority in Bulgaria, Rumania, and Albania. Did Hungary, Poland, and Czechoslovakia become Communist countries because of susceptibility to infiltration (as Oxnam argued) or because of the Red Army and Russian tanks (left unmentioned by Oxnam)? Why did not Austria remain in the Moscow orbit? Was it because Roman Catholics there became enlightened and Roman Catholic Poles, Czechs, and Hungarians did not?

If "freedom-loving Protestant lands" are immune to totalitarian rule, how explain the ease with which Protestant Norway and Protestant Denmark and Protestant Holland (though in fact with a large Catholic population) fell to the Nazis? Was it Protestantism that saved Great Britain (and Ireland) and Australia and New Zealand from conquest?

The absolute separation of church and state was Oxnam's Holy Grail and the union of church and state his Devil. Rarely if ever, however, did he acknowledge the rigorous separation of church and state in such Catholic countries as Mexico, Portugal, the Irish Free State, and France. Rarely if ever did he recognize the historic legal ties between church and state, ties disabling to Catholics, in Britain, Sweden, Finland, Norway, Denmark, Holland, and Greece. While he shredded the situation in Spain and Latin America with the repetitiveness of Ravel's *Bolero,* he was almost mute about the absence of democracy in non–Roman Catholic lands—Chiang Kai-shek's China, Rhee's Korea, Greece, South Africa, for example.

In the matter of the Cold War, Oxnam was certainly correct in warning that the United States should not hitch its foreign policies to Vatican interests, dragging like Vercingetorix behind Caesar's chariot. Oxnam was also right to deem the perfervid voices of Spellman and other Catholic spokesmen dangerous to the preservation of peace and, indeed, darkly adumbrating a call for a Holy War against godless Russia. Nevertheless, unfortunately he defended his position on occasion with asymmetrical arguments that were unmeasured and ahistorical and almost certain to enrage rather than enlighten Catholic Americans.

The Cold War abroad and the "Great Fear" at home are inseparable. As not all American Catholics were Cold War warriors and many American Protestants were, just so not all American Catholics supported "McCarthyism" and many American Protestants did. Notre Dame historian Vincent P. De Santis and Jesuit historian Donald F. Crosby have correctly observed that there was not and could not be a Catholic position on such an issue as McCarthyism. Both professors have properly honored those fine individual Catholics and publications counseling calmness. Civil liberties unquestionably had their Catholic champions. Nevertheless, Oxnam believed the Catholic hierarchy was fueling the "Great Fear" and this belief further intensified his critique of the hierarchy.[17]

After Oxnam's ten-hour ordeal before a hearing of the House Un-American Activities Committee on July 21, 1953, he found comfort in the overwhelming editorial support he received from the Protestant and secular press. With a few exceptions, such support was not forthcoming from the Catholic press. For example, *The Tablet*, organ of the Diocese of Brooklyn, said that an "objective reading of the testimony can result only in the conclusion that Bishop Oxnam is either stupidly gullible or a master of deviousness. It is hard to believe that a stupid person would rise to the eminent post of bishop of the Methodist Church." Oxnam was aware that his brave appearance before the House committee did not cut much ice with Spellman, for only weeks later the cardinal uttered the comforting thought that no American who is "uncontaminated by communism has lost his good name because of Congressional hearings on un-American activities." "Anguished cries," continued the prelate, "and protests against 'McCarthyism' are not going to dissuade Americans from their desire to see communists exposed." (Oxnam probably did not know that Spellman accepted invitations to cruise on the despicable Roy Cohn's yacht and that in return Spellman gave Cohn Catholic legal business in New York.) Oxnam probably did know that ex-Communist informers Bella Dodd, Elizabeth Bentley, and Louis Budenz had been courted into the Catholic Church by Monsignor Sheen and that both Bentley and Budenz found teaching positions in Catholic schools and that Archbishop Cushing appointed Budenz as his advisor on communism. Certainly Oxnam remembered that in *This Is My Life*, Budenz had reported that Oxnam while bishop of the Boston Area had been courted by the Communist Party—a charge the bishop immediately denied.

A feeling of amity was naturally not Oxnam's response when Catholic priests and Catholic organizations attempted to prevent his speaking in their communities.

Repeatedly Oxnam wondered publicly and privately why only Protestant leaders, denominations, and agencies such as the Federal and National and World Councils were being attacked. Was it to clear the field for the further advance of Catholic clericalism? He received a number of letters encouraging this suspicion. To these correspondents he would reply, "I agree with you that there is a fine Italian hand in the background of much that is going on."

An old New England tombstone bears the inscription: "She averaged well for the community." Unfortunately, the record of the Roman Catholic hierarchy in America during the "Second Red Scare" does not merit even that mild accolade. The consequence was heightened Catholic–liberal Protestant tensions.

Oxnam was a member of the Board of Directors of the National Conference of Christians and Jews, an organization formed in 1927 to create interfaith understanding and moderate religious tensions. As early as 1940 an NCCJ officer chided Oxnam for stirring up Catholic-Protestant tensions and received the reply, "One gets the impression that the National Council of Christians and Jews is more concerned to save the Roman Catholic face than to deal with the real issues that lead to division and seek to remove them." In 1948 NCCJ President Everett R. Clinchy alerted Yale Divinity School Dean Liston Pope to a small group of Protestants "who are as bitter and as un-Christlike in their attack upon Catholicism as the darkest minds among the Catholics." On July 8, 1946, Dr. Clinchy had paid Oxnam a call, saying that it was an embarrassment to the conference to have the bishop remain on the board. Would he resign? Oxnam thundered that if he resigned he would present his case to the Methodist Council of Bishops, the Federal Council of Churches, and the general public. Clinchy backed off. Oxnam's temper continued to boil and in 1947 he wrote an angry letter of resignation. The two men continued to correspond to express their disagreements. In November 1948 Oxnam learned that the secretary of the NCCJ in Kansas City had sought to secure the cancellation of his speaking engagement, and Oxnam alerted Clinchy, who in turn rebuked the Kansas City officer: "Personally I consider Bishop Oxnam one of the great churchmen in the world today, one of the most wonderful leaders Protestantism has ever had and a man who should be encouraged to speak at every possible place and time that his energy permits."

Oxnam considered the NCCJ a pusillanimous outfit as did Glenn Archer and E. M. Poteat[18] of POAU and other Protestant leaders. The irony is that Spellman would have no truck with the conference and that in 1950 Archbishop Cushing withdrew his cooperation, saying, "For all practical purposes this whole thing represents indifferentism, or in common parlance, 'One religion is as good as another.' "[19] Indeed, Catholic involvement in the NCCJ had always been minimal, contingent, and tentative.

Oxnam first viewed John F. Kennedy while watching the television coverage of the 1956 Democratic Convention and he liked what he saw. There must be no religious test for the presidency or any public office. But then he added the inevitable qualifier in his diary: "If the hierarchy could leave some of these high minded gentlemen alone and if they could see the wisdom of being an American first and a churchman second when it comes to the political situations, all would be well, but when we see Congressman John McCormack pushing through a bill that gives the Roman Catholics millions of dollars for the Philippines, dollars to which they are in no sense entitled, one wonders just a bit."

Oxnam first met Kennedy on June 16, 1958, in the senator's office and at his request. Present also was President Harold Case of Boston University who had served as intermediary. The bishop found the young senator to be "charming, intelligent, determined, wealthy" and possessing "a certain fundamental integrity . . . that I don't find in Nixon's record." Over delicious steaks, the conversation soon turned (after some bantering about Oxnam as ambassador to the Vatican) to church-state matters. The question of federal funds for parochial schools, said Kennedy, is a matter for the Supreme Court. Such funds are not available and that is that. However, the Court has made it clear that certain services can be supported by public funds, such as transportation, textbooks, and the like. Kennedy then observed that he and his brothers had not attended Catholic schools. He further stated his opposition to McCarthy and noted the embarrassment Spellman caused Catholic liberals. And he would not appoint an ambassador to the Vatican for pragmatic reasons: the political furor would not be worth it. When asked about birth control, Kennedy replied (fibbing as we now know) that he personally did not believe in it, but "my opinion is that the church has nothing to say about this that is binding." Oxnam may have been captivated by Kennedy's "extraordinary charm," but if the senator assumed he had made a prisoner of the bishop he was kidding himself.

In mid-April 1959 Oxnam arranged for the entire Methodist Council of Bishops (fifty-one in all) to meet with President Eisenhower, leading members of his cabinet, and members of Congress. *Time* magazine likened Senator Kennedy to Daniel in the lion's den. Of all the public servants interviewed, Kennedy alone was interrogated on church-state issues, the questions having been prepared by Oxnam. This set John Cogley's teeth on edge. Writing in *Commonweal,* the liberal Catholic imagined the Protestant uproar if the Catholic bishops of the United States had summoned presidential aspirants for an old-fashioned inquisitorial session! "If a group of government officials and potential candidates appearing before a Board of Bishops to answer the Bishops' questions about political matters is not a breach in the wall we hear so much about, I will eat my shirt," Cogley mused. "What assurance does the Methodist Church require from Government officials before it gives them approval? What are the Bishops up to, that they feel it is their business as Bishops to grant or withhold approval from individual candidates? Does the Methodist Church plan to enter the 1960 campaign?" Cogley was still steaming when he recorded his memories for the John F. Kennedy Library's oral history project—steaming at the Methodists for their setting up the interrogation and at Kennedy for permitting himself to be set up. What a fuss would have been raised if Roman Catholic bishops had demanded that Nixon (a Quaker) be grilled on his possible pacifism and its relation to the conduct of foreign affairs! Hugh Sidey in his oral interview recalled that Kennedy was amused by Bishop Oxnam's evasion and that Kennedy finally came to the conclusion that he would never win the bishop's endorsement. (Incidentally, the files of letters in the Kennedy Library suggest that a lot of Catholics—the majority of those who wrote—believed that he was conceding too much to his Protestant questioners and thereby demeaning Catholicism. Henry IV believed Paris was worth a Mass; perhaps Kennedy believed the White House was worth giving up an occasional Mass.

To be sure, in May 1960, one week before the West Virginia primary, Oxnam joined with the Very Reverend Francis B. Sayre, Jr., Episcopal dean of the Washington Cathedral, and several others in an "open letter" to their "Fellow Pastors in Christ." The letter called for "charitable moderation and reasoned balance of judgment. . . . We are convinced that each of the candidates has presented himself before the American people with honesty and independence, and we would think it unjust to discount any one of them because of his chosen faith."

In the May 10, 1960, issue of *Look*, Oxnam and Presbyterian Eugene Carson Blake addressed the question, "A Protestant View of a Catholic for President." They concluded that they would consider voting for a Catholic. "Our votes are not dictated by our religious principles, or by our church," they maintained. "We do not believe that any American's vote should be." Nevertheless, in the course of the article they raised so many nagging questions that one might well imagine that Protestant readers were made more rather than less anxious.

In the late spring of 1960 Oxnam retired as bishop and moved from Washington. He could not have established the necessary residency requirement in New Hampshire to have voted in November. Perhaps it is just as well for he would have faced an agonizing decision. As a liberal Democrat could he have voted easily for Nixon? In light of his principles, could he have brought himself to vote for a Roman Catholic? We will never know.

---

[1] It is a little puzzling to find McConnell present. According to his daughter, Dr. Dorothy McConnell, her father was amused by Oxnam's innocent outrage over the Catholic Church's pursuit of political power. Of course, he observed, Catholics were interested in the game of power, but so were Jews and Protestants—including Methodists. So what else is new? By the way, scholars might wish to know that the McConnell papers are in the sole possession of the daughter, who is writing his biography.

[2] Writing in 1951, Professor Luke Ebersole in his *Church Lobbying in the Nation's Capital* judged that "if Bishop Oxnam were to withdraw his name the movement would collapse."

[3] After Italy declared war on the United States in December 1941, Tittmann moved into Vatican City with the rank of chargé d'affaires. According to historian Gerald P. Fogarty, Tittmann's "move signaled quasi-official diplomatic recognition of the Holy See."

[4] Of course, both the Vatican and Spellman anticipated a more formal and permanent diplomatic relationship.

[5] Pruden, highly respected president of the American Baptist Convention, was in a difficult position. On the one hand, he sought to alert Truman, in the most respectful

manner, to how passionately Protestants felt about the Vatican representation issue, as he himself did. On the other, when a Sunday School class in his church sent the president, without Pruden's knowledge, a petition of protest, Pruden in embarrassment wrote Truman a letter of apology. One source (a biased one) asserts that in anger Truman never returned to worship in the First Baptist Church. I have no way of knowing if this is accurate, but we do have on record Truman's mild reply to Pruden's apology, dated June 6, 1950: "Don't let the communication from the Sunday School Class bother you. I have stacks of petitions on that order every week and it is simply a part of the duty of the Presidential Office to listen to everybody's viewpoint."

[6] Truman, like Oxnam, was a Thirty-third Degree Mason.

[7] Whom Truman approached other than Taft to go to Rome is unknown. Some names that were suggested to him included Daniel Poling, Bernard Baruch, and Jack Dempsey! Some correspondents nominated themselves, including a North Carolina justice of the peace: "I urge that you appoint an ambassador to the Vatican and that you appoint me. I am only 21 but I believe I could successfully fulfill the duties."

[8] Truman and the members of the Senate received, in all, probably millions of letters on the matter, perhaps one hundred to one in opposition. It seems clear that the Catholic leadership did not whip up a mail campaign remotely comparable to the Protestant campaign; indeed, Catholics do not seem to have been of a united mind.

[9] One supposes Fey's allusion is to the prohibition passion of the previous generation. Incidentally, the *Christian Century*'s concern approached clinically paranoid proportions when it editorialized in December 1952: "The worst mistake the new [Eisenhower] administration could make, *short of plunging the world into atomic war*, would be to send an ambassador to the Vatican" (emphasis added).

[10] Truman was to be granted a private audience with Pope Pius XII on May 20, 1956. At a press conference in Rome, Truman continued to espouse U.S. diplomatic relations with the Holy See to "help the peace of the world."

[11] Recall that Charles P. Taft was informed by State Department officials that Taylor's reports were rather insignificant. Is this the explanation?

[12] By a commission vote of thirteen to one the report contained this statement: "Federal funds for the general support of current educational activities and for general capital outlay purposes should be appropriated for use in institutions under public control only."

[13] During the controversy, Representative Barden received thousands of communications, including supporting telegrams from Oxnam and other Methodist bishops. "The fight has taken the lid off a situation that is out of proportion to anything I had ever dreamed of," a shaken Barden reported. Still, his defenders, including some Catholic correspondents, outnumbered his critics about fifteen to one, and he gave the assurance "that the attack made on me personally, as well as on a principle more valuable to the American people than either the Cardinal or I, only serves to make me more determined. I will not quit the fight." To another supporter he ruefully wrote: "Guess you have been reading the papers and it is a fine thing to have Cardinal Spellman and fifteen thousand of his followers praying for me. I might feel just a little bit better about it if I knew just what they are praying will happen to me!"

[14] Glenn Archer, POAU leader, reported that Mrs. Roosevelt told him personally that Spellman told her he was at Hyde Park specifically on the orders of the pope. Archer also reported (on what he considered good authority, that of Edward Pruden, Truman's pastor) that the president wired the pope, "and told him that if he didn't straighten Spellman out, American Catholics would suffer for 30 years of politics." Independent evidence suggests Truman's anger with Spellman.

[15] Amusingly, about this time when Oxnam came to Buffalo to deliver a Reformation Day address he was assigned a motorcycle escort. Protesting, he was informed by the authorities that Spellman earlier had been assigned such an escort and Buffalo did not play favorites. Oxnam secured the names of the four motorcycle officers and later sent them gifts.

[16] Oxnam appealed to General MacArthur to permit Mrs. Sanger to bring her birth control message to occupied Japan. The general replied that the matter was already under control, including government-sponsored birth control clinics and legalized abortion and sterilization.

[17] Among the historians on the subject who have noted the inordinate Catholic contribution to the hysteria are Michael Belknap, David Caute, Kenneth O'Reilly, Thomas Reeves, Peter Steinberg, Ellen Schrecker, Victor Navasky, and Norman Markowitz.

[18] In fact, in 1947 Poteat for that reason declined an invitation to be an NCCJ national cochairman.

[19] Dr. Clinchy continued to lead the NCCJ until 1958 and to this day the group hails him as "the principal 20th Century architect of interreligious cooperation and understanding."

CHAPTER 22

OXNAM AND THE AMERICAN JEWISH COMMUNITY

Oxnam's relations with and attitudes toward the American Jewish community might be symbolized by an event already mentioned. When in 1943 anti-Semitism flared in the Boston area, Oxnam met with Jewish leaders and became convinced that fascism was on the march in America. He called on the authorities, including Governor Saltonstall, to act, and he organized a "Committee on Inter-racial Justice." On November 28 a mass meeting was held in Symphony Hall. He shared the speaking with the governor, a Jewish rabbi, and a Catholic priest. Though given a standing ovation and praised in the press, one wonders if Oxnam's words were entirely helpful. After acknowledging the bigotry of Protestant Ku Kluxers, he added, "If the Roman Catholic Church calls for religious liberty in Russia, let it stand for it in Spain and in Latin America." Then, in an attempt at even-handedness (and as Hitler's ovens glowed with their human ashes), he added, "Our Jewish friends would do better if they would speak less of the persecution they have suffered through the centuries, and center on removing the causes that have in part been responsible." To illustrate his point, he cited Jewish merchants in Washington who refused to serve blacks—as if Jews were uniquely responsible for segregation in the nation's capital. Only days earlier, when visiting Virginia, he recorded a revealing observation, "After one has lived in a community largely Jewish or a community in which the foreign strains are predominant, it is strange how drawn he is to a community that is really American." For the moment, obviously, he had forgotten that his own father had been "a stranger in the land."

Note the ambiguity. On the one hand, Oxnam's loathing of anti-Semitism was unquestionably sincere. More than that, he acted to blunt its thrust for which he was justly honored. On the other hand, he could never quite shake the thought that the Jewish people in stubbornly insisting on being "different" were therefore somehow partially responsible for the persecution they suffered.

How, then, does one explain the scores of invitations to speak before Jewish groups? Why, then, in November 1953 did the Women's Division of the American Jewish Congress tender a banquet in his honor and bestow an illuminated parchment "citation of honor"? Why in June 1956 did he receive the annual Louis D. Brandeis Gold Medal Award from the Jewish Forum at a reception in New York City Hall, Mayor Wagner presiding? And why in 1950 did he receive a formal invitation from the government of Israel to visit the new state? (Reinhold Niebuhr was another American Protestant to receive such an invitation, but ultimately ill-health prohibited both men from accepting.)

In a significant respect the alliance of liberal Protestantism with much of American Judaism, especially Reform and Conservative, was not strange. Oxnam and other liberal Protestants shared with Jews a prophetic passion for social justice. Moreover, to Oxnam, Jews seemed important allies to cultivate in Protestantism's effort to block Catholic hegemony. Especially on questions of church and state, Protestant and Jewish interests often, though not always, coincided. Long popular with Jewish audiences, after Oxnam's challenge to HUAC he became more than popular; he was lionized. Extolled a Jewish leader, "It was he who stemmed the tide of McCarthyism in the land. He will never be forgotten by historians in the annals of civil liberties." Invitations to speak increased and many were accepted, in part because of the generous fees, but primarily because (as he recorded) "the response of the Jewish people is extraordinary. They see through all this McCarthyism and what is really involved." [1]

Moreover, Jews had considerable reason to consider Oxnam a friend. In truth, he counted several individual Jews as personal friends: in Omaha, Rabbi David Wicke; in Boston, Rabbi Joshua Liebman; in New York, Rabbi Stephen S. Wise (on the occasion of Wise's seventy-fifth birthday celebration Oxnam brought the greetings of the Christian churches). Oxnam considered President Louis Finkelstein of the Jewish Theological Seminary an "extraordinarily brilliant person"; on Oxnam's death his older son received from Finkelstein a message: "The news of your great loss has just reached me and is indeed that of the whole community. As one privileged to have known and worked with your father I have some realization of all he meant not only for your family but for the whole world of thought and spirit." No individual of Jewish heritage was closer to Oxnam than David Lilienthal. Of course, there were other leaders, Justice Brandeis and Governor Lehman and David Sarnoff, for example, whom Oxnam met and admired but whom he could not exactly claim as friends.

Not only did Oxnam respect the acumen of his Jewish audiences, on more than one instance he characterized aspects of the Jewish worship service as "impressive," "beautiful," "deeply moving," "dramatic," and one "that never fails to reach my heart." On more than one instance he met a Jew or a Jewish couple whom he liked because of their attributes of courtesy, cultivation, refinement, and modesty.

Nor is this all. Recall his condemnations of Hitler's "Final Solution" and his depictions of the hellish reality of Buchenwald. Recall, too, his denunciations of anti-Semitism in America and of groups especially guilty of this sin such as the Klan, Silver Shirts, Black Legion, and Coughlinites. Moreover, he discerned the dangers of a subtler discrimination. "The man who . . . connives with a real-estate agent," he noted in 1945, "to exclude a Jew from a neighborhood . . . is a nazi."

Oxnam, like most non-Jewish Americans, was prior to 1948 of a divided mind about the establishment of an independent Jewish state in Palestine. In 1943, after reading a volume on the subject, he was "about persuaded" that such a state must come into being. In 1946, however, lunching in London with Sir Lewis Namier, the distinguished historian and Zionist, he disagreed with Namier's position that large numbers of Jews in America and England as well as Europe would migrate to a new Jewish state in the Holy Land, and that those who did not would intermarry with Christians, assimilate, lose their identity—and thus would be solved the "Jewish question." Such an eventuality Oxnam found "inconceivable." American Jews would not migrate in appreciable numbers and those who remained would not disappear. Oxnam's prediction was the more accurate. The existence of the State of Israel has made it clear that the overwhelming majority of American Jews have opted for the Diaspora and do not regard the United States as a land of *galut* (exile).

The birth of Israel in 1948 brought from Oxnam's lips these warm, if vague, words: "In an hour of solemn rejoicing let us hope the moral teachings of the prophets of Israel may come alive in the practices of the new State of Israel and thereby reveal to the world that a people which have given so much in religion to mankind may now give to humanity the leadership essential to the translation of religious ideals into the realities of the common life." In June of that year Oxnam presented a special "Citation to the State of Israel" to Rabbi Israel Goldstein in recognition of his achievement as president of the Zionist Organization of America.

In succeeding years Oxnam retained an interest in events in the Holy Land, including the sponsorship of an abortive curatorship of religious sites in Jerusalem. In 1958 he was invited to extend over the radio a word of greeting to all who celebrated Israel's tenth anniversary. "In gratitude to a people who gave mankind the Ten Commandments, the Psalms, and the preaching of the Prophets, I bring you greeting and pray God's richest blessing upon you," Oxnam sang. Privately he observed, "I deliberately avoided any reference to the Middle East situation. It is a little safer to keep to the field of religion, strangely enough." Oxnam was a brave man, but never insofar as the record reveals did he raise any questions about Israel's influence on the shaping of United States foreign policy or any doubts about the possible divided loyalties of American Jews or any criticism of American Jewish dollars (and non-Jewish tax dollars) flowing out of the country to Israel or any disquietude over

Jewish lobbying in Washington and pressure in elections. To be sure, these are tough issues all, but they are the very ones he called American Catholics to account for.

Mention must once again be made of the ambiguity, not because it convicts Oxnam of hypocrisy, but because it does reveal a disconcerting insensitivity.

Doubtless in his public utterances he thought he was being fair, but was he? In a 1938 address sponsored by the NCCJ he condemned the Klan and also the Catholic school bid for public funds, adding in the interests of symmetry, "When members of the Jewish community reveal arrogance, based upon money power, religious forces are separated." Indiana was a Klan-ridden state. Would not the Hoosier hooded citizens have found comfortable the words coming from the pen of the president of DePauw in his "Facing Facts" newspaper column, April 2, 1936:

> Jews parading in front of Woolworth's carrying placards, "Don't patronize Woolworth's. Woolworth's sell German goods. Down with the Bloody Hitler." At that very moment members of their own race were reaching out with grasping hands for dollars and more dollars, seeking to control wider fields of commercial enterprise. Reaction sets in against all this, and many hate the materialism of the merchant as well as the materialism of Marx. I have great admiration for the Jewish people. Jesus was a Jew. The sources of the life giving waters of my religion are in the mountain peaks of Jewish prophecy. But I know that our splendid Jews, who resent all this as much as the Gentiles, realize the ruthless competition, the grasping materialism and the boorish manners of much Hebrew activity in New York is not forgotten, and the psychological reaction to Jews boycotting Hitler may surprise the placard bearers. Jew and Gentile alike must approach an altar and be cleansed, or perhaps they might well follow the suggestion of a great Jew and be right with their brothers before approaching the altar.

In a 1957 address Oxnam related mediating a strike. The owner of the tailoring company involved reported making only 6 percent the year before from his whole investment. Oxnam continued the story: "I said, 'Now, Mr. Keen, don't misunderstand me. There is no anti-Semitism in me at all, but when a Jewish tailoring contractor tells me that he has made only 6%, I want to see his books.' I did see his books and he had told me the truth. He made only 6% every time he turned over his product, and he turned his product over about 15 times in that particular year." Oxnam's addresses in the 1920s contain unlovely passages, for example a reference to "a hideous being of Shylockian face, carrying a flag to conceal its grasping hand." And: "The Jew fearful of God—will click his heels to the great Cosmic Top Sgt. any time. Doesn't want a message from him. He would send it collect."

Oxnam was quick—too quick—to point out the Jewish identity of an individual, as if this was crucial to the matter at hand. Why note that a "fool director" at NBC was a Jew? Why note a certain chaplain "whose nose told of his faith"? Why describe a symphony conductor as "a smiling son of Israel"? Time and again if Oxnam found a woman "aggressive" he deemed it significant that she was a "Jewess."

Even as late as the 1950s Oxnam used the Jews to make invidious comparisons, describing one individual "gesticulating like a Jew who has lost a sale and yelling at the top of his voice" and in Japan, salesmen who "are as effective as are the Jews but not so offensive in their salesmanship."

One swallow, perhaps a trivial one, does not make a summer, but the diary entries are simply too numerous and too disturbing to be dismissed as insignificant. Would a *sensitive* Methodist bishop make this observation in *1941:* "the streets of New York are filled with Jews, many of whom are bad mannered, creating the very anti-Semitism which they regard as persecution." Would a *thoughtful* Christian make this statement about a New Hampshire village in *1942:* "Bethlehem is Judea. Intense feeling is in the town as the Jew has taken over the once Gentile village. . . . Why does the Jew make himself so obnoxious. Crowding the side-walks, refusing to give an inch, noisy, money [mad], many stopping, congregating like an Oriental Bazaar. No matter what one's real desire and heart may be, these people are part of their own persecution." And: "Bethlehem is Bethlehem indeed! There are five thousand Jews here in season. It appears that Jews have large noses—I had heard that before—and are afflicted with hay fever. There is no hay fever here, so all of them rush to Bethlehem, but few sing Philip Brooks' hymn." (Oxnam later thought more kindly of the Jews visiting Bethlehem.) In 1944 Oxnam was visited by "two high school girls wanting an opinion on international relations, one a young Jewess who knew there was no reason for anti-Semitism." Presumably Oxnam knew that there was. "When will our Jewish brethren learn to be a trifle modest?" wondered Oxnam after a rabbi's prayer at Truman's 1949 inaugural.

No generalization seems more firmly embedded in Oxnam's mind than Jewish aggressiveness as a consequence of a sense of inferiority. "There is an aggressiveness that flows out of being on the defensive that is really very harmful," he noted. "The Jews are an amazing people . . . , but always the sense of inferiority which comes up in a kind of pugnacity that irritates," he observed in 1959. "The Jews run true to type round the world. One finds the same penetrating intellect, the same nervous restlessness, the same unfortunate pushing of one's self forward that may grow out of a desire to overcome an inferiority complex . . . ," he conjectured. One individual was described as having "the inferiority complex that so often characterizes our Jewish brethren." After praising a group of St. Louis Jews for being "courteous, refined, and ladies and gentlemen," he damned in contrast a New York rabbi for having "all of the aggressiveness that irritates the Gentile when he deals with a Jew." In Boston a "fat Jew" was assigned to give Oxnam a driver's license test. Oxnam wondered if the inspector could make the required hand signals in any state: "picture a Jew with his hands palms down." Maybe it is dime store psychology, but one is almost driven to a disturbing conclusion: In ascribing to Jews universally the qualities of aggressiveness, bellicosity, ambition, competitiveness, sensitivity to criticism, and concern for material things, Oxnam was denying through projection the existence of these very attributes in his own nature.

Ultimately, one has the feeling approaching a conviction that Oxnam hoped Jews would become like he fancied himself and other liberal Protestants to be. "These people have genius to burn if they could only learn to adjust themselves to the ways of other people. Down the centuries, they have suffered tragedy, inexcusable persecution, but they never seem to learn that it is difficult to be a separate people and yet have all the privileges of other people," he believed. "Our Jewish brethren do not know what they really do. They want it both ways. They want their own community, separate and no one else in it; they want all the privileges of the other community." "The Jew...everywhere,"

Oxnam explained to himself, "is so sensitive that a single word elicits his immediate combative response. He simply does not know what he himself does in the matter of racial [sic] relations, insisting always that it is persecution. Perhaps I would feel somewhat the same way if I had been through what they have been through, but, nonetheless, the answer does involve certain changes upon their own part. I do not see how the Jew can continue as a separate community, apart from all, and still insisting upon being a part of every community in which he lives. He wishes all the benefits of the larger group, but insists upon a separateness that denies to the larger group the privileges of his own group."

The funny thing is Oxnam was telling the Jews essentially what he was telling Catholics. If you want the privileges of being an American, give up your separateness, join the majority, abandon your claims to being a chosen people (or members of a chosen church), forsake your history and your heritage. Become like us—or rather, like our idealized self-image.

[1] One must be careful here. The Jewish community's resistance to McCarthyism may have been admirable, comparatively speaking, but it was not absolute. Judged Victor S. Navasky: "The Jewish organizations . . . lived up to what they saw as their professional ethic—to protect the reputation of the Jewish community (and thereby curtail the rise of anti-Semitism) and to assist Jewish victims. But they, too, through their back-room dealings, not only ended up strengthening the chief agents of repression but did so at the expense of other Jewish constituents and non-Jewish citizens in the community at large, and at the expense of the broader principles of political and civil rights they were organized to uphold."

CHAPTER 23

AMERICAN BLACKS IN A METHODIST LEADER'S WORLD

As was true in the case of most white Christians in America who considered themselves liberal, enlightened, and prejudice-free, during the opening sixty years of the twentieth century, Oxnam deplored racial bigotry and condemned the injustices suffered by blacks, but it is not self-evident that he fully comprehended the demonic dimensions of racism in the United States. He very clearly grew in understanding, contrition, and sensitivity as the decades passed, but it is also certain that he had considerable growing to do. To be sure, in much of the black community he was judged a friend and there is a substantial objective basis for this assessment. Nevertheless, attention must be paid to Oxnam's silences as well as to his utterances and to his private or casual remarks as well as to his public pronouncements. When this is done the record that emerges is not quite as unambiguously affirmative as his admirers believed.

At a tense Council of Bishops meeting in 1958, Bishop Willis J. King, in a voice edged with emotion, stated that he had never in his life talked to a white man who had not made it perfectly clear that he, the white man, was talking to a Negro. Oxnam immediately protested: "I cannot speak here as a white man speaking to a Negro regardless of what is said. Willis King who is black is my friend and my classmate [at Boston University]. I happen to be his friend and his classmate and I am white. I talk to him just as I talk to anybody else and never think of anything else other than the fact that I am talking to a man." Elsewhere Oxnam denied the existence of discrimination against blacks in the Los Angeles of his youth, although he acknowledged that prejudice did prevail in regard to Orientals and Latins. Oxnam was not wrong to declare a mutual friendship with Bishop King. He was, however, engaging in unconscious self-deception when asserting an unawareness of King's color. And if he remembered the City of Angels at the turn of the century as being color-blind it could only be because the city's blacks were "invisible men" to him. In fact, when the General Conference of the Methodist Episcopal Church met in Los Angeles in 1904, the black delegates were refused service by hotels and restaurants. They suffered "humiliation and shame," "discrimination . . . and reprehensible treatment." Protested one black on the conference floor: "Our reception will ever linger in our memories to remind us that even among angels there are—well—antipodal manifestations serving not only to vex the saints as they pass through the enchanted grounds, but to emphasize the existence of a prejudice which is as cruel as death, and which our immortal founder has declared to be the sum of all villainies."

Oxnam's friendship with King may have begun when they were fellow students at BU School of Theology, but no diary mention is made of blacks either during the seminary years or earlier USC years or at any time prior to 1921. In that year in London Oxnam attended an American Seminar session devoted to race relations and heard Dr. Channing Tobias of the YMCA speak. "He is a fine big fellow," Oxnam recorded, "with a good deal of white blood I think, not quite as temperate in his utterance as he might be, but excusable because of the fires that burn in his soul, fires made hotter by his own tragic experiences." In the 1920s Oxnam, as we know, repudiated the Klan, admitted black children into the Church of All Nations program, and endorsed a 1924 General Conference resolution protesting racial injustice. His little 1928 volume *Youth and the New America* devotes ten pages to the conditions of American blacks. The concern is heartfelt, particularly the anguish over the barbarity of lynching. The section closes: "It is incumbent upon the young American facing the race problem to become acquainted with the data in the field. Not only must he have this intellectual attitude, but he must likewise share the personal sympathy of Jesus of Nazareth. He must remember that 'God is color blind,' and must be Christian enough to see in a man of any color a brother indeed." A 1932 Sunday School lesson from his pen also contains a brief rebuke of racism.

That is about all the extant record discloses prior to Oxnam's becoming a bishop that would warrant his being called the blacks' friend. Even if much of an affirmative nature has been lost from the record, the conclusion is inescapable that economic, political, and international concerns consumed him more completely than segregation. Possibly during his presidency not a single black student attended DePauw.[1] Certainly the diaries fail to note a black presence. Perhaps it is just as well, for occasionally in his chapel chats Oxnam told "darky" jokes and stories. They were not vicious, but they were patronizing and invariably showed blacks in an unfortunate light. If present, no black student would have responded in other than embarrassment and rage. The unhappy truth is that throughout his adult life Oxnam laced his talks and articles and diaries with "funny" stories about "colored folks"—stories innocent of conscious racist intent but ones that reveal the Negro as being superstitious, ignorant, dirty, easily frightened, lazy, a mangler of the language and a walking oddity. Shortly after World War I, in an address he alluded to the cowardice of American black soldiers in France. During World War II, in the Lyman Beecher Lectures, he described at great length a movie scene in which Stepin Fetchit is duped while in uniform in France in the Great War. Oxnam introduces the black actor to the Yale audience as "the Negro who had the emptiness of the ages in his face and the laziness of the centuries in his whines. His conversation was a monotonous cross between a moan and a mumble." When at DePauw, the wife of Dean McCutchan found her maid spitting in the kitchen sink and Oxnam reported the story to his diary: "When the negro had time to find the customary alibi that always characterizes negro conduct [sic], she said, 'Ah work in some homes where they let me spit in the sink, in some houses in which they don't, and my trouble is that sometimes I fo'get which kind of house I'se in.' " Scarcely more edifying is the diary account of a debate between Marshall Field and David Lilienthal as to whether a black sits on his heels or just squats. In the heat of the debate (and in a hotel dining room) both men got out of their chairs to demonstrate their theories. Oxnam sometimes would growl that he felt "like a nigger dodging baseballs in one of those side-show affairs."

Even when condemning racial injustice he managed to take away with one hand what he had bestowed with the other. In a 1922 address he decried lynchings and race riots but then felt compelled to explain that America's blacks had come "from equatorial Africa where nature is rich, indolence a virtue, and those possessing undue sex instinct survive through being prolific. The aggressive die out." Then there are the ambiguous statements, such as found in a 1930s article: "We must keep our racial integrity. Each race must contribute to each other to form a brotherhood." Finally, there are the silences. For example, Oxnam makes no mention of the discrimination suffered by black delegates in the 1932 General Conference in Atlantic City and Ernest Fremont Tittle's condemnatory resolution and the heated debate that followed. Oxnam was present. If to him segregation had truly been a soul-searing issue, surely he might have defended Tittle's resolution in the debate or referred to the matter in his endless public addresses and writings or at the very least made note of it in his private correspondence.

One must not be too severe on Oxnam. Almost all white Americans with memories of that earlier era will recall, if they are honest with themselves, laughing at "darky" jokes and stories and using such expressions as "there must be a nigger in the woodpile" and "I wouldn't take it if a darky boy brought it to me on a silver platter," and finding amusing black characters seen on the silver screen or heard over the radio. Few older white Americans are innocent of (at the very least) thoughtless insensitivity.

The 1936 General Conference at which Oxnam was elected bishop also witnessed a dramatic vote on the Proposed Plan of Union with Southern Methodism and the Methodist Protestant Church, the plan being the result of years of agonizing negotiations, compromises, and prayers. As is well known, the plan provided for a General Conference, meeting quadrennially, and for six new Jurisdictional Conferences, bringing into one church an estimated 99 percent of all white Methodists and 15 percent of all black Methodists in the United States. Five of the Jurisdictional Conferences were based on geography (Northeastern, Southeastern, North Central, South Central, and Western), and one on color (Central); that is, about 95 percent of the blacks in the united church—some 318,000 of 325,000—were to be placed in the Central Jurisdiction. The new arrangement can be defended. Blacks had been segregated in the old Northern Church, having separate local congregations, separate black Annual Conferences, a separate black *Christian Advocate,* and two black bishops elected by separate ballots from which the votes for white ministers were excluded. (Black Methodists in the South [other than those in the Northern Church] were not to be found in the Methodist Episcopal Church, South, but rather were members of the Colored Methodist Episcopal Church, founded in 1870, or the older and larger African Methodist Episcopal Church and African Methodist Episcopal Zion Church.) Under the new plan, blacks would serve on an unsegregated and equal basis in the General Conference and on all national boards and commissions; indeed, they would have more than their proportionate share of representatives. At the national level, white Southern leaders would now associate closely with fellow Methodist black leaders. It was also claimed that black churches in time could request to be transferred into predominantly white conferences and that rigid segregation was not being written into the constitution. Finally, it is true that two black members of the commission, the able Bishop Robert E. Jones and President Willis J. King of Gammon Seminary, gave their endorsement.

Oxnam did not participate in the tense two-hour debate at Columbus on the Plan of Union, a debate in which it can justly be said there were no villains. Bishop Hughes presided with absolute fairness, even permitting the opponents one more speaker than the proponents. Bishop McDowell introduced the plan not as a perfected piece of ecclesiasticism or mechanical or legalistic skill but as the best sixty-five fallible men could devise, a plan looking more toward the future than the past. Bishop Hughes stepped down from the chair to speak that day for the union: the commissioners (he pleaded) did not feel that they had been appointed to reform Methodism but rather to unite its three branches. The problem was not to introduce new features but rather to heal old divisions. We were seeking (he concluded) a Methodist merger and were willing to let Methodist reformations wait upon the prayerful judgment of the future Church.

Lewis O. Hartman of Massachusetts and editor of the influential *Zion's Herald*, perhaps with Whittier's Ichabod ringing in his memory, was the first to rise and speak in opposition. The debate was on, the speakers alternating pro and con. Among those gaining the floor were five blacks: two in favor of the plan, three in opposition. George Lewis, a tall black man from Tennessee, relieved the tension when recognized by Bishop Hughes and asked, "Are you against it?" by replying as he moved toward the platform, "World without end!" President Jones of Bennett College also spoke in opposition, telling the story of being informed by a kindly white lady of her inspired interpretation of the biblical passage "In my Father's house there are many mansions." That means, she sweetly explained to President Jones, that in heaven blacks would have a lovely mansion. "It is going to be separate, and not quite as nice as ours, but it is going to be lovely."

Midway in the proceedings Ernest Fremont Tittle was recognized. "I may truthfully say," he began, "that never in my life have I wanted as much as now to support an organizational plan before the church in which it has been my privilege to serve more than a quarter of a century." He then stated the central issue as he saw it. "All our other jurisdictions are geographic. This is racial. If that is not a concession to race prejudice, what is it? To be sure, by segregating Negroes in a Negro Conference we give them political opportunities which they would not possess as minority groups within our white conferences; but we take away from them the experience of Christian brotherhood which in my judgment, is far more important than is political opportunity." He continued by deploring the effort of the proposed action on young people and on colored people in mission lands. He concluded: "For every other feature of the plan I am prepared to vote. I wish it were not necessary to vote 'yea' or 'nay.' If we could make this one reservation I would be voting with all my mind and all my heart. As it is, my belief is that we should wait another quadrennium, if necessary two quadrenniums, when I fully believe we can have union without compromise; and in that case we will have a church which the living Christ can use, I profoundly believe as he may use no other now in existence." Alas, the proposed plan "does, I think, undeniedly make a concession to race prejudice which would, if adopted, present a church which the Christ could not use without considerable embarrassment."

Soon a standing vote was taken. The plan passed, 407 to 83. Of the 47 blacks present, 36 demurred. As the conference stood spontaneously to sing, "We're Marching to Zion," many of the blacks remained seated, their eyes swelling with tears.

It is impossible to say if unification would have come in one, two, or ten quadrenniums without some major concessions to Southern Methodism on the question of race. (The fear of being swallowed up by the larger Northern branch was also an issue.) It must be said unequivocally, however, that it was possible to favor the plan as submitted without being a racist. Bishop McConnell did—as so did Oxnam.

Yet several points stand out in sharp relief. First, most (but not all) blacks were in opposition. In a caucus of 44 black delegates held before the debate began, 33 agreed to "protest in a mild, but manly way against this Plan." Months later when the plan was submitted to the nineteen Negro Annual Conferences of the Methodist Episcopal Church for ratification, the vote was heavily negative: 583 ministers for, 823 against; 253 laymen for, 477 against. One black spokesman declared, "If the Methodist Church really dared to be Christian, would it humiliate thousands of its most loyal members by forcing them into a Jim Crow jurisdiction?" And Roy Wilkins of the National Association for the Advancement of Colored People penned the bitter words: "We hope God has the Methodists in mind and that He will give compassionate attention to their special needs. They separated a hundred years ago over slavery. Now they have got back together again with old wounds fairly well healed, and with the persistent black man roped off into a separate conference where he will be happy riding to Glory on a sort of Jim Crow car. We trust that if heaven is truly one great unsegregated family, God will not induct the American Methodists in too great numbers, or too rapidly, into a society that would shock them, perhaps, beyond hope of salvation." During the debate David Jones had said it all in one blunt sentence: "Everyone knows the Plan is segregation, and segregation in the ugliest way, because it is couched in such pious terms."

A second point is that Southern Methodists, despite the opposition of Bishops Collins Denny and Warren Candler, did not view the jurisdictional arrangement with alarm. "We are in this Plan, brethren," declared the speaker closing the debate at the 1938 Southern Methodist General Conference, "preserving every essential ideal that we have in the South on the Negro question." And years later the editor of the *Alabama Christian Advocate* confessed, "It is an open secret that there never would have been any unification, so far as the Methodist Episcopal Church, South, is concerned, if some arrangement as this had not been adopted."

The question of the Central Jurisdiction haunted The Methodist Church up to Oxnam's retirement and beyond, until finally in between 1968 and 1973 it was dissolved into the five geographic jurisdictions under the new United Methodist Church Constitution. Oxnam firmly favored the abolition of the Central Jurisdiction, stating to Liston Pope that "any administrative set up that is based on race should be eliminated." As we have seen, however, he passionately believed the entire jurisdictional structure should be scrapped, holding it "regionalism gone mad." We remember, too, his anger at the Southern Methodists who balked at the dismantling. When in 1960, on recommendation of the Parlin Committee, the General Conference did not terminate the Central Jurisdiction, a disappointed but philosophic Oxnam said to the press, "I am personally opposed to the Central Jurisdiction and always have been. But I believe we move to the absolute by way of the relative."

Black Methodists saw the fundamental problem of the Central Jurisdiction as a racist matter. By emphasizing that regionalism, not racism, was the primary structural flaw in the jurisdictional system, Oxnam placed himself at odds with black Methodists. In its report to the 1960 General Conference, the Committee of Seventy (the Parlin Committee) followed the policy of noncoercive gradualism first set forth in 1956 whereby, under Amendment IX, provision had been made for the voluntary transfer of Central Jurisdiction churches and Annual Conferences to regional jurisdictions. Even conservative white Southern Methodists believed they could live with such a measured, gradual, noncoercive and therefore nonthreatening withering of the Central Jurisdiction. It was precisely this projected slow death that disturbed black Methodists. Although Amendment IX became church law in 1958, only twenty-seven churches changed jurisdictions before Oxnam's death.

In 1944 the race question seriously occupied the attention of the General Conference. Meeting in Kansas City, the conference subjected black delegates to shabby treatment regarding eating and sleeping accommodations. Many blacks, including bishops, had to stay in private homes, and one delegate bitterly remembered that he wandered the streets in search of a meal, finally finding food in the only place open to him, a saloon. In anger and humiliation, the blacks were driven to make formal protest, selecting Matthew S. Davage to be their spokesman. Before the protest could be presented, however, Oxnam, acting as secretary of the Council of Bishops, made official apology, assuring the conference that the Committee on Entertainment was taking all steps possible to rectify the situation and hoping that those who had suffered would not think the action "too little too late." Davage withheld the protest. An improvised dining area was set up in the rear of the auditorium, and though the food was miserable, a few white delegates made a special effort to eat there to indicate it was not intended for blacks alone. The conference adopted a watered-down resolution calling for future meetings to be held "only in places where adequate and suitable entertainment can be provided for all delegates and representatives of the Church." It also adopted a report declaring that "no group is inherently superior or inferior to any other, and none is above any other beloved of God." Racial discrimination was then firmly excoriated.

It may be doubted that Bromley and Ruth joined the handful of whites who dined in the makeshift black area, or for that matter, that any white bishop did. If they had, the press probably would have picked up the story. How strongly Oxnam felt about the humiliation of black Methodists in Kansas City, save for the official apology, is unknown. The diary is totally silent on the race issue at the 1944 General Conference. If he had felt intense anger and remorse, would not he have spilled out these emotions as he so often did on other matters?

The 1948, 1952, 1956, and 1960 General Conferences spoke in increasingly stern tones about the sinfulness of racism, now calling not simply for "justice" and "equality" but for the end of segregation itself. Oxnam's conference contribution came in his 1948 Episcopal Address. The single paragraph devoted to the racial situation in America in the fifty-nine-page document reads in its entirety:

> Does brotherhood, does Christianity, within the freedom of democracy justify restricting the vote to the white man while denying it to the red man, the black man? Does the declaration that every human being is of infinite worth as a son of God permit us to deny civil liberty to the American Negro? Is segregation a pattern expressive of the spirit present when, in the name of Jesus, we repeat the Lord's Prayer beginning "Our Father"? What is demanded of Christians when mobs in race riots in North or South kill black men, not because these men are thought to be guilty of a crime but simply because they are black? Is there a duty to ferret out the unpunished members of such mobs? And what of the unpunished murderers who lynch a man, even though they think him to be guilty?

The words are not those of an unconcerned individual, but neither are they the thunderous ones of the Old Testament prophets or even of some Methodist latter-day prophets who spoke on the floor of the 1948 conference. In fact, black Methodists were disappointed in the brevity and vagueness of Oxnam's remarks on race.

It is possible that Oxnam spoke in rather tempered tones because an Episcopal Address should convey the collective thought of the Council of Bishops and he knew that his words would be reviewed in advance by his colleagues. Not even the most reactionary bishops on the matter of race thought to edit out the mild paragraph, perhaps because no bishop then on the council was so deeply racist as to find it objectionable.

Oxnam never acknowledged in public or private the real differences in the status of black and white members of the Council of Bishops. Maybe the thought never penetrated his awareness. Central Jurisdiction bishops were accorded only limited participation in the council inasmuch as they were not general superintendents but rather were limited by election to a particular area. Their voting rights were restricted to issues pertaining to Central Jurisdiction matters. No Central Jurisdiction bishop was privileged to preside in the General Conference or at any Annual Conferences beyond their boundaries.[2] Prior to 1960, no black bishop chaired a general board or agency in the Church. Originally, Central Jurisdiction bishops were allowed travel expenses only to the meeting of the Council of Bishops at the time of General Conference, or perhaps to one additional meeting during the quadrennium.[3] In a word, they were second-class bishops, and although no Methodist historian might employ that ugly term, the memoirs of Bishop Prince A. Taylor, Jr., elected in 1956, suggest that this is exactly the way he felt before the Central Jurisdiction was abolished.

The January 1952 council meeting was a tense affair. Bishop Paul Kern's Episcopal Address draft was under review. The black bishops protested Kern's pointing out the Central Jurisdiction's failure to grow in numbers or progress in other ways. A deletion was demanded. On the other hand, Bishop Arthur Moore insisted that any reference to the question of segregation be expunged. It made for "a long and rather bitterly-contested evening," Oxnam reported, leaving Kern "much dispirited." In the end, the 1952 Episcopal Address did attack segregation but gave no concrete advice as to how Methodists might carry on the fight.

When the council next met in December on Sea Island, Georgia, half the bishops stayed at the luxurious, segregated The Cloisters while the rest, including all the blacks, bunked at Epworth-by-the-Sea. "I doubt we ought ever again to meet in the South until this is really faced up to once and for all," Oxnam believed. Honest though the conviction was, he never pressed the council to act accordingly.

The first meeting of the council following the historic Supreme Court desegregation decision in *Brown v. Board of Education* was held on November 20, 1954, in Chicago. It was an explosive Saturday afternoon. Some southern bishops advised making no public reference to the decision. The black bishops, led by Bishop Jones, spoke eloquently to the contrary. Recorded Oxnam: "The argument for postponement and for silence was one of expediency. It had nothing to do with ethical principles. Some of us had to speak quite a bit and at length in this matter. When the vote was taken, with the exception of the Southeastern Jurisdiction and even some there voted for it, it carried overwhelmingly." The statement adopted, largely from the pen of Bishop Kennedy, opened by affirming that the Supreme Court decision was in keeping with the attitudes of The Methodist Church. It noted that the Court recognized that such a ruling brought with it difficulties of enforcement, and therefore made sufficient time to implement its decision. The statement closed: ". . . the ultimate success of the ruling will be determined in the hearts of the people of the nation. Thus the church is furnished with an unequaled opportunity to provide leadership during this period in support of the principles involved in the action of the court. We accept this responsibility, for one of the foundation stones of our faith is the belief that all men are brothers, equal in the sight of God. In that faith, we declare our support of the ruling of the Supreme Court."

Oxnam as council secretary took the precaution of having each of the bishops sign the statement individually. He also warned them of the danger of acting as a jurisdictional unit in defiance of the majority of the council.

The warning was in vain. Bishop Clare Purcell of the Birmingham Area, doubtless speaking for most of the other bishops of the Southeastern Jurisdiction, immediately in a statement to the press informed the nation that it was not the intent of the council to announce that The Methodist Church was to "lead the fight" against segregation as the newspapers had interpreted the council statement. "The Council recognizes that many thousands of our people are sincerely divided on this issue and differ conscientiously," Purcell reminded. Henry Hitt Crane at once shot a letter to Oxnam expressing the reaction of at least one northern Methodist minister: "Now to have Purcell put out such a statement . . . is ecclesiastical treason or episcopal cowardice of the worst sort—or both. And they must know it—but apparently they are so used to knuckling under to Arthur Moore and he in turn constantly kowtowing to the money boys and the defenders of the status quo, that when the whip is cracked they all howl together."

Oxnam repeatedly in public defended the *Brown* decision, and at a reception in Washington, he told Chief Justice Warren of his gratitude for the Court's wisdom and courage.

The 1956 Episcopal Address's references to race, written by Bishop Corson, were judged by Oxnam to be woefully inadequate, and Oxnam privately expressed the suspicion that Corson had made a deal with the white southern bishops to treat the race issue gingerly in return for their support in electing him to write the address.

An understandably particular concern of Oxnam's was the economic fate of black Americans. Three days after Pearl Harbor, in a Council of Bishops meeting he raised the serious question of race discrimination in the defense industry, and, supported by Bishop Jones, moved that the council appoint a committee to investigate the execrable situation. On July 30, 1944, as the representative of both The Methodist Church and the Federal Council, Oxnam testified before Senator Dennis Chavez's committee on a proposed Fair Employment Practices Act. Although given a courteous hearing, Oxnam accurately observed that "neither party wants to deal with this hot-potato before the election, but it is very necessary to keep this matter to the fore, if we are to avoid race riots when peace comes, not to say anything about practicing our religion." The following month he again took the train to Washington to inform a Senate committee: "The right to work is elementary. Within this right, a man's opportunity should be determined by his character and his capacity, never by his color and his creed. The proposed Act seeks to guarantee this right, and is necessary for the reason that an abstract right must be made enforceable." In November, Mrs. Roosevelt (pointedly not her unenthusiastic husband) invited Oxnam to the White House, joined by Father Ryan, Rabbi Wise, and A. Philip Randolph, to map a strategy to secure the act's passage. In mid-1941 President Roosevelt, under black pressure, had reluctantly established a temporary Fair Employment Practices Committee, and upon his death President Truman unsuccessfully pressed to make it permanent. In 1945 Oxnam addressed a mass meeting in New York in support of a permanent FEPC. In 1946 he was one of the sponsors of a march on Washington to that end. In 1958 he, together with other concerned citizens, mostly black, met with Vice-president Nixon to assert that no government contracts should be awarded to companies that discriminated racially.

As president of the Federal Council, Oxnam helped shape the council's increasingly unequivocal statements on race relations, as for example the March 1946 pronouncement: "The Federal Council . . . hereby renounces the pattern of segregation in race relations as unnecessary and undesirable and a violation of the Gospel of love and human brotherhood. Having taken this action, the Federal Council requests its constituent communions to do likewise. As proof of their sincerity in this renunciation they will work for a non-segregated Church and a non-segregated society."

On a fair number of instances Oxnam was invited to appear before black audiences. The invitations themselves reveal something about his standing in the black community, while his impressions of black culture and black leaders provide clues to understanding the man.

Oxnam delivered baccalaureate, chapel, and Founder's Day sermons at Morgan State, Grambling, Bennett, Howard, Dillard, Tuskegee, North Carolina A.T.&T., Philander Smith, Clark (Georgia), and on rare instances at black high schools. He addressed one General Conference of the African Methodist Episcopal Zion Church and also spoke at that church's Sesquicentennial. Methodist Episcopal churches in Harlem and also outside of New York requested his presence on special occasions, such as the burning of a mortgage. He presided at the South Florida (black) Annual Conference.

More often than not, after these visits Oxnam reported having had a "happy time," a "grand time," "I think I have never had a better time," and "They could not have been more friendly nor more enthusiastic." A service at Saint Mark's in Harlem, at which he preached, drew the accolade: "From the standpoint of careful planning and the expression of every courtesy, this day had been unequalled." The pastor, Dr. Sweeney, was able and his wife a woman of refinement and culture. (Incidentally, Oxnam married the Sweeneys' daughter, the only reported instance of his officiating at the marriage of black persons.)

Viewing a sea of eager young black faces in an Alabama high school audience shook Oxnam up emotionally. A woman soloist in a black church in Boston impressed him more than anything else he had heard "in a long, long time." Hearing sung the spiritual "I Am Going to Sit at the Welcome Table Some of These Days," wrung the admission, "When I thought of the tables that extended no welcome to a person that is black, it was hard to control emotion."

Perhaps inevitably Oxnam found some of these experiences amusing or strange or exasperating. A punctual man himself, he could not abide running on "C.T.—Colored Time"—that is, behind schedule. Why do Negroes always overheat their rooms, he mused? Negro preaching and the congregation's response was a wonderment. Here is a diary description of a mortgage burning service at the Metropolitan Community Church in Harlem: "The emotionalism of our Negro people was evident, some jumping up and shouting, some shrieking, most of them carrying on but singing in a rhythm that before long had that audience ready for somebody to shout 'Forward, march!' or 'Tear him down,' or 'Build him up,' and certainly the orders would have been followed." And here is the final passage of a report of a mortgage burning service at another church: "At last I got the mortgage in my hands, lit it, it was burned, and I had the same feeling you do when little children stand about a Christmas tree. These people are very honest, elemental, emotional."

Oxnam's experience presiding at the South Florida 1938 Annual Conference was not a happy one, but his diary account is scarcely a credit to his own humanity. Arriving at the church on the minute, he found the preachers standing around gabbing, "the chief item of business at a colored conference." Then, "I got through the morning business session learning that negro reports mean nothing, and that nobody is really ready with anything but excuses." The afternoon session convinced him of the importance of "face"—"in this case black face." The reception line ordeal triggered the unfunny barb: "I can testify that the black does not come off. Everybody must shake hands with the bishop. 'Must meet mah bishop.' 'Dis is my little girl, she want to shake hands with our bishop.' Procter and Gamble forever."

Yet, in Oxnam's book, there were blacks and there were other blacks. The congregation of the First Methodist Church in New Orleans was "marvelous," emotionally stirred, to be sure, but also "intellectually acute." After the service he retired to the home of Bishop Robert N. Brooks. "Here one of the most delightful dinners I can ever remember was served," Oxnam rejoiced. "If some of the people who talk about the Negroes as they do were to sit at such a table and become acquainted with the culture, the good manners, the appreciation of the beautiful present there, some ideas would be revised. The table decorations indicated such an understanding of color, arrangement, and appropriateness as I have seldom seen." After visiting the home of a black college president, Oxnam again rejoiced, "It was as beautiful a luncheon as I have ever attended. The conversation was upon a high plane."

Certainly Oxnam respected a lot of black leaders. Among Methodist bishops, he praised Brooks, Edward W. Kelley, J. W. E. Bowen, Robert E. Jones, Willis J. King, Edgar J. Love, and Lorenzo H. King, though he discerned in the last a certain bitterness toward whites and a certain ruthlessness in dealing with Methodists of his own race. "How wise these men are, and how religious, too," Oxnam said of his black episcopal colleagues.

Oxnam highly esteemed President David Jones of Bennett College, giving the major address at Jones's memorial service. Oxnam gave the charge at the installation of Harry Richardson as president of Gammon Theological Seminary and considered him a man of "unusual brilliance." Two blacks with whom he worked on the Federal Council were respected: George E. Haynes, executive director of the Commission on Race Relations, and Vice-president Mays. Outside the church realm Oxnam had some association with nationally known black leaders. In the area of race and labor, he and Randolph joined forces and Oxnam was invited to represent American Protestantism at the twenty-fifth anniversary celebration of the Brotherhood of Sleeping Car Porters. He also met and admired Walter White and Ralph Bunche.

Violence directed against blacks appalled Oxnam. He supported federal antilynching legislation. He was one of the signers of a protest prepared by the NAACP following the bloody 1943 Detroit race riot. He repeatedly warned that racial warfare might explode if the black were not accorded justice, for a "new Negro" was emerging who would no longer passively endure discrimination. When the Daughters of the American Revolution found it impossible to extend the facilities of Constitution Hall to Marian Anderson and when early in the war the Red Cross segregated Negro blood in blood banks, he raged at the stupidity. Learning that the Gideons accepted only white members, he protested and the restriction was eliminated. He was a member of "The Committee of 100" dedicated to a racially just America; one of its activities was to raise funds for the NAACP.

Education was a special concern. In 1944 he made an appeal on behalf of the United Negro College Fund. He sought moneys for Methodism's black educational institutions. When Southern Methodist University's Perkins School of Theology finally in 1957 admitted blacks, he rejoiced. He publicly chastized the Candler School of Theology at Emory for not promptly following suit. Wesley Theological Seminary was integrated from the onset and he lived long enough to see its first black student graduate.

For an entire year Oxnam sought to secure the admission of blacks into the Nurses' Training School of The Methodist Hospital, Brooklyn. Thanks to his persistence, the deed was done and he was able to inform a radio audience: "There are anvil days ahead, perhaps many. But as sure as God's sun rises on the morrow, God's justice will be established, and a cultured and refined Christian Negro young woman will not be denied the right to train as a nurse in a hospital of a Christian church." Under Oxnam's leadership the primarily white New York Annual Conference met in 1952 for the first time in a black church, St. Mark's.

In Washington Oxnam made certain that the doors of the cafeteria in the Methodist Building (Oxnam's office and home) remained open to blacks. (To this day, older black scholars recall this with gratitude, for while researching at the Library of Congress there was then no other place for them to lunch for miles.) At the October 1954 rededication of the renovated Simpson Memorial Chapel in the Methodist Building Oxnam took the occasion to praise the *Brown* decision and say: "Resort to violence and refusal to obey the law is subversive, and does more to undermine democratic government than any traitor Communist. We can deal with him as a traitor; but it poses something of a problem to know how to deal with a man who dares to carry the Stars and Stripes in a parade of persons who march to repudiate the law of the land and to reject the clear teachings of the Christian faith." When in 1958 a group of blacks and a white Methodist minister, Charles Webber, informed Oxnam that the swimming pool in a local Y was open to whites only he used his influence to rectify that situation. When the minister of historic Foundry Church, Frederick Brown Harris, refused Negro children permission to join the church-sponsored Boy Scout Troop 17, Oxnam let him know his position was a repudiation of Christianity and a denial of America's best traditions. (Harris, who was also chaplain of the U.S. Senate, was in Oxnam's opinion vain, self-seeking, reactionary.)

In 1960 a group of ministers (including six Methodists) and rabbis came under fire for criticizing the practice in Silver Spring, Maryland, of excluding blacks from residency. "I am very proud of the Methodist members who signed the statement," Oxnam informed the press. In that year also, Asbury Methodist Church hosted a meeting at which southern blacks testified about their terrible experiences in attempting to register and vote; the intent of the meeting was to secure passage of civil rights legislation at the next session of Congress. Oxnam had been a sponsor of and participant at the assembly. The cry was raised that it was a Communist show. (And once again alert citizens informed the FBI of Oxnam's perfidy.) Far from backing down, Oxnam took the position: "It is high time we took the whole question of denying the vote to the Negroes seriously. . . . Meetings such as that held in the Asbury Methodist Church constitute a blow at Communism rather than cooperation with it."

In fact, as early as 1944 Oxnam had sought to abolish the poll tax. He shrewdly realized, and publicly said, that the end of segregation would come only when the politician had to reckon with a powerful Negro electorate. "When the vote is there, the politicians are going to think in terms of proper treatment of Negroes," he informed the Baltimore Annual Conference in 1958. And in 1960 he added: "This whole question of voting, to me, is incredible—that in 1960 men and women must come here in a democracy and ask for the privilege of voting. . . . I am of the opinion that when the Negro has the vote and exercises his franchise as a free man, political, economic and other problems will fall into line, because there is power in the vote and that is precisely where we need to be upon this issue." Moreover, he repeatedly warned, "The killing of Negroes in a Detroit race riot or the lynching of a Negro in the South, creates more Communists in a day than a committee on Un-American activities can ferret out in many days."

During the Washington years Oxnam worked to raise funds for the building of Hughes Memorial Methodist Church, the first black church to be raised in Washington in decades under the auspices of The Methodist Church; and to this day, the then minister, William Bishop, is grateful. In 1955 the Baltimore Preachers' Conference (white) and the Washington Preachers' Conference (black) merged. Oxnam and Bishop Love together hailed the step "toward the achievement of real brotherhood among the clergy of the two episcopal areas." Finally, Oxnam labored on an agreement between the Washington conference and the Baltimore conference on procedures to be followed for the exchange and development of churches within their bounds.

When in 1947 Jackie Robinson broke the color line in major league baseball, Oxnam confessed his shame "as a churchman to be taught the meaning of the solidarity of the human family by Branch Rickey of the Brooklyn Dodgers." In 1957, as Vice-president Nixon visited Africa, Oxnam suggested that he next "visit Montgomery, Alabama, and call upon the Reverend Martin Luther King, Jr., and look upon the bombed houses of clergymen." Addressing the five thousand delegates to The Methodist Church's National Convocation on Local Church Evangelism, Oxnam lashed Ku Kluxers, adding, "The preacher who pledges himself to follow Christ and then stands silent in the presence of segregation betrays his Lord." And: "The silence of Christians when the vote is denied Negroes, and segregation is enforced, speaks so loud that black men overseas cannot hear what our missionaries say. . . . White Christians counsel patience when they mean acquiescence. The voice of the evangelist is unheard as conscience cries out in condemnation." The black readers of *Ebony* learned from his pen: "For me, segregation is not primarily a political, a social, or an economic issue. It is a religious question. Segregation is a sin. It is as simple as that. Jesus told us to love one another. We do not segregate those we love. When we do we violate a religious commandment, and we sin."

By the late 1940s and 1950s American blacks, not without substantial justification, believed that in Oxnam they had found a friend. In 1946 he was asked to speak at the memorial service for Bishop Lorenzo King and in 1952 at a testimonial dinner honoring Bishop Love. In 1951 Bennett College conferred upon him an honorary degree, and the following year he received a Distinguished Service Award from the African Methodist Episcopal Zion Church. The black magazine *Color* gratefully cited him for his support, as did the famed Mary McLeod Bethune in her newspaper column. The distinguished Dr. Moredcai Johnson said to him, "Bishop, you are the first bishop ever to come to Washington who has stated so that everybody can understand precisely what you mean upon this issue of segregation." A Washington conference leader in bringing greetings to the Baltimore conference extolled Oxnam's matchless nobility, one passage declaring: "Memphis has her Thebes, Paris her Pantheon, London her Westminster Abbey, Washington her Arlington, but no tombs of the earth are rich enough or gorgeous enough to enshrine the deathless deeds of this worthy Bishop, the deathless deeds of this Galahad, this St. George, this Gabriel, this Michael, this Raphael—Bishop G. Bromley Oxnam." On the eve of his retirement Oxnam received the Franklin Delano Roosevelt Memorial Brotherhood Medal from the Interdenominational Ministers of Greater New York, representing thirty-five black Protestant churches.

The most signal thing to observe in Oxnam's record on race is that he clearly grew in contrition for America's deepest sin and in a commitment to rooting out that sin.

[1] Frank Loescher, in research for his book *The Protestant Church and the Negro,* found that DePauw admitted no black students in the period 1939–1944. Therefore, it is possible that none were enrolled immediately prior to 1939, and if there were, surely the

number could not have been large.

[2] However, Bishop Alexander P. Shaw was in the early 1950s finally invited by the California-Arizona Annual Conference to preside, the first black bishop to conduct an Annual Conference of another Jurisdiction.

[3] Incidentally, according to Bishop Roy Short, year after year Oxnam submitted travel vouchers larger than those of any other bishop.

CHAPTER 24

ECONOMIC JUSTICE

The enormity of racial injustice may have come tardily to Oxnam's consciousness, but a passion for economic justice had gripped him almost since his first conscious thoughts: as a youth in Los Angeles concerned with the city's poverty-stricken population; as labor's champion first in Phoenix and then at the Church of All Nations; as a mediator in labor-management disputes in Indiana and author of General Conference economic reports; and as a critic of unfettered capitalism in all of these periods. His election to the episcopacy perhaps banked but certainly did not extinguish the fires of his concern, though at no time was he consumed by the burning Absolute of Marxian socialism either in its Communist Party variant or in the milder Socialist Party form.

Politically Oxnam's concern found expression in the Democratic Party. The record does not disclose how he voted in the presidential elections of 1928 or 1932. After these elections, however, it is certain he supported F.D.R. in 1936, 1940, and 1944; Truman in 1948; and Stevenson in 1952 and 1956. Not only that, he was an original sponsor of Americans for Democratic Action, formed in 1947 to revitalize the liberal wing of the Democratic Party and also hold at bay the Communist Left. Oxnam idolized Roosevelt and extolled the New Deal. His reservations about Truman were not such as to force him in 1948 into Dewey's camp; and Henry Wallace's Progressive Party was too far to the Left for his taste. Adlai Stevenson was held "in very high esteem." Besides, Eisenhower's domestic policies and his backers and advisors (with the exception, of course, of Dulles) troubled him "very, very much." "I think it is going to be better for the country to have a Democratic administration back in power," he held in 1956. "There is a philosophy that underlies the Republican approach that I think in the long run is going to mean disaster." "All of this talk about a business administration," he concluded in 1958, "adds up to the same situation that we had in the Hoover regime. Business men simply don't know how to run the business of government."

Democratic measures won Oxnam's support and some Republican measures, his opposition. While bishop of the Omaha Area he made radio appeals (subsequently distributed in pamphlet form) in support of the 1937 child labor amendment and 1938 National Labor Relations Act. After Pearl Harbor, he served on the National War Labor Board's list of referees and arbitrated a number of disputes. On the eve of Japan's surrender, he testified before Senator Wagner's Committee on Currency and Banking in favor of a proposed Full Employment Act, saying that "freedom to engage in free competitive enterprise is, in the long run, dependent upon another aspect of freedom, namely the right of the individual worker to a job. A man who cannot get a job is not free." (At the onset of the hearing, conservative Senator Warren Austin apologized for the possibility of having to leave at two minutes to twelve, but not because of any lack of interest in Oxnam's statement. "That is all right, Senator," replied the bishop. "You can imagine you are in church.") Late in the fall Oxnam again came to Washington to testify in favor of raising the minimum wage from twenty-five cents an hour to sixty-five cents. The thunderously debated Taft-Hartley Act, a Republican bill passed over Truman's veto, earned Oxnam's condemnation: "Labor's war record deserves praise, not punishment." The Eisenhower administration's support of so-called "Right to Work" laws were judged by Oxnam "neither intended nor designed to guarantee work or to establish the right to work. . . . They are a dangerous proposal, conceived in hypocrisy, and proclaimed in Pharasaic deceit."

The right of labor to organize was axiomatic to Oxnam. Labor's right to strike was "fundamental." "Strikes and picketing as such must not be classified as violence," he held. On one instance he took a bus rather than a cab during a taxi strike, explaining, "I do not wish to ride and add any business to a company that will not deal with organized workers." On another occasion he helped sponsor a fund-raising drive to succor the families of striking General Motors workers. To be sure, if strikers engaged in violent tactics, this was a violation of Christian teaching and counterproductive to boot. If union leadership was corrupt, individuals such as Dave Beck of the International Brotherhood of Teamsters merited ousting. In the civil rights movement, Oxnam had never engaged in freedom marches, never stared into the muzzle of a Kluxer's shotgun, never shared a jail cell with arrested demonstrators. As a bishop, Oxnam never marched in a picket line, risked having his brains bashed by a company goon in Detroit, or caught a police bullet in the groin in Chicago's infamous Memorial Day Massacre, or undertook the dangerous job of helping to organize southern tenant farmers. He did not belong to that little band of ministers and priests who did so. Nevertheless, his concern was genuine and workers knew it.

For example, he respected the Amalgamated Clothing Workers union and considered Sidney Hillman a truly great American. The admiration was mutual, for both in 1948 and 1958 Oxnam was asked to offer the invocation and address the biennial convention of the union. The responses of the three thousand delegates were thunderous on both occasions.

Oxnam's closest union relationship was with the United Automobile, Aircraft and Agricultural Implement Workers of America (UAW) and its leaders Walter Reuther (a Lutheran) and his brother Victor (a Methodist). In 1954 Henry Hitt Crane hosted a testimonial banquet in Detroit in Oxnam's honor. Walter Reuther's expansive tribute contained the praise: "I have long regarded him as one of America's outstanding prophets of social justice." When in 1958 reactionary Senator McClellan's committee grilled Walter Reuther on union and personal matters, hoping to uncover odious malpractices, Bromley and Ruth made a point to be present, judging that the union leader won "hands down."

They then lunched with Victor. Shortly Oxnam heard from Walter: "Just a note of appreciation for the moral support that your presence provided during the recent Senate hearing. Knowing that you had gone through similar sessions and came out with such flying colors strengthened my faith and confidence." Oxnam's address before the UAW's Sixteenth Constitutional Convention left the delegates shouting, "More, more!" The union then presented him with its Freedom Award.

Oxnam was an original member of the seven-person UAW Public Review Board, established in 1957. The board represented the broadest grant of authority over its internal affairs ever voluntarily given by a labor organization—or any other organization for that matter—to an outside body. The board sat as an appellant body, hearing any appeal that came to it constitutionally dealing with the violation of the Code of Ethics of the UAW or of the Code of Ethics of the AFL-CIO. That is, in addition to acting as a body for appeals from decisions of the International Executive Board, it also had broad powers over the moral and ethical standards of the union. The creation of the board is a real tribute to the Reuthers and also a testimony to Oxnam's standing in the House of Labor. His initial colleagues on the board were Monsignor George Higgins, Rabbi Morris Adler, Chancellor Clark Kerr—two jurists and an economist. Oxnam considered this service, for which he received a mere one thousand dollars annually plus two hundred dollars for each case in which he participated, interesting and important, as the diary entries and five bulging folders of case materials attest. When ill-health forced his resignation in 1962, Reuther wrote a long letter, closing, "We deeply regret your leaving us. We want you to know that your presence and your contribution strengthened us. We hope and pray that although this formal bond has been loosened, the labor movement and the whole American community can continue to draw upon your fine humanity for years to come." (One can imagine how the automobile management reacted to Oxnam's 1958 chastisement: "A few more eggheads in the automobile industry to support the blockheads who have designed our recent cars would be in our national interest. Who are the madmen who build cars so long they cannot be parked, so low that an average human being has to crawl in the doors, and so powerful that no man dare use the horsepower available?" In truth, the cars turned out by Detroit in the 1950s do seem to have been designed by beauticians collaborating with morticians.)

Unafraid to take on G.M., Ford, and Chrylser, Oxnam challenged an even more formidable group, the American Medical Association. Denying that he was an advocate of "socialized medicine," nevertheless he informed the five hundred delegates to the 1951 convention of the American Protestant Hospital Association: "There are no better doctors in the world than the American doctors. Let these doctors in cooperation with men acquainted with our national health needs work out progressive answers to the problems, rather than pay their assessments to a little oligarchy that has fought advances for a generation. Protestants want neither the shackles of the omnicompetent state nor the fetters of the incompetent American Medical Association." Naturally AMA issued a rejoinder through its spokesman Dr. Morris Fishbein.

Oxnam was aware of the distance that separated The Methodist Church from any substantial number of labor union members. In fact, it was his understanding that out of the more than seven hundred delegates to the 1956 General Conference, not one was a representative of organized labor.[1] How was rapprochement to be effected? An earlier experience, to be related momentarily, had convinced Oxnam that assigning ministers under special appointment as "Chaplains to Labor" whose salaries were paid by labor was not the answer. Oxnam's solution was outlined in his 1948 Episcopal Address and earlier in *Labor and Tomorrow's World*. Let the Church recruit each year fifty of its finest youth to enter the ranks of labor. Let them receive undergraduate and graduate training in selected universities. Let them then enter the mines, mills, factories. "They are to go to work, asking nothing for themselves, with no assumption that because of their superior education they are to be chosen immediately as the leaders of labor. Let them join the union and rise to such leadership as their talents and service deserve. At first this will be leadership upon the local level, subsequently upon the State level, and finally, in the national and international realm. If fifty such persons go into the labor movement each year for twenty years, out of this thousand will come a leadership of great power. It must be pointed out that this is no plan to tone down the demands for social justice. A person who gives himself to labor, who refuses to accept promotion to the higher paid managerial position, is a person of conviction." The following year the Council of Bishops authorized a new Methodist Commission on the Church and Labor, one of its charges being to implement Oxnam's ideas. For obvious reasons, the plan proved impossible of attainment.

The unfortunate experience alluded to above concerned Charles C. Webber who was as authentically a Man of Labor as any Methodist minister in this century. In 1944 Bishop McConnell, presiding at the New York East Annual Conference, appointed Webber field secretary of the Amalgamated Clothing Workers of America (CIO). The following year Oxnam renewed the appointment with the concurrence of the necessary two-thirds majority of the members of the conference. Originally stationed in Tennessee and Pennsylvania, Webber was transferred to Richmond to organize the employees of the Crawford Manufacturing Company. While there, he was elected president of the Virginia State CIO (serving in all ten years) and director of the CIO-PAC (Political Action Committee).

Unsurprisingly, conservative Methodist laymen and others protested. Oxnam was not at all certain he had the legal right to appoint a Methodist minister to a labor union; if so, what if the National Association of Manufacturers requested the same services of a minister? How could the request be denied? At this juncture Oxnam and Webber talked it over and came up with the idea of Webber's appointment as "Chaplain to Organized Labor." Meanwhile, Bishop W. W. Peele of Virginia was feeling the heat and lamented that Webber was hurting the Church in the Southeast. Bishop Shaw, on the other hand, recognized that the CIO unions had blacks in their locals and embraced Oxnam's statement that "I see more religion in ending Jim Crow than in preaching abstractions about brotherhood." Oxnam, terming Peele "one of the wisest and most devoted leaders of our Church," regretted the embarrassment the appointment had caused. The two bishops then requested the Council of Bishops to render a judgment on the question of special appointments such as Webber's. In 1947 Webber's appointment was withdrawn, but he continued as a member of New York East and as president of the Virginia CIO until he was assigned to UAW-CIO National Headquarters in Detroit where he became a member of the Detroit Annual Conference.

A decade later Oxnam reported to his diary, "Charley has been a courageous man, but has, I fear, been the agitator, certainly not the administrator." This assessment does not do justice to Webber. To begin with, in that era, and especially in that area, if workers seeking to unionize had not "agitated," their chances of success would have been nil. In the second place, the New York East Conference found Webber innocent of all charges brought against him by Methodist minister Rembert Gilman Smith, that hound of hell who continually nipped at Oxnam's heels also. Thirdly, when the House Un-American Activities Committee heard ex-Communist Benjamin Gitlow testify that Webber was one of "the principal individuals involved in the communist conspiracy to subvert the Methodist church," Webber convincingly documented that he had long fought communists in unions and had always challenged the Communist Party Line. The irony is that when Webber's appointment as "Chaplain to Organized Labor" was withdrawn, an FBI agent interpreted this action as lending "credence to information I have received indicating that through pressure being brought on the Bishop [Oxnam] he has undergone a considerable change on [sic] his left-wing views." The long memorandum, dated August 14, 1947, relating the Webber-Oxnam relationship carries at the bottom J. Edgar Hoover's handwritten comment, "I don't believe a leopard ever changes his spots."

A less obtuse individual than Mr. Hoover would not have worried because Oxnam's "spots" had not changed. Indeed they had not. Regarding economic justice, he continued to stand on the foundations of the famous Social Creed of Methodism adopted by the Methodist Episcopal Church in 1908 and later adopted by Southern Methodism and which served as the basis for the Federal Council's Social Creed of the Churches. It was a model of the moderate progressivism of the Theodore Roosevelt-Wilson era.

In succeeding years individual Methodist ministers,[2] groups such as the Methodist Federation for Social Service,[3] journals such as *Zion's Herald*,[4] Annual Conferences such as New York East,[5] and General Conferences, especially that of 1932, moved to the Left, giving a genuine cause for worry to those who equated capitalism with Americanism. But Oxnam always remained in the mainstream of American liberalism—Teddy Roosevelt's New Nationalism, Wilson's New Freedom, Franklin D. Roosevelt's New Deal, Truman's Fair Deal, and Adlai Stevenson's and the Americans for Democratic Action's Vital Center liberalism.

It is impossible to tabulate—or rather it would be hardly worth the effort—the number of words spilling from Oxnam's pen and lips devoted to economic justice. The total must be in the hundreds of thousands. It was the subject of a number of his books, such as *Social Principles of Jesus* and *The Ethical Ideals of Jesus in a Changing World* and *Labor and Tomorrow's World* and *The Christian's Vocation* and *Personalities in Social Reform*. It cropped up even in his books with another focus, such as *The Stimulus of Christ* and *A Testament of Faith*. It was the subject of or figured in sermons, addresses, articles, and newspaper columns almost beyond number. Approximately nineteen pages of his fifty-nine-page 1948 Episcopal Address are devoted, directly or indirectly, to economic questions, surely an important clue to how central these questions were in his understanding of God's will, Christ's life, and the Church's responsibility.

In *A Testament of Faith* he set forth this overarching conviction:

> I would like to consider some of the implications of contemporary theology, namely that the Kingdom of God cannot be realized upon this earth or in history. This, to me, is a shocking and shattering insistence. When I pray, "Thy kingdom come, Thy will be done, on earth as it is in heaven," I am not awaiting the end of history for the consummation of the prayer. When I repeat these words, I mean what I say. The Kingdom for me is a social order in which the will of God is done in all the activities of men. I have dreamed the day when God's will may so rule.

Perhaps the following passage from a 1950 essay, "Jesus, the Great Revolutionist," is fairly representative of Oxnam's utterances on social questions:

> In Jesus's thinking, each individual is of infinite worth. He therefore tests all social institutions by what they do to the individual. This means that

the Christian Gospel can never be identified with any economic system: capitalism, communism or socialism. It stands in judgment upon all such systems, and tests them in terms of what happens to personality. We unfortunately are entering a period in which men put the prevailing economic system before the Gospel.

The Communist admits of no moral law to which the Communist economic order must be subordinated. Too many capitalists are assuming that what is called "the American way" or "free enterprise" is the Christian Gospel and that any criticism of capitalistic procedures is therefore blasphemy. Many socialist leaders assume that the collective ownership and democratic management of the principal means of production, distribution, and exchange is a full expression of the Christian Gospel.

The Church refuses to be silenced by capitalist, communist, or socialist who declares that his particular system shall be free from the judgment of Almighty God. Communism is avowedly atheistic. There are capitalist advocates who argue that God is irrelevant to the economic system, and hold that there are inexorable economic laws at work to which all must bow. The result is a battle in the realm of ideologies; and energies which should be used to reconcile the necessity of brotherhood are wasted upon the fields of conflict instead of being used at the conference tables of cooperation.

We cannot build a moral society by the use of immoral means. The objectives of the moral law must be realized by the use of moral means. The Christian revolution begins in the individual heart. Many are ready to accept God but are unwilling to carry its revolutionary demands into the social order to the end that equal opportunity becomes the lot of all men and brotherhood becomes a practice.

Oxnam was quite capable of other utterances that were far more celebratory than prophetic—they were in fact classics of triumphalism. The great puzzlement is how the man responsible for them could possibly have been branded as an "un-American" as Oxnam was. Witness the following 1953 address:

No man acquainted with the facts can use the same term to describe the economic practices of the United States in 1900 and the economic practices of the United States in 1950. A fundamental revolution has occurred. The immoralities of the robber baron have been supplanted by the moralities of the responsible leader. The moral principles of the Jewish prophets and Jesus revealed in the practices of many strong men of business and competent leaders of labor are further evidence of the change. Conscience

> has a new place in the conduct of enterprise. This, in large measure, has been due to the preaching of the prophets. The Social Creed of the Churches, written in 1908, has become the accepted criterion for the practices of 1948. A Methodist Bishop was attacked in the twenties because he demanded the end of the twelve-hour day and the seven-day week in steel. Is there a businessman in the nation who would advocate a return to such un-American and un-Christian practices? The prophet summons the competent layman to translate the ideals of religion into the realities of the common life.

And the following from a 1954 address:

> The business practices of 1954 and 1900 differ as day from night, and the same term cannot be used to describe them. A man who would corner the wheat market today would not be called a genius. He would be called a gangster. At present the American city-dweller lives in the freest, the cleanest, the healthiest cities man has ever known.

And the following from a 1955 address:

> It is but to state the fact to declare that the practices of American business in 1955 differ so fundamentally from the practices of 1900 that the same term cannot be used to describe them. This amazing change has been wrought in large measure because of the prophetic proclamation of the Christian faith and the clear statement of its demand for justice. Responsible leaders in business and in labor, pledged to the moral principles that lie at the heart of the Christian faith, regard themselves as men upon whom a heavy obligation has been placed. A man who would corner the wheat market today would not be called a genius. On the contrary, he would be called a gangster.

And the following from a 1958 address:

> The Social Creed of the Churches is discounted in some quarters today, but it was the very proclamation of that creed that was decisive in the transformation of American business practice. The morality of contemporary economic enterprise differs today from that of 1900 as day differs from night.

These statements are patriotic pieties, not the bitter, truthful medicine Christian Americans needed to swallow; and coming from a churchman they are self-congratulatory to boot. Thanks to Christian social gospelites, businessmen saw the light, mended their selfish ways, and, save for isolated pockets of unenlightenment, the United States was now a redeemed nation; and churchmen and businessmen were marching onward to an ultimate Kingdom of God to be realized on earth and in history.

Oxnam's social concerns extended beyond the realms of economics and politics narrowly defined. In *The Story of Methodism*, three Methodist historians asserted that "the temperance movement was in many respects the *characteristic* Methodist battle of the century, the one which most fully enlisted the interest and enthusiasm of the church and the one in which Methodism rendered one of its largest services to the nation." Oxnam was not one of Methodism's outstanding leaders in the battle against booze, perhaps because he had too many other parsnips to butter and perhaps because he did not believe alcohol consumption to be *the* transcendent social evil blighting America, in 1930 warning that "it is not right to back an anti-saloon candidate if his only qualification is that he is dry." [6] Nevertheless, he supported the Eighteenth Amendment and opposed Repeal. He was in agreement with the Northern Methodist bishops when they wisely and truly stated, "We fought liquor, not because it has made men happy, but because it has made men unhappy." And he concurred with the spokesman for the Methodist Board of Temperance who accurately observed in 1934, the year after the Noble Experiment ended, "We come now face to face with the original problem, which is not Prohibition, but alcohol." Oxnam practiced abstinence himself. He believed abstinence should be the practice of all Methodists, and that if they in fact did practice it, it would be a marvelous example to other citizens and a near-mortal blow to the liquor interests. After Repeal he did not fruitlessly campaign for a new prohibition amendment, but he did support the passing of laws regarding drunken drivers, alcohol advertising, sale to minors, hours during which alcoholic beverages might be sold, and local option. Oxnam clearly saw and plainly said that drinking was not simply a question of the individual fate of alcoholics but a social problem of vast proportions. Oxnam did not often address the liquor issue, but when he did it was with restrained force, as in his Episcopal Address: "We refuse, in the name of individual liberty, to be estopped from achieving the legislative control of this narcotic necessary to protect the youth of the nation from its ravages. We refuse, in the name of temperance, to condone the use of liquor by clergy and laity. We refuse, in the name of fellowship, to relieve from moral responsibility the individual who makes his own decision to drink. We serve notice upon the liquor industry that we shall seek such regulation as may be necessary to reduce the menace of alcoholism to a minimum and that we shall seek this control through proper legislative channels. We shall seek likewise, through education, to rear a generation wise enough, in the interest of physical well-being, intellectual freedom, and spiritual growth, to realize that the initial stimulation of alcohol soon becomes the fact of eventual deterioration."

Regarding legalized gambling, gaining force in state after state, here, too, Oxnam's opposition was given infrequent voice, but when he did speak it was with persuasive logic and clear conviction.

Nice-Nellys in the Methodist ministry were not unknown, haunted by the fear, as Mencken sneered, that someone somewhere might be happy. Oxnam, happily, is innocent of the charge of bluenosery. To be certain, on rare occasions he made the obligatory condemnations of smut in novels, films, and plays, but his heart does not seem to have been in these infrequent tut-tuttings. Maybe this is because he was himself so cosmopolitan in what he read and saw and heard.

Would that it were possible to state without equivocation Oxnam's attitude toward a matter of truly transcendent significance—the women's movement. Perhaps he favored the Nineteenth Amendment because in 1916 he announced, "During the last few weeks I have been endeavoring to familiarize myself with some of the more notable books that have come from the Feminist Movement. Since I heard Charlotte Perkins Gilman lecture . . . I have been deeply interested in the movement." Beyond that expression the record is silent. Of course he held in esteem such pioneers as Jane Addams and Methodism's own Frances Willard. From time to time he addressed groups of women and found the experience rewarding, not the least because the women were so admirably organized. Especially esteemed was Methodism's Women's Society of Christian Service. "These ladies are remarkable," he noted after a 1950 talk. "1,500,000 women are organized. They are studying, facing the future, rendering constructive service. In fact, they are now so far ahead of the men of the church that there is no comparison at all in what they do." In 1954 he extolled, "The Women's Society . . . is the most remarkable organization in Christendom today. I know of nothing like it among the laity in any Church anywhere." Elsewhere he said for publication, "The most realistic thinking in the church is being done by women instead of men. Most men do not see the pattern as a whole. They are too busy with their jobs to see the picture." Moreover, he publicly affirmed "that a woman is fully entitled to work in any field of labor at equal pay for equal work, regardless of color or creed, and that the issue is not one of man or woman but rather a recognition that a human being is involved and rights are equal because of that fact." While holding that "all political disabilities based upon sex must be removed and doors to all professions must be opened to women on the basis of the equality of the sexes," he concurrently insisted that "the major objective is the preparation of woman for the most influential and challenging service in society, namely that of a mother and home-maker."

Perhaps the argument from silence is permissible here. There is nothing to prove how he felt about the question of granting full ministerial rights to women in The Methodist Church, a matter of much debate, especially at the 1956 General Conference. Oxnam's daughter does not know how her father stood on the question, but she feels certain that he favored the ordination of women inasmuch as his general thought was progressive and forward looking. One senses she is correct. Nevertheless, if his convictions were truly strong, why do these convictions not find expression in his public utterances or letters or private diary entries.

---

[1] Methodism's estrangement from America's industrial workers, increasingly immigrant and non-Protestant, and its growing middle class composition, is evident as early as the turn of the century. Witness the occupations of the lay delegates to Northern Methodism's 1904 General Conference: "Of laymen, there were 55 merchants, 39 lawyers, 34 educators, 27 physicians, 20 bankers, 15 manufacturers, 12 judges, 9 capitalists; 7 each of clerks, contractors, farmers and real estate agents; 6 insurance agents; 5 each of railroad officials, editors and mechanics; 3 stock and fruit growers, 2 business managers of church papers, 1 each of local preachers, State governors, architects, mining operators, students, revenue collectors, undertakers, nurserymen, and 32 miscellaneous and unknown."

[2] According to Kirby Page's famous 1934 poll of 100,499 clergymen, 34 percent of the Methodists who responded named socialism as the most preferred system for America. No other denomination accorded socialism so high a percentage.

[3] Chapter 26 will return to the MFSS.

[4] Editor Lewis O. Hartman (later Bishop Hartman) was a Christian socialist.

[5] Said the conference in 1935: "The twenty-five months of strenuous effort under the New Deal to reform the system has only proved that it is beyond reform. The conviction grows, therefore, that capitalism must be discarded and a planned Christian economy established. . . . The tenderness with which the sacred cow of private profits has been protected, while suffering has been indescribably inhuman, indicts both the intelligence and character of our nation."

[6] Unfortunately too many Methodists agreed with the 1908 Northern General Conference speaker who said, "Wisdom requires the adoption of a plan which will secure to that end [prohibition] the cooperation of every man who desires the thing, REGARDLESS OF WHAT HE THINKS ABOUT ANYTHING ELSE."

CHAPTER 25

THE COLD WAR ABROAD

From the aftermath of World War II to his retirement in 1960 Oxnam anguished over the dangerously developing Cold War. Being the concerned Christian and citizen that he was, being temperamentally incapable of standing on the sidelines, and being confident of his competence as a student of foreign affairs, he was compelled to issue commentaries on the challenge of communism and the policies of the Truman and Eisenhower administrations designed to contain (or roll back) that challenge and ensure the security of the United States and the "Free World." Oxnam did so in his various capacities as a leader of the Federal, National, and World Councils of Churches and of Methodism. His manifold proclamations were not free of internal contradictions and strange omissions. The issues were too complex, his information too incomplete, his hopes too far ahead of reality, his capacity for self-deception too acute, and the advice of the pundits too at variance for his utterances to be otherwise. Moreover, in justice to Oxnam, not even the perspective of three or four decades has enabled scholars to reach a consensus, divided as they are into schools of orthodox, realist revisionist, Cold War revisionist, and postrevisionist. It would be unfair to Oxnam to hold him to too close an accountability for judgments made at the time when much was hidden from him and when later scholars with the record spread before them are unable to agree in their interpretations. Nevertheless, Oxnam was a prominent public figure who felt free to offer advice, loudly, confidently, and frequently, to his Methodist flock and to the public at large—and to that extent he is accountable.

Oxnam's continuing relationship with John Foster Dulles merits extended examination because it is so revealing of Oxnam the man. It will be remembered that the two individuals had worked closely together on the Federal Council's Commission on a Just and Durable Peace. Dulles's increasing commitment to the political realm did not terminate that association. In September 1947 they met in New York, Oxnam seeking advice about his upcoming Town Hall of the Air broadcast. In the course of the conversation Oxnam speculated about a dramatic summit meeting between United States leaders and Stalin. Dulles replied that President Truman lacked the capacity and Secretary of State Marshall lacked the dynamism to stand up to the Russian leader. "I told Mr. Dulles that I hoped that he might be the one to represent us," the bishop reported. "His face lit up immediately, his whole being was electric when he said, 'I'd give up almost anything to sit across the table from Stalin.' " At the conclusion of the conversation Oxnam apologized for intruding on Dulles's busy schedule, and the Presbyterian replied, "You are one of the half-dozen men I want to see at any time. Yours are views that I respect far more than I can express." Is it any wonder that Oxnam used his good offices to have Dulles address the 1948 General Conference and then inform him that he was "superlative"? Oxnam also employed his influence to have Dulles appear before the Federal Council's 1949 Conference on the Churches and World Order. Afterward, dining alone together, the bishop lauded the layman's high moral principles. Dulles's contribution to the Japanese Peace Treaty, as a bipartisan consultant appointed by Truman, drew Oxnam's praise. Explained Dulles piously, "I tried my best to take the Christian principle of reconciliation and write it into the treaty rather than the pagan principle of revenge."

Shortly after assuming command of the Washington Area in 1952 Oxnam wrote Dulles: "I sincerely trust, in fact, pray, that political events may so shape themselves that a new administration in Washington may mean that you will be our Secretary of State. One of the high privileges of serving in Washington would be that of seeking to carry to the largest Protestant communion in the nation an understanding of the ideals and of the policies that we know you would sponsor and direct were you in that high office." Clearly here Oxnam was hedging his bets. He hoped for a Democratic victory in November, and if this transpired there would be no hope for Dulles to be tapped secretary of state. Therefore he was dissembling in praying that "political events" would place Dulles in the new administration's cabinet. Oxnam's private disappointment in Stevenson's defeat did not prevent him from sending a telegram of congratulations to Dulles and another to Eisenhower reading: "The appointment of John Foster Dulles has been received by the churches with enthusiasm and confidence. It is an added assurance with which we face the future under your leadership."

In the ensuing months Oxnam continued to publicly praise his "dear friend" as "a devout man, who loves God, is loyal to Christ, and pledged to the spiritual principles of the Christian faith." Oxnam personally expressed to the new secretary of state his confidence that Dulles's policies "will always be those that are morally right, rather than those that may be temporarily expedient." Nor did the passing of sobering years bring disenchantment to the self-mesmerized bishop. In 1953 a meeting with Dulles found Oxnam gushing with admiration and believing the secretary's assurance that he had no plans for Asia "involving military treaties or anything like a Pacific pact." (Rather shortly Dulles created the feckless Southeast Asia Treaty Organization, still another instance of his pactomania.)

Critics of the secretary received from the cleric a cuffing. (As early as 1947 Oxnam had resigned from the Methodist Federation for Social Action because of its doubts about Dulles.) In 1953 Oxnam lectured representatives of the Associated Church Press to be "very careful" in nicking that "great Christian in that high office" over small matters. Elsewhere he asserted that "Dulles is making a monkey out of Molotov. He is speaking to the peoples of Asia and Africa"—the latter assertion, at least, being quite contrary to fact. A St. Louis audience in 1954 was comforted by the knowledge that Dulles is a "deeply religious, humble but tenacious man who is applying moral principles to the problems of state"—and who in any case was "tired of being pushed around by the Communists." Dulles's book, *War or Peace*, received from a credulous Oxnam public and private praise. On Eisenhower's reelection in 1956, Dulles was pleased to hear from his Methodist friend that his critics were "vicious and uninformed"; that he was following a wise and Christian course; and that he would "go down in history as one whom the people will delight to honor."

There is a note of wistfulness in many of Oxnam's communications to the secretary of state. "I wish you would be perfectly frank and let those of us in the Church who may have some opportunity to develop a public opinion in active support of your principles know what we can do and when we ought to do it," read one plea. A 1955 letter's poignancy is typical: "If at any time you feel that the churches have not come sufficiently to your support, may I assure you that you are held in both pride and confidence by the churches. We do not quite know how to express our approval. I have wanted you to know that those of us who rejoiced in your leadership during the days of the Commission on a Just and Durable Peace and who thank God that you were finally charged with the responsibility of international life are still rejoicing in your leadership and are eager to count wherever we can." Oxnam returned to this lament in a 1957 letter: "I wish the Church could be more effective. Frankly, I do not know how it can be. It is difficult for us to be kept advised of what is going on, and again and again we are confronted with a great issue upon which public opinion should be mobilized but without the time to mobilize it." The letter closed with the familiar wounded moan: Why does the Eisenhower administration seem so cool to the Protestant churches? And the whippoorwill sigh: What can the Protestant churches do to win the president's smile?

These petitions, at once coy and cloying, leave one uneasy. They are suffused with a nostalgia for those moments of past glory when the Commission on a Just and Durable Peace and Methodism's Crusade for a New World Order used their combined moral influence and political muscle in support of the creation of the United Nations and United States membership in it. American Protestantism, led above all by Presbyterian layman Dulles and Methodist Bishop Oxnam, had spoken and

America had listened—or so was the cherished conviction of both men. In effect, Oxnam was begging the Republican secretary of state to permit the Protestant churches to be privy to the government's policy-making in order to give their support to what Washington practiced in the realm of diplomacy.

Perhaps sensing that Oxnam felt like a jilted bride, from time to time Dulles would tender a soothing stroke. In 1957 when Oxnam was recovering from a gall bladder operation he received a phone call from a solicitous Dulles. "I think nothing that has happened to me in recent months," rejoiced the bishop, "has done me more good than the fact that he took time to do this." Oxnam then took Dulles up on his invitation to come to Foggy Bottom for a visit. The secretary expressed regret that there was not a closer relationship between the churches and the leaders of government. "Both the President and I are Christian men. We are humble men, and we find ourselves quite alone. It has been a long time since any churchman has come to see me," he intoned as unctuously as a stage bishop. Oxnam protested that he was not by nature a gate crasher and, anyhow, Dulles's friendliness did not seem to be shared by other members of the present administration. Dulles turned to a little lecture on the necessity of the United States standing firm in Europe and against the communists in Asia, including the "Soviets" in Indochina! He then asked the bishop to offer a prayer and at its close, Oxnam recorded, "when I opened my eyes I saw tears in the eyes of this strong Secretary of State."

In subsequent months Oxnam continued to extoll Dulles. "Your name will take its place among the truly great leaders of our nation," read a seventieth birthday telegram. A fulsome introduction of Dulles in 1958 closed, "But above all, he brings a spirit dedicated to the Christian faith. He seeks to be, and is, a humble follower of our blessed Lord." In turn, the secretary remembered the bishop's birthdays and twice in 1958 called Oxnam in for long visits. At the conclusion of both the secretary asked the bishop to lift up a prayer.

By this time Dulles was feeling intimations of mortality. In 1956 he had undergone an operation for cancer. The doctors claimed a success. Dulles's truly iron will would not permit such painful ailments as diverticulitis, a slipped disc, and a hernia to moderate his awesome pace. In early 1959 cancer returned. Death he now knew was near and would be welcomed, such was his weakened, pain-racked condition. On March 27 Dulles asked Oxnam to come to his home. The meeting lasted ten minutes. The secretary confessed his spiritual, intellectual, and physical exhaustion. He buried his face in his hands and asked the bishop to pray. A Florida trip failed to restore Dulles's strength. He again petitioned for Oxnam's presence on Good Friday. Before words of greeting could be exchanged he said, "Pray for me." At Mrs. Dulles's request, Oxnam went to Walter Reed Hospital on April 15. Dulles beseeched prayer. Tears welled up in the secretary's eyes. He apologized, explaining the radiation treatment had upset him emotionally. "I have never known anyone who could bring the comfort and the strength that you bring, and I really wanted you here," said the thankful dying brave man. In truth, Oxnam was the only visitor not a high official or family member permitted to see Dulles during the last weeks before death. At Oxnam's suggestion, the Council of Bishops sent a message. It closed: "We rejoice in your steadfast and significant leadership characterized by refusal to surrender to tyranny, by loyalty to the ideals of peace and justice and by adherence to Christian principle." Dulles's devoted secretary, Phyllis Bernau, informed Oxnam of her dying employer's gratitude.

The end came May 24. Oxnam gave to the press a statement expressive of his esteem for the departed leader. To Mrs. Dulles he telegraphed the message: "Mrs. Oxnam joins me in a word of understanding, respect, and sympathy. The church, the nation, and the world have lost a great and good man, a patriot, and a peace-maker, and I have lost a highly respected friend." [1]

It is needful to say an additional word about John Foster Dulles not for the purpose of criticizing him but in order to more fully understand G. Bromley Oxnam. Oxnam's praise of Dulles extended unbroken over a period of almost two decades and was virtually unqualified. Why should this be? Three possible explanations suggest themselves. First, Oxnam was uninformed of the Dulles record. If true, this would demolish Oxnam's vaunted reputation as an authority on foreign affairs, a reputation he prized and advertised. He would be the last to plead guilty to the charge of ignorance. Second, Oxnam was bamboozled by Dulles's moralistic, perfervid rhetoric. If true, this would open Oxnam to the charge of naïveté. What then remains of his touted reputation as a "realist"? A third explanation seems more plausible but not less damaging. Dulles was Oxnam's closest link to the center of power in American politics, although the bishop surely overestimated the intimacy of the tie. To preserve that precious link, to forge an even stronger one, the cleric had to shower accolades, in person and in public, on this powerful Presbyterian. Before the accolades could be bestowed they had to be believed, else Oxnam would be guilty of monstrous hypocrisy. To be sure, an element of conscious hypocrisy may be discerned in Oxnam's posture. Yet surely a more persuasive key is Oxnam's infinite capacity for unconscious self-deception. He *had* to believe in Dulles's Christian righteousness, in the ultimately religious basis of Dulles's motivation, in the final morality of Dulles's actions. And so Oxnam did. And so it is now necessary to leave Oxnam for a moment to make certain unhappy points related to Dulles's career after 1946. Only by doing so can we comprehend how wrong Oxnam was. (Certainly not at issue are Dulles's intelligence, mastery of detail, unwhimpering stoicism when gripped by physical disabilities, commanding presence, prodigious industry, unflagging energy, personal courage, or patriotic eagerness to serve his country as did his forebears.)

President Truman for political bipartisan purposes tapped Dulles's services as a kind of consultant-at-large and then, increasingly cognizant of Dulles's abilities and usefulness, promoted him to ambassador-at-large. Dulles was not the architect of Truman's foreign policy—not even the Japanese Peace Treaty—but he did faithfully serve his Democratic masters. Nor was Dulles the sole architect of Eisenhower's foreign policy. Dulles loved the limelight, was highly visible, poured forth torrents of words, traveled world without end, and as a consequence some individuals were misled into thinking that he, not the president, was the dominant figure in foreign affairs. In fact, however, he did not set his own course but rather marched to the orders of Eisenhower, who, confident in his command of himself and the situation, permitted Dulles to puff himself up so long as administration orders were obeyed. Although Eisenhower never sought

Dulles's companionship at the bridge table or on the golf links, he genuinely respected his secretary of state's conscientiousness, ability, and loyalty and felt a deep loss when Dulles died.

What points, then, are at issue?

Item: In the 1948 Dewey-Truman election Dulles urged the Republican leadership to slash away at the Democratic "record" of criminal appeasement of communism and tragic failures in Eastern Europe and China. On the advice of Senator Vandenberg, Dewey did not fully exploit the indictment. The fact remains, however, that originally Dulles recommended an appeasement-baiting campaign even as Truman continued to call on his services.

Item: After serving four months as an appointed United States senator from New York, Dulles lost a bitterly contested special election in 1949 to Herbert Lehman. Even by New York standards it was a dirty campaign, the Lehman forces falsely intimating that Dulles was anti-Semitic and anti-Catholic. For his part, Dulles accused his opponent of walking the road of socialism. Worse, Lehman was charged with being a tool of the Reds: "The half million Communists and fellow travelers who last year voted for Henry Wallace, who will they vote for now? You know the answer." In case there was any doubt, Dulles repeatedly filled in the blanks, darkly catechizing one audience that "if I am defeated in this election, the greatest rejoicing will not be in New York or Washington but will be in Moscow." Dulles acknowledged that Lehman was no Communist, "but I also know that the Communists are in his corner." Oxnam was then bishop of the New York Area. Could he have been unmindful of Dulles's words?

Item: In April 1950 Dulles's *War or Peace* was published. The book depicted Soviet Russia bent on world domination "in order that they may finish us off in quick order." "Thus, the 450,000,000 people in China have fallen under leadership that is violently anti-American, and that takes its inspiration and guidance from Moscow. . . . Soviet Communist leadership has won a victory in China which surpasses what Japan was seeking and we risked war to avert." If the United States temporized with the Russians, the peoples of Indochina, Burma, Indonesia, Africa, and Latin America would suffer the fate of the Chinese and Eastern Europeans. Thus, in Dulles's vision, communism was monolithic worldwide. Oxnam praised the book and therefore presumably shared Dulles's apocalyptic, simplistic scenario of a coming *Pax Sovietica,* just as if the Chinese Communists and Communist leaders elsewhere did not have nationalistic agendas of their own independent of Moscow.

Item: Dulles was in Japan when North Korean forces crossed the thirty-eighth parallel, sending the South Korean army reeling. Being certain the invasion was masterminded in Moscow, he cabled Washington urging U.S. intervention, a course Truman had already decided upon. Truman's later fateful decision to order General MacArthur north to the Yalu, thereby transforming the war from one of defending South Korea to one of conquering North Korea, accorded with Dulles's advice. The entrance of Chinese troops into the war outraged and surprised Dulles. It was Dulles above all of Truman's advisors who led in the opposition to admitting the People's Republic of China into the United Nations. After all, Dulles declared, "Mao Tse-tung is nothing but a puppet" of Stalin's and Chiang Kai-shek was "a Christian gentleman of a very high order" who had steadfastly upheld the faith in a manner that places him "in the category of the leaders of the early Church." On almost every one of these counts Dulles was wrong.

Item: In the late winter of 1952 Dulles left the State Department. He then returned to his Republican home, abruptly discarding the mantle of bipartisanship to become a rough critic of Truman and Acheson (neither of whom liked Dulles personally). He was now invited by Taft and Eisenhower to author the foreign policy plank of the party platform. After Eisenhower's nomination, Dulles with the secretary of stateship in his pocket filled the land with inflammatory right-wing campaign oratory. Truman's containment policy was damned as "negative, futile and immoral" for it abandoned "countless human beings to a despotism and Godless terrorism." Once in power, Dulles pledged, the Republicans would roll back the atheistic tide because Eisenhower would use "all means to secure the liberation of Eastern

Europe." (Adlai Stevenson, not unreasonably, charged that Dulles's line of "liberation" was a "cynical and transparent attempt, drenched in crocodile tears, to play upon the anxieties of foreign nationality groups in this country.") Further, Dulles's platform denounced the "Asia last" policy of the Democrats and said, "We have no intention to sacrifice the East to gain time in the West." Though a Democrat, Oxnam's faith in Dulles remained unshaken. How can this be?

Item: Immediately upon assuming the duties of secretary of state Dulles issued an internal memorandum sternly informing the members of the State Department to demonstrate not only competence and discipline but "positive loyalty" to policies "that our President and Congress may subscribe." His maiden address as secretary contained these ominous words: "Now I suppose some of you are wondering whether the State Department can really be trusted to take a strong lead against Russian communism. There have been shocking revelations which showed that some Communists and sympathizers have found their way into high places and betrayed secrets, even that of the atomic bomb. I can assure you that all the resources of Government, and that includes the FBI, are going to be employed to be sure that any such people are detected and cleaned out." He proceeded to hire a former FBI agent named Scott McLeod to tighten Department security. McLeod hired a squad of goons to ferret out "commies," "pinkos," "New Dealers," "free thinkers," "drunks," "lavender lads," "nymphomaniacs," "incompatibles." A quiet reign of terror demoralized the Department as employees found their desks broken open, private letters read, telephones tapped, off-work movements tailed. Dulles personally completed the gutting, begun under Truman, of the Foreign Service's "China Hands," that core of veteran experts on China who had sought to report truthfully the tragic situation in China in the 1930s and 1940s. The most famous and valuable of those pressured out were John Paton Davies and John Carter Vincent. They met their fate not because Dulles found them disloyal or security risks but because he pronounced their judgments bad. (In commenting on the dismissals and the mealymouthed explanations, Harvard's luminous historian John K. Fairbank spoke of Dulles's "typically two-faced fashion.") Dulles also had no further use for the services of George F. Kennan, recently returned to Washington after being ambassador to Moscow. Kennan had crossed Dulles earlier; the penalty was forced retirement without even a letter of thanks from the secretary for his decades of service to his country. Dulles refused to ride in the same car or be photographed with "Chip" Bohlen when that seasoned and respected foreign service officer came under Senator McCarthy's scrutiny during the confirmation hearings over his appointment as ambassador to Moscow. When in April 1953 Senator McCarthy's ophidian gumshoe Roy Cohn and Cohn's beloved David Schine flew to Europe on their infamous mission of terrorizing America's International Information Agency. Dulles filled the air to Europe with cable traffic to make sure the boys' trip was as comfortable and pleasant as the secretary of state could arrange. Dulles's motives were doubtless multiple: to appease McCarthy, the China Lobby, and the Republican Right by offering up sacrifices to these wrathful idols; to further distance himself from the Truman administration; to weed out veterans who had served under Roosevelt and Truman and who perhaps could not be counted on; to comply with Eisenhower's Executive Order 10450 for tighter security (in turn a sop to the conservative wing of the Republican party); and to free the department from continuing attack so that he could get on with the main business of conducting the administration's foreign policy. Inasmuch as at that very time Oxnam was undergoing vicious accusations of fellow traveling, one would suppose he would be especially sensitive to the plight of those several hundred officers and employees hounded out of Foggy Bottom and the fears of those who survived. If so, one would be mistaken. Not once in public or private did Oxnam relate Dulles's State Department deeds to the larger Great Fear blanketing the nation and not once did he name Dulles as a contributor to that Fear.

Item: On every count Dulles advocated a more massive military build-up than Eisenhower was willing to countenance. During Eisenhower's first term Dulles was the leading proponent in the cabinet for more funds for the Department of Defense, arguing that an effective foreign policy required a clear military lead over the Russians. The secretary of state was far less concerned than the president that heavy defense spending would torpedo the administration's goal of a balanced budget. Dulles pushed a defense policy based on massive overkill capacity. In January 1954 he announced the policy of "massive retaliation"; and then linked this policy to one dubbed "brinkmanship." Eisenhower hoped to reduce U.S. forces stationed in Europe under NATO, but he observed that Dulles "had practically a phobia against raising the question of reduction of these forces." Dulles remained an ardent supporter of A-bomb and H-bomb testing and opposed a moratorium. The president believed there was a limit to what was required for the nation's security and a limit to what the nation could expend without bankrupting itself. Here as in almost all other areas, Dulles was far more the militant war-risking Cold War warrior than was his chief. The voice of restraint was the president's, not the secretary's.

Item: In July 1953 the Eisenhower administration negotiated a military armistice ending the Korean War. Peace came to the bloody peninsula over the strident objections of Dulles, who pressed the president to break off peace talks and go for unconditional victory, driving the Communists north of the Yalu and uniting all of Korea under Rhee while supporting Chiang in an assault on the mainland from his base in Taiwan. Argued Dulles: "I don't think we can get much out of the Korean settlement until we have shown—before all Asia—our clear superiority by giving the Chinese one hell of a licking." Apparently Jesus' seventh beatitude was momentarily forgotten by the secretary.

Item: On April 16, 1953, while the Korean peace negotiations were still uncompleted and shortly after Stalin's death, Eisenhower gave the finest speech of his presidency, "The Chance for Peace." Its eloquence derived from the transparent sincerity of the president's convictions concerning the perils and the costs of continuing the arms race. Dulles had advised against the speech as being too conciliatory, and after its delivery announced that it marked no softening in America's determination to stand firm against communism worldwide.

Item: Dulles bent every effort to turn the United Nations into a useful arm of American Cold War diplomacy, albeit he was following a path charted by the Truman administration.

Item: Eisenhower's summit meeting with Khrushchev in July 1955 took place over Dulles's objections. An hour before flying to Geneva the president appeared on radio and television to share with the people his hope that the meeting would "change the spirit" of Russian-American relations. According to Eisenhower's leading biographer, "Dulles groaned at such overblown language, and groaned again when Eisenhower devoted the second half of the talk to encouraging every American to go to church on Sunday and pray for peace." What Dulles feared most did happen. There emerged a "spirit of Geneva," leaving him bitter but helpless. Dulles remained opposed to a second summit meeting with Bulganin. Because he could not believe there was any possibility of a relaxation between the implacable enemies, he would not even endorse Eisenhower's proposal to invite ten thousand Russian students to come to the United States, at the expense of the U.S. government, to spend a year in American colleges. The idea died, killed by Dulles.

Item: Dulles's younger brother, Allen, was of course director of the Central Intelligence Agency. A biographer of the Dulles brothers has written: "Never before or since has the CIA had more support from the State Department, or because Secretary Dulles was so powerful, more freedom [of action]."

Item: The origins of the Vietnam War are too complex to even outline here. Thanks to the British refusal to go along; thanks to Eisenhower's absolute unwillingness to commit again American troops to battle on Asian soil less than a year after his ending the Korean War; thanks (by a narrow margin) to Eisenhower's ultimate decision not to employ conventional or nuclear bombing to save the French garrison at Dien Bien Phu; and thanks to France's irresolute determination to hold on, the United States did not find itself at war with the Vietminh in 1954. Still, positions were taken, words uttered, policies made that were to bear bitter fruit. Judged a respected biographer of Dulles: "None of Dulles's actions was to bring forth a darker harvest than his refusal to allow United States policy to support or even countenance a diplomatic settlement of the French colonial war in Indochina in the period from 1954 to 1956."

Much, of course, has been omitted from this review. Perhaps it is already overlong. Nevertheless, it is essential. Its justification is that Oxnam's beatification of John Foster Dulles raises so many questions, not about the secretary of state, but about the bishop. Indeed, one must ask: Was there no member of the Council of Bishops or of the National Council of Churches' leadership clear-eyed enough and firm-voiced enough to say, "Bromley, hold on a moment. Have you ever considered this aspect of Dulles's leadership?"

If it is conceded that Oxnam misjudged (for whatever reason) Dulles, it must be stressed that the bishop's concern for the fate of the earth was intense and sincere. The acceptance of war's inevitability was to him a soulless nihilism. Time and again he posed and answered this question: "Suppose every Russian in the world were to die tonight. Suppose the Kremlin walls were to disintegrate and become dust. Suppose Russia as a nation were to cease to exist, her military might disappear. Would our problems be over? Would security and peace be our lot? No, the spectacle of a world in part overfed and in large part hungry; a world with its different standards of living; a world with millions who have never known the meaning of liberty; a world hungry, ignorant and diseased, would still be a restless, seething world. The revolutionary surge would still confront us."

Oxnam attempted to understand Russian fears and explain them to the American people—their ferocious sacrifices in throwing back Hitler, their suspicions when the United States alone possessed atomic bombs. And to understand Russian fortitude, too. "Does any sensible man believe that our sword-rattling will make cowards of men who fought at Stalingrad?" he asked in a memorable 1948 address, "Let's Try for Peace, Mr. President!" The churches must "become so vocal in the face of current war hysteria that our leaders will know that we want immediate steps taken to avert the danger of war with Russia."

The advocacy of a preemptive first strike by the United States was repudiated by Oxnam as the madness it was. Early and late he recognized that the euphemism "anticipatory retaliation" in plain English meant "bomb them first." "Men who think a preventive war is an answer to contemporary international problems," he suggested in 1955, "need their heads examined, and the nation can well afford the psychiatric treatment necessary to bring them back to sanity."

In a September 1947 radio broadcast Oxnam proposed that "two distinguished and qualified plenipotentiaries" be sent to Russia at once to sit with Stalin to negotiate a settlement of outstanding differences.[2] Oxnam repeatedly returned to this idea, including an invitation to Stalin to come to the United States. Not only so, he maintained that "the only way to get rid of an Iron Curtain is to lift it." Therefore, let there be a joint exchange of religious, educational, scientific, artistic, and business leaders. His keynote address before the 1958 Fifth World Order Study Conference carried the appeal: "Would it not be worth the effort to use a few billions to open doors, throw up the windows, and let people and light come in? Let the Russians visit us by the tens of thousands. I think this dear land will stand the scrutiny and prove to be the best answer to Soviet propaganda. Let them see our schools, our factories, our churches, our art galleries, our children at play, and our people at worship. Let us try the hand-clasp instead of the finger-print."

Oxnam of course was not a pacifist. He repeatedly in the postwar years asserted his belief in a "strong national defense"—"a powerful army, navy, and air force." Nevertheless, he desired the discontinuation of the war-time draft and did all in his power to defeat Universal Military Training bills before Congress. The Methodist Church and the Federal and National Councils placed themselves in opposition to UMT, at least in part because of Oxnam.

No thought was lodged more firmly in Oxnam's mind than that communism was an expanding, dynamic ideology that could not be checked with bullets and bombs alone. As he reminded in his Episcopal Address: "Let us not forget that it is less the materialism, dictatorship, and Marxian economics that have attracted masses of men than the promise of more abundant living, the abolition of the exploitation of man by man, and the setting up of a classless society. It is the hope that the masses behold in communism that hypnotizes them." Therefore, peoples worldwide freed from the bonds of colonial exploitation, political oppression, ecclesiastical tyranny, racial discrimination, hunger, and insecurity will turn their faces from communism. America must "give the black man of Africa, the brown man of Southeast Asia, the yellow man of China assurance that he is to be free not only to vote but to live the life abundant." "Let us take up our Christian responsibility," Oxnam cried, "and in cooperation with brothers everywhere, so change the planet that when our first visitors from Mars arrive they will find a society fit to be called the Kingdom of God." The materialism of Marxism, by definition, could not usher in such a Kingdom.

The agonizing question of atomic energy for peace and war much troubled Oxnam, and his true friendship with David E. Lilienthal intensified that concern. In early 1945, when Truman renominated Lilienthal for the chairmanship of the Tennessee Valley Authority, over the protests of Senator McKellar, Oxnam used all of his resources to secure the Senate's confirmation. Then came Hiroshima and the genie was out of the bottle. On April 12, 1946, there assembled in Oxnam's New York office twenty-five church leaders to hear Lilienthal explain a report, popularly known as the Acheson-Lilienthal Report, shortly to be presented to the United Nations Atomic Energy Commission. The group thrilled as they listened to a plan for world cooperation in the peaceful development of atomic energy under the aegis of the United Nations. (The plan, of course, proved unacceptable to the Soviets, and perhaps not without reason. It left the United States free to continue building and testing atomic bombs until the plan became fully operational—that is, in effect it left the U.S. with a monopoly over the bomb for an indefinite period of time. Even then the U.S. could reject it and carry on with its atomic weapons program. The original plan had been toughened by Bernard Baruch and perhaps the judgment of Truman's biographer, Robert Donovan, is the hard truth: "It defies the imagination to think who could have fashioned a plan that would have been acceptable to the Seventy-ninth Congress and Joseph Stalin.")

On November 1, 1946, Lilienthal, having been nominated by Truman, took the oath of office in the Knoxville Federal Court House as first chairman of the new U.S. Atomic Energy Commission. Only a handful were present, including Bromley and Ruth as "special guests," as Lilienthal recorded in his *Journals*. Bromley then proceeded to write every Methodist bishop and every district superintendent who in turn were to contact their ministers urging that the Senate be informed of Methodism's endorsement of Lilienthal's confirmation. The deed was done and Lilienthal was again grateful to Oxnam.

In 1948 Lilienthal and Oxnam hit upon the idea of the formation of an advisory committee to help guide the AEC. The committee was to address the ethical, moral, and religious implications of atomic energy, including weapons. Oxnam, naturally, was to be chairman. However, some members of the AEC demurred and that was that. Oxnam's disappointment was "very real."

Early in 1950, after Truman had announced that the AEC would proceed with work "on all forms of atomic weapons, including the so-called hydrogen or superbomb," Lilienthal, in a mood of deep despair, resigned from the AEC, confessing to an aide that it had become "nothing more than a major contractor to the Department of Defense." Lilienthal masked his true feelings from the public and from Oxnam. Earlier Oxnam had hailed the McMahon Act establishing a civilian Atomic Energy Commission. It never seemed to have penetrated his mind that the touted McMahon Act in reality scarcely served as a restraint on a Pentagon whose appetite was bottomless.

The government's decision to proceed with the building of the H-bomb called forth a statement from the Federal Council's executive committee, of which Oxnam was a member. It was a cool, carefully balanced tripart pronouncement, the third position reflecting Oxnam's own views: "Some of us, on the other hand, believing that our people and the other free societies should not be left without the means of defense through the threat of retaliation, support the attempt to construct the new weapon." Later in 1950, an FCC commission, chaired by Episcopal Bishop Dun, issued a major report, *The Christian Conscience and Weapons of Mass Destruction*. Eloquent in its denunciation of war and warning against any first use of atomic weapons by the United States, its core message was an implicit endorsement of American strategic policy, and one in which Oxnam concurred:

> For the United States to abandon its atomic weapons, or to give the impression that they would not be used, would leave the non-Communist world with totally inadequate defense. For Christians to advocate such a policy would be for them to share responsibility for the worldwide tyranny that might result. We believe that American military strength, which must include atomic weapons as long as any other nation may possess them, is an essential factor in the possibility of preventing both world war and tyranny. If atomic weapons or other weapons of parallel destructiveness are used against us or our friends in Europe or Asia, we believe that it could be justifiable for our government to use them in retaliation with all possible restraint.[3]

The Executive Committee of the World Council of Churches also responded to the prospects of the H-bomb. Inasmuch as Oxnam was a member of the committee and present at the meeting and since the vote was unanimous, he must have given his endorsement. It was less prudential than the Federal Council's. The opening paragraph reads: "The hydrogen bomb is the latest and most terrible step in the crescendo of warfare which has changed war from a fight between men and nations to a mass murder of human life. Man's rebellion against his Creator has reached such a point that, unless stayed, it will bring self-destruction upon him. All this is a perversion; it is against the moral order by which man is bound; it is a sin against God."

Genuinely fearful of the fate of humanity, nevertheless Oxnam remained convinced that America's nuclear shield was a necessity in such a dangerous world until such time as all nations agreed to be left naked also. Asked in 1954 by Henry Hitt Crane to sign an appeal to President Eisenhower, Oxnam declined, explaining: "I think the abolition upon our part of atomic weapons, if that could be done, would be an initial step toward Soviet expansion. The matter will have to be worked out jointly. . . . I think we are dealing [with the Russians] with a type of mind, as far as the ruling class is concerned, similar to the mind we had in Germany. I have always felt that had Gandhi lived under Germany rather than under England he would have been shot."

The fact of the matter is that Oxnam, never an apologist for the Soviet Union and never bedazzled by communism's humane claims, after 1946 grew increasingly tough in his views. Time and again his audiences were warned that "Russia is an expanding imperialism and an infiltrating ideology." Even before the outbreak of the Korean War he alerted the Newark Annual Conference to the harsh fact "that Russia is giving itself to an ideology which, if it becomes regnant in society, will jeopardize —I'll say more—will destroy freedom. . . . There is no question in my mind that Russia intends to conquer the earth if it can do so." After the fighting in Korea began, fifteen hundred Methodists in Indianapolis were alerted: "We see in the expanding imperialism of Russia a threat to freedom everywhere, and we properly cooperate with the United Nations to stop aggression. Some see the Christian mission as an all-out effort to stop Communism, to defeat Russia. Russia does threaten the free society. Its aggression must be blocked." Boston Unitarians were informed that "the world cannot exist half slave and half free. If the forces of freedom triumph, liberty may become the lot of all men everywhere. If the forces of tyranny are victorious, regimentation will be the fate of humanity." An article written for *The Nation* carried this accusation: The Soviet leaders "are actually engaged in a world-wide conspiracy aimed at the eventual overthrow of any government with which they may temporarily negotiate as a matter of expedience. The Soviet government . . . seeks to establish its way of life by invasion or infiltration and the support of a revolutionary group that, puppet-like, dances to Moscow-pulled strings. The so-called dictatorship of the proletariat, once thought of as temporary, has become a continuing dictatorship of a small body of self-perpetuating officials. The assumption that the state will wither away has itself withered away."

These publicly expressed thoughts are confirmed by Oxnam's private diary entries in which Russia is arraigned for "an utter disregard of morality," "willful tyranny," and "actual penetration through treachery" into other lands.

As has been noted, Oxnam advocated a militarily strong America (though his opposition to Universal Military Training remained constant). Naturally he cloaked his position in moralistic and legalistic pieties. Witness this charming justification: "It is imperative that the United States keep itself strong enough to be able *to make available to the United Nations* the proportionate force that may be necessary to restrain aggression. This will be a heavy burden upon the American people, but a light burden when compared to the costs of war. The Russians believe that ideas can be imposed by force. Stalin, who could dismiss the Pope with the question, 'How many divisions has he?' must be made aware of the divisions that are *available to a world agency determined to subject force to law*" (emphasis added). What president, congressman, general or admiral, or American taxpayer believed the billions of dollars being poured into the American military were really intended for the weal of the United Nations? In October 1951 the director of the Office of Defense Mobilization informed Oxnam of the enormous increase in military expenditures and production since the outbreak of the Korean War—300 percent to 400 percent—and concluded that "the nation is industrially strong and must become militarily worthy." Far from dissenting, Oxnam found the presentation impressive and convincing. In fact, in that very year he informed a group of newspaper reporters, "Nothing appears sillier to me than a man getting up on the floor of the Senate to say he's against Communism and then refusing to co-operate in providing the men and arms to fight Communism. Since when have senators been qualified to tell military men how many men they need for necessary operations?" One can imagine the corridors of the Pentagon ringing with praise of "Blank Check" Bromley. Since when in American history up to that point in time have "military men" been judged "qualified" to receive all they demanded without civilian review?

Ultimately, Oxnam found himself not a dissenter from but a supporter of America's foreign policies. Perhaps this is not surprising when we recall that after 1940 he endorsed without qualification Roosevelt's foreign policies, endorsed without reservation Roosevelt's conduct of the war, including obliteration bombing, and justified Truman's unhesitating decision to use the A-bomb on Hiroshima and Nagasaki.

In March 1947 Truman addressed Congress and also the American people via nationwide radio to request that aid be given to Greece, where the Right appeared to be losing a civil war to the Left, and to Turkey, fearful of Soviet pressure on her borders. To secure the appropriations, Truman followed Senator Vandenberg's advice to "scare hell out of the American people." Thus was born the fateful Truman Doctrine which was to define U.S. foreign policy for the next twenty years. "Totalitarian regimes" threatened to snuff out freedom everywhere, warned the president. The conflict between freedom and slavery was universal. Not only must aid immediately be extended to Greece and Turkey, Truman continued in a linchpin sentence, "I believe that it must be the policy of the United States to support free peoples who are resisting attempted subjugation by armed minorities or by outside pressure." Translated, that sentence meant that whenever and wherever an anticommunist government was threatened, by indigenous insurgents, foreign invasion, or even diplomatic pressure (as with Turkey), the United States would supply political, economic, and if necessary military aid to it. All any government, however reactionary, need do to qualify for rescue by America was to claim its opponents were Communists. Truman never mentioned the United Nations.

On hearing the address, Oxnam told reporters that Truman "deserved the gratitude of the free world." Oxnam then requested that he and a small group of churchmen meet with the president. The request was denied. The bishop entered the familiar lament in his diary, "Were the president wise enough to share with church leadership the reasons that underlie his decision, it would enable us to proceed much more wisely in guiding or forming public opinion." Though stung by Truman's inhospitality, Oxnam continued to praise the Truman Doctrine. (The Methodist Peace Commission, however, did not.)

On June 5, 1947, Secretary of State Marshall, speaking at Harvard, outlined what became known as the Marshall Plan or more formally the European Recovery Program. However, it was not until March 1948 that Congress gave its approval and voted the initial appropriations, and it did so spurred by a Communist coup in Czechoslovakia which left the beloved Jan Masaryk assassinated. Oxnam hailed the Marshall Plan when its fate was still pending before Congress. He agreed with the secretary of state when Marshall pledged that "our policy is directed, not against any country or doctrine, but against hunger, poverty and chaos." On March 11, 1948, before the House had voted its approval, the Federal Council convened a conference in Washington on "The Churches and the European Recovery Program." Oxnam and Taft invited Truman to be present and he accepted. On that day, also, Oxnam presented to Senator Vandenberg and Speaker of the House Joe Martin a petition in support of the measure signed by seven hundred clergy. (Russia, of course, rejected economic aid under the plan and ordered her satellites to turn their backs. This did not surprise the Truman administration, although, naturally, this could not be openly admitted. As Truman said, the Truman Doctrine and the Marshall Plan "are two halves of the same walnut." Note that the United Nations is again ignored.)

In the spring of 1949 the North Atlantic Treaty Organization was signed and the Senate gave its approval in July. Britain, France, Belgium, the Netherlands, Italy, Portugal, Denmark, Iceland, Norway, Canada, the United States, and later Greece and Turkey pledged themselves to mutual assistance in case of aggression against any of the signatories. On the very day that Truman signed the NATO Treaty he presented the "bill" to Congress—a request for $1.5 billion for European military aid despite the administration's assurances during the debate that NATO would not necessitate American military aid to Europe or lead to the rearmament of West Germany. The United States had entered an entangling alliance, and many more were to follow—in time, formal alliances to defend forty-three countries and military defense agreements with an additional twenty-one nations. Yet again the United Nations was bypassed. The projected NATO stirred a great debate at the Federal Council's third National Study Conference on the Churches and World Order. Oxnam and Dulles worked out together a compromise whereby the Senate was asked not to act until the nation had had an opportunity to study it more closely. In July, Dulles, then in the Senate, made a strong speech in support of the treaty. Oxnam took that position, as did thirteen other Methodist bishops in a statement issued in May. The bishops spoke only as individuals and not in the name of the Council of Bishops or of the church as a whole.[4]

Oxnam gave a further assist to the Truman administration's waging of the Cold War by accepting General Lucius Clay's invitation to join the Crusade for Freedom and speak over the Voice of America programs. For this service Oxnam received a certificate of appreciation and a warm letter from the general praising one of Oxnam's talks as "the finest program in the entire campaign." Not all Methodists saw it quite that way. "I recall having serious doubts whether Bishop Oxnam or any other church leader should have done this," stated Herman Will in 1984. "Certainly, an ordinary individual might choose to do so. But I questioned whether someone who inevitably would be regarded as a spokesperson for the Christian churches ought to identify himself or herself with the broadcasts of a government engaged in a war of propaganda. How would the bishop have felt if the Russian Orthodox patriarch or the head of the Baptist churches in the USSR had made similar broadcasts over Radio Moscow?" A nice question.

The Korean War makes transparently clear Oxnam's uncritical Americanism and his employment of legalistic and moralistic platitudes to justify that Americanism.

When on June 25, 1950, North Korean forces crossed the thirty-eighth parallel bent on conquest of South Korea, Truman announced that "the attack upon Korea makes it plain beyond all doubt that Communism has passed beyond use of subversion to conquer independent nations and will now use armed invasion and war." Within twenty-four hours he ordered United States air and sea forces to support the retreating South Koreans and ordered the Seventh Fleet to prevent any attack by Red China on Chiang's Taiwan. As the retreat of the South Korean army continued, Truman on June 30 ordered United States ground forces stationed in Japan to proceed to Korea. He formally extended the Truman Doctrine to the Pacific by pledging the United States to military intervention against any further expansion of Communist rule in Asia. He announced that he was extending military aid to the French to help that colonial power crush Ho Chi Minh and his Vietminh, and also increased aid to the Philippine government to suppress the Huks.

On June 27, Russia being absent, the United States pushed through the UN Security Council a resolution branding the North Koreans as aggressors, ordering their forces to withdraw beyond the thirty-eighth parallel, and asking the UN member nations to provide assistance to South Korea. "The resolution was a brilliant stroke," writes the respected historian Stephen Ambrose, "for without any investigation at all it established war guilt and put the United Nations behind the official American version. Its sweeping nature tended to commit the United Nations in advance to any step the United States might wish to take in Korea and, with the help of later resolutions, it gave the United States the benefit of United Nations' cover for military action in Korea." [5]

This understanding is crucial. The Korean War was a United States, not a UN, show. Truman had put in motion interventionist actions long before appealing to the UN. Under the terms of the June 27 resolution, the United States established a military command that took orders from Washington, not the UN. Although MacArthur delighted in calling himself the United Nations Commander, he reported to and took his orders from the Joint Chiefs of Staff. "I had no direct connection with the United Nations whatsoever," he later testified. It is not to disparage the sacrifices and bravery of the soldiers of the sixteen nations who contributed to the United Nations forces to observe that their numbers were relatively small and not decisive to the outcome. America's freedom to act unilaterally, without prior UN approval, is made manifest in Truman's fateful decision to order MacArthur north to the Yalu. To be sure, a U.S. resolution endorsing the action was rubber stamped by the UN (47 to 5), but MacArthur's forces were already on their fatal march.

On August 9, 1950, Truman received this telegram from Oxnam: "Your splendid leadership in the Korean crisis has our fullest support." The press was informed that the president merited the gratitude of the Free World "for his far seeing cooperative United Nations action in Korea." The war was a "morally justifiable exercise of police power under the United Nations." Methodist youth were admonished that the Christian "must participate in the actions of the United Nations, democratically determined and dynamically dedicated. . . ." The Christian "must courageously resolve that mankind shall not be engulfed in materialism nor shackled by tyranny. He is called upon to live dangerously in the spirit of Jesus and in loyalty to the principles symbolized by the cross." How many Methodist youth, inspired by Oxnam's idealistic challenge, took up the cross, volunteered to serve—and kill and die—in Korea, we will never know. There was no doubt in Oxnam's mind that Russia was the source of the aggression by North Korea or about "the clear intent of the Communist forces to spread their power everywhere and, where successful, to establish tyranny." Americans must unite "in the determination to see that through the *United Nations* this kind of aggression, *wherever it occurs*, is met by a control that is effective and final" (emphasis added).

Repeatedly Oxnam returned to the assumption (false as most historians now believe) of a "Russian-planned and dictated invasion of Korea. . . . Negotiation with Russia means that we must deal with a nation whose Korean gamble has been condemned by the world community and whose pawns have been subjected to the restraint of force under law." When former President Hoover suggested the withdrawal of American forces in Korea, Oxnam publicly exploded: "We must think in terms of an offensive. Are we simply to withdraw and wait for the inevitable or are we to gather together with the other nations of the world and meet this threat?" Even in 1957 he continued to hug the comforting illusion of American altruism and United Nations authority when he said, "The United States does not abandon its principles when, in cooperation with other free nations, it supplies the requisite force to the United Nations to block aggression in Korea. On the contrary, this procedure is to hold fast to the principles of the United Nations Charter."

At issue here is not really the wisdom or lack of wisdom of Truman's actions. Nor, really, is the issue Oxnam's support of Truman. Rather, the issue is Oxnam's marvelous capacity to cloak America's intervention in Korea in the robes of benevolent disinterestedness and a sacrificial devotion to upholding the United Nations Charter. Why not admit that a perceived national self-interest was at stake and worth the sacrifice, wounded and killed, of 3.5 million of God's children, on both sides—and then pray for understanding and forgiveness? The

Methodist Peace Commission at least approximated a mood of contrition when it resolved, "Without condoning the unjustifiable nature of the attack by Communist forces which has precipitated the tragic situation in Korea, we believe it to be part of a long sequence of events in which self-interest rather than international concern has governed the policies of nations." [6]

When in late 1949 the Nationalist government of China was forced to withdraw from the mainland and the People's Republic of China was formally proclaimed, Oxnam, as all Americans, was shocked. He was surely in a state of shock when he proclaimed such nonsense as, "We had time enough in China. We had more than 100 years to introduce Jesus there, but we were more interested in teaching our customs than religion. We didn't take Jesus seriously enough in China." We had China, he seriously maintained, but we allowed China to slip through our hands and have watched the people turn to another dynamic ideology and one that will lead them to disaster—communism. "We had China. We didn't come to Christ soon enough." Oxnam's lament is spookily similar to the Republican Party's charge that the Democrats "gave" China to the Communists—as if the world's most populous country had ever "belonged" to Christian America.

While utterances such as these may be dismissed without analysis, the questions of the diplomatic recognition of Red China by the United States and the seating of Red China in the UN are vexing, and one sympathizes with Oxnam's wrestling with them.

In 1957 Oxnam took the position that recognition should be withheld until Red China's conduct was worthy of the term "peace-loving nation"—although one wonders what nation he would cite as having fulfilled that particular condition. In 1958 in a six-page letter to Madame Chiang Kai-shek he reported that neither the Methodist General Conference nor the Council of Bishops had favored the recognition of Red China, and he implied that was also his position. In 1959 he informed an Albany audience that he favored the recognition of Red China with "certain conditions." Among the conditions he listed was the withdrawal of Communists from North Korea, permitting a plebiscite which might result in unification. That is, he was asking Communist China to force the independent Communist government of North Korea to commit suicide. In November of that year in his keynote address at the Fifth Study Conference on World Order he bravely raised the question of recognition. When Bishop Welch in a letter protested, Oxnam replied that he had not recommended recognition but had opened the question for discussion.

Oxnam and the Council of Bishops fully supported the Eisenhower Administration's policy of encouraging independence movements in Communist-controlled nations.7 When in 1956 the Hungarian Freedom Fighters were literally crushed by Soviet tanks, the bishops issued a message honoring "the heroic Hun-garians, who struck down the hand of the aggressor for a brief hour, were once again subjugated by ruthless and overwhelming force, but they stand in their suffering as symbols of the spirit of rebellion that lives forever in the hearts of men created to breathe free." This tribute was sincere. One wonders, however, what the Hungarians thought of the remainder of the bishops' message. President Eisenhower's leadership was lauded. That the United States had not unilaterally used force to succor the doomed resistance fighters was deemed morally correct. "He [Eisenhower] has insisted that force in support of law shall be applied by the only agency legally empowered to maintain peace, the United Nations. Nations pledged to the Charter must not take the law into their own hands. To do so is to sanction the practice of the totalitarian. A nation that acts unilaterally forfeits the moral position that nations which act through the United Nations preserve." One does not have to be a Hungarian to gasp at this canting statement. The United Nations was helpless to throw back the Soviets. The Hungarians were naked to their enemies without military support from the West. The West was unwilling to risk nuclear war with Russia. The West's armed forces were not capable of driving the Red Army out of Hungary. The true immorality was the Eisenhower/Dulles mouthings of "liberation" and "rollback" encouraging revolt and implicitly pledging material assistance and then, when the Hungarians acted, doing nothing. Liberation was a sham; it had always been a sham—and Eisenhower and Dulles knew it. If the

Methodist bishops, including Oxnam, had been less concerned with justifying their moralistic, legalistic leadership, they might better have remained silent while the Hungarians wept.

The penchant of the bishops to identify their nation with righteousness found unedifying expression in their December 11, 1953, message: "Victory over Communism belongs to the triumph of spiritual idealism which has made our nation and given it any leadership it merits among the nations of the world." They would have done better to have quoted Lincoln's warnings against national self-righteousness.

---

[1] Curiously, Eleanor Lansing Dulles, the sister, in her volume *John Foster Dulles: The Last Year*, does not mention Oxnam's name; and in answer to my question, Avery Dulles, S.J., replied that he did not recall his father ever mentioning Oxnam's name. I believe that Oxnam greatly exaggerated in his own mind the closeness of his friendship with and influence on Dulles, although Dulles gave some cause for this misconception. On the other hand, I do not discount the gratitude felt by Mrs. Dulles, Phyllis Bernau, and Dulles himself for Oxnam's comforting presence toward the end.

[2] In the address Oxnam advanced the name of Dulles as his first choice for one of the Americans. Secretary of State Marshall was not deemed acceptable because he was a military man, not a creative leader! It was assumed by Oxnam that Truman would not be the second individual. Recall, just prior to the talk Oxnam had met with Dulles!

[3] Methodist theologian Georgia Harkness was one of only two commission members to dissent from the report. Among the critical points she made was that when speaking of thermonuclear war, "retaliation with all possible restraint" was a contradiction in terms.

[4] The Methodist Peace Commission did not support the treaty. Further, twenty-two Protestant ministers led by Methodists Tittle, Harkness, and Crane declared: "The adoption of the Atlantic pact means continued stockpiling of atomic and biological weapons, continuance of peacetime conscription, increase in the already colossal arms budget, building a world-wide spy network, maintenance of military bases around the world, no relaxation in military influence of education, science, industry and commerce, to say nothing of the periodic waves of national hysteria without which none of these measures could be maintained."

[5] Ambrose is not a historian of the Left; to the contrary, among his works is a splendid and respectful two-volume biography of Eisenhower. Some historians of the Left argue that Rhee started the war with covert support from America and Chiang, a thesis I do not buy.

[6] The Methodist bishops shared Oxnam's interpretations of the war, saying in their 1952 Episcopal Address that America's rescue of South Korea "is the pledge to free men everywhere that the only war we seek is a relentless struggle against despotism, poverty, and human bondage." Both the Federal Council and World Council of Churches condemned North Korean aggression. Incidentally, Truman's firing of General MacArthur in 1951 elicited from Oxnam a supporting telegram and a long statement to the press, closing, "The President deserves the approval and support of loyal Americans."

[7] As did the Board of World Peace. In a cable sent by the board to Dulles in 1955 the secretary was assured of the board's support of his recent proposals for liberating the captive countries of eastern Europe. "Personal greetings and congratulations on your magnificent proposals for eliminating the 'Iron Curtain,' " crooned the cable. "The sweep and challenge of your proposals will hearten the eastern European peoples as well as our own. All possible support will be given by the Methodist Board of Peace. Our prayers ascend for you and for a genuine peace."

CHAPTER 26

"THE GREAT FEAR" AT HOME

The term "McCarthyism" to describe the search for "un-American" "subversives" in postwar America is misleading, unfortunately. The junior senator from Wisconsin, Joseph McCarthy, was in fact more created by, than he was the creator of, "The Great Fear," which antedated his rise to infamy in 1950 and persisted after his censure by the Senate in 1954. Indeed, such was the pervasive fear of global Soviet expansion and internal Communist subversion, including espionage, a consternation sincerely held by many and cynically exploited by some, that the nation would have been gripped by a failure of nerve even if "Tailgunner Joe" had never lived. Moreover, under the guise of anti-Communist rhetoric, Republicans and conservative Democrats, primarily Southerners, launched a counterattack to beat back the reformist impulse that fueled Roosevelt's New Deal and Truman's Fair Deal. After all, even in the 1930s conservative Democrats and Republicans in Congress had created the Fish Committee, the McCormack-Dickstein Committee, and the Special Committee on Un-American Activities (Dies Committee) to ferret out subversives (primarily those on the Left) and thereby taint liberalism, giving point to the witticism that some conservatives opposed communism because it smacked of socialism.

After all, even prior to Pearl Harbor, Congress passed in 1938 the McCormack Act requiring all agents of foreign governments to register with the Justice Department and consequently providing a basis for the Communist registration provision of the 1950 Internal Security Act (McCarran Act). It passed in 1938 the Hatch Act denying federal employment to individuals belonging to groups advocating the overthrow of the government. It passed in 1940 the Voorhis Act requiring the registration of all organizations with foreign affiliations, and thereby forcing the Communist Party, USA to formally dissolve its connection with the Communist International. It passed in 1940 the Alien Registration Act (Smith Act) which provided a basis for the Justice Department's indictments of Communist Party leaders beginning in 1948 and also for the wholesale deportation of alien radicals beginning in 1947.

The explanation for what blanketed the American scene after the war lies not only in a resurgent conservatism or in the sincerely perceived threat from communism abroad and at home. It lies also in the Truman administration's twin motivations: to defend itself from the charge of being tolerant of disloyalty at home and within the ranks of government while at the same time to silence the Left's criticisms of its Cold War foreign policies. Long before Eisenhower's victory in 1952 the Truman presidency had instituted a severe loyalty program for government workers and authorized the attorney general to draw up a list of "totalitarian, fascist, communist, or subversive" organizations, a number totaling 254 and thereby providing the House Un-American Activities Committee with the example to draft its own list of 624. Attorney General Tom Clark was permitted to empanel a special grand jury in New York to investigate possible subversion, the jury hearing the explosive testimonies of ex-Communists Elizabeth Bentley and Whittaker Chambers. The investigative procedures of the FBI were broadened. The Truman presidency secured the conviction of Communist Party, USA members for conspiring to violate the Smith Act and with organizing a group, the CPUSA, to this end; and the convictions were upheld by the Vinson Supreme Court. Truman Democrats naturally exposed the extent of Communist support of and participation in Henry Wallace's Progressive Party in 1948, but in so doing, led to the popular belief that the Progressive Party was a Communist front, which it was not. Therefore, liberal

Democrats, including members of the Americans for Democratic Action (ADA), in their concern not to appear soft on communism, conceded too much both to conservatives within their own party and to their Republican critics. Alas, Cold War liberals failed to appease their conservative foes even though they agreed that Communist Party members were beyond the pale of constitutional protection because the Communist Party was not a legitimate political party but a conspiracy. Or so both conservatives and Cold War liberals believed.

The Eisenhower administration accelerated the firestorm of fear. Following the Republican election victory in 1952, Senate Majority Leader Robert A. Taft rewarded McCarthy for services rendered by appointing him chairman of the Senate Committee on Government Operations. McCarthy promptly appointed himself chairman of its Subcommittee on Investigations—the McCarthy Committee. Eisenhower could have stopped the wild man from Wisconsin in his tracks, but chose instead to mollify the Republican Right by hedging. For example, the order to his cabinet not to criticize McCarthy; the deletion of a defense of General Marshall in his Milwaukee speech; the Voice of America fiasco; the lukewarm support of Army Secretary Stevens on March 7, 1954; and his pussyfooting around the McCarthy issue at his press conference on March 3, 1953, causing columnist Joe Alsop to growl to another reporter, "Why, the yellow son of a bitch." Eisenhower's oft-quoted explanation for his handling—or not handling—of McCarthy, "I will not get in the gutter with that guy," will not wash.

Before the fires of fear had cooled, a chapter had been written in American history that all citizens who cherished the liberties and protections enshrined in the Constitution would wish to forget, but who would do so only at the future peril of their children. Thousands of Americans were immolated in the fires; millions were singed. Inasmuch as there was no place to hide, even for those who had nothing to hide, it is really not surprising that American Protestantism found itself engulfed in the conflagration.

Certainly Oxnam's memories would have averted his being surprised. Memories of the First Red Scare in 1919–20 when the Constitution was concussed as never before in the Republic's history. Memories of the savaging he had received while at the Church of All Nations from Harry Chandler, Colonel LeRoy Smith, and Ralph Easley. Memories of the DePauw years and the indictments of him in E. L. Santuary's 1931 odious *Tainted Contracts* and in Elizabeth Dilling's 1934 looney *The Red Network* and the Reverend Smith's 1936 fantastical *Moscow Over Methodism*. And from these years also memories of whackings at the hands of the American Legion, DAR, *Indianapolis Star*, Henry S. Henschen's concerned Conference of Methodist Laymen, Merwin K. Hart's anxious Church Laymen's Association, the conservative National Conference of Christian Ministers and Laymen, Harry Jung's rancid American Vigilant Intelligence Federation, and of course the tireless Carl McIntire. Finally, Oxnam knew that in 1939 Harry F. Ward had appeared voluntarily before the Dies Committee and that the Methodist Federation for Social Service[1] was under government investigation. He knew too that his own name figured prominently in HUAC's 1944 publication entitled, "Investigation of Un-American Propaganda Activities in the United States—Appendix IX, Communist Front Organizations." [2] (His name also appears in HUAC's 1955 publication entitled, *Cumulative Index to Publications of the Committee on Un-American Activities*.)

Forewarned Oxnam certainly was, but perhaps nothing could have prepared him for the fury of the Cold War onslaught on the Federal and then National Council of Churches, The Methodist Church and groups and ministers related to it, and on himself personally.[3] As the Cold War heated up so did the alarmed warnings. In 1948 HUAC issued the pamphlet *100 Things You Should Know About Communism and Religion*. Among the things concerned citizens should know was that the Methodist Epworth League (which had not existed since 1939) had been infiltrated and that the Methodist Federation for Social Action was a "tool of the Communist Party." Four years later HUAC produced an eighty-seven-page *Review of the Methodist Federation for Social Action* to prove that it had followed the Communist Party line over the years. Then the Senate Internal Security Subcommittee (SISS) released a *Handbook for Americans* which stated that "the Communists have formed religious fronts such as the Methodist Federation for Social Action." Meanwhile a darkly brooding J. Edgar Hoover informed the members of HUAC, "I confess to a real apprehension so long as Communists are able to secure ministers of the Gospel to promote their evil work and espouse a cause that is alien to the religion of Christ and Judaism." Patriotic Americans, ordered "The Boss" (as Hoover was called), must report suspected subversives to his bureau (which, naturally, they did).

In 1949 Verne P. Kaub organized the American Council of Christian Laymen "to meet the need for unified action in opposition to the teachings of communism and socialism in churches and church connected organizations." Enjoying amazing success, this group distributed thousands of copies of *How Red Is the Federal (National) Council of Churches*, a six-page brochure coated with a hammer and sickle superimposed upon a cross; and among the council leaders fingered was Oxnam. In 1951 Captain (later Major) Edgar C. Bundy, chairman of the Church League of America, published *Christianity or Communism*? followed by *Collectivism in the Churches*. Since Bundy branded the Girl Scout handbook "un-American" and the National Council–sponsored Revised Standard Version of the Bible "subversive," his characterization of Oxnam as "the Red Dean of North America" is unremarkable. In 1951 also, conservative Methodist laymen formed Circuit Riders, Inc. with Myers G. Lowman as the indefatigable executive secretary. The sincerity of these laymen is unquestioned, numbering as they did individuals of the stature of Charles C. Parlin. Parlin, however, resigned in 1952, as did others troubled by the organization's increasingly unmeasured allegations. Lowman, for example, charged that Oxnam had "done more to aid communism than Earl Browder or any other six Communists." (Lowman also flooded the FBI with natterings about Oxnam's nefariousness.) In 1952 John Satterfield, a Mississippi Methodist who had been instrumental in organizing the Volunteer Committee of Christian Laymen, joined Lowman in requesting HUAC to conduct an investigation of Methodist radicals.

The Circuit Riders earned the commendation of Robert P. Shuler, fighting pastor of the three-thousand-member Trinity Methodist Church in Los Angeles, who issued his own alarms and who had been suspicious of Oxnam's soundness since the

Church of All Nations years. Tulsa evangelist Billy James Hargis, president of Christian Crusade, began distributing *The National Council of Church Indicts Itself on 50 Counts of Treason to God and Country!* a pamphlet including the interesting assertion that the old Federal Council was responsible for the disaster at Pearl Harbor! The Reverend Gerald L. K. Smith, vicious Jew- and black- and Red-baiter, asserted the presence of "about 20,000 Protestant clergymen who are serving the propaganda purposes of Communism," concluding, "It is easy to understand why Elijah lost his patience and killed 400 preachers." As early as 1951 conservative periodicals such as the *New Leader* were carrying articles with the titles "Communism in the Methodist Church" and "Communism Confuses the Methodist Church."

More threatening to the reputation of American Protestantism were the pronouncements of Herbert Philbrick, who for nine years had served as an undercover agent for the FBI. Philbrick first surfaced into public view when he testified in the Smith Act trial of Communist leaders in 1949. He then wrote *I Led Three Lives*, and from this book came a television series of the same name. An article in the *Christian Herald* from his pen was entitled, "The Communists Are After Your Church!" His syndicated column in the New York *Herald* rang similar alerts. In 1951 and again in 1953 Philbrick testified before HUAC to the existence of a "cell" of Communist ministers in Massachusetts and to his impression that the Council of American-Soviet Friendship used Oxnam's name to "tremendous advantage" in appealing for funds.[4]

Concurrently, government investigating committees were receiving shocking testimony from such ex-Communists as Manning Johnson, Harvey Matusow, Benjamin Gitlow, Louis Budenz, Elizabeth Bentley, Whittaker Chambers, and Joseph Zach Kornfeder. Gitlow, for example, asserted that Communist infiltration of Methodism was highly successful, and Kornfeder estimated there were six hundred ministers who were secret Party members and "2000 were pretty close to the machine."

Damaging as these testimonies may have been at the time, they did not approximate the harm wrought by Chapter X, "The Kingdom of God," in John T. Flynn's 1949 *The Road Ahead*, a book selling almost a million copies, portions of which (but not

Chapter X) were reprinted in *Reader's Digest*. The thrust of Chapter X was not that the Protestant ministry were minions of Moscow, but that powerful forces in Protestantism were promoting a socialist revolution in America. Oxnam, Flynn acknowledged, was not a Communist; "He is a Socialist." [5]

Methodism received a more direct blow when in February 1950 the *Reader's Digest* published the article, "Methodism's Pink Fringe" by Stanley High, one of its editors. The article was read by millions and known by additional millions because the *Digest* sent out a summary of its contents to all newspapers in the country in advance of publication. High, a Methodist minister's son and at one time a candidate for the Methodist ministry, though in 1950 a Presbyterian, did the church of his father incalculable mischief. Judging from the bulging folders in the Oxnam Collection relating to the article, literally hundreds of local Methodist bodies and thousands of laymen individually expressed their disquietude at the presence of a "Red Incubus" in their beloved church. A letter from an Ohio preacher is typical of the legion Oxnam received:

> As a pastor of one of our larger churches in the Middle West, I feel it is my duty to inform you of the seriousness of the crisis which this Stanley High . . . has created. We men down at the grass roots can't do much about it, but we are getting the brunt of this thing in no uncertain terms. I do not know just what the College [sic] of Bishops may feel disposed to do about it. But my laymen are in a state of revolt, and it is serious for our church here. And I believe that ours is a typical Methodist church. . . . But what is worse, many of my loyal and substantial members, who have long been good givers to all our church causes, have reached the place where they are saying, unless our great Methodist church does something about this unwise [leftist] propaganda, their gifts will begin to flow through other channels than our own. These are the pillars of my church, men without whom our church cannot go on, and our whole program will suffer.

Other correspondents pointed out that in their communities the Catholic Church was "making hay" from the article, representing itself as a bastion of Americanism in contrast to the "pink" Methodists. The article accelerated a movement already under way in The Methodist Church to repudiate the Methodist Federation for Social Action and other radical manifestations and to restore Methodism's commitment to the American Way of Life—that is, to the free enterprise system which, it was honestly believed, was the foundation of the American Way. In Texas there was touched to life a Committee for the Preservation of Methodism which published lists of "Methodist Termites" and distributed thousands of copies of a thirty-five-page booklet that inquired in its title, "Is There a Pink Fringe in the Methodist Church?"

By early 1953 HUAC was seeking new fields to conquer, having known triumph after triumph (it claimed) in the matter of Alger Hiss, the Hollywood Ten, William W. Remington, Communist "cells" in the Departments of Agriculture, Commerce, and State, and in the atomic scientist, labor, and entertainment and arts communities. Even the groves of academe were found choked with the weeds of subversion. On March 9 HUAC Chairman Harold H. Velde, a Methodist, in a radio interview in a rather offhand manner allowed how it was "entirely possible" that the committee might get into the "church field." Velde made it explicit that the committee would be investigating individual clergy, not the churches themselves. Initially the idea did not fly. President Eisenhower saw fit to repudiate the suggestion. But it refused to die and on July 21 Oxnam voluntarily appeared before Velde and his comrades, a meeting of such significance as to be the subject of the entire following chapter.

Another bomb exploded in that fateful July. *American Mercury* magazine carried an article entitled "Reds and Our Churches," the opening sentence reading, "The largest single group supporting the Communist apparatus in the United States today is composed of Protestant clergymen." The article went on to report that in the previous seventeen years the Communist Party had enlisted the support of at least seven thousand clergymen—"Party-members, fellow travelers, espionage agents, Party-line adherents and unwilling dupes." Three of the five individuals singled out as the "top pro-Soviet propagandists" were Methodists: Harry F. Ward, Jack R. McMichael, and lay preacher Willard Uphaus. Maybe not many Methodists subscribed to Henry L. Mencken's old magazine. The damage, however, was severe because the story was given heavy play in the national press; it was reprinted and given massive pamphlet distribution by conservative groups; and Representative Kit Clardy (an HUAC member) inserted it into the *Congressional Record* with his commendation.

The author paid a price. Joseph Brown Matthews, known simply as J. B. Matthews, started his adult life as an ordained Methodist minister and missionary. In the 1930s he became a convert to Marxian socialism and a critic of reactionary organized religion. He then swung to the far Right and became a consultant on communism. Such was his new renown that HUAC added him to its staff as chief investigator and the Hearst papers hired him as resident Red hunter. Unsurprisingly, he caught the eye of Senator McCarthy who named him executive director of McCarthy's Permanent Subcommittee on Investigations at almost the moment the *Mercury* article appeared. The Democratic members of the subcommittee denounced the article as "a shocking and unwarranted attack against the American clergy" and threatened to resign unless Matthews was sacked. Protests mounted, even including some from such conservatives as Senator Harry Byrd of Virginia who growled that Matthews "should give names and facts to sustain his charges or stand convicted as a cheap demagogue." The National Council made severe protest. The cochairmen—a Protestant, a Catholic, and a Jew—of the National Council of Christians and Jews telegraphed President Eisenhower of their outrage. In a public statement Eisenhower concurred: "I want you to know at once that I share the convictions you state. Generalized and irresponsible attacks that sweepingly condemn the whole of any group of citizens are alien to America. Such attacks betray contempt for the principles of freedom and decency." (Oxnam telegraphed his gratitude to the president and the message was gratefully acknowledged.) One hour after the president issued his statement, McCarthy announced that he had "very reluctantly" accepted Matthews's resignation. (The resignation did not placate Senators McClellan, Symington, and Jackson sufficiently to prevent their resigning from the subcommittee the next day.)

Matthews's departure from the government payroll did not permanently silence him or permanently derail the search for subversives in the clergy. It is imperative to remember that the hunters were cheered on in their search not only by other men of the cloth on the far Right but also by such respected moderates as Daniel Poling and Methodism's own Frederick Brown Harris, chaplain of the Senate—to say nothing of disturbed lay persons.

Not a few of the barbed arrows unloosed by the hunters were aimed directly at Oxnam himself. Matthews continued to accuse Oxnam publicly of being "one of the 'concentric circles' by which the propaganda apparatus reached from the Kremlin to America." In the spring of 1953 the pertinacious deposed Presbyterian Carl McIntire published *Bishop Oxnam, Prophet of Marx,* in which he charged that "as perhaps no other man, Oxnam represents the popular, radical, pro-Communist element in religious circles in America." This leader of the American Council of Christian Churches repeatedly alerted HUAC of Oxnam's record, describing the bishop as "the most outstanding and dangerous opponent, in Protestant circles, of the House Un-American Activities and its chairman." (McIntire and his associates sent copies of their HUAC communications to the FBI and select congressmen.) Methodist minister Rembert Smith, though retired, remained tireless, publishing in 1953 *Garfield Bromley Oxnam, Revolutionist?* and filing a $75,000 libel suit against the bishop in the U.S. District Court for the District of Columbia, which was set aside by the judge.[6] Another Texas minister, Baptist J. Frank Norris, termed Oxnam "one of the main fifth columnists of Joe Stalin in America."

Meanwhile, hundreds of individuals, as the FBI file on Oxnam discloses, were performing their patriotic duty by keeping the FBI posted, and also HUAC, the SISS, and McCarthy's Subcommittee, on Oxnam's improbities.[7]

Oxnam's relationship to two publications aroused especial consternation. Louie D. Newton, then president of the Southern Baptist Convention, had in the summer of 1946 visited Russia as one of the representatives of the American Society for Russian Relief. His impressions were published by the American Russian Institute in a booklet titled *An American Churchman in the Soviet Union*. Oxnam, in his capacity as president of the Federal Council, wrote a laudatory introduction commending the booklet for "careful consideration by thinking Americans." Newton may have been a little starry-eyed in his account, grateful as he was "for the experience which deepened my admiration for the 200,000,000 people of the U.S.S.R. and calls me anew to prayer that our leaders may find the way to lasting peace," but he was certainly no apologist for Stalin. Nevertheless, Oxnam was to be eternally haunted by his introduction.

In 1947 the Board of Missions and Church Extension of The Methodist Church mailed without charge to twenty-two thousand Methodist ministers Jerome Davis's book, *Behind Soviet Power*. The covering letter, suggesting that the book "will help you to understand the difficult issues confronting us to the end that international peace may be preserved and progress be made toward world order under the United Nations," was signed by Oxnam and Diffendorfer. Actually, the distribution was Diffendorfer's idea, including the picture of Stalin on the book's cover. Actually, also, Oxnam believed (as he informed Davis) that the book was "altogether too sympathetic" to Stalin's Russia (as it was); and it was on Oxnam's insistence that the letter carried the recommendation that the ministers read two more critical items in order to obtain a more balanced perspective. Still, a Methodist agency had authorized the expenditure of Methodist moneys to distribute to the Methodist ministry *Behind Soviet Power* accompanied by a supporting letter signed by two towering leaders of The Methodist Church. The deed made a lot of Methodists mad and the Red-hunters enjoyed a field day.

Increasingly Oxnam found himself the target of conservative newspaper columnists and radio broadcasters. In this group no individual was more troublesome than Fulton Lewis, Jr., an Episcopalian who worshiped in a Methodist church. Lewis, Oxnam moaned, "had long since sold his soul to the devil." Obviously Oxnam could not answer every allegation, but when Paul Harvey, broadcasting over ABC, said that the bishop had lent his support to "a tremendous number of Communist front organizations," Oxnam demanded and received air time to reply. Similarly, when an Alexandria, Virginia, radio station permitted an individual to assert that Oxnam was part of a conspiracy to seize the Christian churches for the purpose of "bringing about the triumph of Karl Marx in America," Oxnam secured rebuttal air time.

Considering Oxnam's controversial reputation, it is unsurprising that many attempts were made to prevent him from lecturing. Two were of particular intensity. In the fall of 1946 the East Tennessee Education Association booked him to speak at its annual meeting. Local patriotic groups, inflamed by a massive campaign conducted by the *Knoxville Journal*, pulled out all stops to muzzle him—without success. It was a tussle of near-epic proportions.

Invited to speak under the auspices of the ACLU on December 11, 1953, in the Philharmonic Auditorium of Los Angeles, he was deemed "too controversial a figure" for permission to be given by the auditorium's owners, the Temple Baptist Church. Rebuked Oxnam: "As an American citizen, I am alarmed; and as a native Californian, I am ashamed. I am sure that the patriotic citizens of Los Angeles will dispose of these would-be Commissars of Culture in their own Western ways." (Exactly a week later Oxnam spoke before a capacity crowd of 3,450 in the First Methodist Church, despite or perhaps because of a protest rally staged by Carl McIntire.)

When on February 23, 1949, Oxnam received The Churchman Award for 1948 from Shipler's *The Churchman,* five hundred people were present. Because of the reputation that both Oxnam and Shipler enjoyed for allegedly being pro-Communist (and anti-Catholic), a raft of individuals, including Hubert Humphrey, Harold Ickes, and David Dubinsky, found it prudent to withdraw their acceptance to be present. (The year before, George C. Marshall first agreed to accept The Churchman Award, then stated he could not be present, and finally refused to receive the award in absentia.[8] Earlier recipients included Roosevelt, Wilkie, and Eisenhower.) When informed in a memo of Oxnam's honor, J. Edgar Hoover made the observation, "The eminent Bishop still seems to be training with the Reds."

Before continuing this account of Oxnam's ordeal by slander and his championship of civil liberties, it is necessary to raise several disquieting questions—questions directed not alone to Oxnam but to many Cold War liberals, a diverse and respected group who favored being known as anti-Stalinists rather than the vaguer term anti-Communists.

These liberals ran with the conservative hounds after the radical hare, only to find their own positions victimized by the yawping pack of Red-hunters. The questions to be asked are: Did not these good liberals comprehend that in legitimatizing the persecution of Communist Party members and genuine fellow travelers and the Radical Left in general they were making themselves vulnerable to attack from the Radical Right? Did they not know that in acquiescing in the denial of civil liberties to Reds they were weakening the constitutional protection of all Americans? Outspoken in their denunciations of Senator McCarthy and HUAC, why did so many of them mute their criticisms of Presidents Truman and Eisenhower, who after all, bore ultimate responsibility for the government's repressions during their administrations? And why did they join in an almost unanimous chorus of liberal praise of Hoover and the FBI?

Less than a month before his appearance before HUAC, Oxnam wrote an article for *Parade: The Sunday Picture Magazine* entitled, "How to Uncover Communists." The article opens: "Communism is a clear and present danger. It constitutes the most menacing challenge to freedom and faith of recent centuries. Governments of free societies are obligated to protect themselves from subversion. That the Communist Party is a conspiracy, no informed man would deny. Conspirators must be discovered, tried, and if found guilty, punished. That is plain truth." Thus, at the onset he concedes too much: the CPUSA has no constitutional right to exist; its members are by definition conspirators; they must be tried (on what charges?) and if found guilty (of what?) be imprisoned. While critical of the procedures of HUAC, Oxnam then concedes the legitimacy of the attorney general's list of "subversive" organizations (254 in all, recall). That list was the yardstick for assessing "loyalty" in almost every department of American working life. It was an instrument of moral terror. It cost countless citizens their jobs and their reputations. The article continues: "The conspirator—the real Communist—must be discovered. Our F.B.I. is qualified to ferret him out. Its thorough work, its loyalty to American traditions, and its spiritual leader, J. Edgar Hoover, *justify the recommendation that the task of discovering conspirators be turned over*

100% to the F.B.I." Again, by definition, the "real" Communist is a "conspirator" who must be discovered (by any means to do the job?) by an omnicompetent FBI led by a peerless "spiritual" leader.

Oxnam then cries: "We should continue to investigate un-American activities. We should continue to pass laws to defeat them." Here Oxnam is clearly giving his approval to a crusade already run amok and to the continuing passage of legislation at the national, state, and local levels of unspeakable danger and folly. Oxnam then opines, "In my opinion, the men best qualified to get at the real menace of Marx are qualified professors, like Sidney Hook, or Reinhold Niebuhr of Union Theological Seminary, or Bishop Fulton J. Sheen of the Roman Catholic Church." Funny that Oxnam should name Sheen, who was regarded as the leading anti-Communist ideologue of the hierarchy famed for courting ex-Communist informers into the Church. Curious that he should name Hook, whose loathing for Communists denied them the right to exist in that bible of the Cold War liberals *Heresy, Yes—Conspiracy, No.* Unfortunately, even Niebuhr was more the hunter than a protector of the hunted in that era.

Oxnam uttered these convictions on dozens of instances before and after they appeared in the June 1953 article. "The communist threat to freedom is so serious that we dare not allow these racketeers to divide us," he intoned. "Let us turn to the F.B.I. for the investigation of subversion, and let us in the light of evidence take those steps in the American way to punish all who violate our laws or who betray the nation. We can trust J. Edgar Hoover and his carefully trained men." [9] American Communists have a lot of sins to atone for, but surely racketeering is not among their mortal ones. What does Oxnam mean by "subversion," the "American way," "in the light of evidence," "our laws"? After all, "our laws" included the 1940 Alien Registration Act, the 1947 Taft-Hartley, section 9 (h) law, the 1950 Internal Security Act, the 1952 Immigration and Nationality Act, the upcoming 1954 Communist Control Act, among others, and the laws in thirty-two states barring "subversives" from public employment and the laws in thirty-two states requiring loyalty oaths of teachers. "I believe the Communist Party is a conspiracy as it is presently organized, and I believe the work that it is doing in this country does seek the overthrow of this free government," became an Oxnam litany.

The truth is that Oxnam was quite willing to see American Communists stripped of their constitutional protections. Writing to Gardner Cowles of *Look* magazine on September 23, 1953, he set forth his position in all its naked force: "Personally I regard the Communist Party as a dangerous conspiracy and do not go along with the American Civil Liberties [Union] brief on the Smith Act. The New Leader, a strong anti-Communist publication, as you know, is also opposed to this Act. It is held that *opinion not criminal action* is being punished. *I disagree* because I don't want conspirators to get their forces ready to move before we fight back" (emphasis added). Oxnam failed to heed Roger Baldwin's warning against the dangers inherent in what he derisively called "'Liberty for Our Side' only." The 141 Communists indicted under the Smith Act were in fact not charged with engaging in the violent overthrow of the government. They were not even charged with teaching and advocating the violent overthrow of the government. They were charged and convicted of conspiring to teach and advocate the violent overthrow of the government, and with conspiring to organize a group to this end, the CPUSA.

Oxnam's complete distrust of Communists is further evidenced when he arranged for the Council of Bishops to hear a group of experts to expound on communism. No actual Communists were invited to enlighten the bishops because, as Oxnam explained, "intellectual honesty and Communist tactics are mutually irreconcilable." Apparently, Communists could not be honest even when discussing what they believed.

When on Friday, June 19, 1953, at minutes before sundown and the beginning of the Jewish sabbath, Julius and Ethel Rosenberg were executed for conspiring to commit espionage for a wartime ally, Oxnam believed justice had been done. Although normally he had reservations about capital punishment, he explained to the press that he had no reservations about the propriety, even the necessity, of imposing upon such persons as the Rosenbergs the most severe penalty which is permitted under the law. When an American Methodist bishop (and Reinhold Niebuhr, too) called for the death of the couple and the pope in Rome pleaded for clemency, one comes to a fuller comprehension of the terror of the times.

President Eisenhower refused to spare the Rosenbergs from the electric chair. Only belatedly and after much harm had been done did he use the enormous power of the presidency to rein McCarthy. But Oxnam was charitable. "The President himself," said the bishop in 1955, "wisely [sic!] refused to be drawn into any personal controversy with Senator McCarthy but it was well known that the deep religious convictions and the unquestioned patriotism of the President were deeply offended."

If Oxnam withheld his tender mercies from Communists, he was evenhanded in withholding them from those he judged American fascists, applauding their investigation by HUAC (limited as it was) and their indictment by the government under the Smith Act during the war.[10] Oxnam was certainly unjustly attacked during the Red Scare, but he himself was a contributor to what historian Leo Ribuffo has termed the "Brown Scare." The sad fact is that in Oxnam's vaunted Vital Center liberalism there was a dangerous core that would not tolerate the existence of radicals either on the far Right or the far Left.

The story of Oxnam's relationship with Hoover's Federal Bureau of Investigation is one of unrequited love. He was not the only liberal who loved the bureau not wisely but too well. Genuinely concerned as he and they were about the erosion of civil liberties, he and they criticized HUAC, the SISS, and of course that loose cannon McCarthy. These congressional investigating committees and individuals, the liberal charge went, were partisan in motivation, sloppy in method, hungry for headlines, and as eager to prosecute innocent liberals as guilty Reds. Still, there was to be faced the existence of a genuine internal Communist menace. What agency could be trusted with the grave responsibility of the ferreting out and fettering of the disloyal? What agency was renowned as a disinterested, professional, apolitical, careful fact-gathering investigative body? The answer almost universally given in the Liberal Establishment was the FBI. As we now know, that blind faith was misplaced. Under Hoover the bureau's ideology was as ferociously reactionary as that of any Red-baiting politico. The Great Fear was fueled by "The Boss" more than it was by even McCarthy or McCarran. It may be that some liberals licked the bureau's boots out of a fear of reprisal.[11] Surely, however, most liberals were like Oxnam in their ignorance of the bureau's ideology and workings. Nevertheless, if most liberals can be absolved of the charge of cowardice, most stand guilty, as does Oxnam, of a will to believe in the bureau's purity and a perhaps unconscious desire to preserve their own innocence of the facts of American life.

The Federal Bureau of Investigation's dossier on Garfield Bromley Oxnam is an unpleasingly plump, though not quite obese, four hundred plus pages filed under the names (in addition to Garfield Bromley Oxnam): G. Bromley Oxham, Bromley Oxman, G. Bromley Oxman, J. Bromley Oxman, One (Bishop) Oxman, Bromley Oxnam, Bromley G. Oxnam, Bromly Oxnam, Frank Oxnam, G. Oxnam, J. Bromley Oxnam, One (Bishop) Oxnam, One Oxam, One Oxdom, One Oxenham, One Oxham, G. Brmley Oxham, Bromley S. Oxman, C. Bromley Oxman, G. Bramley Oxman, G. Bronley Oxman, G. Brumley Oxman, T. Browley Oxman, Bromly G. Oxnam, Browley G. Oxnam, C. B. Oxnam, C. Bromley Oxnam, F. Bromley Oxnam, G. Bramley Oxnam, G. Bremley Oxnam, G. Browley Oxnam, G. Brownley Oxnam, G. Cromley Oxnam, G. Dronley Oxnam, G. H. Oxnam, O. Bromley Oxnam, S. Brownley Oxnam, G. Bromley Oxname, One Oxnom, G. Bromley Oxom, J. Bromley Oxom, One Oxum.

From whence did the information come to fill this bulging file? The respected historian Kenneth O'Reilly in his *Hoover and the Un-Americans: The FBI, HUAC, and the Red Menace,* states that "the Bureau kept anti-communist clergymen like Oxnam under surveillance."[12] Certainly Hoover's bureau did engage in legal and also extralegal break-ins, wiretaps, bugs, burglaries, so-called black-bag jobs, and the shadowing of individuals and the infiltrating of organizations. However, in the case of Oxnam there is no available evidence to suggest that the FBI ever surreptitiously entered his office, rifled his files, tapped his phone, opened his mail, bugged his rooms, tailed his movements. The Oxnam file repeatedly contains such flat statements as, "He has never been investigated by the Bureau" and "This Bureau has conducted no active investigation concerning Bishop Oxnam." That is to say, he was never placed under the *close* surveillance suffered by Dr. King, for example.

Nevertheless, the bureau did keep a weather eye on his utterances and activities. For one thing, FBI headquarters received information on him from at least the following Field (or Division) offices: Los Angeles, Chicago, Omaha, Boston, New York, Washington, San Diego, and Houston. Agents elsewhere also reported what he was up to. Moreover, from time to time the Oxnam file contains such reports as: "In May, 1945, Bureau Agents conducted an unauthorized search of the offices maintained by the American Committee for Spanish Freedom. This search revealed that Oxnam was a member of the Inter-Faith Committee of the American Committee for Spanish Freedom." And: "Through technical sources . . ." and there follows a report on the National Council of American-Soviet Friendship and mention of uncovering Oxnam's name. Further, when in 1940 the Chicago Field Office received news of the bishop's "Red leanings," the Boston Field Office (Oxnam then lived in Boston) was asked to investigate; the Boston Office in turn asked the Boston Police Department to report on the matter. "The inquiry by the Boston Police Department produced no derogatory information." In 1946 Hoover requested "a summary of the background and activities" of Oxnam and on June 20 the report was submitted.

Oxnam's FBI file was further fattened by information on him from at least the following governmental agencies: Office of Naval Intelligence, Military Intelligence Division, Office of Special Investigations of the U.S. Air Force, Office of Censorship (1945), Department of Justice, Department of State, Department of Commerce, HUAC, California Legislature's Committee on Un-American Activities (the infamous Tenney Committee). Reports also came from "a highly confidential source" and from "a highly confidential and reliable source" and from "an outside, unknown source," and the like.

Finally, there was the information supplied to the FBI by concerned private citizens performing their patriotic duty in alerting the bureau to Oxnam's un-Americanism. Some of these citizens were Roman Catholics, but the majority were certainly conservative Protestants. (Not even the deletion of names in the correspondence can mask this fact.) While this information is elephantine in bulk, that portion of a substantive nature could be put in a flea's navel with room left over for two aspirins and an acorn—to steal from Fred Allen.

To whom did the FBI release its file on Oxnam? The bureau received scores of inquiries from private citizens and groups. Some of the inquirers simply wanted the "dirt" on Oxnam to confirm their suspicions of him. Others were his friends who desired assurance of their belief in his loyalty. Still others were genuinely perplexed souls who, having heard so many charges and counter-charges, hungered for the bureau to set the record straight one way or another. On scores of instances the customary Hoover reply was this or something similar:

> Your letter dated March 9, 1956, has been received, and while I appreciate the concern prompting you to write, I would like to advise that information in the files of the FBI is confidential and may not be disseminated outside this Bureau for other than official purposes. Since the FBI is strictly a fact-gathering agency, we are not empowered to make evaluations or draw conclusions concerning the character or integrity of any individual, publication or organization. I am sure you can understand the reasons for these rules and will not infer either that we do or that we do not have information concerning the subject of your inquiry.

Hoover was fibbing as we now know. He did leak privileged bureau files to privileged, that is to say, conservative, private citizens, notably favored columnists and broadcasters, but he did so through "blind memorandums" that left no paper trail. One notation in the Oxnam file reads: "The following references are letters to the Bureau from individuals requesting information concerning the accuracy of allegations, which had come to their attention from various sources, that Bishop G. Bromley Oxnam was a Communist, Communist sympathizer or affiliated with CP front organizations. In the letters of acknowledgment the *majority* of correspondents were advised that the Bureau was unable to be of assistance since FBI files are confidential and available for official use only" (emphasis added). This suggests that in a *minority* of instances information was released, but the available record does not pinpoint a single instance when the

Oxnam file was shared with a private citizen. Certainly it was not released wholesale to the general public.

Another matter altogether was when a governmental agency, the Department of State or the Department of Defense, for example, from time to time requested from the FBI a "name check" on Oxnam. This the bureau quite properly furnished.

Particularly salient to the Oxnam story is the bureau's relationship with HUAC. It now has been proven beyond peradventure that Hoover leaked information on a selective basis to the Senate Internal Security Subcommittee, to HUAC, and to such favored congressmen as Karl Mundt, Richard Nixon, Pat McCarran, and Joe McCarthy—at least until McCarthy's rogue elephant style caused the cautious Hoover dismay. All the while Hoover denied he was doing so and carefully masked his collaboration with these notorious Red-hunters. In 1948 the then chairman of HUAC, J. Parnell Thomas (within the year to be thrown in the clink for extorting kickbacks from his staff) said to fellow committee member Nixon, "The closest relationship exists between this committee and the FBI. . . . I think there is a good understanding between us. It is something, however, that we cannot talk too much about." HUAC chronicler Walter Goodman described HUAC and the FBI as "a pair of mischievously indiscreet lovers," maintaining a formal distance in public, "yet so fond were the glances they exchanged, so endearing the sentiments, that observers could hardly keep from speculating over what they did together when the lights went out." Other historians maintain that HUAC, of all investigating bodies, was the *principal* recipient of FBI assistance.

As luck would have it, the HUAC-FBI dalliance had momentarily cooled at precisely the time when the HUAC-Oxnam controversy was reaching its climax. Harold H. Velde was the newly elevated chairman of HUAC. His vaulting ambition and hunger for publicity disturbed a jealous Hoover, and "The Boss" decided that close association with Velde's HUAC was not in the best interests of the bureau. Moreover, Hoover was a consummate bureaucrat, empire builder, and survivor, and he may have intuitively sensed that becoming involved in the HUAC-Oxnam contest was not in the agency's immediate interest.

In any event, on May 1, 1953, Velde called on FBI officer Louis B. Nichols for help in handling Oxnam. Nichols prepared a memo for his superior, Clyde Tolson, Hoover's second-in-command and inseparable companion, reviewing the conversation with Velde. The final paragraph of the memo reads: "Velde feels the Oxnam campaign will continue to go [on] and something must be done to counter it. I told Velde I simply could not think of any suggestions at the moment. He asked if I would not continue to think about it and see if I could not come up with something. I told him if any thoughts occurred to me, I would get in touch with him. I, of course, will have no suggestion to make." To this Hoover appended the notation, "Right." The memo also contains this significant passage: "The Bishop confidentially advised Velde that in 1948 [sic] he became convinced that the Methodist Federation for Social Action was following the Communist Party line and that the activities of the leadership led him to believe they were not loyal people. The Bishop stated he was satisfied that both Harry Ward and Jack McMichael were members of the Communist Party. The Bishop, however, declined to testify to this." *If* Velde was telling the truth to Nichols and *if* Nichols was telling the truth to Tolson (and there seemed to be no motivation for them to lie on this point), then we have a Methodist bishop reporting his suspicions about two Methodist ministers to both HUAC and the FBI.

On June 26 Velde again sent Nichols an SOS and again Nichols prepared a memo for Tolson. Velde related that HUAC had sleuths in San Francisco, Boston, and New York checking up on Oxnam. Could the FBI lend a hand? "I told [Velde] [13]
we had never investigated the Bishop as such and we could not be of any assistance to him." Another page in the Oxnam file, an internal FBI communication, dated July 15, only six days before Oxnam's scheduled hearing before the Velde Committee, makes it clear that the FBI had no intention of preparing a report on Oxnam for Velde. The communication also contains the statement, "In connection with Bishop Oxnam, Bureau files reflect extensive correspondence between the Bureau and Bishop Oxnam and indicate that cordial relations exist with the Bishop."

At least that assertion is half correct. It will be recalled from chapter 5 that as early as February 1922 the Los Angeles office of the FBI began reporting Oxnam's activities to the Washington headquarters. To the day he died Oxnam had no inkling of the bureau's interest in him. Oxnam publicly praised Hoover ad nauseum. He wrote Hoover's lieutenants praising their chief's holding steadfast to his convictions: "We associate courage with his name." Nor was the bishop posing. To inquiries from private citizens, Oxnam would give the comforting reply, "The work of the F.B.I. deserves our highest commendation. If the same care were pursued by the [congressional] Committees that is exercised by Mr. J. Edgar Hoover, there would be little difficulty." A memo in Oxnam's FBI file reads, "Bureau files also reflect that Bishop Oxnam has occasionally corresponded with the Bureau since 1936. In all of his correspondence and comments to Mr. Nichols, whom he has seen on several occasions, the Bishop has always been cordial and often complimentary of the Bureau and the Director." This is true. Beginning in 1936 Oxnam wrote Hoover letters oozing with flattery, sometimes accompanied by things he had written lauding the FBI.

The director's replies were polite, sometimes accompanied by public statements he had made. From time to time Oxnam would solicit an audience with Hoover. Of course the requests were always denied, Hoover begging off because of the press of duties. The declinations were always courteously phrased. How was poor Oxnam to know Hoover's true reasons? In 1947 when Oxnam sought a meeting for himself and fellow National Council officers, how was the bishop to know that at the bottom of his plea Hoover jotted, "No. This fellow & his outfit are certainly far from being unsympathetic to Communism & as for ——. My statement before the Un-American Activities Committee covers all I intend to say or can say at this time." From time to time Oxnam would invite Hoover to address the Methodist General Conference, the Council of Bishops, and other church groups. Naturally the invitations were invariably declined. The prudent Hoover had no intention of becoming publicly identified with the "pink" cleric, and, besides, there can be no doubt that he honestly believed Oxnam to be too hostile to Catholicism and too sympathetic to communism.

In one of his exquisitely mannered replies to Oxnam, Hoover added, "If at any time you should have any specific problems wherein you think I could be of assistance, I wish you would feel free to communicate with me. In the event I am not available I would be most happy to make one of my assistants, Mr. Louis B. Nichols, who has long been identified with the Methodist Church, available to be of such help as possible. If you desire, I would be glad to have him call upon you the next time he happens to be in New York." [14]

If Oxnam never had a personal meeting with Hoover, he had several of significance with Nichols. Therefore, at the onset it is interesting to note Nichols's assessment of the bishop as set forth in a three-page, typed, single-spaced memo to Associate Director Tolson. The memo was written after Nichols had spoken before the Troy Annual Conference on April 10, 1948 and after having dined with the Oxnams. "Oxnam was very affable," Nichols recorded. "He has an excellent personality, a compelling manner of speaking, and in appearance is everything a Bishop should be. Mrs. Oxnam was equally charming." Nichols then reported that he "made a few general digs at the Bishop" relating to Oxnam's affiliation with pro-Communist movements and organizations and relating to the Communist line followed by the Methodist Federation for Social Action. "I was somewhat pleasantly surprised," the report continues, when Oxnam admitted the error of his ways, "was exceptionally bitter in his condemnation of Communists," and expressed the wistful hope that he was not in Hoover's "disfavor." Nichols further recalled that Oxnam said he was "very sympathetic to the Director's views and position, and despite the fact he himself had been called a 'red,' he did not think he was too far apart from the Director's views on many matters, that he for one appreciated the spiritual note the Director injected into his speeches and appreciated the leadership the Director had given and he thought the Director had not received his just dues and credit and he would like sometime to meet with the Director. I frankly think this would be a good idea." The penultimate paragraph contains this analysis: "I am not prepared to express an opinion on Oxnam. My curbstone guess is that the fellow likes to hear his own voice. I have no doubt as to his brilliance.

He is a great pulpiteer. I think he might be inclined to be superficial in his thought and somewhat on the side of naivete. Either that or he is indeed a sinister character."

After their initial meeting in 1948, Nichols and Oxnam collaborated on several matters which involved a mutual exchange of confidences. In 1950, for example, Dr. Charles Boss, executive secretary of the Board of World Peace of The Methodist Church, charged the FBI with investigating the loyalty of seminarians at the Garrett Biblical Institute and requested that the matter be brought before the Council of Bishops. Oxnam turned to Nichols for clarification accompanying his petition with a copy of Boss's allegations. A considerable correspondence resulted as did a personal meeting. "I will keep after the Bishop until we force [Boss] into a position where he will actually have to shut up and admit that he is wrong," Nichols promised his superiors. Nichols also offered to appear before the Council of Bishops to prove the untruth of Boss's charge. In the end this was unnecessary because Oxnam was convinced by Nichols of the bureau's innocence. (In this instance the bureau was probably innocent.) Oxnam expressed contrition and pledged that in the future, Methodism's leaders would not go off half-cocked. For his part, Nichols was grateful that Oxnam had come to him before bringing the Council of Bishops into the act.

On January 9, 1951, Oxnam again approached Nichols for assistance concerning the minister of the Epworth Methodist Church in the Bronx, a black man named Edward D. McCowan whom Oxnam deemed ineffectual. Oxnam was disturbed because McGowan had attended the Second World Peace Congress, correctly judged by Oxnam to be "Communist-inspired and Communist-controlled." Moreover, the minister was rumored to be a member of the American Labor Party. What facts did the FBI possess? Nichols responded by sending "public source data" on McGowan and the ALP.

A third matter carrying Oxnam to Nichols's office concerned Herbert Fuchs, who over a period of seven years had risen from assistant to full professor in American University's College of Law. On June 6, 1955, a HUAC process-server caught up with Fuchs. Fuchs informed the university of his intent to fully confess his Communist past but that he would not inform on others. President Hurst Anderson urged him to "name names." On June 13 Fuchs testified before HUAC that he had been a Communist from 1934 until 1946 while employed by the government; that he had formed three Communist "cells" in the government; that he had lied to a loyalty board in 1948 about his former party membership. But he declined on grounds of conscience to name his former party associates. On July 10 a committee leak resulted in a full newspaper story. The university sprang to his defense, President Anderson describing him as "an intelligent, loyal and devoted teacher" who would receive the university's support. "To take any other position at this time would be beneath the dignity of an institution with a Christian relationship and commitments."

Unappeased by Fuchs's first testimony, HUAC subpoenaed him again, and this time he named forty-four of his past Communist associates in government employment. The next day, July 16, President Anderson ordered him to apply for a leave of absence, the alternative being summary dismissal. On September 13 the executive committee of the Board of Trustees met, voted, and notified Fuchs his employment would terminate on June 30, 1956, his leave of absence being extended until then. Oxnam was not present, being in Hungary. Six weeks later, on October 29, the full Board of Trustees unanimously confirmed the action taken by the executive committee. Judge R. V. Fletcher, chairman of the board, now denounced Fuchs as a "Communist who had taken the Government's bread and betrayed it," and President Anderson now took the position that Fuchs was a perjurer as well as an atheist or agnostic and that it was unwise to employ even ex-Communists.

As a champion of American University and a member of the Board of Trustees, Oxnam could not escape being caught up in this cause célèbre. He made a point of interviewing Fuchs twice prior to the fateful October 29 action. Further, on October 14 he called on Nichols for his opinion, the FBI officer confirming that Fuchs had fully cooperated with HUAC and the bureau. Nevertheless, Oxnam reached the conclusion that the professor must go and so argued at the October 29 meeting of the board. Oxnam acknowledged to the board the FBI's confirmation to him and admitted that his feelings on the matter were "entirely subjective." Still, he continued, "I have grave doubts in my own mind as to the genuineness of the renunciation." The diary entry for that date ends, "I left before the vote was taken, but I understand the vote was unanimous." (Why he left early the record does not disclose.) The point to be emphasized is that Oxnam wanted Fuchs out not because he had informed on his past comrades and not because he freely cooperated with HUAC and the FBI, but because Oxnam believed that a *former* Communist should not be in the employ of American University.

Fuchs's dismissal called forth a censure from the American Association of Law Schools on Academic Freedom and Tenure. Oxnam reacted with the same outrage he had displayed when DePauw had been censured by the AAUP. The real irony, however, is that the most severe criticisms of American University's decision came from conservative quarters. Congressman Francis E. Walter, then chairman of HUAC, telegraphed his displeasure, the protest closing, "In the view of the Committee on Un-American Activities, former Communist party membership should not be held against an individual whose testimony . . . convinces one that he has completely and finally terminated his Communist party membership. . . . It is detrimental to the work of the Committee, as well as unjust to Professor Fuchs, that he be penalized for the performance of a patriotic duty." Another HUAC member, Congressman Gordon Scherer, publicly charged that Oxnam above all others was responsible for the reversal of the university's original decision to defend Fuchs's right to teach. The American Committee for Cultural Freedom entered the lists on Fuchs's behalf. Reinhold Niebuhr informed President Anderson: "I would like to challenge this decision on moral grounds. If a man has been involved in the Communist conspiracy and has made a clean breast of it, is there any moral reason why an institution should dismiss him? It rather puts all repentant Communists in the category of martyrs, and it incidentally makes repentance a very hazardous adventure." Truth to tell, Fuchs's fate was widely deplored at the time by both liberals and conservatives (and by later historians), leaving only unrepentant Communists to cheer the "justice" done to the "turncoat" by American University. There is no record in either public or private sources that Oxnam ever regretted his large role in Fuchs's termination.

A fourth matter this time carried Nichols to Oxnam's office on September 15, 1950, the FBI officer claiming that he came not as a representative of the bureau but as a loyal Methodist concerned about the weal of his bishop. The FBI, stated Nichols, had been informed that Oxnam was under contract to write a book on church-state relations for Little, Brown, the old, respected Boston publishing house. A senior editor at Little, Brown was a secret Communist, Nichols continued, who used his seniority to secure the publication by his company of books sympathetic to communism. That individual intended to edit Oxnam's completed manuscript to give it a pro-Communist orientation on the assumption that Oxnam would be too busy to note the subtle editorial changes. A shocked Oxnam confirmed that he was under contract with Little, Brown to write such a book, having first been approached by one of his former DePauw students, Angus Cameron. Nichols said that was the name of the secret Communist editor.[15] Should he withdraw from the contract, the bishop wondered? Replied Nichols, "By all means write it; I am only suggesting that you watch very carefully to be sure that no editorial changes are made that will embarrass you." Here Oxnam's diary account of the meeting ends. Understandably he had no wish to relate Nichols's final advice as reported to his superior, Tolson: "I further told the Bishop that it was my personal opinion that he could probably do a lot more for the Methodist Church by emulating John Wesley and get out and preach the message of the Church and to cut out a lot of his extra curricular activities in going after other churches. He stated that in all seriousness he thought there was a lot of merit to what I had to stay." To which Hoover jotted on the memo, "Quite true but I doubt he will follow such advice." (Five years later Oxnam received a visit from the chief counsel of the Senate Internal Subcommittee about Cameron and Oxnam related the same story he had told Nichols.) [16]

The most critical collaboration between Oxnam and Nichols concerned the Reverend Jack McMichael of the Methodist Federation for Social Action. In a moment we will turn to Oxnam's break with the Federation, but here attention will center on the

FBI's role. While dining together at their first meeting in Troy, New York, on April 10, 1948, Oxnam confided to Nichols his disquietude over McMichael's leadership of the Federation even though McMichael had sworn to him on everything holy he was not a Communist and had never been a Communist. "I told the Bishop," Nichols reported to his superior Tolson, "I never had any doubts that McMichael did carry a party card but by using the mantle of the church, he was doing more good for the party than a dozen card carriers. The Bishop admitted this could be true." Nichols then related to Oxnam some putative facts about McMichael. On February 15, 1949, Oxnam called on Nichols for the specific purpose of obtaining from the FBI information on McMichael. "They had a long file and I jotted down a good deal of information that was there, and promised that any references would be kept strictly confidential," the bishop recorded in his diary that evening.

Oxnam then confronted McMichael by mail with the information supplied by Nichols, though withholding the source of his information. McMichael responded by branding the information "brazenly false" and categorically denying he had been in attendance at Communist meetings on the dates and at the places named—or at any other times or places. This denial Oxnam passed along to Nichols on March 10 and on March 16 Nichols replied to the effect that of course McMichael would deny the truth.

On February 16, 1950, Oxnam again wrote Nichols supplying the FBI with a copy of his letter of inquiry to McMichael dated March 2, 1949, and copies of McMichael's defenses dated March 4 and March 25. In his letter to Nichols, Oxnam repeated his doubts about McMichael and asked, "Would it be possible for me to confer with you again and to ascertain whether the reports which you discussed with me are those of an FBI investigator who was actually present at the meetings referred to or whether they came second hand?" Oxnam was entering deeper and dangerous waters and unquestionably he did so because of his absolute confidence in the integrity of Hoover and the FBI.

Then came Oxnam's hearing before HUAC on July 21, 1953. Inevitably he was asked about his relationship to the Methodist Federation for Social Action and its executive secretary,

McMichael, and why Oxnam had resigned from the organization in 1947. Oxnam gave the explanation: "Because, frankly, I believed that Jack McMichael was so tied up with the Communist group that whether or no he were a Communist, I couldn't prove whether he was a member of the Communist Party or not but I was sure that the organization ought not to be under that leadership any more, and I did everything I could. Others talked to Mr. McMichael. He denied this completely." Oxnam was then asked why he had reached the conclusion that McMichael was a Communist? He replied: "Sir, I hope you will not press that question. I will be glad to state to this Committee if I could meet it in executive session. The source of that information was strictly confidential, and I think I would be betraying a trust if I said it in public. I would be glad to convey it to the chairman of the Committee. I am not hedging here at all, but I think I have an obligation because the source was of such a nature—I think the chairman would be the first to recognize this. I will not refer to the source other than that." Chairman Velde understood. Representative Scherer then asked, "Bishop, at the time you got this information, that Reverend McMichael was a member of the Communist Party, you reported it to the F.B.I., did you?" Explained Oxnam: "It was not necessary to report it there. Don't misunderstand me, sir. I am trying to keep a confidence here which I will be glad—" At this point Representative Walter broke in, "You have said it very well, I assure you."

Oxnam had not named the source of his information, but knowledgeable individuals—and certainly the members of HUAC—realized it must have been the FBI. On June 33, 1955, two friendly and courteous FBI agents called on Oxnam at Lake Winnepesaukee to inquire about McMichael. Oxnam reported that he had no firsthand knowledge as to whether or not McMichael was a Communist, but he did share with the agents his grave concern based in part on the FBI file shown him by Nichols. Oxnam wrongly assumed that Nichols had authorized the visitation. In fact, however, the interview had been requested by Assistant U.S. Attorney Hitz, as an FBI memo reveals. Moreover, the memo reads, "The WFO [Washington Field Office] was instructed to advise Mr. Hitz that Bishop Oxnam apparently did not possess any information concerning which he could testify. *Mr. Tolson noted on the memo that the situation was embarrassing to the Bureau and the Director agreed"* (emphasis added). That is, the FBI was embarrassed at the disclosure that it had leaked its file on McMichael to a private individual—Bishop Oxnam—while it was eternally denying that it ever did such a thing.

When on October 14, 1955, Oxnam again met with Nichols, the FBI officer charged the bishop with a breach of confidence. A distraught Oxnam (according to Nichols) profusely apologized. That same day Oxnam wrote Nichols a three-page letter, the heart of which is found in this statement: "I left your office sorely troubled. In my profession, confidences are regarded as sacred. . . . It was therefore with very great regret, not to say shock, that I learned that you felt I had revealed a confidence when I was upon the witness stand before the House Committee on Un-American Activities. I had tried to be very careful that day, and had thought that you would be the first to realize that I had protected the source of information that I had received. I have re-read the testimony, and do not see how I could have protected that source with greater care."

On October 17 in a memo to Tolson, Nichols attempted to cover his tail by relating the "feeble way" Oxnam sought to justify himself and by assuring Tolson that "any information imparted [to Oxnam] was imparted by word of mouth," not by the showing of a file. On the nineteenth Nichols corrected Oxnam to this effect and to this letter Oxnam clipped the note: "The truth is, Mr. Nichols did bring in a file, not in a folder but bound by some kind of metal apparatus, as I recall, which he did allow me to see and from which I did copy three dates and the names of places when and where Mr. McMichael was supposed to have participated in Communist Party activities."

Nichols's letter Oxnam chose not to answer. And thus, apparently, there ended a rather curious working relationship between a Methodist bishop and a Methodist layman.

The Methodist Federation for Social Action and its leadership was clearly a concern to the FBI and HUAC as it was a source of exasperation to all conservative Methodists. As the years passed and the Federation's leadership tacked increasingly to the Left, Oxnam and his fellow liberal Methodists shared in the consternation. This story has already been told in some detail and we must note only those aspects of particular salience to Oxnam's life.

Dr. Harry F. Ward was the driving force behind the Federation for almost four decades, from its inception in 1907, thanks *primarily* to Ward, until his retirement in 1944, in his capacity as both executive director and editor of the Federation's *Bulletin*. To be sure, other socially conscious Methodists contributed mightily to the endeavor, notably Bishop Francis J. McConnell, who served as president until his retirement, also in 1944. Although McConnell and Ward did not always see eye to eye, the bishop never withdrew the support of his towering reputation or the prestige of his episcopal office, believing, as he said to Bishop Welch, another founder and initial supporter, "The Methodist Church ought to be able to afford one Harry Ward." The Federation was never a formal part of The Methodist Church, and conservatives, in particular, never tired of underscoring its unofficial nature. Nevertheless, it was looked upon, as the 1912 General Conference stated, as the executive agency to rally the forces of the church in support of social thought and reform. McConnell described its purpose in more homely terms: that of raising disturbing questions—ahead of time. As late as the 1944 General Conference the Federation was commended for having "a history of achievement in stimulating thought and action of which the Church is proud."

As we know, Oxnam early in his ministry associated himself with the Federation and courageously defended it. However, as we have also seen, in the 1930s he began to discern a disturbing asymmetry under Ward's continuing leadership, the Soviet Union being seen as the world's last, best hope whilst America sank deeper and deeper into fascism—a fear, for Ward, not assuaged by Roosevelt's New Deal.[17] In 1932, Ward's associate, Winifred Chappell, a Methodist deaconess, announced publicly her support of Communist Party candidate Earl Browder for president. In the pages of the *Epworth Herald* she advised Methodist youth: "Accept the draft, take the drill, go into the camps and onto the battlefields, or into the munitions factories and transportation work—but sabotage war preparations and war. Be agitators for sabotage. Down tools when the order is to make and load munitions. Spoil war materials and machinery." At a meeting with Chappell to discuss the situation in Russia, Oxnam was disturbed to hear the deaconess justify the deliberate starvation of the kulaks by Stalin's murderous regime. (Naturally during the HUAC hearing the committee members introduced the name of Chappell to embarrass Oxnam. The truthfulness of his reply is fully supported by his diary entries from the 1930s.)

As for his former teacher Ward, Oxnam's disenchantment became almost complete.[18] In 1936 he informed Bishop Flint: "He [Ward] takes the Communist position as to objective if not as to method. I repudiate it. Too often they prefer a fight to an advance. They would rather throw bricks than build with them, unless we are willing to build in their precise blue-print—I should say, red-print—way." And in 1941 Oxnam made this diary entry. "I was disappointed beyond expression at Professor Ward. His left-wing drift in recent years has destroyed the scientific outlook. This evening what we really heard was a brief for the Communist Party all under the general theme of Present Attacks Upon Civil Liberties."

The Federation was not a Communist front. Its members were socially concerned Methodists, not Communists. The overwhelming majority of its leaders were not Communists either—certainly not the scores of bishop and educators and pastors who held high office. Ward was probably not a Communist Party member. He and his fellow Federationists bravely labored for economic justice and racial brotherhood in America and the world. Yet Ward was a True Believer. One questions not his endless, unmeasured, unrelenting criticism of virtually every aspect of capitalist America—the truly "evil empire" in his astigmatic vision. What one does question, however, is his loyalty to the Communist Party line; his conviction that in the international arena the Communists stood for freedom, justice, equality, and abundance; his belief that capitalism and fascism were virtually one and the same. If ever it is justifiable to designate an individual a true "fellow traveler" that individual is Dr. Ward.[19]

In 1946 Oxnam was elected one of two vice-presidents of the Federation. By this time Jack McMichael had succeeded Ward as

Federation executive secretary. He proved to be as much of a trial to Oxnam personally and The Methodist Church at large as had Ward. We have just reviewed how McMichael figured in Oxnam's relations with the FBI and in the HUAC hearing and now a few additional observations.

The April 1947 issue of the Federation's *Social Questions Bulletin* carried an item entitled "Tarnished Saints?" by editor Alson J. Smith, a Methodist minister well known in Methodist circles for his muckraking (the term is not used pejoratively). The editorial raised questions as to the appropriateness of the haloes which were then being polished for Dulles , Niemöller, Chiang Kai-shek, and the Japanese Christian Toyohiko Kagawa. In early May at a Federation banquet Oxnam exploded in anger, especially at the canards about Niemöller and Dulles. Oxnam then wrote a letter of apology for the Smith article to Dulles. Rather archly Dulles replied that he was principally disturbed because the editorial appeared on the same page listing Oxnam as a vice-president and that a professedly Christian publication should print such libelous statements about him and his law firm, Sullivan and Cromwell. On June 9, 1947, Oxnam wrote Federation president Bishop Hartman, "I regret exceedingly that I must resign as a vice president of the Methodist Federation for Social Action." "I recognize the right of anyone to state his views," the letter continued, "but regret exceedingly that a Christian leader such as Mr. Dulles should be so attacked without so much as a communication being written to him or a conference being sought to test the accuracy of the position taken." Oxnam then informed Dulles of his deed, "I have resigned. . . . It seemed to me that was thc only effective protest I could make in the light of the editorial that referred to you."

There followed a long "Documentary" in the October issue of the *Bulletin* by Smith detailing the business relationships tying Dulles and his law firm to prewar German industrialists and cartelists and the assertion that "now they are back doing business at the old stand" after World War II. Smith not unreasonably concluded: "All I'm saying is . . . Dulles should not be permitted to represent the mind of the Protestant churches on world affairs, particularly on German affairs. If anybody can look at the facts and come up with another opinion, he is free to do so." When Oxnam continued to condemn Smith for his "unconscionable" and "unChristian" attacks on Dulles, the editor allowed how these were "pretty bitter words for a bishop to be using when speaking of his brethren. . . . If you will pardon me for saying so, it is possible to disagree with you, Mr. Dulles, and other Republican party-liners without being either 'unconscionable' or 'unChristian.' " Besides, Smith continued, he was being rebuked for not using a method that Oxnam himself did not use: "I did not talk to Mr. Dulles, but neither did you talk to me, although I am considerably more accessible to you than Mr. Dulles is to me. And you made no effort to see the documentary materials that you told . . . me you would look at."

Meanwhile, in the summer and fall of 1947 Oxnam and McMichael exchanged a series of letters. McMichael pledged that the *Bulletin* would carry any defense of Dulles the bishop cared to write and urged that his resignation be postponed. Oxnam, however, insisted that his resignation as vice-president and as a member of the executive committee take effect as of the date of his June 9 letter to Bishop Hartman.

Oxnam and McMichael continued to correspond and meet, but there could be no meeting of the minds. After one conference with McMichael and Smith, Oxnam sighed, "It is a strange fact, but the man whose views are to the left is just as difficult to deal with as is the man of the right. We don't get anywhere on this basis except where these dogmatists organize and force their views upon people. Then we get somewhere, and the somewhere we get is revolution. We don't want it, from either side."

Finally, on November 15, 1948, Oxnam completed the break by resigning as a member (not simply as an officer) of the Federation. The letter to McMichael followed an article critical of Dulles by the famed journalist gadfly I. F. Stone appearing in the Federation *Bulletin*. "However," said Oxnam, "I do not wish to debate the matter. I simply wish to resign, with very great regret. I believe the Federation is following a course that limits its usefulness and makes it impossible for some of us who have stayed with it through all these years to continue."

That last sentence is certainly objectively true. One does not fault Oxnam, or any other liberal Methodist, for severing ties with an organization now led by McMichael. Nevertheless, it is possible to wish that Oxnam had not made his decision so exclusively on the basis of the Federation's critique of Dulles. Bluntly, Oxnam was blinded by his emotional ties to Dulles. He simply would not countenance his hero being scrutinized critically. As we know, the scales on Oxnam's eyes never fell—not even when Dulles became secretary of state. Moreover, Oxnam held McMichael, Smith, and Stone and the *Bulletin* up to impossibly high journalistic standards. Must it be mandatory for an editor or journalist always to interview the subject of a critical story? And if interviewed and Dulles denied any doubtful Sullivan and Cromwell connections, what then? Does that end the matter—and the criticism? (Later historians have raised identical questions about Dulles and Sullivan and Cromwell and their prewar and postwar overseas clients.) Anyhow, Oxnam himself fired off many public criticisms of individuals without first interviewing them.

During this period, June 1947–November 1948, when Oxnam was cutting his officer and then membership relations with the Federation, turmoil engulfed The Methodist Church. Matters were not calmed when the Federation held its annual meeting in Kansas City in December 1947. Frederick Woltman, columnist for the *New York World-Telegram,* who covered the meeting, began his account with the lead-in sentence: "The prestige of the Methodist Church will be used in Kansas City, Missouri, this week to furnish a national sounding board for communists and fellow travelers to expound the gospel of the communist line." The Federation was said to follow closely the Communist Party and McMichael was described as a former leader in the Young Communist League. Other newspapers picked up the story and the fires within Methodism were fanned (although the *New York Times* retracted statements it had printed.) Oxnam fired off telegrams to seven liberal fellow bishops supporting McMichael's decision to sue for libel, explaining, "This action is really protection of Methodists everywhere who are libelously accused. Do you believe McMichael should proceed? If necessary, could you secure $100 toward expenses?" Oxnam and others conferred with famed civil liberties lawyer Arthur Garfield Hays. Hays agreed that there was no doubt as to the libelous nature of the attack on the Federation but advised against filing a suit, because considering the hysteria in the nation over Reds, it would be difficult to win. Concurrently, Oxnam was informing concerned Methodists: "The Methodist Federation for Social Action has never been communist dominated" and it "is not now and never has been a subversive organization."

Although liberal Methodists were genuinely disturbed by positions taken by the Federation under McMichael and conservatives blazed with anger, all efforts taken at the 1948 General Conference to deny the use of the name Methodist or otherwise seeking to repudiate the organization came to naught. The crisis was weathered—barely. The reason is ironic in the judgment of Dean Muelder who was in a position to know. The General Conference did not wish to appear to be intimidated by Woltman; at that moment it would seem an act of cowardice to throw McMichael to the wolves. Consequently, even those liberals and moderates who had their doubts about him thought that this was not the time to subject the Federation to divisive public debate.[20]

A resolution of the question could not be indefinitely postponed. In 1950 the Board of Publications asked the Federation to move its office from the board-owned Methodist Building in New York in which the organization had rented space for more than thirty years. (McMichael continued to exercise squatter's rights until the board's decision was confirmed by the 1952 General Conference.) In 1950 the Council of Bishops pointedly noted that the Federation did not speak for the Church, deplored certain positions taken by it, and concurred in a recommendation that the word "Methodist" be dropped from its title. The 1952 General Conference passed six resolutions ratifying the bishops' positions and, having greatly weakened the status of an already wounded unofficial group, proceeded to authorize a Board of Social and Economic Relations (later Board of Christian Social Concerns) to provide official leadership in the socioeconomic field. Oxnam and Charles Parlin may well have been the two individuals most responsible for bringing this official agency into being and gutting the Federation's influence.

There is much in this woeful story that need not be retold, but one aspect requires emphasis: the conservative assault on the Federation could have been beaten back if only McMichael's leadership had not forfeited the continuing support of Methodism's leading liberal individuals, groups, such as the National Conference of Methodist Youth, and publications such as *The Christian Advocate* and *Zion's Herald*. Any reader remotely familiar with Methodism's liberal leadership will recognize the names of these individuals (among many others) who believed and stated that McMichael should resign as executive secretary in the interest of Methodism's commitment to furthering the Kingdom of God on earth: H. D. Bollinger, Charles E. Schofield, Owen M. Geer, Henry Hitt Crane, Walter G. Muelder, Ralph E. Diffendorfer, Charles C. Webber, L. Harold DeWolf, Bishop Lewis O. Hartman, Emory S. Bucke, Bishop Edgar Love, Albert Barnett, Wade Crawford Barclay, John M. Mecartney, Harold O. Bosley, Edgar S. Brightman, Clarence T. Craig, Gilbert Hugh LeSourd, Bishop James C. Baker, Bishop W. Earl Ledden, Bishop Matthew W. Clair, Georgia Harkness, Bishop Donald H. Tippett. Some of these individuals resigned as early as Oxnam had. Others did not do so until 1953. But almost all of them parted from the Federation in authentic sorrow, for it had had a long and in many respects worthy history. Under McMichael, pronounced Franklin H. Littell, the Federation had declined "to a crypto-Communist buzzing center," a "sounding board for a political esotericism which is both frivolous and dangerous"; it was his "labored and painful conviction that Jack McMichael" is "genuinely serving party interests." This judgment, it must be remembered, was from the pen of a Methodist who affirmed through word and deed his long conviction "of the need for a radical Christian fellowship within the Methodist Church."

Racked though The Methodist Church was by internal divisions during the Great Fear, with conservative Methodists indicting liberals as well as radicals, and liberals angry at conservatives and fearful of fellow travelers, the Church refused to supinely knuckle under to the Red-hunters. The Council of Bishops adopted statements for the guidance of the people called Methodists warning of the dangers to American constitutional liberties and specifically challenging the charges of John T. Flynn and Stanley High and the methods of HUAC and coming to the defense of their colleague Oxnam. In his correspondence and diary entries, Oxnam makes clear his leadership in the preparation of these statements and regrets only that they were not stronger. When, however, Professor Edgar Brightman angrily informed Oxnam that he was ashamed at the Council's weak, irresolute response to the High article, the bishop calmly replied: "I myself was not at all happy about the resolution adopted concerning the Stanley High article. I assure you it is a much stronger statement than the one that originally came from the committee, weak as it is. Then, too, we must never forget that these are men who hold other opinions and who are as much entitled to their opinions as we are to our own. I think that many Bishops felt that the statement was very weak but from the opposite point of view."

Every General Conference of the era also spoke to the matter of endangered civil liberties. For example, in both 1952 and 1956 the conference warned: "In this time of fear, areas of freedom of speech and thought are being narrowed all over the world. . . . In some lands thought control uses the techniques of absolute censorship, surveillance of secret police, torture, imprisonment, and death. In other lands the techniques are those of social rejection, calling of names, demands for 'loyalty oaths,' denial of employment, irresponsible accusations, and assertion of 'guilt by association.' " The 1960 General Conference adopted by an overwhelming vote a resolution specifically condemning the activities of the conservative Methodist lay group Circuit Riders, Inc.

Many Annual Conferences adopted statements considerably more unequivocal than those emanating from the Council of Bishops or General Conference; in fact, they were truly hard-hitting. And of course groups of ministers signed manifestos. Only the Lord knows how many Methodist preachers examined the challenge to American freedoms in their sermons and in their capacities as private citizens in letters to their elected officials. If The Methodist Church may not excessively boast of its civil liberties record, neither must it be required to hang its head in shame. Certainly few, if any professions, could match the concern and courage of the Methodist ministry, and this conclusion could not be reached if the clergy had not received substantial support from the Methodist lay community.

Thus far, much—perhaps too much—emphasis has been placed on the questionable aspects of Oxnam's role: his disinclination to protect those beyond the constitutional pale—fascists and Communists; his naïve faith in the FBI; his unpersuasive reasons for resigning from the Methodist Federation for Social Action (though not the resignation itself); his silences on essential issues and events; and more generally his unwillingness to publicly censure either Truman or Eisenhower for the things these presidents did or left undone that fueled the Great Fear. Nevertheless, his name is imperishably and rightly linked with those Americans who banked rather than fueled the flames of the Second Red Scare. Resolved the board of directors of the American Civil Liberties Union in 1963:

> The death of Bishop G. Bromley Oxnam removes from the civil liberties scene a distinguished and devoted advocate and defender of human freedom. In his twenty-four years as a member of the National Committee of the American Civil Liberties Union and his numerous religious and educational posts, Bishop Oxnam was a vigorous protector of the libertarian ideals of our Bill of Rights. His devotion was not only to the *concept* of human dignity; he implemented his philosophical and religious convictions on the battlefield of social action, where the rights of the individual must always be won.
>
> Especially during the dark hours of McCarthyism in the 1950's when fear and mistrust pervaded our country, Bishop Oxnam played a significant role in the counter-attack launched against the assault on civil liberties. His testimony before the House Un-American Activities Committee where, with dignity and courage, he answered false charges of Communist sympathy, helped to develop public awareness of the threat to our democratic principles in the half-truth and the accusation based on guilt by association.

When in 1949 John T. Flynn published his really damaging book *The Road Ahead*, containing the assertions that American Protestantism was riddled with socialist tendencies and leaders, specifically, Oxnam, Oxnam wrote the author a five-page, single-spaced letter defending himself, the denominations, the Federal Council, and the World Council. The letter opens, "It is my desire to give you opportunity to make proper correction in subsequent editions of your book. I do not wish to be forced to take the necessary steps to protect my reputation, since I believe that you as a gentleman and an American will wish to record the truth rather than to misrepresent me." Flynn may or may not have been a gentleman, but he was no sissy, for the veiled threat of a libel suit left him unmoved. In his reply he reiterated that he had not called Oxnam a Communist but he had named him a Socialist—and you, sir, are a Socialist! "I do not pretend to know anything about theology beyond the simple chronicles and beliefs of the ordinary Christian. But I do know socialism, its history and its authorities. And I know a Socialist when I see one by whatever name he may call himself." Oxnam then personally spoke to conservative acquaintances who were distributing the book to straighten them out. Oxnam also had a major hand in drafting the April 1950 resolution from the Council of Bishops, printed and widely distributed, condemning the book. Unsurprisingly, Flynn remained unrepentant, bringing out a booklet entitled "John T. Flynn Replies to His Critics," in which Oxnam is again sent to bed without his supper.

Hard on the heels of Flynn's book there appeared the more directly harmful article by Stanley High, "Methodism's Pink Fringe," its contents being broadcast by the press in advance of its February 1950 publication in *Reader's Digest*. This was serious business for the Church. Oxnam on January 24 wired his episcopal colleagues suggesting that the Council of Bishops either authorize the executive committee to make immediate reply or that the council issue a rejoinder at its next scheduled meeting in April. A disturbing number of bishops, especially from the South, answered that High was exposing the Methodist Federation for Social Action, not attacking The Methodist Church itself, and therefore no response was necessary or that if the council did respond in April that the reply limit itself to underscoring the unofficial nature of the Federation. As we know, the council did pass a resolution in April weaker than Oxnam (or Professor Brightman) wished, but stronger than the original intent of the conservative bishops.

Then Oxnam (with the assistance of Charles Parlin) prepared a twelve-page "gentle rejoinder" in the hopes of publication in *Reader's Digest*. When the magazine declined to oblige, the material was published and widely distributed in pamphlet form under the title, "The Reply The Reader's Digest Refused To Publish" accompanied by a statement by Ralph Diffendorfer. Here Oxnam was at his polemic peak. The Methodist Church was magnificently absolved and in the process extolled for its democratic structure and devotion to the principle of freedom of thought for individual Methodists. The brief closed: "Methodists are happy to allow Mr. High to think. They suggest he do so."

In the "Reply," Oxnam had slyly alerted the readers to High's youthful leftist leanings, quoting from his writings and citing his activities. More was to come. On May 23 the bishop and the *Digest* editor lunched together at High's suggestion, the two men having known each other in a friendly way since High's seminary days at BU School of Theology. Although there was no meeting of the minds, they left the University Club in the "friendliest of moods" and shared a cab. During the ride Oxnam said: "You know, of course, Stanley, that you're quite vulnerable, and you may not know that I have received many communications from ladies who question you somewhat from the standpoint of conduct." "Yes, I know all of it's true," sighed the married man. But High hastily explained, he did not approach women "as a cave man," they threw themselves at him. What was a poor man to do? The bishop then assured his companion, "Of course, we never use matters of this kind. We never stoop to references of this kind, but many don't like to have you moralizing in public." Oxnam's diary account of the meeting rejoices, "My objective was to keep him from writing anything further, and I think I was successful."

J. B. Matthews, author of "Reds and Our Churches" in the July 1953 issue of *American Mercury*, was a third inquisitor to earn Oxnam's wrath. Gardner Cowles, president and editor of *Look*, recognizing a hot subject when he saw one, invited Matthews, Reinhold Niebuhr, and Oxnam to contribute statements on "Communism and the Protestant Clergy" to the November 17, 1953 issue of his magazine. Matthews repeated his *Mercury* charges. Niebuhr conceded more than he need have. ("The fact that innocent men are suspected of guilt does not make guilty men innocent," and "Matthews, who is comparatively unscrupulous in handling total figures, is reasonably accurate when he actually names names.") [21] Oxnam's statement, heavily dependent on the researches of Francis Harmon, also made too many concessions; nevertheless, it was not as waffling as Niebuhr's. A Letter to the Editor in a subsequent issue of *Look* carried the fair decision, "It was unfair to permit Dr. Niebuhr to kick Dr. Matthews after Bishop Oxnam had knocked Dr. Matthews out."

When in 1954 the respected Baptist leader Daniel A. Poling asserted in the pages of the *Saturday Evening Post* that Protestant clergymen were citizens too, as accountable for their loyalty as other Americans, and some were fellow travelers, the *Post* invited three churchmen to reply. Methodist Bishop Corson's statement temporized. Reinhold Niebuhr's comment was typically Niebuhrian—that is, ambiguous. Only Oxnam's comment was a strong condemnation of the "pilloring" methods and "below-the-belt punching" and "accusation is accepted as conviction" logic of the Red-hunters.

That Senator McCarthy was a cause of concern to Oxnam is evidenced by the seven folders of McCarthy materials in the Oxnam Collection. Up and down the land, in articles, speeches, and press comments, the bishop characterized the senator as a "clown and a bully." He urged the Washington Area Methodist ministers to inform themselves of McCarthy's dangerous shenanigans.[22] He corresponded with Senator William Benton urging a Senate censure of McCarthy. After the Senate so acted, Oxnam informed the press, "I think all one needs to say about Senator McCarthy is that he is smart enough to know when he is finished, but too stupid to admit it."

Even before McCarthy had appeared on the national scene in February 1950, Oxnam had expressed his concerns over the erosion of civil liberties. In January 1948 he joined in cautioning Seth Richardson, the first chairman of the Loyalty Review Board (established as part of Truman's new loyalty program in 1947 by Executive Order 9835) to exercise the "utmost care" to prevent injustices in the government's loyalty check. In 1948 Oxnam criticized the California legislature's infamous Tenney Committee. When President Truman vetoed the 1950 Internal Security Act, Oxnam wrote the president's secretary,

"All of us rejoice in the care exercised by the President in the preservation of our civil liberties, and in light of his fuller knowledge of the dangers that lie in this bill, may I simply say I am very happy he had the courage to veto it." When Congress passed the measure over Truman's veto, Oxnam publicly termed the action "asinine"; "You cannot fight totalitarianism with measures of a totalitarian nature." In 1952 Congress passed still another dangerous law. Said Oxnam to the press: "The good in the McCarran-Walter Immigration and Nationality Law is submerged in bad philosophy, archaic provisions, and un-American procedures." [23]

The good truth is that not many liberals in this age of suspicion dared to employ, on occasion, the lacerating language of the Methodist bishop. Three illustrations from many:

> Men who declare that in every little red schoolhouse there is a little red teacher, bear false witness that is well nigh treason. There is no more patriotic body of men and women in the nation than the public school teachers in America.

> The vermillion-vigilante must go. I say *vermillion* both because this vigilante does the work of the red, and because there is so much yellow in his makeup the colors mix and become vermillion. . . . The vigilante is forerunner to the police state. Americans who will gladly die to preserve freedom and to destroy every attempt to extend the police state of Russia, will do well to see these vigilantes for what they are, the *vermillions*, or to abbreviate, the vermin, whose red we abhor and whose yellow we disdain.

> A new breed of self-appointed un-American vigilantes threatens our freedom. Profaning our American traditions and desecrating our flag, masquerading as defenders of our country against the infiltration of communism and the aggression of Russia, they play the red game of setting American against American, of creating distrust and division, and of turning us from the problems that must be solved in order to become impregnable. These vigilantes produce hysteria, prepare sucker lists, and live upon the generous contributions of the fearful. They exploit the uninformed patriot. They profiteer in patriotism. These vigilantes do not carry the noosed rope, but they lynch by libel. They prepare their lying spider-web charts. They threaten educators and ministers, actors and broadcasters. Unthinking boards and commissions bow to their tyranny, forgetting that to appease these forerunners of Hitler, of Mussolini, and of Stalin is to jeopardize freedom, and to prepare the wrists for the shackles and the mouth for the gag. In the name of law, vigilantes break the law.

Another chapter would be required to relate the response of the Federal Council of Churches and then the National Council of Churches to the charges that these bodies were infected with socialism and soft on communism, but this important story must be left to other historians. Suffice to say here that the documentation is mountainous that Oxnam played a major role in defending the good names of these councils to which he had given so much of himself.

---

[1] In 1947 the name was changed to the Methodist Federation for Social Action.

[2] Although seven thousand sets were published at a cost of twenty thousand dollars, the full committee membership deemed Appendix IX irresponsible, expunged it from the record, and ordered the existing copies destroyed. Appendix IX was immediately removed from the Library of Congress and government document rooms. A few sets, however, had already been sold to private subscribers and government agencies. In the summer of 1953 I examined the document in the offices of the House Un-American Activities Committee. I also obtained for my personal library the HUAC publication *Guide to Subversive Organizations and Publications*, 1951 edition.

[3] At issue was less the infinitesimal number of actual clerical card-carrying members of the Communist Party (a meaningless distinction in any case) than those individuals judged to be "pinkos," "Soviet apologists," "fellow travelers." The famous Kirby Page poll of 1934 disclosed that out of 20,000 ministers who responded, only 123 favored the establishment of communism in America as defined as that in "Soviet Russia and as represented by the Communist Party in the United States." A poll conducted the following year by the Religion and Labor Foundation found only 36 of 5,000 ministers saying they would actively support the Communist Party. The closest student of communism and the churches, Ralph Lord Roy, himself a Methodist minister, gave as his considered judgment that perhaps as few as 50, perhaps as many as 200, Protestant ministers actually joined the Communist Party. Even if Roy is correct, it might be observed that this handful joined—if indeed they did—during the Depression or during the war, when the United States and the Soviet Union were allied. This was before the government, upheld by the courts, virtually decreed that mere membership was a crime and before the Communist Control Act of 1954 declared the Communist Party an illegal conspiracy. Even so, North Carolinian Junius Scales was the only American ever convicted simply for being a member of the Communist Party. To repeat, the crux of the matter was "fellow traveling," however spaciously defined. At the close of World War II the CPUSA enrolled about 80,000 members. Most certainly churchmen were not commissars in it.

[4] On January 9, 1954, Philbrick requested a meeting with Oxnam. The occasion was not unpleasant, the bishop finding the young man naïve, uneducated, uninformed, but nice: "Down underneath, I really liked Philbrick."

[5] The book delighted some Roman Catholics, but, happily, not the great Monsignor George G. Higgins who tagged it "the most emotional, illogical, inaccurate and probably even libelous book which we have ever been foolish enough to purchase."

[6] In 1952 Smith had brought charges against Oxnam before the New York East Annual Conference. A Committee of Investigation failed to recommend a trial and the investigation was closed.

[7] My memory runs back to the period 1951–56 when I was a young instructor, without tenure, at a university in Texas. My office mate, a senior professor in the Education Department, was turning into the local FBI office the names of his students he deemed to be radicals. This professor was a good, decent fellow who honestly believed he was

performing his patriotic duty. Ironically, at the same time conservative students were reporting to the Texas legislature the names of their professors whom they judged to be leftists. The owner and editor of the local newspaper, for whom I weekly reviewed books without fee, informed my departmental chairman that Robert Moats Miller was a fellow traveler because I had favorably reviewed a book by Kenneth Scott Latourette, and Senators McCarthy and McCarran had charged Latourette with being pro-Communist. Ergo, Miller must be pro-Communist, too. My job hung in the balance. Latourette, of course, was both past president of the American Historical Association and of the Southern Baptist Convention and a distinguished historian of Christian missions. It was a surreal time!

[8] Marshall's most eminent biographer makes no mention of the award so we have only Oxnam's word that it was rejected by Marshall because of conservative and Catholic pressure.

[9] Oxnam had no way of knowing that Hoover favored as FBI agents Roman Catholics, especially graduates of such schools as Notre Dame. Hoover believed their anti-communism to be axiomatic.

[10] If ever the term "poetic justice" is appropriate, it is so in regard to the American Communists and the Smith Act. During the war they had applauded the government's use of the act to prosecute their enemies: the Trotskyist Social Workers Party and assorted demifascist individuals such as Elizabeth Dilling. Then the sword of the Smith Act fell on them.

[11] Hoover's information on the private lives of individuals in and out of government is notorious, including the Kennedys and Dr. Martin Luther King, Jr. The potential for political blackmail was widely, if silently, recognized.

[12] p. 84. O'Reilly bases this assertion on a spot check of the Oxnam Collection in the Library of Congress but not on an examination of the FBI file on Oxnam. I not only believe the term "surveillance" is too loose to describe the bureau's tab-keeping on Oxnam, I am positive that O'Reilly is wrong to state that Oxnam was a "bona fide fellow traveler during the 1930s" and I am certain that he is mistaken to say that the bureau "may have arranged (without Oxnam's knowledge or consent) his later testimony before HUAC."

[13] Here and henceforth when in the copies of the FBI file on Oxnam I received a name has been blanked out, I have supplied it only when I was 100 percent positive that it was the correct name.

[14] Nichols, a Methodist layman, joined the bureau in 1934, rose to the position of assistant director in 1942, and in 1951 was named one of two assistants to the director. He was the bureau's liaison with conservative congressmen and reporters and a public relations man par excellence. He was devoted to his chief, naming his first child after Hoover. When Nichols left the bureau in 1957, he persuaded his new employer, Schenley Industries, to establish and endow the J. Edgar Hoover Foundation. Thereafter, and at a reported salary of $100,000 a year, this good Methodist served Schenley officially and the FBI unofficially as a lobbyist in Washington.

[15] Cameron's name, of course, is deleted from the FBI file I received, but, of course, the individual is Cameron.

[16] According to Victor S. Navasky in his *Naming Names*, Cameron was forced out of his job at Little, Brown in 1951 less because of the undeniable political coloration of his list than because of his well-known leftist politics and his refusal to ratify the rituals of the various committees which subpoenaed him. In fact, in 1953 Cameron declined on constitutional grounds to tell whether he was or was not a member of the Communist Party. Former Communist Party member Joseph Starobin in his *American Communism in Crisis, 1943–1957*, states that Cameron was not a Party member and not even close to the Party. To this day, some former DePauw students are angry at Professor Arthur M. Schlesinger, Jr., for allegedly using his clout in securing Cameron's forced resignation from Little, Brown; others believe (without documentary proof) that Cameron was a Communist; and still others hold the fantastic notion that he was an FBI undercover

agent! After his departure from Little, Brown, he joined with Albert E. Kahn to form the progressive publishing company Kahn & Cameron, and then in 1959 he accepted an invitation to become senior editor at Alfred A. Knopf, a signal honor surely indicative of his skill and loyalty.

[17] As a matter of fact, as early as 1920 the liberal Methodist leader Worth M. Tippy resigned from the Federation, explaining to Bishop McConnell: "The program outlined by Dr. Ward on Monday appears to me to be fraught with danger to the Federation, to the Methodist church and to society; and to be based upon a mistaken estimate of the outcome of the present industrial and political movement. Dr. Ward's program is the one to follow if the revolution is wise and desirable, but not otherwise."

[18] However, as late as 1945 Oxnam's *personal* letters to Ward remained flattering. "Through the years," read one dated December 17, "I have treasured every word I have received from you. You cannot know how much I appreciate your letter of November 20th which was awaiting me upon my return from Germany. . . . Some of these days, I trust in the not too distant future, I hope I may have the privilege of chatting with you for an hour. I would like to see several important issues through your eyes."

[19] I have in an off-and-on fashion since 1950 studied Ward's life and the destiny of the Federation and in three earlier books I have set forth my judgments. A recent (1984) biography of Ward by Eugene P. Link has not changed my mind. Link, a Methodist minister and former Ward student at Union Theological Seminary, views Ward as the peerless knight, *sans puer et sans reproche*. I respect the Reverend Link and his transparent ethical passion and in our conversations about Ward I hope we have disagreed without being disagreeable. (He certainly was always courteous.) Nevertheless, I am not persuaded by his biography that I have been unjust to Ward. What is one to think when he quotes Communist Elizabeth Gurley Flynn, "He [Ward] was fearless in defense of communists and *was ever a friend of the Soviet Union*"? (emphasis added.) What is one to make of this passage: "Church attendance was not among the rituals of Ward's life. Granddaughter Robin Ward Savage asked him, 'Do you go to church?' 'No,' was the quick response, 'I only go when I am giving the sermon.' 'Why?' she pressed, and that brought the reply, 'Because it is often too dull and boring.' *His dislike for trivia, pomp, and escapism surfaced in many ways*" (emphasis added). And: "Then Ward attacked the deficiencies of the social-gospel movement again as *stressing too much church worship and theology, saying these were escapes* that have prevented the proclaiming of a social message in this tragic moment in history" (emphasis added). In my view, it is sad that these words written by a Methodist minister about a Methodist minister are intended to be complimentary.

[20] When Muelder asked aged, retired Bishop McConnell why he did not repudiate McMichael, the answer given was twofold: "I've never been a party to firing a liberal Methodist," and "You have to have a screwball to get the job done." According to a memo in the Oxnam Collection based on a phone call to Dr. Dorothy McConnell, Mrs. McConnell dubbed McMichael "P.B."—the Pesky Boy; and she was aggravated that McMichael was causing her eighty-year-old husband such torment. Dr. Dorothy McConnell, the daughter, agreed with her mother and wished to goodness that McMichael would resign from the Federation. Incidentally, Dr. McConnell did not personally like Harry F. Ward, believing him to be autocratic and abusive, especially of the women, such as Deaconess Chappell, who worked under him. Having said all this, it is important to know that Bishop McConnell wrote a lengthy defense of the Federation appearing in *The Christian Advocate*, November 2, 1950. He may have been eighty, but the statement shows an alert mind and sharp pen at work.

[21] Niebuhr apologized, as he should have, to Guy Emery Shipler, editor of the *Churchman*, for indirectly but clearly naming him a fellow traveler.

[22] Alas, the same episcopal letter included the silly suggestion: "By the way, have you written Mr. Dulles and the President a note of appreciation for their courageous refusal to tolerate Senator McCarthy's attempts to substitute a 'Big Bully' policy in foreign

affairs for the dignified and fruitful 'Good Neighbor' policy. Leaders are often lonely men and a word from a parsonage home means much."

[23] This criticism hardly endeared Oxnam to Representative Walter, a matter of some consequence because he was a member of HUAC.

CHAPTER 27

CALLING THE HOUSE UN-AMERICAN ACTIVITIES COMMITTEE TO ACCOUNT

In calling the House Un-American Activities Committee to account, Oxnam was not tickling a tabby cat. To be sure, the old Special Committee on Un-American Activities, the Dies Committee, had pretty much petered out during the war as the United States and Russia confronted a common foe and when American Communists pressed the war against fascism as furiously as the most fervent patriots. Then in January 1945, Representative John E. Rankin, that troglodyte Democrat from Mississippi (Dies, of course, also fits that description, though from Texas) rescued the almost defunct Special Committee. On his motion the House voted to make it a standing committee and the only permanent investigating committee in the House, enjoying unique subpoena powers, with its members free to sit on other standing committees. At the time, I. F. Stone warned that HUAC promised to be "the John the Baptist of American fascism"—as indeed it almost appeared to become.

As the Cold War intensified, as the committee seemingly went from triumph to triumph, especially in being responsible for sending the Hollywood Ten and Alger Hiss to prison, as committee members were rewarded by their constituencies with elevation to the Senate, as in the case of Karl Mundt and of Nixon, and in the latter case to the vice-presidency, its members had good reason to recall the emperor Ozymandias of Shelley's poem when he cried, "Look on my works, ye Mighty, and despair!" When the Eighty-third Congress met in January 1953, 185 of 221 House Republicans applied for membership to the committee. In February, the House, by 315 to 2, voted HUAC a record appropriation of three hundred thousand dollars. In the Eighty-third Congress (1953–54) there were authorized a record fifty-one investigations into Communism as House and Senate committees vied for publicity and public applause.

In January 1953 Harold H. Velde became chairman of the now Republican dominated (5-4) committee. This amiable former FBI agent from Illinois was neither as vicious as former chairman Dies or as venal as former chairman Thomas. He was, however, politically ambitious and not very bright—a dangerous combination. Witness his bill that would have required the Librarian of Congress to list the books in the library's collection that might be regarded as subversive and his proposal to institute a loyalty oath as a requirement for participation in national elections. Witness his charge that Mrs. Agnes Meyer, wife of the owner of the *Washington Post*, had in 1947 written a pro-Russian letter in a pro-Russian magazine, only to have it pointed out that the letter had in fact been written by a Mrs. Mayer, not Meyer, and she lived in Port Clements, B.C., not Washington, D.C. Witness the fiasco when he subpoenaed former President Truman, former Secretary of State Byrnes, and former Attorney General Tom Clark (and now associate justice of the Supreme Court), all of whom declined on constitutional grounds to testify before HUAC. Witness his reliance (like that of other committees) on professional "expert" witnesses who were as crooked as a dog's hind legs, such as Manning Johnson, who admitted he would lie under oath "if the interests of my government are at stake." And it was under Velde that HUAC began in earnest its investigations of suspect teachers and preachers.

Long before Velde chaired HUAC, Oxnam had tangled with the House's search for subversives. The Dies Committee was formed in 1938, and in that year it heard testimony identifying Oxnam with Communist groups and doubtless Dies received written warnings to that effect. Although Oxnam may have been unaware of this, nevertheless in 1943 he signed a petition calling for the abolition of the Dies Committee. Then he learned for a fact that as early as 1946 HUAC was releasing unverified raw materials in its file to private individuals and these materials were then broadcast by such groups as the American Legion and such individuals as Fulton Lewis, Jr. to "prove" Oxnam's fellow traveling. Protested Oxnam in 1951 to the then chairman of HUAC, John S. Wood: "The material released concerning me contains falsehoods, irrelevant statements, and statements of fact interspersed with expressions of opinion and in some cases accompanied by such vicious interpretation as to amount to false witness." Oxnam accompanied his protests with documentary evidence to support his innocence. The final letter to Wood closed: "I think it unnecessary to take more of your time in extended correspondence. Once again I make formal request of the committee to cease and desist from a practice that is contrary to all of the principles of our American tradition." Wood's feeble justification for any errors in Oxnam's file and their release to the public was that they were "not an attempt to misrepresent you."

Of course HUAC did not "cease and desist" from its unspeakable practices and therefore Oxnam properly continued his criticism of the committee in articles, addresses, and radio broadcasts. "The whole procedure must be reexamined," he informed an American University audience on February 24, 1953. "There isn't a man in this country who cannot be ruined overnight by the kind of procedures followed, wherein a lie is released by a responsible committee and given wide publicity." In that month he delivered another address entitled "The Christian Church and the Threat to Freedom." In it he mentioned by name Velde and McCarthy among the "clowns," "bullies," and "busybodies" who through their "abuses" and "incompetency" were dividing the nation. "The 'investigatism' plague is a disease that is paralyzing the normal activities of the government." The procedures of HUAC "constitute a threat to freedom" and "some members of this committee appear to capitalize upon hysteria for political advantage." When HUAC member Kit Clardy was asked if he knew that many Methodists did not agree with Oxnam, he prayerfully replied, "If that isn't so, then God save the United States."

Clardy was not the only member of HUAC to feel the stings of the bishop's barbs and not the only one to change his mind regarding Velde's hint in early March that the committee might turn to the investigation of individual churchmen. The die was cast when on March 17 Republican Representative Donald L. Jackson of California, an individual more ruthless and stronger-willed than Velde, arose on the floor of the House to unburden himself. Midway in the oration Jackson uttered the words making war irrepressible. After identifying Oxnam as "a gentleman who now presumes to criticize the work of your House committee in its investigations of identified Communists," the Californian continued:

> Bishop Bromley has been to the Communist front what Man O' War was to thoroughbred horse racing, and no one except the good bishop pays much attention to his fulminations these days. Having served God on Sunday and the Communist front for the balance of the week, over such a long period of time, it is no great wonder that the bishop sees an investigating committee in every vestry. If reprinting Bishop Oxnam's record of aid and comfort to the Communist front would serve any useful purpose, I would ask permission to insert it here, but suffice it to say that the record is available to any Member who cares to request it from the committee.

Jackson pledged to support Velde's earlier call for an investigation of individual churchmen, not, he promised, for a "blunderbuss, overall investigation of any church, any creed, or any denomination." (It is not to accuse Jackson of cowardice to merely note that he could not be sued for libel for any words he uttered on the floor of the House.)

As Jackson sat down, the members of the House of both parties (presumably including at least some of the ninety Methodist members) rose to give him the greatest ovation received by any member during that session of Congress, an ovation Jackson naturally found "heartwarming" and the "greatest tribute" a Representative can receive, as he informed the press. He then reported being flooded with supporting telegrams from all sections of the country.

Oxnam immediately released to the press a rejoinder: "Congressman Jackson should know that there is no Congressional immunity from the Biblical injunction, 'Thou shalt not bear false witness.' It is to be regretted that he should have used the floor of the House to broadcast a lie. When the Committee on Un-American Activities releases falsehoods and rumor which it admits it has not investigated and which does not represent a conclusion or judgment of the committee and does so to silence criticism it becomes a party to slander and justifies the mounting nation-wide criticism of its methods." To his diary Oxnam confided, "If some of these men have become so vicious that they now wish to attack an individual in this fashion, it may be necessary to let them know what it is going to cost. Methodism happens to be an organization of some power, too. These Republicans seem to be mad."

If Jackson had his cheering section, Oxnam also had champions. Immediately he, too, was flooded with supporting telegrams, letters, and phone calls from Methodist and National Council leaders and "just folks." Newscasters of the stature of Elmer Davis and Edward R. Morrow and newspapers of the reputation of the *Washington Post* and *Christian Science Monitor* came to his defense. Oxnam was grateful for the assurance that he did not stand alone, especially when he was alerted by a Methodist laywoman of the reply given by Representative Leslie Arends, Republican Whip of the House, to her question, "What are you going to do about this vicious attack upon Bishop Oxnam?" "We are going to do nothing," said Arends. "We are going to cut that bishop down to his proper size."

The most important of Oxnam's immediate defenders proved to be the *Washington Post*. On March 19 Jackson declined to supply the *Post* with the committee's file on Oxnam, reneging on the offer made in his speech on the seventeenth, explaining that "the detailed documentation is very voluminous and would be much too lengthy to include in a letter of this kind." The *Post*, using its investigative resources, somehow managed to obtain the file, and on March 23 J. R. Wiggins, managing editor of the newspaper, came to Oxnam's office, file in hand. Reading it, Oxnam was rightly outraged. The editor then proposed that the *Post* print the file with its twenty-four charges together with the bishop's comment on each. Oxnam slaved preparing his rebuttal ("It is like being caught in flypaper"), and the April 5 issue of the *Post* prominently featured the material. One-by-one HUAC's charges were refuted, thanks primarily to Oxnam's habit of having preserved in his own massive files documentation extending back decades. Editorialized the *Post* in that issue:

> The *Washington Post* published today a calm, factual, detailed analysis by Bishop G. Bromley Oxnam of a dossier on himself in the files of the House Committee on Un-American Activities. Bishop's point-by-point refutation of the accusations, innuendos, and insinuations contained in the dossier, his exposure of its slovenliness and downright fraudulence, reveal a dangerous sort of evil which the House of Representatives ought not to countenance. What is a committee of Congress doing with a compilation of this sort of groundless gossip about a distinguished minister of religion? Read Bishop Oxnam's full statement. . . . The committee apparently regards as "subversive" any opinion of which it disapproves. The dossier complied on Bishop Oxnam is the kind of dossier compiled by the political police behind the Iron Curtain. It does not represent investigation; it represents a naked and ugly attempt at intimidation.

This *Post* story is important not only in itself but also because the Council of Bishops requested that the full seven pages be reprinted in *The Christian Advocate* and because it was picked up by other church and secular publications across the land and because the respected Unitarian Beacon Press in June used it as a basis for its widely distributed booklet "Bishop Oxnam and the Un-American Activities Committee."

On Sunday, April 26, HUAC received another cuffing when Oxnam and Jackson accepted invitations from NBC's American Forum of the Air to debate the subject, "Is Criticism of the House Un-American Activities Committee Methods Justified?" with Frank Blair as moderator. Oxnam believed he shredded Jackson, later noting in his diary the congressman's apparent nervousness, "wiping his forehead and drinking water" and generally being "flabbergasted." An "avalanche of mail" informed the bishop that he had won the debate hands down. The transcript of the radio and television debate supports that decision. After the program Oxnam suggested to Jackson that he was misunderstood and that the two men should have a good chat. The congressman agreed, saying he would soon run over to the Methodist Building. "It is too much to hope he will apologize, but we will have a try at it," reads the final diary entry for the day.

Naturally Jackson never apologized. The belief that HUAC was the injured party in the controversy is clearly expressed in a series of letters between Kit Clardy and a Methodist minister, Marcius Tiber, in May. All the publicity concerning the bishop originated with him, Representative Clardy explained. It was

Oxnam, not the committee, which made his full file public—a reference to the *Post* article. In fact, "the Committee did not 'go after' the Bishop or make any charges against him as you seem to think. It did not 'release' anything about him. [This was an untruth.] But the Bishop in a most unchristian manner has been guilty of smearing this committee since its inception. Are we supposed to remain silent under its continued venomous attack?" Clardy closed the correspondence with the observation: "The Bishop lacks a spirit of Christian charity insofar as this Committee is concerned. He can see no good in any committee investigating subversive activities. He has a right to this viewpoint. But he should not object if the members of his own church rise up in indignation. And, believe me, my mail shows that he does not represent the true spirit of the Methodist Church."

Meanwhile, since March 6 Oxnam had been seeking a negotiated redress of grievances with Velde that would obviate the necessity of a hearing before the full committee. The correspondence between the two men makes clear that Oxnam, pugnacious though he was, was not spoiling for a fight. On that date Oxnam wrote Velde requesting a personal conference. The letter emphasized Oxnam's sympathy with the committee's efforts to expose communism; only its methods were questioned. "I think it would be mutually advantageous," the letter concluded, "for us to meet each other and at least to understand the other's points of view." Velde replied on the thirteenth: "Certainly, I would be most happy to meet with you. However, I feel that such a meeting, if ex-officio, would be of little value in clarifying certain problems raised in your letter. I definitely feel that if there is any error or unjust information contained in the files . . . , relating to you, you should have the opportunity that the Committee affords to any individual to correct, clarify or rectify this material. I definitely feel that such information given under oath before myself and other members of the Committee would be incorporated in our records and insure against any misinformation being disseminated as you mentioned." On the nineteenth Oxnam responded. He still hoped for an informal interview with Velde alone. "I do not care to appear before the Committee as a witness if the appearance in any way assumes that my patriotism is in question. It is not my patriotism that is involved, but rather the practice of a Committee that cuts right across fundamental American principles." However, if Velde wished other committee members present at an *informal* meeting, that would be acceptable.

Meanwhile, Oxnam was being warned by Wiggins of the *Post* and others to prepare himself should a formal, full hearing be necessary. A diary entry reveals his growing concern: "I presided at the meeting of the Commission on Chaplains all day. It is hard to give hours when under such pressure. I am trying to get all the files ready so that in the event I ever have a run in with the House Committee on Un-American Activities we can settle the matter for once and for all."

On April 16 Velde invited Oxnam to a private, informal meeting, and on the twenty-second the two men conferred for over an hour. The affair went so pleasantly that Oxnam pocketed the statement he had prepared for the press and suggested that he and Velde issue a joint statement. After all, the nation was informed, the congressman was a staunch Methodist, and the bishop was, after all, his bishop. After all, the churches in teaching theism were striking a mortal blow at atheistic communism. Finally, if Oxnam wished to draft a list of committee procedural reforms Velde would submit them to the committee for consideration. In letters to friends Oxnam affirmed the affability of the meeting and the hope that "substantial good will result." The diary entry for the twenty-second closes, "I think we have made substantial progress. I may be naive." He was.

On May 5 Oxnam submitted four reforms, actually ones prepared by five National Council of Churches leaders. Oxnam (as he reported to David Lilienthal) felt a chill when he read Velde's cool acknowledgement: "I will take this matter up with the other members of the Committee in Executive Session, along with the criticism and suggestions made by other American citizens. I want you to know, Bishop, that your suggestions and criticism will be given the same consideration as the suggestion and criticism of any other American citizen." Small comfort this!

During the Oxnam-Jackson American Forum of the Air debate on April 26 the congressman had piously intoned that "in the case of any citizen who feels that he has come under public censure as a result of House Committee action, he has redress before the greatest forum, I believe, in the entire world, the forum of the Congress of the United States. Before its committees he can answer any allegations and refute any charges which he feels are not founded in fact." Oxnam may have won the debate by any objective standard, but Jackson's challenge left the bishop with no further room to maneuver. To save his reputation, defend his Church, and protect the liberties of all Americans he now virtually had to wire Velde on June 5: "Respectfully request opportunity to be heard by your committee to answer false allegations regarding me appearing in your files and released by your Committee. Please advise when I may be heard." A number of telegrams, letters, and meetings with HUAC's newly hired counsel, Robert L. Kunzig, followed.

The date was set for July 21 without disagreement. Also uncontested was the televising of the hearing. However, two matters were contested and Oxnam won both. Having lost all faith in the fairness of the committee, even in Methodist Velde (and never having had any faith in the likes of Jackson and Clardy), he insisted on an open, rather than a closed, hearing in order that what transpired would be public knowledge. And he insisted on the right to make an unchallenged preliminary statement. During the weeks preceding July 21 Oxnam wondered as to the wisdom of requesting a hearing. The two individuals who most influenced his decision to do so were Mr. Wiggins of the *Post* and Ruth.

Oxnam's uncommitted hours preceding the hearing were spent in preparation for the ordeal. His diaries fairly scream with the frustration of pouring over old records in an attempt to second-guess the committee's line of questioning. Fortunately, such friendly newsmen as Eric Sevareid, Martin Agronsky, and Elmer Davis warned him of HUAC's ruthless methods. Happily, Patrick Malin and other American Civil Liberties Union officers offered oral advice and supplied him with materials which he found "extraordinarily helpful." The greatest assist came from his friend Parlin, whose conservative partners at the powerful New York law firm of Shearman and Sterling granted him time off to help prepare Oxnam's defense, believing a precious principle at stake. Parlin quickly discovered that the committee operated by its own rules. He tried to obtain without success a list of the items on which his client would be questioned. Nor could he pry loose a specification of charges. "Bishop Oxnam and I were forced to go to the hearing room completely in the dark," he later recalled, to face "for rough techniques . . . a new mark for my thirty-one years out of Harvard Law School." Parlin did his best and it was not bad. He had the sharpest young members of Shearman and Sterling comb files of the *Daily Worker* on the Left to fundamentalist church journals on the Right for references to Oxnam. He had these junior lawyers pound the bishop with questions the committee members might ask. "That's a dirty one!" Oxnam once exclaimed. "Yes," agreed Parlin, "and that's what you can expect."

On the evening of June 24 God again demonstrated that he moves in mysterious ways, his wonders to perform. Representative Jackson was at the National Press Club bar knocking back a few. A reporter, the respected Frank Hewlett (a Catholic, as it happens), overheard the boozed-up Jackson boast that his committee was going to nail Oxnam by springing revelations of his un-American, pro-Communist activities dating back to the 1930s and 1920s DePauw years, and worse, back to the early 1920s Church of All Nations period. Hewlett passed the word to his office mate Glen D. Everett, a reporter for the Religious News Service. The next day Everett scurried to Oxnam's office, persuaded the formidable Christine Knudsen that he was there not to get but to give an important story to her boss, and the reporter was given the opportunity to alert the bishop. Oxnam could scarcely credit what he heard. Surely, Velde, a fellow Methodist, would not stoop so low. Yes he would, insisted the battle-scarred reporter, and besides Velde could not control Jackson and the rest of the scurvy HUAC crew. Oxnam then informed Parlin and Parlin agreed with Everett. If Jackson had been a teetotaler it is entirely possible that when Oxnam came to the hearing his bulging brief cases would not have contained his files for those early years—and the consequences for him might have been near-fatal.

What happened that fateful July 21 has been related by Oxnam in his book *I Protest*. The transcript of the hearing was conveniently published in full in the August 7 issue of *U.S. News and World Report* for those interested individuals who did not wish to wait for its official publication by the United States Government Printing Office in 1954. Major newspapers such as the *Washington Post* and *New York Times* carried substantial extracts. A taped recording of the hearing is available.[1] Here, only a few specific points will be noted, leaving to the next chapter a general assessment of the entire hearing. Some of these items have not before been revealed.

Item: The Committee on Un-American Activities met, pursuant to call, at 2:30 P.M. on July 21, in the Caucus Room, Old House Office Building. Present were nine members of the committee, five staff members, Oxnam and his counsel Parlin, media personnel, and over five hundred spectators (with many turned away), the largest crowd since Whittaker Chambers confronted Alger Hiss in the same room. The hearing was adjourned at 12:20 A.M., Wednesday, July 22. It was a long ordeal made only slightly less grueling by an hour dinner break and three briefer recesses to permit the committee members to return to the House for roll calls.

Item: Parlin, seated next to Oxnam, was not allowed to make any statement beyond giving his name, address, and the fact that he was a member of the New York bar. Moreover, the battery of microphones on the desk at which Oxnam was seated made it difficult for him to spread out his papers; the crowded conditions made it difficult to retrieve items from his brief cases; the bright klieg lights necessary for television were directly behind the elevated committee members and almost blinded him. HUAC counsel Kunzig repeatedly played the game of asking Oxnam a question and then using the question as an excuse to break in and read into the record large chunks of materials that were tangential or irrelevant to Oxnam's life. It was mightily frustrating. Nevertheless, Oxnam appeared to be "the coolest person in the room," in the judgment of the *New York Times* reporter.

Item: Although Representative Jackson had reserved front row seats for five representatives of the fundamentalist American Council of Churches, which had secured one hundred thousand signatures to a petition asking Congress to investigate radical clergy, actually the audience was overwhelmingly in Oxnam's corner. On four occasions Oxnam's rooters broke into jeers or cheers despite Chairman Velde's opening ban on demonstrations, banging the gavel, and orders to the marshall.

Item: Oxnam was permitted, as promised, to give an uninterrupted opening statement, although he found the allotted fifteen minutes far too few to do an adequate job.

Item: Chairman Velde initially accorded Oxnam cautious courtesy, and never in fact became truly venomous, but he did become prickly whenever Oxnam questioned the procedures of his committee.

Item: The only Roman Catholic member of the committee, Republican Bernard Kearney of New York, sat mute during the afternoon session and failed to appear for the evening session.

Item: Jackson was the bishop's toughest questioner, followed by Walter. The few words which Ohio Republican Gordon Scherer directed at the witness were strong with contempt.

Item: Republican Kit Clardy of Michigan got in the act, a reporter observing that a Republican congressman who wouldn't shut up for President Eisenhower wouldn't remain silent when the opportunity was presented to grill an HUAC critic. However, the newsman witnessed this scene during a hearing recess: "You big stiff," said Clardy, slapping the bishop fondly on the back, "why didn't you come up and see me when I told you to? We'd have straightened all of this out." Parlin recalled that after the hearing Clardy said to him, "You and the Bishop may think you're getting a rough deal but when you see him, give him my regards and tell him that I'm a good churchman, a member of————church." Parlin reported this to Oxnam and received the reply, "When you see Mr. Clardy give him my regards. Tell him that church passed out of existence by merger 23 years ago." (Clardy, and Scherer, too, later joined the John Birch Society.)

Item: When the committee sprang questions dating back to the 1920s, another reporter whispered to a colleague, "The next question will be pre-natal." As Oxnam adroitly fielded accusation after accusation dealing with the distant past, Jackson's face was observed to drop and drop.

Item: During the dinner break Walter treated himself to a preprandial martini or three, returning to the hearing obviously worse for the wear. "What a sight!" one newsman said to another. "A drunk congressman interrogating a Methodist bishop!"

Item: During the dinner hour Oxnam and Parlin hailed a cab to take them to a quiet restaurant for iced coffee and a sandwich. After their quick repast they luckily found an available cab waiting at the restaurant door to carry them back to the hearing. "Aren't you the fellow who brought us here," Parlin asked the young black cabbie. "Yes. I have been listening to my cab radio all day. I knew the Bishop had to be back by 8 P.M. so I waited; I thought you might need me."

Item: At approximately midnight, California Democrat Clyde Doyle, who had supported Oxnam, albeit within limits, throughout the hearing, moved "that the record show in these hearings that this committee has no record of any Communist Party affiliation or membership by Bishop Oxnam." The motion was seconded by Jackson (an indication of its emptiness) and passed unanimously. A second motion by Dole to have HUAC's files clearly state where Oxnam denied their accuracy was defeated 5-4 on a strict party line (an indication of the true feelings of the Republican members). In the closing minutes Oxnam and Clardy exchanged pleasantries, agreeing they would have a good talk on the bishop's return from Europe. Oxnam then turned to Velde, saying, "I would like to thank you personally for your courtesy throughout the day. I know at times I have talked at length. At no time have you rapped the gavel, and I appreciate it very much." Velde sighed that being a committee chairman was no easy task and hoped that the bishop was appreciative.[2] The bishop said he was. The two men then smiled at each other as they shook hands while the cameras clicked.

After adjournment as Bromley and Ruth waited for a car, the bishop turned to reporter Glen Everett and said in a dejected tone, "Tell me the truth. I did a rotten job, didn't I?" Everett replied, "You have struck a marvelous blow for American democracy" and then added as he pointed to the flag flying by the capitol steps, "Thank God, the Stars and Stripes are still flying."

Back at the apartment sleep would not come. Oxnam lay on the carpeted floor, his heart missing every fourth beat. Ruth urged that a doctor be called; that their trip abroad be cancelled. She feared that the strain of the hearing might prove fatal to her cherished husband's already overworked heart. As Oxnam lay on the floor, engulfed in an exhaustion he had not felt during the emotional high of the hearing, the rage he had repressed during the ordeal mounted. Had his strategy of remaining calm, unprovocative, rational, objective, respectful been wise, he now bitterly speculated? This is not to suggest that he made a passive witness. He was not. His voice was firm and clear and occasionally laced with emotion. On several instances the tartness of his wit brought applause from the audience and flushes to the faces of the committee. He did not permit himself to be bullied. It is to suggest that he kept his anger reined, did not engage in uncontrolled outbursts, did not resort to counterproductive name calling. His strategy may have been mistaken, but if so it was due to misjudgment, not to cowardice.

Morning came, the doctor uncalled, the trip still on. He now faced the aftermath of the most signal experience in his life.

---

[1] As noted in the bibliography, NBC televised the entire hearing in order to present a thirty-minute program consisting of clips of the highlights, but, alas, this television coverage is no longer to be found in NBC's archives.

[2] Such unctuousness was not confined to Velde. Groaned Clardy to Oxnam at one point, "We have sat here and taken abuse day after day and week after week and month after month and if you had gone through the fire and the furnace that we have you would understand what we have gone through."

CHAPTER 28

THE AFTERMATH OF THE HOUSE HEARING

Scarcely more than twenty-four hours after the adjournment of the hearing, the Oxnams departed for Europe to attend a meeting of the World Council. With his astonishing recuperative powers, Bromley managed to muster the energy to dictate a seven-page, typed, single-spaced letter to "My dear, dear Friends"—Area Methodist ministers and others— prior to the voyage. By the hour of the dictation his spirits had soared, buoyed up as they were by the widespread and overwhelmingly laudatory newspaper coverage of the hearing and by a torrent of supportive telegrams and phone calls. The letter reviewed in considerable detail his experience before HUAC. Although the letter closed with the suggestion that his friends communicate to Representative Doyle their appreciation of his fairness to Oxnam, its general tone was not irenic. Witness one passage:

> In these hearings, there is no real attempt to understand an individual's life or his contribution to a church or to country. The real purpose, it seems to me, of the technique of using citations which themselves are subject to serious question, is to prove an individual is guilty. Of course they say they are not a court, but an investigating body. I take it that is true. But the procedures are . . ."damnable." The Committee members can lecture you from the bench. They can state you were a "sucker." You can't answer back. Men whose intellectual qualifications in some fields are distinctly limited nevertheless sit there and lecture a representative of a church who is like a boxer going into a ring with his arms tied behind his back.[1]

Here Oxnam was echoing his opening statement at the hearing when he had pointed out the dangers of this "new and vicious expression of Ku Kluxism, in which an innocent person may be beaten by unknown assailants, who are cloaked in anonymity and at times immunity, and whose whips are cleverly constructed lists of so-called subversive organizations and whose floggings appear all too often to be sadistic in spirit rather than patriotic in spirit."

Oxnam was justified in finding comfort in the nationwide response to his ordeal. Hundreds of newspapers carried the story, often on their front page and often giving it a banner headline. The great papers had their own reporters at the hearing; the smaller ones generally relied on the wire service, especially Associated Press, for their stories. The stories were backed up with editorials, 80 percent of them favorable.[2] Without pausing to cite the names of the publications (and without the capitalization), a few representative cheers: "Bishop Oxnam victor for self and country"; "Red-hunters rapped"; "Oxnam strikes a blow for liberty"; "The bishop hit a mighty blow for decency in investigations"; "Bishop Oxnam renders valuable service to principles of Americanism and fair play"; "Millions of Americans must have asked themselves: What is the purpose of this inquisition and whither is it taking us as a nation?"; "Investigators take care!"; "The two-fisted counterattack by Bishop Oxnam on the House Un-American Committee points the way for that body to mend its ways and get on the right track"; "Despite appearances, it wasn't the bishop on trial. It was the committee, on trial before public opinion. And that trial is rapidly going against the committee"; "Bishop Oxnam had the facts and the courage to talk back to the committee"; "It is to be hoped the good bishop's vigorous replies to the committee will help clean up this practice of congressional sadism"; "The bishop proved resolute and strong enough to defeat his detractors, but it should never have been necessary to put him through such an ordeal"; "Oxnam is a rare individual with the mental skill, courage, personality and confidence required to combat a technique against which lesser men might falter and become afraid."

Columnist Doris Fleeson darkly observed, "For the first time in the history of the United States the church power has been called to account before the civil power for its political opinion." Columnist (and historian) Bruce Catton hopefully opined, "Perhaps some kind of corner has been turned at last. Not only was the House Committee on Un-American Activities forced to eat its words in the matter of Bishop G. Bromley Oxnam; it got laughed at to boot, with the mikes switched on, the cameras whirring, and the press tables jammed." The *Christian Century* held "that the committee fared so poorly in its encounter with the bishop that it has never recovered the prestige it lost when the truth came out as the nation looked and listened."

Radio newscasters were in Oxnam's corner, including such respected individuals as Charles Collingwood, William R. Stringer, Elmer Davis, and Eric Sevaried. Listeners to George Hamilton's ABC broadcast were informed, "Bishop Oxnam comported himself with dignity and calm and gave categorical answers to such specific questions as were propounded by the committee. It seemed to me that in every respect his testimony was explicit, straight-forward, and devastating to his critics." Martin Agronsky's commentary deserves extended quotation:

> A contemporary re-enactment of "Daniel in the Lion's Den" was successfully played out before the House Un-American Activities Committee in an extraordinary ten hour long day and night session. . . . The part of Daniel fell to the lot of Methodist Bishop G. Bromley Oxnam. And like his Biblical predecessor, the Bishop ended with the lions eating out of his hand. . . . Never for a moment during the long ten hour grind did the Bishop retreat an inch. . . . Rarely has the redoubtable House group, accustomed to being on the giving rather than the receiving end in the accusation business, received such a tongue lashing.

Oxnam did not need to rely solely on media coverage to sense that he had not witnessed in vain. The Oxnam Collection is choked with supporting letters, Official Board resolutions, Annual Conference resolutions, ministerial association resolutions and copies of communications of protest to Velde. On August 30 the Council or Bishops issued a statement which included the paragraph: "In recent weeks, one of our esteemed colleagues has been subjected to accusations that were untrue and by methods that were manifestly unjust. Bishop Oxnam needs no defense at our hands. These recent accusations and insinuations have been answered in detail by him through the press and over the radio and television, and his statements, clearly and forthrightly made, are convincing to all unbiased and fairminded men." Shortly the National Council of Churches' Committee on the Maintenance of American Freedom (which Oxnam had assisted in forming) let Velde know of its wrath. Council officer Cavert expressed to Oxnam the conviction: "I have no doubt that the way in which you stood up to the Committee . . . was the most important single incident in turning the tide against McCarthyism of the post-war era."

David Lilienthal flashed the message: "You did your country and your church a magnificent service, taking on an evil thing as you did. It was a most moving and manly picture, and may well prove to be an historic turning-point." The HUAC hearing, Princeton University President Harold W. Dodds later revealed to Oxnam, was a principal reason why Princeton bestowed upon him an honorary degree in 1954.

From Japan, Methodist Bishop Yoshimune Abe reported much interest in the hearing, closing, "Righteousness is not dead and is victorious." In Europe Bishop Berggrav informed Oxnam (at a World Council meeting) that he was "the hero of Norway." In Britain, France, and Germany, Oxnam learned, interest was also keen, leading him to ruminate: "These people see this in a way we do not. They see these Committees as the precursors of Hitlerism. They have been through this, and thus anybody who stands up to what they regard as a menace, not only to freedom but to themselves, is one they wish to commend. I can scarce believe the reaction."

Approbation was of course not universal. Some Roman Catholic papers and spokesmen, as chapter 22 noted, did not concede that Oxnam was cleared of the charges of fellow traveling. Conservative newspapers, such as the *Chicago Tribune*, observed that he "spent 10 hours defending a 20-year record of connections with Communist movements." Wrote Oxnam's nemesis, columnist Fulton Lewis, Jr., "He had been accused, widely, of being a vain and gullible old joiner, who lacked the precautionary responsibility to find out what he was lending his name to, before he lent it, and on that score he proved the case against himself in very conclusive fashion."

Surely more troubling to Oxnam were the questions raised by the non-Communist Left. I. F. Stone in his prickly *Weekly Letter* believed that in naming names Oxnam conceded too much to the committee, thereby giving "the witch hunt open season to the pulpit." Humanist and pacifist Milton Mayer in the *Progressive* charged, "To get the pack's fangs out of his neck, he threw Harry F. Ward to them—Harry Ward, that fighting old fool for Christ, who would have gone Communist or anywhere else his good heart led him." Asserted a writer in *The Nation:* "For clearing his own name, Bishop Oxnam let himself be induced to discuss two of his fellow ministers [Ward and McMichael] with the committee in such a way as to confirm its allegations regarding these men's 'subversive' attitudes" and that the bishop would be responsible if McMichael should have "to go to jail in the present inquisition." A. Powell Davies, the pastor of All Souls' (Unitarian) Church in Washington, in the pages of the *New Republic* praised Oxnam's gift of self-expression, dignity, courage, and patriotism. Nevertheless, Davies was concerned that a churchman of such high stature should have felt obliged to explain his actions to a Congressional committee. "He was not accountable to the committee for any of these actions; nor would he have been accountable for other alleged actions if the allegations had been true. He was accountable as to all these matters only to his own conscience and to his church." Martin Agronsky had earlier raised this same crucial point. In the end, Oxnam had salvaged his own reputation, but his was a special case. Agronsky continued, "Bishop Oxnam after all has behind him the great power of the Methodist church and it seems fair to wonder how many of those persons whose reputations are similarly and daily damaged by the committee's files, are capable of playing Daniel so courageously and skillfully to these contemporary Congressional Lions. It's not the Daniels who need the protection but those whose position is such that it is not in their power to force upon the Committee a special hearing such as was granted Bishop Oxnam."

A very few individuals communicated their reservations directly to Oxnam. Let one three-page, typed, single-spaced letter stand for several.[3] The correspondent informed Oxnam of her "dismay which deepened into acute nausea" as she read the transcript of the hearing in the *U.S. News and World Report.* "Most of your testimony was a verbal fugue on a recurrent theme: 'I am not—NOT—NOT—' a Communist." This "vain oblation" was none of the government's business. She gagged on reading Oxnam's explication of his spiritual convictions, "surely a work of supererogation since the sine qua non of your position as a Methodist Bishop should furnish more than tacit proof of your adherence to its theological tenets." She was shocked by his "failure sternly to rebuke its [the Committee] invitation to cooperation in the naming of names. And since the smallest taste of blood to a tiger excites a compulsive appetite for more, on your return from abroad the Committee will inevitably invite you to expatiate on their introduction of other names." Why was it necessary for Oxnam to justify his wartime positions on American-Soviet friendship by trotting out the names of General Eisenhower *et al?* "Dare to stand alone." As to Oxnam's identification of communism with atheism and Christianity as a bulwark against atheistic communism, was he unaware that "the world has known many avowed atheists and agnostics who have served their fellow-men worthily." Finally, she charged, the bishop's strictures on Communists, in America and Italy, "were a compendium of every canard now being circulated with such feverish industry."

Eighteen years later Eric Bentley in his *Thirty Years of Treason,* a documentary history of HUAC, returned to a troubling point when he judged "Bishop Oxnam was one of those who claimed to be more effective in their anti-Communism than HUAC, more royalist, as it were, than the king. Hence there is rivalry rather than true enmity in their confrontation." Bentley concluded that HUAC, being masters of a certain kind of showmanship, proved the victor. At the close of the hearing Oxnam thanked Velde; Velde wished the bishop Godspeed upon his journey abroad; the two men, beaming at each other, shook hands for the photographers; and Clardy reminded Oxnam about their anticipated "little private session" and Oxnam replied, "We will have a good time, and you told me you were Irish, and we will have a wonderful time."

A far more extensive and searching explication of this critical point was advanced by David E. Gillingham.[4] The thrust of

Gillingham's critique is the theological and intellectual bankruptcy and political naïveté of Oxnam's defensive position. Oxnam agreed so completely with the committee on the existence and peril of a Communist conspiracy and on the necessity of exposing this "disease," he had no substantive grounds on which to protest. He could only assert that the spiritual message of the churches was the more potent antitoxin to make the nation immune to the virus of Marxian materialism; that American values found their foundation in the Judeo-Christian tradition; that clergymen were as patriotic and as devoted to the splendid American way of life as congressmen; that his quarrel was not with the committee's right and need to investigate, but only with its methods; that all might be well if only HUAC accepted his proposed procedural reforms. As shall be seen momentarily, the reforms proved unacceptable and the unrepentant committee went on its merry way. In Gillingham's judgment, the crucial matter is not Oxnam's failure to secure procedural reforms but his positing the Church as the true defender of the American Faith during the Cold War at home and abroad. When on November 12, 1953, the Council of Bishops issued a Pastoral Letter, a perfect illustration was given of the pure popular piety required by the Cold War cult:

> Under God this nation grew and prospered, and if today it be great and strong, as nations are counted strong, we know that the greatest factor in bringing her preeminence has been not alone the multitudes brought here from other lands, not alone our resources, or our industrial skills, but the faith of our fathers. If we are to remain strong and discharge our obligations to the peoples of the earth we can best do so by renewing our faith. *A faith which will restore self-reliance, personal responsibility, a conscience about debts, a disinterested love of country so characteristic of those in our armed forces, and a determination to be satisfied with life's essentials.* (Emphasis added.)

Is *this* really the "faith" of the people called Methodists?

The surface cordiality of the last moments of the hearing quickly evaporated. It is true that Representative Morgan Moulder, Missouri Democrat, said, "After hearing and careful consideration of all the evidence, it is my opinion that Bishop Oxnam is not and never has been a Communist or a Communist sympathizer. On the contrary, he has convinced me that he has vigorously opposed Communism, and has fought hard against the philosophy and conditions which breed Communism. However, I do believe Bishop Oxnam to be a liberal, but not more so than Thomas Jefferson or Theodore Roosevelt. It is my opinion that he is a loyal American citizen and is intensely possessed with the spirit of God and the work of the church he serves." Congressman Doyle affirmed that "not one scintilla of evidence was presented to show that he was a Communist or willingly or knowingly a member of any Communist front." True enough, but also accurate is Jackson's explanation to the press that "no accusation of Communist Party membership had ever been leveled against the witness by any member of the Committee or its staff." How could the press conclude, Jackson wondered, that Oxnam was "cleared" of a charge never leveled against him? Over a year later, in seeking reelection (successfully) Jackson told his constituents that he intended to make his controversy with Oxnam a major issue in his campaign. Far from backtracking, Jackson maintained that "the hearing accorded the bishop . . . points up, in our opinion, the extent of aid and comfort lent by the 'pink' bishop to the Communist Party and its front organizations in this country since the 1920's."

Far from being contrite, Representative Walter asserted, "I think we demonstrated very clearly that the Communists are using well known and highly placed people willing and otherwise, as dupes and that the bigger the name, the better for their cause. I place Bishop Oxnam in that category." Representative Scherer, in an open letter to the Cincinnati *Enquirer*, set forth his interpretation of the hearing. It was Oxnam who demanded the hearing, desired it to be public, welcomed the television cameras, packed the audience with his Methodist supporters—who, Scherer recalled, during recesses verbally assaulted and villified him. Scherer claimed that he had opposed the hearing because he knew that "the Bishop's demand for this hearing was for the purpose of obtaining a forum to attack us, and not, as he claimed, to correct misinformation about him in the file." Representative Clardy admitted to the press his regret that he had voted for the Doyle motion for the motion was likely to be misunderstood by the public. While Oxnam was not a Party member he "had been made a sucker of by Communist and Communist-front groups." Velde stood by his position that

Oxnam had not been an effective fighter against Communism; that he "knowingly or unknowingly" had been associated with a number of Communist front groups; that he had been vociferous in his denunciations of HUAC; and that (!) his "concept of government . . . is not based on religion as should be expected from a Methodist Bishop, but rather on economic and political viewpoints." [5]

That left only Doyle out in left field, so to speak. But did it? Doyle's mental processes may be judged by the final paragraph in a cordial letter he wrote to Oxnam in reply to the bishop's letter of gratitude to him:

> When I was in Korea several months ago, and other places in the Far East, the unanimous reply to my inquiry made of top authorities in such matters, was that the military aggression in Korea by the Communists, was part and parcel of the same international conspiracy as exists in the United States of America and which is being carried on in America by subversive, un-American persons and programs, which would not be unwilling to stoop to the use of force and violence if needs be, in order to turn over all freedom loving peoples to totalitarian slavery in a Godless world.

Oxnam could not have quarreled with that statement because it was almost precisely his own belief.

Between the hearing in July 1953 and April 1954 a series of negotiations took place between Oxnam and his lawyer Parlin and Velde and HUAC counsel Kunzig concerning what would be in the official government transcript of the hearing. This tedious, dispiriting but unsurprising story need not long detain us. Oxnam's political innocence and his obtuseness about human nature once again revealed themselves. Even the shrewd Wall Street lawyer Parlin might have benefited from a tincture of Calvinist understanding of man's depravity. How could they possibly continue to place hope in the committee's sense of fair play? How could they fail to discern that Oxnam's continued criticism of HUAC would only stiffen the members' resolve not to appear to knuckle under. It was inevitable, psychologically, that the politicos would justify themselves to the voters by defending their records. How could Oxnam and Parlin suppose that an understanding with the not unsympathetic paid counsel

Kunzig would prevail over the wishes of the likes of Jackson and Walter?

Anyhow, in April the official government transcript of the hearing was published. In their naïveté, the Methodist bishop and Methodist lawyer were outraged. Oxnam ticked off his "shocked" futile dismay in a letter to Velde on April 23, 1954. One, he and Parlin had not received for correction and approval printer's proof before final printing in violation of a written agreement between Parlin and Kunzig. Two, the committee had inserted new material without warning. Three, changes were made in the text which radically altered the meaning. Four, the transcript failed to include the bibliography on Oxnam's writing on communism, which he had submitted, to make his position on communism clear. Five, the transcript omitted items submitted by Oxnam which he had not been permitted to present orally in the hearing. Six, the transcript failed to distinguish between the exhibits of the committee and those which Oxnam personally filed. Moreover, there was no indication that the committee had any intention of correcting the falsehoods in its file on him. "I am of the opinion that the printing of this record," Oxnam righteously scolded, "in violation of a written agreement is below the standard one has the right to expect from an agency of government." In the minds of Oxnam and Parlin, as their exchanges make clear, the perfidy of the committee was proven—as if there ever should have been any doubt.

The widespread prediction that after its setback in the Oxnam hearing (something the committee never admitted), HUAC would wither away was about as accurate as Marx's prediction concerning the fate of the state after communism's triumph. The committee and its subcommittees rode into town after town like a sheriff's posse, literally from Connecticut to southern California and from Florida to the Pacific Northwest. Masters of show business, the committee conducted well publicized hearings that were really purification rites. The hearings were not intended to uncover secret Communists present or past, for the names of these individuals were already known to the government. Rather they were intended to secure—by wheedling or bullying—public confessions, public pleas of contrition, and as proof of repentance, the public naming of names of others (also persons already known to the government.) Moreover, the committee continued its practice of equating support of liberal causes with fellow traveling. By the year of Oxnam's retirement, HUAC's budget (by unanimous voice vote of the House) was the highest ever and its permanent staff had swollen to forty-nine.

The aftermath of the hearing brought not only continuing blows from HUAC but also chastisements from a completely different quarter. During the hearing, Oxnam had been compelled under questioning to state that Harry F. Ward had once been his inspirational teacher, dear friend, and admired social gospel prophet, but that in the 1930s he had found himself in profound disagreement with Ward's politics. At no point did the bishop identify Ward as a Communist, but he did acknowledge his belief that Ward "takes the Communist position as to objective." Ward's continuing admirers let Oxnam know that they considered his performance an act of betrayal. Ward himself dismissed his former pupil as a "trimmer." "Oxnam's dealings with Ward," judged Ward's biographer Link, "involved hedgings, double meanings for words, and clever dodges such that his behavior . . . became disappointing to Ward."

A second Methodist, Jack McMichael, figured even more prominently in the HUAC hearing, as has been noted. It will be recalled that it was the committee, not Oxnam, who first introduced McMichael's name, and that it was the committee who (based on the testimony of FBI paid informers Manning Johnson and Leonard Patterson—both liars) flatly charged that McMichael was a member of the Communist Party. It will be recalled also that Oxnam testified as to why he sought to remove McMichael from the leadership of the MFSA. Inevitably, if not exactly fairly, Oxnam was accused of fingering the young radical minister. McMichael's wife in a rather restrained letter informed Oxnam, "I hope that you will not feel that I am of an unforgiving nature and one who bears malice. Those who know me would tell you that I am not. However, I feel that I wish you to know the harm that the newspaper reporting of your testimony against Jack is still causing." [6] The letter from the minister's mother was scorpian in sting: "Do you think you are a Christlike Christian? I do not. I feel sure that Christ would never have stooped so low. It was so entirely unnecessary. You did not have to say anything when Jack's name was mentioned." Oxnam's reply, gentle but not hair-shirted in tone, closed, "I recognize fully as Jack's mother you must feel very deeply concerning any word that I spoke. I hope you may have the opportunity to read the testimony in its entirety. I tried to speak with Christian charity and at the same time to tell the truth."

The mother's letter to Oxnam had been written on the eve of her son's appearing before HUAC on July 30 and July 31, a two-day hearing lasting a total of eleven hours. Having found Oxnam's hide rather tough, HUAC subpoenaed McMichael hoping to feast on tenderer fare. To Parlin's and Oxnam's credit, both men believed McMichael should have the benefit of legal counsel and sought to raise funds for that purpose, Oxnam calling (from the dock in New York before sailing for Europe), McMichael's bishop in California, Donald Tippett, to that effect. Tippett announced to the press that "until civil charges are brought against him—and proved—we will support him." The real credit for raising money, securing the services of the famed civil libertarian lawyer Frank Donner, and rallying support must go to Lee H. Ball, who related to MFSA members the details in a five-page, typed, single-spaced letter dated August 4.

McMichael's performance before HUAC was as nimble-footed as any by Nijinsky, though unlike the dancer he did not leave his audience cheering.[7] Murray Kempton, liberal columnist for the *New York Post*, no admirer of the Red-hunters, described McMichael as a "folksy, weedy, balding Georgia boy . . . the soul of irreverence, sniggling, and weasling and larding his auditors with every Packsniffism of the lower Protestantism." Kempton charged that the Methodist had followed "the Communist line for 14 years, that he knew exactly what he was doing and that he used every trick in the book (ad nauseum) yesterday to avoid admitting it." After noting that McMichael offered to take a lie detector test on whether he ever belonged to the Communist Party, the columnist continued: "We'd all be better off if the Un-American Affairs [Committee] would go home. A fellow-traveler's opinions are his own business, but there is such a thing as service to the truth and this McMichael is a bum; and he is no less a bum for being in trouble with Harold Velde. It is not the business of Congress to inquire into the confusions of a minister of God, and it is not the business of a minister of God to set out deliberately to confuse a committee of Congress. There is such a thing as coming clean. Yesterday Jack McMichael chose the alternative." [8]

McMichael's supporters, and McMichael himself naturally,[9] interpreted the hearing differently. Oxnam had sought to be dignified; McMichael was consciously outrageous and outraging. Oxnam had sought to be cooperative; McMichael was cleverly obstructive. Oxnam had sought clarification; McMichael was bent on obfuscation. Oxnam had sought to be courteous to the committee members; McMichael was openly contemptuous of them. Oxnam had challenged the procedures of HUAC; McMichael repudiated its very right to exist. Oxnam's hearing ended with at least a surface appearance of cordiality; McMichael left the committee members like bulls studded with banderillas, quivering with frustration and snorting with fury. By their own testimony they found the Methodist the "most obtuse," the most "contemptuous," the most "clever" witness ever to appear before them. Grumbled Clardy, "I practiced law for pretty nearly 30 years. If this witness had appeared in any court in which I had practiced during all that time he would have been in jail." Poor Velde pounded his gavel, threatened to order him removed forcibly from the room, and at one point with no trace of irony announced to McMichael, "The chair will allow you two minutes to make any derogatory statements you may want concerning this Committee." The hearing ended with Velde turning the pesky parson over to the Justice Department for a possible perjury indictment—but no such action was taken.

The most obvious point to be observed about this controversial hearing is that it did not receive a fraction of the public attention accorded Oxnam's hearing. The bishop had the massive organization of The Methodist Church behind him. He had the supportive cooperation of the National Council of Churches, the ACLU, the *Washington Post,* the legal talent of Parlin and his law firm and the friendship of power brokers in and out of Washington. On whom could McMichael count? A badly weakened and fragmented MFSA then without office, telephone, secretary, money. A concerned, competent lawyer, Donner. A few sympathetic journalists such as I. F. Stone and a few supportive church journals such as Shipler's *The Churchman*. A small bank of parishioners at Upper Lake, California. A mother and a wife and two young children. This is not exactly to say that McMichael was thrown to the wolves. Witness, as noted, the concern of Parlin and bishops Oxnam and Tippett.[10] It is merely to note that the attention paid to the minister's fate did not remotely approximate that accorded the bishop's.

At his hearing, Oxnam had been interrogated by the committee about his relationship to the *Protestant Digest* (in 1941 becoming known as simply the *Protestant*), edited and published by a Canadian Baptist layman, Kenneth Leslie. HUAC asserted that the magazine "was Communist in origin and inception and in practice" and in 1947 it was cited as subversive by the attorney general. Oxnam explained that he had accepted Leslie's invitation to become a member of the editorial board in March 1940. He accurately noted that the other board members were among the most respected figures in American Protestantism (George Buttrick, Rufus Jones, Reinhold Niebuhr, Bishop McConnell, among others) and carried the endorsement of Mrs. Eleanor Roosevelt. Oxnam then quoted from his letter of resignation dated February 11, 1942, giving the justification, "So far, there have been no meetings of the group [of editorial advisors] associated with the *Protestant*, and the material that appears is never considered by this group." However, Oxnam's name continued to appear on the magazine's masthead through the October-November issue, and on November 30 he again asked Leslie to drop it. When pressed by the committee to elaborate on the reason for his resignation, Oxnam responded that Roger Baldwin of the ACLU had warned him that he thought the magazine had Communist support. Oxnam continued: "I resigned because of what he had told me, after having looked into the matter. Interestingly enough, one of the most influential church men, Edwin Holt Hughes . . . was . . . an advisor. I called him and told him immediately [sic] upon receiving this information from Mr. Baldwin that he ought to get his name off the list. That is my relationship with the magazine." Oxnam did not mention the considerable friendly correspondence he had had with Leslie between 1940 and 1946. Not even the two letters of resignation referred to Baldwin or hinted at Baldwin's suspicions. Nor did any of Oxnam's letters suggest that he thought the *Protestant* was excessively critical of the Roman Catholic Church, a point raised during the hearing, to which the bishop pledged to the committee that "there is no anti-Catholicism in my spirit whatsoever." The committee also noticed that the magazine had printed with Oxnam's permission his address, "Monsignor Sheen and Clerical Fascism." (Actually, it was run as a front-page editorial and Oxnam was pleased.)

Leslie felt betrayed by the bishop and so bitingly informed him in personal letters, as he did the dwindling faithful readers of the *Protestant* (September 1953) and the renamed *One* (September 1954). Leslie raised several penetrating questions. Why during the hearing had Oxnam accepted as fact HUAC's assertions that the *Protestant* was both Communist and anti-Catholic, based on the testimony of ex-Communists Benjamin Gitlow and Manning Johnson? Why, on being warned by Baldwin, had not Oxnam shared his concerns with Leslie for clarification and correction? Why had Oxnam "immediately" called Bishop Hughes? Why had he masked from Leslie his reasons for resigning from the editorial board? Why for years did Leslie continue to receive letters of commendation from Oxnam? "Since the Bishop was there to correct falsehoods *about himself* how was it that he swallowed *gratefully* falsehoods about others?" Leslie mused. "Baldwin and Bishop Oxnam did not lie, but they allowed the lie to defame a man's character." In *One* Leslie thrust home savagely: "Bishop Oxnam was big and wanted to be bigger. And so this bishop became not only a victim of this terror but also its perpetrator, just as a sick rodent involuntarily carries the plague. . . . Terror is the road on which a coward becomes a killer." After praising Oxnam's early career as a crusader for social justice, Leslie questioned, "Can it be that, as the young Bromley Oxnam grew older, the bright rewards of conformity distracted him so that he stumbled off the narrow Cross-bound road?" The last personal letter from Leslie to Oxnam closes, "Your statement to the Committee that I am reduced to begging for funds reminds me to tell you that I am now engaged in driving a taxi for sustenance. Hope you will approve of this and give me your blessing."

It is not necessarily to defend Oxnam to make three final observations. Although Leslie may be believed that he was never a Communist and his magazine was never a tool of the Party, the fact is that the *Protestant* was hopelessly uncritical of the Soviet Union. Secondly, no Catholic would agree that the magazine was not relentlessly critical of the Church. Thirdly, virtually every respected Protestant leader who served on the editorial board ultimately severed the relationship in disappointed dismay, Niebuhr scolding Leslie, "You are determined to follow the line of Russia as closely as possible."

During the course of the hearing the name of a fourth churchman had surfaced when counsel Kunzig asked Oxnam if he knew the Reverend Stephen H. Fritchman and if he had given an address in Fritchman's First Unitarian Church of Los Angeles on April 4, 1952. The bishop replied "yes," explaining:

> I had no knowledge whatsoever that Mr. Fritchman was in any way related to the Communist Party. May I say this, that since that time and I will not name the men, but two prominent officials of the Unitarian Church have conferred with me and gave me information that gave me grave doubts concerning Dr. Fritchman, and had I known what they informed me I would, of course, not have lectured at his church.

Representative Jackson broke in to say that "there is perhaps no individual who has been as closely associated with the Communist Party or Communist front organizations over a period of many years as has Reverend Fritchman. He appeared before the committee and declined to answer questions as to his membership in the Council on the grounds of the Fifth Amendment."

Fritchman, a Unitarian minister (though ordained a Methodist) had long been a cause of consternation to the American Unitarian Association, first as director of American Unitarian Youth and then as editor of the respected Unitarian journal, the *Christian Register*. In 1947 after a bitter battle he was ousted from the editorship post and the following year he accepted an invitation from the First Unitarian Church in Los Angeles, famed for its liberalism.[11]

Considering the reaction of Ward, McMichael, and Leslie to Oxnam's testimony before HUAC, it is not surprising that Fritchman also voiced his dismay. Writing to Oxnam on August 10, he noted that he had twice appeared before HUAC. In 1946 he had stated under oath that he had no connection whatsoever with the Communist Party. In 1951 he refused as a matter of principle to answer this same question again or any questions concerning his church. "You have a right to ask for hearings before this infamous Committee if you wish, but you have no ethical or moral right to place your finger upon fellow ministers. . . . This disassociation of yourself from others long active in the Protestant cause is a tragic failure on your part to maintain the freedom of the church from government impertinence," the letter continued. Fritchman closed: "Since you protested rightly the use of unverified and unchecked material by the Committee regarding yourself, it seems you might have used the same logic in accepting from 'two Unitarian officials' material I have not been shown by them or you." He then demanded that Oxnam supply the names. Oxnam replied that "I spoke reluctantly and without any thought at all of doing you harm." He then put to Fritchman a list of the Unitarian's alleged Communist ties and bargained that if Fritchman would answer, he in turn would supply the names of the two Unitarian accusers.

Responding on September 15, Fritchman categorically denied each allegation about his Communist associations or loyalties. He made no apology for his record, a matter of public property, snapping, "I find no reason to ask permission of the Attorney General before joining a cause or signing a petition, nor to repudiate any such action on pain of his displeasure. . . . In this time of grave threat to the whole Protestant social gospel, there must be ministers who will stand up and say that every man's ideas or affiliations are his own business, and only his. I learned this lesson from Bishop McConnell who ordained me, and I do not see any reason for bartering it away." In his brief reply, slightly injured in tone, Oxnam kept his word and offered the names of the two Unitarians—Arnold and Eliot. The injured tone stemmed from Oxnam's reading of an address by Fritchman which contained the criticism: "We read six [sic] hours of Bishop Oxnam's supplication to the committee to clear his name; this rather than an effort to explain the moral and constitutional independence of the church in measuring and criticizing Congress and our society or a defense of a minister's right to choose his causes freely and without apology. It led to his placing the finger on other religious workers in an effort to clear himself." Fritchman then set forth his personal belief that the wisest path for churchmen to follow was that of "remaining silent and refusing to recognize the Committee's right to inquire into religion, into church affairs, or the activities of ministers so long as they break no law and commit no crime."

As is well known, Oxnam gave his full account and interpretation of the hearing and its background in a 186-page book entitled *I Protest* published by Harper & Brothers in 1954. He appeared on eight radio and television shows to publicize it. The reviews were generally favorable. Letters from grateful readers poured in. It remains an important document for understanding the times. Is it a self-serving work? Of course. But it would be unreasonable to expect Oxnam to write from an angle of vision other than his own; that is from that of either HUAC at one pole or Ward, McMichael, Leslie, and Fritchman at the other. In light of what has preceded in these pages it would seem unnecessary to summarize the contents of *I Protest*. However, perhaps notice might be taken of a thoughtful 1954 diary observation entered after speaking before a Unitarian group: "I talked on the 'Procedures of the Investigating Committees.' I am getting a bit tired of this, but the people continue to be interested. Whether or not we can really reach the masses who are duped by politicians?, and the Hearst papers, and the like, I do not know. Sometimes, I think we are fooling ourselves in assuming that because we get great responses in the audiences we face that therefore the people are beginning to change." And also this 1955 entry: "I began to think about our Senators, and it is a little startling to notice the men that Methodism has contributed to the United States Senate. Of course, there are some strong people, such as Alben W. Barkely, Mrs. Margaret Chase Smith, but when I note the other names, Allen Bible of Nevada, John Marshall Butler of Maryland, Dworshak of Idaho, Eastland himself, Hickenlooper of Iowa, Jenner of Indiana, Knowland of California, Mundt of South Dakota, and Potter of Michigan, one begins to wonder just a little about our religious education."

Over the years one of Oxnam's most searching criticisms of the methods employed by congressional investigating committees was their reliance on the sworn testimony of ex-Communists who were, in fact, often paid "professional witnesses." In this gang was an individual named Harvey Matusow. Oxnam had a principal role, though quite by chance, in exposing this quite possibly demented soul, and thereby helping to discredit the whole informer system. This convoluted story must be cut to the bone, but it is too revealing to be omitted entirely.

Matusow joined the Communist Party in 1947. Disillusioned, he offered his services for a price to the FBI as a spy until 1951 when the CPUSA expelled him as an "enemy agent." After a stint in the Air Force he emerged as a "surprise witness" at the 1952 trial of secondary Communist Party leaders, where his testimony filled some seven hundred pages. From this point his career was meteoric. He was available for a fee to HUAC, SISS, the Department of Justice, the Subversive Activities Control Board, the McCarthy Committee, and several Congressmen. The Ohio Un-American Activities Commission, the New York City Board of Education, the *New York Times*, the Hearst Press, and the American Legion all contracted for his services. He peddled subscriptions to *Counterattack* and found employment as a disc-jockey and nightclub entertainer.

In 1952 Oxnam was informed that in a talk before a college audience Matusow had named the bishop as a fellow traveler. Oxnam inquired into Matusow's status with the FBI and was informed by the bureau that Matusow had been employed as an "informant" from June to December 1950, but that he had never been a special agent.

On the evening of April 27, 1954, Oxnam was approached in the lobby of the Waldorf-Astoria by a man who identified himself as Harvey Matusow who confided he had had a profound religious experience and confessed that he had lied again and again in his testimonies as a government witness and that he wanted to go to each individual about whom he had falsified to ask forgiveness. The conversation because of the late hour lasted only ten or fifteen minutes. Matusow next contacted the bishop by letter on April 28, again asking forgiveness for his unforgivable perjury, and on May 31 the two men talked for over an hour in Oxnam's office. Much the same story unfolded with Matusow now asking for a financial contribution to underwrite the publication of a book exposing the government's investigation. (Oxnam did not do so.) In June Oxnam informed a Methodist audience of Matusow's recantation, the press picked up the story, and quickly Matusow was hauled before HUAC where he assured Velde and Co. that the bishop was lying. Luckily for Oxnam, Matusow earlier had also confessed what he had confessed to Oxnam to two members of the law firm of McGrath and Brown. Former Attorney General McGrath alerted his friend Charles Parlin and offered to substantiate the truth of Oxnam's account.

Oxnam was then subpoenaed to appear on October 18, 1954, before the Subversive Activities Control Board relative to Matusow's reliability. The Justice Department's attorney grilled Oxnam unmercifully, but the bishop could back up his testimony with that of McGrath's and the board members were courteous, and in the end Oxnam was informed that that would be the end of Mr. Matusow. Shortly afterward, Oxnam wrote a polite but firm letter to Attorney General Brownell urging that the government exercise greater care in its reliance "upon the testimony of some former conspirators" such as Matusow and Manning Johnson.

Oxnam was again subpoenaed to appear on March 21, 1955, in the Federal Court in New York relative to Matusow because of his false testimony in the 1952 trial of thirteen secondary Communist Party leaders. While on the witness stand for ninety minutes Oxnam simply restated the account of his two meetings with Matusow. At the close of the day Oxnam recorded in his diary the true words: "I hope I am done with the Matusow business. I think a service has been rendered in bringing his name to the public in such a fashion that he has been discredited and the whole question of using unreliable professional witnesses has been raised." [12]

---

[1] One of the hundreds of copies of the letter ended up in the FBI file and on it in the longhand observation was written, "Gee! Bromley Oxnam at his best."

[2] Ralph Stoody, director of the Methodist Commission on Promotion and Cultivation and Methodist Information, and Francis Harmon, of the National Council of Churches, compiled a scrapbook of newspaper and magazine clippings devoted to the hearing, including 226 editorials which appeared in daily newspapers from coast to coast arranged by states alphabetically. The two men dedicated the volume to Oxnam with admiration and affection, "a HAPPY WARRIOR 'Whose strength is the strength of ten.' "

These items complimented the vast number of clippings Oxnam received from his own sources. Stoody and Harmon were also responsible for preparing a twelve-page "tabloid" (printed under Methodist auspices) devoted to commentaries on the hearing. Copies were sent to 25,000 Methodist ministers and an additional 10,000 copies were mailed by the National Council to newspapers, councils of churches, ministerial associations, members of Congress, state governors, and others.

[3] Actually, this letter to Oxnam from Muriel I. Symington dated August 8, 1953, is not in the Oxnam Collection, but a copy is in the Harry F. Ward papers, Union Theological Seminary.

[4] David E. Gillingham, "The Politics of Piety. G. Bromley Oxnam and the Un-American Activities Committee." Unpublished senior thesis, Princeton University, 1967.

[5] Poor Velde had some reason to be miffed as Oxnam publicly stated Velde was made "from the same cut of cloth as McCarthy"; cut a "sorry figure" as HUAC chairman; and no doubt faced the stern judgment of the people of Illinois in the next election. As a matter of fact, Velde won, but when ranking Democrat Walter succeeded him as HUAC chairman in 1955, Velde "resigned" from the dissension-torn committee. (Mrs. Velde, the committee's "official reporter" "resigned" with her husband, and counsel Kunzig was given the gate.)

[6] In the hopes of setting up an interview to obtain his angle of vision, in March 1985, I wrote McMichael, only to receive this sad reply from his widow: "I am sorry to tell you Jack McMichael died Dec. 7, 1984. He will not be able to share with you his views of Bishop Oxnam."

[7] As it happens, I was in Washington on a research trip in the summer of 1953 and attended the open hearing for several hours, although I do not remember whether it was the first or second day.

[8] On May 8, 1985, in Washington Joseph Lash shared with me his opinion of McMichael whom he had known when Roosevelt was president and McMichael was chairman of the American Youth Conference. Lash described the young minister as being tall, slim, blonde, handsome, intelligent, articulate—and a true fellow traveler. Probably McMichael was a not a card carrying member of the CPUSA, said Lash, but the Party was not dumb and realized that the magnetic Methodist was of more value out of than in the Party. Lash, who surely was in a position to know, recalled that Eleanor Roosevelt, once a McMichael benefactor, lost all confidence in him and broke all ties with him.

[9] See Jack Richard McMichael, "My Experience with the Velde Committee," a twenty-six-page typed manuscript in the Harry F. Ward Papers.

[10] The record does not disclose the size of the sums, if any, actually contributed by the wealthy Parlin and affluent Oxnam to McMichael's defense fund. All we know for certain is that they favored the raising of such a fund. In September Oxnam and Parlin were informed by Kunzig and another HUAC staff member that it was not necessary for Oxnam to appear before the committee in executive session to reveal the sources of his information about McMichael. The committee knew perfectly well the source was the FBI, said Kunzig. He also reported that his bosses were still tearing out their beards in anger at McMichael.

[11] Melvin Arnold, director of the Unitarian division of publications, and Frederick May Eliot, president of the American Unitarian Association, led in Fritchman's dismissal as editor. The bitterness surrounding Fritchman is suggested in a 1946 letter from John Haynes Holmes to Reinhold Niebuhr: "The situation in the Unitarian body as regards the Communists is alarming. At the same time it is so incredible, that Beacon Hill should be taken over by the Reds, that I have to shake myself awake from a nightmare. The *Christian Register*, staid old organ of the Unitarians, is now definitely in the hands of the Communists under Fritchman's leadership. The young people's organization is being slowly but surely captured. And here you send me proof positive that the Unitarian Service Committee has been taken over and the amazing thing is that most of the ministers and laymen are so innocent that they haven't the slightest idea as to what is

going on. I have been bombarding Fred Eliot for months with facts and charges, but seem as yet to have made little impression."

[12] In 1955 Matusow wrote a volume entitled *False Witness*. It was published by the firm of Kahn & Cameron. Oxnam shared his diary notes with the two publishers. The government pulled out all stops to prevent its publication. In the book Matusow claimed to have been coached in his perjury by U.S. Assistant Attorney General Roy Cohn. The story becomes increasingly surreal. The Justice Department, HUAC, SISS, and the FBI were spurred to nail Matusow. He did not stand a chance. He was eventually convicted and received a five-year sentence in September 1956 for lying under oath when he had confessed that he had lied under oath as a government witness. Was he a scamp? Deranged? A sinner who bravely confessed his sins and served his prison term without whimpering? Who knows? What can be stated with assurance is that Matusow seriously underminded the confidence of the American people in the government's informer system.

CHAPTER 29

FINAL TASKS AND FINAL FAREWELLS

As we know, Oxnam's sense of responsibility committed him to accept assignment in 1956 to a second four-year term as bishop of the Washington Area in order to bring to fruition a number of goals he had set, notably those surrounding American University, Wesley Theological Seminary, and Sibley Hospital, but other Area needs as well. We have seen the energy and passion he gave to these challenges. We have seen also the continuing service given to The Methodist Church at large. We have noted that while not quite as active as in the past in the leadership of the National Council of Churches and the World Council of Churches, he by no means dropped completely out of the affairs of these organizations. WCC matters especially occasioned tiring trips abroad. His interest in public affairs—peace in the world and social justice at home—remained undiminished. During this last quadrennium he cut back on his public speaking appearances, it is true, and now made "merely" several score addresses annually rather than several hundred. The volume of his writing also dropped off; still, there continued to flow from his pen a stream, if not a torrent, of words, including a major book, *Testament of Faith*, in 1958.

Nevertheless, with the passing of each quadrennium year, Oxnam's thoughts increasingly and naturally turned to retirement and beyond—to death. He began to notice the absence of familiar faces, even at meetings of the Council of Bishops, as death or retirement claimed old friends. He was both touched and troubled when the younger men insisted on carrying his suitcases or suggested that he take the elevator rather than climb the stairs. He and Ruth looked into places they might spend their retirement years. Washington, D.C., was out because they did not wish the new Area bishop to feel haunted by their presence. Los Angeles was out because it was no longer the city they loved as youths, and besides none of the three children lived on the West Coast. Ultimately, in 1959, they rented a beautiful apartment on the sixth floor of The Cragswold on Garth Road in Scarsdale, New York. Their adored daughter and her family lived in the community and it would be heaven to have Bette near. Their thought was to live less than 180 days a year in Scarsdale in order to escape paying the New York income tax, establishing instead legal residence in New Hampshire. This would enable them to spend the late fall and winter months in New York in order to take advantage of the cultural opportunities afforded by Gotham and the spring and summer months at the Pine Island cottage. They also intended to travel several months of the year. An alternate plan seriously considered was for Bromley to enroll in the Harvard Law School and win a degree, for the idea of studying law had always keenly appealed to him.

Being the man that he was, Bromley gave much study to their financial situation, not only for retirement purposes, but so that "things would be in decent order just in case." And "just in case," cemetery plots were investigated. "Strangely enough, as we drove about the peaceful lanes of this lovely cemetery," he recorded, "the peace that has come to those who lie there seemed to come to me and I thought it altogether fitting and very beautiful to think seriously of a last resting place."

Oxnam's thoughts also turned to his possible successor and he shared them with Parlin, chairman of the Northeastern Jurisdictional Conference Episcopal Committee. Oxnam's first choice as the new bishop of the Washington Area was Gerald Kennedy if he could be persuaded to leave California. If not, John Wesley Lord would be perfectly fine. These individuals, judged Oxnam, were preferable to the ambitious Fred Corson.

In all this it is necessary to observe and underscore again that Oxnam in 1956, 1957, and 1958 did not live in the future to the neglect of his present duties. Nor did the increasing health problems, noted in chapter 10, including the warning signs of Parkinson's, immobilize him. He not only continued to work harder than did most young men in excellent health, he also drove long distances, dined out at restaurants, attended movies, plays, and concerts. At least one of his secretaries could not recall any marked diminishment of his normal life-style. That is, until December 24, 1958.

On that day Bromley and Ruth were in New York to spend Christmas with son Robert and his family. At noon a cab dropped them off at a favored Chinese restaurant. After helping Ruth out, Oxnam unknowingly closed the cab door on his overcoat. The unaware cabbie roared off dragging the sixty-seven-year-old man many feet before stopping. Oxnam was knocked unconscious when his head struck the curb. An ambulance rushed him, now having regained consciousness, to Roosevelt Hospital. He was to have no memory whatsoever of the accident. He suffered a brain concussion, a head wound requiring stitches, a fractured left arm, a severely bruised jaw, and broken teeth. (The dental treatment required five hours of excruciating pain.) After four days of hospitalization, the Oxnams returned to Washington by train. "I have been here since, wondering what it is all about," he shortly informed his diary. When news of the accident appeared in the national press, condolences poured in.

The medical profession does not conclude that the accident necessarily aggravated Oxnam's deteriorating Parkinson's condition; the injuries suffered and the Parkinson's are independent of each other. In the absence of medical records we cannot be precisely certain what that "condition" was. Was it true Parkinson's disease, a very specific disease, or was it Parkinsonism or Parkinson's syndrome, a less severe symptom complex? Indeed, perhaps not even an examination of the medical records would prove conclusive inasmuch as today's knowledge is so much further advanced than it was thirty years ago. All that can be said with certitude is that the final eighteen months as bishop of the Church were a physical and emotional ordeal for G. Bromley Oxnam.

The diary entries for this period relate visits to the Lahey Clinic in Boston and to Sibley Hospital. They relate the taking of "rather severe sets of tests." "The truth is not too much is known of this Parkinson's difficulty. They are exploring, that's about all," reads one passage. "We are going to have a try at a new remedy for Parkinson's which may be helpful," reads another without specifying the remedy. In fact, if drugs were prescribed they go unmentioned. "The doctors generally left me knowing that I have got to watch my step or I'll not step at all," reads a third.

There are no reports that at this time Oxnam's speech became slurred. There are no reports of "stickiness" of mind or bradyphrenia, the thought stream as slow and sluggish as the motor stream, as would be the case in true Parkinson's disease.

On the other hand, there was a severe tremor in his right hand that grew progressively worse, observed by all and acknowledged by Oxnam in his dictated letters. Son Philip recalled that Oxnam referred to his condition as "my friend Parky," but Philip and everyone else observed that to lose control was especially frustrating to a man of Oxnam's temperament who for a lifetime had willed his body to obey. Once when a church secretary offered to help him button his robe before a service, he declined the assistance and struggled for ten minutes to perform the task himself. On another instance, a young minister asked him to autograph a book, and Oxnam fell to his knees, placed the volume on a low table, steadied his right hand with the left, and painfully scrawled his signature. In the Oxnam Collection the notes written by hand as late as 1958 were reasonably steady; by 1960 they became virtually illegible.

Moreover, on several instances while giving addresses in 1960 his famed memory failed him, to the intense concern of Ruth, who now pleaded with her husband to terminate, or at least moderate, his speaking career. Crane spoke feelingly for all of Oxnam's friends when he observed Oxnam in the pulpit in 1960, "What a tragic thing to see him now. It is like watching a great ship go down."

Compounding his Parkinson's condition was an angina heart condition. The doctors ordered him to lose weight, of course, but also not to exert himself climbing stairs or walking slopes, particularly after eating. This meant, to his vexation, that he could no longer perform the necessary chores on Pine Island and had to hire the labor done.

An earlier bursitis condition worsened to the point that he almost passed out from the pain on occasions that required him to wear a heavy robe.

Many diary entries in 1959 and 1960 are bleak. "I find that no matter how buoyant one is in the morning, all of the nervous energy is used up by noon," he confessed. Even holding office hours or placing phone calls made "demands upon the nervous system that are very hard to bear. But the regular work goes on." A March 1959 passage laments, "The days are quite drab." In November a series of morning conferences brought the admission: "It is strange how exhausted I am at the close of a morning's conferences which I used to take in stride before the day really began. Browning was nuts when he talked about 'Grow old along with me, the best is yet to be.' " He then recalled the long days and nights of work he formerly put in, adding, "All of which I think was quite stupid."

To Lilienthal he wrote, "I am trying to do the best I can between now and my retirement on June 19th. I am really counting the days." When he reported to Crane that he was trying to keep on top of the work despite the doctors' orders to cease all work for three or four months, his friend replied, "I wish to goodness you would take it easy for a while instead of driving yourself like a mad man. As you well know, all your friends are deeply concerned over the fact that you so relentlessly continue to do your usual incredible stint of work instead of deferring to your doctors' request." In January 1960 Oxnam told a reporter, "Above all, I want to try to get my health back. I'm looking forward to the day when I won't have any responsibilities."

On the third of that month Oxnam delivered one of his last, though not the very last, major addresses from the pulpit of the Lovely Lane Church, Baltimore, on the occasion of the 175th anniversary of the founding of The Methodist Church in America. One of the less lyrical passages in Crane's praiseful introduction reads, "He wants, longs for, just one thing—to hear his Master's voice and to obey. And yet his heart as big, as brave and tender as a whispered prayer, it is. Seeking his Master like a creeping flame and folding one woman with a passion ever youthful and to his children and his friends a city of refuge. God, how he loved us!" Oxnam rose to make a prediction:

> Before another 175 years have passed, we will have conquered space and come to know the thinking, the culture, the dreams, the problems, the limitations of the people who populate the great planets of the universe. Surely God the Father Almighty did not devote all of His creative power to an unpopulated universe and did not place the climax of creation, which we believe is the human being, solely upon the earth. Is Methodism ready for the intellectual stretching necessary to re-examine its missionary program and to ask, Must the old command be revised to read, 'Go ye into the universe and preach the Gospel to every creature'?

He repeated the substance of this prediction in a statement for *Parade* magazine and in his final General Conference address. And also to the press when asked what would be the most significant event in the religious field in the next ten years:

> The decade's most dramatic event will be The Interplanetary Conference of Religious Faith to be attended by the finest minds of all the planets of the universe. It will be the first "universal" conference on religion, made possible by scientific mastery of space travel. Teachable humility will characterize the delegates who will make known the revelation of God to all. Fundamentalist dogmatism and papal infallibility will have no place among men who love one another and seek the truth in freedom. It will be a "sharing" conference. How did God make Himself known to the inhabitants of Mars? Through incarnation in a Person, by revelation in a Book, through the thinking of a scholar and saint? Is there evidence for immortality? The sessions will be televised, and the universe will come to know the universal truth that frees.

One may refrain from asking how in heaven's name the most famed bishop in American Methodism could possibly paint such an Edward Hicks peaceable interplanetary kingdom where fundamentalists and papists would have no place. One must, however, ask how American Methodists could pronounce Oxnam's prediction profound.

In late April–early May, the Oxnams attended the General Conference in Denver. On May 6 Bromley presided and reported having "a very good time of it." The high moment was a testimonial dinner held in the Brown Palace hotel. The guest speaker was Parlin whose words were heartfelt. Dr. Asbury Smith presented the Oxnams with a testimonial scrapbook containing photographs, letters, and tributes. They were truly touched, for admiration and affection were revealed on every page.[1]

On May 22 Oxnam presided for the last time at the Peninsula Annual Conference in Wilmington. Again a farewell banquet was tendered, words of respect uttered, and a large gift of money bestowed. "I shall be leaving many, many friends in the Peninsular Conference," the bishop grieved. [2]

In early June Oxnam presided for the last time at the Baltimore Annual Conference. A gala "service in recognition of the distinguished career of Bishop G. Bromley Oxnam" was held. Among those who spoke in tribute were Parlin (again), aged Bishop Welch, and Arthur S. Flemming. Oxnam judged Welch's tribute "the finest piece of work from a literary and friendly standpoint I have ever heard." He and Ruth were overwhelmed by the words from a hundred lips and even more by the visible tears in a hundred eyes.

In mid-June a last banquet was tendered at the Shoreham Hotel in connection with the meeting of the Northeastern Jurisdictional Conference. Ralph Sockman was the principal speaker and his oratorical powers were brilliantly displayed.

Even as Oxnam found understandable satisfaction in these occasions, his diary also reveals his troubled thoughts. "If I were built differently I would toss in the sponge today," he wrote on May 15. "It has been a very difficult and trying week. . . . There are but 35 days until retirement, but they seem about 35,000 as one contemplates them. However, I suppose there is nothing to do but take it a day at a time, and to cease resenting the growing inability to use my right arm effectively, and to keep going at anything like normal speed."

In June the Oxnams went to Pine Island where they spent July, August, and September. In the fall they took up residence in Scarsdale. Oxnam continued to embrace the hopeless hope that his health might return. Ruth, without a shadow of self-pity or bitterness, tended to her husband's increasing needs.

On December 6 the Oxnams flew to San Francisco where Bromley addressed the triennial assembly of the National Council of Churches. He could not summon the necessary physical reserves to avoid a poignantly imperfect performance. The sympathetic audience understood. Dr. John McLaughlin observed Ruth's face as her husband stumbled on and it was clear to him that she was devastated. Never again did Oxnam attempt a major address.

[1] As it happens, I was at the conference to interview individuals in connection with my then projected biography of Ernest Fremont Tittle. Although I recall seeing Oxnam, I did not seek an interview. I did, however, interview several Methodist leaders, including Charles C. Parlin. Dr. and Mrs. Smith generously shared with me the contents of the scrapbook.

[2] The Reverend Ralph Minter told me the money was intended to go toward the purchase of a new Cadillac (with other conferences chipping in), but Minter believed the car inappropriate and lobbied to secure the use of the money for another more seemly gift.

CHAPTER 30

"AWAITING THE DAY OF NEW BEGINNINGS"

Writing to David Lilienthal on January 5, 1962, Oxnam said, "As you may have heard, I retired a year ago last June and have been trying to make the days of retirement count, although illness is not the best way to count for the most." That statement might stand as a summary for the years 1961 and 1962. Parkinson's proved a harsh jailer. On rare occasions, perhaps only two, he appeared at church-sponsored events. "He was a pitiful shadow of the mighty man he had been," recalled a Methodist minister, not touching the banquet food on his plate for fear of dribbling it. He now ceased eating in restaurants altogether. With a granddaughter he saw his last movie, "The Birdman of Alcatraz." Inferential evidence suggests that even letter writing largely ceased. According to the FBI file, the Oxnams applied for passports in order to spend six weeks in England in early 1961; the trip was never made. A letter written by Ruth to a dear friend, Rachel Smith, dated June 16, 1961, is revealing: "The days here at the lake are very full, keeping house, getting meals, reading, playing Scrabble, and listening to the T.V. (when the T.V. behaves itself). Mr. Oxnam needs a great deal of attention these days, finding it more and more difficult to do for himself—which of course, you will understand, hurts his pride. He has always, in all ways, been self-reliant and to depend on anyone else depresses him. But we'll take it in our stride. When you write don't mention this. I know you will understand."

Oxnam's condition cruelly continued to worsen. In late December 1962 he underwent a rare brain operation in New York City's St. Barnabas Hospital, the surgery being performed by Dr. Irving S. Cooper, originator of a deep-freezing technique to help palsy victims. The initial post-operation reports were favorable. They were wrong. Parkinson's was not checked. There followed a stroke.

Now Ruth, even with her total devotion, could no longer cope with caring for her husband at home. Oxnam entered the Burke Foundation Rehabilitation in White Plains. He literally wasted away, his weight dropping to less than 100 pounds according to son Phil. The Reverend J. Edward Carothers, pastor of the local Memorial Methodist Church, frequently visited the bishop, finding that while Oxnam retained an interest in church affairs he was so weak that he could concentrate for not more than two or three minutes. "I wish you would stop preachers from coming in here to pray over me," Oxnam once requested Carothers.

On March 12 death released Oxnam from the prison of his tortured body. He was ready to be released, believes son Phil.

The family gathered for a simple liturgical service led by Carothers. At Oxnam's wish, his body rested in the least expensive casket the funeral director could supply. With her unfailing thoughtfulness, Ruth expressed her gratitude to Carothers by placing in his hands a precious Wedgwood bust of John Wesley, saying, "This was Bromley's dearest treasure and I think he would want you to have it."

On March 25 American and ecumenical church leaders from near and far filled Christ Church, New York, in a service commemorating the life and labors of Bishop G. Bromley Oxnam.

On April 1 a Service of Commemoration was held in the overflowing Metropolitan Memorial Methodist Church, Washington.

Oxnam Chapel, Wesley Theological Seminary, on April 11 was the appropriate scene of a "Service of Enshrinement of the Ashes of the Mortal Body of Garfield Bromley Oxnam."

The extraordinary words of tribute paid to the lost leader at these services and in editorials in the religious and secular press and in letters of sympathy to Ruth and the children, Robert, Philip, and Bette, would fill another book. Let the words of one-hundred-year-old Bishop Welch symbolize the praise: Behind the courage there was no ferocity; behind the positiveness of leadership no selfish meanness; behind the conflicts no hatred; rather within the militant champion a tender heart of compassion and eager love, with a deep devotion to all things true and beautiful and good. He has thought creatively, planned largely, led boldly and achieved greatly. "Here is a man, take him for all in all, we shall not look upon his like again."

I N D E X